WITHDRAWN

**to my beloved family
Rupert, Dom and Dani**

and to my dearest parents

Brindar
verb. To drink a toast, to wish happiness
or good health to someone by raising your glass

Brindis
noun. masculine. Toast

Sociedad Anónima (S.A.)
noun. feminine. Joint stock company

Brindis + SA = Brindisa

BRINDISA

THE TRUE FOOD OF SPAIN

Monika Linton

with Sheila Keating
Photography by
Pippa Drummond

4th Estate
An imprint of HarperCollinsPublishers
1 London Bridge Street
London SE1 9GF
www.4thEstate.co.uk

First published in Great Britain by 4th Estate in 2016

1 3 5 7 9 8 6 4 2

Design and Art Direction by BLOK
www.blokdesign.co.uk

Patterns by BLOK and Jerry Sweet

A catalogue record for this book is available
from the British Library

ISBN 978-0-00-730718-0

Printed and bound in China

MIX
Paper from
responsible sources
FSC www.fsc.org   FSC® C007454

FSC™ is a non-profit international organisation established
to promote the responsible management of the world's
forests. Products carrying the FSC label are independently
certified to assure consumers that they come from forests
that are managed to meet the social, economic and ecological
needs of present and future generations, and other
controlled sources.

Find out more about HarperCollins and the environment at
www.harpercollins.co.uk/green

THE STORY
OF BRINDISA

Brindisa began, not so much with a plan, more on a shoestring and with an idea, as a salute to the real, largely undiscovered artisan food of Spain. The name, which comes from the Spanish *brindis,* means 'to make a toast', or 'raise your glass'; and what began over 28 years ago with a few stunning cheeses never seen in the UK before just gathered momentum, as more like-minded people jumped aboard and helped to propel a kind of Spanish food revolution.

People always ask me: why food, and above all why *Spanish* food? And more commercially hard-nosed people have often said, 'How on earth did you make it work?' given the hoops we had to jump through in the early days, before Spain was a part of the EU. I would travel hundreds of miles to seek out small producers and growers in remote regions and mountains, to try to convince them to be brave and let us sell their produce in Britain, where, in the late eighties, the popular notion of Spanish food and drink was still largely limited to holiday resort *paella* and *sangría.*

My answer is that, although when I was younger I would never have dreamed my future would be that of a trader, a kind of pioneering spirit, entrepreneurship and lust for travel seems to have run through the generations in our family. My grandfather on my mother's side, Eric Popper, known as Opa, was a truly inspirational figure who managed a trading post in Kota Kota in Malawi, which eventually became the country's biggest agricultural/rice co-operative society, while my paternal grandfather, Augustine Lavery, was an old-fashioned, cautious bank manager from Leytonstone, who instilled a judicial understanding of money and business into myself, my twin siblings, Mark and Michele, and sister Moyna.

We were privileged enough to have all our grandparents with us until we were in our twenties, and the stories that echoed among the older folk conjured up pictures that still stay in my mind. Opa's tales, especially, were rich and wonderful. He was a German of Jewish extraction. All his family seemed to be traders, and his wife's family were mariners of Norwegian origin. He was trading silk in Hamburg when in the early thirties life in Germany began to become uncomfortable, so they headed for Cyprus, where they bought some land. Opa dug an irrigation system and planted a citrus farm, working with the local communities. When he later found himself a job with the government of Nyasaland (now Malawi), much of what he did involved teaching local rice growers to develop new techniques. Again he introduced a proper regime of irrigation, this time to the natural swamp plains, for the cultivation of rice. He built a mill, traded the rice, and managed the Kota Kota Produce and Trading Society. As the quality of life improved for the growers, Opa set up small general stores in the district, the largest of which became like an old-fashioned department store where the local community could buy everything from sugar, flour and tinned sardines to cloth, haberdashery, needles and watches.

By all accounts he was a fantastic employer with considerable entrepreneurial spirit, and when he and my grandmother eventually returned to the UK, they brought back files which documented everything Opa had done: the measurements of the fields, all the tasks, everything recorded in unbelievable detail.

I suppose what I took most from his story was the idea of working the land from scratch, respecting the food that it gives, the skills it supports and the livestock it nurtures. His enterprise was a good model: he created jobs, opened up new markets, and used trade to feed money directly back into rural communities, to help sustain and regenerate family livelihoods. In recognition he was awarded an MBE.

Add to Opa's influence my father's great love of Spain, which rubbed off on our whole family; my mother's wonderful, healthy home cooking and her love of sharing it, often with crowds of people, which she inspired in all her children; my own childhood in Africa and Asia, which opened up my senses to a diversity of ingredients; and the seeds of Brindisa were all there.

Everything really began to crystalise when, after taking a degree in Spanish, Iberian and

Latin American Studies, I moved to Spain, where I taught English for three years and immersed myself totally in Spanish life. I was completely knocked out by the air-dried hams, sausages, cheeses, olives, anchovies and other foods, but above all, it was people's intrinsic understanding of food that was so mind-blowing. In the markets every Spanish housewife would know which of the mounds of exquisitely coloured dried beans were the best, which fish were the freshest of the catch, or which tomatoes the sweetest, whereas at that time back in England, people were buying ingredients because a celebrity cook said so, or because a magazine told them it would change their life. It wasn't part of the British culture to *know* and *feel* about food in the same way.

Spain on a Bantam 125

I had always felt the call of Spain, perhaps because my father had a yearning to be there and immerse himself in the language, the food and culture. Spain, post-war, was a country full of mystery and wildness, recovering from the experience of its own gruesome civil war, which was little understood by the rest of the world, and my father was fascinated by it all.

Dad had learned to speak Spanish when, during his military service, he had found himself convalescing from polio in a military hospital in Kuala Lumpur and, to while away the time, had asked for one of those old yellow and blue *Teach Yourself Spanish* books. After he returned to the UK in 1953 and went to read law at Oxford, he hankered to visit Spain, so on his first vacation the following year he borrowed a Bantam 125cc motorbike from a student friend and, with a small grant from the Oxford Society and little else, like Laurie Lee in his famous book *As I Walked Out One Midsummer Morning*, pointed the bike in the direction of San Sebastián. Imagine: all the way to the Basque coast!

From there, in the space of a month, he took in Salamanca, Ávila, Madrid, Valencia, Barcelona and Ripoll, sleeping under the stars or in hay lofts and empty barns wherever he met generous farmers in hospitable villages, and occasionally managing to afford a basic *pensión*. On his next university vacation he travelled to Andalucía by train, and in his final summer he found himself a job in Galicia teaching a nine-year-old boy English. In three summers he had covered almost all the regions of mainland Spain. Dad's stories of his adventures were full of the joy of discovering Spanish hospitality and companionship, the literature and the landscape, and his infectious enthusiasm rubbed off on the rest of the family. So it was probably inevitable that I and my brother, Mark, chose to study Spanish.

Food of the streets

After military service my father joined the Colonial Service – which is how I came to be born in Malawi. When independence came and my parents returned to the UK – by now with three children in tow – he flirted with the idea of the Spanish wine trade, but in the end he chose to work for a multinational company in Nigeria and then Brunei, where I was brought up, travelling back and forth to convent boarding school in Essex from the age of nine.

Even at an early age I understood that you learn about people and culture as much through the way they shop for food and cook and eat, as through their houses and history. Food is a language that illustrates a place, people, seasons and values better than anything else I know. I can still recall the intoxicating concoction of sights, smells and colours in the market of Lagos in Nigeria: a heady mix of street food, ripe tropical fruit and drains. I would eat paw paws and mangoes among the noisy chatter and bartering, surrounded by women with beautiful, block-printed Adire cloth wrapped around their hips and heads. African cloth has a unique smell that I can still find in the fabric shops of Brixton.

I loved the sweet, dense loaves at the bread stall, and once I sneaked around the back to watch the enormous baker working an old tin bath of dough. The buckets of sweat were running off his big, black, muscley body into the bath, and I thought half the bread that was baked from the dough must be made of him!

Once Dad was working in Brunei I couldn't wait to leave drab school meals behind for the school holidays, which meant wok-cooking in the markets: pak choy and grilled langoustines, delicate chicken satay, beef rendang, or *char kway teow* – spicy wide, flat noodles, with prawns, chicken, bean shoots and chives, which we often ate out of newspaper on the go, and which, I later discovered, makes an excellent hangover breakfast!

Lunch on a rubbish dump

One memory, from a few years later, really stands out, because it underlines for me the generosity of sharing food even in dire circumstances – something that underpins so many of the simple, sustaining dishes in this book, dishes that are born of the need to feed family and friends, even in hard times. As part of my university studies, my friend Annabel and I spent time at Lima's Católica University, then travelled around Peru and Ecuador, discovering yet another world of food and flavour. On a memorable Palm Sunday we were invited to family lunch with cousins in 'the country' by a local woman called Isabel and her daughters, who all looked like Diana Ross. Isabel first befriended us after we bought single cigarettes from her kiosk in Rimac, a suburb of Lima which at that time was known as *'un pueblo joven'*, a poetic way of describing a semi-slum.

We bumped along a dirt track, with stones bouncing through the holes in the floor of her old car, towards the beach and what looked like sand dunes stretching for miles, until we got closer and realised that they weren't dunes, but mountains of rubbish. These were the city rubbish dumps and the cousins lived in two brick houses in the middle of them, making their living *Slumdog Millionaire* style from selling whatever of value they could sift from each new batch. While the children were outside picking through the rubbish, looking for pieces of leather, metal, or whatever they could salvage, Annabel and I

were given seats at a canvas-covered table, and lunch of rice, avocado and steak: only us; no one else ate. Over 30 years later I still remember that food vividly, because every mouthful was intertwined with the local shapes, sounds and smells and the touching embarrassment of this lovely family going hungry themselves, while they cooked, waited on and welcomed guests they had never met before.

Costa Brava to Barcelona

Of all the places I have come to know in Spain, Catalunya is the most familiar and perhaps closest to my heart, since I lived there for three years and my brother lives there still. The land, the people I met and stayed with, and the places and producers I got to know, are all an integral part of why Brindisa happened in the first place.

The summer I finished my degree I had some time on my hands before starting a teaching course in Barcelona in the autumn, so I went with my parents for a holiday to the beautiful town of Begur on the Costa Brava. Because I spoke Spanish, I quickly made friends locally, and, though I had planned to move on and work as an au pair in Valencia, they said: 'You can't go – stay here!' One of the friends was Pepa Salvador, who gave me a job in her restaurant, La Salsita, despite the fact that I was very green, and my previous job experience was limited to working in a toy factory and helping with the hop and fruit harvests near my parents' home in Hampshire.

The dishes of the coast, with their natural emphasis on fish and seafood, tend to be more colourful than the typical sausage, bean and vegetable dishes of inland Catalunya, which taste delicious, but often look brown and dark; and Pepa always tried to make her dishes visually stunning. Favourites included her *gazpacho* and *suquet de peix* (the famous, glorious fish stew), along with *suquet de rascassa i congre* (made with potato, scorpion fish and crab). Hake would be served with bright parsley sauce, or monkfish would be pan-fried in butter with slices of apricot, roasted pine nuts and raisins.

There were stand-out meat dishes too, such as pork loin with prune sauce, and *conejo al 'jas'*, a juicy rabbit stew sweetened with carrots and tomatoes (see page 422).

I started work at La Salsita at six every evening and finished at around two in the morning. My job was to hand-write the menus, prepare the starters, serve the puddings and make coffees. We had a crazy mix of culture and dialect in the kitchen. Pepa's business partner, Marta Aramburu, was from Uruguay, and so we always had *matambre* on the menu, a Uruguayan dish of slices of beef, rolled up and stuffed with hearty local ingredients such as *chorizo*. There was an old lady who did the washing up and spoke in old Catalan, which at that time was almost unintelligible to me – and almost everyone else – and Jeti de Swart, who was the waitress and Catalan-Dutch. She and I shared lodgings in a little beach house. It was a memorable and hedonistic summer in this era of liberation after the Franco years, when good food, drink, freedom of expression and friendships without boundaries were all becoming central to life again and the people I knew were compellingly optimistic.

La Salsita also serviced a *chiringuito* (a little bar) on the beautiful Platja Fonda in Aiguablava, one of the wilder local beaches, which offered the usual snacks, such as *pan con tomate* (tomato bread), with ham, *chorizo* and cheese. The beach could only be reached by a long flight of steps down the cliff, so all the ingredients had to be taken around in a little speedboat by a wonderful, sadly late friend, Alex Veiga Sol, the dynamo of our group, who ran the *chiringuito* by day and helped in the restaurant at night.

At midnight at La Salsita the tables would ease off and we would serve ice creams and sorbets, drinks and coffees, usually to a bunch of our friends who would linger on in the bar's beautiful little stone courtyard. When we closed up, there was no thought of going to sleep. Instead we would all head for the nightclubs until about five in the morning, stagger back down to our little lodge on the beach and finally sleep

until midday. Then for myself and Jeti there would be a few hours in the sun and back up the hill to the restaurant again for work at six.

Sometimes after these crazy nights we would wind up breakfasting at Alex's *masia* (farmhouse) in Pals, watching the sun come up, or we would gather there for long Sunday lunches in the sunshine, sometimes twenty of us around the table. In between courses someone would inevitably break into song, because Alex's passion, other than the best food and wine, was serious flamenco music, and many of his friends were guitarists, singers and dancers.

Our impromptu get-togethers inspired him and his sister to set up a restaurant at the *masia*, where he built an outdoor terrace for musicians to play, while people danced. It was tough, though, to turn spontaneous good times into a business, and when Alex's ill-health took over it all ended in 1986. But the community of friends still gathers in his memory every Thursday at the house of one of the gang. I joined them recently at Pepa's home, where she prepared a nostalgic Salsita menu, which included her famous *conejo al 'jas'* (see page 422).

Finally, though, I had to leave the beach and head to Barcelona, where I trained to teach English as a foreign language. Fortunately many of my coastal friends were returning to the city too, so I shared a flat with some of them in a part of the city called Tres Torres, where one of the closest of the friends, Alex Sardà, ran the Dos Torres bar with its triangular garden of palms, cacti and bright flowers. Alex knew Barcelona intimately and introduced me to amazing late-night places to eat, to guitar bars and tapas bars such as El Xampanyet in the narrow stone streets of the old town, where they served such wonderful anchovies, and on Sundays he and I would seek out hillside places overlooking the city where the cooking and eating took place outside under the tall trees. He was one of seven children and his mother, Rosa, was always ready with weekday lunch for any or all of them, their families and friends – including myself and my brother, Mark, on a regular basis. Any time that you pitched up between 1 p.m. and 4 p.m. there would always be food for you. I still visit her, and nothing has changed.

Cottonwool city

Once I got my teaching qualification, I wanted to get out into the countryside. I was lucky in that one of my sister's friends lived in the same village as the former politician and writer Matthew Parris, whose mother, Terry, along with a local lady, ran the Anglo-Català School in Manlleu, north of the town of Vic, in inland Catalunya, approaching the Pyrenees. Both Terry's daughters, Debby and Belinda, were teachers there and expecting babies so they needed help at the school. When I arrived in Manlleu the whole family 'adopted' me. They were so kind, and I stayed at first with Debby and her husband Manel, a dairy farmer.

Manlleu sits in La Plana de Vic, an undulating plain that has a microclimate all of its own, and at certain times of the year it is enveloped in a mist so thick that Vic itself – the capital of the region – becomes like a cottonwool city, in which you can't see anything as you walk around. My friends elsewhere in Spain all talked about this mist, known as *la boira* – and either they had seen old Sherlock Holmes films and assumed I was used to a permanent and worse fog in London, or they would throw up their hands and say: '*La boira, la boira!* How can you live with this?' But it is *la boira* that is partly responsible for the special conditions in which it is possible to cure the very best *salchichón*, and while I was with Debby and Manel I learned how to make these traditional cured sausages.

Each year the family carried out the annual slaughtering of their pig in the winter months, and Manel's mother, Isabel, had the task of butchering the carcass on the large cellar table for the making of the year's supply of *salchichón de payés* (country sausages) and thin *fuets*. All hands were needed for the big task-list of chopping, piecing-up, mincing, salting and seasoning with black pepper, then stuffing the sausage casings and tying up the ends, while over the huge fire, a blackened pot, about 2 metres in diameter, bubbled away with the ingredients for the *morcilla* (see page 76).

Since I was the tallest, my job was to climb on to the high stool to hang the *salchichón* and *fuets* from the long nails which had been driven into the beams decades ago. I must have hung around eighty sausages that afternoon. How things have changed. Debby and Manel have since become vegetarians and animal rights activists campaigning against bullfighting. These days their only farm animals are rescued, and the house is free of milk and cheese as well as meat.

I couldn't live with Debby and Manel for ever, so I moved out to the nearby village of Roda de Ter, to share a flat with one of my students, who was about the same age as me, Núria Mayans Pla. Although still so young, Núria had already been widowed for five years and still wore her widow's black on Sundays. She was working as a seamstress, making clothes for designer shops, and had never held dinner parties before – at the time it wasn't a very Spanish thing to do – but I had so many friends and family members visiting that she began to rediscover the fun-loving person she used to be, as we cooked and entertained constantly.

On Sundays we would go to the family house where her mother, María, would cook lunch for us, along with Núria's sister Rosa, and brother Josep, who worked the nightshift in the local slaughterhouse. I was considered one of the family, and I have never forgotten the way María included me in these wonderful meals. There would be plates of cold grilled vegetables, dressed in vinegar and oil, then a big dish which would reflect the season. My favourites included chicken with wild mushrooms (see page 414) and duck with local wild pears (see page 420), which would take her two days to prepare.

In all I spent three years living and working in Catalunya, sharing meals and cooking with inspirational friends. Then, when my parents eventually returned to Hampshire, after living in Africa and Asia, I decided it was time to come home too. So in 1986 I came back with a vague, idealistic idea of introducing people to the wonderful diversity of foods I had discovered on my travels, some of which had never been seen in Britain before, and telling the stories of the artisans who produced them.

Small beginnings

In an odd twist of timing, I came home just as my brother, Mark, having spent a couple of years climbing the City ladder, decided that he wanted to jump off and set up his own business in Barcelona, which he was certain was the liveliest and fastest up-and-coming city in Europe.

For four decades, under General Franco, Spain had been cut off from trade with the rest of the world, but since he had died in 1975 there was a huge sense of possibility and, little by little, produce from abroad, such as basmati rice, began appearing in shops for the first time. Mark saw a great opportunity to introduce high-quality, traditional British foods such as Scottish salmon, Stilton cheese and English biscuits to good food shops in Barcelona. The licensing for the Stilton, in particular, was very complicated, as Spain was not yet a member of the EU. Mark might order 200 kilos of cheese and apply for a licence for it, and then the Spanish authorities would come back with permission for only 30 kilos, so I would help him sort through the bureaucracy – though not always successfully.

Franco had industrialised, standardised and compartmentalised the production of certain foods such as pork and wheat with a view to higher yields. But now an idealistic 'neo-rural' movement of sons and daughters of farmers, who had left the land and taken city jobs, were taking their commercial skills back to the countryside, setting up small businesses, growing organic vegetables, making raw milk cheeses and rediscovering local grape varieties for unusual wines. So after a year of importing British foods to Spain, Mark realised he could also send some of this produce to Britain, and we agreed to set up a company together. First he found a supplier

of table Rioja, the first pallets of which I stored in the garage of my parents' home in Hampshire, and I began selling the wine in London. Then he met one of the first Spanish suppliers to select traditional artisan cheeses from around Spain. He was able to gather together cheeses from six different regions, including Idiazábal, made with sheep's milk in the Basque country; Menorcan Mahón, from cow's milk; and a goat's milk cheese from Trujillo, Extremadura. On a memorable night in London, Mark, my sister Michele and I devoured an entire box of these cheeses, along with the Spanish wine, and we were thrilled at the excellence of what we were tasting. But who would I sell these hitherto unknown cheeses to?

My first port of call was Products from Spain, then in Charlotte Street, a company which had been importing Spanish foods since 1950. I asked the sons of the founders, George and Robert López, if they would be interested in buying some artisan cheeses, since they only sold Manchegos and blended cheeses, and they said yes. My first order. So in 1989 I invested around £800 in cheese and my father helped me with the weighing for my first despatch. It was the widest range of Spanish cheese ever seen on British soil.

A cheese in a tin

My next order, the one that really crystallised in my mind what Brindisa should stand for, was my first raw sheep's milk Castellano cheese, similar to a Manchego, but made in the north with a different milk, and matured in olive oil. I discovered it in among some bottles of Ribera del Duero wine on a stand at a trade fair in London. It was made by Ambrosio Molinos in Burgos, in the middle of Castilla y León. Ambro was a discerning cheese-maker and a ball of fun, who has become a lifelong friend.

Small-scale sheep farming was nothing new to me. Dad had always hankered after being a farmer and when we settled back in England my parents bought a house with four or five acres and started buying traditional breeds. So for 15–20 years we ate all our own lamb, and occasionally supplied mutton to friends. The whole family was involved in the lambing and sometimes if it snowed, we would bottle-feed newborns next to the Aga in the kitchen if they caught a chill. The idea of making cheese from sheep's milk, however, was considered quite an unusual thing in Britain. I am sure that when people first began buying Pecorino they were unaware that it was made with milk from sheep, and not cows. So it was of great interest to me to realise that in most areas of Spain and the islands, traditional breeds were valued as much for their milk and cheese as for their meat.

From the moment I first visited Ambro, his family and his herd of 100 per cent Churra sheep (see page 154) at his farmhouse, with its beautiful barns and carved feeding troughs – such workmanship – I was bowled over. The Churra sheep are the prettiest creatures: white, with black-tipped ears, eyes and hooves, and I felt so at home among the animals and in the maturing cave, with its eating space and chimney. Ambro would grill unweaned Churra lamb chops over vine prunings and pour red wine. Right from the start, I realised that one of the principles of Brindisa must be to do its utmost to help keep such small rural businesses alive and thriving.

Ambro's cheese was stunning – creamy with hints of toasted caramel and almond, with a long elegant finish – and it came in a simple but beautiful tin which specified that it was made with the milk of Churra sheep. Even now people remember it; it took on an almost mythical status because it was such a novelty at a time when virtually no one had seen Spanish raw milk cheese, let alone one from a specific breed of sheep – and in a tin, too. Buying that cheese was one of those strokes of luck that can put you on the map. I knew it was something extraordinary, and with the arrogance of youth I boldly rang up some of the innovative, creative chefs who were making their mark at the time, such as Alastair Little, Simon Hopkinson at Bibendum, and Rowley Leigh at Kensington Place, to ask if they would be interested in tasting it, and they all bought it.

I really didn't have any money but I was quite fearless. My parents, who had been our first customers, emotional backers and common-sense advisers, continued to offer storage and office help, but the boxes of cheese were now way too big for a domestic fridge, and what I needed was some proper, free warehousing. So I asked the local milkman if he had any space in his fridge that I could use for a few months, while I worked out what to do next. Amazingly, he obliged. It could only be a short-term solution, of course, because all my clients were in London, but then came my next stroke of luck.

Flicking through a magazine I spotted a photograph of a chap in a smart Burberry suit in his London loft. The caption read, 'Michael Day, director of the Huge Cheese Company, London'. Michael was very well connected and supplied most of the restaurants in London, so I called him up, told him my story and said, 'Would you look after my cheese?' He said yes, and so I had my first base in London. I used to go out at 6.30 in the morning with his van and visit the chefs in their kitchens, telling them about my cheeses.

By now I was sleeping and working in the living room of the flat that I shared with my two sisters in Maida Vale, and taking orders from chefs like Mark Hix at 2 a.m. but I still had no proper commercial base.

Fortunately, two friends, Vicky Fuller and Robert Lyle, who had an office in Tite Street, SW3, offered to field calls and type letters. My brother, Mark, continued to invest in our big idea, but I needed a working partner, and by chance I bumped into Emma Ranson, another old friend who had been born in the same hospital as me in Malawi. We had known each other as teenagers in West Africa, and again at university. Emma spoke Spanish and had just returned to London after working in Madrid. She was game to join me, and together we worked like Trojans, badgering chefs and shops all over the country, and commuting between London and Spain.

From cheese we began importing peppers, anchovies, vinegars and olive oils, cured meats, sausages and turrón from producers whose foods we tasted at fairs and markets, or spotted in good food shops in Madrid and Barcelona, forging relationships with farmers, cheese-makers and artisans which remain firm to this day.

Space-hopping

Back in London, Emma and I constantly moved from space to space, as our needs grew. First we found a corner of a warehouse in Bermondsey (just a stairwell and a fridge, really), then a funny little triangular-shaped building in Crouch End that one customer said was just like a wedge of cheese. We shared it with a French food importer, and the snails that he housed in nets would often escape and leave glistening trails all over our beautiful bottles of estate olive oil. There was no heating and it was so cold in winter we wrapped ourselves in blankets and wore thick socks and woolly hats. At lunchtime the guys in what was Florians restaurant opposite would sit us down next to heaters and thaw us out with big bowls of soup. Then we moved to Bankside, and finally to Park Street in Borough Market. I was still selling mainly to chefs such as Steve Carter and Richard Corrigan, who were working with Stephen Bull at his bistro in Blandford Street and his restaurant, Fulham Road, respectively. They were among the first to start serving *chorizo* and carving cured Serrano hams in front of customers and, as the fashion grew for chefs to source really good olive oils, Richard, especially, was something of a pioneer. He and Steve loved the Arbequina oil from Tarragona, with its tropical banana taste.

Next I targeted R. García & Sons, on Portobello Road, where Rafael García told me he was only interested in Spanish staples, and that the artisan and farmhouse speciality products I was offering – goat's cheese in olive oil, fruit wheels, estate oils, etc. – were far too expensive, and his customers would never buy them. It took two years of me visiting the shop every few months, begging him to give in and allow me to feature some of the produce in his window on a strictly sale or return basis, before he relented. Within days he rang me up asking for more, and became one of our best customers.

Borough beginnings

It is hard to imagine now, when Borough Market and its surrounding shops and restaurants are a bustling, colourful, eclectic magnet for food lovers, but in 1992, when we moved into a warehouse around the corner in Park Street, this was a desolate area, a forgotten island in a big city, with tumbleweed and many empty cages inside the market gates. So much so that I felt unsafe walking to the tube station at night.

Gradually, though, things began to change, and on Saturdays we opened up the doors of the warehouse to friends, family and anyone who had shown interest in our foods over the years, to come and taste. Scott Boden, who during the nineties was Brindisa's finance director and business partner, set up a barbecue outside, grilling mini *chorizos* and spearing them with cocktail sticks for people to dip into bowls of *Romesco* sauce, and before long the word had spread and people were travelling across London, attracted by an event that only a few people knew about, and going home with whole cheeses, trays of jarred *sofrito* (see page 316) and 5-litre cans of olive oil.

Next, along with Neal's Yard Dairy and Turnips vegetables, we took an extra retail and storage space in the market itself, and in 1998 the food writer Henrietta Green held her first Food Lovers' Fair there, the success of which convinced the trustees to regenerate the place. It was all new and very exciting. Our cage was right in the centre of the market, and as well as cheese, cured meats, tinned fish and oils, we began selling homemade strings of dried *ñora* and *guindilla* peppers, and bouquet garnis known as *farcellets* – these were things unseen in a British market, and turned out to be so popular that friends all knuckled down and made hundreds of them by hand. You could visit any one of their homes and find dried peppers and *farcellet* strings hanging everywhere.

From the stall we opened the Borough Market shop on a corner of the market; we also moved our wholesale and logistics operation to a warehouse in Balham and, finally, launched the tapas bars and restaurants – the opening of the first of which was a mammoth moment for all of us. After over 15 years of importing the best Spanish food we could find, I wanted a showcase for it. I had dreamed of bringing these wonderful hams, sausages, cheeses, olives and conserved fish together on plates for customers to relax and enjoy, along with authentic Spanish cooking and a glass of fine Spanish sherry or wine. At first I was fearful of moving from warehouse to table, but our long-term friend, Mark Hix, came to see the space in Southwark Street, and at once we visualised a tapas bar there. He put me in touch with his then-colleague at Caprice Holdings, Ratnesh Bagdai, who had years of experience in setting up restaurants, and with him on board, I found the courage to press on.

And so suddenly in October 2004 it all came together. I had a team of chefs, led by José Pizarro, who was then cooking at the Eyre Brothers restaurant and was a long-time customer of Brindisa. He was looking for a new chapter in his life and from day one we were full. Since then we have opened more restaurants and bars, even in Barcelona, and from the beginning I loved the energy of them, and the feeling that even though it might be a big red London bus that passes the windows, people can enjoy the true food of Spain in its proper context.

The never-ending journey

All of us at Brindisa are still constantly learning. You can never sit back and think you have got there. There is always more to discover or improve, and the excitement of both is intoxicating. My own journey has been a series of light-bulb moments, of discovering that, in the hands of skilled and passionate producers, ingredients we are so familiar with, like anchovies or olives, are capable of being elevated to new levels of excellence and sometimes quite

extraordinary heights. And I never stop being struck by the deep culture of respecting food and tasting and identifying flavours that is ingrained in families who have passed their extraordinary skills down through the generations. The last time I visited our honey supplier, Ferran Alemany, and his family in the hills of Lleida outside Barcelona, some of the young children of the honey packers arrived home from school. When they saw that a new batch of the great drums of honey had arrived, they were so excited they ran over, threw off the lids, peered in and tasted some from each barrel with little spoons, saying: 'Hey, the orange blossom is tasting good.' It was stunning to realise that they could recognise immediately which honey was which, and I was reminded how close people in the Spanish countryside, particularly, are to the source of their food, when sometimes our supermarket culture can make us feel quite distant and removed.

I like to think that by supporting such dedicated smallholders and artisans we play a small part in helping to preserve traditions, jobs, rural environments and ecosystems that might otherwise be lost or abandoned.

Recently my husband, Rupert, and I went to Zamora, to see a cheese-maker friend, Sarah Groves-Raines, who is married to a Basque wine-maker, Patxi, and makes her cheese in the smallest of dairies near the Portuguese border. The tiny place where they live is almost like an African village, with the houses camouflaged under the rock, and the heat in summer is almost as intense. As we arrived an old woman in a heavy skirt and wellington boots was sweeping her yard with a branch of broom shrub; and there was a little store with a formica counter and a wood-burning stove where you could warm yourself when the temperature dropped in winter, and buy everything from matches to sardines. The scene reminded me of my grandpa Opa's stories and how the seeds of the Brindisa journey were sown all those years ago. Of course, I never saw Opa's store in Kota Kota, but this was just the way I had always imagined it to be.

A Way
of Eating

I think there is often a misconception about what Spanish food is all about. People have an image of dishes full of vivid, hot colours and fiery spices. But this isn't the everyday reality in Spain, any more than flamenco dancing.

In fact, many traditional recipes can seem very plain to the modern multicultural British palate, and the use of seasoning, spicing and decoration tends to be quite restrained, mainly because the emphasis is on using full-flavoured ingredients, from local vegetables to seafood, wild game, new season pulses, and hams and sausages made from specific breeds, and letting them stand up for themselves without the need for the condiments we use so freely in the UK.

Spain is evolving, like most European countries, and supermarkets have infiltrated the towns and cities, but I don't believe that its food and producer markets will ever be replaced. Where supermarkets exist in smaller towns or villages, especially, they frequently sell local breads and regional specialities and often avoid selling meat, so as not to compete with the independent butchers.

Changing times and work patterns have inevitably impinged on traditional meals, as they have all over Europe. Years ago when I first lived in Spain I would have laughed at the idea of people snacking on the run, and I still find it odd to see a British-style sliced white sandwich encased in a plastic triangle in a Spanish shop – but neither would I have imagined British families holding tapas parties. That said, even though there is no rule book, in general the Spanish still have their own way and pace of eating, since the working day typically starts at 8 a.m. (much earlier in farming communities), stops at 2 p.m. for a two-hour lunch, and finishes at around 7–8 p.m.

This means that *desayuno* (breakfast) and/or the mid-morning snack are still very important meals in Spain, whether they involve coffee or hot chocolate, *churros* or pastries, or a hearty sustaining farm-worker's meal. I've eaten silky bacon from acorn-fed Ibérico pigs in the forests of the Dehesa, tucked into chunks of country bread, cured meats and red wine with smallholders on perishingly cold hilltops, and eaten porridge made from *gofio* (toasted grain flour) with cheese-makers in the sunshine of the Canary Islands. On our numerous visits to the olive mills of Núñez de Prado and Olivar de la Luna in Córdoba in Andalucía, we have been treated to the typical mid-morning feast of warm farmhouse bread from the wood-burning oven, sun-ripened tomatoes and oranges dressed with freshly pressed olive oil and honey, cracked green Manzanilla olives, eggs from the local farm, ham, cheese, oven-baked salt cod and sauté potatoes. And in Catalunya I have breakfasted with dairy farmers on runny, creamy yogurts made from goat's and sheep's milk, and sheep's milk junket (*cuajada de leche de oveja*), similar to Italian *panna cotta*, but made with whole milk set with rennet and eaten with fresh fruit and honey, sometimes pine nuts.

Then there is often the pre-lunch *vermut* or *aperitivo*, a well established indulgence which involves popping into a local bar for a vermouth and perhaps a tin of cockles, before the main meal of the day.

However, the meal that is almost sacrosanct in Spain is lunch. I would be devastated if the Spanish lost their desire to lunch in a spectacularly slow and generous way. In England this indulgence is usually relegated to Sundays. But in Spain, on any day of the week, it is so enjoyable to feel no guilt about taking more than an hour's break from work and to allow yourself to relax over good food and conversation. It might be a simple meal in a local restaurant – often a plate of vegetables or lentils, followed by grilled fish or meat: steaks or chops and a salad – or a visit to the family home where a mother or grandmother would have lunch prepared. In small towns and villages, especially, the whole week's lunches are often mapped out in a time-honoured pattern. Monday might be *croquetas* or *canelones* using up leftovers from the big Sunday meal, then there might be a stew day, often involving beans or pulses; a rice day, a fresh fish day, a meat day, and a salt cod day, depending on the locality and markets.

Since during the week the evening meal is usually just a light supper, children coming home from school love and need *merienda* (tea) at 5–6 p.m. It could be a wedge of bread, dredged with olive oil and a sprinkling of sugar, María biscuits with a slice of *membrillo* (quince paste) inside, or a square of cake. Many of the recipes that are popular for *desayuno* can also double up as *merienda*.

Of course, the aspect of Spanish eating and drinking that has truly caught the imagination all over the world is the tradition of tapas. In the towns and cities, workers typically drop into a bar for a beer or sherry and a series of small snacks at the end of the working day. Then they will go home for something simple like soup, salad – perhaps with tinned fish or seafood – or small fresh fish or cuts of meat popped on the *plancha* (hotplate or grill). Or mothers and grandmothers might make big *tortillas* (see page 160), *empanadas* (see page 400) or savoury *coques* (see page 70) so that everyone can help themselves to a slice.

Sundays are the days when families and friends gather together for big meals: usually a series of tapa-like small plates, followed by shared casseroles, rice dishes or roasted meats. Sometimes it will be a family effort of home cooking, at other times everyone will gather in a favourite restaurant. In the villages in mountainous regions, families will often have converted ancient caves into weekend and holiday dens where they set up tables and chairs, wine stores and grills for barbecuing.

ROOTS AND REGIONS

Many of the ingredients we consider to be cornerstones of Spanish eating were originally introduced by the people who settled there over the centuries. The Romans, who arrived in 218 BC, brought olives and grapes; and the Moors, who invaded in 711 AD, introduced almonds, saffron and other spices and herbs, such as cumin and coriander.

Religion played its part, too. In 1492, when the Jewish people were expelled from Spain and the Moorish people faced persecution, one of the ways that Christians demonstrated their faith was by the conspicuous consumption of pork, a food culture that has embedded itself ever since. And Catholicism gave rise to Lenten recipes involving much salted fish and other suitable foods during days of abstinence, as well as celebratory Easter dishes.

The sixteenth century saw another major sea change in the flavours and colours of Spanish food when tomatoes, potatoes, chocolate and, importantly, peppers – which eventually came to be dried and ground to make *pimentón* (paprika) – were first brought back by explorers from the New World.

Some of the foods and recipes from the north of Spain have a noticeably French or Italian feel to them, as at one time Catalunya stretched into France as well as Italy, so inevitably there were crossovers of influences, techniques and ingredients; so, for example, while the cooking of the Mediterranean usually involves olive oil, in the north you often see the use of local butter and cream.

Closer to current times, people still have vivid memories of the hunger and poverty after the civil war, and many recipes that make good use of basic ingredients, such as bread, potatoes, milk, olive oil and garlic, date from this time when nothing could be wasted.

Before improved transport and refrigeration enabled ingredients to be distributed all around the country, typical dishes were necessarily local, developed around whatever was able to be grown, farmed or fished – and those traditions still shape the cooking in each region, city, town, village and family.

The great Catalan journalist and writer Josep Pla observed: *'La cocina de un país es su paisaje puesto en la cazuela'* – 'the cooking of a country is its own landscape put into a cooking pot' – and the regional foods and dishes of Spain still reflect a whole gamut of different landscapes and microclimates from the Atlantic to the Mediterranean, from hot, dry and dusty to rich, green and fertile, from sun-drenched beach to cold and remote mountain, cut with icy rivers, sometimes so remote that the night sky is absolutely pure, with no unnatural light.

And in some regions, such as Castilla y León, the biggest in Spain, there is something of everything, which is why it has been one of the greatest sources of ingredients for Brindisa. It is hard to imagine anything that you can't find in this vast area, which covers the wild forest of Palencia, verdant valleys such as that of the Tiétar river; open country; and mountains, including parts of the Picos de Europa range, the Sierra de Francia and the Sierra de Gredos, where eagles, owls, black vultures and peregrine falcons fly and the climate is harsh: biting winds and cold temperatures for about eight months of the year and baking, suffocating heat for the rest of the time. But the drying winds and high altitude have always been perfect for the slow curing of meats – though changing weather patterns are beginning to confuse things, making it harder to cure foods naturally.

Since the region is also blessed with seasonal rain, the rich pastures, where goats and sheep and cows graze, help to create the best milk for some famous cheeses such as the goat's milk Monte Enebro, sheep's milk Zamorano and Castellano, and blue cow's milk Valdeón. The meadowland, watered by springs and dried by the winds, is also perfect for growing legumes, particularly the maroony-coppery-coloured *alubia de Ibeas*, the typical bean used for *olla podrida*, a hearty stew originally made with any meat that could be had. And in El Bierzo, the area to the south of the Picos and bordering Galicia, with its high altitude and fertile river valleys, the red peppers and vine-ripened tomatoes are exceptionally concentrated in flavour and colour.

THE ISLANDS

Both the Balearic and Canary Islands lend a different perspective to Spanish food and since as a family we visit them often, the foods of the islands feature throughout this book.

Mallorca, in particular, is an island of huge contrasts between luxurious converted farmhouses owned by wealthy people from Madrid and abroad, and smallholdings where a few fruit trees or beehives might be kept to make jam or honey, or small groves of fig, almond, chestnut or olive trees can be harvested for local sale and subsistence. Often small farms will be high up in the mountains in stunning but rough terrain, where families live so remotely that they struggle even to get enough water without bringing it in by mule. Most jobs are done manually and sometimes old traditional stones are still used for milling corn. Visiting producers in these unspoilt pockets in the warm sun, with the eagles circling above, is always magical, but then I am not bound to make a living in such challenging circumstances.

Menorca, home of Mahón or Maó cheese (see page 530), is the island I know best, and I have included many of my favourite local recipes: the *ensaimadas* I love to have with a mid-morning coffee (see page 48), *banyetas* made with *sobrasada* (spreadable spicy sausage similar to the Italian *nduja*), *flaons* (cheese puffs, see page 25), *pastissets* (crumbly biscuits, see page 38), the simplest of tomato soups, *oliaigua* (see page 153), and *perol de cordero*: oven-baked lamb with tomatoes and potatoes (see page 436).

By contrast, even though they belong to Spain, the Canary Islands are an intoxicating mix of Africa, the Americas and Europe. La Palma is home to the biggest cheese in all of Spain, Palmero (see page 531), as well as to the salt pans of Fuencaliente on the southernmost tip of the island, where the salt from the sea is evaporated through a series of ponds, and finally piled into pyramids of beautiful pure crystals ready to be sold to shops throughout the islands. In the brightly coloured food markets there are stalls full of avocados and papayas, mangoes, *duraznos* (peaches) and *cherimoya*, dried peppers and dried herbs and plants that are used for teas and herbal remedies. *Cola de caballo* (horsetail) – a long, hairy plant that pre-dates the dinosaurs – is one of the best known for making into a tea or infusion, said to help ease stomach ache. At the fish stalls the evocative names on the labels next to the varieties are often completely different from those you find on the mainland. *Lenguado sahariano*, for example, means Saharan sole –the idea of a desert fish might sound odd, but since the Canaries are closer to Africa than Spain, it makes some kind of sense!

Canarian bananas were the first to be exported to Britain, which is why the quay and warehouse where they unloaded at West India Docks was given the name Canary Wharf. There are a number of varieties that are grown, and the smoothies and juices that you can make from them are irresistible. Green bananas (*polines*) are often boiled, mixed with potato and then eaten with green coriander *mojo* (the famous pesto-like sauce made with herbs, spices and sometimes hot peppers, pounded together with oil, see page 298); or they might be fried to eat with the local dish of *Arroz cubano*: rice, tomato *sofrito* (see page 318) and fried egg.

Although a typical Canarian meal will inevitably include a red or green *mojo,* usually served with fish, potatoes or grilled cheese, in the winter parts of the island can be very cold, and rural work needs sustaining food. So as well as sunshine food there are also hearty soups such as *potaje de berros,* made with beans, potatoes and watercress (see page 222), and stews such as *rancho canario.* Typically they will be made with vegetables like *choclos* (maize cobs), peppers and cabbage, perhaps with some salted pork ribs added and enriched with starchy vegetables, such as potato, pumpkin, *bubango* (a pale green, spotted courgette) and green bananas, or bulked out with pieces of *fideo* (pasta, see page 366). And whereas in mainland Spain such big meals are usually eaten at lunchtime, in the Canaries people often eat these slowly-cooked one-pot dishes for dinner to warm them before going to bed.

RECIPE COLLECTING

The recipe-gathering for this book has frequently provoked passionate arguments between friends, cooks and chefs from different regions, towns and villages, all insisting their own version of a particular dish is the one and only, which just underlines how much, even today, Spanish cooking is influenced by both history and geography.

Many of the recipes have been given to me by long-standing friends who have cooked them for their families all their lives but in most cases never written them down before. Others are dishes introduced by our Spanish chefs to the Brindisa restaurants and tapas bars in London.

As for me, I am not a chef, but an avid cook who has grown up with the love of feeding and gathering family and friends around the table that my mother inspired in all her children, and during the writing of this book our kitchen at home has been full of Spanish friends and chefs, helping to test and tweak favourite recipes – some new, some old.

Brindisa is all about the best produce that Spain can offer, and ultimately that is what I wanted the recipes to celebrate, so I have also included a handful of recipes from the close circle of leading non-Spanish chefs, like Sam and Samantha Clark, Fergus Henderson, Mark Hix, Peter Gordon and Jeremy Lee, who have supported me since the crazy early days, accompanying me and my colleagues on memorable trips to Spanish farms, vineyards and olive groves, and becoming firm bean, *chorizo*, Ibérico ham or anchovy 'friends'.

They haven't necessarily used these ingredients in Spanish-style dishes on their menus, but they have chosen to showcase them in their own way, not only because they love the quality and flavour, but, in common with everyone at Brindisa, they have a great respect for the care, skills and heritage that have gone into the production of beautiful food.

DESAYUNO Y MERIENDAS

Breakfast and
afternoon snacks

Among all the pleasures of eating in Spain, the many snacks of doughnuts, small cakes, pastries and biscuits that are popular in the morning (*desayuno*) or afternoon (*merienda*) are some of the greatest for me. I love them so much that I really have to hold back, otherwise I could happily munch my way through a mound of buns and pastries with a coffee or hot chocolate – possibly because although most of these snacks are sweet (though I have included some savoury recipes too), they tend not to be overly sugary, with their sweetness typically coming from the dough or sponge, rather than elaborate icing or pastry cream. Even so, mindful of the concern over eating too much sugar in the UK, I have often asked Spanish friends whether they would think of adapting a recipe to include less, but their answer is absolutely not, as a certain ratio of ingredients is needed to produce the right result. And since, in general, the Spanish still cook far more with fresh ingredients, rather than buying sugar-heavy processed food, a sweet mid-morning bun or pastry is considered much less of an issue.

Mallorcan *ensaimadas*, silky, soft coils of dough (see page 48), are my absolute favourite treat, although *churros,* the long, ridged, deep-fried doughnuts that originated in Madrid, are probably the most famous (see page 28) and other regions have their own versions, from the halo-shaped Manchegan *rosquillas* to the little round Catalan *buñuelos* (see page 27).

In Seville *desayuno* might be coffee accompanied by a *torta de aceite* – one of the famous thin round biscuits, made with extra virgin olive oil and a hint of anise, shaped by hand so each one is slightly different, and individually wrapped in waxy paper. And everyone I know who has moved to the UK from Cantabria, in the north of Spain, pines for the speciality sponge and cheese cakes of the region that are sold in every baker's shop for *desayuno* or *merienda*. Cantabria really is the land of milk and butter, where herds of dairy cattle feed on the lush pastures, and the people all seem to have rosy cheeks, smiles and a contented, well-nourished look about them. Some of the most appealing cakes are *sobaos*: charming, deep yellow, buttery sponge oblongs with toasted orange-coloured tops that sit glistening in their waxed white paper origami cases in the bakers' shops.

In the Balearic Islands, in particular, many people celebrate afternoon teatime in a similar way to the British tradition, since the British occupied the islands in the eighteenth century. Whenever we visit our cheese suppliers and *afinadores* (maturers), Nicolás Cardona Enrich and Rosa Gornés Vinent, on a family holiday we are always treated to an indulgent late-afternoon array of goodies at La Palma, their country farmstead. Inevitably this will include flower-shaped *pastissets* (see page 38) and star-shaped *flaons crespells*, mellow cheesy 'buns' that are a little reminiscent of cheese scones, but involve yeasty pastry pressed around balls of cheese mixed with egg and olive oil. Traditionally they were made for Christmas, Carnival, Easter and local festivals, but nowadays many bakeries offer them every day. Rosa and her mother make their own with young Mahón cheese in a quite elaborate process, which involves putting it through an old-fashioned nut grinder to grate it into loose 'crumbs' the night before baking so that it dries out a little. When the puffy golden- brown *flaons* emerge from the oven the cheesy filling has risen up through crosses in the pastry lids, giving a volcano effect, and they are delicious eaten warm, especially drizzled with a little honey.

DULCES

Sweet snacks

Buñuelos de Viento
Sugared brioche fritters

You will find variations of *buñuelos* all over Spain: doughnuts about the size of a new potato. In the Empordà area of Catalunya, they are typically rolled in sugar and anisette (anise liqueur) and are also known as Lenten doughnuts. Eggs were banned during Lent in the Middle Ages, but when they later became permitted, the doughnuts were traditionally made in the run-up to Easter. In Valencia similar *buñuelos* are made with pumpkin added to the dough.

These are the ones favoured by the family of our head chef at Brindisa, Leo Rivera, and I love them, as they are much lighter than most: beautiful airy little fritters, crispy on the outside and hollow inside; so light in fact that their name translates as 'puffs of wind'. Leo rather sweetly calls them 'intelligent' because they flip themselves over in the hot oil as they fry so that they become golden brown all over.

Makes enough for a big plateful (around 30) of bite-sized puffs

250ml milk or water
100g butter
150g plain flour
approx 4 eggs
caster sugar, for coating
vegetable oil, for deep-frying

Bring the milk (or water) and the butter to the boil, then take the pan off the heat, add all the flour at once and work into a soft dough with a spatula, until the mixture comes away from the sides of the pan. Put back on a low heat for about 2 minutes, stirring to keep the mixture moving around. Take off the heat, then add the eggs one at a time, working them in with a whisk. Don't add the next egg until the previous one is completely absorbed into the dough. Four eggs is usually enough, but you may need 1 or 2 more to give you a loose mixture (similar to that of a sponge cake).

Have ready plenty of caster sugar in a shallow bowl.

Pour some vegetable oil into a deep pan – it should not come more than a third of the way up – then heat to 170ºC (or, if you don't have a thermometer, test by dropping in a little of the mixture – it should sizzle). Taking 2 lightly oiled teaspoons, make 'quenelles' by scooping some of the mixture on to 1 spoon, then on to the other so that the mixture is smooth and egg-shaped, then use one of the spoons to ease the mixture from the other into the hot oil. Repeat, frying in batches, so that the mixture doesn't lower the temperature of the oil.

As the *buñuelos* fry, they puff up to double their size, and as if by magic they do a little somersault in the oil, thanks to the expansion of air inside. As soon as they are golden brown all over, lift them out carefully and dip them straight into the bowl of sugar, coating them well.

Churros
Long fritters

One of my most memorable *churros* experiences was in the walled town of Benavente in Castilla y León, where Rupert and I were staying one New Year. It is an area that often gets neglected by visitors, as it is so isolated, with its quite stark, flat meadowland, dotted with round *palomares* (dovecotes): squat, circular houses, with red-tiled roofs and portholes around the top. When we woke up on New Year's Day the temperature had dropped to sub-zero and the mist had come down so thickly we could only see a few metres ahead of us, but we headed for the only bar that was open. It was a perfect old-fashioned snug, lined with dark brown wood, a cross between an Irish bar and a Rennie Mackintosh café from the 1890s, where they were serving steaming hot chocolate that was thick and beautiful, perfect for dunking the sugary *churros*.

Originally these little ridged tubes of doughnut were a speciality of Madrid cafés and specialist *churro* bars. Here, big circles of batter are extruded into hot oil through a metal pipe, using a revolving handle, and deep-fried until crispy, then they are cut into lengths and sprinkled with sugar. They do a roaring trade in the early hours, satisfying the all-night clubbers' need for a surge of sugar and oil on their way home, before gearing up for office workers, mothers and children buying their *churros* on the way to school, then the mid-morning wave of people coming in for a snack.

Though *churros* are an irresistible café and street snack, they are rarely made at home, since the batter is quite solid and hard to push out into tubes thick enough to sizzle for a while in the oil without burning. Some committed mothers do make their own, and this recipe is from the mum of our head chef Leo Rivera. He says that when he was growing up she would spoon the *churro* mixture into a funnel, holding her finger over the narrow opening and then releasing it when she wanted the mixture to flow into the hot oil – that is real dedication.

At a push, you could use a piping bag with a wide, ridged nozzle (about the size of a £1 coin), but to be honest, it is very hard work, and you are better off buying a dedicated *churrera*. These are similar to the kind of pumps sometimes used for piping icing, and you can find them in some kitchen shops and online. If you prefer an easier, oil-free alternative, try the baked *melindros* (opposite).

Makes about 6 coils

around 100g caster sugar for finishing, mixed with a little ground cinnamon (about a heaped teaspoon), if you like
½ teaspoon salt
a strip of lemon peel
about 2.5cm of a vanilla pod
25g butter
250g plain flour
1 teaspoon bicarbonate of soda
500ml sunflower oil, for deep-frying

Have ready a big plate of caster sugar (and cinnamon, if using).

Pour 500ml of water into a pan with the salt, lemon peel, vanilla pod and butter and heat until the water starts to break into a boil. Take out the lemon peel and the vanilla, take the pan off the heat, add the flour and bicarbonate of soda all in one go, and whisk it in as fast as you can until you have a smooth paste. The heat in the pan will cook the flour a little.

Spoon the mixture into a *churrera* or piping bag.

Pour the sunflower oil into a deep pan – it should not come more than a third of the way up – then heat to 180ºC (if you don't have a thermometer, test by dropping in a little of the mixture – it should sizzle gently).

Carefully pipe about a sixth of the *churro* mixture into the oil, forming it round and round in a big coil. Repeat this with the rest of the mixture.

There should be enough for about 6 coils, and depending on the size of your pan, you will probably need to fry them in batches. Fry each coil for around 2–3 minutes, until rich golden brown.

Lift out the *churro* coils, quickly cut them into lengths of about 10cm, then press each piece into the sugar so that it is well coated, turning it over to coat the other side. Serve with hot chocolate for dunking (see page 32).

Melindros
Catalan lady fingers

The first time I ate *melindros* was a great moment for me, as I had been looking for an alternative to *churros* that would be easier to make at home. And these are as simple as baking a tray of biscuits.

They are typical of Catalunya, where the pairing with hot chocolate is known as *melindros amb xocolata*. There is a café and chocolate shop in Barcelona called Cacao Sampaka, where they serve them in a very sweet way. They leave them attached to the strip of baking paper on which they were baked, which they roll up, so that when you unroll it you discover the *melindros* lined up like little soldiers inside.

This is another family recipe from Leo Rivera.

Makes 24–30

3 eggs, separated
125g caster sugar
125g plain flour
1 teaspoon baking powder
caster sugar, for dusting

Preheat the oven to 200°C/gas 6. Line a baking tray with greaseproof paper or use a silicone mat.

Whisk the egg yolks, adding half the sugar a little at a time, until double in volume.

In a separate bowl, whisk the egg whites until they form snowy peaks, then carefully fold in the rest of the sugar. Take half of this and mix into the yolk mixture. Combine the flour and baking powder and fold in, bit by bit, using a spatula.

Finally, fold in the rest of the whisked egg white, taking care not to over-mix, as you want the mixture to be as light as possible.

Spoon into a piping bag (we use a freezer bag with the corner cut off) with a nozzle about 1cm in diameter, and squeeze out lengths of the mixture (7–8cm long) on to the lined tray. Sprinkle well with caster sugar – you want this to form a crust – then put the tray into the preheated oven and bake for around 6–8 minutes, until light golden (the colour of a sponge finger). Don't over-bake, as the *melindros* need to be a little tender inside, like a macaroon. Try to wait for them to cool a little before you eat them!

CHOCOLATE A LA TAZA

'an agent of sorcerers'

Thick, dark and substantial, like a liquid mousse, Spanish chocolate is a world away from the rather tame milky drink we are more used to in the UK. It was first brought to Spain from Mexico in 1528 by the conquistadors, led by Hernán Cortés, much earlier than it appeared in northern Europe. At that time chocolate was always made into a drink, and while the northern Europeans later started adding milk to it, there was no tradition of milk in Spain, so the Spanish made their hot chocolate thick and dark like the Aztecs, simply by roasting the beans, grinding them coarsely and adding cornmeal and hot water and sometimes spices such as cinnamon and chilli. At first it was such an expensive luxury that the drink was reserved for the Spanish court and the political figures of power and wealth who were concentrated in central Castilla and Extremadura (the seat of the *Reyes Católicos*, the Catholic Kings).

It was prepared to secret recipes by monks (who later sometimes added sugar), despite the fact that the church denounced chocolate as an agent of sorcerers – an association with wickedness that it has never entirely lost, and which only increased its allure. In 1580 the first factories for grinding cocoa were set up, and by the seventeenth century Spain was monopolising cocoa production in Venezuela, and the drink became more widely available, though the

earliest commercial chocolate houses were naturally Castilian.

These days hot chocolate in Spanish cafés is more often made with milk, but it is headily rich and dark. There is a famous old bar in Barcelona, Granja M. Viader on Xuclà Street, one of the narrow little streets near the Boqueria market, where they have been serving hot chocolate in the same way for a century. *Granja* means dairy farm, and the café began as a milk shop back in 1870, with cows kept outside at the rear of the shop, which must have been quite a sight at a time when Barcelona was emerging as a busy new commercial and industrial city.

In the early twentieth century it was taken over by Marc Viader, the M. Viader in the 'farm's' name. He had a big family, and he and his sons and daughters started exploring and developing *derivados de leche*, different ways to consume milk and cream. So they began offering *mató* (fresh cheese), which they still serve with honey and almonds, as well as yogurt and, perhaps most famously, hot chocolate drinks. In 1931 they developed the chocolate drink Cacaolat, which is popular all over Spain.

People would stop and have breakfast or snacks in the little bar – apparently the likes of Picasso would drop in for a *xicra* (the old Catalan name for the measure, or special cup, used for hot chocolate). The place still has the same

marble tables, old tiles and fixtures, and of course hot dark chocolate and *suizos* (chocolate with whipped cream on top).

Real, traditional Spanish drinking chocolate can be wonderful, when made by serious makers of solid chocolate. The two examples that we chose for Brindisa are vastly different in terms of their background and approach, but they share a total commitment to quality and individualism. At one end of the spectrum are the traditional makers, the Sánchez García family from Navatejares, a municipality close to El Barco de Ávila in Castilla y León; and at the other, the modern artist, our good friend Enric Rovira, the chocolate 'sculptor' from Castellbell i el Vilar in Catalunya.

El Barco is a town that was well known to me from the very early Brindisa years, as I first travelled there to meet Julián Sánchez García, our supplier of beans (see page 386) – and ended up discovering that his family have been making sweets and chocolate since the end of the nineteenth century. Their business, which was officially founded in 1905 by Julián's great-grandfather, has evolved on the site of an old mill that was built at that time, with a wood-burning stove for roasting, and a series of wheels made with poles that were turned with leather belts and which powered the separator and grinders. Julián, who now runs the operation, selects and grinds all his own cocoa beans, and is hoping to renovate the old mill into a workshop that will pay tribute to the arrival of cocoa in Spain and his own family's extensive history of working with it.

Enric Rovira's philosophy couldn't be more different. Along with the likes of Ferran Adrià, who used his chocolate at El Bulli, Enric is one of the *vanguardistas* of experimental Spanish food. When he shows our children around his *atelier* in Barcelona they are just mesmerised. He is a magic box of a person, intellectual and intense, buzzing with ideas. There is something quite extraordinary about the way he can sculpt and flavour chocolate that seems to owe something to *el duende*, a Spanish expression that is hard to translate, but that flamenco dancers often talk about, as the spiritual invocation they need in order to perform the ultimate dance.

Enric's beautiful carved Easter eggs have been much copied – and many of his innovative flavour combinations have now become accepted in the wider chocolate world. He was the first to put the special Cabernet Sauvignon and balsamic vinegars produced by Forum in Tarragona in Catalunya into chocolates, in the way of traditional liqueurs. He has made chocolates inspired by Gaudí and encapsulated aromas inside chocolates that look like lipsticks.

Enric's commitment to the finest chocolate is total, and he has been working with a small cocoa producer, Claudio Corallo, on the island of Príncipe, off the west coast of Africa. Corallo has been restoring and cultivating derelict plantations of the first variety of cocoa that was introduced from Brazil by Portuguese sailors around 1822, so the trees have never been hybridised and the beans have the pure flavours of the original fruit.

How to choose and use drinking chocolate

Drinking chocolate can vary as much as solid chocolate. In Spain it is so popular that in supermarkets you can buy it in every shape or form, from chunky blocks to be melted in hot water or milk, to flakes and powders. In most Spanish cafés and households children will have chocolate drinks at breakfast time, particularly in winter.

Some of the best drinking chocolate is made with chocolate flakes or 'vermicelli' rather than powder, to give a rich, creamier taste.

The main thing to decide, when you buy, is how you want to drink it: straight, as a milky drink, or thicker, for dipping *churros* or *melindros* into (see pages 28 and 31). Also remember that when cocoa is the first ingredient listed on the label, as opposed to sugar, the chocolate will have a deeper, possibly more bitter flavour.

A la taza

This essentially means 'in a cup', but this is dunking chocolate, thickened with cornflour and designed to be mixed with milk, so that it is almost sauce-like: perfect with *churros* – or my favourite *melindros* (see page 31) – to dip into it. Sometimes it is sold as 'vermicelli' (flakes), sometimes powder. It can be *amargo*, which means bitter, and contains 66 per cent cocoa solids; or *tradicional*, which is less strong, containing 42 per cent cocoa solids.

A la piedra

Chocolate as the ancient Mexicans would have recognised it: a dark, solid block with a high cocoa content and unrefined sugar glistening through it. It may also have chilli added. You grate it, and then add milk and water according to taste – for the real authentic Aztec experience water is best, in which case it makes a dark, dark brown drink. It is quite bitter, so it is an acquired taste, but it has a dedicated following because it is considered to be pure and healthy. Dark chocolate contains a good level of iron, in particular, which the addition of milk counteracts.

Cacao desayuno

This tends to be sweeter, with a higher ratio of sugar to chocolate, and is aimed at a younger audience, typically for breakfast.

Carquinyols
Hard-baked almond biscuits

These twice-baked biscuits, similar to the Italian *cantuccini*, are famous in Catalunya, especially in the mountain village of Rupit, about half an hour's drive from Vic, in the region of Ausona. When I lived in Catalunya I often used to visit Rupit, with its feisty river running through it and its stone streets, where the shops do a roaring trade in freshly baked *carquinyols*. Athough mostly people buy, rather than make, the biscuits, my friend Núria Montiel bakes her own, and this is her recipe. She uses whole almonds with the skin still on, so that when she adds the nuts to the dough before baking, it sticks to them. Mellow rather than sweet, and very crunchy, the biscuits are excellent with a mid-morning coffee, or a sweet aged sherry or Moscatel wine after dinner.

The trick is to get the timing right so that the dough, when baked the first time round, is not so hard that you can't slice it into rounds for the second baking.

They keep well, up to 4 weeks in an airtight container, so Núria makes them in big batches.

Makes around 60

400g plain flour
½ teaspoon sea salt
1 tablespoon baking powder
3 eggs
250g caster sugar
grated zest of 1 lemon
2 teaspoons Grand Marnier,
  Cointreau or Triple Sec
175g whole almonds, skin-on, preferably Marcona

Preheat the oven to 180°C/gas 4. Line a baking tray with baking paper.

Place all the ingredients, except the almonds, in a bowl and mix to a dough, then add the almonds.

Moisten your hands and divide the dough into three. Shape each piece into a *ciabatta* shape about 3cm wide and with a curved top, and lay on the lined baking tray.

Bake in the middle of the preheated oven for 20–25 minutes, until the tops are golden.

Take the tray out and turn the oven off. Leave to cool for about 12 minutes, then cut each piece horizontally into slices about 1cm wide. Put these back on to the lined baking tray – laying them flat – and return it to the cooling oven for around 12 minutes, turning once halfway through, until the biscuits have dried out and are crunchy.

Pastissets

Menorcan flower biscuits

These pretty flower-shaped biscuits are one of the highlights we have enjoyed with our friends Rosa and Nicolás in Menorca (see page 25). I haven't seen *pastissets* anywhere else in Spain, and their similarity to shortbread may be a hangover from the two British occupations of the islands in the eighteenth century. Our daughter Daniela loves to tuck into these, as they aren't overly sweet, but mildly spiced, quite rich and crumbly. The traditional recipe uses lard, which in Spain is far superior to the British equivalent (see page 40).

In Menorca you can buy special *pastisset* cutters which come in different sizes, but you could use any flower-shaped cutter. I use some that are around 4.5cm in diameter. However, if you don't have any you can just make round biscuits, or any shape you like. Daniela likes to shape them like little people.

Makes around 30

2 egg yolks
125g caster sugar
125g Spanish pork lard
  (ideally Ibérico, see page 40)
¼ teaspoon vanilla extract
¼ teaspoon ground cinnamon
250g plain flour, plus extra for dusting
icing sugar, for dusting

Preheat the oven to 165°C/gas 3.

Put all the ingredients, except the flour and icing sugar, into a bowl and mix into a paste with your hands. Add the flour and work in until you have a supple dough – like a shortbread dough.

Lightly flour your work surface and roll out the dough to about 7mm.

Lay the dough on a sheet of greaseproof paper, then cut out using a flower-shaped or round cutter (about 4.5cm diameter) and put on to a baking tray.

Bake in the preheated oven for about 20 minutes, keeping an eye on the biscuits to make sure they don't burn. They should still be pale, like shortbread.

Remove from the oven, cool, then dust the biscuits well with icing sugar – as if they have been in a light snowfall.

Galletas de almendra
Almond puffs

This is a recipe devised by Scott Boden, who was my co-director during the nineties at Brindisa along with my brother, Mark. Scott is a dedicated gourmet who loves to cook and is always tinkering away intelligently in the kitchen, refining his ideas relentlessly with great attention to detail until he has a recipe just as he wants it. He was constantly looking for ways in which to use favourite ingredients such as Ibérico pork lard and Marcona almonds, both of which come together in this recipe. The puffs store very well in an airtight tin.

Makes 48

100g salted almonds, preferably Marcona
200g plain flour
½ teaspoon ground cinnamon
150g Spanish pork lard (ideally Ibérico,
   see page 40), at room temperature
200g icing sugar
½ teaspoon vanilla extract

Preheat the oven to 175°C/gas 4.

Line 2 baking sheets with baking paper.

Put the almonds, flour and cinnamon into the bowl of a food processor and process until the nuts are very finely chopped.

Put the pork lard and half the icing sugar into the bowl of an electric mixer fitted with a paddle beater and mix on medium speed until fluffy (about 3 minutes), then mix in the vanilla extract.

Scrape down any mixture from the side of the bowl, add the chopped almond mixture and mix on low speed until just combined into a dough.

Form the dough into 48 balls about 2.5cm in diameter and arrange them on the baking sheets 3cm apart.

Bake in the preheated oven for about 25 minutes, swapping the baking sheets over and turning them around halfway through, until the biscuits are very lightly browned around the edges.

Remove from the oven and place the baking sheets on cooling racks until the biscuits are cool enough to handle.

Put the remaining icing sugar in a bowl and gently roll the warm biscuits in it, then place them on the cooling rack for about 15 minutes, roll them in icing sugar a second time and return them to the rack to cool fully.

Store in an airtight container. Note: the biscuits improve for a day or two after baking.

MANTECA

'a pronounced taste'

At one time most home baking in Spain was done with pork lard (*manteca*) rather than butter (*mantequilla*). This was partly because there was no proliferation of cows, as in the UK or France, and in the countryside most people would have kept a pig instead; and partly because, before refrigeration, butter would go off too quickly. As a result, recipes such as *ensaimada* (see page 48) and many *coques* (see page 70) and biscuits rely on lard for texture and flavour. It is produced from all breeds of pigs but, if you can find it, it is worth choosing the more expensive Ibérico lard as it can be sweeter, and has a wonderful distinctive flavour and aroma – that said, I am aware that in the UK, where our own lard is completely different and relatively tasteless, its pronounced taste is not everyone's cup of tea.

In the old pre-fridge days lard had an additional use: cured meats would be put inside earthenware pots and covered in the lard, which would keep the meat in good condition. Many of the old jars that we have collected on our travels were used in this way: one in particular still has a slight tackiness where the lard has penetrated the terracotta.

Some cheese-makers smear the rinds of their cheeses with *manteca*, either to help any further coatings such as spices or cereals to stick, or as a way of protecting them, allowing them to be cured for longer. Hams can also be coated with it as they cure, in order to seal any cracks in the leg, and all hams are lard-coated as they leave their curing chambers to be sold.

Manteca is made by rendering down cuts of bacon or *panceta* until you have a liquid, which then solidifies as lard. It is naturally white in colour; however, there is also a particularly fine Andalusian *manteca colorá* or *colorada*, which is seasoned, coloured bright red-orange with *pimentón* (paprika), and sometimes has pieces of meat or offal added to it. It might also be flavoured with oregano, bay and orange peel. Served on bread or toast, it is a popular tapa in the mountain villages of the south.

The residual hard pieces of rind that don't liquefy are known as *chicharrones*, which are an equally vital ingredient in the traditional Spanish kitchen. Unlikely as it might seem, they are widely combined with sweet ingredients. In Catalunya they go into the square-shaped *coca de llardons*, a popular breakfast or teatime snack that is also traditional for Mardi Gras. Two sheets of puff pastry are studded with *chicharrones* that have been smashed into small pieces with a rolling pin, then baked, sprinkled with sugar and pine nuts, cut into pieces and eaten with goat's cheese and fig jam.

Chicharrones can also be ground into a powder that can vary in colour between a mottled golden yellow and a chestnut brown,

and is used in traditional crumbly 'sand' cakes, known as *mantecados* and *polvorones*.

When I ate at El Bulli, one of chef Ferran Adrià's famous dishes (a version of which has since been repeated at his brother Albert's 'tapas' bar, Tickets, in Barcelona) consisted of wafer-thin *tacos* (slices) of raw tuna belly, which he had painted with Ibérico lard. Of course, the deep red tuna belly streaked with fat and laid out on waxed paper looked just like Ibérico ham, and the *manteca* disguised the aroma of the fish and replaced it with the sweet, complex, meaty aroma that is characteristic of the best acorn-fed Ibérico ham. So you were fooled into thinking it was meat. Then you tasted it, and there was a burst of tuna flavour. I can just imagine the fun they must have had in the El Bulli development sessions, deciding how to delude and delight the diner by fusing and confusing these two favourite Spanish ingredients.

Bollo de limón y nueces
Light lemon and walnut muffins

This recipe comes from our friends Mercedes and Pepe (see page 80). As the muffins are not too rich or sweet, they are a mainstay of their children's lunchboxes and light snacking at their house. Many of the recipes I have collected from friends in Spain use coffee cups or glasses as convenient measures in the way that was typical of Spanish households before everyone had kitchen scales, and Mercedes told me that at one time when she was making cakes, after she had broken the first egg, she would use half an egg shell (*cascarón*) to measure out the rest of the ingredients.

This recipe uses yogurt pots in a similar way. I think it is a great idea, but I have given the quantities in more conventional weights and measures too.

Makes 12

1 lemon yogurt (125g)
3 eggs
2 yogurt pot measures of caster sugar (285g)
3 yogurt pot measures of plain flour (255g)
1 teaspoon baking powder
½ a yogurt pot measure of vegetable oil (75ml)
50g chopped walnuts

Preheat the oven to 180°C/gas 4.

Line two 6-hole muffin trays with paper cases.

Pour the yogurt into a bowl, then wash out the pot and dry it. Break the eggs into a separate bowl, then use the yogurt pot to measure out the sugar, add it to the eggs and beat together. Stir this mixture into the yogurt.

Fill the yogurt pot with flour. Add this to the yogurt mixture and continue to beat.

Add a second yogurt potful of flour together with the baking powder and stir in with a wooden spoon. Add the last yogurt potful of flour, then half-fill the pot with oil and mix in until smooth. Lastly, add the walnuts.

Pour the mixture into the paper cases and bake in the preheated oven for around 25 minutes, until risen and golden.

Horchata de chufa
Tiger nut milk

Horchatas are nut milks, and this refreshing, sustaining and healthy one made with *chufas* (tiger nuts) is one of my husband Rupert's favourite drinks. So much so that he has a dream of setting up a machine to make *horchata de chufa* in our shop at Borough Market.

Chufas resemble wrinkled brown chickpeas and are the tubers of a species of sedge that above ground looks like a grass with long, flat, quite fibrous leaves. They are an ancient food that was first introduced by the Arabs to the area of Alboraia, just north of Valencia. Sorting the harvested, mud-covered nuts from the pebbles in the fields of Valencia was one of the unusual agricultural holiday jobs that Rupert took up when he was a teenager in Madrid (where his family lived at the time) to escape the boredom of the city and connect with the land.

The *chufas* have a tough, woody texture and milky, earthy flavours, and though you see them prepared as a snack at fairs, they are mainly pressed for their almond-like milk, which is a favourite served chilled during the hot summers in Valencia in particular, where the drink is known by its local name, *orxata de xufa*. The tradition there is to serve it with *fartons*, sponge fingers dusted in sugar, for dunking into it – something I find quite odd, as it is such a lovely, thirst-quenching drink, why pair it with something so dry and sugary? We like it just on its own, and whenever we are in Spain and find a bar selling it we always taste and compare, since the quality and especially the sweetness can vary enormously. Most often you find that it is not actually made from scratch on the premises, but from pre-prepared concentrate. The best we have found so far was actually not in Valencia, but in Mahón in Menorca, where in the heat of the summer we would knock back huge glasses of the homemade drink in a little café-bar that specialised in *horchata* and ice cream.

Because they are so small, the *chufas* consist mainly of skin, but what flesh there is, is bullet hard, white and as fibrous as a coconut, so you need to soak them for about 12 hours or overnight before using them.

How much sugar, if any, you add to the drink is really an individual thing. We often make batches to which we don't add sugar at all.

Once you have experimented, you might find you prefer a stronger flavour. In which case reduce the water added to the chopped nuts to 600ml and you will end up with around 400ml of a more concentrated drink.

Makes about 800ml

500g *chufas* (tiger nuts)
100g caster sugar, or more to taste

Wash the *chufas* well, a number of times, and put them to soak in 1 litre of water for 12 hours. Wash them again and drain well. They will increase a little in weight after soaking.

Pulse-chop in a blender, until the nuts are the texture of desiccated coconut – it will take about 5 minutes, but it really is best to pulse-chop, as even when the nuts are soaked they are very hard, and could easily burn out your blender if you left the motor running.

Add another litre of water and leave for 3 hours to rest, but no more or the nuts will ferment (I once left them overnight, and in the morning it was as if there was a beer monster in the kitchen!).

Using muslin or a clean tea towel, strain well into a bowl or wide-mouthed jug, twisting the muslin or tea towel around the *chufa* mulch so that you push as much liquid out of the *chufas* as you can manage.

Add the sugar to taste, and put into the fridge to chill before drinking.

Coca bamba de Menorca
Raised dough spiral

This is related to the *ensaimada* that follows, in that it is a similar coiled shape, but it rises in a different way and is more cake-like, similar to an Italian *panettone*.

For the islanders a *coca bamba* any time is special, but it is also the typical treat during the summer horse festival when crowds fill the streets to see the horse-races, jousting, and the spectacular *jaleo*, in which the majestic, pure black Menorcan horses, guided by skilled riders in black tailcoats, jump and dance on their hind legs to music.

The recipe was given to me by Rosa Gornés Vinent, wife of our cheese supplier on Menorca, Nicolás Cardona Enrich. She is a wonderful, generous, cheery and affectionate woman, and as soon as I asked her for some recipes she told me she was racing home to go through a bunch of them with her mother, who cooks lunch for the family during the week and often gets up at dawn to bake. Then, at weekends, they cook together. Her mother is an authority on traditional recipes and handed-down wisdom in the kitchen and knows all about the best ingredients and where to seek them out.

A little like the *coca tovada* on page 65, the dough contains potato, but, as Rosa explains, in spite of this it is meant to be sweet and airy, so her mother's trick is to add some saccharine to the potato water, and then use some of this to make the potato purée. This allows her to get sweetness into the dough without weighing it down with lots of sugar, so it rises well and stays light.

To get the timing of the rising of the dough right, she swears by putting a walnut-sized piece of leftover dough in a glass of water. When it rises she knows that she will need to rest the dough for 30 more minutes before baking!

Makes 4

170g peeled potatoes
5 saccharine tablets
3 eggs, beaten
175g caster sugar
250g strong white bread flour
250g plain flour
50g fresh yeast
75g white pork lard, cut in pieces,
   plus a little extra for greasing your hands
75g butter, melted plus a little extra
   for greasing the tray
40g icing sugar

Boil the potatoes in unsalted water until soft and drain into a bowl, so that you reserve the water.

Dissolve the saccharine tablets in a tablespoon of the potato water, then add this to the rest of the water.

Put the potatoes into a separate bowl and mash them, adding 85ml of the potato and saccharine water, then leave to cool.

When the potato purée is cold, stir in 2 of the eggs, then add the sugar and mix well. Sift the flours together and work into the mixture.

In a small bowl or cup, mix the remaining egg and the yeast well, using a fork. Pour this on to the potato mixture, and with your hands mix it in, adding the pieces of lard and melted butter as you go, until you have a homogeneous paste. Cover the bowl with a clean cloth, then put a large freezer bag over the top to keep in the moisture, and leave overnight in ambient temperature.

By morning the dough should have risen, so that if you gently move the bowl, the dough trembles. If this doesn't happen, leave it a little longer.

Preheat the oven to 170°C/gas 3. Grease a baking tray with butter.

Ensaimada
Soft dough spiral

Grease your hands with a little lard, then divide the dough into 4 pieces and roll them into long cylinders about 3cm in diameter and 75cm long. Try not to handle the dough too much, so that you don't interrupt the fermentation process. Coil each cylinder into a tight snail and place on the greased baking tray. Leave to rest, uncovered, for 45 minutes.

Sprinkle each coil of dough with 2 teaspoons of icing sugar, then put into the preheated oven and bake for about 30 minutes, until a skewer inserted into the middle comes out clean.

Remove from the oven, sprinkle each coil with another 2 teaspoons of icing sugar, then leave to cool and enjoy with a hot chocolate (see page 32) or café con leche.

A really properly-made ensaimada is my absolute favourite breakfast. Sometimes we rent a boyera (converted barn) in Menorca, and early in the morning I escape to the fish market in Mahón, where I watch and learn from the expert local shoppers as they select the best of the catch. Once I have bought my fish, I slip down to the port, where in the cafés and bars they serve the lightest, squidgiest ensaimadas: coiled buns of airy, yeasty dough, dusted with icing sugar, that you can tear into soft strands to eat with your coffee while you sit and watch the people coming and going in their yachts.

Ensaimadas were originally a speciality of Mallorca and the ones made there are still considered the ultimate, even though you can find them everywhere nowadays. I like ensaimadas plain, but often they are split and filled with a confit of pumpkin or spaghetti squash, or custard.

The locals claim it is the damp atmosphere surrounding the islands that makes the dough more moist, so the finished buns stay soft for longer, and they insist that you can't make them properly anywhere else. They are made with pork lard (saim in Mallorquín means lard), which gives a silky texture to the dough. Made with a different fat they tend to be puffy and don't melt in the mouth in the same way. We use a fantastic Ibérico lard (see page 40), which is very different from British lard, and you really do need its ultra-silkiness in order to stretch the dough – if you can't find it you could try substituting it with English lard blended with some olive oil.

You do have to do quite a lot of kneading, and much of the finished result depends on how thinly you stretch the dough – it should be almost transparent. It is actually quite astonishing how the addition of the pork lard enables you to stretch a tennis-ball-sized piece into a sheer sheet of dough that will take up most of your kitchen table or work surface. What this size and thinness does is allow you to create more layers as you roll it up, and the more layers you have, the lighter and softer the finished ensaimada will be.

This recipe comes from Rosa María Company Bauza, who is the partner of our Spanish cheese adviser, José Luís Martín. They live on the island of Mallorca with their son, and some of the other recipes in this book, such as the *coca* bases (see page 70), are also from her family's repertoire.

Makes 6 small *ensaimadas* or 2 large ones

50g fresh yeast
500g strong white flour, plus extra for dusting
150g caster sugar
15g salt
3 large eggs
olive oil, for greasing your work surface
about 150g pork lard (white or Ibérico),
  at room temperature, for smearing the dough
icing sugar, for dredging

To start, you need to make a 'mother'. Melt the yeast in 3 tablespoons of warm water, add 200g of the flour plus enough water to bring the mixture together into a soft dough, and shape into a ball. Put into a bowl and leave to rest for 30 minutes, covered with a damp cloth (don't let this touch the dough) until doubled in size.

Lift the dough out. Put the sugar, the rest of the flour, the salt and the eggs (unbeaten) into the bowl and mix together. Then return the dough to the bowl and work it into the flour, salt and egg mixture with your hands – you may need to add a little water or extra flour to help it form a smooth, workable dough.

Flour your work surface, turn out the dough and knead it for 30–45 minutes, until it is glossy, silky and extremely elastic. Once you have reached this point, roll it into a ball again and leave it on your work surface, covered with a clean tea towel, for 30 minutes.

Divide the dough into 6 (if you are making small *ensaimadas*) or 2 (if making large ones) and roll each piece into a rough ball.

Lightly oil the surface on which you will be working – you need a large work area. Also grease a tray or trays with lard.

Roll out each ball individually in one direction only, so that it resembles a long tongue of dough – it should be as long and thin as possible (preferably about 2mm).

With your hand, smear the surface of the dough generously with lard (this will help you to stretch it more easily), then with your fingertips pull and stretch it in all directions, but particularly widthways, as this will allow you to make more turns once you start to roll up the dough). Keep stretching as much as you can, until the dough is almost translucent. This is the fun bit – you will be surprised how much the lard allows the dough to stretch! It will be a bit uneven and wavy around the edge – this doesn't matter at all – and don't be scared of making little tears or holes. This doesn't matter either, as they will mend themselves when the dough rises overnight.

Fold over the long edge by about 1cm to give you a good grip on the dough, then roll it up into a long, thin, snake-like sausage.

Now loosely coil each sausage into a spiral shape on your greased tray or trays, making sure that the edges of the sausage don't touch each other as you wind them around – you need to leave a gap of 2–3cm, as you are going to let the dough rise again overnight, and it will spread out. If you don't leave this gap you will lose the definition of the spiral shape as the dough rises.

Put the trays into a closed, switched-off oven overnight (you don't want any heat, just to keep the air out). By morning the dough will have risen and the gaps in the spirals will have filled up.

Preheat the oven to 170°C/gas 3 and bake for around 12 minutes for small *ensaimadas* or 15 minutes for large ones, until light golden, with a soft-baked top. Dredge with icing sugar.

A Tale of Two Jam-makers

Over the last two decades I have enjoyed so many stunning jams made by Spanish friends and artisan suppliers, as wherever you have fertile land and sunshine, you have glorious fruit, and everyone wants to capture its flavour in a jar – but two people stand out above the crowd.

I first met Juana Cerezo at a market in Madrid. I was searching the stalls trying to spot a particular cheese-maker when this dark-copper-skinned woman with a long pony-tail insisted that I taste her jams, which are truly stunning. Juana lives in the tiny village of Herguijuela de la Sierra in the middle of nowhere in the province of Salamanca. She comes from a family of twelve siblings and her surname means 'cherry tree' (Salamanca is an area famous for cherries). A captivating woman with an infectious energy and un-compromising standards, she has studied to be a teacher and is involved in rural development and community issues.

The valley in which she lives has a very privileged alpine climate, situated as it is in the national park of Las Batuecas in the Sierra de Francia mountain range, and she uses wild fruits from the woodland and valley as well as her own orchard fruits (cherry, pear, apple, quince, plum, olive, peach, fig and chestnut) and strawberries, raspberries, pumpkins and onions from her garden. Then she puts them together in interesting combinations, such as chestnut and chocolate, coconut and nutmeg, green tomato and apple, and an amazingly deep orange pumpkin with almond.

It was May time when I first visited her at her home, where she keeps chickens and a goat called Lola, and the surrounding countryside was covered in flowers and fruit blossom. She makes her jams and seasonal *membrillo* (quince, see page 511) at a little work-station with her daughter, who has helped her pack the jars since she was very small. I very badly wanted to sell her jams at Brindisa, but her production is tiny and her recipes so instinctive that I couldn't even coax her to write them down for this book.

I did, however, succeed in collecting some wonderful recipes from Teresa Cotorruela Rodríguez, another of the finest jam-makers I have come across. Teresa makes her jams in the remote area of Sayago in Zamora, only a few miles from Los Arribes del Duero (the canyons of the Duero river), which cross over the border into Portugal. She uses local fruit and calls her little business

Oh Saúco – saúco means elderberry. In the jam-making room of her beautiful low, stone cottage with its walled garden, she has a collection of ports and homemade cherry liqueurs that she adds to many of her jams, which, by their very local nature, can only be made in relatively small batches.

The three recipes that I have included on pages 52–53 are my favourites – remember, though, that the ultimate secret of great jam-making is to do as Teresa does, and only use the very best fruit, in season.

Mermelada de guindas
Cherry jam

JAMS

The combination of *tostada* (toasted white bread) with preserves is as popular in Spain as it is in Britain. The Spanish love jams, but as in Italy or France they tend to be much looser, more runny and made with less sugar than 'set' British jams, so the flavour of the fruit comes through more strongly.

To prepare and fill the jars
Always use new jars and lids.

For home consumption Teresa Cotorruela Rodríguez, whose recipes follow, prefers to sterilise her jars before filling them, either by boiling them in a metal pan for ten minutes or putting them through a dishwasher cycle. Then she fills them right up to the top with jam while it is still hot, closes the lid and gives a gentle twist to seal it tightly. She then turns the jars upside down, so they create a vacuum, and leaves them like this until the jam cools. At this point they are ready to eat, but will last for up to three years unopened.

The alternative, more conventional, way is to use the *baño maría* (bain-marie) method. Fill the sterilised jars to within a centimetre of the top, put the lids on and then place the jars upright on a small rack or tea towel in a large pan of water, so that the jars are not resting directly on the base of the pan. Wedge a tea towel in between the jars to stop them from bumping into each other. Bring the water to the boil for ten minutes, then lift the jars out carefully, using tongs. The important thing with this method is not to over-fill the jars, or the seal can leak as the contents expand. Check that the domed lid has been pulled down tightly. If it springs back, this shows that the seal has not worked, in which case you can cool the jar, keep it chilled in the fridge and eat the jam within a month.

It is up to you whether you put in the cherry liqueur at the end – but it is an excellent addition.

Makes around 900g

1kg stoned cherries
450g sugar (half granulated, half caster)
1 cinnamon stick
juice of 1 lemon
cherry liqueur (optional)

Put a plate into the fridge to chill, ready to test whether the jam is set, and prepare your jars (see left).

Put the cherries into a preserving pan and add the sugar and cinnamon stick plus about 200ml of water – enough to keep the fruit from sticking to the pan. Stir constantly over a low heat and once a small amount of the juice has evaporated, turn up the heat to its highest, add the lemon juice and stir without stopping until the jam reaches its setting point, then take off the heat.

The time this takes can vary, but begin to test when the jam starts thickening. Spoon a teaspoonful on to your chilled plate. Put it back into the fridge for a minute, then push the jam with your finger. If it forms a crinkly skin, it is ready. If not, continue to boil and test again.

Remove the cinnamon stick and then, using a hand whisk, squash the cherries so that they are half 'chopped'. If you prefer the jam to be smoother you could blend them instead. If you want to add a small amount of cherry liqueur, this is the moment.

Leave to rest for 5 minutes, then fill the prepared jars (see left).

Mermelada de melocotón a la lavanda
Peach jam with lavender

Mermelada de fresas al oporto
Strawberry jam with port

Makes around 900g

1kg ripe peaches
400g sugar (half granulated, half caster)
2 sprigs of lavender
zest and juice of 1 lemon

Put a plate into the fridge to chill, ready to test whether the jam is set, and prepare your jars (see opposite).

Wash the peaches well, peel and chop them, then put them into a deep, heavy-based pan. Add the sugar and let the fruit macerate for 12 hours.

Wash the lavender sprigs, dry them with kitchen paper, then tie them in muslin.

Once the sugar has completely dissolved and formed a syrup, put the pan over a low heat, add the lavender parcel and stir occasionally. Once the syrup has evaporated enough – it will thicken, become brighter, and come away from the sides of the pan – add the lemon juice and zest, turn up the heat to its highest and stir constantly with a long wooden spoon, to avoid burning, until the jam reaches its setting point, then take off the heat.

The time this takes can vary, but start testing when the jam becomes shiny and thickens. Spoon a teaspoonful on to your chilled plate. Put it back into the fridge for a minute, then push the jam with your finger. If it forms a crinkly skin, it is ready. If not, continue to boil and test again.

Remove the lavender parcel and leave the jam to rest for 5 minutes, then fill the prepared jars (see opposite).

I know we are all familiar with strawberry jam, but the addition of port makes it very special – the area of Sayago where Teresa lives is only a few miles from the Portuguese border, so port is a very familiar drink locally. Sometimes she uses lemon instead of port but we decided to try it using both, and found it worked really well.

This is a silky, rich jam, especially if you are using over-ripe fruit, but if you prefer a firmer texture you could add a little more lemon juice. As well as serving it in conventional ways, it is also delicious with pâté.

Makes about 700g

1kg ripe strawberries
450g sugar (half granulated, half caster)
zest and juice of 1 lemon
65ml good-quality port

Put a plate into the fridge to chill, ready to test whether the jam is set, and prepare your jars (see opposite).

Put the fruit into a large preserving pan with the sugar and allow to macerate for about 30 minutes, until the fruit has released its juices.

Stir over a low heat to release more juice and once most of this has evaporated (about forty minutes), add the lemon juice and zest. Increase the heat to its highest and boil until it reaches its setting point. The time this takes can vary, but should be about 15–20 minutes, so start testing after ten minutes. Spoon a teaspoonful on to your chilled plate. Put it back into the fridge for a minute, then push the jam with your finger. If it forms a crinkly skin, it is ready. If not, continue to boil and test again a few minutes later – but be careful not to let the jam begin to burn on the bottom of the pan, or the colour will become dark and the taste more caramel-like.

At this point, add the port, stir briefly and turn off the heat. Leave to rest for 5 minutes, then fill the prepared jars (see opposite).

Crema de almendras marcona
Almond butter

Not traditionally Spanish, perhaps, but made with beautiful Spanish almonds and olive oil, this is gorgeous on toast, and even better with some orange blossom honey (see page 56) drizzled over the top. This is another recipe from Scott Boden. I guess being Anglo-American, his mission was to make an equivalent to peanut butter using a Spanish almond (and at home we also use it in any way you might use peanut butter or tahini, in a satay-style sauce, in cookies, even a spoonful added to a bean or vegetable stew or curry). Scott made various versions with different varieties of nut, which we compared and decided that, although expensive, the Marcona delivered the richest, most pronounced almondy flavour. Any of the butter that you don't use immediately will keep in a cool larder (or a fridge in summer) for 3 months – but Scott recommends you just eat it all straight away.

Makes about 500g

**500g good blanched almonds,
  preferably Marcona**
1 tablespoon good olive oil, such as Arbequina
1 tablespoon vegetable oil
½ teaspoon sea salt
**½ teaspoon bittersweet smoked paprika
  (*pimentón agridulce*)**

Preheat the oven to 150°C/gas 2.

Spread out the almonds on a large shallow tray and toast for 10–12 minutes until lightly golden brown, turning them once halfway through.

While the almonds are still warm from the oven, combine half of them with the other ingredients in a food processor. Process until very smooth and runny (approximately 4–5 minutes).

Add the remaining almonds and process for about 45 seconds, or longer if you prefer a smooth rather than crunchy texture.

Smear thickly on toasted country bread.

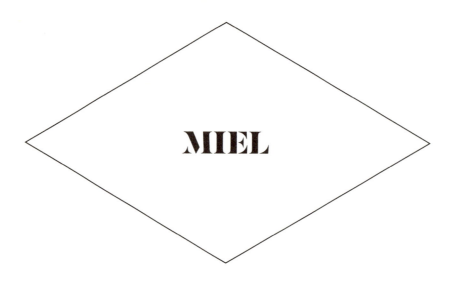

MIEL

'from flowers, woodland trees or mountain shrubs'

Spanish artisan honey can be amazing since the bees have such a vast expanse of unspoilt countryside to forage on, from forest and wilderness to hills and meadows filled with a whole range of aromatic flowers, shrubs and trees. The honeys truly reflect the countryside in which they are collected, unlike those made by large-scale commercial companies which combine honeys from different sources. Where producers situate their hives in areas of mixed flora, their honey is labelled as 'diverse', while honeys that come from regions where one particular flower, herb or tree dominates can be labelled as 'single varietals', and will have an especially distinctive flavour.

In the early days of Moro restaurant our friends Sam and Sam Clark served their homemade yogurt with three of these very special honeys: the almost-black *madroño* (strawberry tree), the copper-coloured *castaño* (chestnut) and the golden *azahar* (orange blossom). It was such a lovely, simple way to highlight their flavours and very different hues, which showed beautifully against the bright white of the yogurt.

Honey is a food with a long history and ancient importance in Spain. There is a famous painting in the Cuevas de la Araña, the Spider Caves, near Bicorp in Valencia, which is around 8,000 years old and shows a figure, known as the 'Man of Bicorp', climbing high up to raid *miel de serrania* (wild honey) from a nest of bees.

We select our honey from Ferran Alemany and his family, who live up in the hills of the province of Lleida outside Barcelona in the foothills of the Pyrenees, a place full of almond groves and horses, and quite magical when the trees are in blossom and there are young foals gambolling around. Ferran's grandfather, Miquel Alemany, began collecting honey back in 1929, and every year the production builds up to a crescendo when they make their beautiful *turrón* (nougat) with honey and almonds in time for the Christmas season.

In addition to their own honeys, they also collect diverse and single varietals from other producers around Spain. Some, such as the heather honeys, are processed 'raw', i.e. they are extracted from the comb without any pasteurisation or heat treatment, only enough warmth to allow the honey to move. They are not filtered either, so may contain small amounts of pollen, then they are simply jarred and settled. As a result they are very different from fully pasteurised honeys, which may have been heated to as high as 85°C and then chilled down fast to about 25°C. This harsh treatment can cause the honey to lose nutritional value and much of its complexity: caramel and vanilla notes will fade, floral and herbal aromas will evaporate, and the

quality will be short-lived. By contrast, a gently handled, artisan honey will retain its natural, individual flavour – more aromatic than sweet – its high mineral and protein content, and the energy-giving and antiseptic properties that country people have long valued in tonics and natural remedies.

How to choose honeys
As a general rule, tree honeys are darker than the more golden flower ones, partly because there is a higher protein content in their nectar. This, combined with the natural sugars, creates a darker pigment and a toasted aroma, which makes the honeys excellent for homemade granola and nut-based recipes.

The most distinctive tree honey comes from the *castaño* (chestnut), which blooms in larger forests around Galicia and Asturias, and in smaller quantities in the Montseny mountains of Catalunya. It produces dark greeny-amber-coloured, slightly malty, aromatic honey with a strong dry-wood intensity and a mild, bitter finish.

The evergreen holm oak produces a honey that is very viscous, almost black in colour, but with a mild flavour, in Aragón, Salamanca and Catalunya.

Then there is *madroño*, from the strawberry tree, which has no relation to the fruit as we know it, but does produce little berries that are not dissimilar in appearance to the wild strawberry. The tree is so well known in Spain that the coat of arms of the city of Madrid actually shows a bear reaching up for the berries. The honey produced from *madroño* pollen is the darkest of all, and has an unusual, especially bitter flavour that is good with yogurt.

Eucalipto (eucalyptus) honey tastes almost like good medicine, and its balsamic properties give a strong soothing finish that nurses the back of your throat.

Brezo (heather) is a plant we associate more with Scotland, but it can be found in a certified organic area of the Cantabrian mountains, where the hives are positioned 1,100 metres above sea level in areas of mixed woodland and meadow. The honey is collected from five different varieties of heather and has a unique thick, jelly-caramel-like texture that is similar to the famous manuka honey from New Zealand. It has an exceptionally high protein content – close to 2 per cent, compared to 0.5 per cent for most honeys.

The lavender (*espliego*) plant, with its grey-greenish leaves, strong camphor aroma and violet flowers, blooms in the summer around La Mancha, and the honey is light amber and very aromatic, wonderful for making cakes or spreading on toasted bread.

Rosemary (*romero*) honey comes from Catalunya, Aragón and Valencia, and has a mild sweetness with a touch of acidity and definite bitter tones.

Azahar (orange blossom) honey from Valencia and Tarragona is beautiful with fresh cheeses such as Mató and young goat's cheeses.

Royal jelly is sometimes added to the honey, but be aware that 90 per cent of this is sourced in China. If you find a honey made with local Spanish royal jelly this will add quite a bit to its price.

The Canary Islands produce some excellent honeys, and here you may also come across *guarapa*, or '*miel de palma*', which is not bee honey but the sap of the Canary palm tree, more like maple syrup (you have to tap the tree for it in the same way). However, it is used just like honey, especially with junkets, fresh white cheeses and *gofio* (see page 60). Like honey, too, it is high in mineral content and is often used in remedies.

Coca de yogur
Yogurt cake

This recipe is from a friend of Àngel Puigsellosas, who makes our *coca* breads in Catalunya (see page 70), and in this case, as is typical in his region, he also uses the word *coca* to describe a cake. Although the ingredients are similar to those in the recipe for muffins (see page 43) the texture is much lighter and fluffier, almost pillowy, thanks to the addition of meringue. Again, the idea is to use a 125g/150ml yogurt pot for measuring, but I have also given the equivalent standard weights and measures.

Makes 1 cake, around 32cm x 22cm

a little butter, for greasing the tin
3 large eggs or 4 small ones
2 yogurt pot measures of caster sugar (285g)
1 natural yogurt (125g)
1 yogurt pot measure of olive oil (150ml)
a dash of vanilla extract
3 yogurt pot measures of plain flour (225g),
   plus a little extra, for dusting the tin
1 teaspoon baking powder

Preheat the oven to 180°C/gas 4.

Grease and flour a cake tin (roughly 32cm x 22cm).

Separate the eggs and beat the whites until you have soft peaks, then beat in the sugar until you have a quite stiff meringue.

Mix in the yolks, then incorporate the yogurt, olive oil and vanilla extract.

Finally, fold in the flour and baking powder and spoon into the tin, levelling the top.

Bake in the preheated oven for about 30 minutes, until a skewer inserted into the centre comes out clean. Leave in the tin for a few minutes until cool enough to handle, then turn out and cool on a rack.

GOFIO

'vital and sustaining'

Gofio is maize flour that has been toasted so that it is almost caramelised. Occasionally you find it in recipes in mainland Spain, but there its presence is quite limited. In the Canary Islands, however, it is a vital and sustaining carbohydrate, the rough equivalent of mealie meal in many African nations (in fact, much *gofio* is sold to Africa), and is similar in taste and texture to *tsampa* from Tibet.

In times gone by, if you were a shepherd out with the goats in the hills you might have some cheese in your pocket and some *gofio* to mix into a paste with water, and that is how you would get by. At one time you might even have eaten it from a leaf, in the African way. And when villagers went off to work in the banana or tobacco plantations they would take with them a nourishing mid-morning drink of *gofio* and honey or sugar, mixed into goat's milk, along with dried figs and nuts.

Most children grow up eating *gofio* porridge, perhaps mixed with honey and bananas; but it is also added to soups or stews as a thickener; mixed with water, nuts, rum or olive oil and kneaded into a loaf-shaped dough (*pella de gofio*), which is sliced, rather like polenta (though not baked); or used like fine breadcrumbs or flour for coating fish before frying. On one visit to Gran Canaria, farmer and cheese-maker Juan Alonso took me up into the hills to see the sheep, goats and the few cattle he farmed. His wife worked

the night shift in the local hospital and so when he came home after working the land all day, he told me that for a quick supper he would make *agua hervida*, which basically means 'boiled water', with a bit of thyme or *hierba luisa*, lemon verbena from the garden, then he would throw in some *gofio* to thicken the liquid into a kind of soupy paste.

However, *gofio* is also being re-invented in ever more interesting and experimental ways in contemporary restaurant cooking, where it is appearing in *tortillas*, mousses, meringues, ice creams, milkshakes, savoury purées and fish and vegetable dishes. At one island restaurant I was served *gofio* mixed with meat stock, parsley and spices to make a dip called *gofio escaldón*, which is similar to the traditional *gachas* (pastes) you find in La Mancha. I was given a big slice of raw, sweet Spanish onion to scoop up the dip, so the crunchy, juicy, clean onion flavoured the relatively flavourless paste. At the end of another meal I also tried *mousse de gofio*, in which the toasted *gofio* was mixed with whipping cream, egg whites, sugar, ground almonds and cinnamon to make a light nutty mousse which was quite sweet and really delicious – it reminded me of Horlicks or the inside of a Malteser.

The tradition of *gofio* in the islands goes way back to the times when the Canarian aborigines, the Guanches, inhabited the islands, living in the

volcanic caves. They were said to have been tall and blue-eyed, possibly a mixed race of Berbers from North Africa and Vikings. In the museum in Las Palmas de Gran Canaria you can see the old utensils they used for making and eating *gofio*: storage containers, roasters for toasting the grain, large *tinajas*, or jars, with wooden lids for storing it once it was pounded, and ceramic *ganigos* (flat bowls for making stews).

When you wander through the hills of Gran Canaria, you can often see small, stunningly beautiful patterns made up of geometric lines and shapes marking the rock over doorways that lead into old caves where the islanders once kept their stores of *gofio* and sometimes cheese. Each clan created their own little emblem and would make stamps, called *pintaderas*, out of baked clay or sometimes wood, into which they cut the geometric patterns. The stamps were dipped in dye and were also used to brand animals and any other treasures the people owned. The designs are so central to Canarian history that you often see them reproduced on T-shirts for selling to holidaymakers.

These days many of the old caves have a chimney poking through, because a popular thing to do here, as in mountainous areas of mainland Spain, is convert them into dens for big family gatherings on Sundays and holidays. People put in a grill for barbecuing, a long table and chairs and maybe even a little wine store.

Over the years *gofio* has been made from many different grains and sometimes legumes such as dried *arvejas* and *chicharos* (types of pea) and *habas* (broad beans). *Trigo* (wheat) and *millo* (maize/corn, which has arrived more recently from America) are the most popular these days. In general, *gofio de trigo* is lighter in colour and finer, so is more suited to breakfast porridge made with milk, while the heavier *gofio de millo* is often used for making a paste, and for adding to stews and soups.

Many local mills now provide a full bespoke service of stone milling and toasting the grains to individual requirements. Outsiders to the islands might find it difficult to understand why the Canarian people are so particular about a certain variety or grade of *gofio*, but once you have tasted a few, you begin to understand the difference and develop a preference.

Juan was very insistent about which *gofio* I should bring home with me. The one he recommended, Buen Lugar, was a *gofio de millo* made from Argentino (an Argentinian strain of corn) and it was a revelation to me: a beautiful soft beige/golden colour with a taste full of all those Horlicks flavours with hints of toffee. We mix it with porridge or make it into a paste with water and add it to yogurt. We have even used it to make brunch pancakes – not typically Canarian, but just making good use of a very typical ingredient.

Gofio isn't easy to find in the UK, but if you come across it, try these childhood favourites of a former Canarian colleague, Eduardo.

Breakfast shake

This also makes a great after-gym drink. For one person blend 2 dessertspoons of *gofio* (no more as it thickens the drink very quickly) with 1–2 teaspoons of muscovado sugar or organic honey, 1 sliced banana (or half an avocado or a wedge of fresh coconut, chopped), a handful of blanched almonds and 200–300ml of milk, until smooth. Substitute almond milk, coconut or soya milk, as you like.

Gofio amasado

These are little rounds of *gofio*, fruit and nuts, a favourite childhood snack for days out with the family in the countryside. For enough for 4 people, infuse 3 cloves in 300ml water for 15 minutes, remove the cloves and mix 4 tablespoons of honey into the water. Put 500–700g *gofio* in a bowl and slowly add enough honeyed water to work into a firm but sticky dough. Mix in 2 handfuls each of chopped nuts and dried fruit of your choice, form into little balls and then dust in a little more *gofio*.

Pan perdido de Adolfo
Adolfo's 'lost' spiced loaf

Adolfo Zuazua Iglesias and María Valdés García have a 'vegetarian casa rural' in Cabo de Gata in Almería in Andalucía – an unrenovated eighteenth-century farmhouse, where the ceiling is made from woven bamboo, and swallows fly freely through the house. The whole place smells of the rosemary and orange blossom which grows all around and the wild scenery is mind-blowing.

The couple have a simple, healthy philosophy when it comes to eating: use the best-quality ingredients that cause little or no harm to the environment and combine them with *mucho amor*.

When Rupert and I stayed there, Adolfo, who does most of the cooking and baking, was delighted to give me the recipe for this loaf made with ginger, spice and dried fruit. He calls this the lost loaf because he always keeps back a little of each loaf he bakes, which might otherwise get left over or 'lost', and then uses it as the stale bread required to make the next one. It is an ancient habit that our generation, with our wasteful kitchen habits, would perhaps do well to follow. As well as being thrifty, the stale bread adds that extra little bit of flavour to the new loaf. It is especially delicious toasted and spread with goat's curd or crème fraîche.

Makes 1 loaf

200g stale wholemeal bread, torn into chunks
275ml milk
3 cloves
a little oil or butter, for greasing the tin
a little flour, for dusting the tin
130g strong bread flour
150ml olive oil
2 eggs, beaten
200g apricot jam
¼ teaspoon baking powder
½ teaspoon ground cinnamon
1½ teaspoons ground ginger
70g chopped dried prunes
1 good eating apple, peeled, cored and chopped
70g mixed raisins/sultanas and dried berries, such as blueberries, cranberries, sour cherries, blackcurrants, etc.
50g blanched almonds, preferably Marcona

Soak the dry bread in the milk with the cloves for 1–2 hours until it is pliable, then drain off the milk and keep to one side, removing the cloves. Squeeze out the bread.

Preheat the oven to 200°C/gas 6. Grease a 21cm loaf tin with oil or butter and dust with flour.

Put the soaked, squeezed bread in a bowl and mix in the flour, oil, beaten eggs and the jam. Beat, adding as much of the drained milk as necessary, until you have a light dough/batter.

Add the baking powder and the rest of the ingredients. Leave to rest for 10–15 minutes, until the dough has risen a little.

Spoon the dough/batter into the prepared tins. Put into the preheated oven and bake for 10 minutes, then lower the temperature to 180°C/ gas 4 for about 25 minutes. The loaf will be solid, with a bread pudding-like texture. Leave to cool in the tin for about 15 minutes, then turn out and finish cooling on a wire rack.

PLATOS SALADOS

Savoury snacks

Coca tovada de sobrassada
Light *sobrasada* and plum loaf

This is a savoury-sweet *coca* (see page 70) from Mallorca, made from a potato dough with pieces of *sobrasada* (soft *chorizo*) – spelled *sobrassada* in the local Mallorquín dialect – pushed into it, along with fresh fruit. It is astonishingly light despite the quantity of potato, lard and egg, and makes a great weekend brunch when you might have a little more time on your hands, as it does require a bit of work.

You really need to eat it on the day you make it, as it will become stale quite quickly – but actually it is so good, that is not difficult!

Serves 6–8

300g floury potatoes
30g fresh yeast
4 medium eggs
175g caster sugar
150g lard
pinch of sea salt
500–600g strong flour
150g *sobrasada*, ideally *de Mallorca*, broken up
2 fresh plums or apricots, sliced (skin on)

Boil the potatoes in their skins until they are tender and the skins are splitting, then drain and leave in a colander to steam. Once the potatoes have cooled enough to handle comfortably, peel off their skins, remove any 'eyes' or discoloured parts, and keep the potatoes to one side.

In a cup, dissolve the yeast in 1½ tablespoons of warm water.

Break the eggs into a large mixing bowl, add 150g of the sugar and beat together.

Put the lard into a pan and heat gently to melt it, then add to the eggs and sugar. Stir in the dissolved yeast. Next add the salt and the warm boiled potatoes, breaking them up with your fingers as you put them in, and mix all together well with a wooden spoon. It doesn't matter at this stage if the potatoes are still lumpy.

Weigh out 500g of strong flour initially, and with one hand add it slowly to the mixture while you work the dough with the fingers of the other hand. Keep adding handfuls of flour until you have a soft dough – you may need to add a little more flour.

Turn out the dough on to a floured surface and knead for 5 minutes, again adding extra flour if the dough feels too sticky.

Line a deep baking tray with baking paper and press the dough out over the surface. Arrange the pieces of *sobrasada* and plum or apricot over the dough, alternating them in a chequerboard fashion (or as decoratively as you like), and leave to rise in a warm place for 2 hours.

Preheat the oven to 200°C/gas 6.

Mix the remaining sugar with a tablespoon of water and brush over the top. Put into the preheated oven, then lower the temperature to 180°C/gas 4 and bake for around 30 minutes, until risen and the crust is golden. The paprika-soaked fat will have run out of the *sobrasada* and down the sides of the *coca*. Take out of the oven and lift from the tray using the baking paper; leave to cool on a rack.

Banyetes de sobrassada
Sobrasada pastry horns

A speciality of Menorca, *banyeta* is Menorquín (a dialect of Catalan) for 'little horn', which refers to the shape of the pastry and also to a children's storybook character of the same name who sometimes appears as a puppet and looks like a little devil with horns. The soft, spreading *chorizo sobrasada* (see page 260) is a great ingredient for baking, and can be used in the same way as sausage meat.

This recipe makes a lot of *banyetes*, but once made up, you can freeze what you don't need immediately, then just defrost and bake them.

You could also make an alternative 'pinwheel' version, which is a little easier to shape, and which Scott Boden came up with when experimenting with this recipe. He suggests rolling out the dough into one rectangle, 2–3mm thick, then turning it so that the short side is facing you and spreading the *sobrasada* over half the dough. Sprinkle with some dried oregano, then roll up firmly like a Swiss roll, slice into rounds of 1–1.5cm thick, using a sharp knife, and bake as in the recipe here.

Makes around 65

250g *sobrasada*
125ml olive oil
125ml *fino* sherry
½ teaspoon salt
½ teaspoon caster sugar
425g plain flour, plus extra for dusting
1 egg, beaten

Preheat the oven to 170ºC/Gas 3.

Roll the *sobrasada* into a thin sausage, about 2cm in diameter, and with a sharp knife cut into rounds about 8mm thick. Keep to one side. Mix all the ingredients, except the *sobrasada* and beaten egg, into a firm dough, then roll out on a floured surface to 2–3mm thick.

Use a cutter or small glass (about 5cm in diameter) to stamp out circles. Place a disc of *sobrasada* on each circle, just to one side of the centre, damp all around the edge with a little water, then fold the dough over to make half-moon shapes. Press all around the edges to seal, then take each end between your fingertips and twist and pinch them, curving them inwards to create the 'little horns'. Place on a baking tray, or trays, and brush with beaten egg.

Bake in the preheated oven for about 18 minutes, until light golden. Leave the *banyetas* to cool on the tray before lifting them off.

Bollos de chorizo a la parrilla
Hot grilled *chorizo* rolls

At our Chorizo Grill outside the Borough Market shop, we have been making *bollos de chorizo a la parrilla* – hot rolls with sizzling grilled *chorizo* and *piquillo* peppers (see page 275) – from mid-morning to lunchtime for over fifteen years and they are one of the most popular things we sell: world famous in fact, since, amazingly, they have even featured in newspaper articles in America, Italy and Japan. For each person, you need a bread roll, cut in half, a cooking *chorizo*, cut in half lengthways, a *piquillo* pepper from a jar and a handful of rocket leaves.

Preheat the grill, then toast the bread. Grill the *chorizo* halves for about 3 minutes, turning halfway through (if you have a griddle pan, you can get a nice criss-crossing effect as you do this). Sandwich the bread around the rocket leaves, pepper and *chorizo* and eat immediately.

Panecillos de mantequilla
Mini butter rolls

Pilar, of the Gutiérrez de la Vega winery in Valencia (see page 190), makes these rich little rolls with a touch of sugar, which are a perfect foil for *foie gras* topped with her Moscatel jelly. They are also excellent with Ibérico ham, pâtés and blue cheeses.

Makes around 25

2 large eggs
500g strong white flour
50g fresh yeast
50g caster sugar
½ teaspoon salt
about 275ml milk
10g unsalted butter, softened

Beat one of the eggs. Place the flour in a bowl, make a well in the centre and put in the yeast, sugar, salt and the beaten egg. Warm the milk to tepid – don't overheat it, or the heat will kill the yeast – and add it slowly to the flour mixture, mixing to a soft dough that you can knead easily (you may need more or less milk).

Transfer the dough to a bowl. Cover with a clean cloth and leave in a warm place for 30 minutes, until doubled in size.

Now add half the softened butter, working it into the dough, then knead it again, put it back into the bowl, and rest it, covered as before, for another 15 minutes, until it doubles in size again.

Preheat the oven to 180°C/gas 4.

Work the remaining butter into the dough, knead it again and put it back into the bowl. Cover with the cloth and this time leave the dough to rise for 30–45 minutes, until its size has increased by half again (i.e. it is now three times its original size). Take walnut-sized pieces of the dough and form them into rounds. Place on a greased baking tray. Beat the remaining egg and brush lightly over each round, then bake in the preheated oven for about 20 minutes, until a rich golden brown.

PAN ARTESANO

'it can be a revelation'

Often it is hard to discover the true diversity of Spanish breads, hidden as they tend to be by more standardised loaves. Since Franco's time many traditional varieties of grain have been supplanted by newer more 'productive' ones, and modern factory techniques dominate, so local, handed-down recipes are sometimes hard to find outside the home or small bakeries, and some have been forgotten completely, or are only made on special saints' days. However, many do still exist, and when you come across a real regional *pan artesano* (artisan bread) it can be a revelation. I am thinking particularly of the beautiful *pan de coca* of Catalunya; or, in Castilla, the golden *pan sobado* with its distinctive patterns marked in the crust, and a tight, absorbent texture that is perfect for the typical garlic and bread soup of this part of Spain, *sopa castellana*. Here too you find the light and airy *pan de hogaza*, and *torta de aceite*. Not to be confused with the thin Andalusian biscuit of the same name, this *torta* is a flat, bronze-coloured spongy loaf about 5cm high, which can either be round or long. It is similar to an Italian *focaccia*, as it is made with olive oil in the dough, then coated with more oil before baking, to give it an attractive gleam.

At one time, in every region the style of bread would have been dictated by the variety of cereal that was traditionally grown there. Wheat was often supplemented by barley (*cebada*), rye (*centeno*), which was popular in the high mountains of the north; oats (*avena*), millet (*mijo*), or maize (*maíz*), which was introduced from central America in the sixteenth century, particularly into the green land of Galicia with its abundant rain. And on the north coast flour would often be made from chestnuts from the forests, as well as with grains.

The Galicians, Castilians and Levantines were particularly known for their speciality breads, and the regions are still dotted with mills – originally wind-driven in La Mancha, and water-driven in Galicia and most other areas. In Galicia many of the old breads, including corn bread and potato bread, still survive, and they boast the only Protected Geographical Indication (PGI) bread in Spain, a country-style loaf with a thick crust called *pan de Cea*, made with one of the many local varieties of wheat. Cea is a little village in the province of Ourense, and the bread has a documented history stretching back to the thirteenth century.

The province of Zamora in Castilla y León was especially renowned for its exceptional wheat and flour, and this is possibly why one area is called Tierra del Pan, 'the land of bread'. Until around 30–40 years ago the variety of wheat grown throughout Castilla y León was the local and historic *candeal*, which produced

high-quality, very fine white flour that made very close-textured, dense, bright-white bread capable of lasting a good 10–15 days. However, in recent years the bread-making industry has designed more productive strains and crosses and it has become harder for farmers to justify growing *candeal*, which works out at around 30 per cent more expensive to use. So it has reduced considerably in cultivation and will only increase again if it can gain more recognition in specialist breads such as *pan sobado*.

In the old days wood-fired baking ovens were sometimes owned communally, or by the local baker, who would take in the trays of dough made by each family and bake the bread for an entire village. On Saturday night you might also take along a lamb or suckling pig to be roasted in the wood-fired oven. In some places you can still do this. My brother, Mark, had his wedding meal of roasted local lamb baked in this way in the bakers' oven in Santa Maria d'Oló in Moianès in Catalunya.

Coca
Flatbread or 'cake'

Coca is a broad term given to a host of different flatbreads made to many recipes along the whole of the Levantine coast, from the French border to south of Alicante, and reaching inland to Lleida.

Some are very simple, some quite complex, some are made with savoury toppings, like pizza, others are sweet, perfect with coffee mid-morning, and might be flavoured with anise and/or slender, creamy Mediterranean pine nuts (*coca de pinyons*). Often in bakeries a *coca de pinyons* will be in the form of one long, doughy piece, shaped a little like a tongue, so known as *una lengua*, which will be cut into pieces for you, whatever size you want – and you will be charged by the weight. A popular variation is to add an extra layer of dough to the base to create a slim pocket filled with *crema catalana* (custard). Or, especially in Catalunya, you see more brittle versions that snap like *langues de chat* biscuits.

Sometimes they are sprayed lightly with anisette before baking, which gives a lovely refreshing edge to the flavour.

Our friend Pilar, of the Gutiérrez de la Vega winery in Alicante, makes *coca de mollitas*, a local variation in which the base is spread with melted chocolate and a crumble-type topping flavoured with white wine.

Other *coques* are more cakey in texture – in fact, in parts of Spain the word *coca* applies to some kinds of cake (see page 59, *coca de yogur*). And there are often special ones for celebrating a saint's day, such as the *coca de San Joan*, made with a puffy, round, brioche-like dough, pine nuts and sugared fruit.

However, you can also find the plain bread, *pan de coca*, which is shaped like an elongated espadrille and is usually made with a yeasty 'starter culture' or 'mother', so it puffs up quite thickly. For a while it was a somewhat forgotten bread, much harder to find than its sweet or pizza-like counterparts, but a handful of artisan bakers are spearheading its revival, notably one unrelenting perfectionist, who is the baker and *coquero* (*coca* maker) in the village of Folgueroles near Vic. Since a good *pan de coca* is quite the most heavenly bread I have ever eaten it is very appropriate that his name is Àngel!

Àngel Puigsellosas makes his *pan de coca* a full metre long. Soft and delicate, yet typically crispy-crunchy on the outside, it is sweet yet salty, somewhere between a *focaccia* and a *ciabatta* in texture, but really a bread that has a character all of its own. It is perfect for tomato bread (see page 72) because it is so long-lasting – especially if you keep it in the fridge, and because it freezes beautifully, Àngel is able to send us his breads all the way to Brindisa. You can slice the bread widthways along its full length if you are really skilled, or cut it into 15cm slices and then split it and toast it ready for painting with tomato and extra virgin olive oil.

Àngel comes from a long line of *panaderos* but has really pioneered his own signature *coca*, made with his special bespoke mix of cake flour with a blend of sugars and salts. The dough is mixed slowly and gently, using purified water at a specific temperature. Àngel likes to employ women in the bakery, as he believes they have a softer touch; and his philosophy is also that the well-being of the baker is reflected in the bread, so everyone works a more sociable eight-hour day, while still baking two batches of bread, rather than the extreme hours that bakers are often required to keep.

Once the dough is mixed and portioned for the first fermentation stage, the room becomes quite magical and silent, with a special whiteness about it from the flour dusted over the work surfaces and the white light filtering through the blinds. Next, the characteristic *rombo* marking is pressed into the top of each loaf, then these are rested again before being carefully stretched to more than double their original length. This is the most delicate stage of the process, as any heavy-handed touch could cause the bread to lose the air that gives it its special texture, and damage the creation of that firm but light crust.

Once stretched, the breads are rested again and at last the quiet of the bakery is broken by the sound of the *dosificadora* machine sprinkling them with olive oil ready for baking.

Leftover bread

Many recipes in Spanish cooking were originally designed to use up dried-out bread, as, especially in rural areas, it wasn't possible to buy fresh loaves every day, so they would be eked out. Tomato bread (see page 72), *gazpacho* and *salmorejo* (see pages 144 and 149) are all based on using up bread that is a few days old, as is *torrijas de leche,* in which the slices are soaked in cinnamon and lemon-scented milk until soft, then drained, coated with beaten egg, deep-fried in olive oil and sprinkled with sugar.

Stale bread is also important for making breadcrumbs (*migas*, see page 79), and there is even a word, *rebozados*, which describes something that is coated in breadcrumbs and fried, such as *croquetas* (see page 241).

PAN CON TOMATE

'a universal food'

If there is such a thing as a universal breakfast and any-time snack, it has to be *pan con tomate*: tomato bread, or *pa amb tomaquet* as it is called in Catalunya and *pamboli amb tomàtiga* in the Balearics. Originally the addition of tomato to bread and oil was the choice of the north, but over the years it has become fashionable in homes all over the country, where each morning families are busily rubbing toasted bread with halved tomatoes and olive oil before going off to work or school. Then later in the day in the tapas bars and restaurants it will appear again, topped with the likes of anchovies, cured ham or grilled meats and vegetables (see pages 131–134).

You might think that not much variation is possible, given so few ingredients are involved, but inevitably everyone in every region has a different view on how to make tomato bread. Sometimes the bread is toasted, sometimes not. I prefer the tomatoes to be squashed into the bread, but in some regions the tomato might be grated or puréed and then treated as a spread, and if you ask for *pan con tomate* in some parts of the country, be aware that you might simply get bread with sliced tomatoes on top!

Sometimes garlic is a feature, often depending on the time of day you eat it. In Navarra at the olive oil mill of Hacienda Queiles in Tudela, I was given toasted country bread with a bowl of grated tomato with tender raw garlic shoots (*ajetes*)

finely chopped and mixed in almost like a herb, which you spooned on top: wonderful.

Tomato bread is so simple that everything depends on the quality, ripeness and flavour of the tomatoes. Spain is endowed with exceptional tomatoes throughout most of the year, but in the Levante, the area of the east coast that stretches from Catalunya in the north down to Murcia, they specialise in a small, strong-skinned variety of 'hanging tomato', *tomaquet de penjar*, which is cultivated exclusively for the purpose of making tomato bread. The tomatoes are harvested just as they start to turn red, then are matured and ripened in a cool dark place such as an attic or cellar. Typically their stems are sewn in bunches on to knotted strings that are stretched from ceiling to floor, though the father of Leo Rivera, our head chef, has developed a horizontal system for the tomatoes he grows in the family allotment, in which he twists the whole plants around wires stretched across his roof space.

Tomaquets de penjar contain more bright red juice and less flesh than other varieties, and thanks to their strong skin they won't fall apart when you press them on to your slice of bread or toast. They paint the bread a beautiful colour, their flavour is rich and deeply aromatic, and they are so highly regarded that people will pay easily three or four times more than for other varieties in the Catalan markets.

Alubias al horno en salsa de tomate

Homemade baked beans in spicy tomato sauce

Traditionally, for *pan con tomate* people used bread that was a day or two old, which would come to life with the juice of the tomato. My favourite is *pan de coca* (flatbread, see page 70) or alternatively *pan de payés* (country loaf); or a slice of sourdough. In the Basque country they often use a baguette, though this wouldn't be my first choice, as once rubbed with tomato the soft texture can become too pasty. Look for bread with a good crust and quite an open airy texture – not dense and solid – that will crisp up nicely if you are toasting it. Industrial sliced bread won't do, as it will just become a mush.

You also need good olive oil, something fruity but not overpowering, such as *Arbequina*, which will complement the sweetness of the tomato. Use as much as you like, but remember that you might end up with oil running down your arm as you eat.

Inevitably, there is always an argument over which of the few ingredients should go on to the bread or toast first. At home the way we do it is to toast a pile of good bread, then put out the halved tomatoes, cut cloves of garlic (for those that want them), a bottle of good extra virgin olive oil and some sea salt, and let everyone help themselves. If you are happy using your fingers this is really the best way, however messy.

If you are using garlic I would say only do so if the bread is toasted, and then rub it on *before* the tomato, as the roughness of the toast's surface gives you something to grate the cloves against, and it will embed itself better if the bread is not already soaked in tomato. Next I would squeeze the juice into the toast until it is coloured bright red and all that is left of the tomatoes is their skin. Ideally, you will have more juice than flesh on the toast, so it looks as if it has been painted red.

Some say salt should come next, then oil, as this helps the salt to impregnate the bread, but I like to drizzle on the oil first and rub it in, then scatter on sea salt, as I love the crunch it gives.

Eat straight away, neat, or with whatever topping you like, from slices of cured ham or sausage to anchovies, or *Manchego* cheese. Freshly cooked kippers are good too.

This is baked beans taken to a whole new, spicy level, which we serve for breakfast at our London Bridge restaurant, using small white *arrocina* beans – a Spanish twist on a British tradition. We make the *brava* sauce with a little more sugar than when serving it in the traditional way with potatoes, which makes it a bit more syrupy when it reduces down during cooking. The quantity of liquid might seem a lot when the dish goes into the oven, but I promise you this works – we cook these beans regularly at home and they are a big favourite.

Serves 4–6

500g *arrocina* beans
***salsa brava* sauce (see page 295),**
made with 2 tablespoons of demerara
sugar, rather than just a pinch
1 rice *morcilla de Burgos* (optional, see page 76)
1 tablespoon olive oil

Soak the *arrocina* beans in cold water overnight.

Preheat the oven to 180°C/gas 4.

Drain the beans, put into an ovenproof dish and cover with 2 litres of fresh cold water. Stir in the *brava* sauce and put into the preheated oven, without a lid, for 3 hours, until the beans are tender and the liquid is syrupy and has reduced down to just about a centimetre above the beans.

Slice the *morcilla*, if using, into 1 cm rounds, then heat the olive oil in a small frying pan and brown each slice on both sides. Serve on top of the beans.

MORCILLA

'varied in shape, flavour and texture'

The black puddings of Spain are very varied in shape, flavour and texture. Like *chorizo*, they can be small like a regular sausage, fatter and more salami-shaped, or hooped, and they might be poached before being sold, or hung up to cure, and sometimes even smoked. Some are best suited to grilling or frying; some are texturally better for adding to a one-pot dish, usually with beans, or the cooked *morcilla* might be taken out of its casing and eaten as a spread.

The traditional way of making the sausage is to heat the pig's blood in a big cauldron, then mix in fat, salt and spices, plus any other recipe ingredients, before stuffing into natural casings. Many *morcillas* will have around 50 per cent pork meat added as well as fat, and across the regions you find a vast variety of added flavours and different textures. In Galicia, there are some curious *morcillas* made with dried fruits such as minced figs, walnuts and breadcrumbs; or in the Canaries sweet potato, currants, thyme, almonds, bread and sugar might be added. In the Basque country leeks, pumpkin and rice are used (here they even have a *morcilla* called *mondejos*, made from sheep's blood), and in Aragón, herbs, spices and nuts. The special sausages made in this region for the feast of San Antón (Saint Anthony, hermit and patron saint of animals) on 17 January are flavoured with cinnamon, ground aniseed, walnuts, almonds, hazelnuts, pine nuts and rice.

How to choose *morcilla*
Pick the *morcilla* best suited to the way you want to eat it. Smaller, softer *morcillas* that have thinner casings and look like normal sausages (about 15cm long and 2.5cm in diameter) have usually been poached before you buy them, and will just need to be finished by grilling, frying or breaking up to make a soft mince or *migas* (crumbs) that can be added to dishes.

I think the ideal breakfast *morcilla* is the fat sausage from Burgos, as it contains rice, which makes it quite dense, and as it is always poached before being sold it is very easy to slice, then fry or grill in fat rounds that hold together. Also, it is not as strongly flavoured as those from some other regions, but just lightly spiced with cumin or nutmeg.

Other *morcillas,* especially those which contain onion, and often also pine nuts and cinnamon, are quite soft, and should not be sliced before cooking, but grilled whole, or added at the end of a long-cooked dish, typically of beans, otherwise they will disintegrate. This softer style is also ideal for *migas*.

Firmer ones, such as those from Asturias in the north, are often smoked after curing and therefore a fair bit drier, almost wrinkled

and leathery-looking (often they are thin and hooped), so they need more rehydration in the cooking process. These are ideal for long, slow-cooked dishes, as they will happily plump up and hold their shape while they are simmering in the pot for a couple of hours. They impart a deep smoky flavour to the dish, and because they stay intact, they can be neatly sliced at the end of the cooking.

Some *morcillas*, such as those made with the meat, fat and blood from *Ibérico* pigs (see page 168) are not poached, but are cured for around 50 days and can be eaten sliced, like any other cured sausage. Their texture can be quite coarse and they look very dark but with redder *pimentón*-coloured chunks. They are high in fat and I feel they are almost too rich for adding to one-pot dishes, but they are great grilled.

Migas de la casa
Breadcrumbs with *chorizo*, *panceta* and black pudding

Migas (breadcrumbs) are an old country breakfast favourite to eat with good bacon (*baicon*), or *chorizo* and eggs; or, in the south of Spain, topped with a tin of good sardines, or roasted peppers. Traditionally, they were an essential shepherd's sustenance, eaten in the field in early morning by the campfire: pieces of old, dry bread, fried in a little fat, with maybe some garlic, paprika or herbs added, if they were available. When the men were lucky there might have been some cured ham or sausage to eat with them.

Friends at one of our olive oil suppliers, Olivar de la Luna, told us about a local rhyme that would be sung by olive harvesters, frying up *migas* in the groves:

> *Sartenes tostando migas*
> *están repicando al alba*
> *sartenes tostando migas*
> *anuncian la madrugada . . .*

which translates as:

> Frying pans toasting crumbs
> pealing out at dawn
> frying pans toasting crumbs
> herald in the morn . . .

One of our former head chefs, Esperanza Añonuevo Heys, worked with me on this recipe, which is more luxurious than the old shepherds' or oil harvesters' fare, incorporating *chorizo*, *panceta* and *morcilla*. I would use a *morcilla* from Burgos, which is milder than some, and if you can find *panceta ibérica* (see page 394), so much the better.

If you like, you can leave all the ingredients to soak in a bowl overnight in the fridge – if you do this, you will need to add a little extra stock.

Serves 4

250g stale country-style bread
2 tablespoons sherry or dry white vermouth
130ml chicken stock
100g cooking *chorizo*
1 small soft onion *morcilla* (see page 76), around 70g
50g *panceta*, finely diced
½ a green pepper, finely diced
sea salt and freshly ground black pepper
2 tablespoons olive oil, plus extra for frying the eggs
4 eggs

If you wish, cut the crusts from the bread then put it into a food processor and pulse a few times to make the breadcrumbs. They should be medium to fine, and don't need to be completely regular.

Put the crumbs into a large bowl and sprinkle them with the sherry or vermouth along with the chicken stock.

Skin the *chorizo* and *morcilla*, break them up into very small pieces and add to the bowl, along with the *panceta* and green pepper. Season and mix together lightly. Cover the bowl and leave for a minimum of an hour. The mixture should feel damp and sticky to the touch.

Heat the oil in a wide, deep frying pan over a low to medium heat, then add the breadcrumb mixture and turn about in the oil. Cook for a few minutes, then stir and turn the mixture again. Continue in this way for about 10 minutes, until warmed through and lightly golden – the crumbs should not be crisp, but more the consistency of a cooked grain, such as bulgar wheat.

Meanwhile, heat a little more oil in a separate pan and fry the eggs, making sure you keep the yolks soft. Serve some *migas* on each of 4 plates and top each with a fried egg.

Life and Cooking with Pepe and Mercedes

I first met Pepe Buitrago, an abstract installation and holographic artist, and his partner, Mercedes Laso, a puppet-maker, at an art exhibition in London when I had just started Brindisa and they were living in the capital for a few years before returning to Madrid. Pepe was establishing a market for his art, and Mercedes was selling her puppets in small art outlets. Beyond their crafts, they are great intellectuals who love music and food, and gathering friends around them to cook, eat, drink and discuss the world.

One of the first words I learned in Spanish literature was *tertulia*, which refers to a small gathering of academics, artists, writers and historians who get together regularly to share thoughts and enrich the mind on a range of scholarly topics and ideas over an afternoon or evening, and often into the small hours – something akin to the Bloomsbury set in London in the early twentieth century. Across Spain there is a network of *tertulias*, which hold this old tradition as something precious and a little removed from modern life, in which there is so rarely time to sit and ruminate on philosophical or literary matters.

Pepe and Mercedes are part of a *tertulia* circle who are also great cooks – including Raul Domingo, his wife Carmen Dalmau (see page 111), and Margarita and Asunción Almela Boix, jolly, funny, anarchistic and academic sisters (see page 98) in their sixties who have very strong opinions on food. Consequently, they often hold their *tertulias* in the bars and restaurants of different Castilian towns, so that good cooking, good drink and good thoughts are always on the agenda.

From the start Pepe and Mercedes were so interested in my fledgling plan to bring Spanish foods to the British table that we connected immediately, and Mercedes put her puppet-making skills to amazing use for me, making the strings for hundreds of dried peppers and *farcellets* (see page 14). One of our earliest Brindisa success stories, these were made up of dried *ñora* and *guindilla* peppers, alternated with little parcels of dried thyme and savory wrapped up in bay leaves, which provided the perfect rustic mix of flavourings for casseroles.

Both Castilians (Pepe is originally from Tomelloso, La Mancha, and Mercedes from Salamanca city), they have been invaluable in teaching me about the mood and food of central Spain. They showed me how to make my first *cocido madrileño* (see page 446) for a big tableful of family and friends at my parents' house in Hampshire, and from them I first learned about the likes of *caldereta*: shepherd's lamb stew (see page 435), *morteruelo*, a spiced game and meat pâté, and *zarajos*. A favourite in the villages of La Mancha, these are milk-fed lamb intestines, stretched and twisted by hand in tidy loops over small vine twigs, knotted, roasted in a hot oven for about an hour, then split into two and grilled just before serving, still on their twigs, so you eat them like kebabs on skewers. They look beautiful to the eye, but are quite a heady and aggressive experience for the nose and palate: not for the faint-hearted.

In the late eighties when Pepe and Mercedes were travelling between Spain and London, they would bring me produce such as *tortas cenceñas* for serving in the herb-scented stock of *gazpachos manchegos* (game stew, page 456). Each giant unleavened biscuit, similar to a water biscuit, came in individual bright, retro-style wrapping, featuring Don Quixote characters.

Time spent with Pepe and Mercedes is always uplifting and no trip to Madrid is complete without a visit to them at their apartment in the area that used to be the medieval city, in a street with the wonderful name of Mediodía Grande, 'the big midday'. The apartment was converted from shops, and Pepe has created a series of simple living spaces in which to celebrate his renowned art and holography, food, family and cooking, which all seem to happily co-exist. I remember one Christmas time, when Pepe's sons from his first marriage visited, he built a huge nativity set for them, with lights and music, half the size of a dining room, but it was so typical of him that in addition to the scene around the manger he had created streams and fields, with models of villagers harvesting, plucking chickens and baking bread.

Pepe also gave me his recipe for a lemon salad 'hangover' breakfast: a Manchegan cleansing recipe made by villagers in Castilla La Mancha after a big meat and red wine fest – when actually it is usually the quantity of meat, rather than alcohol, that is consumed in excess. The idea is that the salad cleans the system and allows everybody to embark on more of the same by midday! In fact, it is absolutely delicious, and so well worthy of its inclusion in this chapter, hangover or no hangover.

ENSALADA DE LIMÓN

Finely (and quietly if necessary!) chop 1 mild onion, spring onion or shallot with 2 garlic shoots, then peel a lemon and carefully squeeze as much juice as you can over the top without destroying the segments of flesh (don't throw the lemon away). Leave for 10 minutes to mellow the flavours. Chop the pieces of the lemon flesh left after squeezing and add to the mixture. Season and add 2 tablespoons of olive oil. Mix together and finally add 2 tablespoons of cold water. Mix again, serve with good bread and recover.

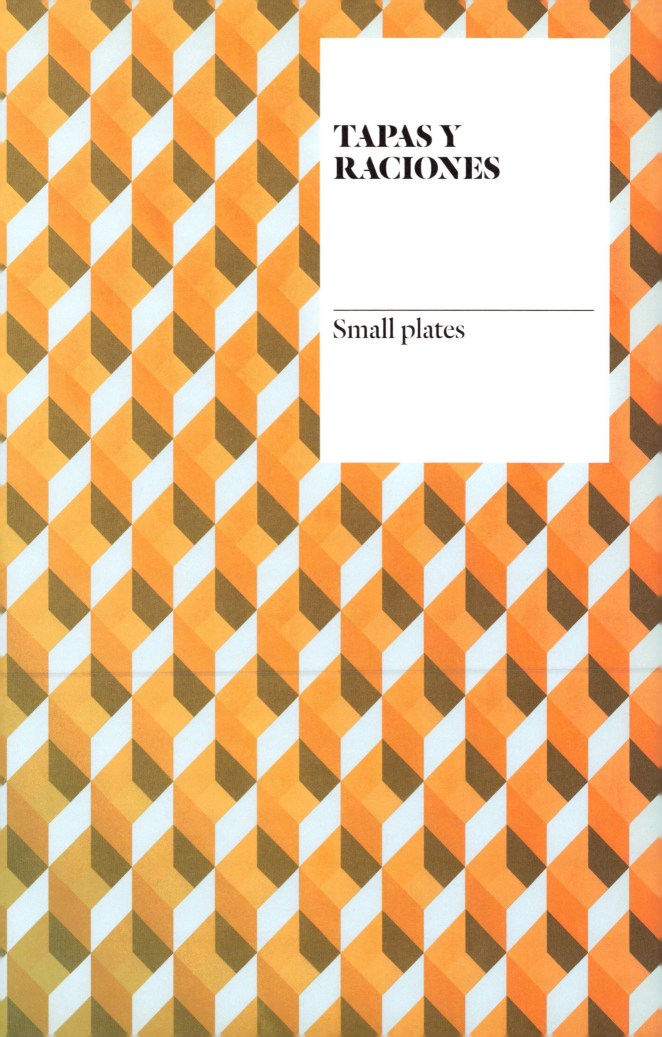

TAPAS Y RACIONES

_____

Small plates

Sometimes I want to stand on the rooftop and shout: 'Tapas are not the only Spanish food!' Outside Spain these snacks are so famous, and tapas bars so fashionable, you could be forgiven for thinking that this is the be all and end all of Spanish eating.

That's not to say that I don't love tapas. I do. They represent a relaxed way of sharing food, drink and gossip with friends that is typically Spanish. But it is only one aspect of the way people eat. Also, defining *tapas* (little snacks) as distinct from *raciones* (small shared plates) can be quite spurious. The squares of *tortilla*, saucer of olives, plate of air-dried ham and dish of local beans or wrinkled potatoes in a spicy sauce that you eat with a glass of sherry or a beer, standing or sitting on a stool in a bar, could equally be starters in a restaurant. They could be little plates that you put on the table before the big Sunday meal, or a collection of dishes that make up lunch or a simple supper.

Our good friend, chef and writer, Pep Palau, cooked in a restaurant in Orís in Catalunya for a number of years. It was actually a rectory attached to a church and there were only four other houses in the village. His food was fantastic and one year he put on a spectacular New Year's Eve dinner with dish after dish leading up to roasted *isard*, the local name for the Pyrenean chamois, or goat-antelope.

In between each course on the menu, Pep had written the word *flostis*, which, he explained, was an old-fashioned Catalan word meaning 'thingamijig'. His delicious selection of *flostis* included various *croquetas* (see page 241); a local farmhouse cheese coated in crushed nuts; *sobrasada* (see page 260) and honey toasties, homemade pâtés and sautéd wild mushrooms.

I thought it was a brilliant word, and something about the sound of it conjured up a sense of nostalgia and forgotten language that amused the table and had everyone talking about favourite *flostis*. Maybe that is what I should have called this chapter, as it is really about a collection of small 'thingamijigs' you can group together or serve alone, as you like.

APERITIVOS

Nibbles to serve
with drinks

Galletas de queso manchego
Scott's Manchego cheese biscuits

These beguiling little biscuits with a big flavour make a great *aperitivo* with *cava* or extra dry Martinis. The recipe comes from Scott Boden, one of my earliest partners in Brindisa. He makes the biscuits with a variety of Spanish cheeses, but recommends Manchego for the most impact and reckons they are also good without the saffron, if you prefer not to use it. When Rupert and I got married, Scott very generously made around 400 of the biscuits to serve with drinks at the party afterwards, and everyone loved them.

The biscuits are ready to eat once they are out of the oven and have cooled to room temperature, but are better after a couple of days, kept in an airtight container.

Makes around 60 biscuits

125g mature Manchego cheese, finely grated
175g strong white flour
6 strands of saffron (optional)
125g unsalted butter, softened

Mix the grated cheese with the flour.

Grind the saffron, if using, very finely using a pestle and mortar, then incorporate into the butter and rub into the flour and cheese.

Form into 3 rolls of 2.5cm in diameter – working the dough as little as possible. Wrap in clingfilm and chill for at least 1 hour in the fridge.

Preheat the oven to 160°C/gas 2.

Remove the rolls of dough from the fridge and slice into rounds, 1.5cm thick, then arrange them, well-spaced, on baking trays. Bake in the middle of the preheated oven for around 20 minutes, or until the biscuits are lightly golden brown and the centres are fairly firm to the touch, turning the trays around once during the baking time, so that the biscuits bake evenly.

Remove them from the oven and place on a rack to cool.

Almendras al horno o fritas
Salted roasted or deep-fried almonds

Of course, you can buy wonderful-quality, ready-salted almonds, but it is also pretty satisfying to do your own. In theory, this is one of the easiest *aperitivos* of all – but you do need about ten minutes of calm and patience in the kitchen – as it is vital to make sure the almonds don't burn.

The Spanish will always use the best nuts for serving with drinks. The ultimate almond is the round, fat, rich, buttery Marcona (see page 90). These are almost always sold blanched, i.e. out of their skins, and then usually they are fried in olive oil, which gives the nuts a stronger flavour and fabulous crunchy texture – though I also like them oven-roasted, and they feel healthier this way.

The longer, slender and more brittle Largueta variety of almonds can also be roasted in the same way in or out of their skins (they tend to be more flavoursome this way than deep-fried) and are a touch drier, for times when you don't want the full-fat creaminess of a Marcona.

Whichever method you choose, find yourself a good dry sherry to wash down the almonds.

Makes a good bowlful

200g whole blanched almonds, preferably Marcona
2 tablespoons olive oil if roasting; 500ml if deep-frying
around 2 teaspoons sea salt, crushed

Have ready a shallow bowl, lined with several pieces of kitchen paper.

For roasted almonds, preheat the oven to 180°C/gas 4 and spread the almonds on a large baking tray. Pour 2 tablespoons of oil over them and gently tilt the tray so it is well lined with oil and all the almonds are coated. Put into the preheated oven for about 10 minutes, making sure you watch carefully and turn the tray if necessary to keep the nuts that are at the edges and the back from getting burnt. Give the tray a gentle shake after about 5 minutes and again after about 8 minutes.

Once the nuts are golden in colour, take them out of the oven and tip them into the prepared bowl. Sprinkle with around 2 teaspoons of crushed sea salt and mix well, then cover with more kitchen paper and leave to cool completely. They should be ready to eat in about 15 minutes.

For deep-fried almonds, heat 500ml of olive oil in a deep pan (making sure it comes no further than a third of the way up). It needs to be around 180°C, but if you don't have a thermometer, put in an almond and if it sizzles the oil is hot enough. Fry the rest for about 2 minutes (moving them around), then lift out with a slotted spoon into the paper-lined dish. Immediately sprinkle with the salt as before, shake well to distribute it and leave to cool completely.

ALMONDS

'stone fruit, eaten as nuts'

Something we tend to forget is that almonds are actually stone fruit, eaten as nuts. There are around 200 varieties of almond in the world and many of them are native to Spain, where the acreage of almond trees is over three times that of California, yet the Spanish production is less than half that of the American state, which says a great deal about the different philosophies. In California, production is on a massive, hi-tech scale, with the orchards often being sprayed from the air. In Spain almonds are primarily produced on thousands of small farms on marginal land next to the Mediterranean, where the trees will often share their pockets of territory with olive trees, grapes and occasionally some cereal crops. The main growing areas are around Barcelona, Tarragona, Lleida, Castellón de la Plana and Valencia, where the soil tends to be quite poor. Since the land is not often irrigated, the trees rely heavily on rainfall and are very sensitive to weather changes, especially during the flowering season.

Despite the tough conditions – and perhaps partly because of them – Spanish almonds, particularly the highly prized Marcona, have a natural fattiness that is lacking in their counterparts grown in California, which tend to dry out more quickly and so are less versatile and not ideal for use in Spanish recipes. Inevitably, though, Spanish growers are now experimenting with planting newer, higher-yielding Californian varieties in Spanish soil, with some good results: for example, the Guara produces a good, sweet, round and soft almond.

Almond harvesting and processing in Spain begins in coastal areas around August and finishes inland around October, depending on the weather and the size of the crop. The almonds are either harvested manually by knocking the fruits from the branches, or by mechanically shaking them. Typically the nuts are left to dry on the ground for about 7–10 days, then swept into heaped rows where a mechanical picker gathers them up and delivers them, stones, soil and all, to the almond seller for shelling, grading, blanching, etc.

Varieties of Spanish almond vary considerably in flavour, from the buttery creaminess of the Marcona, grown on the Levante coast, to the more brittle nuttiness of the Largueta, grown in inland Aragón. These two are the best known, but older varieties include the Planeta, a sweet and oily almond that is very flat in shape and grows around the Alicante region, but is in danger of disappearing due to droughts; the Mallorca, grown on the island of the same name, and rich in fats, with a mild flavour; and the Comuna, which is usually long and slim but can vary in shape as well as flavour – occasionally you might find a bitter one. You might also come

across the Ramillete variety from Murcia, which is very sweet and perfect for marzipan, and Esperanza, a very versatile, good-quality almond that can be fried like a Marcona. If you can find it, it is probably the next best to its more famous relation, but again it is limited in production and in danger of disappearing, as the trees yield only a low quantity of fruit.

The Marcona almond
This is the most loved and revered of all almonds and the best known outside Spain. However much growers may experiment with new Californian varieties, it is hard to imagine the Marcona being supplanted as the king. Small, plump, round and pale-coloured, the nuts flourish all along the south-eastern Levante coast, and connoisseurs will buy their nuts from the particular villages that they believe produce the best. The selection of the nuts is crucial, as bees can transfer bitterness from one tree blossom to another. Marconas are graded by their size and proportion, and the best you can buy is a perfectly shaped nut measuring 16mm.

What makes the almonds special is their high oil content, so they are luscious and aromatic when they are fried and salted and served as an *aperitivo*. The fat content is also crucial in making *turrón* (the famous Spanish nougat). As the natural oil comes out of the nuts it helps bind the ingredients, compacting and sticking the elements together without the need for any added fat. One of my fondest food memories is the cosy smell of recently roasted almonds, mashing slowly with warm honey on an autumn morning at the home of *turrón*-maker Ferran Alemany, in the Lleida hills in Catalunya (see page 15).

Across the regions of Mediterranean Spain Marcona almonds might also be used in cake-making and baking; coarsely chopped into a rice dish; crushed with garlic and parsley in a *picada* (see page 320); toasted and served with *mojama* (salted and dried tuna) to give a different, crunchy texture to the cured fish; or made into

ajo blanco, the famous cold garlicky almond soup (see page 147).

I'm told that when the almond trees blossom, the flowers point upwards, which is why you can't grow Marcona almonds further north or inland because the dew that collects inside the petals might freeze overnight, and then the crop of nuts is ruined. That is why in the north and inland areas they favour the Largueta, as its flowers point downwards and the dew can drain away before it freezes.

MARINATED AND STUFFED OLIVES

All of the following, except the *gilda,* make a good bowlful, enough for four people with drinks, to put out with bread before a meal, or as part of a tapas selection.

If your olives come in brine, rinse them quickly under running water and dry them, before adding your own marinade.

Aceitunas empeltre con alcaparras
Black olives with capers

80g good capers in brine or salt
300g good black olives, such as Empeltre (see page 97), stone in
chopped thyme, to taste
1 tablespoon good olive oil
½ teaspoon *pimentón de la Vera dulce* (smoked mild paprika)
½ teaspoon *pimentón de la Vera picante* (smoked hot paprika)

Soak the capers in water for an hour to remove the excess salt, changing the water twice, then drain and put into a bowl with the olives, thyme and olive oil and mix together well. Marinate overnight or for at least 6 hours at room temperature. Sprinkle with the paprika just before serving.

Aceitunas empeltre con vino y naranja
Black olives in wine and orange marinade

1 orange
300g good black olives, preferably Empeltre (see page 97), stone in
2 teaspoons sugar
2 cloves of garlic, crushed
2 teaspoons chopped flat-leaf parsley
2 bay leaves
enough white wine to cover the olives
2 tablespoons Moscatel vinegar
4 tablespoons extra virgin olive oil

With a peeler, take off the orange zest and cut into rough strips. Separate the flesh into segments, then cut the flesh into chunks (around the size of the olives). Put into a bowl with the rest of the ingredients and mix together well. Leave to marinate for at least 6 hours at room temperature.

Aceitunas verdes con naranja y miel
Green olives with orange zest and honey

This was the idea of James Robinson, my long-time colleague at Brindisa, and a big fan of casual gatherings of friends sharing lots of small plates. His idea was to add some sweetness to the Caspe, which is a bitter olive. Once marinated, these will keep in the fridge for several days.

400g green olives, such as Caspe (see page 96), stone in
1 tablespoon finely grated orange zest
1 teaspoon honey
2 cloves of garlic, crushed
½ teaspoon dried thyme
a pinch of ground allspice
¼ teaspoon coarse salt
¼ teaspoon coarsely ground black pepper
1 tablespoon chopped flat-leaf parsley
4 tablespoons extra virgin olive oil

Put all the ingredients into a bowl and mix together well. Marinate overnight or for at least 6 hours at room temperature.

Aceitunas gordal con anchoa
Gordal olives with anchovies

This is one of my favourite ways of serving olives, but since we are talking about only two main ingredients, success depends on selecting the best quality olives and anchovies. We use the big, beautiful green 'queen' Gordal olives from Andalucía, which because of their size are a real feast for the eyes, stuffed with whole, hearty Cantabrian anchovy fillets, and drizzled with a robust extra virgin olive oil. The result is a world away from industrially produced anchovy-stuffed olives, where the pitted olives are mechanically filled with pulped anchovy paste.

around 30 large Gordal olives (see page 97)
around 15 best-quality cured anchovy fillets –
**   Cantabrian or Mediterranean if possible**
**   (see page 122)**
2 teaspoons chopped marjoram (preferably
**   with flowers) or rosemary**
a little good, robust extra virgin olive oil

Carefully make a slit in each olive lengthways and remove the stone, making sure you don't break the olive completely in half.

Halve the anchovy fillets lengthways, roll up and gently push one inside each olive. Arrange in a bowl, sprinkle with the chopped marjoram or rosemary and drizzle with oil.

Aceitunas y alcaparras aragonesas
Aragonesa olive mix

So called because we combine three ingredients from Aragón: Empeltre and Caspe olives and wild capers from the Monegros mountains.

50g good capers in brine or salt
2 teaspoons dried marjoram, preferably
**   with flowers**
3 teaspoons dried thyme
peel from 2 oranges
1 tablespoon sherry vinegar (see page 186)
4 tablespoons extra virgin olive oil
200g good black olives, such as Empeltre
**   (see page 97), stone in**
200g good green olives, such as Caspe
**   (see page 96), stone in**
2 cloves of garlic, crushed

Soak the capers in water for an hour to remove the excess salt, changing the water twice, then drain.

Cut the orange peel into thin strips about 1cm long.

Mix the vinegar and oil in a bowl, add the herbs and orange peel and leave to sit for 1–2 hours at room temperature before adding the olives, garlic and capers. Toss all together and leave to marinate at room temperature overnight, or for at least 6 hours before serving.

Gilda
Olive and anchovy tapa

The classic Basque 'lollipop' tapa varies in its combination of cured fish and pickles – this is my favourite.

Per person

1 pitted Manzanilla olive (see page 97)
1 cured anchovy fillet in oil or *boquerón*
**   (marinated anchovy, see page 127)**
1 pickled *guindilla* chilli
1 *pepinillo* (cornichon)

Spear the ingredients in any order you like on a cocktail stick.

OLIVES

'for a long time I searched for the consummate olive'

You can still see small rustic groves of olives dotted around Catalunya and on the hillsides of Mallorca, but these days the harvesting of local crops on a small scale is often only for pure subsistence, or for the romance of it. Small commercial growers frequently fight against tough odds to keep going, while the majority of Spain's olive production, which is the biggest in the world, is done very professionally on a large scale (mostly in Andalucía), featuring over 250 varieties in many, many different shades and flavours.

Introduced to Spain by the Romans, the cultivation of olives was developed by the Arabs. Roughly speaking, olives harvested early are green and firm. When they are more mature they turn a more yellow colour, and when they are allowed to ripen further, they turn 'black', a bit wrinkly and shiny with their own oil, which intensifies as the olive matures. In reality there are no olives that are truly ebony-coloured – all mature 'black' olives are really a deep purply-brown. When you see the dense, boot-polish black ones that are sold quite cheaply and used on top of pizzas or sometimes chopped in salads, they often seem unreal. That is because they are unreal. They are actually green olives that have been soaked in water with oxygen running through them, an industrial process that is used a great deal around Extremadura and which turns them black. The colour is then fixed with ferrous gluconate, which appears on labels as E579. The argument is that this gives you the firmness of a younger olive, which can be pitted easily, without the pronounced quite bitter and intense olive-y taste of the ripe, naturally cured, 'black' fruit. However, the oxygenating process strips the olive of pretty much all its flavour, so that they taste of virtually nothing at all.

In southern Spain, most particularly around Sevilla, the olives are a yellowy-green colour, the result of steeping them in a caustic soda solution, which is used to turn the bitterness of the olives to sweetness.

They are drained and refreshed with citric acid, to neutralise the caustic soda. This process manages to penetrate about two-thirds of the flesh and the olives require repeated washing before transferring to barrels, where they are left to ferment in salt water of 8–9 per cent salt.

By contrast, olives that have been naturally cured really taste of olives and still have a bitterness that we at Brindisa love. However, I have realised that outside Spain this taste is not always to everyone's liking, initially at least, since people have got used to the neutral character of olives which have been cured with chemicals and added ingredients, and so it often takes time to convince them that this is not what a real olive is about.

All olives contain oleuropein, which is the compound that gives them their bitterness, but since this is water-soluble, naturally cured olives are initially put into water, which is changed regularly over many days, to draw out the bitterness. Then, as they sweeten up, you can start the cure by adding salt as well as any flavourings, such as wild fennel, to the water.

I have a romantic idea of curing olives at home, so we have planted two small olive trees in our garden in London, and while I have no illusions that we will be handing out home-cured olives to friends and family, as my sister-in-law does in Catalunya, I look forward to harvesting and attempting to cure even the smallest batch of fruit. The notion gives me a feeling of being part of the long and great history of the olive tree, and, in a very small way, extending the line.

Green Caspe

For a long time I searched for the consummate green olive, and finally I found it in Aragón in north-eastern Spain. Caspe olives have the most amazingly clean, sharp, pure olive flavour and a quite crunchy texture, since they are harvested relatively young. They are grown in groves outside the town which gives the fruit their name. We buy them from a family business, Conservas Calanda, run by olive-curer Ismael Coneso and his son, also called Ismael, who specialise in both olives and peaches. The olives are cured and packed in their beautiful old beamed building, which was once a wine warehouse, while the peaches are processed in a modern facility nearby.

They source their Caspe olives, as well as the black Empeltre (see opposite), from their own land and from local families, who are often related to each other or come together in co-operatives, and who have been growing and harvesting the fruit for generations. Typical are the Cardo family. In mid-September the father, Demetrio, now in his eighties, still harvests the lower branches of their 500 or so 40-year-old trees by hand, while his son Ezequiel uses a mechanical shaker for the higher branches.

The olives drop into tarpaulins under the trees, then they are classified by the local *almacenista* (storer) before Ismael Coneso Senior cures them in the traditional way in brine (for the Caspe, he adds wild fennel picked from the hillsides), for a minimum of one month. After this they will have acquired a natural shine, and their characteristic crisp, sharp, deep and 'proper' olive taste.

The Caspe is a fragile olive, which needs constant storage temperatures and must remain wholly immersed in brine, otherwise the fruit will discolour. The olives also continue to lose some of their sharpness over time, so that the strong bite of the autumn becomes much softer by the following summer. Sometimes white specks appear on the olives that have thinner skins – this isn't a fault, but denotes the fruits that are the nicest and juiciest.

Green Gordal Reina (Queen)

At Brindisa these huge, oval, green Andalusian olives have been the most popular variety ever: their size helps, as they are a real feast for the eyes – a single olive can weigh around 8–12g – and the indent at the stem can sometimes give them a heart-shaped look. But they also deliver in terms of their firm yet juicy texture and the rich, intense flavour that bursts out of them. As with the Caspe olives, a white speckling often appears on the thinnest-skinned, juiciest olives.

Despite their lusciousness, their oil content is relatively low, so they are rarely pressed for olive oil. Instead they are perfect for curing. We launched our first Brindisa tapas bar with a winning combination that was a favourite of our chef of the time, José Pizarro: pitted Gordal olives, opened up and stuffed with pieces of orange, closed again, then drizzled with olive oil and sprinkled with salt and wild, flowering marjoram or dried oregano.

The substantial nature of the olives also lends them to being speared with a few other ingredients on a cocktail stick, and in the *pintxos* (local tapas) bars of the Basque country, a typical favourite is the *gilda* ('lollipop', see page 92), a combination of a single olive, anchovy and various pickles, which you down in one mouthful.

Green Manzanilla

Great dressed with some extra virgin olive oil, crushed garlic and thyme leaves and served with sherry, this is also the perfect Martini olive: fresh and green, firm, crisp and juicy, with a light, sweet flavour. Also from Andalucía, the Manzanilla grows in Pilas and Albaida del Aljarafe, close to Sevilla, and is harvested between September and October. As a tapa, the olive might be served as a *banderilla*, i.e. wrapped in a *boquerón* (marinated anchovy fillet, see page 127) and speared with a cocktail stick.

Black Empeltre

The Coneso family (see opposite) also cure aromatic, sweeter, purply-black Empeltre olives, which are not unlike the Greek Kalamata. Most come from their own groves, where they are allowed to mature on the tree until late winter, so their texture is softer than the crunchy Caspe.

They are harvested between November and February, then cured in brine for a minimum of 6–8 months. Because their flesh clings firmly to the stone, they stay a perfect oval shape: very, very pretty.

Ismael Coneso Junior also makes the Empeltre olives into a pâté or tapenade, which contains the best fruit and nothing else, unlike many olive pâtés which use a strong preservation process, colouring and herbs or other ingredients, either to mask lesser-quality olives or to add unnecessary dimensions of flavour. Ismael simply washes the ripe olives, leaves them to drain, then removes the stones, before crushing the flesh into the pure pâté, which is allowed to rest overnight so that the rich oil separates out. The excess oil is skimmed off and sold separately, then the pâté is packed, after which it will oxidize and darken a little and the oil that remains will rise to the surface. So before you serve it, you gently mix it back in.

The Tapas
Tradition

What really defines a tapa is not the ingredients or recipe, but the cultural aspect, the social occasion in which it is eaten. Traditionally, you go out for tapas, usually in the evening after work and particularly at the end of the week. Typically, you meet at one bar, then move on to another, and another, and until not so long ago many bars would automatically serve a complimentary tapa whenever you ordered a drink, though that is a rarity nowadays. In towns and cities the bars are often clustered together, and in the best places it is first come first served, so you have to fight for your space. That said, tapas are not about fast food on the go: just the opposite. They are about a slowing of time, in which to share conversation and cement friendships over a few drinks and a leisurely procession of snacks.

There are so many stories about the origins of tapas that I consulted the two grand food-loving, historian sisters, Margarita and Asunción Almela Boix, who, along with other friends in Madrid, are members of the local *tertulia* (circle of intellectuals, see page 80). Margarita, known as Marga, is a literature professor, and Asunción, known as Maicha, is an archaeologist – and according to them the word tapas probably comes from the Gothic *tappa*, which arrived with the Visigoths, the Germanic tribes who came to Spain in the fifth century. It referred to something that 'covered or closed', and the first tapas were probably pieces of cheese or ham used to cover open bottles and serving vessels, to stop any foreign objects falling into them.

Some popular stories suggest that tapa culture really took off in the thirteenth century when the Castilian King Alfonso the tenth, having been advised by his doctor to take small mouthfuls of food with a glass of restorative wine, passed a law saying that all drinks in inns had to be served with a snack. In seventeenth-century literature, Cervantes's character Don Quixote, as well as Don Pablos, the swindler in Francisco de Quevedo's novel *El Buscón*, talked of certain salty snacks that would need a drink with them. These would have been the likes of olives, almonds and caperberries, which could not be used in themselves as a 'cover' but were just placed on a small plate and were not called tapas, but *llamativos*, in the case of Don Quixote, and *avisillos* in the case of Don Pablos.

However, the sisters confirmed that tapas as we know them today really evolved in Andalucía around the nineteenth century. Again, there is a popular story that pins the spread of the fashion throughout Spain on a particular royal moment when King Alfonso (the twelfth this time) visited an Andalusian inn. Suddenly gusts of wind started blowing dust through the door, so he asked for a slice of ham or cheese with which to cover his glass of wine.

Whatever the truth or legend, it is generally accepted that around this time in Andalucía people would gather outside the local bars on hot evenings enjoying a glass of sherry, and to keep away the insects that were attracted to the sweet drinks, they would cover their glasses with little saucers (*tapas*). It became the custom to add a few olives, almonds, slices of sausage or ham to the saucers, and gradually the idea spread throughout Spain, evolving over the decades.

Of course, everyone in Spain is an authority not only on the history of tapas, but on the best kind of tapas bar – but with seventeen regions, and who knows how many thousands of bars throughout the country serving tapas from the traditional to the daring and contemporary, there is no one story and no rule book.

The fun of the best and busiest bars is watching streams of amazing little dishes coming towards you, one after the other – particularly if a bar specialises in the kind of skilfully fried seafood and fish tapas that are quite tricky to do really well at home, because they have to be cooked *al momento*.

On the other hand, some of my favourite places are little more than tiny tiled rooms that haven't changed in hundreds of years, in which the locally cured hams hang above you from the ceiling, and with no space for a slicing machine they have to be carved vertically. Apart from the ham, there might be *tortilla*, olives and salted almonds, and that is all. Or there might be one hot tapa of the day, such as the delicious little bowls of oxtail served along with cold beer, ham and olives that we discovered in the tiniest of bars in the highest village of the Sierra Nevada on a climbing and camping trip.

Barcelona is famous for its new wave of stylish, often quite elaborate and avant-garde tapas, influenced by Spain's culinary alchemist Ferran Adrià, but these often sit alongside the city's classic old-style bars, full of soul, like the famous El Xampanyet, on calle Montcada, the same street as the Picasso Museum. The bar is lined with beautiful old tiles and crammed full of jugs, photos and pictures, as well as a good mix of locals and tourists. In its present incarnation it has been in the same family since the 1930s, though they say some kind of bar has been there for centuries. They serve only what you see on the counter: the biggest and best of anchovies, dressed with olive oil in a big bowl ready to be spooned out on to saucers, along with olives, *tortilla*, cheese, slices of sausage and *pan con tomate* (see page 72).

Around Spain you might find bars that specialise in *montaditos* – ingredients 'mounted' on pieces of toast or bread (see page 131) – perhaps a slice of black pudding or pork loin cooked on the *plancha* (grill plate), with a sliver of roasted green pepper. A very popular tapa is *montadito de sobrasada mallorquína y manchego*: grilled soft, pâté-like *sobrasada* sausage (see page 260), topped with grated Manchego cheese. Simple, yet really tasty.

By contrast, in bigger bars, there may be long lists of both hot and cold tapas with more substantial big plates to follow. In the most cutting-edge venues, inventive and architectural-looking tapas often give a contemporary twist to classic ingredients and sometimes mix in influences from other cultures such as tempura and sushi, Eastern spices, or – strangely very popular – French Brie. In Madrid I was taken by friends to La Musa de Espronceda, where along with beautiful tapas they celebrate flamenco, story-telling and film. The restaurant is named after Teresa Mancha, who was the muse of the romantic poet José Espronceda and lived in the building until she died in 1839. On the menu the traditional and experimental sit side by side, so that you can order old favourites like garlic mushrooms and *croquetas* at the same time as the likes of cabbage rolls filled with pork and raspberry.

Usually tapas reflect the region you are in, and whether it is known more for meat or fish. In Galicia, famous for its seafood, both fresh and conserved, you would expect to find bowls of mussels, and the local speciality of poached *pulpo* (octopus), sprinkled with oil, infused with paprika, salt and garlic. Or there might be clams and *zamburiñas* (queen scallops), put on the *plancha* in their shells until they open up. Then they are brought, sizzling, to the table and served just as they are, with a lemon, olive oil and garlic dressing.

In central Spain a popular snack with the first beer of early evening is mackerel on the bone (known as *chicharro*, *verdel* or *caballa)*, fried in olive oil and preserved in vinegar and garlic, accompanied by slices of raw sweet young onion and often hard-boiled eggs and fresh red peppers.

In the Canaries stand-out tapas include pieces of very lightly smoked white cheese made with a blend of sheep's and goat's milk, grilled on the plancha in a similar way to the Greek halloumi, or chunks of grilled fish with bowls of the famous green or red sauce, *mojo verde* or *mojo rojo* (see pages 298–300).

Alicante is famous for its *salazones* (salt-preserved fish), which are a speciality at La Taberna del Gourmet, owned by María José San Román, a champion of regional foods whom I first met many years ago at a food event. We agreed to spy amicably on each other's ventures and over the years she has been a great source of local knowledge. Included on her amazing menu of *tapas y raciones* are *mojama* (see page 121), *huevos de atún* (pressed tuna roe), lightly cured and marinated mackerel, and *visol*, the name in Alicante for a sardine which is salted, only lightly dried, then neatly sliced. María José serves it in her *salazón* selection with roasted Marcona almonds and a glass of chilled white Catalan Priorat wine. It is exceptionally good, as the flesh, with its tones of blue, yellow and grey, retains its oily texture and the flavour is relatively mild, not unlike an unpressed anchovy.

In the Basque region the name for tapas is *pintxos*, and the bars there often have wonderful baroque displays. In the busiest ones the hot plates fly out of the kitchen to the bar and the food is devoured in seconds. I would always go for the freshly grilled *pintxos* straight from the *plancha*: prawns, green Basque *guindilla* peppers, and doorstep slices of beef, grilled very, very rare, then thickly sliced, along with *gildas*, 'lollipop' tapas on a stick, typically consisting of little pickles, chilli and anchovy (see page 92).

Ultimately, wherever you are, it is the quality of the ingredients that makes or breaks a tapas bar. No one wants to be served *boquerones* (marinated anchovies) so vinegary they bring tears to your eyes, Russian salad turning crusty, or meatballs that have been congealing under lights on the counter for hours. The best and busiest bars are constantly feeding people, so the tapas are always freshly prepared to order, and in these, you can eat food that is truly sublime.

TAPAS FRÍAS

Cold tapas and
other small plates

Since tapas and relaxation are supposed to go hand in hand, the important thing, if you are making tapas at home, is to keep things simple and make good use of cold ingredients. Trying to produce half a dozen hot snacks simultaneously, without a kitchen brigade of helpers, can be stressful – just ask my husband. When I took maternity leave before our son Dominic was born, he decided to do a tapas party for everyone from Brindisa at our house, using an amazing old book of recipes from the Basque region which had pictures and instructions for every conceivable style and shape of tapa, from classics to the kind of elaborate concoctions that edged into the world of seventies' *hors d'oeuvres*.

I was instructed to do nothing while Rupert ran around madly doing intricate things like mixing salt cod with béchamel sauce, then stuffing the mixture into tiny red peppers, dipping them in batter and deep-frying them. It was a huge success and Rupert was very pleased with himself at the end of it all, but he said it was like cooking six entirely different three-course meals, only for people to devour everything in a matter of minutes.

So, I would say stick to just a few things that need cooking, and for the rest, do as everyone in Spain does as a matter of course, which is to make good use of excellent quality cured hams, sausages, chorizo and cheeses, together with vegetables, peppers and fish prepared by artisans and packed into jars and cans. If you go to a friend's house in Spain, they will invariably offer you a glass of wine or sherry and whichever of these foods they happen to have, with no adornment, because none is considered necessary.

When we visit our friends Ambro and Asun in Burgos, in Castilla y León, as a prelude to Ambro's famous Sunday lunch of *bacalao* (salt cod) *al pil pil* (see page 332), Asun will put out a wonderful selection of small dishes, which always involves something from the profusion of jars and pots of home conserves she keeps in her store cupboard, such as peppers under oil or tomato, onion and pepper jams.

White asparagus is a favourite ingredient, highly prized because it is very tender, juicy and subtle in flavour; however, it is rarely sold fresh in Spain, as the local growing season is short, so it is almost always canned or jarred. White asparagus imported from places such as Peru and China is also canned in Spain, which massively undercuts the local product, but the spears tend to be more stringy, less juicy and relatively flavourless. Spanish asparagus is grown to different sizes, but the bigger and fatter the better – in fact, the giant spears prepared by Conservas Navarrico in Navarra are labelled *cojonudos*, which is the colloquial expression for something awesome and ballsy.

TENTEMPIÉ
Quick and easy tapas

The following make quick and easy tapas that require no cooking (other than boiling some eggs or potatoes):

Little Gem lettuce leaves filled with anchovy fillets and white asparagus spears and *piquillo* peppers from jars.

Good Serrano ham with *picos de pan* (mini breadsticks).

Wedges of Manchego cheese topped with *membrillo* (quince paste).

Rounds of cured sausage such as *salchichón de Vic*, each topped with a pickled *guindilla* pepper from a jar.

White asparagus in a dish, topped with grated hard-boiled eggs, a drizzle of extra virgin olive oil, wine vinegar and a sprinkling of sea salt.

Torta de Barros from Extremadura or Cañarejal cheese from Pollos in Castilla y León (see page 524), served at room temperature with the top cut off and savoury *tortas de aceite* (olive oil biscuits) to scoop out the creamy cheese. The cheeses are also tasty with boiled potatoes and caperberries on the side.

See pages 117 and 131 for more quick ideas.

PESCADOS Y MARISCOS EN CONSERVA
Conserved fish and shellfish

Spain has a long and rich heritage of fish and seafood, conserved either in salt (*salazón*), oil, or by cooking and storing in a vinegar and spice marinade (*escabeche*), which, chosen well, makes for outstanding small plates.

I know that not everyone will be convinced to pay a premium for a tin of fat Cantabrian anchovies, Galician clams from the Rías Gallegas (the local estuaries), or luscious *bonito del norte* from the Bay of Biscay, but I can honestly say that discovering how good fish in tins can taste has been a life-enhancing experience not only for me, but for the very many Brindisa customers and curious chefs who have come to understand and appreciate its luxurious nature.

Some of the best conserved fish is produced by small and medium-sized, usually family-run, businesses such as Conservas Ortiz, now in their fifth generation and still run by three brothers. The family began preserving fish in the days when it was impossible to send it fresh to cities such as Madrid, and so they started putting sea bream in barrels of 'spoiled' vinegary white wine – the beginnings of the *escabeche* recipe that is still used for their tinned tuna and mackerel.

Similarly, Conservas Nardín are now in their fourth generation and run by daughter Milagros and her husband, Sebastián. The company was begun in the small Basque fishing village of Getaria at the beginning of the twentieth century by Leonardo Oliveri, one of many Sicilians who settled in the area. At that time, the local Basque people tended only to fry anchovies, or use them as livebait when fishing, whereas the Sicilians prized these little fish and were skilled at salting them. Leonardo found that the ones that could be caught in the colder seas of this northern coast were big and fatty and so perfect for this form of preserving.

The great beauty of the notion of conserved fish, both gastronomically and ethically, is that you can capture the best local fish in season, obeying the fishing regulations which govern licences and monitor and control the volumes and sizes of fish caught in order to preserve the long-term populations, particularly of endangered species. Then you have the luxury of making the fish last as long as you like, so you can eat it whenever and wherever you please.

Of course, that is the ideal. The reality is that we sometimes forget that conserved fish begins with a fresh product. We expect to see tins on the shelves all year round, irrespective of the fact that the quantity and quality of fish and shellfish available for conserving is very volatile. As always, fishermen are at the mercy of whatever the oceans can provide. In lean times, therefore, producers of canned fish must decide whether to accept fish taken from other seas, often far away and possibly of lesser quality, to satisfy demand; or do as many small, select operations do, and stick rigidly to a policy of only using locally caught fish. Often there is no indication on the can – but the best clue is in the price. Exceptional, locally caught conserved fish will always be more expensive.

Conservas en 'hojalata'
Fish presented in tins

Our first menu back in 2004 at London Bridge had a section called 'fine fish from a tin' – though I had actually wanted to call it 'fish *in hojalata*', as I have always loved the sound of the word *hojalata*, which means tin can. Instead of arranging Ortiz Cantabrian anchovies on plates, we served them in their colourful, elegant tins with the tops rolled back, surrounded by piles of brown toast, with unsalted butter and finely sliced shallots. It was an idea that was ahead of its time and not really understood, but I wanted to emphasise the quality and sheer breadth of choice of the preserved fish from Spain, as opposed to fresh seafood. Eventually the fish in tin cans evolved into plates of different conserved fish with fruit, nuts and olives (see page 117), but recently we decided that it would be fun to revisit the idea of presenting anchovies and other seafood, using their tins as serving 'dishes'.

Because the seafood is so rich and concentrated in flavour, a small tin is fine for two people with added ingredients. Of course, when you take out the fish and combine it with these, the mixture won't necessarily all fit back into the tin, so just mound the rest alongside or serve it separately in a small bowl. I think if you are feeding more people it is fun to put out a selection of different *hojalatas* and let people help themselves.

All of the following recipes are for two.

Filetes de anchoa con pan tostado
Anchovies with shallots and buttered toast

For long, fat anchovies, the ultimate tin to buy is the 78g tin from Ortiz. Remove the anchovies, then rinse out the tin and dry it well before putting the fillets back in, so that the fishy oil does not take over the combination of flavours. Finely chop 1 shallot, along with some parsley and chervil. Mix together and sprinkle over the fillets. Put the tin on a big plate with a stack of buttered toast alongside on which to arrange the anchovies.

Filetes de anchoa con escalivada
Anchovies with roasted vegetables

Again the 78g tin of Ortiz anchovies is perfect. In Spain many people have homemade *escalivada* – roasted vegetables in vinaigrette (see page 284) – permanently in their fridge, so it is a very easy thing to combine them with anchovies, which pair really well with the sweet juiciness of the vegetables. However, you can make a quick version by slicing half a red pepper and a small aubergine quite thickly, drizzling with oil and grilling the slices until the pepper is charred and the aubergine browned. An even simpler alternative is to use some jarred *piquillo* or *bierzo* peppers (see page 275), together with jarred grilled slices of aubergine.

Cut the vegetables into strips roughly the size of the anchovies, then dress lightly with Cabernet Sauvignon vinegar or another good red wine vinegar (if you are using jarred vegetables, you could add some of the conserving juices). Layer up the dressed vegetables with the anchovies in the tin, as far as you can, and arrange the remainder neatly alongside.

Anchoas con ensalada de remolacha
Smoked anchovy fillets with beetroot

This is based on a recipe from Mark Hix's book *Fish etc.* Ideally, use smoked anchovies from Conservas Nardín (see page 106). Mark marinates the anchovies in the fridge for 24 hours, which of course doesn't make it a quick snack – but 4 hours is fine.

Take the anchovy fillets out of a 100g tin and put into a bowl. Wash out the tin and dry it. Make a marinade by mixing together 1 teaspoon of lemon juice, 1 teaspoon of Moscatel vinegar, 1 finely chopped clove of garlic, 50ml of olive oil, ½ tablespoon of sea salt and some freshly ground black pepper, and pour over the anchovies. Leave in the fridge for 4–24 hours (see above).

Boil 2 medium raw beetroots in their skins in salted water until just tender (about 1 hour), then peel them while still warm and cut into squares of about 0.5cm. Keep to one side. Lift the anchovies out of their marinade and dry them, then layer them up with the beetroot in the tin, as far as you can, arranging the remainder alongside. Discard the marinade, as you want the zing of a fresh-tasting dressing. Make this using 1 finely chopped shallot, 1 teaspoon of chopped chives, 1 teaspoon of white wine vinegar and 2 tablespoons of olive oil and pour it over the layered anchovies and beetroot.

Verdel ahumado con ensaladilla
Smoked mackerel with potato salad

We use tins of smoked mackerel produced
to quite a secret method by the Nardín family
in the Basque country for this. The fish is quite
special, pale-looking, and tender in texture, more
like the raw fish used in sushi.

For one 100g tin of smoked mackerel, boil
150g new or salad potatoes in salted water, drain
them and refresh under cold water. Halve or
quarter according to size, then put into a bowl,
mix with 1 tablespoon of good mayonnaise,
1 teaspoon grain mustard and 10 small capers
(soaked in water for an hour to remove the excess
salt and drained), and season with sea salt and
black pepper. Arrange the potato salad next to
the open tin of mackerel.

Navajas con chorizo y habitas razor clams
Razor clams with *chorizo* and broad beans

Mark Hix likes to use the irresistible combination
of *chorizo* with razor clams and this recipe is
another from his book, *Fish etc*. While he cooks
fresh razor clams, tinned ones work equally well,
and we have adapted his recipe to serve from
the tin. It is best to use baby broad beans when
you can, as they look more elegant than big ones,
and their bright green colour contrasts well with
the whiteness of the razor clams (to get the same
effect with large beans you would need to slip off
their skins once they are cooked).

The Galician razor clams we buy have been
selected when they are at their most tender, and
are packed into tins by hand, doused in lemon-
and bay-infused spring water. Because they are
so delicately flavoured, our chefs prefer to use a
mild *chorizo* which won't overpower them.

Remove the razor clams from a 118g tin, drain
the brine to use later, then clean the tin, dry it
and return the clams. Cook 50g of broad beans in
boiling water for 2 minutes, then drain and rinse
under cold water to stop them cooking further.
Keep to one side.

Heat 1 tablespoon of olive oil in a small frying
pan, add 30g of mild cooking *chorizo* (cut into £1
coin slices and then into quarters) and cook on
a low heat until softened and browned on the
edges. Drain the oil from the pan and discard.
Add 2 tablespoons of the reserved clam brine.
Bring to the boil, then add the reserved beans
and heat through for 2 minutes over a medium
heat. Add 1 tablespoon of chopped parsley, stir
through for another minute, then add 10g of cold
butter, straight from the fridge. Stir quickly to
emulsify the sauce, then taste and season
as necessary.

Spoon the *chorizo* and bean mixture over the
clams in their tin – if you can't fit it all in, mound
some alongside – and serve.

Mejillones en escabeche con picadillo de piparra
Escabeche mussels with tomato and red pepper salad

It might sound strange, I know, but these are brilliant served with really good, thin, olive oil-fried crisps, which give a great salty, crunchy contrast to the tender mussels.

The combination was introduced to me by our friend Raul Domingo, an excellent cook who lives in Madrid with his wife, Carmen. I was working away on this book at their home, when Raúl brought me a tray with a glass of wine on it, a plate of potato crisps as thin as butterfly wings, and a bowl of the mussels. He told me this was a favourite Madrid tapa – you topped a crisp with a mussel and downed it in one – and it was a glorious pick-me-up.

The plump, golden, almost orange mussels of the Galician region are farmed, but nourish themselves on sea water as they cling to the ropes of the wooden platforms (*bateas*) in the Arosa inlet, near the O Grove peninsula. They are harvested between July and February and, as with most shellfish, the bigger the better. The largest can measure over 4cm long and 1.5cm wide and the best will go to be canned as *mejillones en escabeche*. They are first fried in olive oil before being put into the marinade, which includes vinegar, oil, paprika, bay leaves, peppers and cloves.

To add a touch of freshness and colour, drain the mussels from their tin, keeping the marinade to one side. Finely chop 1 medium ripe tomato or 2 cherry tomatoes, ¼ medium red pepper and the white of a spring onion and mix into the marinade. Put the mussels back into the tin, and spoon the marinade over the top. Serve with good crisps.

Berberechos aliñados
Dressed cockles

In Vilassar de Mar, just north of Barcelona, there is a famous taverna, the Espinaler, which has been in the same family since it was founded in 1896. In the 1940s they made a name for themselves by selling glasses of *vermut* (vermouth) in addition to wine, then in the 1990s they expanded into seafood, travelling to Galicia to select the finest, which is canned under their own label. Cockles in salsa and a *vermut* became a typical midday snack after Sunday Mass.

The combination was a novelty at the time, but *vermuterías* – bars serving vermouth and small tapas, especially conserved fish – have since become very fashionable in Barcelona. However, people still commute from the city to the Espinaler to eat their cockles, razor clams, mussels and squid at the bar, as well as buying tins to take away.

Cockles have a delicate flavour, so you have to be careful not to overpower them, and our executive chef, Josep, makes a light, fresh salsa using the brine from the can, mixed with extra virgin olive oil, sherry vinegar, lemon juice and mild paprika. The result is absolutely delicious, and the title of 'dressed cockles' really can't convey the quintessentially Mediterranean freshness of the flavours, especially when served with a glass of chilled *fino* sherry or vermouth.

Open a 112g tin of cockles in brine and place a spatula over the fish so that you can drain the brine into a bowl, leaving the beautifully arranged cockles in place. Keep the brine to one side. To make the dressing, combine 1½ tablespoons of a good, well-balanced extra virgin olive oil such as Arbequina with ½ tablespoon of smooth sherry or Moscatel vinegar, 1 teaspoon of lemon juice, 1½ teaspoons of the reserved brine, and ½ teaspoon of *pimentón dulce* (mild paprika) and pour this over the cockles in their tin. Serve with good bread to dip into the dressing at the end.

Seafood Saints
and Witches

When my Galician friends and colleagues get together to swap tales from home, the talk inevitably turns to old stories of the sea, the wonders of the local seafood and the perils of searching for *perce-bes* – the weird, strangely beautiful 'goose' barnacles that are found clinging to some of the most precarious rocks around the coastline – and witches! Galicians love to talk about the mysticism of their homeland, which has a unique historical mix of the magic prac-tised by its early pagan inhabitants and the later Catholic religion, so witches and saints are both paid homage in the region's festivals. And it is true there is a spookiness sometimes in the narrow valleys and misty forests which becomes even more eerie when, as is tradi-tional during festivals, the bagpipes are played.

The legend of the *meiga*, the good witch, is still strong. Most likely this was really the wise woman of the community who made healing potions, but the *meiga* is still called upon to bring good luck, watch over fishermen, ensure a good harvest, and help families not to fall out with each other. If the fishermen don't come back, or the crops fail, there is still a generation who will blame the evil spirits.

Equally, there are festivals appealing to the saints or the Virgin of the Sea for the same kind of help and good fortune that is asked of the *meiga*. On 16 July Galicians celebrate the feast of Virxe do Carme (Our Lady of Mount Carmel), one of the many advoca-tions of the Virgin Mary, protector of fishermen and the local navy, with processions of boats, and flowers thrown into the water for all those who have been taken by the sea. The King of Spain often attends the procession and celebrations at the naval base and school in Marín, during which officers carry a statue of the Virgin from the church to the boats.

One of Galicia's most magical nights of the year is 23 June, when the tradition is for everyone to go down to the beach, where each group of family and friends will light a fire and heat up *la pota da queimada,* a three-legged clay pot of moonshine, or 'witches' brew', made with *caña blanca,* a clear spirit distilled from wine (known elsewhere in Spain as *orujo* or *aguardiente*), to which you add lem-on and orange peel, coffee beans and sugar. (There are other *cañas,* such as *caña de hierbas,* flavoured with herbs, and *caña tostada,* which has caramelised sugar added to it, but these are traditionally drunk by fishermen to keep them warm as they put to sea.

As the alcohol begins to burn from the heat of the fire, some of the drink is lifted high up with a big ladle and then poured slowly back into the pot, creating a streaming blue flame, while everyone chants the *conxuro de queimada*, the spell to ward off witches and evil spirits. The brew is poured into clay cups and everyone drinks and dances around the fire while sardines are barbecued and the bagpipes are played. Then at the end of the night, when the fire has died down to embers, everyone has to jump over it in a final gesture of defiance against the witches.

Personally, when I think of Galicia, it is seafood, rather than witches, that comes to mind, since the Costa do Marisco (shellfish coast) stretches all the way around three of its four provinces and the famous Rías Gallegas offer a unique environment in which Atlantic sea water meets river and rain water in a series of estuaries, which provide one of the richest environments possible for seafood, so crustaceans, molluscs, cephalopods and fish all grow and thrive here, especially in the months of high rainfall.

Local restaurants are known for the *mariscada*: big displays of seafood from mussels to oysters and crab, prawns, langoustines, *percebes* and lobsters, which pair beautifully with the local white wines such as Albariño, Godello or the headier Ribeiro, which you traditionally drink out of white ceramic bowls.

In olden days the *marisqueo,* the mollusc harvest, was a purely seasonal event. The *veda* or 'campaign' was declared open on the first full moon at the end of summer, and as soon as the tide was low, often as early as four in the morning, whole families, young and old, would pile on to the beach in the cold and dark, buckets in hand and small rakes at the ready, to reap the bounty of *berberechos* (cockles) which live in the shallow sands.

Nowadays, however, most molluscs are seeded, and can be harvested almost all year round, although they will have their optimum moments and quotas are strictly controlled.

Cockles are still collected by hand, mainly by women. Also in the sand, but in somewhat deeper water, you find *almejas* (clams). Harvesting of these is done with a boat. Razor clams need a depth of water of about ten metres, and are collected by divers throughout most of the year. Their quality and size can vary depending on where they grow. In the more sheltered waters of the Rías they will be more delicate in flavour and texture than those that grow in the more open and wilder waters of the Finisterre peninsula.

Once harvested the shellfish go to the local auction houses, the *lonxas*, where some will be sold fresh, and those of the right variety, condition and price go for the delicate work of conserving. While for Galicians fresh fish and seafood is the ultimate, for quick tapas and snacks at home they will always have a store of the highest-quality local seafood conserved in cans or jars.

Around the coastline you will inevitably hear stories of brave locals who have battled treacherous waves to prise a haul of *percebes*. Pinky red and black, with pale green, dragon-like, pointy claws that shimmer like mother of pearl in the light, they look like crazy pieces of jewellery.

Although some can be accessed by land at low tide (the mother of one of our Galician colleagues at Brindisa used to regularly collect them in this way), sometimes you have to knot your rope to a safe rock and lower yourself down the cliffside to reach them, which is physically demanding and slippery, and there are many tales of tragic accidents. Other *percebes* can only be reached from the sea by swimmers (*percebeiros*), who dive from boats and head through the thrashing waters towards the cliffs to cut them away from the rocks. Inevitably the best, shorter, fatter, juicier and pricy barnacles are the ones that have had to grow strong in the wildest waters, and to reach them you need a deep understanding of the sea, its tides and wave patterns to avoid being slammed against the sharp rocks. As the locals say, *el mar es un toro, no te puedes fiar*: 'the sea is like a bull; you cannot trust it for a moment'.

In past times Galician foragers risked life and limb, without even wearing wetsuits, to gather *percebes* to stave off hunger – perhaps to add to a tortilla, to make it stretch further – or to sell for a few hundred pesetas per kilo, but the barnacles are now considered a great and expensive delicacy on the tapas menus of smart restaurants and bars. They are most popular at Christmas time, when they can grow to 5cm long and up to 1cm wide, and since inevitably the best *percebes* are becoming scarce, smart restaurants in Madrid and Barcelona will pay hundreds of euros per kilo. It is very similar to the oyster story in Britain, where once there was such a profusion of oysters in the Thames that Londoners packed them into meat pies to help them to go further, whereas now they are a luxury.

These days, also, the collection of *percebes* is much more regulated. To be a *percebeiro/a* you need to have one of a limited number of licences issued by the regional government. You must also comply with quotas which specify a maximum catch and minimum sizes of barnacles in certain areas and during specific times, in order to protect stocks. The *percebes* must then be auctioned at the *lonxa*, the auction house run by the *cofradía*, a society of locals who make sure everyone complies with the licences.

As with most exquisite seafood, little needs to be done to prepare the *percebes*. Traditionally, they are cooked for just 30 seconds in boiling sea water (or for a maximum of 1 minute in plain water with 'a fist and a half' of salt added to every 2 litres of water to mimic the sea), plus a bay leaf or two, then drained and wrapped in a clean cloth, as they will be very hot. To eat, you grasp a *percebe* at each end and twist it, peel and tear away the leathery reptile-like skin and bite and suck out the flesh from the inner tube. The taste and aroma is of pure sea: there is no other way to describe it.

EASY CONSERVED FISH COMBINATIONS

Our special plates combining cured fish, such as mackerel, *boquerones* (marinated anchovies), small sardines and *mojama* (tuna loin), each paired with a fruit, nuts or olives, have become a signature of the Brindisa tapas bars. They make the easiest of starters, requiring little or no preparation, as they simply rely on the quality of the seafood, and the various combinations of flavours.

The pairings that we like best are as follows – we usually serve four different types of fish with their partners – but you could just focus on one or two. Add a mound of fresh toast and some soft herbs, such as parsley and chervil, for scattering over the top.

Smoked mackerel with sliced green apple (skin on) – the quite fleshy, oily fish goes really well with the sharp, crisp apple.

Boquerones (marinated anchovies, see page 127) with Manzanilla olives. What you are looking for is a good contrast between the mellow vinegariness of the tender marinated anchovies and the salty, fruity crunch of the olives. So beware of the kind of ferociously sharp, vinegary *boquerones* that you sometimes find in supermarkets. If necessary, drain off the marinade and make your own, with just a few drops of good vinegar and a light olive oil – light is always best with fish so as not to overwhelm it. A little chopped garlic and parsley scattered over the top can be good too.

Mojama (cured tuna, see page 121) with sliced fresh pears. *Mojama* has a dry texture and quite a fishy, savoury taste, so you need really fresh, sweet, juicy pears to go with it: not hard, woody ones. Ideally, slice the *mojama* as thinly as you can (about 1mm), then marinate it briefly in olive oil. Mango and pineapple also go well with *mojama*, as do whole or chopped and roasted almonds.

Sardinillas (small sardines) with good tomatoes and chopped parsley – the sweet and sour of the tomatoes cuts through the oiliness of the sardines.

Bonito ventresca (see page 118) with jarred *piquillo* peppers (see page 275). Fry the peppers very briefly in garlic and olive oil, to bring out the flavour and juice. Top with some *ventresca* and drizzle with a little PX vinegar (see page 188). The intense, slightly smoky, fruity flavour and the thinness of the pepper are very good with the silky, subtle *bonito*.

Razor clams with lemon zest and some lemon juice squeezed into the brine, served with *encurtidos* (pickles) such as pickled garlic or green pickled *guindilla* peppers (see page 275). The quite neutral flavour of the clams is really enhanced by the vinegariness of the pickles.

Huevas de atún (pressed tuna roe, see page 120) with *frutos secos* (a selection of unsalted skin-on almonds and dried fruit, such as apricots and dried peach halves (*orejones*), soft fruit such as strawberries; or tomatoes, dressed with a little balsamic or PX vinegar (see page 188).

Hueva de verdel (mackerel roe) with radishes and tomatoes. Mackerel roe has a very delicate flavour. We buy our tins from the Nardín family, who pack it with *guindilla* peppers in olive oil, seasoned with salt and pepper, so you need to add very little dressing, otherwise you will overpower it. Arrange some cherry tomato slices (about 10 tomatoes to one 95g tin of roe) in a circle on a plate with some thinly sliced radishes on top (about 3 radishes will do it). Carefully lift the roe from its tin, gently break it into pieces of about 1cm, and scatter these over the top. Sprinkle with 1 tablespoon of chopped parsley, 1 tablespoon of extra virgin olive oil, and about ½ teaspoon of Moscatel vinegar. Finish with a twist of salt and pepper.

SALAZONES

'a largely forgotten art'

In the tapas bars and restaurants of the coastline that runs from Alicante to Cádiz you will usually see *salazones* on the menu. The process of curing and drying various fish, along with their roe and other tripe, to give them longer life and enhanced flavour, is very much a skill that is associated with this stretch of coast, and apart from *mojama* (salted and dried tuna loin, see page 121) and *huevas de atún* (pressed tuna roe), most *salazones* have not travelled much further into Spain than this stretch of coast. So they have become a largely forgotten art.

I first came across them when I met María José San Román (see page 101), who invited me to Alicante to see her incredible tapas bar and restaurant where she served salted fish, rice dishes and vegetables in abundance along with superb wines of the region: Moscatels and the famous Fondillon. She advised me to visit a unique shop in the city market owned by Vicente Leal, who is the fourth generation of his family business. It was a mysterious and curious place that felt like the belly of a ship, with pieces of fish hanging from bars and a strong deep-sea aroma lingering in the air. On the counter there were dark-coloured dried octopus and tuna intestines contrasting with the whiteness of salt cod. Ever since that visit I have been fascinated by the history and skills involved in salting and drying fish.

Salazones

These have a strong flavour so you don't need large quantities of them. They are typically sliced thinly (about 2–3mm), drizzled with olive oil and served on baked savoury biscuits with tomatoes, or with some almonds and/or dried fruit and a selection of other small plates, salads, fresh cheese and fresh or pickled vegetables. We present them in this way in combination with other conserved fish, and they are very popular, albeit with a relatively limited audience.

Around 80 per cent of *salazón* production involves tuna. The cure can be dry *(salazón seco salado)* or wet *(salazón húmedo)*. Dry-curing simply involves washing and then drying either in natural air or adapted chambers. Wet-salting involves either an initial soaking in brine, followed by air-drying; or a longer cure, in which the fish is covered in salt over a few months, before being washed, dried and then stored under oil.

Ventresca salada

Also known as *ijada de atún* or *tronco de atún en salazón*, *ventresca salada* is the belly or flank of either the bluefin or the yellowfin tuna, which is wet-salted whole for 2–3 months in a similar way to salt cod, then filleted, washed, dried off and placed in olive oil. It is one of the most delicate

preparations I have ever savoured, on its own or in a salad. Silky and tender, with a pronounced, but refined flavour of tuna, it melts in the mouth. In the Alicante region it is favoured on the feast of San Juan, on 24 July, and is famously made into *coca amb tonyina,* a kind of pie made with *coca* dough sweetened with *anís,* filled with the cured tuna and a generous amount of slow-cooked onion and pine nuts, which is served with fresh summer figs.

Huevas

Huevas, or roe, is salted and pressed and is similar to the Italian *bottarga,* and though most comes from bluefin tuna, the roe from yellowfin tuna, as well as other fish, such as sea bass, ling, hake and mullet, is also sought after along the southern and eastern coast of Spain. The roes can often be quite an acquired taste – though I think they are delicious sliced thinly and eaten in salads, with tomatoes or fresh fruit.

Buche

This is salted tuna tripe, an old-fashioned preparation that is less popular nowadays, and fewer people know how to use it. The stomach of the tuna is salted in the same way as the belly, but only for a number of weeks. It is sold salted and you need to wash it well with water before using it in stews and dishes that require long cooking, such as *buche de atún con cebolla* (tuna tripe with onions and potatoes), as the texture will only soften properly with heat and time.

Bonito seco

This comes from a small species of *bonito* that is caught in the Gibraltar Strait, to which a small part of *salazón* production (only about 5 per cent) is devoted. It is filleted and salted for 24 hours, then dried for four days in a chamber with natural airflow, and a full slice will only be the size of a small sardine. It has a strong flavour, more of the fish than of the sea, and the flesh darkens to mahogany as it cures. It is eaten on its own and if you can find it I would suggest a dry sherry or a beer to accompany it.

Sarda

Sarda is something that I only discovered when I was looking for specialities for the coastal menu at our restaurant in Shoreditch. Somewhat confusingly it is called *albacora* in Castilian, certainly in the southern area of Andalucía, and it looks a little like a small tuna; however, it is not from the same family. It is fished along the coast of Cádiz and Gibraltar and cured in a similar way to anchovies. It is first filleted, then pressed and cured under salt for 3 months before being preserved in oil ready for serving as an outstanding tapa.

Mojama

Mojama continues to be the best-known tuna *salazón*, especially outside Spain. Eaten thinly sliced in the same way as cured ham, it has a dedicated following among chefs and customers. In Spain it is most popular with roasted almonds or fresh tomatoes but it is occasionally dressed with rosemary and pairs extremely well with eggs. A slice of *mojama* with a fried quail's egg is an excellent tapa.

The warm, dry, coastal breezes of the Cádiz coastline make it the perfect place to dry-cure the fish to preserve it for eating throughout the year. The most sought-after *mojama* is made with bluefin tuna; however, due to the scarcity and protection of the species, most is now made with yellowfin caught in tropical seas, frozen then and there and brought into harbour for curing. Even the elite and most established local buyers will only manage to produce a tiny amount of *mojama* made with bluefin tuna caught in the traditional *almadraba* (see page 204), which will be sold to their most discerning of customers, to whom price is no object.

Successful *mojama* requires cuts of tuna that have a lower fat content, so it is made from the four loins known as *descargamentos* or *descargados*. *Descargamentos,* the highest grade, are closer to the spine and are of a slightly superior quality for curing and drying.

The pieces are washed, then stacked and pressed in sea salt for 24 hours, washed again, dried briefly and, finally, hung up in special rooms to air dry naturally and slowly for anything from 15 to 25 weeks, depending on the particular piece of fish. As the fish loses moisture it firms up and shrinks and develops its characteristic deep red-amber colour and intense flavour.

ANCHOAS

'a vital and much cherished ingredient'

In the UK we have something of an obsession with these little fish, yet oddly we frequently use substandard ones – the kind of crusty powdery brown specimens that turn up on cheap pizzas, or the flabby white *boquerones* (see page 127) that can be overpowered by a sharp vinegar marinade.

In Spain, however, anchovies are a vital and much cherished ingredient, used in many, many ways, but often simply combined with the likes of olives, tomatoes and sweet peppers and piled on to *pan con tomate* (see page 72) or added to salads.

A forage fish related to the herring, the European anchovy (*Engraulis encrasicolus*) is found not only around the coasts of Spain, but also of Portugal, Morocco and the Mediterranean, and is a different species to the one you might come across from Latin America, which, although it can look bigger and more impressive, often has yellowy flesh that is hard and chewy, with little flavour of fish.

It is the Cantabrian anchovy, caught in the Atlantic ocean along the whole of the Cantabrian and Basque coastlines, that is the king of them all. One of the world's great foods, this is a fish to convert the most serial anchovy-sceptic into a believer in one mouthful. The very best fish are fat and fleshy, with an aroma of the sea and a taste that is intense, rounded and meaty, with

a real savoury nuttiness. Even when cured, such anchovies should taste more of fish than of salt, and still be tender in texture.

I still remember my own moment of discovery back in 1991 when my colleague of the time, Emma Ranson, first brought me some Cantabrian anchovies cured by the Ortiz family, whose tinned fish are famous in the region. I realised I had no idea how they should taste, having only really eaten anchovies that ranged from mediocre to quite horrid – but the moment I tried them a new chapter opened up for me that would involve multiple visits to the north coast of Spain to learn how anchovies were treated in order to be so valued.

It is the temperature of the Bay of Biscay, locally known as *el Mar Cantábrico* (the Cantabrian Sea), combined with the salinity of the plankton-rich waters, that contributes markedly to the quality of the fish.

The anchovies make their annual journey from the bay all the way to northern Europe during the winter, swimming in deep waters where the colder temperatures help their fat to develop and protect them. Then, as the weather warms up in spring, the plump shoals swim south on the return journey along the French coast back to the bay. Here the turbulent waters with a temperature of 14–18°C are full of algal blooms, which are a great food for the fish, and the

underwater shelf edges provide a protected area for spawning.

The best fish tend to be caught in April (traditionally with circular surface nets) and their flesh is smooth, thick and firm-textured, almost like a tender meat.

When the fishermen land their catch, some anchovies will go fresh to fishmongers and restaurateurs, typically to be boned, split, butterflied-out, coated in flour and fried like sardines – delicious – but in general they are cured.

As with so many species of fish, however, stocks of Cantabrian anchovies are running desperately low, thanks to years of over-fishing (with some fleets fishing all year round) combined with a reduction in fishing grounds, the use of pelagic nets (towed behind big freezer-trawlers) and environmental factors such as changes in temperature, wind and the salinity of the sea. All of this has affected the anchovies' food supply and their spawning grounds. In 1965, 80,000 tonnes of anchovies were fished in the Cantabrian Sea, but between 2002 and 2004 the average annual catch had fallen to only 10,000 tonnes. To try to get things back on track after this dramatic fall, the fishery was closed for five years. Since it re-opened in 2010, although quotas have virtually doubled each year, the permitted season for fishing is short, just from April to June.

The scarcity of Cantabrian anchovies has meant that, for a few years now, even those anchovy specialists most respected for the integrity and the quality of their produce have sometimes had to look beyond Cantabrian waters for their anchovies. The closest to the Cantabrian fish is the Mediterranean anchovy, and when it is fished in cooler areas and transported quickly to the salting houses, the difference in quality may not be that great. However, the temperature of the Mediterranean varies considerably, and if the fish come from warmer waters, possibly even other countries, where they live in different environments, they may not develop their size, flavour and texture in the same way.

People often think that anchovies packed in salt or oil have been through different processes. In fact, they both start off in the same way, whole (though with heads and guts removed) in salt. The difference is that only the biggest and best fish are destined to remain in salt, since only these can stand up to a long salting and pressing. Those fish that are of average size are given an initial salting and pressing in large barrels, then they will be taken out, cleaned, filleted and canned in oil. A small quantity of smaller fish might be lightly salted, then smoked; or marinated in oil and vinegar – in which case they are known as *boquerones*.

Anchovies in salt

The biggest, fattest anchovies are salted and pressed in the large *salazón* (salting) tins in which they will be sold – a technique that was started along the Cantabrian coastline in the 1880s by the Sicilian community that had settled there. The fish are arranged in their tins in layers of either ten or fourteen – the fewer per layer the better – in a criss-cross pattern, with each layer of fish separated by a layer of rock salt. A plastic neck disc goes over the top and the tins are placed in rows underneath huge weights which gradually press down on to the discs as the fish exude water and volume.

On average the anchovies will lose half their weight as they are pressed and aged in this way over 6–8 months, until the discs become almost level with the tops of each tin. At this point the discs are removed and the tins are sealed and labelled according to the number of fish they contain (the fewer the better, as this indicates the biggest, fattest anchovies).

These are the anchovies that are sought after by chefs, because when you fillet them not only are they sumptuous looking and tasting, but they have a lovely pinky colour which is lost when the fillets are kept under oil. The late Rose Gray of the River Café used to love the biggest of our Ortiz anchovies, which she and her chefs would just clean, fillet and drape over a salad. I will never forget the mutual appreciation on the day I took Javier Ortiz to the restaurant to meet her, which culminated in her insisting that he carve his signature with a knife into one of the huge, iconic, bright, slightly retro-looking Ortiz anchovy tins. I know people who love these so much they have clocks and all kinds of artefacts made from them, and I have some big lids at home that have been machine-edged so that they are no longer sharp, which I sometimes use as platters for serving seafood starters and tapas.

Anchoas de l'escala

L'Escala anchovies from Catalunya

The Catalans are famous for the anchovies (*anxoves* in Catalan) from L'Escala near Girona, where the preserving process has remained virtually unchanged since the days of the Greeks and Romans. You can still see the remains of an ancient salting factory a few kilometres from L'Escala in Empúries, where the fish were prepared, left in salting tanks and then packed into *amphorae* (jars).

Fished from the Mediterranean, L'Escala anchovies are smaller and rounder than their Atlantic counterparts, and have a lower fat content. After a lighter pressing, they are typically sold whole, in salt, in jars – though there is beginning to be some diversification into fillets under oil. Typically they are served in a salad with Little Gem lettuce, or piled on to toasted tomato bread (see page 72).

The catch is smaller than in other fisheries, and while the fish are cured for 2–6 months, depending on the season (higher summer temperatures can speed up the process), they are pressed more gently than their Cantabrian counterparts and so are juicier and plumper-textured; more like fresh or smoked fish and less salty in taste. They are similar to the famous French style of anchovy fished and cured in the village of Collioures near Perpignan – the ones that you find on a traditional *pissaladière*.

How to choose anchovies

If you are looking for Cantabrian anchovies, unfortunately labels don't always tell you everything you want to know. Even the best canners often take the attitude that their customers will trust them to choose the very best anchovies they can find, even if this means sometimes buying from outside the local waters, and you have little choice but to go along with this, as the provenance of the fish will not necessarily be obvious from the tins. Labels on preserved fish, unlike those on fresh fish, don't need to declare its origin, so while the production or packing site might be in Cantabria, the anchovies may have come from somewhere else.

To counteract this uncertainty, some smaller Basque producers are now banding together to label their tins *Conserveros Artesanos de la Costa Vasca*, which is a new guarantee (that also applies to tuna) certifying that the origins of the fish are on the Costa Vasca, the stretch of Basque coastline around the Bay of Biscay, and that the fish is caught and processed in season. All fishermen, boats and processors are registered and audited twice a year to guarantee traceability of origin and quality, and to keep out fraudsters. For small companies, choosing to impose these standards might be tough, but it can also allow them to stand out from the bigger concerns.

I am always asked which are best, whole anchovies in salt, or fillets in oil. Well, ultimately, you can't beat a long, fat anchovy that has stayed in its salty sea environment right up to the moment that you fillet it. The advantage of buying whole fish kept under salt is that these will be the biggest and most sturdy of the catch, whose scales and density of flesh can stand up to the salting and tight pressing so they remain rich and meaty, with a surprising ability to retain the aroma of the sea. The very best will always be those preserved in the largest tins, usually of 5 or 10kg, but whereas in Spain specialist market stalls and fish counters will dispense anchovies from these tins, as we do at Brindisa, in the UK it isn't always easy to find delicatessens willing to do this, and so the biggest tins tend to be bought only by chefs. Currently, the smallest tin of salted anchovies you can buy is around 850g – so you still either need lots of anchovy-eating friends or, once the tin is opened, you can transfer any fish you don't need to a bowl, cover them with wet salt and keep them in the fridge for up to a week.

The good news, though, is that more and more producers are looking at different ways of packaging whole salted anchovies that should make it easier to buy whole, big fish in smaller quantities. Already at Brindisa we are occasionally able to receive small batches of vacuum-packed sleeves containing around four or five anchovies in rock salt brine.

To prepare whole anchovies in salt for eating

Wash off the exterior salt, then, starting at the tail end, split the fish in two by running your fingernail along the backbone, which can then be pulled away from whichever fillet it clings to. The flesh will be pinky-brown and there will be a deep red line where you have pulled away the spine. The finest fish, caught at the right time in the best environment, will have compact flesh and an aroma and flavour that are a delicate balance of fish, salt and sea.

You can rub off the scales, if you prefer, then dress the fillets simply with olive oil and eat them alone, or on a slice of *pan con tomate* (see page 72), add them to a salad, or use them in whatever recipe you have chosen.

How to choose anchovy fillets in oil

Because they are more convenient I always have tins of good anchovies in oil at home – which have the added advantage that you don't have to fillet them. Do go for the best and biggest grade you can afford, though. Big is always beautiful where anchovies are concerned, and as with anchovies

under salt, the bigger the tin, the bigger the fish. Or again, buy them loose, if possible.

Anchovies in oil look more brown than pink in colour and ironically can be a little saltier than the ones that stay packed whole in salt. This is because they will always be relatively smaller fish, so they will absorb more salt when they are in the barrels for their initial curing.

All anchovies stored in oil are hand-filleted, but the better canners will do this using a knife, rather than scissors, removing all the tiny bones inside, so the fillets should have a tidy shape, well-trimmed, with no 'hairy' edges of fine bones.

If a fillet conserved in oil has yellow tones or streaks on the flesh, this shows the fat content has oxidised and turned rancid during what might have been an ineffective pressing process, i.e. not heavy and long enough to expel all the fat from the fish and give the best flavour. White tones in the fillet are also not a good sign, as they show that the anchovy has suffered from exposure to heat at some point in the pressing or canning process. And dark markings show that the fillets haven't been handled carefully enough to avoid bruising.

The best producers often prefer to pack premium fillets carefully in jars of oil rather than tins, so that customers can recognise the quality – since most defects can be seen. Just be careful not to break the fillets when you remove them.

Choose fillets in olive oil rather than vegetable oil, which can taint the fish. Some canners suggest that they are adding value by using extra virgin olive oil, but my view is that you don't want a stunning oil, especially if it is strongly flavoured and deeply coloured, as it will detract from the taste and appearance of the fish, which shouldn't need any disguise.

People assume that, just like baked beans, you can keep tins or jars of anchovies in your cupboard and they won't change, and in UK supermarkets they will be stacked on the shelves at ambient temperature, but over time the anchovies will alter and become stronger-tasting. In Spain all good retailers will keep their tins of anchovies chilled in the fridge, as we do at Brindisa.

Anchoas ahumadas
Smoked anchovies

One of the alternative techniques of conservation is smoking. The anchovies are salted briefly first – just enough to draw out some of the water in the fish – but not pressed. Then they are cleaned and smoked over wood before being filleted and packed in oil. Their flavour is less salty but fishy and rounded, the smoky flavour is gentle, and because they have not been pressed the fillets stay plump and juicy, so the experience is more like eating a fresh fish.

We buy ours from the Nardín family in the Basque country, who pioneered the art of smoking with beech, a typical Basque wood that is also used for the light smoking of the famous Idiazábal cheese.

Smoked anchovies pair well with beetroot in salads, or red peppers on toast, and are quite a favourite with chefs. Heston Blumenthal has used them with beef, or with roast marrowbone, parsley and pickled vegetables on toast.

Boquerones
Marinated anchovies

The other very popular method of conserving is to fillet the anchovies, clean them with water and then steep them in a mild vinegar marinade which 'pickles' them.

The flesh is naturally bleached white by the vinegar, so boquerones are often known as white anchovies. They are very versatile and have a wide appeal because they are not at all salty, and when they are done well, with good fish and a gentle marinade, they can be a real treat: mild and fresh-tasting with a unique aroma, perfect as a tapa on their own, in salads or combined with cured anchovy fillets on toast (see matrimonio, page 131). However, the downside can be that once in the marinade it is harder to detect the quality of the fish. Also, the vinegar used can sometimes be overpoweringly harsh.

How to choose boquerones
Boquerones tend to be sold by the weight or in plastic trays, and tasting for the strength of the vinegar is rarely an option before buying, so it is best to find a shop that sells them to your taste, and stick with it. Rarely are boquerones sold in tins, except for the perfect ones labelled anchoa a la vinagreta, made by Conservas Nardín.

When buying boquerones, look for silky-textured, slender white fillets with tones of grey. They shouldn't be big and fat, as in Spain large anchovies usually go for salting, so if they are very big, this is a clue that the fish are a different variety of anchovy from South America, which will not have the same flavour and delicate texture. Colour-wise, a more yellow anchovy may again signify a variety that is not Spanish.

Despite being stored in vinegar, boquerones do not last as long as salted ones, so it is best to buy them early in their date 'window' or they can lose texture and become pasty.

If you find the taste of the vinegar too strong, you can usually rescue this by adding your own dressing. Drain the anchovies of their vinegar, then replace this with a combination of olive oil and a gentle, sweeter vinegar such as Moscatel or Chardonnay, some chopped parsley and garlic. Add a few Manzanilla olives if you like.

Like all anchovies, whether tinned, jarred, under salt or smoked, boquerones should always be stored in the fridge.

SARDINAS

'a tin of good sardines is a great lunch or supper'

I think there is almost no wrong way to eat sardines: they are so good, whether fresh, conserved, big or small. A tin of good sardines with some sliced tomato and chopped parsley inside slices of fresh bread, accompanied by a bottle of beer, is a great lunch or supper.

The very best are caught in colder waters off the Galician coast (where they are known as *xoubas*), as they swim from Asturias towards Porto in Portugal, and where there are strict regulations and quotas to protect stocks. The sardines are netted after spawning and in this stage of their life-cycle they are carrying maximum levels of fat, which gives the flesh great flavour. This is thanks to the abundance and rich variety of plankton in these areas, which allows the sardines to feed well and grow fat and strong to withstand the cold waters and turbulent currents. The sardines are fished close to the coast rather than in the open sea, using nets that allow some fish to escape, so they don't get too crowded and crushed, and by-catch such as dolphins is avoided.

La Noche de San Juan, the night of St John, on 23 June, signals the start of the sardine harvest, which will run until September. At midnight fires are lit and families grill the first of the season's fish. The best producers of canned sardines, however, will be waiting to purchase their fish at just the right moment when the quality is exactly what they are looking for. Often this is in a very small window, maybe only 2–3 weeks; sometimes only one week. Producers will often attend the auctions of the landed fish themselves, or they will have their own paid watchman on the floor of the *lonxa* (fish market), selecting the best batches only from fishermen they trust, who readily show their records of each journey and the time spent at sea, which has an impact on the quality of the catch. Once bought, the fish, if it is to be conserved, needs to go for processing immediately, to retain its best characteristics.

By law sardines must be a maximum of 25cm, and smaller fish between 10cm and 16cm must be called *sardinillas*. On average these are around 11cm and can be exceptional, especially during the window when the real cream of the catch is coming through.

Both sardines and *sardinillas* are gutted and their tails removed by hand in one swift movement (the verb for this is *esmojar*), then they are processed by steaming at a high temperature, so that the fat is retained within the fish, and, finally, they are packed, either in olive oil or a variety of preparations, from plain brine to tomato sauce (*a la Americana*), *escabeche* (with vinegar and/or *pimentón*), or black ink. If you buy *xoubas picantes* there will be red chilli and a slice of carrot and cornichon beneath the fish.

Both sardines and *sardinillas* improve their flavour in the tin, so the longer you keep them – up to three years – the better they will taste once opened.

Sardinas anchoadas
Cured sardines

Some fish in the sardine family – we know them as pilchards – are sold 'anchovified', i.e. they look very similar to large anchovy fillets.

The conservation process is different, however, as the fresh fish are cured in brine and turned daily over a period of 5 days, then they are filleted, scaled, washed and air-dried in a room with high humidity for 7–12 hours, before being seasoned and packed in sunflower oil.

They have a wonderfully intense flavour of the sea and a very meaty texture, perfect in a salad of peppery leaves such as watercress, with a squeeze of lemon and olive oil. They are also good served on toast as a *montadito* (see opposite) with *piquillo* peppers or fresh cheese.

MONTADITOS, LLESQUES I COQUES CATALANS
Mini bread tapas, Catalan toasts and flatbreads

Some tapas bars specialise in these quick and easy combinations of ingredients that are literally 'mounted' on bite-sized pieces of bread or toast.

Quick anchovy *montaditos*

Matrimonio (marriage). The name of this one speaks for itself. It brings together cured anchovy fillets in oil, or salt, prepared as on page 126 (or you could even substitute smoked fillets), with *boquerones* (see page 127) – just alternate them on pieces of toast that have been rubbed with a cut clove of garlic or a halved ripe tomato.

Criss-cross anchovy fillets with strips of *piquillo* peppers from a tin on squares of *pan con tomate*.

Grill some good bread, drizzle with a little olive oil, cut into squares, add a few thin slices of hard-boiled egg and some anchovy fillets, and finish with a little grated lemon zest.

Arrange some slices of Manchego cheese on pieces of toasted bread, put under the grill until the cheese melts, and top with anchovy fillets.

Llesques

These are more hearty than the typical *montadito*. *Llesca* is Catalan for a slice of country bread, usually toasted, grilled or charred over coals, and in Barcelona specialist *llesquerías* serve these with a fantastic range of cold or hot toppings. The cold version will usually involve slices of *pan con tomate* (see page 72) topped with cured foods, such as ham, anchovies, cheese, *salchichón* (salami), chorizo or *lomo* (pork loin). The hot version can be equally simple, or at its most elaborate it will involve sharing platters of roasted meats, such as grilled chops, maybe half a rabbit, a quarter of a chicken, sausages, or even steak, accompanied by grilled vegetables and/or a bowl of beans, and a pot of *alioli* (see page 136) for people to assemble themselves.

I love this way of eating, which was the inspiration behind the menu in the café/bar of our Brixton Food Rooms, where we have a varying *llesca* menu.

Brindisa Food Rooms *Llesques*

Cold

All of these are served on substantial slices of tomato bread:

Manchego cheese and a slice of *membrillo* or tomato jam.

A drained tin of *bonito del norte* or good tuna, with some strips of *piquillo* pepper and capers, sprinkled with wine vinegar.

Jarred artichokes and a handful of rocket (or other salad leaves), tossed in extra virgin olive oil and topped with a spoonful of *romesco* sauce and toasted pine nuts.

Sliced *salchichón* with sweet *guindilla* peppers from a jar.

Spears of white asparagus (*cojonudos navarricos*) on top of a chopped gherkin mixed with mayonnaise, topped with grated hard-boiled egg and *piquillo* peppers, if you like.

Slices of well-ripened tomato, topped with cured sardines and a thinly sliced *piquillo* pepper from a jar, finished with a drizzle of extra virgin olive oil.

Hot

Food Rooms Grilled *botifarra*

For 2 people, slice an onion and cook very slowly in olive oil in a heavy-based pan until caramel-brown, then lift out the onion and keep to one side. Cut a *botifarra* sausage into 3 and cook in the same pan for 10–12 minutes, until browned all over. Turn off the heat and add the sliced white bulbs of 2 or 3 spring onions, stirring for a minute before adding the green stems. Top 2 slices of tomato bread with the caramelised onions and strips of *piquillo* peppers from a jar (1 pepper per person is fine). Slice each piece of *botifarra* in half lengthways and arrange on top, skin side upwards, top with the spring onion, season with salt and pepper and finish with a drizzle of extra virgin olive oil. Serve with salad and *alioli*.

Food Rooms Presa *ibérico* or pork loin

For 2 people, slice and caramelise 1 onion as in the recipe above. Heat some olive oil in a pan, season 2 slices of pork loin, preferably *Ibérico*, that are around 5cm thick and cook over a high heat. Allow to rest for a few minutes before slicing at an angle. Spread the onions over 2 slices of tomato bread, add some strips of *piquillo* peppers from a jar (again, 1 pepper per person is enough), top with the slices of pork and drizzle with extra virgin olive oil.

Food Rooms—Monte Enebro cheese with walnuts

For 2 people, you need 2 slices of Monte Enebro goat's cheese (about 70g and cut 1.5cm thick). Mix a small handful of raisins and walnuts with a little olive oil, honey (we use orange blossom) and Moscatel vinegar. Preheat the grill to medium, place a slice of cheese on each of 2 slices of tomato bread, and put under the grill for about 3 minutes, until the cheese begins to bubble and colour. Remove and top with the walnuts and raisins in their dressing.

Asun's *pimentón* chicken

This is based on the marinated and grilled chicken that our friend Asun (see page 154) prepares in Burgos. For 2 chicken breasts, mix 2 crushed cloves of garlic, a handful of chopped parsley, ½ teaspoon each of *pimentón picante* and *pimentón dulce* (hot and mild paprika) with 1 teaspoon of honey, 1 tablespoon of sweet, aged balsamic PX vinegar and a sprinkling of salt. Marinate the chicken for a few hours (or overnight), then slice and cook under a hot grill (Asun cooks her chicken on the *plancha*, the flat grill plate). Serve on good toasted bread, with some chopped rocket and sliced *piquillo* pepper from a jar.

Llesca de sobrassada mallorquina i Maó
Sobrasada on toast with Mahón cheese

Even though the 'spreading chorizo', *sobrasada*, hails from Mallorca (see page 65), it is eaten all over the country, and is a typical *llesca* topping in the bars of Barcelona. We always keep some in our fridge at home, because combined with some good cheese, such as Mahón, it makes a great, quick snack. In the restaurants we also make this with Manchego cheese.

For two people, gently dry-fry around 20g of *sobrasada* to remove much of the fat in the meat. Drain off the fat. Preheat the grill. Toast 2 large slices of country bread on both sides, then drizzle with olive oil and spread with the *sobrasada*. Lay some slices of cured Mahón or Manchego cheese over the top (you need around 50g). Put back under the grill to toast for 4 minutes, until the *sobrasada* is hot and the cheese has melted and is turning golden. Drizzle with a little honey.

Llesca de pencas de acelgas con manchego tierno
Rainbow chard stalks with Manchego cheese on country toast

One day when I was working on this book, a photo pinged on to my mobile phone from chef Barny Haughton, a dear friend known affectionately as the godfather of Bristol chefs. After many acclaimed years at Bordeaux Quay in the city, he now runs the Square Food Foundation there, with its cooking school and café, and is an ambassador for Slow Food. The picture was of a shallow pan, filled with golden, pink, green, yellow and purple stalks. The chard season had arrived and Barny was braising the juicy stems ready to pile on toast and sprinkle with shavings of young Manchego cheese. This is his recipe, which is really tasty – though sadly the chard stalks don't look quite as brightly coloured at the end of cooking.

The juices from the chard soak into the toasted bread, so you need at least a serviette and maybe even a knife and fork to eat the *llesques* easily.

Serves 4

olive oil
1 small red onion, finely sliced
a few dried chilli flakes
1 clove of garlic, finely sliced
400g rainbow chard stalks, cut into 3cm lengths
sea salt
juice of ½ a lemon
4 large thin slices of sourdough or other good bread, cut into 4 pieces
100g young Manchego cheese or some *alioli* (see page 136)

Heat a little olive oil in a large frying pan, add the onion and chilli flakes and cook gently until the onion is soft but not coloured. Turn the heat up, add the garlic and fry a little bit more, but take care not to burn it, or it will turn bitter. Add the chard stalks. Once they have started to sizzle, add the smallest amount of water – just enough to stop the chard stalks frying – and a generous pinch of salt. You may need to add a little more water as the stalks cook.

Have a warm bowl ready and once the chard stalks are tender, put them in the bowl and toss well with the lemon juice.

Meanwhile, toast the sliced bread and drizzle it with olive oil.

Transfer the slices of bread to plates, top with the chard stalks and, with a potato peeler, shave the Manchego over the top, if using, or serve with a small bowl of *alioli*. Finish with a drizzle of olive oil.

ALIOLI

'garlic and oil'

The original *alioli* is made without eggs – the Catalan *all i oli* means *garlic and oil* – and purists will always make it this way. However, it requires a lot of work and immense patience and skill, because you can overdo the blending and the sauce will split in a fraction of a second. Even when you make it with eggs, just like making any mayonnaise, it needs to be done carefully to avoid splitting. So if I am making the quantity here I admit I use a food processor (it needs to be one where the blades reach right to the edge of the bowl so that it pulls in the oil better), or you can use a blender – in which case you can just chop the garlic and let the machine do the rest.

If you want to make a half quantity, using 200ml of olive oil, 1 clove of garlic, just 1 small egg (no added yolk) and ½ teaspoon of salt, the safest way to make sure the emulsion works is to crush the garlic to a pulp in a pestle and mortar first, then whisk in the egg and salt, before slowly adding the oil.

Depending on what you are serving *alioli* with, you might like to make it stronger or lighter in flavour. We prefer stronger oils for meat dishes and lighter ones (plus a dash of lemon juice) for fish or vegetable dishes.

It is surprising how many variations on the classic recipe you come across; for example, some people add honey, dark chocolate, or even squid ink. Perhaps more unusually I have come across quince as an addition, for which I have given two recipes following this one.

Makes around 400ml

2 cloves of garlic
a dash of lemon juice (optional)
 if serving with fish or vegetables
1 small egg
1 small egg yolk
1 teaspoon sea salt
400ml extra virgin olive oil

Halve the garlic cloves, remove the centre germ if it is large and green (this removes any bitterness), then chop the cloves.

Put the garlic into a food processor or blender with the lemon juice, if using, and blend, add the eggs and the salt and blend again, then slowly start adding the olive oil. Stop as soon as all the ingredients have emulsified and the *alioli* is thick and yellow. Taste and add more lemon juice if necessary.

Alioli de Codony
Quince *alioli*

Alioli de Nadal
Christmas *alioli*

Joan Puigcercós is a fiery, eloquent, tall, dark and imposing ex-politician who is a neighbour and friend of my brother in the village of Santa Maria d'Oló in Catalunya. A man with a deep love of his surrounding countryside and the Ripollés mountains where he grew up, he supports the independence of Catalunya, and represented the ERC (Esquerra Republicana de Catalunya) at the Spanish parliament. Whenever I meet him, however, we always talk about food, as he is also an outstanding cook, with a library of cookery books at his weekday base in Barcelona and his home in Santa Maria, where at weekends he takes over the cooking from his wife, Núria.

Joan aims for an *alioli* with a jelly-like texture, which can actually be sliced rather than spread, but since that is quite challenging to achieve, we came up with a variation which is much easier and is more of a fruit purée than an emulsion. It is surprisingly tasty and, because of its resemblance to apple sauce, goes well with tapas of grilled *botifarras* or *pintxos*, as well as roast pork and game dishes.

1 quince
30ml olive oil, plus a little extra
 for rubbing the quince
½ teaspoon sea salt
½ teaspoon sugar

Preheat the oven to 200°C/gas 6.

Rub the quince lightly with olive oil and wrap it in aluminium foil. Place it in the preheated oven for around 25 minutes, until the flesh is soft and you can pass a skewer through it smoothly without meeting any woody resistance. Let the quince cool down, then peel and de-seed it, discarding any tough fibrous lumps.

Put the quince flesh into a blender, add the salt and sugar and blend while pouring in the olive oil, slowly and a little at a time, until it is all absorbed and you have a smooth sauce.

This is a more elaborate quince *alioli*, bulked out with walnuts, again from Joan Puigcercós, who explained to me that it was once an essential part of the *Noche Buena,* the Christmas Eve vigil that used to be celebrated in his mountain village (*Nadal* is Catalan for Christmas). All the villagers would gather at midnight in the eleventh-century stone church and keep watch until 6 a.m., not an easy thing to do on a bitterly cold night in the days before central heating. To keep everyone going the people would take with them big *panes de coca* – traditional Catalan flatbreads (see page 70) – baked in the communal village oven, which would be anointed with this *alioli de Nadal* to help bulk it out, and they would drink glasses of strong red wine or Moscatel.

Even though the vigil is no longer practised, Joan still makes this alioli every Christmas. We like it as a dip for crudités or with roasted vegetables as well as an accompaniment to darker meats such as beef or game, lamb chops or sausages.

Because of the addition of bread, quince and walnuts this is easier to make using a pestle and mortar than the classic *alioli*, but you do need a big mortar, and it works equally well done in a food processor. If you prefer a more textured *alioli,* however, chop the walnuts, rather than blend them, and mix them in at the end.

Joan also likes to add a sweet potato, but this is optional. If you want to try this, roast the sweet potato in the oven and then add as much as you like, to taste, pounding or pulsing it along with the other ingredients.

You can use quince paste rather than freshly poached quince: if you do this you will need 50g. In order to really bring out the quince and walnut flavours it is important to use a mild olive oil, as a strong extra virgin one will be too overpowering.

Serves 8 as a dip or accompaniment

1 quince
4 peppercorns
1 teaspoon sugar
½ a cinnamon stick
100g walnuts
3 cloves of garlic, peeled
1 slice of bread (about 50g) with the
   crust taken off, torn into pieces
½ teaspoon Moscatel or PX sherry
4 egg yolks
350ml mild olive oil

Preheat the oven to 180°C/gas 4.

Put the whole quince into a pan with the peppercorns, sugar and cinnamon and enough water to cover. Bring to the boil, then turn down the heat and simmer for about 25 minutes. Check that the quince is cooked through by piercing it with a skewer: there should be no sense of woody resistance as it passes through the fruit. Drain (discarding the peppercorns and cinnamon) and allow to cool.

Lay the walnuts on a tray and roast them in the preheated oven for about 7 minutes, until browned. Remove and leave to cool.

Peel and de-seed the quince, discarding any tough fibrous lumps of uncooked fruit.

Remove any green shoots from the garlic to prevent a bitter aftertaste in the *alioli* and then either pound the cloves with the walnuts to a rough paste using a pestle and mortar, or pulse briefly in a blender. Add the quince flesh and pound/pulse until smooth. Next, add the bread and pound/pulse again, then pour in the Moscatel, or sherry, and the egg yolks and continue to pulse/pound until smooth again.

Finally, pour in the olive oil, slowly and a little at a time, pounding or pulsing until you have a firm and smooth mixture that resembles hummus.

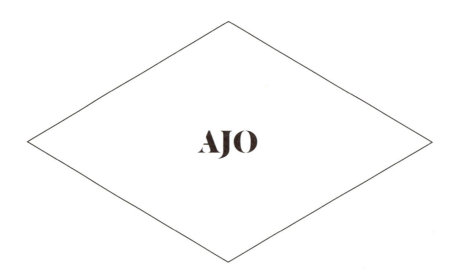

AJO

'the key to some of Spain's most iconic and ancient preparations'

The earliest garlic harvest in all of Europe begins in Andalucía in May, while June and July are the harvest months for the growers of Castilla y León, who celebrate with a festival in the city of Zamora on 28 June, St Peter's Day. The streets are lined with pyramids of garlic strings, stacked on pallets and way taller than their vendors, their aroma hanging assertively in the air.

Although originally from Central Asia, garlic has been cultivated around Spain for over 2,000 years and the country is now Europe's leading producer. The most famous variety is the purple *ajo morado* from Las Pedroñeras in the province of Cuenca in La Mancha, which has fragile white outer layers with tight purple-wrapped cloves inside, and a sweet flavour with a strong punch.

Garlic is the key to some of Spain's most iconic and ancient preparations, such as *alioli* (and all its variations with saffron, quince or walnuts); *gazpacho* – which existed as a garlic, water and bread soup before the arrival of the tomato in Spain – and *picada*, the crushed paste made with garlic, herbs and nuts, etc. (see page 320). Beyond this, its use varies from region to region.

In Catalunya and the Levante, sometimes before being added to a sauce or *picada*, a whole head of garlic or individual cloves (still in their skins) will be lightly roasted first, either in the oven or over a flame, which gives a smoky aroma and soft creamy flesh.

Francisco Juan Martínez Lledo, one of the chefs from Alicante at our restaurant in Shoreditch, introduced me to a method that he particularly likes to use. He crushes the garlic cloves still in their skins and fries them gently in hot olive oil in the corner of a pan that he has tilted slightly to provide a deeper well of oil. The skins shrivel and he discards these, but the little crushed pieces of garlic flesh in irregular shapes and sizes cook slightly differently, so some are toastier, some fresher. Thin, straggly strips will begin to caramelise, while larger chunks will remain almost raw in the middle and these can be crushed with the back of a spoon. When he scoops the pieces out and adds them to his *picadas* they give more complex layers of flavour.

In the UK, the green garlic shoots (actually flowering spikes) that sprout from hardneck varieties of garlic in March and April tend to be pulled off and thrown away to encourage the growth of the bulb, but in Spain these *ajetes* (or scapes as we call them) are a very short seasonal treat, pounced on in a similar way to wild garlic from the British woodland (though this is a different family). If there is a surplus the scapes will be frozen, as they are excellent in scrambled eggs, sautéed and scattered over green vegetables, chopped into salads or pounded into *picadas* or pestos. In the UK, you can sometimes buy them from garlic farms in the summer.

Coca de recapte
Catalan flatbread

Of all the many recipes for *coques* – flatbreads, which can be sweet or savoury (see page 70), the pizza-like ones are perfect for slicing and serving with other small plates. Sometimes I feel as if these *coques* are a forgotten piece in the jigsaw of Spanish food, since the Italian versions have taken over the world.

The name *recapte* really means 'made with things in the house', in other words the base is topped with whatever you have to hand, but most usually this would be *escalivada* (roasted vegetables). In villages where few people had ovens, the local baker would go around the houses collecting whatever ingredients each family was able to contribute, then make a selection of *coques* to be shared out among the whole community.

Toni Chueca of La Bauma dairy in Catalunya, who gave me this recipe, remembers that in the time of his grandparents this *coca* was made to welcome the 'sunshine season', when juicy onions, peppers, aubergines and tomatoes would be in abundance in the vegetable plot. Olive oil would be poured over the stretched dough, then the vegetables arranged in strips. On to this base you could add anything else you had, such as chard, sardines, anchovies, tuna, or slices of sausage. Once in the oven the base puffs up like a pillow, and is firm around the edge and light, soft and juicy in the centre beneath the vegetables and other ingredients.

Unlike the typical Italian pizza, a *coca* typically doesn't involve cheese. That said, Toni likes to break with tradition by shaving a little of his semi-hard Garrotxa over the top – and I have to say it is really very good!

Coca is delicious just warm after baking, but the old-fashioned way is to eat it cold the next day – it is up to you.

As it is easier to make the dough in relatively large quantities, this recipe will make two *coques*, each big enough to serve four people, but if you don't want to make them both immediately, you can freeze half the dough for another time.

**Makes 2 *coques*, each big enough
to serve 4 for tapas**

15g fresh yeast
500g plain flour, plus extra for dusting
1 teaspoon sea salt
100ml olive oil

For the topping
4 red peppers
2 aubergines
4 large sweet onions
6 tablespoons olive oil
**12 fresh sardines, filleted and each
    fillet cut in half lengthways**
sea salt
2 teaspoons chopped parsley

For the base, dissolve the yeast in 2 tablespoons of warm water. Put the flour into a bowl, make a well in the centre, and pour in the yeast and warm water. Sprinkle the salt around the edges of the flour and pour in 100ml of water. With your hands, begin to mix the ingredients into a dough, adding another 100ml of water when it starts to come together, then turn out on to a lightly floured work surface and continue to knead until the dough has a uniform, smooth, elastic consistency (you may need to add a little more water or flour).

Dust a clean bowl with flour, put in the dough, sprinkle the surface with a little more flour, then cover with clingfilm to prevent any draughts forming a crust. Leave somewhere warm for 30 minutes, then allow the dough to rest for a further hour or two at room temperature until it doubles in size.

Towards the end of the resting time, make the topping. Preheat the oven to 200°C/gas 6.

Rub the peppers, aubergines and unpeeled onions with the olive oil, making sure they are well covered. Put into an ovenproof dish, cover with foil, then put into the preheated oven for

40 minutes, removing the foil halfway through and turning the vegetables, so they brown equally on both sides. Remove them when they are tender (the onions may need a bit longer – possibly another 20 minutes).

Turn down the oven to 180°C/gas 4.

While still warm, peel the skin from the peppers and cut them into thin strips. Peel the aubergines and de-seed if necessary. Slice the flesh into thin strips, and then into small dice. Peel and finely slice the onions.

Remove the clingfilm from the bowl of dough and add the olive oil slowly, a little at a time, squeezing the dough initially to help the oil blend in, and then kneading vigorously until it is completely absorbed. Cover again with clingfilm and leave to rest at room temperature for another 30 minutes. The dough will rise some more, though not as much this time.

Line two 40cm x 25cm oven trays with baking paper.

Generously flour your work surface – you may need flour on your hands as well as your rolling pin, as the dough will be very sticky. Roll out the dough into two rectangles of around 40cm x 25cm, and 5mm thick. Roll each around your rolling pin and then unroll on to the trays.

To each, add a layer of sliced onion, leaving a 2cm rim around the edge of the dough. Next, add the aubergine and sprinkle with a pinch of salt. Finally, alternate the sardine and pepper strips diagonally on top – lay the sardines skin side up, so that this will turn crispy – and put into the top of the oven for 25–30 minutes until the dough is firm and golden brown.

Remove from the oven, sprinkle with parsley and serve warm.

SOPAS FRÍAS
Cold soups

Gazpacho

Although these days *gazpacho* seems to be universally understood as a cold soup made with tomato, it existed long before the tomato arrived in Spain, and the name really refers to an idea rather than a specific recipe. Originally it was devised as a way of using up old bread by combining it with the kind of rustic essentials that most people would have at home: garlic, olive oil, vinegar and salt. If there were nuts to be had these would be ground and added, sometimes with onion and any other available vegetables. When the tomato and the pepper began to appear in the sixteenth century these made perfect additions – but not all *gazpachos* contain either.

In Spain it has become the fashion for chefs to rediscover and rework old recipes for *gazpacho* and also to invent new ones. Often these, especially ones made with fruits (see page 148), are made without bread. You only have to browse through chef Alberto Herráiz's beautiful book, *Gazpacho*, to get the picture. Originally from Cuenca in Castile-La Mancha, Herráiz set up his restaurant Fogón Saint Julien in Paris, re-interpreting not only *gazpacho*, but tapas and other Spanish dishes. He adds all sorts of ingredients to his *gazpachos*, from strawberries to beetroot, even anchovies, and Rupert and I have enjoyed working our way through his recipes at home.

Gazpacho andaluz
Chilled tomato soup from Andalucía

Some *gazpacho* notes
If you are using bread it should be 1–2 days old, so that it absorbs all the flavours. You need a dense loaf that won't turn to mush.

As a rule, most tomato-based *gazpachos* benefit from being allowed to infuse for a few hours before blending. We put all the ingredients together in a plastic food container in the fridge.

If using a liquidiser, choose a slow speed to preserve all the nutrients and the bright colour.

Where water is added, Spanish chefs will often use spring water for its purity. As far as tap water goes, hard water without calcium gives the best results.

Add the olive oil slowly so that it properly emulsifies. *Gazpachos* offer a good opportunity to experiment with different oils, which can subtly affect the flavour.

If you are not using the *gazpacho* straight away, keep it chilled in the fridge and use within 3 days.

This is the summer classic in our tapas kitchens. You need ripe tomatoes, which will give the aroma and colour that a good *gazpacho* needs.

Serves 8–10

1kg ripe tomatoes, cut into large chunks
200g cucumber (about ⅓ of a cucumber), peeled and cut into large chunks
1 medium onion, cut into large chunks
2 cloves of garlic, cut in half
2 *piquillo* peppers (optional)
100g bread, chopped
2 tablespoons sherry vinegar
200ml extra virgin olive oil
a pinch of ground cumin (optional)
sea salt, to taste
200g ice cubes

To serve
pieces of bread, fried in olive oil
finely chopped cucumber (optional)
finely chopped red pepper (optional)

Put the tomatoes, cucumber, onion, garlic and peppers, if using, into a bowl or plastic food container, add the chopped bread, vinegar and half the extra virgin olive oil and put into the fridge to infuse for 2 hours.

Add all the rest of the ingredients apart from the remaining extra virgin olive oil, and begin to blend with a hand blender, adding the rest of the oil a little at a time until you have a creamy, soup consistency, then pass through a fine sieve.

Serve with the fried bread scattered over, and, if you like, some finely chopped cucumber and red pepper.

Gazpacho de tomate y pimiento choricero

Tomato and dried red pepper *gazpacho*

This is our executive chef Josep's variation on an idea in Alberto Herráiz's book *Gazpacho*, and one that we particularly like to make at home, where we are always looking for ideas for the dried peppers which we have in abundance, particularly the *choricero*. One of our favourite peppers, it is used particularly by the Basques in their thick pepper sauces, and here it adds a hearty, deep background flavour to the freshness of the ripe tomatoes.

Although you can prepare the bread and the peppers an hour or so before you want to serve the soup, the aromas won't be as profound as if you do it the night before.

Serves 4

4 *choricero* peppers
700g tomatoes
1 large shallot (100g)
100g light dry white bread, crusts cut off
75ml olive oil
around 1 teaspoon sherry vinegar
¼ teaspoon *pimentón dulce* (mild paprika)
sea salt and freshly ground black pepper

Soak the *choricero* peppers in a bowl of water overnight, then remove the stalks and seeds and carefully scrape the flesh away from the skin with a teaspoon. You should have around 70g of *choricero* flesh. Discard the skins.

Roughly chop the tomatoes, shallot and bread and mix them together in a bowl or plastic food container with the olive oil, sherry vinegar, the *choricero* flesh, the *pimentón*, a pinch of salt and a twist of black pepper. Knead the mixture briefly to help the tomatoes release their juices. Cover the bowl with clingfilm and let the mixture marinate for at least 2 hours. Add a little more sherry vinegar if you like.

Blend the mixture with 300ml of water for at least 2 minutes, until the *gazpacho* is completely smooth. Add another 200ml of water, blend again and taste, adding salt and possibly a drop more sherry vinegar if necessary.

Pass the soup through a sieve or conical strainer and then put into the fridge for about 2 hours, until cold.

Ajo blanco
Almond 'gazpacho'

Contemporary gazpachos

Although this cold almond soup has a name of its own, it is really part of the *gazpacho* family and, in fact, predates the better-known tomato one. Since I can't resist almonds in any form, I love this soup, and during the summer we always have it on the menu at Tapas Brindisa, London Bridge.

If you want to add more oil, feel free – though make sure it is a really good, fruity, aromatic one. Rupert remembers the first time he made *ajo blanco*, many years ago, confusing millilitres with decilitres and ending up using a litre of Núñez de Prado olive oil, which he said made the soup absolutely delicious, if a little extravagant!

Serves 4

100g stale white bread, crusts cut off
200g blanched almonds
1 clove of garlic
2 teaspoons sherry vinegar
4 tablespoons olive oil
sea salt and freshly ground black pepper

To serve
a few green grapes, halved

Put all the ingredients except the seasoning into a food processor and pulse until the almonds and breadcrumbs are finely ground. Keep the processor running and pour in 600ml of water a little at a time. Taste and season as necessary and put into the fridge to chill. Serve very cold, garnished with the grapes.

These next few recipes for *gazpacho* move closer to our modern approach to fruit and vegetable juices and smoothies. Creative Spanish cooks are preserving the essential fresh, cool simplicity of the classical soup, but taking out, or elaborating on, the subsistence elements of dry bread and oil, and replacing or enhancing them with more relevant modern twists.

While more traditional tomato-based *gazpachos* tend to benefit from being started the night before, fruit soups need to be made closer to serving – you just need to allow around 2 hours for chilling – as they lose colour, aroma and flavour very quickly.

Gazpacho de melón
Melon *gazpacho*

This is a very fresh *gazpacho* which our head chef, Leo Rivera, ensures is always on the summer menu at our South Kensington tapas bar, where he used to be in charge. It is delicate, thirst-quenching, mildly sweet and smooth with a luxurious edge from the fat of the cream: a nice light way to start a meal. I suggest serving it from cups and glasses for people to drink from, rather than bowls.

It should be made with a Galia or the elongated, green-skinned *piel de sapo* ('toad skin') melon, as a Cantaloupe or watermelon won't produce the same consistency. You could try it with a Charentais melon, but the *gazpacho* will tend to be thicker, more like a *salmorejo* (see opposite), and you will most likely need spoons to eat it.

Serves 4

1 large melon, such as Galia or *piel de sapo*
¼ teaspoon grated nutmeg
750ml single cream
a pinch of black pepper

***To serve* (optional)**
small pieces of melon (either scooped into balls, or cut into cubes and dipped, if you like, into a little port to give a contrasting colour)
small pieces of bacon, dry-fried until crispy

Peel and de-seed the melon (keep a wedge back if using some for garnish) and blend until very smooth, then add the nutmeg and blend briefly. Strain through a fine sieve and put into the fridge to chill.

Just before serving, beat in the cream and season with black pepper. Serve, if you like, with the melon pieces in port, if using, and/or small pieces of crispy bacon.

Gazpacho de manzana
Apple *gazpacho*

This recipe was passed on to me by Rocío Muñoz González-Meneses, wife of Felipe Núñez de Prado of the pioneering olive oil family in Córdoba, with whom we have worked since the early nineties (see page 218). It is a favourite, made by a friend of hers, which seems perfect for the British table, since excellent apples are so much more abundant than ultra-ripe tomatoes.

Serves 4 generously

650g green apples such as Granny Smith, sharp ones such as Braeburn, or a similar local and/or heritage variety, peeled, cored and de-seeded
100g cucumber, peeled and de-seeded
1 clove of garlic
4 teaspoons Moscatel vinegar
a pinch of salt
1 tablespoon delicate olive oil, such as Arbequina
70g stale bread

To serve
50g pine nuts
50g raisins
50g pomegranate seeds

Toast the pine nuts in a dry pan until just golden, then lift out and keep to one side.

Blend all the ingredients, except the pine nuts, raisins and pomegranate seeds, in a food processor. Slowly add around 250–300ml of water, until you have the consistency of double cream – you may not need all the water.

Put into the fridge to chill.

To serve, garnish with the toasted pine nuts, raisins and pomegranate seeds.

Salmorejo
Chilled cream of tomato from Córdoba

The home of *salmorejo* is Córdoba in Andalucía. Superficially it seems very similar to a tomato *gazpacho* – cold and tomato-red – however, the difference is that while it is still refreshing and nutritious, it is much thicker. Rocío Muñoz González-Meneses, of the Núñez de Prado olive oil producers in the region, defines *salmorejo* as a cream of vegetables, whereas she considers *gazpacho* to be closer to vegetable juice. I consider it almost a tomato spread, too thick to be drunk from a cup in the way that *gazpacho* can be served. So much so that it is often scooped up with additional pieces of bread, rather than with a spoon.

I have tasted many different *salmorejos*, some of which involve longer soaking of the bread, tomatoes and oil, but I have chosen this one from Ana Barrera (see page 442) because I love the fresh simplicity of it. In her Madrid restaurant she garnishes it only with some watercress, whose pepperiness works brilliantly with the flavour of ripe tomatoes (choose the ripest, most plump ones you can find). However, I also love the way that Rocío serves her *salmorejo* at Núñez de Prado, with chopped hard-boiled egg and *taquitos* (small pieces) of cured ham, with some of the family's wonderful oil drizzled in a cross shape on top.

The quality of the olive oil you use is important. It should be stronger as opposed to mellow, and adding it very slowly is the key to a brighter colour and creamier texture.

Serves 8–10

1.5kg tomatoes, quartered
½ an onion, chopped
1 clove of garlic, green centre removed, crushed
2 tablespoons sherry or wine vinegar
50g (1 small slice) white day-old bread
sea salt
½ teaspoon sugar
around 150ml extra virgin olive oil

To serve
either a big bunch of watercress, or 1 hard-boiled egg and/or 80g good Spanish cured ham, preferably Ibérico

Put all the ingredients except the oil into a bowl or plastic food container and put into the fridge for an hour to allow the bread to soak up the liquid and the aromas of the vinegar and the tomatoes.

Blend, adding the oil a little at a time until you have the required texture in terms of thickness and silkiness – you may prefer to add more than 150ml – then put through a fine sieve. Chill for about 2 hours in the fridge.

Serve in small bowls, scattered with the watercress. Or, if garnishing with egg and/or ham, grate the egg finely and scatter one or both over the *salmorejo*.

Salmorejo de cerezas
Cherry *salmorejo*

This a simple contemporary fruit version of *salmorejo* given to me by Sandra Salcedo, the chef daughter of our vegetable and pepper supplier Conservas Navarrico, and it is a great way of using cherries during the wonderful, if short, British season. It pairs amazingly with the red Recóndita Armonía wine made by Felipe Gutiérrez de la Vega in La Marina Alta (see page 190), which tastes like the ripest red plums you have ever eaten.

Serves 4

200g crisp ripe cherries, without stones
200g ripe tomatoes
1 clove of garlic
sea salt, to taste
1 tablespoon sherry vinegar
100g light dry white bread, crusts cut off

Mix all the ingredients in a bowl, cover with clingfilm, and leave to marinate for an hour at room temperature.

Blend, adding 300ml of water, taste and adjust the salt if necessary, then add 200ml more water and blend again. The consistency should be quite thick. Strain through a sieve and chill in the fridge for about 2 hours before serving in small bowls or glasses.

Salmorejo de tomate con almendras 'zoco'
Almond and tomato *salmorejo*

Another variation on one of Alberto Herráiz's recipes, which combines my two absolute favourite soups: tomato and *ajo blanco*. The closest I have come to finding out why the dish is so called is that there is an Arabic word *zoco*, meaning a market, and as almonds were brought over by the Arabs to Spain this makes sense to me.

Choose the ripest, tastiest tomatoes you can find. Traditionally, the soup is served with grapes or little cubes of *piel de sapo* melon.

Serves 4

420g tomatoes
60g bread, ideally a fluffy white bloomer, crusts cut off
4 tablespoons good olive oil, such as Arbequina
1½ tablespoons sherry vinegar
100g blanched almonds, preferably Marcona
1 clove of garlic
¼ teaspoon ground cumin
sea salt and freshly ground black pepper

To serve
a few green grapes, halved, or little cubes of melon, preferably *piel de sapo*

Quarter the tomatoes and put into a mixing bowl. Wet the bread, then squeeze out any excess water and add to the tomatoes, along with half the olive oil, 1 tablespoon of sherry vinegar and the rest of the ingredients. Sprinkle in half a teaspoon of salt.

Briefly knead the mixture to allow the juices of the tomato to meld with the other flavours, then cover the bowl with clingfilm and put into the fridge to marinate for at least 2 hours.

Blend, then slowly add 450ml of water, blending for at least 2 more minutes until the *gazpacho* has a completely smooth consistency.

Continue to blend as you add the remaining olive oil, to form an emulsion. Taste and add another pinch of salt as necessary, together with the rest of the sherry vinegar, briefly blending them in.

Pass through a fine sieve into a serving bowl, and put into the fridge for about 2 hours until well chilled.

Serve in bowls, accompanied by the grapes or cubes of melon, and a twist of black pepper.

Oliagua amb figues
Rustic tomato soup with summer figs

This simple, but quite unusual, soup with its contrast of salty and sweet flavours is unique to Menorca. It is a favourite recipe given to me by our cheese *affineur* friends on the island, Nicolás and Rosa (see page 25), and it caused quite a stir of interest and approval when Rupert made it with the chefs at Brindisa.

Traditionally, many people would have had most of the fresh ingredients growing in their gardens, so this was a quick, economical and nourishing soup, which was often eaten for breakfast as well as supper.

Light and fresh, it must be related to *gazpacho*, but it is something of a halfway house between a hot and cold soup, as it is cooked – but mustn't be allowed to boil – and then cooled until it is just tepid, but not chilled. What makes it especially distinctive is that it is served with fresh figs. The preferred local variety, common to both Menorca and Mallorca, is a slightly spiky fig known as *paratjal*, which is harvested quite late in September to October, when, thanks to the heat of the summer, tomatoes are still good and ripe – but, of course you can make the *oliagua* with any summer fig.

The soup is usually poured over lightly toasted garlicky bread in the base of the serving bowl (although you can cut the toast into croutons for garnishing if you prefer) – the reason for toasting the bread is to stop it from swelling and disintegrating when it is topped with the soup.

Try to use small, very ripe, super-red vine tomatoes, a flowery olive oil and very sweet figs.

Serves 4

7 tablespoons olive oil, such as a fragrant Arbequina
1 large onion, diced
2 cloves of garlic, roughly chopped
sea salt
1 green pepper, diced
800g very ripe tomatoes, quartered
½ teaspoon sugar, plus extra if necessary
1 sprig of thyme

To serve
4 slices of white bread, toasted
2 cloves of garlic halved, for rubbing the bread
8 figs

Pour the oil into a deep ceramic dish or heavy-based pot, warm gently, then stir in the onion and chopped garlic along with a pinch of salt. Let the oil bubble gently, stirring the onion for 5 minutes so that it poaches, rather than turning brown or crispy. Add the green pepper and let it poach in the same way for another 2 minutes.

Stir in the tomatoes and squash them gently with the back of a spoon to help release their juices. Sprinkle in the sugar, pour in 600ml of water and submerge the sprig of thyme in the soup. Taste and adjust for salt or sugar.

Place the pan on a diffuser, preferably, or otherwise the lowest heat possible, and allow the soup to heat through very gently for 30 minutes, stirring occasionally. The secret is to make sure that it doesn't come to the boil. After 30 minutes, remove from the heat and allow to cool, during which time the flavours will develop.

Rub the toast with the halved cloves of garlic and place a slice at the bottom of each bowl, then ladle in the soup. Slice the figs and serve on the side.

Life and Cooking with Ambro and Ásun

I met cheese-maker Ambrosio (Ambro) Molinos when I bought my first raw sheep's cheese from him in the village of Guzmán in Burgos province in Castilla y León, back in 1990. The cheese came in a tin and Ambro called it after the plateau where it was made: Páramo de Guzmán, 800–900 metres above sea level, where the winters are cold, the summers hot and dry, and where they also harvest grapes to make wine. In springtime the rain is frequent, but comes and goes quickly, driven on by the wind, and the velvety, undulating, green pasture underneath a big, open, clear sky reminds me more of Ireland than Spain.

That tin had a whole world inside it: Ambrosio's world. Larger than life in every way, he is a great bear of a man, seven feet tall, the youngest and tallest of three brothers (one of whom is a hunter), with a big, booming voice. A generous-hearted rebel and philosopher, he plays the *charango* (a South American kind of lute) and is an outspoken upholder of his values and beliefs, from the superiority of the Churra breed of sheep to the abstinence from vegetables in his diet, or the need to patiently spend two hours making the best *bacalao* (salt cod) *al pil pil* (see page 332).

He also eats an extraordinary number of eggs. At twelve he won his first egg-eating competition – devouring 45 fried hen's eggs, and in a later contest took the title after eating 245 quail's eggs. These days he is famous for his hearty tortillas (see page 160).

His elegant wife, Asun (short for Asunción), tells the story of how in the seventies the teenage Ambro, looking a bit like Che Guevara, with his long wild hair and beard, and in his bell-bottoms and *zuecos* (clogs), proclaimed his feelings for her in the middle of the street in Aranda de Duero, her home town. She told him he had no chance looking the way he did, so he tidied himself up and they were married six months later.

Both of them love to cook for friends and their family, which includes their spirited daughter, also called Asunción, whose stunning looks and clear vision of right and wrong turned heads when she spent time working with us at Brindisa in London. Now back in Spain, she creates installation art, whose theme is often a campaign for the rights of farmers and the rural economy, and a protest against intensification and pesticides. Her brothers, Enrique and Josué, care for the vines and make the wine as well as harvesting cereal crops, fixing the tractors and doing all the back-breaking work around the farm.

It broke my heart when Ambro attempted to grow his cheese business and it all backfired, but the arable farming continues, and both he and Asun know they are lucky to have children who are committed to the land. While many of the elderly people in the village still work the fields in the way they have been doing since they were twelve or thirteen (in times when school was not obligatory), in a fast-changing world with different priorities and aspirations few of the young people want to stay and toil the land.

The family remain a great inspiration for me, and when I was researching recipes for this book, Asun and I spent a week cooking and swapping notes. With three big strong men with hearty appetites to feed every lunchtime, she has her work cut out, so we set off with our bags to the local weekly market to buy onions bigger than grapefruits, beautiful green tomatoes with streaks of red, voluptuous peppers, and big chickens *de corral*, strong free-range birds that require long cooking to tenderise the meat, ingredients for many different meals in one expedition. The butcher cut fresh pork from a vast leg, which we would marinate for kebabs, as well as fattier *aguja* (rib meat), minced for *picadillo*, and diced lamb, which would be served with a baked potato dish. He also deboned two legs of lamb for us to make *caldereta* (lamb stew, see page 435).

In customary local fashion, before we could get home laden with our purchases we were invited for a mid-morning snack by friend and neighbour Manolo (Manuel) Pérez Pascuas, one of the three brothers who with their families run the Pérez Pascuas winery, and have been Ambro's friends and neighbours since their youth, when they broke out of the local co-operative system to go their own way. Manolo's 'snack' consisted of *lomo ibérico de bellota* (acorn-fed cured loin), artisan Zamorano cheese and *pan sobado,* the typical Castilian shallow and close-textured white loaf, with a seal pressed into its significant crust, together with a glass or two of their fine 2001 and 2003 Reservas. Finally, it was back to the house to begin cooking.

It is lamb that is the prime meat of the Burgos area and everything centres around it. Ambro remembers that when he was growing up in his village, where only about 100 people lived, the children were divided into three groups: north, east and south of the village, and each had their own games. Ambro believes that just as the history of man so far has been divided into BC and AD, in the future it will be marked as before and after TV. Before TV, a favourite of the children in his part of the village was *el juego de las tabas,* a bit like jacks, but played with the four small articulating knee bones (the *tabas*) of a milk-fed lamb, which you threw up in the air and scored points according to the way they landed. It was such a famous game in the region that there is a square in Valladolid decorated with *tabas* inset into the stones.

Among the many dishes Asun and I cooked over the week were *caldereta, chilindrón* (chicken with red peppers) and *pepitoria* (a chicken dish, in which the sauce is thickened with almonds and hard-boiled egg yolk). She also showed me how she prepares *adobados* and *salmueras* – meats that are seasoned or marinated over a short or long time (at least 24 hours), depending on the way she wants to use the meat. In particular, she prepares her own salt cure for *costillas* (pork ribs), then keeps a stash of these in the freezer, ready to pull out whenever they are needed. We cooked some marinated ribs with chorizo and lentils and they were delicious (see *lentejas Asunción*, page 398).

The tradition of marinating, flavouring and semi-curing fresh meat at home goes back to the times when the family pig would be slaughtered once a year. Beyond the obvious curing of the legs for hams and the making of sausages, which would also be cured and dried, you needed to preserve other cuts since in those days before refrigeration, fresh meat would not last long. It would be cut into the required portions: chops, ribs, loin steaks, and the cures would either be dry (*adobos*) or wet (*salmueras*) – the wet-curing would generally be used for meats that needed to be kept for longer. Once prepared, the meat would be stored in large ceramic jars, covered with lard or olive oil, or smoked and stored in the rafters in regions such as León and Asturias, where the smoking of hams and sausages was traditional.

These days, of course, there is no necessity to use these preparations, but many families like Ambro and Asun's still do, as it is a way of tenderising the meat, and either mellowing the flavour in the case of game (the phrase is *quitar el bravio:* to take out the wildness) or adding flavour to industrially produced meats. You can also buy *adobados* done for you at some butchers' counters in Spain.

EASTER IN BURGOS

Our family spent one of our most memorable Easter holidays with Ambro and Asun. My only previous experience of a Spanish Easter was when I was in my twenties at the end of a road trip with friends from Catalunya to Sevilla. Easter in Sevilla was a huge thing – solemn, magnificent and emotive – whereas in the Burgos countryside the celebrations were much more modest, though just as heartfelt, involving days of preparation and cooking, followed by much feasting.

When we arrived at the house Ambro gave us a piece of rosemary branch that had been blessed in the church on Palm Sunday to be kept in the home for the rest of the year.

Then on Maundy Thursday we prepared generous quantities of *limonada*, the lemon aperitif made with *vino tinto* (red wine) that is traditionally drunk in the run-up to Easter Sunday – of course, *limonada* is the name for lemonade, which makes it sound far more innocent than it is. In Ambro's cellar a fair amount of early tasting is a serious task, and the men of all the local families heroically dropped by to test and check the balance of flavours, while Ásun prepared another of the special Easter treats, *torrijas de leche* (see page 480): slices of the local *pan sobado* soaked in warm milk, infused with sugar, cinnamon and lemon, ready to be dipped in beaten egg and fried, then sprinkled with more sugar – similar to French toast and full of flavours that remind you of childhood. *Sobar* means to knead, and *pan sobado* is bread that is hand-kneaded so that it has the right texture to absorb lots of milk without becoming mushy.

Maundy Thursday dinner was in the nearby town of Roa with Manolo Pérez Pascuas and his wife Juani González. We started in their *merendero*, the outdoor bar and eating space at their *bodega* in the village of Pedrosa, drinking our first cups of *limonada* with the ladies of the village before they attended the evening church service. Then it was into the back room of the local bar, for slow-cooked *bacalao a la taverna*. This is grilled salt cod in an emulsion of olive oil and garlic, similar to *pil pil* (see page 332) but made with fish still on the bone, from which the cod just falls away into the unctuous, tasty sauce. Adorned with slices of roasted red peppers, it was served in one of the vast earthenware dishes that are a speciality of the Zamoran town of Peruerela, along with a fresh salad and some fascinating vintages of Pedrosa wine.

Also dining were some of the local hunters, including Isidro el Bartolo, considered one of the best hunters of the village. A quiet man of the land, his name is really a mote (a nickname or byword), since he is the son of Bartolo, but no one actually knows his surname. With barely a word he passed me a bowl of the hare casserole the hunters were sharing: an amazingly dark, mysterious dish, full of tender, aromatic meat. It was so good that I have included a version of it on page 464.

After midnight the whole village congregated in the front bar to play the traditional Maundy Thursday game of *chapas*, using *alfonsinas,* ten cent coins from the time of Alfonso XII. It was a riot of noise as the players bet on heads or tails as the coins were thrown in the air, sometimes losing and leaving, then returning again with a fistful of money, to try their luck in new rounds. When we left at 3 a.m. the game was still going strong.

At midday on Good Friday we headed to Ambro and Asun's own *bodega*, overlooking Guzmán village and the flat-topped Manvirgo mountain. These *bodega*/caves abound in hilly regions throughout Spain. As with the *gofio* caves of the Canary Islands (see page 60), they usually have a chimney built into them, a fireplace to cook on, a gas ring, table and chairs and, as in this case, stone seats and tables outside to create a *merendero* for sunny days. Typically, they also have steps that lead down into a cool storage space, where families keep homemade preserves and olives, wines and *orujos* (liqueurs). At one time Ambro and Asun used to age their cheeses in their *bodega*, almost breaking their backs carrying them up and down the steps. These retreats are favourite places for family and friends to gather, eat, drink, play music, sing and relax at weekends and on special holidays. Sometimes just the men of the village will escape to them for a few hours to sit around and tell stories in the way that people often sit around their sheds on allotments in Britain.

On Good Friday we sat outside on the warm stones, drinking *limonada* and dipping hunks of bread into our Easter lemon aperitifs (see recipes opposite) before cooking the traditional *revueltos* (scrambled egg) over an open fire – one pot with the addition of young garlic, just in season (see page 140), the other with tuna – and washed them down with tumblers of red wine, while Ambro played guitar and everyone sang.

On Easter Sunday morning we joined the procession around the village in which the men, in their best suits, carried the statue of the resurrected Jesus from the church, while the women carried the statue of the mourning Virgin Mary, her face and figure covered in a black cloak (*manta de luto*), in the opposite direction. When eventually they were reunited the women sang, while, according to tradition, a representative of the church asked who would bid the most money to remove the mourning veil from the statue of Mary. After an intense auction the ladies who had pledged the winning bid removed the veil, kissed the Virgin – no longer *dolorosa*, but *feliz* in her newly revealed, brightly coloured dress – and the procession returned to the old church with its beautiful rickety wooden porch, for the Easter Mass.

And so finally, after *aperitivos* of *vermut* (vermouth) and a game of cards with the villagers, we sat down for the Easter meal, a feast of roast milk-fed lamb, shared once again with the Pérez Pascuas family.

LIMÓN DE PASCUAS
EASTER LEMONS

Makes 450g

Peel 4 lemons and remove as much pith as possible. Break into segments, then slice each segment crossways into three chunks.

Put the chunks into a bowl with 250ml of olive oil and cover with a layer of sugar about 5mm thick (about 100g). Mix, then cover and leave for 24 hours in the fridge.

Eat with slices of country bread or baguette as an *aperitivo* – each person just dunks their slices of bread into the bowl, sliding on some lemon chunks and bitter-sweet juice.

LIMONADA
EASTER DRINK

The traditional Easter drink of Burgos is served either as an *aperitivo*, or with *torrijas de leche* (see page 480) at the end of a meal.

Makes 4 litres

500g lemons
a pinch of ground cinnamon
250g sugar
4 litres red wine

Remove the rind and as much pith as possible from the lemons and cut into quarters. Put them into a big jug or bowl and add the cinnamon and sugar. Crush the lemons so that their juice comes out, then top with the wine. Leave to macerate for 2–3 days in the fridge, then bring the jug out before serving, to take off the chill. Strain through a sieve and enjoy.

TORTILLAS
Omelettes

In Spain the combination of eggs and fried potatoes can move people to a passion that verges on the poetic. *Tortillas* have their place any time of day in the Spanish kitchen, but more often than not they are cut into slices or squares and served with drinks as a tapa.

Our friend Ambro (see page 154) makes a famous *tortilla* with 12 large eggs, which he proudly calls his *buenona*, an expression all of his own that conjures up something beautiful, warm and friendly. And Spanish cooks talk about the *cuajada*, a word borrowed from cheese-making that refers to the coagulation of the milk. In terms of a *tortilla* it describes the solidifying of the eggs to give just the right balance of firmness and *babosidad*: juiciness.

The problem is that there are too many experts all over Spain for us to know if there really is a definitive way to make a *tortilla*. Despite the fact that the classic recipe uses only four very basic and accessible ingredients – eggs, potatoes, onions and oil – a good *tortilla* is so much greater than the sum of its parts, so everybody has something to say about it: the ratio of eggs to potato, the kind of potato to use, the oil, whether to lightly fry the potatoes and onions so they retain the texture of a boiled potato; or whether to colour them so that they are slightly golden, or darker.

Knowing my fascination with the subject, Ambro and his wife, Asun, took me to meet Ciri González of La Encina restaurant in Palencia, Castilla y León, who is a three-time winner of the national *tortilla*-making competition known as the Campeonato de España de Tortillas de Patata. Her husband is also a stunning *asador* (specialist in roasting and grilling meat), who cooks suckling lamb in the traditional manner in a wood-burning *adobe* oven at the restaurant.

Ciri happily parted with some of the secrets that help her win championship after championship. She is totally specific about every ingredient. Because she wants as little moisture in the potatoes as possible, she uses only the Kennebec variety, grown locally and aged for a month after harvesting to dry the flesh out a little, which she says gives just the right texture and a proper full potato flavour. The potatoes are also very thin-skinned, so she patiently rubs off the skins with a cloth, rather than using water, again to keep them as dry as possible, and she seasons them before cooking, as she says the seasoning penetrates better.

Ciri uses 8 eggs to 500g of potatoes (and half an onion), whereas most people use a lower proportion of eggs. Ambro uses 12 eggs to 1kg of potatoes for his *buenona*, and in our Brindisa kitchens we use 14 eggs to 2kg of potatoes. Ciri insists that the eggs must be *de corral* (see page 164) and at room temperature, and she beats them very well.

The potatoes and onions for a *tortilla* should always be fried using olive oil. While some people like a neutral one, Ciri uses Picual de Jaén olive oil, which is a strong, characteristically bitter oil made from Picual olives in Jaén in Andalucía that is excellent for frying potatoes, as it enhances their flavour – at Brindisa we have some potato crisps fried in Picual oil, and they are unbelievably good.

She also likes her potatoes to be well 'bronzed', so she fries them for longer than most Spanish people I know. Our chefs at Brindisa, for example, insist that the potatoes should be more 'cooked' than 'fried' so they have the texture and taste of a baked potato – rather than a chip encased in egg – but Ciri goes for the opposite. However, she does it very slowly and cleverly so that she still retains the all-important juiciness inside the sliced potatoes. Then she drains them and the onions very well before adding to the beaten egg and leaves the mixture to amalgamate for at least 3 minutes before making the *tortilla*.

The method I have given in the recipes that follow is the way I make *tortilla* at home, based on an amalgamation of tips from Ambro, Ciri and our own Brindisa chefs, who make around 100 *tortillas* each week, using more than 1,200 eggs and almost 150kg of potatoes.

I suggest that if you can't find Kennebec potatoes, or the Galician Pataca, which also works well, you should try Yukon Gold, preferably,

or Maris Piper, and when you peel them, dry them very well to reduce the moisture, as this really helps the texture. Personally, although I understand the attraction of a stronger oil, like Picual, I have always preferred a good but mild olive oil, such as Arbequina.

Some tortilla notes

Use the very best eggs you can find and cook the onions in the traditional Spanish long, slow way, so that they become very, very soft and sweet. The onions and potatoes need to be drained very well after sautéing and before adding to the eggs, so that you don't make the mixture too oily. I learned a good tip from one of our former head chefs, Esperanza Añonuevo Heys, who always uses a fine sieve, rather than a slotted spoon, to scoop the onions and potatoes from the oil, then balances this over a bowl, to let the oil drain away well.

A very good, big frying pan of around 28cm diameter and 3–4cm deep is fundamental, and the other thing that is vital is to make sure that there is a good film of oil all around the sides of the pan, not just the base, to prevent sticking – but at the same time, be careful not to have too much oil, or the *tortilla* itself will become greasy, unless you are using a non-stick pan.

The recipes that follow are for *tortillas* 3–4cm deep, but in our tapas bars we also make ones that are 10cm deep. If you want to make them this size, then a good tip from our chefs, to make sure the *tortilla* cooks all the way through without burning at the bottom, is to pour only half the mixture into the pan at first and stir it until it has the consistency of a nearly-cooked but still runny scrambled egg, then tip this back into the rest of your raw egg mixture and stir. Remove any egg that may have stuck to your frying pan, heat a little more oil and then put in all the egg mixture, flattening the surface gently with a spatula. Continue to let the *tortilla* set, and flip it over in the usual way.

Tortilla buenona de patatas
Hearty potato omelette

You need a very large flat plate or a wooden *tortilla* turner for flipping over the *tortilla*. You can buy a *tortilla* turner in good kitchen shops or online. It is shaped like the lid of a pan and has a knob which you hold while you place it over the top of your frying pan, turn the two over so that the *tortilla* sits on the turner, then slide it back into the pan to cook the underside. Of course, you can do the same thing using a plate, but having the knob of the turner to hold on to just makes the movement easier and protects you a bit more against the heat of the pan and the *tortilla*.

As I say, there is no steadfast rule about the ratio of potatoes and eggs – everyone has their own opinion. The recipes that follow give the ratio we use in our own Brindisa kitchens – but feel free to experiment and adapt.

Whatever you settle on, making a really good *tortilla* takes practice, so I would recommend making it often and keeping it as a standby food for the next couple of days for everyone to tuck into a slice whenever they like – because that is the thing about *tortilla*: you need people to share it.

As a variation on this classic, Ambro sometimes adds half a green pepper, cut into thin strips. You can also add saffron – 6 saffron threads in 1 tablespoon of warm milk –mixed in along with the eggs.

Makes 1 x 28cm *tortilla*

1kg potatoes, such as Yukon Gold or Maris Piper
250ml olive oil
1 large onion (about 500g), sliced into half-rings
sea salt and freshly ground black pepper
7 good, large eggs

Peel the potatoes and slice about ¾cm thick.

Heat around 3 tablespoons of the olive oil in a large frying pan or wok, then add the onion and cook very gently for at least 30 minutes, until all the water has been drawn out of them and they are soft, light golden and very sweet. The longer you cook them the sweeter they will be, so you can leave them for up to 1 hour if you have the time and a heat diffuser to place under the pan. Lift out with a slotted spoon, or preferably a small sieve, leaving the oil for cooking the potatoes. Drain the onion over a bowl, as you want it to be as free of excess oil as possible.

Add the rest of the oil to the pan (it needs to be about 2cm deep). To test whether the oil is the right temperature, put in a small piece of potato. It should sizzle gently. Put in the potatoes, season and cook very slowly for about 20 minutes, moving the pieces around regularly from the middle to the edges so they cook through evenly, taking care not to let them burn. Some slices will break and stick to the pan, but that is inevitable. If you feel the potatoes are cooking too fast and getting too crispy, put a lid over the pan to allow them to steam a little and slow things down.

When the potatoes are light golden and tender if you pierce them with the tip of a sharp knife, remove the pan from the heat, lift the potatoes out, again preferably with a small sieve, then place this over a bowl, to drain off the excess oil. Measure around 4 tablespoons of the oil from the pan and pour it into a non-stick 28cm omelette pan 3–4cm deep.

Once the potatoes are well drained, transfer them to a clean bowl. Beat the eggs, season and add them to the bowl, together with the drained onions.

Heat the oil in the omelette pan, tilting it gently to make sure that the oil coats the sides as well as the base of the pan. Pour in the egg and potato mixture and begin to cook gently over a medium heat. For the next minute, keep moving some of the mixture from the centre to the outside to help it to cook evenly, then leave it alone to cook slowly, for about 10 minutes, keeping an eye on the edges to make sure they don't burn, until the base is sealed and light golden – lift the base a little every so often to check whether it has reached this stage.

Hold the pan over the sink, in case of leakage, and place a large plate or *tortilla* turner over the top. Turn the two over together so the *tortilla* lands on the plate or turner, cooked side upwards, hopefully with no pieces stuck to the pan.

Make sure you still have a good film of oil in the pan – add a little more if necessary – then slide the *tortilla*, uncooked side downwards, into the pan and cook gently for 5 more minutes.

When it is ready, the *tortilla* should be just firm, but still creamy inside. To check, press the surface near the centre, to make sure that no uncooked egg seeps out. Alternatively you can insert a skewer into the centre – it should have no uncooked egg on it when you withdraw it.

Once the *tortilla* is ready, slide it on to a big, flat serving plate – or if you think the underside looks better, you could flip it over again – but don't worry about perfect looks, it is the taste that matters.

Tortilla de chorizo con patatas y pimientos con alioli
Chorizo, potato and pepper omelette with *alioli*

In our bars and restaurants this is an immensely popular variation on the traditional potato *tortilla*. The key is to try to choose a good cooking *chorizo* made with no additives, so that you have a clean flavour, and not to use too much of it, so that the other ingredients have a chance to play their part.

Makes 1 x 28cm *tortilla*

1kg potatoes
250ml olive oil
½ a large onion, sliced into half-rings
sea salt and freshly ground black pepper
1 red pepper, cut into thin strips
1 green pepper, cut into thin strips
1 clove of garlic, finely chopped
300g good cooking *chorizo*,
  cut into small squares
7 large eggs
200g *alioli*, to serve (see page 136)

Follow the previous recipe for the hearty potato omelette, but once you have cooked your potatoes and onions, then drained the oil into a bowl or container, take 4 tablespoons of the oil and heat it in the same pan.

Put in the peppers, garlic and *chorizo* and fry gently until the peppers are soft and the *chorizo* lightly coloured. Lift out, preferably with a small sieve, drain them over a bowl to remove the excess oil, then transfer them to a bowl with the potatoes, onions, eggs and seasoning.

Now heat another 4 tablespoons of the reserved oil in a non-stick 28cm omelette pan 3–4cm deep and continue with the recipe.

Serve with the *alioli*.

HUEVOS

'by the Easter weekend you would have masses'

At one time in Spain, when you bought eggs, you typically had two choices: *de corral* or *industrial*. *De corral* refers to the free-range, naturally reared and fed hens which run semi-wild in the enclosed yards or fields in and around Spanish villages and tend to be sold locally. Rupert remembers that when he was growing up in Madrid you hardly ever saw a proper country egg, except that occasionally a man used to come by his family's house on a *vespino* (little motorbike), selling a basket of them, along with honey and *chorizos*, as well as offering haircuts!

These days good free-range and organic eggs can still be hard to find beyond the villages and small towns where they are produced, but they are slowly becoming easier to source and gradually beginning to command the price they deserve. This is often because more young people are going back to family land that they had previously abandoned, focusing on alternative and specialised food production, and selling via websites, as a small rebellion against the supermarkets that have grown up in Spain as much as anywhere else.

Quail's eggs are also popular in tapas, either hard-boiled and dipped in a spicy mixture of salt and *pimentón* (paprika), or fried and served on top of a strip of fried green pepper, or spicy *picadillo* (minced pork), on toast to make bite-sized *montaditos*.

Hen's eggs used to be almost seasonal, because light stimulates the birds to lay, and before the invention of electric lighting it was daylight that they set their laying clocks by. So from spring, when the days started to grow longer, through summer, there would always be more eggs. Add to this the fact that it was forbidden to eat eggs during Lent in the Middle Ages, and by the Easter weekend you would have masses to use up. There is a tradition of cooked eggs at Easter time – either hard-boiled or, on Good Friday, *revueltos* (scrambled eggs), sometimes made with young garlic shoots (see page 140) and sometimes with tuna, washed down with red wine.

One autumn when I was staying at the hotel Convento de Santa Clara, a converted convent in Alcázar de San Juan, La Mancha, I saw bowls of eggs everywhere. When I asked their significance, I was told that whenever there was a family wedding being planned, the villagers would traditionally bring eggs to the convent, in exchange for prayers to keep the rain away. The belief was so strong that in years when the countryside was very short of rain, notably during the droughts of 2007, the convent would not accept any eggs for fear that they would prolong the drought.

Pastel de escorpora con albahaca
Light 'loaf' of gurnard with tomato
and basil dressing

Pastels or mousse-like 'loaf' cakes are rather out of fashion in the UK, having been a big hit in the seventies, but they are still very popular in parts of Spain. Pepa Salvador had this one on the menu at La Salsita on the Costa Brava when I worked there, and making it again after all these years has convinced me that such recipes are due a comeback. It is full of the subtle, delicate flavours of egg, tomato, fish and basil and it makes a great wholesome family lunch or supper, put out with other small plates, as everyone can simply help themselves to a slice or two.

If you have good ripe, flavoursome tomatoes it is worth the effort of making your own tomato *sofrito* as in this recipe, rather than using a jarred one, as the fresh flavours will contribute to the lightness and sophistication of the mousse. If you do use a jarred one, however, you will need about 300g.

Serves 4

5 eggs
a pinch of salt
120ml full-cream milk
120ml double cream

For the tomato sofrito
2 tablespoons olive oil
1 large onion, finely chopped
500g tomatoes, grated
a pinch of sugar, to taste
sea salt, to taste

For the poached gurnard
½ teaspoon salt
1 onion, cut in half
1 carrot, cut in half
2 cloves of garlic, each cut in half
1 whole gurnard (600–800g), cleaned

For the dressing
1 tomato
1 tablespoon chopped basil
2 tablespoons olive oil
1 teaspoon lemon juice
sea salt and freshly ground black pepper

To prepare the loaf tin
10g butter
2 tablespoons breadcrumbs

First make the *sofrito*. Heat the oil in the pan and add the onion. Cook very gently over a low heat until golden brown. Add the grated tomato, bring to a boil and then turn down the heat and allow to simmer for 1 hour, until you have a sauce that has reduced by around a third to a half in volume. Taste and adjust with a pinch of sugar or salt if necessary. Take off the heat and leave to cool.

Preheat the oven to 180°C/gas 4.

To poach the fish pour 2 litres of water into a large pan, add the salt, vegetables and garlic and bring to just under the boil – to the point where you can see bubbles beginning to form on the base of the pan – then put in the gurnard. Keep at a gentle simmer for 15–20 minutes, depending on the size of the fish (don't let the water boil or it will break up the fish). The fish is ready when the flesh peels away from the bone.

Drain off the water, lift out the fish carefully and gently take the fillets from the spine. Flake the fish into pieces of around 2cm, removing any smaller bones, and keep to one side.

Grease a loaf tin of around 23cm x 12cm with the butter. Tip in the breadcrumbs and tilt the tin until they cover the whole of the inside. Put the tin into the roasting pan.

In a large bowl, beat the eggs, adding the salt, then begin to fold in the *sofrito*, flaked gurnard, the milk and the cream. Make sure the ingredients are mixed well, but go gently so that you keep the flakes of fish intact. Spoon into the prepared loaf tin.

Fill the roasting pan with hot water until it reaches about three-quarters of the way up the outside of the loaf tin. Put into the preheated oven for about 20 minutes, until a skewer inserted into the centre comes out clean.

To make the dressing, grate the tomato into a bowl, add the chopped basil, olive oil and lemon juice, season with a pinch of salt and a twist of black pepper, stir and adjust to taste.

Turn the loaf out of its mould, slice, and serve with the tomato dressing.

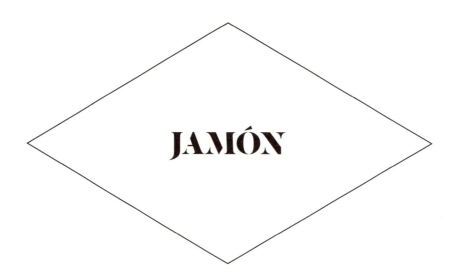

JAMÓN

'a big story'

The simplest tapa of all is a plate of finely carved Spanish ham – the quintessential one being *de bellota Ibérico*, which comes from the special black-footed, acorn-fed pigs that roam the forests and hills of the Dehesa in south-west Spain. I don't think the ham needs anything else to adorn it, except perhaps a bowl of almonds or olives, put out separately. I like it with just a good *fino* sherry, but typically it is also paired with wine or champagne, which curiously I think works better with it than *cava*. However, our good friend and expert on hams, Germán Arroyo Duque, who comes from the heart of the Dehesa, likes the ham served in the local way, with good bread and a refreshing beer.

If I could total up the number of hams that I have seen hanging in silent rooms across Spain it would run into hundreds of thousands. Over the years, I and my colleagues have visited some of the most prestigious, as well as the most humble of curing rooms, and experience has shown us that great hams or average hams can be produced in both. The whole process of curing and hanging can take up to four years or more, and every stage counts, so it is possible for the ham from a great animal to be spoilt by poor practice, while that from an ordinary animal might be immensely improved by diligent attention to detail.

For us, ham is a big story which really began in 1992, when the EU was formed and in Brussels the bureaucrats were finalising the details of the invasion of Spanish ham into member states – at least that is the way its arrival was perceived by its competitors in the world of charcuterie. Although I am sure some ham slipped quietly across the borders, until 1992 no ham was officially allowed to be exported from Spain, so the owners of Spanish bars and restaurants in other countries had to use Italian Parma ham. Even when the first shipments of legal Serrano ham arrived from Spain, many such establishments continued to use the name Parma on their menus because it had become accepted and synonymous with quality, and they feared they might lose custom if they mentioned the hitherto unknown Serrano.

It has to be recognised that in Spain the production of pork, hams and sausages is on a very large scale, so inevitably when we ordered our first Serrano hams approved for export in 1990, these were not produced by small artisans, but by bigger companies which had the resources to expand and tick all the right boxes.

There was also a long and frustrating wait for them. A ham takes at least a year, sometimes three, to cure, and the legislation said that the meat had to be from animals slaughtered after 1990, so it was two more years before we received the hams. Later, in the mid-nineties, when we began importing our first Ibérico hams we had

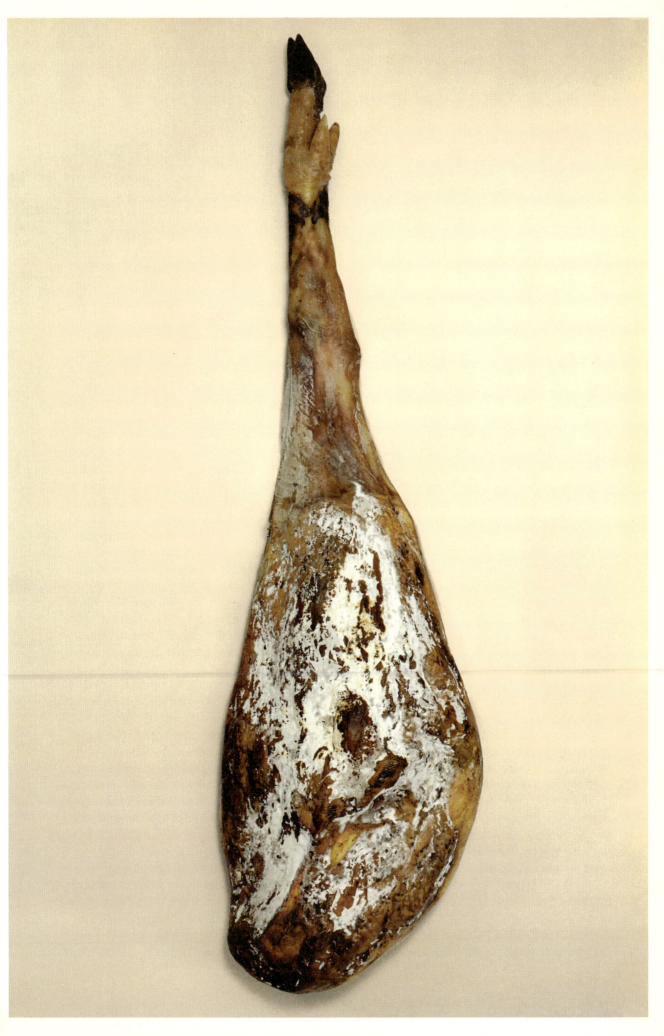

to go through a similar waiting process, only receiving our first prized hams in 1998.

As incompatible as these semi-industrial hams felt alongside the farm-made Churra sheep's milk cheeses and other artisan produce that we were bringing in from Spain, I badly wanted to sell Spanish ham. And although those early examples, from Large White pigs crossed with Durocs, may not have been as specialist as those we can source today, they were still a delightful, novel experience for most British people: a rich red colour, with a more pronounced flavour than their Italian equivalents.

Steve Carter and Richard Corrigan, who were then the chefs at Stephen Bull's restaurants, were the first to offer platters of Spanish hams and other cured meats, along with cheese, olives and peppers, which were a big success.

Once the market opened up, we were able to become properly selective and begin forging real relationships with favourite producers. Ultimately, there is no substitute for this. Only through getting to know the farming, husbandry and curing processes can you understand what makes a truly great ham.

An ancient technique

Wherever ham is cured the process is similar, and in essence the process hasn't substantially changed since the days when villagers would fatten up a piglet each year, slaughter it in winter, salt a leg in a stone basin in the coolest part of the house, then hang it up in the eaves to cure and mature, ready to feed the family.

Traditionally, cured hams were more the product of mountainous regions, where, at altitude, the dry winds naturally cured them slowly and fully. Nowadays, however, it is possible to create any environment you want to cure the meat to your own specifications.

What varies from region to region, and producer to producer, is the breed of animal, its diet and quality of life, whether it has run free or lived in a shed. It may have foraged for wild food, or been given compound feed, or a mix of the two. These factors will affect or determine the length of time that the ham will improve during curing, and the characteristics and organoleptic qualities it will develop. The way the animals are handled immediately before and during slaughter will also have an effect, since stress produces lactic acid in the meat, which is not conducive to good curing.

In the time-honoured way, the process of curing begins with the selection of a fresh back leg from the pig, which is placed in salt. Non-Ibérico hams tend to be salted for one day per kilo, so an average 9kg leg will be salted for nine days; whereas an Ibérico ham will be salted for 12 days. The salting has the effect of separating the protein filaments and weakening the muscle fibres, which in turn dehydrates the meat, darkening it and beginning the process of fermentation, which concentrates the flavour.

After salting, the legs are washed, then dried off for a period of time in chilled chambers, before being hung in the curing rooms.

Originally, ham-curing was done according to the seasons, which 100 years ago were more reliable and distinct. The ham would be hung up in winter, in chambers with windows which could be opened and closed to control the cold winds blowing through, and the flora that had built up in the building over years and years would develop naturally on the skin. Then, when the temperature rose in spring and summer, the hams, while still protected from decay by the salt, would start the *sudado* (the sweating), or warm phase, during which the flavours of the ham really begin to open up and develop and the hams lose fat – over a third of their original weight. In the old days the floors of the curing rooms would be covered in so much shiny fat that they looked like ice rinks until sawdust was laid down in order to soak it up.

Nowadays, though some traditional producers still follow the seasons, opening or closing shutters, depending on the dryness or dampness of the air and the strength of the wind and its temperature, the climatic change is mostly mimicked in false – though usually less picturesque – chambers in which the temperature and humidity can be accurately controlled. Even if the outside air is blown through, using fans, it contributes less to the curing process than in the old, seasonal days. For most producers the benefits of being in total control of the environment in which their hams cure far outweigh the romance of seasonality.

Finally, the ham is taken to the natural cellars for *asentamiento,* or 'settling', at a constant temperature. This will be at least nine months, but could be up to four or five years for the finest acorn-fed Ibérico hams, after which time even the best will not improve, but may even begin to dry out. At the end of the process a skilled *calador* pierces the ham in three strategic places with a thin veal bone called *la cala,* which picks up all the aromas inside, enabling the *calador* to check that there are no faults.

Serrano ham

This is air-cured ham from a selection of cross-bred white pigs, such as the Duroc. The name Serrano simply means mountain ham, coming as it does from the word *sierra* (mountain range), and although it has become quite a loose colloquial term for any cured ham other than Ibérico (see page 172), the name is protected by the EU under the term TSG (Traditional Speciality Guaranteed).

After many years we have settled very happily on the traditional area of Aragón for our cured Serrano ham. It is one of the most undiscovered areas of Spain, a landlocked province stretching from the French border in the Pyrenees to Valencia, underpopulated and wild. The high plateau of the Teruel province, where the hams are produced, has the perfect climate for producing hams – biting winds and dry air in winter, and open uninterrupted landscape so the curing rooms can be lined up at the best angle for introducing the air at the first stage of curing.

Being so isolated, the committed Teruel ham community has built a kind of self-sufficiency that is very productive: they grow and mix their own feed for the pigs (which are kept in barns to protect them from sunburn in these shadeless areas), and even run a co-operative system for the purchasing of domestic items such as washing machines, allowing income to flow fairly and help life run more smoothly.

How to choose Serrano ham

Within the TSG mark, local regulating boards can set their own criteria, and you will see many different labels which will be more or less demanding, so the quality can range from ordinary to excellent.

When you buy Serrano ham you should be looking for a deep pink colour, with less of a marbling of fat than an Ibérico ham, a sweet aroma, a strong savoury umami taste and a distinct presence of salt.

Although sliced ham, interleaved in packets, is convenient and easy to find, it is always better to buy it freshly sliced if you can. The slices will keep for a few days in the fridge, wrapped in clingfilm, and won't have the plastic look and smell of packaged ham.

If you do buy a ready-sliced pack, ideally choose one that has the origin stated on it – for example, Teruel or Trevelez – and preferably the age of the ham. As with many foods, you will often see rather vague terms on packets, such as *bodega*, air-dried, special reserve, or farm assured, which are genuine attempts to communicate the characteristics of the ham; however, they don't actually guarantee all the quality criteria required for an excellent ham. Ultimately, it is a case of tasting to discover the one you like best.

Whichever way you buy your ham, always bring it to room temperature before eating, in order to experience the full flavour.

Ibérico ham

This is the most highly prized air-dried ham, from animals descended from the ancient breed of wild black Ibérico pig, which has characteristically long slender legs, a long snout to forage with, and a dark skin to help protect it in the sun. The ham it produces is popularly known as *pata negra*, referring to the black hoof which stays on the slim leg like a pointed shoe throughout the curing process and makes it look very different from other hams.

Pigs with 100% Ibérico parentage, brought up in the wild and fed on acorns, can produce hams that are quite sublime. However, not all Ibérico ham is produced from pure-bred, acorn-fed pigs. Nor does it necessarily taste sublime. The demand for Spain's most luxurious meat is growing fast and methods are intensifying, so while you still have small farmers producing only a few thousand hams in a year and controlling everything from the breeding and rearing of the animals to the curing and maturing, there are also big companies slaughtering 1,000 animals a week.

In these more intensive systems the pigs may still have access to some acorns, but others will have been raised solely on industrial feed. Even if they have been outdoor reared on farms they will not have had to course the hills foraging for food in the way of those labelled *de bellota 100% ibérico*, and without this phase of their development leading into the *montanera* (acorn-fattening), the ham won't be as elegantly streaked with translucent fat, nor will it have the aroma or sublime, naturally nutty flavour, with all its small but important nuances.

However, since genetics and breeding still play a big part, the hams will often be very good, although due to the lesser quality of their fat they cannot be cured for as long as those from animals who have fed in the wild and foraged on acorns. Eighteen months is a good length of cure for the best of the hams, and those from animals reared out of doors will be reddish in colour and gently marbled, with a fruity aroma – peachy with a hint of golden plums or melon – and will be mildly sweet while retaining a good touch of salt, so the flavour is round in the mouth with a long finish. Ultimately, however, the quality may not be that different to an excellent Serrano ham.

To help give consumers more information about the way the pigs have been reared and fed, Ibérico ham is divided into four classes: *de bellota 100% ibérico, de bellota ibérico, de cebo de campo ibérico,* and *de cebo ibérico.* New regulations are also being phased in, which will colour-code each whole ham slaughtered since 2014. In addition to displaying the name, race and rearing and feed details of the pig, the hams must be colour-coded with non-removable tags in the slaughterhouse: black for *de bellota 100% ibérico*, red for *de bellota ibérico*, green for *de cebo de campo ibérico* and white for *de cebo ibérico*. However, the best *de bellota* hams, which have the longest cures, will not appear with these coloured tags until around 2018.

De bellota 100% ibérico

This is the ultimate ham, from a pig that has 100 per cent Ibérico parentage. The animals must have been brought up wild in the oak forests without any grain supplements during their autumn *montanera*, when they gorge and fatten on acorns. They will have also been slaughtered immediately after the *montanera*. This is ham that has to be tasted to understand just how aromatic, silky, sweet and long-tasting it can be, and to appreciate that it is all about the 'good' fat which is the key to the texture and flavour. Yes, it is expensive, but you need only a few ultra-fine slivers to savour the experience.

The pigs spend all their lives in the wild of the Dehesa, a vast ecosystem encompassing swathes of forest, pasture, hills and plains in south-western Spain where the pigs forage on acorns from the *encina* (the evergreen holm oak), the *quejigo* oak and the *alcornoque* (cork oak), along with grasses and herbs and other natural forest food, which build up the silky, tasty translucent fat that streaks through the deep crimson and light purple colours of the finest hams.

It is the varied topography of the Dehesa that is crucial to determining the quality of the animals, and ultimately the hams. The best scenario for a producer of *de bellota ibérico* ham is to have a good extent of land both up in the hills, with big distances between water pools, and down in the plain, with access to the best acorns. This way the nimble, agile pigs can spend their summers rummaging and foraging on the hilltops, keeping fit running up and down, negotiating rocks, and sometimes covering as many as 40 kilometres in a day as they search for something to eat and scurry from water pool to water pool in heat that can reach 40°C. As a result they develop strong thin legs, big thighs and a bone structure that will support their weight once they are moved down to the plains for the *montanera,* or fattening phase, in which they spend the last three or four months of their lives gorging on acorns.

During the *montanera,* producers use skilled swine herders to guide the pigs towards the concentration of the best and sweetest acorns that have fallen from the oak trees. Following their energetic summer, the superbly fit pigs go crazy for them, gorging not only on the acorns, but on grasses from the *gramíneas* plant family, and clover, in particular, which is important in producing the best fat, along with wild purslane and legumes such as lentils, which have been strategically planted in the wild. At this stage of their lives the pigs are bulking up for winter, when the temperatures can plummet to below zero, and an average animal will eat 7kg of acorns and 3kg of grasses a day, sadly not knowing that such luxuries makes them perfect for the January slaughter and curing process.

In this crucial fattening phase the animals are expected to double their weight and the increase is monitored weekly to ensure the pigs are taking up the maximum amount of food needed. Quaintly, their weight is measured in *arrobas,* the old Spanish unit that country folk still use sometimes – each *arroba* equals about 11.5kg. Amusingly, the younger generation in Spain know the word as the @ symbol for emails.

The two classifications of acorn-fed ham refer mainly to the breeding of the pig. The highest classification, *de bellota 100% ibérico,* signifies that both parents were also 100 per cent Ibérico, while *de bellota ibérico* allows for a lower percentage of Ibérico in the breed, which is reflected in the quality of the ham. The purer the breed, the better the pig will be at absorbing the all-important acorn oils and allowing the fats to infiltrate the meat.

The best hams also vary with their 'vintage' or season, just like good wines, oils and cheeses. When you talk about a ham's season, this is the winter in which the pig was slaughtered (even though it may not actually be on sale for another two or three years, after the curing process), and a pig farmer is always hoping for ideal conditions in the autumn leading up to slaughter: gentle temperatures and enough rainfall to produce lush grasses, forest flowers and emerald green acorns which will mature to dark brown as the season goes into a dry, cold winter.

It is the acorns that are the real key to the intense, sweet, nutty aromas of the ham and the characteristic low-cholesterol, silky, melting, lubricating fat that runs through the finished ham in thin lines. This is what makes the flavour of the ham so complex and unctuously tasty, so it should always be eaten along with the lean, and never cut out or thrown away. When we first started bringing in *de bellota ibérico* ham, before there was any real acceptance or understanding of it in Britain, I gave a wonderful ham to chef Simon Hopkinson, then at Bibendum, who was very excited by the arrival of this delicacy. His instincts were right: he simply sliced it and sent it out to diners, but the plates came back with the fat trimmed off and customers wanting to know why it was there. I was duly called over to the restaurant to confirm that the ratio of fat to lean was perfectly normal and exactly as it should be.

It was an absurd misunderstanding of a fine product that seemed so characteristic of modern meat production and consumption, which has all fat marked out by many people as almost criminal. Simon did, however, have one customer who genuinely appreciated and understood fine fat: the late great artist Francis Bacon. Simon saved up all the trimmings that the other customers had eschewed and offered them to him to top up his own slices of the ham, and they were enjoyed with great gusto.

De bellota ibérico

This denotes cross-breed animals, i.e. Ibérico crossed with Duroc pigs. A pig can have as little as 50 per cent Ibérico genes (it must have a 100 per cent Ibérico mother, but could have a father who is 100 per cent Duroc or an Ibérico–Duroc cross) but this information, including the percentage of Ibérico, must appear on the ham's labelling. Apart from their breeding, however, these animals will have enjoyed the same exceptional lifestyle as the *de bellota 100% ibérico* pigs.

De cebo de campo ibérico

A ham from a cross-breed animal that has been raised outdoors but not necessarily across the large hills and woodland enjoyed by *bellota* pigs. Often the animals will have been brought up on a farm that is more intensive and without the space or acorn-quota per animal that the two *de bellota* grades require. The pigs will have been given a compound feed of cereals and pulses during the *montanera* fattening season, even if they have some access to acorns.

De cebo ibérico

This is the label for hams which originate from cross-breed animals that are reared intensively and are entirely grain-fed with very limited space in which to move, both of which factors are significant in terms of the quality of the hams.

How to choose *de bellota ibérico* ham

First of all be sure that what you are buying is genuine Ibérico. Until the new labelling system is fully phased in, the safest way is to actually see the ham being carved in front of you, as you can tell an Ibérico ham by the long elegant leg ending in a pointed black hoof. If the ham has a fat ankle and no black hoof, it doesn't mean it is a bad ham, but it won't be the genuine article.

Beyond this, you can tell that the ham is *de bellota ibérico* by the quality of the fat, which should melt at body temperature. Ask for a sliver of ham to be cut for you, warm it between your fingers and the fat should become meltingly soft.

All *de bellota ibérico* hams must be produced to official and traceable criteria; however, the very best producers will choose to exceed these, taking their hams to an eating experience that really blows the mind and makes the high price seem almost irrelevant. In the best vintages, a ham will have a deep crimson/purple colour and a delicate marbling of fat with a smooth, silky texture that melts on the tongue. In exceptional hams, when they are warm, experts sometimes claim to identify anything from 70 to 120 different aromas, from fresh hazelnuts, crisp apple and sweet melon to flowers, butter and grasses.

Depending on whether you buy ham from the north or the south of the production area, the flavour will tend to be subtly different. As a general rule, the further south of the production area you go, the slightly saltier the ham will be.

Due also to the cooler temperatures, northern hams can be cured for longer than in the south and will maintain their juiciness more easily. Ours come from the area of Guijuelo, where the hams can be cured for about four years and will continue to improve during this time. The very best hams from Guijuelo have always been my favourite, as they are balanced and aromatic with a long flavour: not as immediately appealing as the southern hams, perhaps, but more subtle.

The meat is deep red and well marbled, almost as sweet as honey on the palate, with some flavours of walnuts and almonds coming through. The hams tend to have a very silky texture and a fat that is translucent when warm and which literally melts away on your palate.

Hams from the south have an extraordinary ability to instantly impress, but lesser ones may turn out to be one-dimensional and often a little dry; however, the good ones carry the initial savoury experience on into a greater complexity and long flavour. Our hams, from Extremadura and Huelva, are deep burgundy red and well marbled, with a profound aroma that is a combination of honey, chocolate and coffee, with hints of smoky nuts and earthiness, and the flavour is markedly more savoury: sun-dried tomatoes, hazelnuts and chestnuts. The fat is very silky, and the finish slightly peppery and complex. In one slice you can experience sweetness, saltiness, creaminess and nuttiness.

Occasionally you might see *tirosinas*: white dots that appear in the lean meat of Ibérico ham – these are just amino acids of proteins that are part of the meat and have crystallised as a natural consequence of the disappearance of water and humidity during the later stages of curing, which has stopped them from dissolving. They can be a sign of maturity and decent curing.

Carving and serving
De bellota ibérico ham should always be served at room temperature, around 20–25°C, so that the fat can warm up and soften and lubricate the flesh, making it beautifully succulent and allowing all the extra dimensions and nuances of sweet flavours and aromas to develop and travel throughout the ham. In Spain the hams that are in use will always sit on the carving stand on the bar or in the restaurants, and when one is becoming close to the bone the next one will be taken from the cellar or ambient store and be waiting and warming, ready to take over. After

the first carving, the cut surface of the ham will be rubbed with the removed outer layer of white fat and covered with it, and then the whole ham will be tightly and completely wrapped in layers of clingfilm to press the fat on to the cut surface and prevent the meat from drying out.

At Brindisa we were the first to bring Spanish hams on the bone into the UK, so we also had to convince the environmental health officers that this is the way whole hams should be kept, rather than in the fridge. We had to supply a wealth of technical information from Spain to show that dramatic changes in temperature are the enemy of hams on the bone, drying them out; while, conversely, refrigeration can let damp into the bone via the hoof, which will spoil the flesh.

The carving of these hams is an art which takes into account the anatomy of the leg and an understanding of where the more sweet or savoury cuts lie. So we also brought over a string of Spain's best carvers, who were wonderful, colourful characters, quite diva-like, since they are celebrated as superstars at home and abroad. Since then we have set up our own school at our Borough Market shop, run by master carvers, which is hugely popular with customers who want to buy whole hams.

Most people, however, buy their ham carved for them in the shop. Once off the bone, you can keep it in the fridge, but always take it out around 4–6 hours before you want to serve it, so that it can warm up slowly to room temperature.

Tacos and taquitos de jamón
Often in Spain butchers and deli counters will sell the offcuts from the end of carving a Serrano or Ibérico ham. These are called *tacos*, or *taquitos*, depending on their size. The bigger *tacos* are perfect for adding to *revueltos* (scrambled eggs, see page 264), *croquetas* (see page 241) or stews, while the smaller *taquitos* (almost minced), are great for filling out meatballs or garnishing *salmorejo* (see page 149), etc. Of course, you can cut up pieces of ham yourself; however, because its texture is so soft, it is not easy to do it finely.

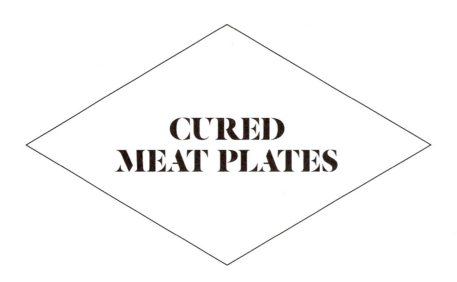

CURED MEAT PLATES

'every region will have its local favourites'

Ham is inevitably the hero of every cured meat plate throughout Spain, but also every region will have its local favourites which will feature alongside it. This is a selection of some of the most interesting.

Lomo en manteca colorá or blanca

This is pork that is marinated in black pepper, garlic and sometimes vinegar to tenderise it, then slowly cooked, confit-style, in lard, which is either white, or seasoned with *pimentón* (paprika). Alternatively, paprika may be included in the marinade to avoid any bitterness from overheating. Then the pork, which by now is incredibly tender, is cooled and stored in the lard. In days gone by families would have kept it in an earthenware jar (*orza*) where it would last for a number of months. This would have been a typical way to use up the trimmings of prime loin after the winter slaughter of the family pig. *Lomo en manteca* can be just sliced cold and the lard spread like butter on crusty bread.

Lomo doblado or doblao

This is stunning, especially when made from acorn-gorging Ibérico pigs. The loin is folded, or doubled – hence the name – over a piece of lard which is seasoned with salt, pepper and a touch of garlic, so that as the meat cures it melds together and becomes almost like a wide sausage that is shorter but twice as thick as the usual cured *lomo*. Because of this extra thickness, *lomo doblado* requires longer curing of at least 6 months, and as a result it is quite luxurious with its marbled lard centre and a flavour that is reminiscent of ham.

Lomo embuchado

The back loin of pork, seasoned with salt, paprika and oregano, then lightly dried over oak fires, which give it a gentle smokiness. When the cut comes from an Ibérico pig (see page 168) it is usually known as *caña de lomo*, and can be sublime, delicately streaked with sweet fat. It is eaten thinly sliced, on its own.

Cabezada de lomo

The end of the back loin which attaches to the shoulder of the animal. It is cured in the same way as *lomo embuchado* or *caña de lomo,* but because of its smaller size the curing is done

over a shorter time and as a result its flavour is less developed, and its texture less consistent, so while it can be very silky it can also be a little dry.

Morcón

This can include lean and fat from anywhere on the pig, especially the head and neck cuts, coarsely chopped and then cured in a stomach or bladder casing. It is typical of western areas such as Extremadura.

Cecina

This is cured beef, and it is unique to Castilla y León. The hind legs are cured for 14 months, then lightly smoked, and the result is somewhere between a ham and Italian cured beef, *bresaola*. *Cecina* is served sliced, and I have seen it presented with shavings of *foie gras* over the top, but my favourite way is sprinkled with pomegranate seeds. It is also good in salads, or, for a quick and tasty tapa, wrap strips of *cecina* around jarred *higos agridulce*: 'bittersweet' figs preserved in mustard syrup.

Salchichón

This is dry-cured pork sausage, which is the equivalent of the French *saucisson* or the Italian *salami*. Not surprisingly, it is most typical of Catalunya (where it is called *llonganissa*) which borders France and is across the water from Italy, areas of which it once ruled. While this style of sausage is made all around Spain, it is really only worth seeking out in Catalunya and south-west Spain (where it is made with meat from the Ibérico pig), as elsewhere it is often a very standard industrial *salami* made from indifferent meats and offal. In these two regions, however, *salchichón* can be superb, designed to highlight the meat, so that the spicing, which might be black or white pepper, nutmeg, coriander, oregano and/or garlic, is used to enhance, rather than dominate, the flavour of the pork. In Catalunya *salchichón (llonganissa) de Vic*, from the city of the same name, is a guarantee of quality.

Variations on *salchichón*-style sausages range from the thinner *Ibérico longaniza* (the Castilian spelling) to the Catalan *llonganissa de payés*, the very thin *fuet* (which can be hoop-shaped or candle-shaped), *secallona*, *tastet*, *espetec* or *sumaya*, but all of these are extremely rare outside Catalunya.

Ibérico salchichón

The very best *salchichón* from the south-west will have been made from the acorn-fed *de bellota* pigs that have roamed outside for most of their lives, so the meat will be infiltrated with acorn-rich fat and the sausage is so good that I often prefer it to *chorizo*. It is even more irresistible in the season immediately following the winter slaughter, when it is known as *salchichón vela*. This is thinner – about 3cm in diameter as opposed to 6cm for regular *salchichón*, and is cured for a shorter time, only a matter of weeks, so it is quite fresh-tasting, juicy, melting and velvety, with an aroma of the acorns and forest foods on which the pig will have fed.

Four Storeys of Sausages

The city of Vic sits on a high plateau surrounded by table mountains in the foothills of the Pyrenees, and when you drive towards it, invariably you go from bright sunshine into a thick mattress of cotton wool mist, known locally as *la boira*. It is this misty moistness, where cold crisp mountain air meets warm humid lowland air, that creates a unique microclimate in which the high natural bacterial activity is perfect for the curing of *salchichón*. As a result they develop a special aroma and flavour that makes them as desirable as any sausages made from the highly prized *Ibérico* pork at the other end of the country.

The *salchichón* we buy for Brindisa is made by the Riera family in a beautiful old town house with wrought-iron balconies, decorated with frescoes and a sundial, overlooking a square in the centre of Vic. Joaquim Comella Riera, who now runs the business, is the sixth generation of the family, who have been making and curing their salami-like sausages to the same recipe at Casa Riera Ordeix since 1852.

From the outside you would have no idea that, apart from the old living quarters that have been preserved from the days when it was also the family home, the four storeys are given over completely to the natural curing of sausages. The floors have loosely fitted boards over wooden beams, so that when the master curer adjusts the humidity and air flow by opening or closing the louvred windows, the air can circulate freely through the four levels. Even the wood itself, with its capacity to absorb moisture in this damp climate, is an essential element of humidity control.

Once I had returned to London in 1986 and was setting up Brindisa, my brother and any other relatives or friends who happened to be coming to the UK would always be instructed to stop in at Vic first to collect a box of the sausages for us from Joaquim's father, who was then in charge. We couldn't sell them until 1992, when Spain finally opened its doors to exports. Then, when the EU began to impose new standards on producers, we were all concerned that the town house would have to change. However, thanks to a mixture of determination and good sense, this hasn't happened, and these glorious sausages are still allowed to be made in the time-honoured way.

The family's small team of skilled butchers prepare the best pork leg or loin (depending on the recipe), together with belly. To make a genuine *salchichón de Vic*, you only use meat from sows of 2½ to 3½ years old, who will have had six litters by then. This more mature meat ensures a more active and dark cure, so there is no need to add any sugars or colouring to the recipe.

From Monday to Thursday the fresh meat is chopped by hand and the fat removed, and on Friday the mincing is done by machine. Some of it will be done more finely to make *salchichón de payés,* the 'country' sausage, which at Brindisa we simply call *llonganissa* in order to distinguish it from the *salchichón de Vic.* Once minced, ground black pepper, whole peppercorns and cubed belly fat are added and the mixture is left to settle and marinate over the weekend in the fridge. On the following Monday and Tuesday the natural tripe skins are filled to form sausages in various styles, including the stick-like *bastonet* (named after the wooden stick that is used in the traditional dance of the *bastonets* – a kind of Catalan equivalent of Morris dancing). In season, the family also make a special sausage in which the minced pork is mixed with black winter truffles.

Next, the sausages are taken up to the curing rooms to hang. This is very much an instinctive affair that relies on handed-down knowledge. Joaquim tells me that he often wanders through the rooms during the quiet of the night, checking on his *salchichones* and soaking up the feeling of history that pervades the old family house. In summer the sausages are hung higher in the house where there is more ventilation, while in winter they have to be moved around according to the damp. The curing time can be anything from two to six months, as again, so many factors come into play, from the size of the sausage to the thickness of the tripe casing, the positioning of the sausage in the hanging rooms and the climate outside.

My absolute favourite of their sausages is the *salchichón de Vic,* but any one of the range is fantastic with tomato bread, as one of a selection of small plates before a main meal, for tapas, or even for breakfast.

Ensalada de queso de cabra
'Luna Negra' con frutos secos
Goat's cheese, dried fruit and nut salad

ENSALADAS
Salads

There was a time when ordering *ensalada mixta* (mixed salad) in a Spanish restaurant could be a minefield. You might easily receive a plate piled high with everything from tuna *escabeche*, olives and tinned white asparagus to tinned corn, diced beetroot, carrot, the inevitable chunks of hard-boiled egg and slices of raw onion. Even in the best restaurants a salad would often be considered a showcase for speciality regional food, so in Catalunya *ensalada catalana* would inevitably be full of hearty slices of cured and poached meats and sausage, and in Alicante *ensalada de la tierra* would be loaded with *salazones* (cured fish, *mojama* and roe, see page 118).

In recent years, though, much has changed, and I have eaten many fine, restrained salads around Spain, particularly in Catalunya, that feature local produce such as citrus fruits, salt cod, anchovies, capers and beans in a more delicate way. Such salads combine well with other small plates, and I have included some of my favourites here.

A note on oil
For salads that feature salty or sharp ingredients, such as salt cod or citrus fruits, I would recommend a peppery oil such as Núñez de Prado or Olivar de la Luna. Where cheese or fresh seafood are involved, or for green salads, I would go for a sweeter oil such as an Arbequina. Both styles of oil work well for salads involving grilled fish or poultry.

Luna Negra is a lactic, ash-coated, round soft goat's cheese, which we really wanted to introduce and show off at its best in the tapas bars and restaurants, so our executive chef, Josep, created this utterly delicious salad. You could, however, use another Spanish cheese such as Monte Enebro from Ávila, or substitute an English goat's cheese log, such as Golden Cross.

Serves 4

1 tablespoon sweet olive oil, such as Aubocassa
1 small clove of garlic, finely chopped
1 tablespoon pine nuts
1 tablespoon almonds
1 tablespoon hazelnuts
25g raisins
2 tablespoons PX vinegar (see page 188)
250g baby mixed leaves
5 cherry tomatoes, finely sliced
150g soft goat's cheese, such as Luna Negra (see above), cut into small squares

To make the dressing, heat the oil very gently in a pan over a low heat and add the garlic and all the nuts. This oil will become part of the dressing, so be careful not to let it get overheated or burn, or it will turn bitter. When the nuts are light golden, lift them out and keep to one side.

Put the raisins into the pan of oil and shake them around so that they are all coated. Heat gently for about 3 minutes, by which time the raisins will have swollen with the oil, then pour in the vinegar and let the mixture bubble and reduce for about 4 minutes, until it caramelises. Take off the heat and allow to cool.

Arrange the leaves and tomatoes on a serving plate with the squares of cheese and the toasted nuts on top. Drizzle with the dressing.

Cogollos con anchoa y tomate

Fergus Henderson's anchovy,
Little Gem and tomato salad

Fergus Henderson of St John Restaurant is one of our longest-standing customers and supporters from way back in the days when I was operating solo; so when we celebrated Brindisa's twentieth anniversary it seemed only fitting that we celebrate with Fergus, his wife, Margot, and all the St John crew in their inimitable style in an arch in Shoreditch, amid tables heaving with food that they had prepared, and dancing to the music of Roberto Pla and his twelve-piece Colombian band!

Fergus included this salad in his first book, *Nose to Tail Eating,* and it is similar to a popular starter salad in Catalunya which shows off fine *anchoas de L'Escala* (see page 125), filleted at the last minute so they retain all their deep-sea-and-salt flavour, which contrasts with the light freshness of the young green lettuce halves, or 'cogollos', on which they are served. Fergus includes tomatoes and parsley, which the Spanish would not add, but in my view they bring colour and juice to something that might appear a little plain for the UK taste. And I love the way, in his book, he asks you to use the happiest tomatoes you can find – i.e. those that have seen the sun.

Serves 4

6 good sweet tomatoes on the vine
sea salt and freshly ground black pepper
olive oil
a handful of chopped parsley
16 good anchovy fillets in oil
2 heads of Little Gem lettuce, washed and separated into leaves

For the dressing
1 clove of garlic, finely crushed
1 teaspoon Dijon mustard
a pinch of sea salt and freshly ground black pepper
juice of ½ a lemon
1 teaspoon white wine vinegar
150ml sweet extra virgin olive oil, such as Aubocassa or L'Estornell

Preheat the oven to 180°C/gas 4.

Slice the tomatoes in half lengthways, sprinkle with salt, pepper and olive oil and roast in the preheated oven for about 20 minutes to soften and slightly dry them, intensifying and sweetening their flavour. Allow to cool, then mix with the rest of the ingredients in a serving dish.

Combine all the ingredients for the dressing, except the oil, then slowly mix this in until the dressing emulsifies. Toss through the salad. You may not need all the dressing, but what you don't need you can keep in the fridge for about 5 days.

Salpicón de rape y gambas
Seafood salad of monkfish and prawns

A few years ago I took a group of erudite cheese experts and food writers on a trip through the high villages of the Picos de Europa mountains, hunting for local cheeses with the help of a valued colleague, María Cobo. Before we flew home, we stopped off at Somo, an unremarkable-looking coastal town facing Santander, but with a stunning beach. We stayed in a gorgeous rural house called La Casona de Suesa, and the owners recommended a restaurant called El Galeón de Somo. When we arrived for dinner we found our table was next to the kitchen counter, where we could see the chef proprietor, Agustín Bedía, preparing the fish for service – enormous turbots, vivacious lobsters and the spooky-looking *percebes* (barnacles, see page 112).

Agustín is an imposing character, with a big smile and a head brimming with facts about the local fish and seafood he serves. He comes from Astorga, in the deepest hills of the province of León, in northern Spain, which is probably the country's biggest meat-eating region, a land of beans and pork, so it is interesting that he is a fanatical expert on the fruits of the sea and all its complexities. We were so overwhelmed by his food that our party returned for lunch the next day, and now whenever we take a family holiday in the region we always make time to stop for a meal at El Galeón de Somo before flying home. Since the restaurant is so close to the airport, it is the perfect way to round off a trip.

We especially love this *salpicón*, as it is a dish that can so often be ordinary, and Agustín generously gave me the recipe. His trick with the monkfish and prawns is to cook them separately and fast for just 2 minutes in a very large amount of water – he suggests 1 litre per 100g of fish (however, this isn't always practical in a domestic kitchen, so just fill the biggest pan you have) – before lifting them out and putting them into iced water to keep the texture good and firm.

Agustín prefers to use a mild vinegar and oil which won't overwhelm the flavour of the seafood, so I suggest a very delicate, sweet PX vinegar *en rama* (see page 188), and an olive oil such as Arbequina.

Serves 4

3 eggs
400g monkfish, cut into pieces about 2cm square
400g king prawns, peeled
around ½ a green pepper, or to taste, finely chopped
around ½ a red pepper, or to taste, finely chopped
around ½ a shallot, or to taste, finely chopped
150ml sweet extra virgin olive oil, such as Brindisa Arbequina
50ml good-quality sherry vinegar PX *en rama* (see page 188)
sea salt

Boil the eggs for 10 minutes until hard, then cool under running water and peel. Leave to cool, then cut into thin slices lengthways.

Bring some water to the boil in the largest pan you can find and have ready a bowl of iced water. Add the monkfish and boil for 2 minutes, then lift out with a slotted spoon and put into the iced water. Put the prawns into the same boiling water, also for 2 minutes, then lift out and add to the bowl of iced water.

Arrange the fish, prawns and slices of egg on the plate and mound the chopped peppers and shallot in the centre.

Combine the oil and vinegar and season with salt. Drizzle over the dish and put into the fridge to rest for an hour before serving, as the salad is at its best when chilled.

VINAGRE

'crafted with immense care, patience and respect'

Where there is alcohol there will eventually be vinegar, and Spain has an ever-growing array of stunning examples made from both sherry and wine. Back in 1991 we sold our first sherry vinegar to chefs, produced by the family-run Valdespino *bodega*. It was complex, balanced and special, and it had a massive impact on restaurant kitchens. Since then more and more wine co-operatives and estates have begun developing excellent vinegars, often from single grape varietals, and the most outstanding ones are crafted with immense care, patience and respect. Some of the most stunning I have tasted are the Casta Diva vinegars made by Pilar Sapena on the wine estate of Bodegas Gutiérrez de la Vega (see page 190).

Traditionally, in Spain families would often make their own vinegar from leftover wine, which would be used both to enhance flavours and extend the life of fresh foods such as fish, vegetables and meats, especially game. In contemporary cooking, however, the more sophisticated vinegars that are now readily available are used with fresh fruit, in sauces, or rice dishes; while a generous drop in a soup or a dish of beans and lentils can bring flavours together and add an extra dimension in a way that few other ingredients can.

Vinagre de Jérez
Sherry vinegar

The vinegars produced by the sherry estates of Spain have become much better known and understood over the last two decades. They must be made within the 'sherry triangle' of the towns of Sanlúcar de Barrameda, Jérez de la Frontera and El Puerto de Santa María and are matured using the *solera* method, which involves mixing older and newer vinegars in partly-filled wooden barrels and allowing them to mature and evaporate for at least 6 months, after which time the vinegar becomes dark, with aromas of liquorice, salty almonds and yeast. When aged for 2 years the vinegar can be labelled *reserva* and after 10 years *gran reserva*. The longer it is matured the more dense, dark and smooth-flavoured it will become.

The particular character of the vinegar depends on the grape varietal. Typical of the good, traditional sherry vinegars is the dark, intense and deeply aromatic cask-aged Gran Reserva from Valdespino, made from wine of the Palomino grape, which is most commonly used to make the dry, straw-coloured *fino* and *manzanilla* sherries.

Vinagre de Pedro Ximénez (PX)

The origin of this vinegar is the subject of great debate, but the popular story is that when King Carlos I (who was also Charles V of Germany and Holy Roman Emperor) arrived in Spain he was accompanied by an army recruited from peasants from the banks of the Rhine, and among them was a wine-maker called Peter Siemens, who brought with him grape varietals unknown in the Iberian peninsula. The vines were planted around the sherry towns and evolved into the white varietal known as PX. Once harvested the grapes are dried in the sun so they become raisin-like and will produce a rich, sherry vinegar.

There are many fine examples, but at Brindisa we support two which we believe to be the most remarkable. Both are offered by producers of quite special olive oil, who are able to apply their skill and understanding to the selection of superb vinegars.

Sotaroni is a delicious balsamic PX vinegar from the south of Spain, aged for 12 years and selected by the Torrevella estate, which produces excellent olive oils in Valencia. It has a sweet and sour quality, with flavours and aromas reminiscent of dried fruit and nuts.

Ximénez Paula Coll de Acetum Flumen *en rama* is selected and finished by Martí Terés i Ríos, owner of the Catalan olive oil producers Oleum Flumen. Since 1983 the vinegar has been made on the family-run Ximénez Spinola estate in Jérez de la Frontera, where Martí shares barrels and cellars with the Spinola family and produces and monitors limited editions (only around 1,500 half bottles a year) of his stunning vinegar.

En rama refers to grapes that are ripened on the vine and once harvested are matured and dried further in the sun, so they will have intensified in flavour and have a low water content. A hundred kilos of these sun-dried grapes, known as '*pasificadas al sol*', will be reduced to 30 litres of must, which is aged for up to 25 years through a series of oak barrels to make the PX sherry wines that then feed the vinegar barrels. The oak lends a little woody smokiness to the rounded, sweet and mellow flavours of the vinegar, with its good balance of sharpness and roasted aromas.

How to choose vinegar

As with wine or olive oil, so much is down to individual preference and the context in which you want to use a vinegar.

The best way to taste vinegar is in a wine glass, but leave it for a minute after pouring, as the aroma can seriously tickle the nasal passages. A good vinegar should be smooth and dense, with a careful balance of acidity and sugar.

When buying wine vinegars look for ones made with slow cold methods of acetification, which allow them to retain most of the qualities of the original grape variety. The most famous of these is the Schützenbach 'trickling' method, which was developed by a German chemist in 1823.

In many of the recipes in this book and in dressings, especially for warm salads, I recommend Moscatel vinegar, as it is balanced with a mellow, bitter-sweet flavour of fresh apples, pears and jasmine flowers, which will add character to a dish without any harshness. Sprinkle it on fruit salads and even chocolate puddings. Two teaspoons of Moscatel vinegar with a heaped tablespoon of orange blossom honey (or other light floral honey) and a pinch of sea salt in a mug of boiling water is also a fabulous remedy for sore throats, which our former Brindisa colleague Scott Boden would unfailingly produce for anyone ailing, with instructions to stir well, relax the mouth and throat and sip slowly.

A good Cabernet Sauvignon vinegar made using the Schützenbach method should be elegant and dense, with aromas of plums and red peppers –

perfect for sprinkling over *escabeche* dishes and using in marinades and reductions for sauces, especially to go with steaks and other red meats.

Merlot vinegar aged for 12 months in oak is bittersweet and smooth, with notes of red berries and spice. It pairs well with fresh tomatoes, or add some to apple sauce for serving with roasted meats.

Good vinegars made with the fruity Chardonnay grape according to the Schützenbach method will be crisp and flowery with some sweet almond notes; ideal for fish and salads.

Riesling vinegars aged for 2 months are refreshing, with hints of exotic fruits and citrus – good with fruit salads and duck dishes.

Vermut vinegar is as complex as the drink of vermouth itself, and with its herbal undertones it suits marinades for olives and *boquerones* (see page 127).

Balsamic apple vinegars from northern Spanish regions such as Lerida, Asturias and the Basque country are sharp yet honeyed, and have a sweet and sour tone that pairs well with sautéd leaves such as spinach, chard or red cabbage, fruity salads and puddings.

Sherry vinegar is good for meat marinades and in *gazpacho* soups.

The more dense, dark and aged vinegars, such as PX sherry vinegar and Casta Diva Fondillon wine vinegar, are excellent with cheese, sprinkled over fried eggs, a bowl of steamed clams or mussels, or roasted potatoes, red meat and pâté; and also pair well with ice cream and soft fruits, such as strawberries and cherries. Cut the fruit in half and sprinkle with sugar first, leave them for 2 minutes or so, then sprinkle them with the vinegar. Leave them for another 10 minutes, then drizzle with some good olive oil, such as Arbequina, just before serving.

Life and Cooking with Pilar and Felipe

On a winter evening in a bar in San Sebastián, back in 2006, our friend and supplier of wonderful conserved fish from the Rías Gallegas in Galicia, Ángel Delgado, introduced me to a small group of seminal people: Imanol Jaca, who has provided us with his exceptional beef ever since (see page 438); María José San Román, restaurateur and 'Saffron Queen' (see page 101); and Felipe Gutiérrez de la Vega and his wife Pilar Sapena of Gutiérrez de la Vega wines in the village of Parxent near Javea in La Marina Alta. We all settled in for a session of fine *pintxos* (tapas) and the evening went on and on into the night, as we were having so much fun.

The willowy Pilar and arts lover Felipe make a striking couple. Felipe produces exceptional red, white and dessert wines, and is recognised as the first wine-maker in Spain to make dry, as well as sweet white wine from the famous local Moscatel grape, with his Casta Diva Cosecha Dorada. And Pilar produces a golden early harvest extra virgin olive oil, as well as a late harvest one, which is such a deep mossy green that it reminds me of a Tuscan oil. Both are simply stone-pressed and bottled (for more on the oils see page 216). She also makes luxurious wine vinegars in tiny batches (see page 186) and wine *gelées* (jellies) which are lovely with cheese, cold meats and pâtés, or can be coated in sugars and eaten as sweets. After I first met the couple Felipe would send me his wines regularly to taste, and in one consignment he included some of Pilar's vinegars – it only took one drop for me to know that I had to visit Parxent to see how she created such jewels and, if possible, bring some back to Brindisa.

Felipe's father was Basque and his mother from Sevilla, and he was brought up in Madrid, steeped in the city's art, music and politics, so he has dedicated each of his wines to a great artist, writer or musician. Soprano Montserrat Caballé and novelist Camilo José Cela feature on the labels of the sublime Casta Diva Cosecha Miel, James Joyce on Viña Ulises, and Italian writer Giuseppe Tomasi di Lampedusa, author of *The Leopard*, is quoted on the label of the red Príncipe de Salinas, made from the Monastrell grape.

La Marina Alta is a very small, unusual and special *comarca* (district) of Alicante, which has the same average rainfall as Bordeaux, but more sunshine to dry off the grapes and vines, so there is little risk of rotting. Close to the Levante coast, Spain's most mountainous coastal area overlooking the Mediterranean, it has a humid, fresh, breezy and sunny microclimate. This, combined with the growing of local grape varietals on old vines in sandy, chalky soil, makes it possible to produce the range of Casta Diva wines, with their unique balance of natural sweetness and *la fescura* (freshness), as well as the dry Cosecha Dorada.

When Felipe and Pilar first returned to the area to settle, after living and marrying in the Canary Islands, they would join with her family in making a barrel of wine a year. Gradually, though, with the help of Tío Raimundo, Pilar's uncle and viticulture expert, Felipe learned about the land, the vines and the wine-making process, so they took over a small *bodega* that had been used for pressing olive oil in nearby Parxent, and set about extending the wine production. Felipe concentrated on the white Moscatel de Alejandria grape, which is synonymous with La Marina Alta, and the meaty, robust local Monastrell grape, though he also grows Giró (a varietal of Garnacha, or Grenache) and has a small plot of Shiraz.

The Moors, who followed the Romans in the region, built an ingenious system of irrigated terraces known as *bancales*, stretching from the dominating Montgó mountain to the beach. Sadly most of these, along with the old family *huertas* (allotments) and patches of mountain farmland, have been bought by developers, but Felipe is determined to pursue his wine-making in the traditional spirit of the *huerta* by taking on the care of old vines on the remaining small parcels of terraced groves.

These days the wine-making has moved to a bigger site in the village, while the old *bodega* is used for Pilar's vinegar-and-oil-making. Pilar is a wonderful cook who was brought up in Javea, where her family made a living growing, selling and exporting the famous Moscatel raisins of the area, as well as harvesting olives and grapes, and making oil, wines and vinegars for their own consumption. She learned to cook from her grandmother, who mostly brought her up while her mother was at work, and who also taught her the skills of the *huerta*. Every school summer holiday from the age of eight, she would watch and help her grandmother grow vegetables and herbs and prepare the family meals. Nowadays she makes wonderfully healthy dishes for visitors to the *bodega* and bakes her own bread, as well as producing her vinegars and oils, and when I began writing this book, to which she has generously contributed many recipes, I spent some time cooking with her.

Our first stop was the beautiful stone-built covered market that had been designed by her family. As always, even after so many years of living in Spain, I found myself initially having to shake off the very English need to plan before buying food and give myself up to Pilar's very Spanish attitude of buying *sobre la marcha* – on the hoof, going for what looks good and then working out what to do with it later.

Pilar thinks nothing of beginning the day's cooking and baking at 5 a.m., to a background of whatever operas or symphonies Felipe has selected for the day, played through the sound system that delivers music throughout their work spaces. In the beamed kitchen there is a wood-burning oven set in the wall, where she bakes her *coques,* both breads and cakes (see page 70), sweet bread rolls and *empanadillas* (see page 250). There is also an area for cooking over wood and vine trimmings, where special holders allow a big paella pan and the traditional, tall, four-legged, long-handled pan for making *gazpachos manchegos* (see page 456) to sit comfortably at the correct height over the flames.

The flavours in Pilar's food are exquisite but always subtle, and what elevates her simple-sounding dishes beyond excellent home cooking are the special touches. Her bread doughs will have a dash of Moscatel wine in them; she insists on manually grinding almonds with their skins on to give her almond tarts just the right texture; she will toss onions in salt and leave them for 30 minutes, then rinse, drain and dry them to soften the taste before adding them to a salad (these drained onions are known as *sevas escorregudas* in Valencian), or go out with a pair of scissors looking for particular wild herbs. She will squeeze orange juice into a dressing only when the fruit is from the early crop, because the flavour of their juice has just the right sharpness. In August she will harvest *ñora* peppers from the *huerta*, then lay them out in the full sun to dry on *cañizos* (cane mats) covered with netting at night to protect them from insects. This slow drying produces a fresh flavour and bright red colour totally unlike commercially dried peppers.

Each day we would cook until 2 p.m., when Pilar would put out the foods we had made for lunch, and Felipe and the couple's daughter, Violeta, now a qualified oenologist herself, would join us. A different bottle of wine would be opened each day: sometimes the red Príncipe de Salinas, minerally and dry, reflecting the sandy soil in which the vines grow; the Recóndita Armonía, a sweet berry-rich red that tastes like ripe Victoria plums; or the semi-sweet, ruby red Fondillon, the traditional wine of Alicante made from a combination of fully ripened and overripe Monastrell grapes and aged in barrels for 10 years or longer, which I think is amazing with chocolate desserts.

Pilar told me that she insists on a daily glass of Fondillon for good health, as her grandmother and mother used to give her a glass of it every day with bread and sugar when she was a child, and she believes the combination to be the perfect match and medicine.

THE CASTA DIVA VINEGARS

Pilar's wonderful vinegars are an extension of Felipe's ability to craft some of Spain's very best wines. She makes three kinds, a Moscatel vinegar, a balsamic vinegar from the must of the Moscatel grapes, and balsamic vinegar, which is made from the must of the Monastrell grapes.

The Moscatel vinegar is made using the slow, continuous

Orléans method, originated by Louis Pasteur in the nineteenth century. To start the process off, the Moscatel wine is aged for 6 years in aerated barrels to which a special *madre* or 'mother' bacteria that is viscous in texture is added, which 'feeds' the wine and turns it to vinegar. This mother grows inside the barrel and some of it is transferred to other barrels to start new batches. The vinegar barrels are monitored regularly and fresh wine is added to keep the acidity down and produce a delicate rusted-pink vinegar with a touch of sweetness and a taste of wine. When it is ready, the *madre* stays behind in the barrel and new wine is added, so the process can begin again.

The Moscatel balsamic vinegar is called *agrídulce* (sweet and sour) and is made from the second picking of very ripe grapes, the *sobremadura*. The bunches are hung for about 2 months from rafters in a shady, arched porch where the air can circulate and slowly dry them, so that they darken but don't dry out or rot in the rain as they would if left on the vine. The grapes are then pressed manually to extract their juice, now highly viscous and honey-like, which is taken to the vinegar cellars in the old family *bodega*. Here Pilar cooks it down until reduced by half to create a rich must which is then aged for at least 10 years, starting in a large 125-litre barrel and then passing through a series of barrels of different woods – chestnut, cherry, acacia, juniper, oak and cedar. These decrease in size down to 10 litres and each adds its own tones and layers to the flavours and aromas. The cherry wood, for example, gives chocolate notes, while chestnut adds a degree of acidity.

Throughout the long and exacting process, Pilar monitors the aromas and flavours in order to move each batch of vinegar on at the right moment, then select and blend from the different barrels and finally bottle limited quantities, unfiltered, into small dark glass bottles.

The Fondillon balsamic vinegar is made using a similar process, but using the rich dark must from the Monastrell grapes. However, these are not hung after picking, and the barrel-ageing extends for up to 30 years, so that the resulting vinegar is dense, with spicy and sweet and sour overtones, reminiscent of dried figs and aromatic herbs.

From both these balsamic vinegars Pilar makes her special *gelées*, setting the vinegars with apple pectin. The Moscatel *gelée* is great with shellfish, fish, cheese and pâtés, while the Fondillon *gelée* is also perfect with pâtés, aged cheeses, certain salads, cured *salchichón* and red meats like roast lamb.

ALCAPARRAS Y ALCAPARRONES

'piquant, floral and citric'

There are about 345 varieties of caper bush in the world, which can either be cultivated or found wild throughout the western Mediterranean. Spain and Italy are the biggest cultivators in Europe, and both the buds (the capers) and the fruit (the bigger caperberries) are widely used in the Spanish kitchen, combined with anchovies, olives, tinned tuna or cured meats; in salads and sauces, and fish and rice dishes, to which they add piquancy, floral flavours and a citric vibrancy. However, their flavour can vary subtly according to factors such as the variety, the composition and the mineral content of the soil in which they are grown, and the degree of rainfall.

Both capers and caperberries are graded by size, whether cultivated or wild. The size affects texture, not flavour, and smaller ones are the most desirable, since these will be the firmest in the case of capers; while the smaller caperberries will be softer (though they should still have a little crunch when you bite them) and have less seeds than larger ones.

Both capers (*alcaparras*) and caperberries (*alcaparrones*) can be preserved in brine or vinegar. Capers can also be preserved in dry salt, which removes the sharpness and condenses and intensifies the flavour (it is rare to find Spanish caperberries packed this way). This is my preference as the capers retain their fresh flavour the best. Whichever way they are destined to be sold, they are all initially put into sea salt for two weeks to draw out the moisture and create a brine. Then they are rinsed and put into more sea salt for a further two weeks, before being drained, graded according to size and packed in salt, brine or vinegar.

How to buy and use

When buying capers in dry salt, check that the harvest date is shown on the packaging, and buy ones that are as close to this as possible, as they will be the freshest tasting.

The salt should look good and white, rather than beginning to discolour around the capers.

Capers in salt and capers and caperberries in brine need to be rinsed and soaked for 10 minutes, then drained before using, or they will add too much salt to your dish. Don't soak them for longer, however, or you will leach the flavour from them.

Capers and caperberries in vinegar only need rinsing and draining.

They are best added raw, or, if added to hot dishes, this should be at the end, as too much heat will cause them to lose flavour.

Miguel and the Wild Capers of Ballobar

Up in the arid mountains above the village of Ballobar in Aragón grow some of the most distinctive wild capers and caperberries you will find in Spain. Although wild caper shrubs (*Caperis espinosa*) grow in arid areas of Lleida, the Balearics and Valencia, it is the Ballobar capers that grow in this, the biggest desert in Europe, that were once valued so highly they were said to have been given to the Russian Czar in exchange for caviar. Now they have become treasured again, so much so that they have been identified as a *baluarte* (Spanish Slow Food) product. And the man who chose to make a hero out of them is Miguel Ángel Salas.

Until a decade or so ago Miguel was a civil servant working on construction projects in the region, but when he saw the shrubs growing he decided to dedicate himself to harvesting and curing the buds. He set about learning the skill from the older ladies of the village and one of these venerable women, Señora Antonia, whose recipe he still uses, continues to taste each new harvest to give her opinion on the crop.

The first time I tasted the capers I was struck by their amazingly distinctive fresh, citrussy and earthy flavour. Even eaten straight from their jar of brine, their taste was so wonderful I was determined that at Brindisa we should help champion this very individual ingredient. So I decided to go over for the harvest in the Monegros Desert, where they are collected entirely by hand between June and August/September in temperatures that can rise to a scorching 50°C.

Although the bushes freeze in winter when the temperatures drop below 10°C, they recover and flourish in the heat of summer, and their roots can extend down 30 metres in search of water. Such extreme conditions create beautiful buds of grey-green with white and pinky flecks, and a characteristic, concentrated flavour and exceptional freshness, with no bitterness on the finish at all; and the berries that follow are more crunchy than other cultivated varieties. Such quality, however, comes at a price, since each bush produces only around 3 kilos of capers per plant, as opposed to 6–8 kilos for other varieties.

As Miguel drove me deep into the nether regions of Aragón towards Ballobar village there seemed something bleak but gripping about the scenery that reminded me of the open roads of the southern states of America, where tumbleweed blows around, as we passed storks' nests and the occasional itinerant hitch-hiking harvester looking for a lift to the next patch of work.

From the village we drove further up the barren, windswept mountain to the exposed areas where the shrubs were growing, seeming to love the hot dry wind that buffeted the thorny stems mercilessly as the pickers, who had been out harvesting since 6 a.m., tried to negotiate them without being prickled. Most of the varieties of caper found around the world are less thorny and much easier and cheaper to harvest than those from Ballobar, but there are none quite so amazing.

Many of the harvesters are Africans, who have built up a great reputation for the excellence of their work and travel through the region from one harvest to the next, saving up their money to send home to their families. In the heat, you can sustain only about 4 hours of back-breaking work, so by midday the pickers would begin bringing their shopping bags filled with capers into the sheds, where Miguel carried out a visual check, weighed and paid for each batch – then the capers were put through his homemade grader, which consisted of a series of rolling tubes with different sized holes which allowed the buds to be channelled into one of four different boxes, according to size. Leaves and bits of debris were removed, then Miguel sealed each grade separately in a plastic bag full of salt brine, ready for the transfer to the curing house in the town of Calanda, where the capers would be cured until October, before being packed into jars.

Remojón
Salt cod carpaccio and
orange salad with capers

Wafer-thin 'carpaccio' slices of de-salted cod loin
are the most elegant for this salad, but if you find
the loin tricky to cut this finely, just use small
pieces instead. In Spain people are lucky enough
to be able to buy the carpaccio already coated in
oil, so they don't have to do the work themselves.

The capers can be in brine, or salt, whichever
you prefer – if you can find wild ones (see page
194) these will be in brine.

Serves 4

20g capers in brine or salt
200g salt cod (loin or fillet),
  de-salted (see page 328)
½ a large orange, or 1 small one
½ a red onion or shallot, finely sliced
8 good black olives, such as Empeltre or Aragón
sea salt and freshly ground black pepper
a pinch of fresh oregano
1 tablespoon good olive oil, such as Arbequina

Soak the capers in water for an hour, to remove
the excess salt, changing the water twice, then
drain them.

Remove any small bones from the cod and
either cut into small pieces, or with a very
sharp knife cut into thin slices (about 1–2mm)
crossways. Peel the orange and cut it into thin
round slices.

Lay the slices of cod on a plate, then lay the
orange on top, followed by the onion or shallot,
capers and olives. Season with a pinch of salt and
pepper, sprinkle the oregano over the top and
drizzle with olive oil.

Xatonada
Catalan salt cod and frisée salad

Another Catalan salt cod salad, which has a
number of variations. Although it is traditionally
done with salt cod, I have also seen it with tuna
and/or anchovies, taking it closer to a Caesar
salad, albeit with a nut sauce. This is our head
chef Leo Rivera's way of presenting it, which I
particularly like, as he chops the spindly frisée
(or escarole) lettuce quite finely, making it easy to
eat, and dresses it with *xató* sauce and olives.

Xató is very similar to *romesco* sauce (see
page 303), and there is much debate about how to
distinguish the two, depending on the particular
recipe you choose. The nuts in the sauce also
tend to vary according to what is grown locally
throughout the region, so in Tarragona it will
usually be made with more, or only, hazelnuts,
which grow in abundance there; while in Sitges
the sauce will be made using more, or only,
almonds. Leo uses half and half, but you can vary
the proportion as you like.

Serves 4

150g salt cod fillet, de-salted
½ a frisée or escarole lettuce, chopped very finely
around 4 black olives, such as Empeltre,
  stoned and halved
1 x quantity *xató* sauce (see page 303)

With a very sharp knife, remove the skin and
then either slice the salt cod as thinly as you
can or with your fingers break it up into bite-
size pieces.

Mound the frisée neatly on a serving plate and lay
the salt cod slices or chunks over the top. Add the
olives and dress with the sauce.

Esquiexada
Catalan salt cod salad

This is a famous and very refreshing Catalan salad. *Esqueixar* means 'to tear', and you combine long, thin, torn strips of white salt cod with black olives and red and green peppers, which makes the dish quite dramatically colourful. It is also very light on the stomach.

If you don't have olive paste, you could stone and crush around 3 good black olives using a pestle and mortar.

Serves 4

200g salt cod (ideally loin, or *morro*),
   de-salted (see page 328)
½ a green pepper
½ a red pepper
6–8 cherry tomatoes
½ a shallot or sweet onion, finely sliced
about 12 good olives, preferably black,
   such as Empeltre or Aragón

For the dressing
2½ tablespoons extra virgin olive oil
1 tablespoon good vinegar, such as Spinola PX
   sherry vinegar (see page 188)
1 teaspoon *olivada* (Aragón olive pâté), thinned
   with a little extra virgin olive oil

Remove the skin from the cod and carefully pick out any bones, then tear the flesh into long, thin strips.

Slice the peppers into julienne strips and cut the tomatoes into quarters or sixths, depending on their size. Mix all the salad ingredients together loosely in a serving dish.

Combine the oil and vinegar and dress the salad with it, then drizzle with the thinned olive pâté. Put in the fridge for an hour to marinate, and serve chilled.

Empedrat
Catalan white bean and salt cod salad

Our executive chef, Josep Carbonell, cooked for us for over five years in London before moving back to Barcelona, from where he now travels back and forth, overseeing the menus in the tapas bars and restaurants. When his daughter, Judit, was born I went to visit him and his family, and knowing how much I love the Catalan *mongetes del ganxet*, as a little gift they gave me a special bag filled with these shiny white hooked beans which have quite thin, delicate skins, so need less soaking and cooking time than other varieties, and quickly become creamy, delicate and beautiful.

Inside the bag, written on a tiny piece of paper, was a recipe for *empedrat*, the simple, nourishing salad of *mongetes* and salt cod that is famous in Catalunya, and this is the version that we now have on the menu at Casa Brindisa.

If you can't find *mongetes*, you could substitute other small white beans, such as *arrocina* or *planchada* (see page 381).

Serves 4

300g white beans, such as *mongetes*
2 eggs
200g salt cod *migas* (see page 330),
   de-salted (if you can find them),
   or de-salted fillet, broken into pieces
2 ripe tomatoes, diced
1 shallot or sweet mild onion
10–12 mixed black and green olives,
   stones removed

For the dressing
2 tablespoons white wine vinegar,
   preferably Chardonnay
80ml olive oil
1 teaspoon chives
1 small clove of garlic, crushed

Soak the beans for 12 hours at least, then drain. Put into a pan of cold water, bring to the boil, then turn down to a simmer for 45 minutes, and cook until just tender. Drain and allow to cool.

Put the eggs into cold water and bring to a simmer gently so that the shells don't crack, then cook gently for 10 minutes. Drain and run under cold water, then peel, remove the yolks and discard them (or keep for another recipe). Chop the whites and keep to one side.

Mix together all the dressing ingredients and stir to emulsify.

Combine the cooled beans with the rest of the salad ingredients and the reserved chopped egg whites, and toss carefully with the dressing.

LOS TÚNIDOS

'a big family'

The tuna family (*los túnidos*) is a big one and there are many different species. In the UK we are most used to the relatively cheap, brownish and quite strong-tasting skipjack, which comes from tropical seas and is mainly canned to meet world demand. However, in terms of Spanish fish, you have three main choices: yellowfin, which in Spain is known as *atún claro*, the supreme but very threatened bluefin, which thanks to its rich red flesh is rather confusingly known as *atún rojo*; and the prized *bonito del norte*.

Atún claro
Yellowfin tuna

This can reach around 20–50kg in weight and has pink meat with a pronounced, but not strong flavour. It is mostly canned for the speciality markets not only of Spain, but of Japan, Italy and other Mediterranean countries.

It is usually fished in tropical, rather than local waters, and is frozen at sea. On average only about 20 per cent will be eaten fresh (from frozen), and about 80 per cent will go on to be preserved: either in tins, or salted and dried to make *mojama* (see page 121). The content of fat is what determines how a piece of the fish is used: the fatty pieces, notably the *ventresca* (belly), are the most coveted for eating fresh, smoking or canning; the least fatty will be used for *mojama*, though occasionally the *ventresca* is salted over a very long period of time (a couple of months), then pressed and hung, and can be exceptional.

How to choose canned tuna
Price is the main clue. Pole-and line-caught tuna will suffer less in the fishing and so the meat will be less damaged in terms of bruising, and the best and most expensive fish is cut and packed by hand, so that the processors can more easily keep a visual check on quality.

The larger the tin the more intact the tuna – 2kg tins, for example, will have large cuts, whereas in cheaper, smaller tins (about 120g) you find a mix of pieces of ends of loins, large flakes or chunks.

Usually tuna is packed in a conventional vegetable oil or a light olive oil, which is better than extra virgin olive oil, as the delicate flavour of the fish should be able to shine rather than compete with a more distinctive oil.

Most canned tuna can also be found in brine and spring water – lighter, healthier preparations containing no fat which are excellent for special diets; however, you will not experience the luxurious texture of fish stored in oil.

Atún rojo
Bluefin tuna

Fished in the Atlantic and most famously in the Mediterranean in the month of May, bluefin tuna is renowned for its high fat content, which gives luxuriously marbled, oily-textured, deep red meat with a very, very silky texture and almost ethereal flavour. This is the tuna that is loved by chefs and especially the Japanese, who will pay high prices for it for sushi and sashimi. Though it is usually eaten fresh or raw, it is also found preserved in jars of olive oil.

Spanish bluefin tuna is fished in Spain either in the Bay of Biscay or in the Mediterranean sea, but its stocks have decreased dramatically (largely because of the Japanese appetite for it) and fishing limitations have been established, so most canneries no longer conserve it in tins, opting instead for yellowfin or *bonito del norte*.

The oldest, most controversial, and some would say barbaric form of fishing for bluefin tuna is the *almadraba*, which still takes place each year around Barbate on the south coast, though on a much smaller scale than in the past.

La almadraba
The *almadraba*, which translates from Andalusian Arabic as 'the place where one beats something', is the famous, bloody capturing-ground for the great bluefin tuna in a tradition that goes back at least 3,000 years and was devised by the Phoenicians, who valued tuna so highly that they featured the fish on their coins. However, it was truly perfected by the Arabs.

Every year between May and June, usually on the first full moon of the month, the shoals of fish migrating from the cold Atlantic to the warmer Mediterranean to spawn pass close to the coastline at Barbate near the Straits of Gibraltar. Here the local boats are waiting to drive them through a series of nets that are placed along the route of the fish until they become trapped in a central pool or *copo* near the water's edge, where they are speared by the waiting fishermen.

The fish on this stage of their journey are known as *atún de derecho* and are at their prime and rich in fat, which gives the flesh a very visible marbling. Tellingly, this is known as *tocino,* which is also the name used for pork back fat, and the Spanish often call this tuna *el cerdo del mar*, the pig of the sea, not only because of its size but also because of the desirability of this fat, and also the fact that both have traditionally offered nose-to-tail eating for families.

Those who support the *almadraba* argue that for centuries it has been a sustainable form of fishing since only a certain number of fish are captured, and in their view this is preferable to the massive-scale plundering of bluefin tuna using vast, sophisticated trawlers often guided by spotter planes that is endangering the stocks, and in turn has caused the demise of all but a handful of the *almadrabas*.

Once slaughtered, those *almadraba* fish destined for the local market are taken to the auctions and then cut up in a process known as *el ronqueo*, or 'hoarseness', which represents the sound of the knife as it hits the spine of the tuna and cuts along the length of it. The very best fish fetch prices two or three times higher than the rest, and their flavour will be so clean-tasting it needs no condiments. A small quantity still goes to be preserved as *mojama* (see page 121) in the traditional way; however, the Japanese are so enamoured of bluefin tuna that 90 per cent of the *almadraba* catch leaves Spain for Japan, sold even before the boats have returned to shore.

Some tuna which escape the May cull are caught around September, again using the *almadraba* method of trapping, when they pass by the coast on the reverse trip – these are known as *de vuelta* (returning) – but by now, having spent time in warmer waters, they are about 30 per cent leaner and their meat is drier, so they are not highly rated gastronomically.

Bonito del norte
This is in a class apart from any others in the tuna family: elegant, subtle, with a sublime, delicate

flavour and white flesh. Expensive, yes, but just a small tin excites and satisfies the palate in the same way as a few slivers of the most expensive acorn-fed Ibérico ham. That said, I frequently find that initially the taste is quite surprising and foreign to the UK palate, more used to feisty skipjack. In the early days at Brindisa I would hold blind tastings of different labels of tuna and *bonito del norte* with both Spanish and English colleagues, and the reactions were very different. The Spanish would immediately recognise and prefer the *bonito del norte*, while the English would veer towards more familiar skipjack or yellowfin. Once converted, however, I find that people love the *bonito del norte*, even if its high price makes it a treat, rather than a regular food.

It is important to call the fish by its full name, *bonito del norte*, as there can be confusion with the Portuguese *bonito*, which is similar to a mackerel and is more often cured as a *salazón* (see page 118). Although its name means 'of the north', this just refers to the species, not the geographical origin, even though the best are actually landed in the north of Spain.

It is a very distinctive-looking fish, with silvery blue scales, huge round eyes and a large mouth with tiny teeth; it is much slimmer and smaller than yellowfin and bluefin tuna (typically weighing 6–8kg) and has whiter flesh, with a beautifully smooth, delicate flavour. The silky *ventresca* (belly), in particular, is in a league with the finest cured hams, caviars or *foies*, and although the fish is often eaten fresh, even when canned it is considered a real luxury.

The fishing season is June to September, and while *bonito del norte* can be fished in other seas such as the Pacific or the Indian Ocean, to which the fish often migrate, the very best are caught around the Bay of Biscay, where the fish come in search of food (sardines, anchovies and mackerel) having wintered in the Mar de los Sargazos (the Sargasso Sea), passing by the Azores on their journey, before returning south again to spawn. By now, although they are small to medium size, they are rich in the prized fat that makes them such an exquisite,

tender delicacy. The fat settles particularly in the *ventresca*, the belly, giving the cuts from this part of the fish its special silkiness. Because they are caught locally they can be landed fresh, whereas those from further afield and in other parts of the world may be older and bigger, have a drier, less sought-after meat and will be frozen at sea.

In the old days around the Bay of Biscay the fish were caught in hazardous conditions using a method called trolling, which involved small rowing boats towing hooked lines behind them. The towing of lines is still done sometimes, but mostly about 20 fishermen fish from bigger boats, with fixed poles and lines, using live bait (anchovies) – a system introduced by the French Basques in the 1950s. Since each fish is caught individually, the fishermen can select the best and at the same time avoid catching other species, such as dolphins, or damaging the sea bed, as can happen with big trawlers using nets.

How to choose *bonito del norte*

Often the name of the harbour where the fish was landed appears on the labelling: so you might see ports such as Getaria, Burrela, Arila, Lequeitio or Ondarroa listed. This shows that the fish comes from the prime waters of the Bay of Biscay.

At the packing house the fish is divided into different cuts: *ventresca* (the velvety belly), whole loin, chunks of loin, and small pieces, known as *migas* (crumbs). The most prized *ventresca de bonito del norte* will consist of long *láminas* (fillets) of fish which should melt on your tongue and be beyond comparison with any other tuna – a luxury that will be reflected in the price.

The best producers will also offer whole tuna loins in tall jars rather than tins, which allow you to see the quality: look for perfect, pale, undamaged flesh with no blood spots.

Migas in oil are 'crumbs' of *bonito del norte* which are a fantastic, cheaper alternative for something like *empanada* (see page 401).

Ensalada de bonito del norte con piquillos, huevos y garbanzos

White tuna salad with *piquillo* peppers, eggs and chickpeas

This is a very simple, summery, colourful salad that we serve at Casa Brindisa, which is designed to showcase the delicate flavour of *bonito del norte* (see page 204), though you could substitute yellowfin tuna.

Serves 4

1 tablespoon capers in brine or salt
2 large tomatoes
2 eggs
100g tinned *bonito del norte*
  (see page 204) in olive oil
2 tablespoons olive oil
1 clove of garlic
1 shallot, finely chopped
100g jarred *piquillo* peppers
  (see page 275), cut into strips
200g good jarred chickpeas, drained
2 teaspoons parsley, chopped

For the dressing
100ml extra virgin olive oil
30ml good red wine vinegar,
  such as Cabernet Sauvignon
sea salt

Soak the capers in water for 10 minutes, to remove the excess salt, changing the water twice, then drain them.

Either grate the tomatoes or, if you prefer a smoother, more elegant texture, de-skin and de-seed them. The way to do this is to cut a cross in the top of each tomato and put them into a bowl. Pour boiling water over them, leave for about 10 seconds if they are very ripe, or up to a minute if not so ripe – just enough to loosen the skin, but no more, or the tomatoes will begin to cook – then cut them in half, scoop out the seeds with a teaspoon and chop the flesh.

Put the eggs into cold water and bring to a simmer gently so that the shells don't crack, then cook gently for 10 minutes. Drain and run under cold water, then peel and slice.

Drain the *bonito del norte* of its fishy oil, put it into a bowl and mix in the capers, together with 1 tablespoon of the olive oil.

Gently heat the rest of the olive oil and add the whole garlic clove to flavour it – once the clove starts to colour, take it out, put in the shallot, allow to soften, then put in the *piquillo* peppers and chickpeas and warm them through.

Layer up the salad in a serving dish, beginning with the shallots, peppers and chickpeas, then the *bonito del norte* and capers and finally the tomato. Combine the dressing ingredients and drizzle over the top, but don't toss through, as you don't want to disturb the layering of the ingredients. Arrange the sliced hard-boiled eggs on the side or on top of the salad. Finish with the parsley.

Ensaladilla
Russian salad or white
tuna and potato salad

In Britain Russian salad often has a bad name, thanks to the tinned versions that were popular in the sixties, but in Spain people love it, and when it is made carefully with fresh ingredients and good, preferably homemade, mayonnaise, it can be lovely, a bit like coleslaw really, in that it makes a good dish to have on the table with other small plates or to take on a picnic. My good friend Ambro, the cheesemaker in Burgos (see page 154), says it is a salad that makes him happy, and he packs it into a lunchbox to take with him when out on the family farm, or into a much bigger box to take to their *merendero* (converted mountain cave) for weekend get-togethers.

The salad was first created by French chef Lucien Olivier at the Hermitage restaurant in Moscow in 1860, combining freshly cooked vegetables and pickled vegetables in the Russian tradition, adding cooked meat and eggs, and mixing everything in mayonnaise, the fashionable dressing of the time.

The salad arrived in Spain during the twentieth century and its popularity may have grown partly out of a Spanish affinity with the Russians, who supported the Republican effort during the civil war, so much so that Franco's government insisted that it be re-named 'national potato salad'.

At its most basic the salad is made with chopped cooked potatoes, carrots, peas and possibly green beans, bound in mayonnaise, but there are endless embellishments that are often added, from cauliflower, cucumber and *piquillo* peppers to sliced apple, capers and olives, chopped hard-boiled eggs, even prawns, langoustines or tuna in oil or *escabeche*.

This particular recipe is a fishy variation from Ana Barrera (see page 442) that is a staple on her restaurant menu in Madrid, and while, of course, you can add other ingredients if you like, I feel the merit of Ana's salad is that she keeps it simple, and her customers love it for that.

If you can't find *bonito del norte en escabeche*, substitute tinned tuna in oil (drained very well, so that it is not too oily) with a little lemon juice squeezed over it.

Serves 6

6 tablespoons olive oil
25–30 Marcona almonds (see page 90)
6 eggs
4 carrots, skin on, washed
10 small potatoes, skin on
sea salt
**250g Ortiz *bonito del norte en escabeche*,
  or tuna in oil, well drained and mixed
  with a little lemon juice**
200ml good mayonnaise – preferably homemade

Heat the olive oil in a deep frying pan, add the almonds and fry gently, turning until golden, then lift out and drain on kitchen paper.

Put the eggs into cold water and bring to a simmer gently so that the shells don't crack, then cook gently for 10 minutes. Drain and run under cold water, then peel.

Cook the carrots and potatoes together in boiling salted water with their skins on until just tender. Be sure not to overcook them, as they need to retain their texture. Drain and cool, then rub off the skins. (If you are in a hurry you can cook the eggs, carrots and potatoes all together.)

Chop the eggs, carrots and potatoes as finely as you can, so that they almost appear to be grated. This way you will stop the salad becoming too heavy once the mayonnaise is added. Add the fish and mix all the ingredients evenly. Mix well with the mayonnaise, and garnish with the almonds.

Barny's butter bean, piquillo pepper, artichoke and olive salad

This is another recipe from chef Barny Haughton. Being one of ten siblings and the father of five children, he embraces that wonderful, generous ethic that I also grew up with – and that is very Spanish – of welcoming everyone to come and eat. He made this salad with one of his favourite varieties of dried bean, the *judión*, as part of a many-course meal for myself and about twenty friends at his family home.

If you buy good olives marinated in oil, vinegar and herbs, you can use this marinade for the dressing, otherwise you will need a little extra virgin olive oil and sherry vinegar.

Serves 4

500g *judión* beans (see page 383)
1 onion, quartered
3 sticks of celery, chopped into large chunks
2 carrots, chopped into large chunks
2 leeks, each cut into three
1 *farcellet* (see page 80) or bouquet garni
12 peppercorns, tied in muslin
1 small aubergine
a little olive oil
a pinch of sea salt
1 x 250g jar of *piquillo* peppers, cut into strips
250g chargrilled artichokes in oil,
   drained and cut into small pieces
200g black olives, such as Aragón, either plain,
   or marinated in oil, vinegar and herbs
a little extra virgin olive oil, if necessary
a little sherry vinegar, if necessary
8 spring onions, chopped
a bunch of fresh coriander, finely chopped

Soak the beans for 24 hours in plenty of water (as they will expand).

Drain the beans, put into a large pan of fresh water and add the onion, celery, carrot and leek, along with the *farcellet* and the peppercorns. Simmer gently for about 2 hours, until the beans are tender.

While the beans are cooking, slice the aubergine, brush with a little olive oil and char-grill (preferably), or grill, until golden. Keep to one side.

Once the beans are tender, take off the heat, put the pan under the cold tap and run water into it until the beans are cool, then drain them to avoid their skins cracking. Take out the vegetables and herbs and discard them. Season the beans with a pinch of salt.

Put the beans into a serving bowl. Add the peppers, aubergine, artichokes and olives, with their own dressing and/or a little extra virgin olive oil and sherry vinegar, and mix well. Sprinkle the spring onions and coriander over the dish.

Ensalada de lentejas con piquillos y anchoas
Lentil salad with *piquillo* peppers and anchovies

Ensalada de alubias, garbanzos, chorizo y alcachofas
Chorizo, artichoke, chickpea and bean salad

Good jarred or tinned lentils are fine for this and mean that you can make the salad quickly and easily. Sometimes, however, I find the tinned ones can be a little soft for salads, when you are tossing them with other ingredients, so when I have time I usually pre-prepare my own. If you want to do this, use 300g of Castilian green or dark Pardina lentils, or their equivalent. You don't need to soak them, just wash them well, put them into a pan together with a whole carrot, a small onion, a bay leaf and some peppercorns, cover with cold water, bring to the boil, then turn down the heat and simmer for about 20 minutes until tender. Drain and discard the vegetables, herbs and peppercorns.

When we had our shop in Exmouth Market we wanted to offer good, healthy food for people to take away, but we had virtually no kitchen space. So Scott Boden (see page 39) created a selection of salads such as this one, which could easily be assembled from the jarred beans and other ingredients on our shelves and in our fridges.

Serves 4

2 medium tomatoes
225g jarred white haricot beans, rinsed and drained
225g jarred chickpeas, rinsed and drained
1 spring onion, thinly sliced
½ a medium red onion, finely chopped
1 hot pickled *guindilla* pepper (see page 275), thinly sliced
120g artichoke hearts in oil or brine, drained and roughly chopped
100g cured *chorizo*, cut into small pieces
several sprigs of flat-leaf parsley, finely chopped

For the dressing
5 tablespoons good olive oil, such as Arbequina
1 tablespoon *fino* sherry
1 *piquillo* pepper (see page 275), with its juice
2 tablespoons good red wine vinegar, such as Cabernet Sauvignon
1 clove of garlic
a pinch of thyme leaves

Serves 4

1 tablespoon capers in brine or salt
400g good jarred or tinned lentils
6 *piquillo* peppers (see page 275), cut into strips
½ a red onion, sliced
3 tablespoons olive oil
1½ tablespoons good red wine vinegar, such as Cabernet Sauvignon
sea salt and freshly ground black pepper
12 anchovy fillets in oil
a handful of mixed fresh herbs, such as mint, chervil and parsley

Soak the capers in water for an hour, to remove the excess salt, changing the water twice, then drain.

Mix the lentils, peppers, onion and capers in a serving dish. Mix the oil and vinegar and use to dress the ingredients.

Season to taste with salt and pepper, bearing in mind that the anchovies and capers will also give salt to the dish. Lay the anchovies on top and sprinkle with the herbs.

Either grate the tomatoes or, if you prefer, de-skin and de-seed them (see page 206). Put the beans and chickpeas into a large bowl, add the onions, *guindilla* pepper, tomatoes, artichokes, *chorizo* and parsley and mix well, taking care not to break the beans.

For the dressing, blend all the ingredients well. Add to the mixture, turning well to coat.

Salmorejo de conejo al extremeño
Roasted rabbit and red pepper salad

This is a deconstructed version of the cold soup on page 149 which makes for a wonderful, fresh, succulent and colourful salad, perfect for summer, and shouldn't be confused with the similarly named *conejo al salmorejo*, which is a typical rabbit stew in the Canary Islands in which the meat is marinated in garlic, herbs and *pimentón* (paprika).

Ask your butcher to cut the rabbit into six, giving four legs and two loins, and keeping the lard from around the kidneys. Dotted on to the rabbit pieces, this will melt in the oven, keeping the meat succulent and moist and helping it to brown nicely.

The salad can be served warm or chilled – either way it is good with some country bread and a glass of dark, aromatic red wine from El Bierzo in the province of León.

Serves 4

1 farmed rabbit (around 1.6kg), cut into
  6 pieces (see above), plus the lard from
  around the kidneys
sea salt and freshly ground black pepper
½ teaspoon dried oregano
6 tablespoons olive oil
4 red peppers
1 head of garlic
1 medium tomato
4 spring onions
2 tablespoons sherry vinegar

Preheat the oven to 180°C/gas 4.

Put the rabbit pieces in a roasting pan and season with salt, pepper and the oregano. Break up the lard and dot some on each piece of rabbit, then drizzle with 2 tablespoons of the olive oil.

Put the peppers into an ovenproof dish and smear with another tablespoon of olive oil. Wrap the head of garlic in foil.

Put the roasting pan containing the rabbit, the dish of peppers and the foil-wrapped garlic into the preheated oven and leave all three for 20 minutes, until the rabbit is golden, the skins of the peppers have darkened and are beginning to char and the garlic is soft.

Halfway through the baking time, put the tomato into a separate dish and put into the oven for 10 minutes. Add the spring onions to the dish of peppers for the last 5 minutes.

Take everything out of the oven, cover the red peppers with a tea towel and let them sweat to make peeling them an easier task.

When cool enough to handle, strip the rabbit meat from the bones and put into a serving bowl. Peel the peppers, cut them into strips and add them to the rabbit. Peel the tomato and chop it finely, strip off the outer layers of the spring onions and slice diagonally, then add these two ingredients to the bowl. Peel 2 of the cloves of garlic and mash them with a fork, then add this pulp to the bowl, along with the rest of the whole roasted cloves.

Combine the rest of the olive oil and the sherry vinegar and toss through the salad. Taste, season with salt if necessary, and serve.

OLIVE OIL

'surely the best gift of Heaven'

Olive groves seem to bring out the philosopher and the romantic in their owners, perhaps because the olive tree is so elemental, its history so vast and its pace of life so slow that only poetry or fine prose can express the emotion of becoming its guardian. One inspirational olive grower, Joan Miralles of Finca Treurer in Mallorca (see page 217), likes to quote Thomas Jefferson on the subject: 'The olive tree is surely the best gift of Heaven.' And olive oil, says Joan, 'is an investment in health, a pleasure for the senses, a feast for the palate and balm for the soul'.

Often the most stunning olive oils, the ones that stand out against the crowd, are produced by people with a story to tell, and I think ultimately I make a connection with an oil when I know and relate to the people who make it, why they do it, where, and under what circumstances. Sometimes these are families making oil on a small, artisan scale in the most challenging circumstances; sometimes they are wine-makers, who can bring their skills of cultivation and blending (coupage) to a different fruit. Or they might be engineers or businessmen looking for a new way of life, who can combine old-fashioned methods and utter respect for the land with cutting-edge technology. For example, they might grow their olives in groves filled with wild flowers and grasses, irrigated only by rain water, then harvest them by hand, vibrating the trees and catching the fruit in an inverted umbrella to avoid bruising, before cold-pressing them in innovative, state-of-the-art mills.

Some of my favourite oils have the most lyrical of names that relate to their history; for example, in the Sierra de los Pedroches in Córdoba, Jesús Fernández de Castro and his wife, Tránsito Habas Sánchez, make an oil called 'Olivar de la Luna' – olive groves of the moon – which is a tribute to all the people who worked in extreme conditions in the previous three centuries to establish and nurture the olive groves in the tough, dry terrain of the remote and beautiful mountains. On nights of a full moon they would carry on working and the locals say that the leaves of the olive trees reflect the moonlight as a sign of appreciation.

Olive oil is quintessential to the Spanish table, vital for marinating, cooking and drizzling on to toasted bread, cured meats, cheeses, roasted vegetables, grilled fish, salads and soups. It is the essential ingredient of the classic garlic mayonnaise *alioli*, and is becoming more and more popular in sweet dishes, especially added to red fruits such as raspberries, strawberries and cherries, or used in ice cream, chocolate desserts and yogurts.

The average Spanish household gets through around 9.66 litres per capita of olive oil in a year, and Spain is the leading olive oil producer in the

world in terms of quantity (producing more than double that of Italy). However, if you compare the perception and appreciation of the oils from each country, both at home and abroad, there is a big gulf. In Spain olive oil is considered an all-purpose fat, and only around 30 per cent of the oil consumed is extra virgin. By contrast, in Italy 70 per cent is extra virgin, since it is revered as a delicate complement to exceptional dishes. On average Italians are prepared to pay two to three euros more per litre than the Spanish.

Until relatively recently most Spanish oil came from gigantic mills run on the principle of economy of scale, whereas in Italy there may be many more producers, but the majority are small estates whose image is of integrity and individuality.

In the UK, if there is a choice of Spanish or Italian oils on a supermarket shelf, the chances are most people will choose an Italian one. Although I like to think that at Brindisa we have helped to turn around this perception, there is still a long way to go, and it is a subject I have often discussed with Roberto Gracia of La Maja, the family mill where we produce our own-label pure varietal oils and blends.

Roberto believes Spanish oils are every bit as good as their Italian counterparts, but, while Italian producers have valued and marketed their oils supremely well, the Spanish have lagged behind. 'Even 30 years ago, if you went to a food trade fair the Italian brands already had a certain level of design, image and care taken with their product,' he says. 'They spent money on presentation, which cost them, but they valued their product because they were proud of the quality, so they put the little Italian flag on it. The Spanish went with plastic bottles, cheaply priced and badly presented, with ugly labels.'

Roberto went on to explain that many Spanish producers simply sold their oil to Italy in bulk to be bottled and marketed there, as they could make the same money as they would selling to the home public, but without the additional work of bottling the oil.

Over the last 15 years, however, a band of smaller Spanish producers have begun to take a leaf out of the Italian book, making high-quality characterful estate oils in smaller quantities, and taking care and time with the design of bottles and labels. As Roberto observes, however, it takes time to change the instinctive attitude of consumers who say, 'If I am going to pay your price, I would rather have an Italian oil.'

Frustrating as this can be, Spanish olive oil has come a huge way since I bought my first bottles from Núñez de Prado in 1990, the year that the estate achieved organic certification: a first in Spain. I had stopped off in Madrid on my way to Burgos to meet cheese-maker Ambrosio Molinos, and inevitably I went food shopping in the city, where I spotted these beautiful bottles with their informative labels. I bought some of the oil, tasted it, immediately called the telephone number on the bottles and spoke to Paco, the eldest of the Núñez de Prado brothers and head of the operation. We agreed that I should make my way south to Baena. Coincidentally, I was also interested in the cheeses made in a tiny dairy in the village of Zuheros nearby, so I managed to visit both producers, and only months later, I and my earliest Brindisa colleague, Emma Ranson, were selling both the oils and cheeses in London.

We knew that initially we would have to convince people to try the oil, since only a decade earlier the industry had been in real crisis after a consignment of *colza* oil, made from brassica seeds and meant to be used as an industrial oil, had found its way into street markets and was being sold as olive oil. It coincided with the sale of tomatoes that were over-fertilised with chemicals, and in households where these two contaminated ingredients came together, many people suffered toxic syndrome, and around 600 died. At that time Spanish tomatoes were a great source of income abroad, so it suited the authorities to divert blame from the tomato crops on to the oil alone.

It was against this backdrop of tainted reputation that Emma and I began selling our first bottles of Núñez de Prado. 'Are you sure this won't harm anyone?' was the inevitable question, but the fear faded once people got to know and trust this stunning oil, which we sell to this day. And over the years I have discovered many, many more exceptional Spanish oils, made by dedicated people who are championing local olives and sustainable or organic methods. I only wish I could bring all of them to Brindisa.

How to choose and store olive oil
Various indicators help to show the quality of an oil: for example, it might have a PDO (Protected Denomination of Origin) label, the bottles might be numbered as part of a limited production or notes on the bottle will state that methods satisfy environmental criteria. The best oils will usually be estate bottled, since this shows that the producers are involved in every step of the process, in which they will take great pride.

Ultimately, though, it is all about the organoleptic qualities of an oil, and the only way to find your favourite is through tasting. The correct way to taste an oil is to use a blue glass with no stem, which allows you to warm it in your cupped hands, and not be prejudiced by its colour before smelling or tasting. Breathe in the aromas deeply, then taste a small mouthful by pressing the oil to the top of your mouth with your tongue and then swilling it around gently and swallowing slowly. The sensations of aroma and flavour that you experience might be anything from apples to tropical fruit to freshly mown grass: the important thing is to find a character you like, but also that suits the way you want to use it.

When possible, look for new season oil and use it within its first year. Although you can keep oils longer, they don't improve with age like wines, and their potency and impact reduces over time.

Good oils are normally in dark bottles, to keep out the light in order to preserve the properties of the oil. If in doubt, keep your oil in a cupboard. These are notes on some of my favourites:

Núñez de Prado, Flor de Aceite and extra virgin olive oil
The pioneering Núñez de Prado brothers (see page 218) produce their wonderful oils in Córdoba in Andalucía. The three main varietals of olives grown on the estate are the floral Picual, Hojiblanca (for sweetness) and Picudo (robust and more bitter), which, when combined, give the oils their distinctive character.

The limited production *Flor de Aceite*, 'the flower of the oil', is pure, raw and unfiltered. Instead of being pressed, the olive paste is allowed to seep naturally through a mesh, so it retains all of its intense character. The precious oil from each olive variety is kept separately and then the *coupage* is made of all three, to give the right combination of spicy fruit flavours and peppery aftertaste. Finally, the oil is bottled by hand, unfiltered (so it has some sediment) in numbered bottles, each with a red wax seal. The remaining paste is sandwiched between round mats (sadly, the original and beautiful mats made from *esparto* grass have had to be replaced by regulation EU plastic ones that are easier to wash). Then it is pressed to make the extra virgin olive oil, with the temperature not exceeding 20°C, so none of its character is lost.

Both oils have similar qualities of intense aromas of Cox's apples, melons, passion fruit, papaya and a touch of lemon, and rich complex flavours of tropical fruit and herbs, and a good bitterness and pepperiness, which linger in the aftertaste of almonds and lemons. However, in the Flor de Aceite, these are more exaggerated.

Olivar de la Luna, Pozoblanco, Córdoba, organic single-estate extra virgin olive oil
An unfiltered green oil with golden hues made according to biodynamic techniques by Jesús Fernández de Castro and his wife, Tránsito Habas Sánchez, using native Nevadillo Blanco olives, supplemented by Lechín, Picudo or Manzanilla. The olives are stone-pressed immediately after harvest at room temperature, and the oil has an exceptionally pure flavour, rich in polyphenols,

antioxidants and vitamin E, with aromas of orange, spicy lemon and mango. It has a fruity taste with spicy nuances of apples, almonds and freshly cut grass, and is long, soft and sweet in the mouth, with a slightly bitter fruit flavour on the finish.

Marqués de Valdueza, Extremadura, estate-bottled extra virgin olive oil

Alonso, the Marqués de Valdueza, and his son Fadrique planted their olive groves with four varieties: the local Morisca, cultivated by the Romans who once inhabited Extremadura, the Hojiblanca, a variety grown in the neighbouring region of Andalucía, and the more widely grown Arbequina and Picual. These are harvested separately, pressed in the modern mill on the farm, and blended to give an elegant oil with a great balance between the aromas of mango and deeper tones of tomato leaves. It has a lovely creamy texture with sweet almond and cobnut flavours, and a walnut-skin bitterness on the finish with some gentle pepper.

Aubocassa, Manacor, Mallorca, single estate extra virgin olive oil

Owned by wine-makers Bodegas Roda of Rioja, the estate reflects the philosophy of a wine chateau applied to an olive grove, in that the oil is respected and treated as a fresh fruit juice that requires minimal processing to preserve its qualities. The oil has PDO status and is made solely from Arbequina olives, grown on a small family estate with an ancient Moorish farmhouse dating back to the twelfth century. The oil has citrus notes on the nose, with sharp apple, tomato, salad leaves, herbs and fennel, and flavours of almonds, dry hay and fresh vegetables, with a silky finish.

Casta Diva extra virgin olive oil, Parcent, Alicante

Produced by the Gutiérrez de la Vega wine-making family (see page 190). The olives – Picual, Grosal, some Blanqueta and a little Arbequina – are collected from sheltered groves in the area of La Marina Alta, pressed at a low temperature in a small stone mill in what was their original wine bodega, and the oil is bottled without filtering.

The early harvest oil is golden yellow in colour with green tones, rich on the nose with floral notes, eucalyptus, mint, basil and rosemary. Its taste is soft, with some sweetness on the palate and a peppery finish. The late harvest oil is pressed from double the quantity of olives, which produce a fresh-tasting, deep green oil with aromas of fennel and mint, and a flavour that is grassy and fruity, with subtle spicy and bitter notes and an intense finish.

La Maja, estate-bottled extra virgin olive oil, Mendavia, Navarra PDO

Brindisa and La Maja have a strong collaboration in that not only do we buy their premium estate oils, but our own-label pure varietal oils and blends are produced at their mill. Historically, the Gracia family were successful grape growers in Rioja; however, in 1977 the current generation, brothers Roberto (who studied chemistry and has a master's degree specialising in oils and fats), Mateo (in charge of the land), José Luís (an architect) and Carlos (an engineer), decided to give up the vineyards and pioneer the cultivation of olive trees in this fertile plain which is the highest olive-growing region in Spain. Here they developed a highly innovative and technically progressive olive oil operation dedicated to making a high-quality oil at an affordable price.

Their own estate-bottled extra virgin olive oil, produced from Arbequina olives, with 30 per cent of local Arróniz and 10 per cent of juicy, medium-sized Empeltre olives, is yellowish-green, with a clean, intense aroma, reminiscent of fresh green fruit, with banana-skin tones, tomato plant, grass, artichoke and apple, and a touch of kiwi, green coffee bean, almonds and caramel. These notes are reaffirmed in the flavour, which has a medium bitterness and a slight late 'bite'.

Treurer, Mallorca, Spain, extra virgin estate-bottled olive oil, PDO

Mallorca produces excellent oils, and when I first tasted this one from the tiny estate of Finca Treurer, I was bowled over by its floral nose.

Joan Miralles is a Mallorcan businessman who changed lifestyle from the tourism industry to olive oil when he bought the estate back in March 2000 and began planting Arbequina trees for this single varietal oil. Treurer means treasure in Mallorquín, which perfectly describes the result: liquid gold, noted for its sublime fragrance and medium-fruity flavour, reminiscent of green almonds, hazelnuts, tomato plant, artichoke, fennel and banana, with a touch of bitterness and moderate piquancy.

Ninou, Oleum Flumen, Lleida, Catalunya, extra virgin olive oil estate-bottled

The name Ninou comes from the Latin *annum novum* (new year) and reflects the idea of facing the different challenges that each harvest brings. The small production of numbered bottles is made by Martí Terés i Ríos, who supplements the olives from his own groves by working with a tight selection of local growers. The olives are predominantly Arbequina, with a small percentage of local Vera and Salze Fulla, all of which are harvested manually in the traditional manner. The oil is a deep straw yellow, with fruity aromas of ripe green olives which give way to notes of green grass, tomato, avocado, banana, green almond, artichoke, fennel and green walnuts. The flavour is intense, but with an elegant balance on the palate, a long finish and a sweet and nutty aftertaste.

Vea, Lleida, Catalunya, early harvest

The fourth generation of the Vea family to be producing oil is Gerard, who along with his father, Avelino, runs their mill in the little village of Sarroca de Lleida, which is surrounded by 200-year-old olive trees, all of the local Arbequina variety, some of which are harvested in late October or early November to produce this oil. Although the Arbequina is a quite high-yielding variety, when picked this early the harvest is small, but the quality is very high and the oil is particularly aromatic and flavourful.

Aromas of smoky olives mingle with light dried herbs and some deeper earthier tones, and attractive nutty flavours combine with the freshness of green apple skins, balanced by a long finish of gentle pepper.

The Oils of Núñez de Prado

'The earliest and purest memory I have is the smell of freshly prepared olives on entering the mill with my father,' says Francisco Núñez de Prado (known as Paco), whose family's oils are made in Baena, in the province of Córdoba in Andalucía. 'It was a smell full of fragrance, innocence and purity and it is engraved forever in my memory. My dream is that the paradise of the olive grove, the greatest magical forest planted in the history of mankind, becomes a kind of cultural and geographical heritage, because it is a source of wealth and health and helps to prevent desertification. My dream is that it becomes almost eternal, that this landscape will not change and that it will always be a source of human nutrition.'

Núñez de Prado was the first olive oil to receive organic certification in Spain in 1990. Although the estate has produced olive oil since 1795, it wasn't until 1986 that the three brothers – Paco, Andrés and Felipe, the seventh generation of the family – made the bold move to pioneer high-quality organic oil.

It was the late Andrés, an agricultural engineer, who recognised that the increased use of pesticides in Spanish agriculture left a residue in the olives, and so he drove the conversion to organic farming, bringing together traditional techniques and innovative technology in order to nurture the land and crops that he and his brothers had inherited. Now the estate is recognised all over the world for the family's dedication to purity and perfection, and they have achieved PDO (Protected Denomination of Origin) status, but in 1990 this was the first time that the family had exported their oils, and I felt we shared the same pioneering spirit, and a similar ethic of mutual respect for the chain that links land, farmers, suppliers and customers.

The *almazara* (oil mill) is on the edge of Baena town, and a painting of Santa Lucía, patron saint of the mill, greets you as you pass under the arched entrance into a vast courtyard, surrounded by whitewashed buildings where the oil is produced and stored. Nowadays visitors come every year to see the groves, taste the oils and enjoy a traditional miller's breakfast of olive oil, oranges and honey, or lunch of a variety of dishes, all laced with estate oil.

The qualities of a good oil are mostly defined by the land in which the olives grow. All the way through the process, producers have to make decisions according to the philosophy they have chosen for their crop and their business, and it is out in the groves that the Prado brothers really come alive. At heart they are farmers, from a long line of farmers, and the land is what they know and love. Instead of ploughing the groves, which can cause soil erosion, they allow wild grasses and flowers to grow and only cut these back manually once a year, near the base of the trees. The cuttings are then left as a mulch to capture rain and retain moisture.

The belief is that every small detail contributes to great oil, so the trees are trimmed by a skilled pruner, one of a long line of pruners who have worked only for the estate. A good pruner looks to protect the tree bark from the sun, to keep the height moderate, so that the sap can reach across the width as well as the height of the branches, and to balance the trees' shape, size and density to allow the olives to fall easily through the branches at harvest time. The trimmed branches are left where they fall, as, like the cut grasses, they help to retain the humidity of the soil.

The olives are picked by hand with a 'milking motion', to avoid bruising, then washed in the groves to remove leaves and twigs, which go into natural compost to feed the trees. Then, since speed is of the essence, in order to retain the highest properties of the olives, they are mashed within three hours of picking, using the traditional granite cones first introduced by the Romans. From here the resulting paste goes to make the mill's finest *Flor de Aceite* and cold-pressed extra virgin olive oil (see page 215).

Everything that the olives have to give is maximised. After the oils have been produced the paste is sold off and sent away so that plain olive oil can be extracted from it. A further treatment produces characterless pomace oil, and finally the leftover pulp and olive stones are compressed into slow-burning stones which are used for fuel. On patios and in restaurants you can see these being used in the ingenious *mesas de camilla* – round tables which have a shelf at foot level, with a round hole cut in the centre, in which, during the winter, a wok-like pan of the coals gives out a smokeless heat. The tables are draped in heavy cloths, and you sit with your feet tucked underneath, resting on the shelf and keeping snug and toasty.

TAPAS CALIENTES

Hot tapas
and other
small plates

SOPAS CALIENTES
Hot soups

There is a Valencian name I love, *sopa cubierta* ('pantry' soup), which to me sums up the way that simple soups, often served before or alongside other small plates, are very much a part of day-to-day eating in Spain. Few, except for some fish soups which border on stews, are very elaborate.

At one time bars and cafés would always have a bowl of stock on the counter, often made with a ham bone, so that people could take a cup or bowlful to warm them up on an icy day, and many soups are little more than that: good stock, perhaps with some *fideo* (fine noodles), cooked beans or chickpeas added; quite basic, though very healthy, such as *sopa de farigola*, Catalan thyme soup. Essentially, it is crunchy bread soaked and then whisked in hot water, and infused with branches of thyme, garlic cloves and a pinch of salt. Sometimes an egg is added or whisked into the soup before pouring into bowls. Sounds easy, but like so many supposedly simple things it is deceptive: thyme that isn't properly aromatic or bread that is too soft, for example, can easily spoil it.

Castilian garlic soup is a similar quintessential and inexpensive bowl of sustenance that is entirely dependent on good stock to carry the flavour, and is usually served over a poached egg, which you break up and mix in as you eat. However, you will find more sophisticated contemporary versions, for example garnished with slices of fried *chorizo* or *panceta*, and a handful of parsley for colour. In its traditional form it is a soup I have often eaten with our friends Ambro and Asun and their family in Pedrosa de Duero (see page 154), and if any was left over, by the next morning the bread would have absorbed all the stock, making it thick enough to slice, so Ambro would have it this way for breakfast with a glass of wine!

Potaje de berros
Gomeran watercress,
bean and potato soup

The interior of the island of Gomera, the second smallest of the Canaries, is very damp, so watercress grows in abundance, which comes as a real surprise when all you see at first is beach.

On Gomera this dish is considered a *potaje* (stew), but although the watercress is bolstered with potatoes and beans, and the *panceta* and chicken stock give a meatiness to the base flavours, it is still quite light, so I think of it as a soup. If you use vegetable stock and omit the *panceta* it makes a good dish for non-meat-eaters, too.

I first came across it some years ago on a family holiday. On a tropical morning we hiked for about three hours through the shade of the damp green forest of the Parque de Garajonay, with its moss-velvet trees, until we came to a valley filled with mist and found a little lodge where we were served the *potaje* in wooden bowls, like lengths of little hollowed-out tree trunks.

It is easiest to use good, jarred beans, drained, or tinned ones, well rinsed. However, if you want to cook your own dried beans, leave 100g to soak in water overnight, then rinse them, put them in a pan with copious amounts of cold water, bring them to a simmer and cook for 1–2 hours – you can add a piece of pork belly, an onion and a bouquet garni for flavour if you like. When the beans are tender, drain off the excess water.

Make sure you remove any green shoots from the garlic to avoid bitterness.

Serves 4

50g *panceta*, cut into lardons
1 tablespoon olive oil
2 cloves of garlic, finely chopped
200g potatoes, peeled and diced (about 1cm)
sea salt
1 litre cold *caldo de pollo*
  (dark chicken stock, see page 468)
250g watercress, roughly chopped
250g cooked beans, preferably *alubias*
  (white beans)

Put the lardons into a dry pan and fry until they release their fat and become crispy, then lift out and keep to one side. Add the olive oil to the same pan, stirring it into the hot fat released by the *panceta*, and when hot add the garlic, letting it sweat briefly.

Before the garlic turns golden, add the potatoes with a pinch of salt to help them sweat along with the garlic. The potatoes don't need to brown either, so keep stirring them around the pan for 4 minutes, just to allow them to become coated in oil and garlic.

Pour in the chicken stock and, keeping the pan on a medium heat, simmer until the potatoes are cooked through. Add the watercress and cook on a low heat for a further 5 minutes.

Spoon around half of the soup into a bowl and purée with a hand blender, then return this to the pan, add the cooked beans and heat through over a medium heat for a couple more minutes. Taste and season with salt if necessary, bearing in mind that the stock will have its own saltiness, and if you are using jarred beans they will have been kept in brine, so the soup may not need more salt.

Pour the soup into bowls, garnish with the reserved lardons and serve hot.

Crema de calabaza y castañas
Chestnut and pumpkin soup

La castañada is the chestnut festival that is celebrated in the first week of November in many villages of Spain. The nuts are often roasted and served with grilled *chorizo* washed down with cider, young wine or Moscatel, as well as being used to make soup, since the chestnut and pumpkin season coincide.

Make sure you select pumpkin or squash with brightly coloured flesh, so that when blended with the chestnuts the soup keeps as much vibrancy as possible.

Serves 4

4 tablespoons olive oil
20g butter
400g pumpkin or butternut squash, chopped, around 1cm
1 small onion, chopped, around 1cm
1 carrot, chopped, around 1cm
1 stick of celery, chopped, around 1cm
sea salt
around 600–750ml hot *caldo vegetal* or *caldo de pollo* (vegetable or dark chicken stock, see pages 466–468)
400g peeled and cooked chestnuts, chopped
3 tablespoons double cream (optional)
2 tablespoons chopped parsley

Heat the olive oil and butter over a high flame in a large pan, and when the butter has melted and begun to sizzle add the vegetables. Stir until they begin to turn a light golden colour, then turn down the heat to low, add a pinch of salt and allow to sweat uncovered for 10 minutes, checking regularly to make sure the vegetables are still *al dente* – don't let them overcook.

Pour in 400ml of the hot stock together with 400ml of water, and add most of the chopped chestnuts, reserving a few for the garnish.

Bring to the boil, then turn down to a simmer for 5 minutes to heat the chestnuts through and finish cooking the vegetables. Taste and season if necessary, then blend, using a hand blender.

The chestnuts will act as a thickener and turn the soup a brown colour. Add another 200ml of hot stock, bring back up a simmer, and add the double cream, if using – this will lighten both the colour and texture of the soup and bring out the creamy flavours of pumpkin and chestnut.

If the soup feels a bit too dense (some chestnuts absorb the liquid more than others), add more hot stock and serve immediately, garnished with the reserved chopped chestnuts and the parsley.

Menestra de verduras
Spring vegetable bowl

Menestra de verduras is often served in little bowls in fashionable Madrid bars, but probably the best I have ever had was made for me by Raúl Domingo, when I stayed with him and his family in the city. Raúl is a history lecturer, his wife, Carmen, a photographer, lecturer and archivist, and their student daughter Livia is a jazz and classical violinist. The shelves of their home groan with incredible books and the walls are covered with extraordinary paintings, and when it comes to food, Raúl is in charge of the kitchen and his cooking is excellent. While I was writing up recipe notes he brought me a Madrid tapa of fine crisps and *escabeche* mussels (see page 111) and then a little bowlful of this light, delicious, nutritious *menestra*.

The key is in the initial brief and individual blanching of the green vegetables, apart from the courgette, which is fried. It may seem a lot of fuss, but it really is worth it, so that you keep all the flavour, texture, bite and particularly the bright colour of each vegetable. You can use frozen peas – but full-sized ones, not petits pois,

Serves 4

2 small eggs
2 small-medium artichokes
250g fresh or frozen garden peas
150g Brussels sprouts
6 green asparagus spears
100g fresh broad beans
2 tablespoons olive oil
2 spring onions, white parts only, chopped
2 cloves of garlic, chopped
2 carrots, sliced
1 courgette, cut lengthways, central
  seed part scooped out, cut into slices
1 aubergine, chopped, around 1cm
sea salt and freshly ground black pepper
250g *tacos* (see page 175) of Serrano ham
½ tablespoon plain flour
1 tablespoon chopped parsley
6 mint leaves
2 red *piquillo* peppers from a jar,
  cut into thin slices

Put the eggs into a pan of cold water and bring to a simmer gently so that the shells don't crack, then cook gently for 10 minutes. Drain and run under cold water, then peel and keep to one side.

Trim and quarter the artichokes (see page 350).

Have ready a bowl of iced water. Blanch the green vegetables one at a time. Boil the peas in 2 litres of salted water for about a minute, then lift out with a sieve and put into the iced water. Cook the Brussels sprouts in the same water for about 3 minutes, until just tender, then lift out with the sieve again and add to the bowl of iced water.

Repeat the process with the asparagus, cooking the spears for about 2 minutes, the artichokes, for 3 minutes, and finally add the broad beans, for about 2 minutes. Keep back 1 litre of the cooking liquid and discard the rest.

Heat the olive oil in a deep sauté or frying pan and add the onions, garlic, carrots, courgette and aubergine. Season and cook gently until soft but not coloured. Add the ham and cook briefly, then sprinkle in the flour and move everything gently around the pan, so that the flour brings the vegetables together, but take care not to burn it. Add a little of the reserved vegetable cooking water and cook briefly to thicken the liquid a little.

Drain all the green vegetables from the bowl of ice through a colander and add to the pan, stir well, then add the parsley and the rest of the reserved vegetable stock. Bring to the boil, then turn down the heat and simmer gently, uncovered, for about 10 minutes, until all the vegetables are just tender and the stock is slightly thickened and aromatic.

Taste and correct the seasoning if necessary, and add the mint leaves just before serving. Serve in a big shallow dish, topped with the *piquillo* peppers and slices of the reserved hard-boiled eggs.

Porrusalda de la casa
Brindisa vegetable broth
with salt cod and fennel

This is a lovely, wholesome and light broth which
in Spain is often made just with garlic, leeks,
onions, squash and potatoes. However, when our
head chef, Leo, decided to put it on the menu at
Casa Brindisa, he added some fennel and salt
cod and people love it. The quality of the stock
is important, so it is worth making your own.

Serves 4

3 tablespoons olive oil
4 cloves of garlic, finely sliced
2 leeks, sliced quite chunkily
1 medium onion or 1 shallot, sliced quite chunkily
¼ of a butternut squash, peeled and
  roughly chopped
1 bulb of fennel, sliced
2 large potatoes, roughly chopped
1.25 litres hot *caldo vegetal* (vegetable stock,
see page 466)
200g de-salted cod (optional) – ideally
  an inexpensive cut such as *cola* (tail),
  ***migas* (crumbs) or *tacos* (chunks)**
  (see pages 329–330)
sea salt and freshly ground black pepper

Heat the oil gently in a large pan, add the garlic
and cook for a couple of minutes until softened
but not coloured, then add the leeks and onion
or shallot and cook for 3 minutes. Add the squash
and fennel and continue to cook for another
3 minutes. Finally, add the potatoes and let
everything cook gently for 10 minutes until
lightly coloured.

Add the hot stock, cover the pan and simmer
over a medium heat for 20 minutes.

Meanwhile, if adding de-salted cod, blanch it in
a pan of boiling water for about 3 minutes, then
drain under the cold tap – just until the fish
is cool enough to handle. Put it on a chopping
board, remove the skin, and flake carefully to find
and remove any bones. Add the flakes to the soup
5 minutes before the end of the cooking time.
Season to taste and serve.

Sopa de pescado
Fish soup

This is an amazing, light soup made with prawns and squid and a delicate *fumet* (fish stock) whose flavours are beautifully balanced by the sweetness of the carrot and the acidity of the tomatoes. We owe the recipe to Sandra Salcedo, chef and daughter of José Salcedo, of Navarrico in Navarra, who prepare superb jarred vegetables and *piquillo* peppers, and with whom we have worked for almost 25 years.

Serves 4

4 tablespoons olive oil
½ an onion, finely chopped
100g tomatoes, grated
sea salt
100g squid, cut into 2cm pieces (or squid rings)
1 small potato, chopped, around 1cm
1 carrot, coarsely grated
1 litre *fumet blanco* (white fish stock,
**   see page 466), at room temperature**
200g peeled prawns, cut into 2cm pieces
1 tablespoon chopped parsley

Heat the oil in a deep pan or casserole on a low to medium heat. Add the onion, stir and leave to sweat for 2 minutes. Mix in the tomato and a pinch of salt, coating the tomato in oil and onion and allowing the mixture to continue sweating for 4 more minutes.

Add the squid and stir into the other ingredients, then fry over a medium heat until the squid and onion just start to brown.

Add the potato and carrot, stirring and frying for 2 more minutes, then pour in 200ml of the stock, stir and turn up the heat, mixing the juices from the bottom of the pan into the stock. Pour the remaining stock into the pan and bring gently back to the boil. Turn down the heat, skim off any froth with a spoon, and simmer until the potato is cooked through.

Take the pan from the heat and add the pieces of prawn. Leave the soup to rest for 5 minutes, which will allow the prawn pieces to cook through in the hot liquid while preserving their texture and flavour. Taste and season with a little more salt if necessary.

Serve immediately in soup bowls, sprinkled with parsley.

Gambas al ajillo
Large garlic and chilli prawns

SEAFOOD

This is one of the all-time favourite combinations in our tapas bars and restaurants. There is something irresistible about the smell of the chilli and garlic sizzling in the hot terracotta dishes. Buy the biggest and best prawns or langoustines you can afford.

Serves 4

20 tiger prawns or langoustines, fresh, or if frozen, defrosted
extra virgin olive oil
5 cloves of garlic, sliced
3 dried *guindilla* peppers (see page 275), finely chopped, or 2 teaspoons crushed chilli
a pinch of sea salt
a little chopped parsley

Remove the heads and shells from the prawns, but leave the tails on. Heat 2.5cm of olive oil in a flat-bottomed heatproof terracotta dish or a frying pan and once very hot put in the garlic and chilli. Sauté briefly, then add the prawns. Cook on one side for 90 seconds, then turn over and cook for another 40 seconds – that is all you need, as the prawns will continue to cook after you take the terracotta dish/pan from the heat.

Scatter with sea salt and chopped parsley and serve immediately, straight from the terracotta dish/pan.

Calamar frito al pimentón
Fried squid with paprika

In summer, rather than deep-fry the squid, you could barbecue it, without the floured coating, and serve it with this quick, fresh, slightly spicy sauce.

Serves 1–2 people

200g cleaned squid
100g wholemeal flour, for coating
500ml vegetable oil, for deep-frying
sea salt and freshly ground black pepper
½ teaspoon *pimentón de la Vera dulce*
   (sweet smoked paprika)

For the dressing
1 tablespoon olive oil
2 cloves of garlic, finely sliced
2 spring onions, sliced
1 fresh large red chilli, finely sliced
a pinch of chopped parsley leaves

To make the dressing, heat the oil in a pan, add the garlic and cook gently until it just begins to turn golden, then add the spring onions and cook for another 1–2 minutes. Lift out the garlic and onions with a slotted spoon and reserve, take the pan off the heat, let the oil cool down, then mix in the chilli and parsley, so that they coat in the cooling oil. Mix in the reserved garlic and onions and keep to one side.

Cut the squid into 1cm strips and have the flour ready in a shallow bowl.

Pass the strips of squid through the flour. Heat the oil in a pan, making sure it comes no higher than a third of the way up. If you have a thermometer it should be 180°C, otherwise drop in a few breadcrumbs, and if they sizzle the oil is hot enough.

Put in the squid and fry until golden and crispy, lift out, drain on kitchen paper, then season.

Arrange on a plate, drizzle with the dressing, and finish with a sprinkling of *pimentón*.

Tortilleta de camarones
Crisp little shrimp pancakes

I had these wonderful, elegant morsels served as a tapa when I was staying at the Posada Rural Ríoturbio, a country house hotel outside Comillas in Cantabria. Crisp, lacy and golden, they almost snap when you break them to find the fragments of shrimp inside (you can also use prawns). The secret to the crunch is the chickpea flour.

Makes around 15

55g chickpea flour
1 teaspoon bicarbonate of soda
½ teaspoon salt
½ teaspoon *pimentón picante*
   (hot paprika) (optional)
200g peeled shrimps, chopped
1 spring onion, white only, chopped
   very, very finely
3 tablespoons very finely chopped parsley
2 cloves of garlic, very finely chopped
vegetable oil, for frying

Put the flour and bicarbonate of soda into a bowl and slowly add about 130ml of water, mixing until you have a creamy, pancake-like batter. Season with salt and paprika, if using, then put into the fridge to chill for about 30 minutes.

Mix the shrimps with the onion, parsley and garlic, then add to the batter.

Pour enough oil into a large frying pan to give a depth of around 7mm. When medium-hot, fry in batches, taking dessertspoonfuls of the batter and dropping them carefully into the oil, quickly spreading the batter out so that it flattens and becomes lace-like and crispy as it fries. Turn each *tortilleta* once, until light golden on each side. Lift out, drain on kitchen paper and eat straight away.

PIMENTÓN

'colour and flavouring'

Along with Hungary, Spain produces and consumes the most paprika (*pimentón*) in Europe. It is added to soups and stews; it provides the colour and flavouring for chorizo, and it is ubiquitous as a condiment, often sprinkled on eggs or salads for colour or used in dressings and dry marinades.

So it is sometimes easy to forget that the spice didn't actually exist until the end of the seventeenth century, since peppers, from which *pimentón* is made, only arrived in Spain with Christopher Columbus in the sixteenth century. They were first cultivated by monks at the Monastery of Yuste in Cáceres, Extremadura, and by the end of the seventeenth century it was realised that they could also be smoke-dried and that their skins, and sometimes seeds and veins, could be ground to make a spice. Once discovered, *pimentón* began to be used as a seasoning and marinade for almost every dish in Spain, as well as for colouring and flavouring sausages and other meats. The main production centred around La Vera in Extremadura, and at first the peppers were ground in water-powered flour mills; however, once electricity arrived in La Vera, production grew and improved significantly.

The species of the Capsicum genus from which *pimentón* is made is *Capsicum annuum*, which includes fruit spanning from the large mild Bola varietals through to the bittersweet *Capsicum longum* and the smaller hot Ocales, each of which produce *pimentón* of different character and heat from *dulce* (sweet and mild) to *picante* (quite sharp and hot). You might also see *agridulce* (bittersweet and medium hot), and cooks in different regions will select the style best suited to the dish they are preparing. While *dulce* and *agridulce* tend to be the most popular around Spain, as they give a dish good balance without being too fierce, hotter varieties are favoured in the Canary Islands, Galicia and Extremadura.

The ripeness of the fruit, the soil and climate in which they are grown, and the production method all help determine the character and quality of the finished spice. A paprika producer will want his peppers to be well ripened in good fertile soil, then selected carefully before the process of drying, using smoke, sun or air, begins. Preferably this will be done slowly, since if the peppers are overheated or dried too quickly the paprika can be bitter and the colour very dark.

The two main styles are *pimentón de La Vera* from Extremadura and *pimentón de Murcia*.

Pimentón de La Vera
Protected and watered by the Sierra de Gredos mountains, the privileged pepper fields of La Vera produce excellent fruit, which is harvested

at the end of the summer and usually smoke-dried on the farmers' holdings. The gentle process harks back to the seventeenth century and takes about two weeks, during which time the water content of the peppers is reduced from about 80 per cent to 15 per cent before the fruit is ground in stone mills.

Look out for the DOP label and the typical oblong tins which are beautifully lithographed.

Pimentón de La Vera paprikas have a deep smoky flavour and their colours can vary from coppery to dark red. They suit bolder dishes such as game, meat and potatoes and of course are used in the cures for *chorizo*.

There are three styles: *dulce* (mild) has a sweet flavour and is made primarily from Bola and Jaranda pepper varietals. *Agridulce*, or *ocal*, is a semi-sweet paprika with a touch of heat on the finish made from Jaranda and Jariza varietals. *Picante* is hot paprika made mainly from Jeromín, Jariza and Jaranda varietals.

Pimentón de Murcia

This orangey-red paprika from the Mediterranean coast is ground predominantly from the Bola family of peppers: small, round, bright red, aromatic and sweet with a good fruity flavour. They are either dried for a few days under the sun or in warm air chambers for 8–10 hours. The sun-dried peppers will be redder and more aromatic. Once dried, the fruit is stone-ground to a fine powder which has a fresh, almost tomatoey flavour, well suited to the more delicate dishes of this coastline where rice, vegetables and fish predominate.

This paprika also comes in hot, mild and *agridulce*/bittersweet versions.

How to buy, store and use *pimentón*

Jars of the generic spice with no country of origin will be a mix of paprikas of different origin and may not offer the best quality.

The spice starts to deteriorate almost as soon as it has been ground, so buy it in small quantities and store it in an airtight container, so it is out of the light.

The colour of the paprika will vary according to the style and some will be more or less ground. The aroma, however, should always overwhelm your senses. If it is dusty or flat it has been sitting on a shelf too long.

Be careful not to overheat the spice when adding to hot oil, especially, as it burns easily and can turn bitter.

Tiras de calamar con judías verdes
Squid strips with green beans

Esperanza Añonuevo Heys, who was our chef at Tapas Brindisa until her first child was born, created this beautiful, colourful combination.

Serves 4

600g squid tubes, cleaned and opened out
400g French green beans
sea salt
4 tablespoons olive oil
4 cloves of garlic, sliced
1 dried red *guindilla* pepper
(see page 275), sliced
2 tablespoons red wine vinegar,
preferably Cabernet Sauvignon

Cut the squid tubes into strips about 4cm long and 0.5cm wide.

Cut the beans into lengths of a similar size to the squid, then blanch in boiling salted water for a minute or two – they should still be crunchy. Drain under the cold tap to halt the cooking, then make a slit along each bean lengthways and open out like a book – this will help them to absorb the flavours when you add them to the squid, garlic and sliced pepper.

Heat the oil in a pan, add the garlic and squid, and then the slices of pepper. Sauté briefly until they all colour a little. Then add the beans and toss all together until the beans are heated through. Add the vinegar and continue to heat through for 1 minute more.

Serve with good bread to mop up the juices.

Pulpo a la gallega
Octopus Galician-style

Our executive chef, Josep, cooks whole octopus for this, using a technique that he calls *asustar el pulpo*: scaring the octopus. He fills a large pan to just over halfway with water, adds the carrots, shallots and peppercorns, then brings it to the boil and dunks in the octopus with the head upright, counts to ten and lifts it out, drains off the water, then repeats the process twice more. This helps to soften and curl the tentacles, and after the final dunking the octopus will have visibly shrunk. Finally, he removes the tentacles (the head can be kept for a seafood salad), returns them to the pan and cooks them as in the recipe below.

For ease, however, I have suggested you buy ready-prepared octopus.

Serves 6–8

2 carrots
2 shallots
4 peppercorns
about 400g raw, frozen octopus pieces
200g whole baby potatoes
1 tablespoon *pimentón dulce* (mild paprika)
3–4 tablespoons olive oil, for drizzling
a pinch of sea salt (optional)

Bring a pan of water to the boil, add the carrots, shallots and peppercorns, put in the octopus, turn down to a simmer and leave to cook gently for 40–45 minutes, until tenderised (check by pricking the chunky parts of the tentacles). Lift out with a slotted spoon, and cut the tentacles into 1cm slices. Reserve the pan of cooking water, but discard the vegetables and peppercorns.

Cook the potatoes in the same water for 20–25 minutes, or until just tender, then cut in half lengthways and arrange in a serving dish with the octopus slices on top.

Sprinkle with the *pimentón* and drizzle with olive oil and a light scattering of sea salt, if you like (remember, though, that the octopus will be quite salty).

Chipirones al romesco
Baby squid in *romesco* sauce

Romesco sauce is typically served on the side of barbecued or pan-fried squid, octopus or cuttlefish, but in this recipe, which uses baby squid (*chipirones*), the ingredients are all cooked together to create a warming, homely little stew which is thickened at the end with a *picada* (see page 320), in this case a paste of crushed fried bread, nuts and sautéd garlic. Traditionally, the stew would be made in a *barro*, or clay pot.

If *chipirones* aren't available, you can use small squid (*calamares*), up to about 6cm. It's best to get the fishmonger to remove the black ink sac for you, while keeping the little tentacles intact and in place.

Serves 4

4 *ñora* peppers (see page 280)
3–4 ripe tomatoes
3 tablespoons olive oil
3 cloves of garlic, peeled
1kg *chipirones*, or small squid, cleaned
  (about 1.5kg uncleaned)
250ml *fumet rojo* (red fish stock,
  see page 468)
1 tablespoon sherry vinegar

For the picada
1 medium slice of country bread without
  crust, fried in olive oil until golden,
  then drained on kitchen paper
15g toasted hazelnuts, chopped
15g blanched almonds, preferably Marcona,
  toasted in a dry pan and chopped
2 tablespoons olive oil

Soak the peppers in warm water for 30 minutes, then scrape out the flesh and set aside, keeping the skins too.

Either grate the tomatoes, or, if you prefer, de-skin and de-seed them (see page 206).

Heat a little oil in a deep pan or casserole, put in the whole pepper skins and garlic cloves and cook gently until coloured, then lift out, discard the pepper skins and keep the garlic to one side for the *picada*. Keep the pan ready to cook the squid.

If you are using *calamares*, open them out and score them with a sharp knife diagonally in one direction and then the other to form a diamond pattern, making sure you don't cut all the way through (*chipirones* don't need scoring). Put the pan back on the heat, and when hot add the *chipirones* or *calamares* and fry quickly until coloured on all sides. Remove from the pan and keep to one side.

Add the chopped tomatoes to the pan and cook for 10 minutes until softened, then add the reserved pepper flesh, the *chipirones* or *calamares* and the stock and leave to simmer for 10 minutes, until reduced by half.

To make the *picada*, break up the slice of fried bread and either pound with the nuts and reserved garlic, using a pestle and mortar, or pulse in a blender, then add the olive oil a little at a time until you have a rough paste. Add the picada to the stew to further thicken the sauce, and then at the final moment stir in the vinegar.

Sardinas fritas con pipirrana
Pan-fried sardines with *pipirrana*

Pipirrana is a refreshing combination of tomatoes, onions, peppers and hard-boiled eggs which balances out the stronger flavour of the pan-fried sardines very well.

Serves 4

2 eggs
1 onion, chopped very small, about 2–3mm
2 tomatoes, grated
1 green pepper, chopped
** very small, about 2–3mm**
½ a cucumber, central seeds removed
** and chopped very small, about 2–3mm**
seasoned flour
4 fresh medium sardines, butterflied
2 tablespoons olive oil
a handful of micro herbs, such as
** purple radish, to garnish (optional)**

For the dressing
1 tablespoon good-quality sherry vinegar
3 tablespoons olive oil
sea salt and freshly ground black pepper

Put the eggs into cold water and bring to a simmer gently so that the shells don't crack, then cook gently for 10 minutes. Drain and run under cold water, then peel and chop finely.

In a bowl, mix the onion, tomato, pepper, cucumber and hard-boiled eggs. Mix the dressing ingredients and add to the bowl, toss all together and leave to marinate in the fridge for an hour.

Have the seasoned flour in a shallow bowl, and coat each sardine in it. Heat the olive oil in a pan and fry the sardines for no more than 2 minutes on each side until golden.

Serve the sardines with the *pipirrana* alongside, and garnish, if you like, with micro herbs.

Filetes de anchoa con brócoli, migas de pan y huevo
Anchovies with sprouting broccoli, fried egg, breadcrumbs and smoked anchovy dressing

This is a recipe from our friends at the Dehesa tapas bar in London, who reckon that the metallic-tasting sprouting broccoli combined with the salty umami of the anchovies is a match made in heaven. They dry out the salted anchovies until they are brittle, so that their flavour is intensified, and when they are mixed with the *migas* (breadcrumbs), they give a crunch to the tapa. As well as salted anchovies, they use quite sweet and subtle beech-smoked anchovies, combined with sweet wine vinegar in the dressing.

Serves 4 with other tapas

400g sprouting broccoli, trimmed of any woody ends and cut into bite-size florets
olive oil, for frying
sea salt and freshly ground black pepper
2 eggs

For the migas
2 whole salted anchovies
100g fresh breadcrumbs
olive oil
1 clove of garlic, sliced

For the smoked anchovy dressing
5 smoked anchovy fillets
1 small shallot, finely chopped
50ml Moscatel vinegar
lemon juice, to taste
100ml extra virgin olive oil

For the *migas*, rinse and dry the salted anchovies, then split each one in two and carefully remove the backbone (see page 126) so that you have 4 fillets. Chop these finely and mix with the breadcrumbs. Place on a tray and put in a cool dry place, such as the oven on its lowest temperature, for 3–4 hours to dry out until crisp.

Take a medium pan and pour in enough olive oil to cover the surface. Add the dried-out anchovies and breadcrumbs, together with the garlic, and cook over a medium heat until the breadcrumbs are lightly browned. Season well and drain on kitchen paper.

Bring a pan of salted water to the boil and blanch the broccoli florets for 3–4 minutes, then refresh in cold water, drain and keep to one side.

For the dressing, chop the smoked anchovies and mix with the shallot. Pour the vinegar over and add a squeeze of lemon juice. Pour on the extra virgin olive oil. Mix everything together well, season to taste, and keep to one side.

Put the drained broccoli in a sauté pan with some oil and warm through over a medium heat. Transfer to a serving bowl. Season well, then spoon the smoked anchovy dressing over the top.

Heat a small non-stick pan over a medium heat and add a lug of olive oil. Crack the eggs into the pan and lightly fry them, ensuring the yolks are still runny. Season and place on top of the broccoli and anchovy dressing. Spoon the anchovy crumbs over the top and serve, breaking up the eggs as you do so.

CROQUETAS Y BUÑUELOS
Croquettes and fritters

I know people in London who are *croqueta* obsessives and have been around every Spanish restaurant or bar, trying them out, comparing notes and looking for new variations on the typical chicken and/or ham recipe, which is traditionally a way of finishing up leftover pieces of meat from the Sunday *cocido* (stew). Done well, these little croquettes, made with thick, creamy béchamel paste, coated in breadcrumbs and deep-fried, can be wonderful, and in Spain every good cook feels they are going to be judged on how well they can make them – though it is equally acceptable to buy them ready-made from a good food shop. Whenever you get a bunch of chefs together they will argue over the precise detail – inevitably, of course, each one will insist that their mother makes the ultimate *croqueta*. I always find that quite funny, as for me there is something deliciously sinful about *croquetas*, and my own mother would never have fed us such a thing: far too rich, heavy and fatty!

I have eaten every style of *croqueta*, from delicate, sophisticated ones in the sixteenth-century Echaurren Hotel in Ezcaray in Rioja, to miniature versions with roasted partridge and quail meat made by our friends at the Núñez de Prado oil mill in the Sierra Madre, and massive hearty ones at Café Melo's, a Galician bar that keeps the hungry night-time crowd going in downtown Madrid.

The recipes that follow are a selection of favourites.

Some croquetas notes

Using full-fat milk in the béchamel paste makes for a creamier *croqueta*. We call it paste rather than sauce, because this is something much heavier and more sturdy than the kind of béchamel sauce you might serve with a vegetable or fish dish – more like a dough or a base that you can shape.

Always use warm milk when making the béchamel mixture, and equally, when you add the stock later, make sure this is warm, as cold liquid can create lumps as you stir.

The fat used to make the béchamel paste may be butter, olive oil or even lard, according to personal taste, family or local tradition and the ingredients you are going to add. On the whole in Spain the emphasis is more on oil, which gives a bolder flavour than butter, but as the key feature of a great croqueta is the creaminess of the paste and the method is based on the French béchamel sauce, the use of butter is very in character. However, you can experiment with either in an equal ratio (for example, 120g of butter can be replaced by 120ml of oil).

You need patience and a strong arm, as you have to stir the paste pretty continuously for at least 20 minutes for the quantities given in the recipes that follow, and up to around 40 minutes if you are making a larger quantity. This is necessary in order to cook out the flour properly and reduce the milk down to the right consistency, at which point the mixture comes away from the sides of the pan. Many Anglicised recipes tend to shorten the cooking time for convenience, but don't be tempted to cut corners. If the flour is not cooked through the paste will have an unpleasant aftertaste.

Let the béchamel rest for at least two hours before using. This allows the flavours to meld together and the mixture to bind, so that it will be easier to shape. In our bars and restaurants we leave it overnight in the fridge. You also need to cover the surface of the béchamel with clingfilm to stop it oxidising and forming a crust on the top, which would make it harder to work with.

We use large Japanese *panko* breadcrumbs to coat the *croquetas*, as they give a really good colour and crunch when deep-fried. Alternatively, you can buy natural breadcrumbs from bakeries, which are also very good.

Although I wouldn't normally recommend olive oil for deep-frying, it is a luxury that can make the *croquetas* very tasty – though its flavour is quite strong. If you prefer something less extravagant and more neutral, use sunflower oil.

Always keep an eye on the *croquetas* as they fry, as they only need to be cooked long enough for the outside to turn lightly golden and crisp and the inside molten – all the ingredients that you add to the béchamel are already cooked.

The recipes that follow will all make around 1kg of béchamel, enough for 22–24 *croquetas*, either about 7cm long and 3cm in diameter, or shaped into balls. As they are quite rich and filling, two each is a reasonable serving – though it can be very easy to eat more, depending on whether you are serving them with other small plates or alone with drinks.

Because making *croquetas* is a time-consuming process, most people will make a large quantity at a time and freeze what they don't need immediately. Either they will freeze the béchamel in one piece, then defrost it to make the *croquetas* in the usual way; or they will make the *croquetas* in their entirety, coated in breadcrumbs, before freezing, then defrost and fry them. I have tried both ways, and they are equally good.

Brindisa croquetas de jamón ibérico
Ibérico ham croquettes

These have been loved since the first Brindisa tapas bar opened. They are very creamy and quite irresistible. We make the *croquetas* with Ibérico ham, but you could use Serrano instead.

Makes around 22–24

600ml full-fat milk
75ml chicken or ham stock
120g butter
½ a leek, very finely chopped
120g *taquitos* (trimmings) of Ibérico
  ham or good Serrano ham, finely chopped
120g plain white flour
a small pinch of salt
freshly ground black pepper
a pinch of freshly grated nutmeg
sunflower oil, for deep-frying

For the coating
50g white flour
2 eggs, beaten
70g large breadcrumbs, preferably
  ***panko* (Japanese crumbs)**

Warm the milk in a pan, but don't let it boil. Warm the chicken/ham stock separately.

Melt the butter in a tall, non-stick saucepan, add the leek and cook without colouring for 2 minutes, then add the ham and continue to cook, stirring, for 3 minutes.

Add the flour and stir very well over a low heat until it is a light brown colour. The longer you can cook the flour at this stage, the less you will have to cook the mixture once you have added the milk and stock, but be careful to keep the heat low, as the flour can burn very easily.

Slowly add the warmed milk, stirring continously until it is all incorporated, then add the warmed stock – again do this slowly – and keep stirring until it is all mixed in. Season with salt, pepper and nutmeg and continue to cook gently for at least 15–20 minutes, stirring all the time, until the mixture comes away from the sides of the pan of its own accord. Alternatively, check by denting the mixture with your finger, and if it doesn't stick, it is ready.

Spoon this béchamel paste into a shallow dish or tray, place a sheet of clingfilm over the top, and as soon as it has cooled, put into the fridge for at least 2 hours or overnight.

When you are ready to make your *croquetas*, have the flour, beaten eggs and breadcrumbs ready in separate shallow bowls. Take the béchamel out of the fridge and divide into 22–24 equal pieces. Oil your hands lightly and roll each piece into a ball. If you like, elongate them until they are around 7cm long and 3cm in diameter.

Coat each *croqueta* first in flour, then dip into the egg and put into a sieve to drain off the excess. Finally, coat well in breadcrumbs.

Heat the oil for deep-frying in a large pan, making sure it comes no higher than a third of the way up. If you have a thermometer it should be 180ºC (if you don't have a thermometer, drop in a few breadcrumbs and if they sizzle gently the oil is hot enough).

Fry the *croquetas,* in batches if necessary, for 3–4 minutes, turning until golden on all sides. Drain on kitchen paper and serve.

Asun's croquetas de pollo y champiñones
Chicken and mushroom croquettes

This is a variation on the chicken *croquetas* that our friend Asun makes in Burgos in Castilla y León. She cuts her chicken very, very small, but when our head chef, Leo, makes his version he prefers to tear it into small pieces with his hands, as he thinks it gives more texture to the *croquetas*. If you prefer, you can substitute the mushrooms with the same weight of chopped cured ham.

Makes 22–24

4 tablespoons olive oil
1 shallot, chopped
175g mushrooms, cleaned and chopped
1 clove of garlic, chopped and crushed
175g fresh chicken breast, chopped to the size of petit pois
4 tablespoons plain white flour
840ml warm full-fat milk
salt and white pepper
sunflower oil, for deep-frying

For the coating
50g plain flour
70g large breadcrumbs, preferably *panko* (Japanese crumbs)
2 eggs, beaten

Heat 1 tablespoon of the olive oil in a frying pan and add the shallot. Fry gently until it begins to soften, then add the mushrooms and continue to cook until both shallot and mushrooms are soft and the liquid from the mushrooms has disappeared. Add the crushed garlic and cook for a minute or so more. Keep to one side. Heat the rest of the oil, put in the chopped chicken and sauté until cooked but not browned. Sprinkle in the flour and cook for a few minutes, stirring all the time. Gradually add the milk, continuing to stir and fold until you have a thick béchamel paste. Add the sautéed vegetables to the paste and continue to cook gently, stirring all the time, until the mixture comes away from the sides of the pan of its own accord. Alternatively, check by denting the mixture with your finger, and if it doesn't stick, it is ready. Season with salt to taste, and around 2 teaspoons of white pepper, and take off the heat.

Spoon this béchamel paste into a shallow dish or tray, place a sheet of clingfilm over the top, then follow the rest of the instructions as for the recipe on page 243.

Brindisa croquetas de chorizo
Chorizo croquettes

I spotted *chorizo croquetas* on a menu in Santander, made with sausage from Liébana, which is strong and quite smoky. I was hesitant about ordering them, as I suspected they would be incredibly rich, but gave in to temptation, and yes, they were rich, but delicious, and excellent with a cold beer. So back home we set about coming up with a recipe. The method is slightly different to the previous *croqueta* recipes, because you need to compensate for the additional fat that comes from the *chorizo*. For this reason we make the béchamel paste with butter rather than olive oil, which might seem to be contributing to the richness, but just achieves the usual result, without the béchamel splitting due to the *chorizo* fat. For the same reason we add the cooked *chorizo* pieces to the béchamel once the paste has been mixed, rather than at the beginning of the process.

Makes 22–24

500ml full-fat milk
250ml vegetable stock
1 cooking *chorizo*, weighing 100–120g,
  cut into cubes (about 5mm)
100g butter, cut into small cubes
¼ of a leek, white part only, finely chopped
120g plain white flour
sea salt, to taste
sunflower or olive oil, for deep-frying

For the coating
50g plain flour
70g large breadcrumbs, preferably
  ***panko* (Japanese crumbs)**
2 eggs, beaten

Warm the milk in a pan, but don't let it boil. Warm the stock separately.

Put the *chorizo* into a dry pan over a medium heat and fry for 2 minutes, until cooked through. Lift out the cubes with a slotted spoon and keep to one side.

Add the butter to the coating of *chorizo* fat in the pan, then put in the leek and cook for about 4 minutes, until soft and transparent, but not coloured.

Add the flour and stir very well over a low heat until it is a light brown colour. The longer you can cook the flour at this stage, the less you will have to cook the mixture once you have added the milk and stock, but be careful to keep the heat low, as the flour can burn very easily.

Slowly add the warmed milk, stirring continuously until it is all incorporated, then add the warmed stock – again do this slowly – and keep stirring until it is all mixed in. Stir in the reserved *chorizo* pieces. Taste and season with salt if necessary. Continue stirring on a medium heat for a further 10 minutes, until the mixture comes away from the sides of the pan of its own accord. Alternatively, check by denting the mixture with your finger, and if it doesn't stick, it is ready.

Spoon this béchamel paste into a shallow dish or tray, place a sheet of clingfilm over the top, then follow the rest of the instructions as for the recipe on page 243.

Brindisa croquetas de queso, manchego y espinacas

Manchego cheese and baby
spinach croquettes

I was determined to perfect a vegetarian *croqueta* that, in the tradition of cooking with leftovers, would make good use of the pieces of cheese and bags of salad spinach that our family inevitably has in our fridge at home. Our former Brindisa chef Esperanza Añonuevo Heys helped me to come up with this recipe, which we liked so much we have since put it on the Brindisa menus.

The charming feature about these *croquetas* is the colour the spinach leaves bring to the béchamel – you can see some of the leaves beneath the breadcrumbs.

Makes 22–24

600ml full-fat milk
75ml vegetable stock
120ml olive oil
¼ of a leek, very finely chopped
sea salt and freshly ground black pepper
150g plain white flour
150g grated Manchego cheese
100g fresh baby spinach leaves
sunflower or olive oil, for deep-frying

For the coating
50g plain flour
70g large breadcrumbs, preferably
  ***panko* (Japanese crumbs)**
2 eggs, beaten

Warm the milk in a pan, but don't let it boil. Warm the stock separately.

Heat the oil in a pan, then add the leek and cook without colouring for 2 minutes. Season, then add the flour and mix briefly. Start adding the warm stock and keep mixing until it is all incorporated. Slowly add the warmed milk, and cook gently for at least 15–20 minutes, stirring all the time, until the mixture comes away from the sides of the pan of its own accord. Alternatively, check by denting the mixture with your finger, and if it doesn't stick, it is ready.

Add the cheese and mix very briefly – a maximum of a minute – so as not to let the fat come out of the cheese, then take the pan from the heat and mix in the baby spinach leaves. As soon as they have softened, turn the paste out of the pan.

Spoon this béchamel paste into a shallow dish or tray, place a sheet of clingfilm over the top, then follow the rest of the instructions as for the recipe on page 243.

Buñuelos de bacalao
Salt cod fritters

The batter here is known as *al monjàvenes*, derived from the old Andalusian Arabic word *almuyabbanat* in the region around Valencia, and is similar to that of a profiterole. It is difficult to be exact about the quantity of eggs, as much depends on the absorbency of the flour, so it is best to do as suggested in the recipe and work in the eggs one at a time, until you have the right consistency.

For an interesting variation, add ½ a teaspoon of *pimentón dulce* (mild paprika) and 1 tablespoon of finely chopped parsley to the batter just before forming it into quenelles for frying.

The *buñuelos* are good served with a tomato salad and some fresh mayonnaise.

**Makes enough for a big plateful
(around 30 bite-sized puffs)**

**400g de-salted cod *migas* (pieces, or 'crumbs')
(see page 330), or salt cod fillet
250ml fish stock or water
100g butter
150g plain flour
about 6 eggs
vegetable oil, for deep-frying**

If you are using *migas*, just break them into pieces 1–2cm square. If using cod fillet, peel the skin from the flesh with a sharp knife, then feel for any bones with your fingers and remove them with tweezers or a knife before flaking it into pieces 1–2 cm long. Keep the pieces to one side.

Bring the stock or water to the boil in a pan, then add the butter and let it melt. Take the pan off the heat and add all the flour at once, whisking continuously, then add the eggs one at a time, working them in vigorously with a wooden spoon. Don't add the next egg until the previous one has been completely absorbed into the dough. Six eggs is usually about right, but you may need more or less. The dough is ready when it comes away from the sides of the pan easily.

Gently stir in the flakes of cod so that you avoid breaking them up too much. It is much nicer to find some good mouthfuls of cod inside the *buñuelos*, rather than tiny bits.

Pour some vegetable oil into a deep pan – it should not come more than a third of the way up – and heat to 180°C (if you don't have a thermometer, test by dropping in a little of the mixture – it should sizzle). Taking two lightly oiled teaspoons, make 'quenelles' by scooping some of the mixture on to one spoon, then scooping it on to the other and passing the mixture back and forth between the two spoons a few times until the mixture is smooth and egg-shaped. Finally, ease the quenelle gently into the hot oil with the help of the free spoon. Fry in batches, so that the mixture doesn't lower the temperature of the oil.

As the *buñuelos* fry, the batter will puff up. As soon as each batch is golden brown all over, lift them out carefully and drain on kitchen paper. Eat hot.

Buñuelos de queso de cabra con miel y almendras
Goat's cheese fritters with honey and almonds

Chef Peter Gordon has been a champion of Brindisa ingredients for many years. A New Zealander himself, he is inspired by the food of Spain and the small-plate way of eating. As well as his London restaurants, he also has a Spanish tapas bar in Auckland called Bellota (acorn) as a tribute to the *ibérico de bellota* ham that he serves there. These delicious fritters have been on the menu since opening day, back in 2006.

Makes 12 balls

300g goat's cheese, such as Monte Enebro
3 tablespoons plain flour
1 small egg, beaten
50g large breadcrumbs or *panko*
  (Japanese breadcrumbs)
vegetable oil, for deep-frying
2 tablespoons runny honey,
  preferably orange blossom
12–15 very small mint leaves (or small basil leaves)
a small handful of salted Marcona almonds
  (see page 90), roughly chopped

Divide the cheese into 12 even-size pieces and roll each one into a ball. Have the flour, egg and breadcrumbs ready in separate shallow bowls.

Gently toss the balls of cheese in the flour, then coat in the beaten egg and, finally, roll them in the breadcrumbs, making sure you press the crumbs on firmly. Put into the fridge for at least an hour to firm up.

Pour a 5cm layer of vegetable oil into a pan large enough to hold at least half the balls in one layer without overcrowding (make sure the oil comes no higher than a third of the way up the pan). Heat to 180°C. If you don't have a thermometer, put in a few breadcrumbs and if they sizzle the oil is hot enough.

Lower the first batch of balls into the hot oil with a slotted spoon and cook for 2 minutes or so, turning them over gently as they fry, until they are a lovely golden colour all over. Lift out and drain on kitchen paper for a few minutes while you cook the next batch in the same way.

Arrange all the balls on a platter, drizzle with the honey, then scatter with the mint or basil leaves and the almonds. Eat while hot.

EMPANADILLAS

Originally a speciality of Galicia, *empanadas* were the equivalent of the British Cornish pasty, in that farm-workers would take them into the fields for their midday meal. I have included some hearty versions in the Big Plates chapter, but these much smaller *empanadillas* make great tapas.

Empanadillas de txangurro
Spider crab parcels

These little half-moon-shaped parcels are often deep-fried, but here they are baked, and so make a perfect, light *aperitivo*. I was given this recipe by Agustín Bedia of El Galeón de Somo, in Cantabria (see page 184). When I called him for his *salpicón* (seafood salad) recipe he insisted on giving me this too. He included a great deal of detail on how best to select and prepare a live crab, but I suggest you do as I do, and buy hand-picked white crabmeat instead.

Makes around 24

2 tomatoes, grated
50ml olive oil
2 small shallots, finely chopped
3 spring onions, finely chopped
1 small leek, finely chopped
½ a medium carrot, finely chopped
2 cloves of garlic, finely chopped
¼ teaspoon sea salt
125ml *fino* sherry
1 bay leaf
150g white crabmeat
flour, for dusting
500g good butter puff pastry
1 egg, beaten

Preheat the oven to 180°C/gas 4.

Either grate the tomatoes, or if you prefer, de-skin and de-seed them (see page 206).

Heat a little olive oil in a pan, add the vegetables, garlic and salt and cook gently without colouring. Add the sherry, tomato and bay leaf. Bubble up and reduce the liquid for at least 30 minutes, until it has the consistency of a moist, soft porridge. Remove the bay leaf and stir in the crabmeat.

Lightly flour your work surface and roll out the pastry to 4mm thick. Using an upturned glass or cutter, cut out around 24 circles of about 9cm in diameter.

Spoon some filling into the centre of each round, dampen the edges with a little water, then fold over the top to make half-moon shapes. Pinch the edges together to seal. Place on a baking tray, brush with beaten egg and bake in the middle of the preheated oven for around 20 minutes, until golden.

Empanadillas de espinaca
Mini spinach pasties

This recipe is from Pilar Sapena, wife of wine-maker Felipe Gutiérrez de la Vega, who naturally uses wine in her *empanadillas*, in this case their Casta Diva Cosecha Dorada, a dry wine made from local Moscatel grapes grown on ancient vines (see page 190).

Makes around 24

100ml olive oil
60ml dry Moscatel wine or light sherry
½ teaspoon sea salt
450g plain flour, plus extra for dusting
1 egg, beaten

For the filling
50ml olive oil
2 cloves of garlic, chopped
75g pine nuts
50g small raisins
500g baby spinach
½ teaspoon sea salt
freshly ground black pepper
a few scrapes of fresh nutmeg

Preheat the oven to 180°C/gas 4.

To make the dough, combine the oil, wine and salt in a bowl, then add the flour and mix, kneading gently until everything comes together. Form into a ball and rest it in the fridge for 20 minutes.

To make the filling, heat the olive oil, add the garlic and cook gently for a few minutes, then add the pine nuts, raisins and spinach. Season with the salt, pepper and nutmeg to taste. Cook gently, being careful not to burn, until all the liquid has evaporated. Take off the heat.

Lightly flour your work surface and roll out the dough to 4mm thick. Using an upturned glass or cutter, cut out around 24 circles of about 9cm in diameter.

Spoon some filling into the centre of each round, dampen the edges with a little water, then fold over the top to make half-moon shapes. Pinch the edges together to seal. Place on a baking tray, brush with beaten egg and bake in the middle of the preheated oven for around 20 minutes, until a light rich golden brown.

BROCHETAS Y TAPAS DE CARNE
Meat skewers and tapas

Brochetas are little skewers made with small marinated cubes of lamb, pork, chicken, duck or whole prawns, which are typically grilled on the *plancha*, the barbecue, or cooked under the grill.

Makes 4

½ teaspoon chopped garlic
1 teaspoon fresh oregano (or ½ teaspoon dried)
½ teaspoon ground cumin
½ teaspoon sweet paprika
2 tablespoons olive oil
sea salt and freshly ground black pepper
400g tenderloin or Ibérico pork
  (see page 168), cut into 2.5cm cubes

Mix all the ingredients except the pork in a bowl. Add the pork and rub the mixture into the meat so that it is coated all over. Put into the fridge to marinate for 3 hours, then thread on skewers and cook under a hot grill or on a barbecue until the juices run clear.

Brochetas de cordero
Lamb skewers

Makes 4

1 medium red onion, sliced very thinly
½ teaspoon ground cumin
½ teaspoon grated ginger
1 teaspoon chopped garlic
½ tablespoon chopped rosemary leaves
1 tablespoon chopped parsley
2 tablespoons olive oil
sea salt and freshly ground black pepper
400g lamb leg, cut into 2.5cm cubes

Mix all the ingredients except the lamb in a bowl. Add the lamb and rub the mixture well into the meat so that it is coated all over. Put in the fridge to marinate overnight, then thread on skewers and cook under a hot grill or on a barbecue until browned on the outside, but medium rare inside, or for a little longer if you prefer.

Chorizo al vino o a la sidra
Chorizo poached in wine or cider

When I tried to think of hot *chorizo* tapas that I have enjoyed, I could recall very few, since *chorizo* is usually served in a very straightforward way. The cooking sausages are either just chopped and sautéd with squares of potato until golden, or poached, as here, in wine or cider, to make one of the simplest and most tasty of tapas: especially warming for winter evenings. Poaching, however, does require a very good *chorizo*. Don't pierce it, as you want it to retain its juices and fat and flavour; however, some of this will leach into the poaching liquid, flavouring it richly.

Serves 4 as a tapa with other dishes

1 onion, sliced
1 x 250g fresh cooking *chorizo*,
  such as *Alejandro barbacoa*
450ml red wine, such as Garnacha, or cider
1 bay leaf

Put all the ingredients into a pan over a medium heat (keeping the *chorizo* whole) and simmer for 15–20 minutes, to reduce the wine or cider and poach the *chorizo* and onion. Turn the *chorizo* from time to time so that it colours evenly. Lift out the *chorizo* and slice it, then serve it with the poached onions and sauce, and some crusty bread.

CHORIZO

'almost a national emblem'

Across the world, the ruddy-coloured *chorizo* flavoured with *pimentón* (paprika) is probably the most popular and recognisable food export of Spain. It has almost become a national emblem, offering a fast route to a Spanish experience: a magic ingredient with an immediate 'wow' flavour, whether on its own or in any number of dishes.

In Spain itself, however, people tend to be far more judicious in their use of *chorizo*, the argument being that not only is it quite rich and fatty, but if they are combining the sausage with other more subtle ingredients they don't want these to be blasted by its powerful flavour. While in the UK pairing *chorizo* with fish or seafood, such as squid (or razor clams, as in Mark Hix's recipe on page 110) is popular, in Spain this is a contentious subject. I remember once, when I was in Madrid, someone mentioned having seen a dish of cod cheeks with *chorizo* being made on a cooking show on British TV. My Spanish colleagues were horrified. In their view fish was far too delicate and subtle to cope with pork and *pimentón*.

Pilar Sapena, of the wine and vinegar estate in Alicante (see page 190), who typically uses very delicate flavours in her cooking, has this rule about *chorizo*: 'in a sandwich great, with potatoes and legumes, great, but never in rice and never with seafood'. And Ana Barrera echoes this philosophy at her wonderful little restaurant in Madrid (see page 442), in that she only ever uses *chorizo* with beans or chickpeas, which she feels can cope with the fattiness and spiciness of the sausage.

In Alicante and Valencia, where the food is generally much lighter than in other regions, they use *chorizo* very little, and in the Basque country and Catalunya they don't even have a traditional *chorizo* of their own.

Also, given its iconic status abroad, it is strange to realise that while the history of sausage-making in general goes back to Roman times, *chorizo* is a relatively recent development. Almost all *chorizo* is now made with pork (though in Asturias, venison *chorizo* is a speciality); however, its origins are not with the pig at all, but in the flavouring of lamb meat, goat and small game with aromatic herbs and spices such as cumin and coriander, which was favoured by the Moors who arrived in Europe in the eighth century and whose religion prohibited them from eating pork. These meats were often made into sausages, and the recipes for their spicing and marinades became absorbed into the local communities. It was only later, during the persecution of the Moors in the fifteenth century, that Christians began making a point of eating pork to demonstrate their faith, while keeping the inherited tradition of herbs and spices.

At this point, however, there were still no peppers in Spain, and therefore no paprika. It wasn't until the sixteenth century that the monks at the monastery of Yuste, in Cáceres, Extremadura, first began cultivating peppers brought in from the New World and realised these could also be dried and ground to make a spice. As the cultivation of peppers spread, this *pimentón* began to be used in the flavouring of sausages throughout central Spain.

Like almost all Spanish foods, *chorizo* isn't made to a single recipe. It spans around fifty recognised styles which vary from region to region, often according to the kind of paprika used (see page 232), which can be *dulce* (mild) or more *picante* (spicy). Some regions add a little garlic or herbs to the basic *chorizo* mix of pork meat and *pimentón*, and in Extremadura cooked potatoes can sometimes be added.

The sausages are either fresh, in which case they must be cooked before eating, or they are cured and air-dried, ready to slice and eat like salami. They might be made on a very small, artisan and local scale, or produced industrially by brands who sell them all over Spain.

Chorizo fresco

Fresh, cooking *chorizos* are usually a similar shape to British sausages, though in some regions they are hooped, mini-sized, or long and thin – like the 60cm-long hooped *chistorra* typical of the Basque country.

In Spain you might find a butcher who is making his own fresh *chorizo* on a daily basis – sometimes people buy these and strip off the skin, then use the seasoned pork as a stuffing or *picadillo* (mince). More usually, though, 'fresh' actually involves a few days of curing – typically up to a week. This brief curing concentrates the flavour but still allows the juices to come out of the sausage and flavour any other ingredients in a dish. It also firms up the meat a little, so that if you put the *chorizo* into a dish such as a casserole with beans that requires long, slow cooking, it won't disintegrate. Some, like the famous *chorizo*

de León, are also lightly smoked over oak.

Fresh *chorizos* are incredibly versatile. They can be sliced and grilled or fried for breakfast dishes, for example *huevos a la flamenca*, a combination known all over Spain in which the whole *chorizos* are coloured in a terracotta dish (as with a good meaty British pork sausage, if you are grilling, frying or barbecuing fresh *chorizos* whole, don't prick them first, as you will leach out the fat, and with it a lot of the flavour). They are then lifted out, and some tomato *sofrito* is spooned into the dish, cooked peas are added and the *chorizo* put back on top. Some good eggs are broken over the top and then the dish is put into the oven at 180°C/gas 4 for about 12 minutes, until the *chorizo* is cooked through and the white of the egg is firm – how soft you have the yolks is up to individual taste. Then it is eaten with toasted country bread to mop up the eggy-tomatoey juices.

Fresh *chorizo* can also be poached whole for tapas (see page 255), as well as added to rice dishes, stews and casseroles. Of course, you could use cured *chorizo* in these slow-cooked dishes, but a Spanish person wouldn't, because they want the juiciness of the fresh sausage.

How to choose fresh *chorizo*

Look for few ingredients and no additives. The fresh Alejandro *chorizos* that we sell, for example, list only three ingredients: pork, spices and salt. Those made without preservatives and colours will have a duller, more rusty-orange colour than the more pinky-orange, industrial ones. The joy of these natural sausages is that they have a full taste that is deeply peppery and mildly smoky, without being spicy-hot, whereas the industrial versions often have a slight taste of chemicals and an unattractive metallic after-flavour.

Cured *chorizo*

Cured (ready to eat) *chorizo* is graded according to meat, fat and humidity content. At one time you might have seen many different grades, including *puro* (pure), *primera* (first), *segunda* (second) and *extra*. However, these days *extra* is considered the highest grade, and is the only one you are likely to see on a label; otherwise, there will usually be no grade stated. Sometimes you might also see *natural* on a label, which simply indicates no additives.

The best *extra chorizo* begins with the quality of the meat. The choice cut is the redder lean meat between the belly fat and the ribs, as well as that from the foreleg, which is much juicier than the hind leg, and good producers tend to cut the meat by hand. Cheaper *chorizos*, not labelled *extra*, tend to be more gristly, as they have been made from less fine cuts of meat.

You also need fat, so some *panceta* will be added. An *extra chorizo* will have a percentage of around 60 per cent lean meat to 30 per cent fat, with the rest made up of flavourings. In thicker *chorizos* the meat tends to be coarsely minced, whereas in thinner ones it is more likely to be finely chopped.

The sausages can be small, the shape of a normal sausage, long, or hooped. Once made, they are hung up to cure for 1–6 months, depending on the size, ingredients, the kind of casing used and the environment in which they are being cured.

Generally speaking, the longer they are cured, the firmer the sausage, and the more expensive they are likely to be. In the colder, wetter, northern areas of Spain, such as Galicia, Asturias and León, the *chorizos* tend to be smoked as they are curing, as this helps them to keep longer, and deepens the flavour. *Chorizo de León* is the most famous example of rich, smoked, cured *chorizo*.

Sometimes, finding a brilliant food is really down to a stroke of luck, and the day I met our Riojan *chorizo* producers, the Rituerto brothers, Roberto and Alejandro, was one of those moments when the gods were smiling on me. Back in the early, heady days of Spain's EU membership, in the lead up to the Olympics in Barcelona, the Spanish were investing heavily in launching themselves as a serious exporter of excellent food and wine. At Brindisa we were already a step ahead, but most of the world was not really plugged into what Spain had to offer, so a motley selection of foodie people and buyers, including myself and my colleague Emma Ranson, were invited aboard an extravagant promotional cruise ship sailing from Barcelona to Cádiz for Expo 1992. Various regional wine-makers, cheese-makers and other local Spanish producers had been selected to set up stands on board, and among them were Roberto and Alejandro, with their Riojan 'Alejandro' *chorizo*, made with very high-quality *pimentón*, a touch of garlic and no additives or preservatives.

Tasting that *chorizo* was the start of a long and great relationship. At first we insisted that the *chorizo* needed to be hotter to suit the British taste, but Roberto refused to adapt the recipe, as he said it would unbalance the flavours. In his view a good *chorizo* should be mild, so that the quality of the meat and other seasonings are not overpowered. Over the years he has been proved right, since his traditional *chorizo* is a best seller. Whenever possible the brothers come over from Spain to join us at events, and everyone loves them. Invariably they burst into song as they hand out slices of their cured *chorizo* and poach fresh ones in wine and cider for people to try.

How to choose cured *chorizo*

Look for the grading *extra* on labels. If you also see the word *natural* this shows that no preservatives or colours have been added. Next, what is important is the casing used, as this affects the quality of the curing. The *chorizos* should have a quite thick skin, as this indicates they are made from animal casing, rather than man-made. These *chorizos* will usually have a better flavour, as the skins are permeable both ways, allowing the sausage to be cured more naturally and for longer, intensifying the flavour. They will also be irregular in shape.

By contrast, industrially made *chorizos* tend to be much bigger – sometimes 6–8cm in diameter, and more uniform-looking, inside man-made casings, and they are more likely to have been fast-cured in special drying rooms. They may contain preservatives, which can give a chemical-like petrolly aftertaste; or strong, dried garlic flavourings, often designed to enhance an otherwise unremarkable flavour. They are also likely to contain colourings, which makes them look pink, rather than the natural-looking rusty-coppery colour that comes from using only *pimentón*.

Sobrasada mallorquina

In the Balearic Islands and some Levantine coastal villages where the local air is too humid to produce firm *chorizos*, the Balearic islanders opt for this popular soft orange-red 'spreading *chorizo*', which is more like a pâté (locally it is spelt *sobrassada*). Instead of chunks of meat, it is made with very finely minced pork and belly fat and is truly delicious. It is mostly eaten as it is, taken straight from the skin and spread on bread, or it can be spooned on to toast, with some Manchego cheese and grilled (see page 134), used in *banyetas* (see page 66) or to fill *empanadas* (little pasties). You could even use it to make a Spanish twist on little sausage rolls. Often it is used to make the sweet and savoury *coca tovada*: little pieces of *sobrasada* and fruit such as fresh

apricot are pushed into focaccia-like dough which rises up around the *chorizo* and fruit as it bakes (see page 65).

These days industrially made *sobrasada* may contain pork from white pigs, but traditionally the meat comes from the herds of native black Mallorquín pigs with their distinctive dangly bits of skin at the base of their necks (*mamellas*), which are descendants of the Ibérico pig and have been indigenous to the Balearic Islands for around seven centuries. Unlike their mainland cousins which are fattened on acorns before slaughter, the Mallorquín black pigs have a year-round diet of beans, alfalfa grass, acorns, carobs and figs, and the sweetness of the figs, in particular, comes through in the meat.

Once the pork and fat mixture is seasoned and flavoured with *pimentón*, it is stuffed into natural skins to make bulbous sausages which are tied with string and hung up on poles to cure for 1–8 months or longer, depending on the casing, weight and shape.

How to choose *sobrasada*

For the authentic and very superior product, look for *sobrassada de Mallorca de cerdo negro* on the label.

Each size and shape of *sobrasada* has a different name. These include the largest, *bisbe*, which can weigh as much as 30kg. It is cured for up to a year, hanging from three strings – so it looks almost like a baby in a sling. More popular, however, are the wrinkly bulbous *rizada*, which cures in 6–12 weeks; the *poltru*, larger than the *rizada*, but similarly shaped and cured for 2–6 months; and the ball-shaped *bufeta* (also cured for 2–6 months). As an indicator of the flavour (not always reliable), the milder sausages are tied with white string, and the hotter, spicier ones with red string.

Often some of the best *sobrasada* is sold in delicatessens, where they will slice soft chunks from a large sausage for you.

Chorizo con judiones y tomates
Hot *chorizo* with butter beans and tomatoes

Sam and Samantha Clark of Moro restaurant have long been supporters of Brindisa produce, and this recipe combines some of their favourite ingredients: fresh cooking *chorizo* and plump, luxuriously creamy *judión* butter beans. They included it in their *Moro Cookbook* (Ebury), and Sam tells me their customers love it. When they cook their beans (and also chickpeas) they add a little bicarbonate of soda, to help soften them.

You could also make this with good, jarred butter beans, warmed through in their brine in a pan, and then drained.

Serves 4

100–150g dried *judión* beans,
  butter beans, or cannellini beans
a pinch of bicarbonate of soda
sea salt and freshly ground black pepper
20 sweet cherry tomatoes, cut in half
½ a red onion, thinly sliced
1 medium bunch of flat-leaf parsley,
  roughly chopped
a drizzle of olive oil
250g mild or spicy cooking
  chorizo, cut into little pieces

For the dressing
1 clove of garlic, peeled
sea salt and freshly ground black pepper
1 tablespoon sherry vinegar (or red wine vinegar)
a squeeze of lemon juice (optional)
4 tablespoons extra virgin olive oil

Soak the beans overnight in plenty of water with a pinch of bicarbonate of soda added.

Drain and rinse the beans, then cover with 2 litres of cold water in a large pan. Bring to the boil, then reduce the heat to a simmer, skimming off any froth that comes to the surface. Cook gently for 1–2 hours, until the beans are tender. Pour off some of the cooking liquid until it is level with the beans, season and keep to one side – this stops the skins from wrinkling or splitting.

Meanwhile, make the dressing. Crush the garlic to a paste with a good pinch of salt, using a pestle and mortar, then add the vinegar and lemon juice, if using, and whisk in the olive oil. Season to taste.

Drain the beans and put them into a shallow serving bowl with the tomatoes, red onion and parsley. Allow to cool until warm, then pour on the dressing and mix well. Leave to sit for at least 5 minutes to let the flavours mingle.

Meanwhile, set a frying pan over a medium to high heat. Pour a drizzle of olive oil into the pan and add the *chorizo*. It will only take about a minute to cook – it really just needs to sizzle quickly until it is crisp on both sides. Lift out the cooked *chorizo* with a slotted spoon and serve on top of the beans.

Fabes a la catalana
Catalan broad beans with
black pudding

Pochas con morcilla y acelgas
Fried white beans with black pudding
and Swiss chard

In Castilian broad beans are *habas*, whereas in Catalan they are *fabes*, hence the name of the dish. You can use good sausages if you prefer, rather than the black pudding. *Cansalada* is the Catalan for *tocino* (back fat, see page 394) and is similar to *panceta*, so you can use either.

Serves 4 with other small plates

3 tablespoons olive oil
125g *cansalada* (see above) or *panceta*,
   rind removed, sliced into 1cm x 0.5cm batons
1 onion, finely chopped
2 cloves of garlic, finely chopped
400g fresh (or frozen) shelled broad beans
100g *morcilla* with onion or *botifarra negra*
   (see page 450), skin removed
2 tablespoons anise liqueur,
   such as Anis del Mono Seco
1 tablespoon chopped fresh mint

Heat 2 tablespoons of the oil, preferably in an earthenware, flameproof dish, then put in the *cansalada* or *panceta* and sauté until the fat becomes translucent. Add the onion and garlic and cook slowly until the onion is translucent but not coloured. Take care not to let the garlic burn. Bring some water to the boil in a pan and put in the beans, lower to a simmer and cook for about 10 minutes (depending on their size), until tender.

Meanwhile, heat the rest of the oil in a frying pan, add the *morcilla* or *botifarra negra* and sauté for a couple of minutes, breaking it up into small pieces with a wooden spoon. Add the anise – be careful, as it is likely to flame, and stir for another minute or so to burn off the alcohol.

Transfer the *morcilla* or *botifarra negra* to the pan containing the beans and allow to simmer for another 8–10 minutes, until the beans are completely tender, then add the chopped mint. Stir through, simmer for another 2 minutes, and serve.

This recipe was created for the London Bridge tapas bar menu by our executive chef, Josep. Colourful, iron-rich and nourishing, I have enjoyed it on so many occasions.

Serves 4

250g fresh white beans, such as *pochas*,
   alubias or *mongetes* (see page 381),
   or 200g dried white beans
1 carrot, peeled
1 bay leaf
2 cloves of garlic, peeled, one left
   whole, the other chopped
3 tablespoons olive oil, plus a little
   extra for cooking the beans
1 shallot, chopped
200g Swiss chard leaves
salt
4 *morcilla* or *botifarra negra* (see page 450)
chopped parsley (optional), to finish

If using dried beans, soak them overnight in plenty of water. Put the soaked or fresh beans into a pan with the whole carrot, bay leaf and whole clove of garlic. Cover with plenty of cold water. Add a drizzle of oil. Bring to the boil, then turn down the heat and simmer until tender (around 20 minutes for fresh beans or 45–60 minutes for dried). Drain, reserving some cooking water, and discard the garlic, carrot and bay leaf.

Heat 2 tablespoons of the oil in a sauté pan or wok, add the chopped garlic and shallot and cook gently until golden, then add the cooked beans, together with the Swiss chard, and fry quickly, adding a tablespoon of the reserved cooking water. Let the liquid bubble up and reduce a little, then taste, and season with salt.

Meanwhile, heat the rest of the oil in a frying pan, add the *morcilla* or *botifarra negra* and sauté for a couple of minutes, breaking it up into small pieces with a wooden spoon. Serve the beans topped with the *morcilla* or *botifarra negra*, and a sprinkling of parsley, if you like.

REVUELTOS
Scrambled eggs

In the hands of the Spanish cook scrambled eggs (*revueltos*) are really taken to another level, and only the best ingredients are added. These are not dishes for using up leftovers.

Whereas *tortilla* slices or squares tend to be served as a tapa, scrambled egg dishes are more often eaten as starters. They are more like broken omelettes, only lightly beaten and stirred slowly over a low heat, so the egg stays quite soft and moist, rather than the drier, grainy, quite quickly cooked eggs that used to be traditional in Britain. When my brother and sisters and I were young and my mum made scrambled egg, I remember there were always little crispy bits where the eggs had caught at the bottom of the pan – which we all wanted in our portion, but in the Spanish kitchen eggs like this would be considered a dry disaster.

Some *revueltos* notes

Start with the very best eggs you can afford. In Spain the *huevo de corral* (see page 164) is the ideal. In the UK, choose a good farm egg, preferably with a deep orange-coloured yolk, which shows that the hen has been allowed to forage properly outside.

Only beat the eggs very lightly with a fork: 2 seconds, that's it.

Good *revueltos* are cooked slowly, so that the eggs remain moist. So use a heavy-based pan, or preferably a non-stick wok, which allows you to move the eggs around to cooler areas, so that they don't get too hot and cook too quickly.

Always turn down the heat under your pan of oil before you add the lightly beaten eggs. Then quickly take the pan from the heat, stir and fold the eggs and put the pan back on the heat. Continue with this on-and-off-the-heat process, which will stop the eggs drying out and keep them creamy.

Revueltos con ajetes
Scrambled egg with fresh garlic shoots

This is a typical Good Friday dish in Spain, when the fresh garlic shoots, or scapes as they are known in the UK (see page 140), are in season. Our friends Ambro and Ásun pick their shoots straight from Ambro's brother's garden, and when we visited for Easter, Ambro cooked a huge *revueltos* made with around 20 eggs in a massive pan over a gas ring at their *bodega*/cave up in the hills.

This is what I call a 'yellow scramble', because the garlic shoots are light in colour and there are no added ingredients to darken the colour of the eggs.

If you can't find fresh green garlic shoots, or scapes, you could substitute very small, mild-flavoured leeks.

Serves 4

12 fresh garlic shoots (scapes) or 6 thin leeks
8 medium eggs
sea salt
2 tablespoons olive oil
2 tablespoons chopped parsley

Chop the garlic shoots or the whites of the leeks, if using (discard the green parts), into 2cm lengths on the diagonal.

In a bowl, beat the eggs very lightly with a fork for 2 seconds and season with salt.

Heat the oil in a small wok or heavy-based pan, add the garlic shoots and sauté gently for 2 minutes, then lift out with a slotted spoon and add to the beaten eggs. Turn down the heat.

Pour the egg and garlic shoot mixture into the pan, take it off the heat and stir gently, then put the pan back on the hob and for 1–2 minutes keep taking it on and off the heat as you stir and fold, to stop the eggs drying out and keep them creamy. Stir in the parsley at the last moment, off the heat.

Revuelto de morcilla
Scrambled egg with black pudding

This dish may lack beauty, as the egg will blacken with the pudding, but it more than makes up for it in flavour. Ideally, use a soft *morcilla* made with onion – typically these have a very thin skin (see page 76).

Serves 4

2 tablespoons olive oil
1 tablespoon pine nuts
200g *morcilla* with onion or black *botifarra*
**   (see page 450), skin removed**
1 shallot, finely chopped
a pinch of ground cinnamon (optional)
8 medium eggs
sea salt
4–5 mint leaves, chopped or torn

Heat the oil in a small wok or heavy-based pan, put in the pine nuts, moving them around to brown them slightly, then lift out and keep to one side. Put the *morcilla* or *botifarra* into the pan and sauté until heated through. Add the shallot and cinnamon, if using, and sauté for 2 more minutes. Turn down the heat.

In a bowl, beat the eggs very lightly with a fork for 2 seconds and season with salt. Add to the pan, take it off the heat and stir gently, then put the pan back on the hob and for 1–2 minutes keep taking it on and off the heat as you stir and fold, so that the egg envelops all the ingredients (the sausage will blacken the eggs). Stir in the pine nuts and mint at the last moment, off the heat.

Revuelto de setas
Wild mushrooms in
scrambled egg

Obviously this is far more interesting if you can use seasonal wild mushrooms rather than cultivated ones.

The eggs in this scramble will remain yellow and the colour will contrast really well with the mushrooms.

Serves 4

2 tablespoons olive oil
100g mixed wild mushrooms, cleaned
1 shallot, finely chopped
2 large cloves of garlic, finely chopped
8 medium eggs
sea salt
2 tablespoons chopped parsley

Heat the oil in a small wok or heavy-based pan. Add the mushrooms, shallot and garlic and sauté for 3 minutes. Turn down the heat.

In a bowl, beat the eggs very lightly for 2 seconds and season with salt. Add to the pan, take it off the heat and stir gently, then put the pan back on the hob and for 1–2 minutes keep taking it on and off the heat as you stir and fold, so that the egg envelops all the ingredients. Stir in the parsley at the last moment, off the heat.

Revuelto de espárragos
Asparagus in scrambled egg

This only works with fresh green asparagus, rather than jarred white asparagus, as it is not only the texture but the colour of the spears that really makes this an exceptional combination. It is such a favourite dish in Spain that in asparagus season everyone talks about it. I have frequently spent long journeys listening to Madrid taxi drivers regaling me with romantic stories of collecting wild asparagus from the hills when they go back to visit their mothers in their home villages, in order to make this *revuelto*.

Serves 4

2 bunches of fresh green or wild asparagus
   spears (about 24 spears), ideally thin ones
2 tablespoons olive oil
8 medium eggs
sea salt

Chop the spears into 2cm lengths on the diagonal, leaving behind the woody stems. If the asparagus isn't thin, boil the pieces in salted water for 5 minutes, then drain and reserve.

Heat the oil in a small wok or heavy-based pan, and if you are using thin spears put them in and sauté for 2 minutes. Turn down the heat.

In a bowl, beat the eggs very lightly for 2 seconds and season with salt, and if you are using thicker asparagus which you have cooked in water, add the pieces to the egg. Add the eggs to the pan, take it off the heat and stir gently, then put the pan back on the hob and for 1–2 minutes keep taking it on and off the heat as you stir.

Tortilla de bacalao
Salt cod omelette

I have included this here, despite it being called a *tortilla,* as it is somewhere between scrambled egg and an omelette. Since it is relatively thin and doesn't contain any potato to soak up the moisture from the eggs, the texture is quite soft and creamy, so it is impossible to turn, and is sometimes served folded in the French style.

It is a menu staple in the cider houses of the Basque country, where it will be followed by exceptional, super-thick rib-eye steaks, cooked over coals. To finish there will be Basque sheep cheeses with walnuts on the side and, naturally, cider to drink.

This is our head chef Leo Rivera's version of the omelette. You don't need to buy expensive salt cod loin, you only need the '*migas*', or 'crumbs', which are the small pieces left after the loins have been cut out (see page 330 for more about salt cod).

Serves 2 hungry people

500g de-salted cod *migas* (see page 330)
2 tablespoons olive oil
2 medium onions, finely chopped
2 cloves of garlic, finely chopped
1 tablespoon chopped parsley
5 eggs

***To serve* (optional)**
a little olive oil
1 clove of garlic, thinly sliced
4 *piquillo* peppers, from a jar (see page 275)

If serving with *piquillo* peppers and garlic, prepare these first. Heat a film of oil in a 28cm frying pan, add the garlic slices and cook briefly but don't allow to colour, add the *piquillo* peppers and heat through, then take off the heat and keep to one side.

Separate the *migas* into small pieces with your fingers, then heat 1 tablespoon of the oil in a frying pan on a medium heat, add the onions and garlic and cook gently for 10 minutes, until softened but not coloured.

Add the cod and cook for 3 more minutes, then add the parsley and cook for another minute. Remove from the heat.

Beat the eggs in a bowl, then add the cod mixture.

Wipe out the pan with kitchen paper, heat another tablespoon of oil and swirl it around so that the sides as well as the base are oiled, then pour out the excess.

Pour in the egg mixture and cook in the style of a French omelette, drawing the sides of the egg mixture towards the middle as you cook it. When just set underneath but still soft like scrambled egg on top, either slide it out on to a plate, or fold it over first. If serving with red peppers and garlic, spoon these on top.

Remanat de camp
Country scrambled egg

Llorenç Petrás has a famous stall in the Boqueria market in Barcelona, where his *fruits del bosc*, wild woodland produce, is a stunning sight. You have to go to the market early, though, if you want to see the scale of his treasure, as by the end of the day it will all have sold out. We often use his book, *La Millor Cuina dels Bolets*, at home since it is full of ideas for wild mushrooms – Catalunya in autumn is a mushroom-picker's paradise – and this colourful combination of squash, peppers and mushrooms is incredibly tasty. It is really more of a mix of vegetables with eggs than a creamy scrambled egg dish.

Llorenç adds snails to his *remanat* (the Catalan name for scrambled egg), which he collects and cooks himself; however, I admit I shy away from snails. If you do want to add them, however, you can buy them in tins or jars.

When ceps aren't available, Portobello mushrooms give an excellent flavour, though they give off a lot of moisture and darken the final dish. A combination of chestnut and chanterelles is very good too and keeps a more golden colour.

Try to use a sweet, thin-skinned green pepper.

Serves 4

2 ripe tomatoes
150ml olive oil
200g potatoes, peeled and chopped, about 1cm
200g pumpkin or squash, peeled
  and chopped,about 1cm
1 green pepper, roughly chopped, about 1cm
sea salt and freshly ground black pepper
1 slice of country or sourdough bread (about
  100g), crusts cut off, cut into small squares
250g ceps, cleaned and cut into
  slices of about 4cm
1 small onion, finely chopped
1 clove of garlic, finely chopped
300g freshly cooked or jarred snails (optional)
6 eggs

Either grate the tomatoes, or, if you prefer, de-skin and de-seed them (see page 206).

Heat 4 tablespoons of the oil in a deep frying pan and add the potatoes, pumpkin or squash and the green pepper. Season with a pinch of salt and sweat over a medium heat for 10–15 minutes, until the potato is just tender and beginning to brown, then lift out and keep to one side. Wipe out the pan for later.

Heat 2 more tablespoons of the oil in a small pan, put in the bread and fry until the cubes are nicely browned, to make croutons. Lift out and keep to one side. Heat a further 2 tablespoons of oil in the pan, put in the ceps and briefly cook through. Take off the heat and keep to one side.

Return the deep frying pan to the heat with the rest of the oil, then add the onion, garlic, tomato, the snails, if using, and a pinch of salt. Allow to sweat on a low heat for around 10 minutes, until the onion is transparent. Add the reserved potatoes, pumpkin or squash and peppers, together with the mushrooms, and heat everything through on a medium heat. Taste and season as necessary.

Meanwhile, in a bowl, beat the eggs very lightly for 2 seconds and season with salt. Add to the pan, take it off the heat and stir gently, then put the pan back on the hob and for 1–2 minutes keep taking it on and off the heat as you stir, to stop the eggs drying out and keep them creamy. Sprinkle with the reserved croutons and serve immediately.

TAPAS DE VERDURAS
Vegetable tapas

If you were to give a Spaniard a plate of boiled or steamed vegetables their attitude would probably be: 'Why would you do that? They don't taste of anything.' In Spain so much more consideration and attention goes into the cooking of vegetables, and they really come into their own as small plates. For example, in Catalunya and all along the Mediterranean coast, greens such as spinach are especially popular cooked long and slow, or just lightly tossed through hot oil in a pan with sautéd shallots, pine nuts and raisins.

In Alicante, at La Taberna del Gourmet, María José San Román serves a wonderful platter of individually prepared vegetables, laid out like a colourful fan: baby artichokes lightly coated in chickpea flour and fried until crispy, baked whole tomatoes and chunky slices of roasted squash, grilled courgette, aubergine, asparagus and large slices of mushroom, all sprinkled with sea salt and olive oil. Such combinations are typical of this southern Levante region and also of Murcia, where vegetables are often cooked on hot stones.

Garden vegetables coated in tempura-style batter have also become very fashionable. On a visit to the Núñez de Prado brothers at their olive oil mill in Baena, at the foot of the Sierra Madre mountains (see page 218), they arranged an elaborate early lunch in the private restaurant which included irresistible mounds of peppers, courgettes and aubergines, cut into delicate matchstick pieces whose green and red colours peeped through their light batter. I went downstairs to the kitchen to watch the cook prepare the vegetables for frying – naturally using their wonderful oils – and I was fascinated by the simple and ingenious device she had next to the deep fryer – a version of which our executive chef, Josep, has since bought for the kitchen at our Shoreditch restaurant. Essentially, it is a metal box with a sliding sieve at the top. You fill the box with flour, put the batter-coated vegetables into the sieve, scatter them with some of the flour, then slide the sieve up and down to shake the excess flour back into the box, leaving the vegetables thinly coated. Of course a normal sieve will do the trick, but the tin is more fun!

While in many regions vegetables are eaten in abundance, you won't necessarily encounter the same reverence towards them all over the country – in inland Spain in particular, the diet is often heavily weighted towards meat. Even though vegetarianism is growing, it is still very much in the minority, and a vegetarian is often taken to mean someone who likes vegetables a lot, rather than someone who doesn't eat meat or fish. The thinking is that you might not want half an animal on your plate, but a little bit of ham is fine. So a vegetable such as red cabbage, Swiss chard, cauliflower, green beans or asparagus might be blanched until just tender, then sautéd in oil and garlic and finished off with a sprinkling of roasted nuts and chopped cured ham, or *panceta*, fried until crispy. Or, in a mix of traditional and new, you might find the likes of chard stalks sandwiched around Ibérico ham and cheese, covered in tempura batter and deep-fried.

While stuffed tomatoes and peppers might seem a little passé in the UK, they are still all the rage in Spain. In Navarra, the garden of Spain, Sandra Salcedo, one of the daughters of the family who supply us with many of our jarred vegetables, makes a lovely cosy dish of big, ripe, ruby-red tomatoes, filled with spinach and ham mash. And *piquillo* peppers make perfect receptacles for all kinds of combinations, from cheese to rice or *morcilla* (see pages 276).

PIMIENTOS

'flavour over heat'

A sun-ripened Mediterranean pepper is a world away from the hydroponically grown ones we tend to see in supermarkets in the UK, and Spanish varieties range from small to big, mild to spicy, though in general they are valued for their flavour over their heat. There is a huge appreciation and understanding of all of them, and the best ways to use them – some fresh, others dried, preserved in oil, or pickled in gentle vinegars.

We started buying dried peppers very early on in the days of Brindisa. I first saw *ristras* (strings) of them drying on the balconies of homes across Rioja and Murcia and they were irresistible – they seemed to me to be a way of bringing sunshine into the kitchen. So we began combining *guindilla* pepper strings with *farcellets*, the very pretty Catalan version of bouquet garnis (two bay leaves rolled around herbs such as thyme and savory), with Brindisa colleagues and friends all helping out with the stringing. From there we progressed to bringing in *ñora* and *choricero* peppers.

In Spain these days most dried peppers are sold in boxes of about ten, with a clear window in the lid so that you can see the peppers inside, but we feel that the strings are more visually exciting, so I asked the growers if these could be made locally. Yes, I was told, but I was also warned that pepper-stringing is a dying art which may not remain viable in the future.

Many of the peppers we sell dried are grown by the García family, based in Quel in south-eastern Rioja, away from the main wine-growing areas, close to the southern tip of Navarra and the barren hills where you can follow the ancient dinosaur trails, which of course we have visited with the children. Their business was set up back in 1935, and as well as growing *guindillas* and *choriceros* (see pages 275 and 281) in Rioja they also cultivate *ñora* peppers (see page 280) on another five hectares they own in Murcia, as these benefit from a drier climate in which to ripen.

Herbón (Padrón) peppers, PDO
The bright green, pointy, triangular-shaped variety of pepper from the municipality of Padrón in Galicia has become Spain's most recognised and loved pepper in the UK, since it is a staple of the tapas bar, flash-fried in olive oil and served hot, sprinkled with sea salt (see page 274). I like to think that its popularity gives renewed hope for the green pepper in general, since for so long in Britain we have known only the green bell pepper that is relatively flavourless.

It can, however, be grown in other areas of Spain such as Almería and Murcia, and in countries such as Morocco (allowing the peppers

to be still available when the Galician harvest is over or in short supply). Some are even grown in small volumes in Cornwall, so one way or another you can usually find them fresh in UK shops. Peppers grown outside Galicia, however, are usually larger, possibly lighter in colour and may be drier in texture and less flavoursome.

Peppers from the town of Herbón, where, on the first Sunday in August, they celebrate the Fiesta del Pimiento, have PDO status. This guarantees the varietal and dictates that the peppers must be grown and picked to traditional methods in five villages of the municipality during the season (May to October). The area here benefits from generous rainfall and very fertile soil which produces peppers that are small – about 2cm in length – and are a bright, deep green, with juicy flesh. In the UK it can be almost impossible to find peppers bearing the mark of the Herbón PDO, but you can at least check that the peppers have been grown in Padrón.

Usually the peppers are mild, but you can play Russian roulette with the prospect of occasionally being hit with a more fiery one. Mostly they are harvested young, at only about 4–5cm in size, as at this stage only a minority will be spicy hot, whereas if they grow bigger there is much more chance of heat on the finish. As well as being a favourite tapa, the fried peppers are sometimes packed into tins of the small sardines (known as *xoubas*) in Galicia to add spice to them.

Pimientos de Padrón
Small flash-fried green peppers

The simplest and most delicious tapa. Serve 60–100g per person, according to whether or not you are serving them with something more substantial to follow (or how mad about them you are).

Serves 4 with other tapas

olive oil, for frying
around 300g fresh small green Padrón peppers, preferably Herbón PDO
sea salt

Heat a film of oil in a frying pan, put in the peppers and fry, moving them around, for about 4 minutes, until they blacken, then remove from the pan, sprinkle with sea salt and eat hot.

Gernika peppers (fresh)
These are in season between April and November and are similar to the Padrón, but bigger, around 6–9 cm long, and fairly thin with a more delicate skin, more tender flesh, a stronger flavour and more seeds.

How to use
These are typically eaten as a snack in the same way as the Padrón, flash-fried whole in olive oil and sprinkled with salt (see above).

Guindilla (eaten fresh locally, but mostly jarred or dried)

The best green *guindilla* peppers are grown in Ibarra, in the Basque country, where they are nicknamed *langostinos* (prawns) *de Ibarra* (or *ibarrako piparrak* in Basque), partly because of their long thin shape (they are 5–12cm long), and partly as a term of endearment, as both the peppers and prawns are among the best-loved foods of the Basques.

The peppers are famous for their mellow, fruity flavour – this is not an area that considers *picante* (hot) peppers desirable – and when they are in season, around July to October (earlier with greenhouse cultivation), freshly picked ones are pan-fried and sprinkled with salt, like the Galician Padrón in Basque homes and local bars. Ibarra is a gentle, verdant lowland, and the limited production of *guindillas* that grow there are of a strain that has been nurtured specially for the area. This microclimate is key: the small difference in temperature between day and night and the ample rainfall at 400 metres above sea level makes for sweet and juicy peppers that are collected by hand once they reach the length of a French green bean.

However, they are also very delicate, and once picked their life is short – which is why fresh ones don't travel to the UK. Since they won't keep, some are dried on long strings; however, the bigger tradition is to pickle and jar them in good wine vinegar.

In Rioja, a different, more strident variety of *guindilla* is grown and allowed to ripen to red on the plant, then dried and strung – we buy ours from the García family in Quel (see page 272). It is longer and fatter than the Ibarra *guindilla* and is used to add warmth and spice to dishes such as *gazpachos manchegos* (see page 456).

How to use

The jarred peppers are speared with olives, gherkins, and/or anchovies to have with drinks. They are also the essential complement to a plate of one of the Basque country's most typical dishes of slow-cooked Tolosa beans and bacon. The vinegary flavour and fresh crunch of the peppers makes a fabulous contrast to the velvety creaminess of the dark beans.

Piquillo (mainly charred in jars)

Roasted and conserved red *piquillo* peppers, the small version of the larger *pico* ('tail'), were unheard of in 1990 when Brindisa began to bring them in from Lodosa in Navarra, a region which carries its own label of Denomination of Origin. Of course, most of our customers said, 'But I can roast my own peppers' – however, most of the red peppers in the shops at the time were being grown hydroponically in Holland, and had so little flavour compared to the *piquillos* grown in the fields of Navarra. Here the clean waters and good soil combine with the sunshine to create a pepper with a delicate, thin skin that is intense in flavour and red colour and gives off an amazing aroma as it roasts in kitchens, garages, or over fires in the garden all around Navarra, as families make the most of the season.

Occasionally at Brindisa we have brought over a few sacks of fresh red *piquillos* and grilled them on our barbecue to share with customers as a way of celebrating harvest time. And in the local Navarra markets you sometimes also see fresh green ones that have been picked early, but they tend to be less popular than the ripe red ones, as they are a little bitter in comparison – though they are excellent lightly fried on a *montadito* (toast) with some grilled pork loin. The majority of the harvest, however, is grown for charring and preserving in jars.

Ours are grown by Pepe Salcedo Soria. At harvest time, the bright red fruit peeps out from lines and lines of low plants stretching towards the horizon. Nimble pickers pack the peppers into huge wooden crates, then they are washed and sorted. Traditionally, they would be tumbled on to a conveyor belt that took them through a funnel filled with burning beechwood, but the world moves on, and the process now uses gas flames – a shame, as I feel a little of the picturesque romance has been lost, even though the taste difference is minimal. The peppers are charred in a flash, losing around 60 per cent of their weight, so their flavour becomes even more concentrated. Then the belt carries them on to the warehouse, where they are gently and patiently hand-peeled by the women of the village – no use of an industrial water bath here that would strip the skins quickly but dilute their flavour in the process.

Once peeled, the women pack them one by one into jars and tins, placing the first ones flat against the outside of the jar or tin, then working inwards, and finally sealing them in nothing but their own juices. When you taste the peppers, their flavour is as intense as if they were still on the plant: sweet initially, then warm, slightly peppery and smoky on the finish.

At one time *piquillos* were cultivated and processed intensively in other regions of Spain, but outside Navarra production has largely transferred to countries like Peru, who can compete on price. Many Spanish companies are now packing Peruvian peppers – though not necessarily declaring the country of origin, in the way that we do at Brindisa. Their size is similar to the Spanish *piquillo*, the flesh fairly thin, and their flavour is as good as any other industrially produced pepper of this type; however, since they will usually be peeled using a water bath rather than by hand, they cannot compare with the exceptional quality of the traditional Lodosa *piquillo*, protected by its PDO.

How to use
Quick and easy
In Spain *piquillos* are used a great deal for decorating plates; for example, a rice dish might come with five of them arranged to form a star on top. The beauty of the peppers is that they have already been roasted before being peeled and put into a jar or tin, so they are ready to stuff (see right) or slice as you like, and they go well with so many ingredients, from tuna and capers (great as a sandwich filling) to soft cheese, to British pork sausages or steak. All of us at Brindisa hate to be without a jar in the cupboard and my colleagues are always swapping ideas on how to use them. This is a selection of our favourites:

To make a simple *tosta*, spread a layer of fresh curd or cream cheese on toast and top with the peppers. Or chop the peppers, then either pound them using a pestle and mortar or whiz them in a blender with garlic and enough extra virgin olive oil to form a paste. Spread on a slice of toasted bread, and top with Manchego cheese and some chopped chives.

I particularly like chef Peter Gordon's recipe for *piquillo* pepper harissa, for spreading on a slice of toasted bread topped with roasted vegetables, or spooning into a stew or soup. He toasts 2 teaspoons of cumin seeds, a teaspoon each of toasted fennel and coriander seeds, a stick of cinnamon and 2 star anise in a dry pan, grinds them, then blends to a paste with 300g of *piquillo* peppers, 3 cloves of garlic, 2 chopped chillies, a handful of fresh coriander, 2 tablespoons of dried mint, the juice and zest of 3 limes and around 150ml of olive oil.

Chop the peppers and scatter them over a *tortilla*, or use as a pizza topping, along with slices of aubergine and wild mushrooms.

Whiz some peppers with hummus in a blender and serve with grilled meats or burgers. Although the peppers don't need heating, they are also good sautéd very briefly. I often use up

Pimiento de piquillo
con meloso de setas
Piquillo peppers stuffed with
'creamy' wild mushroom rice

peppers from opened jars in this way, adding a little crushed garlic and sprinkling with a little PX vinegar, sherry vinegar or red wine vinegar, to serve alongside grilled meat or put into a grilled *chorizo* sandwich (see page 67). If you like, you can blend the peppers, garlic and vinegar to turn them into a smooth dipping sauce. Or add some capers and chopped herbs.

The peppers are also good cut into strips and pan-fried with cooked butter beans in a little olive oil, to serve alongside other small plates.

Stuffed *piquillos*
These are mainstays on tapas bar menus around Spain, featuring many fillings from the traditional to the experimental, easy or complex. Manu, one of our early chefs at the Food Rooms, likes to fill the peppers quite simply with a mixture of tuna, chopped hard-boiled egg and thinly sliced spring onions – great for a summer's day.

When filling the peppers, you just need to handle them with care, as they are very thin and delicate. Carefully open each one out, then spoon in the filling of your choice.

In tapas bars, stuffed *piquillos* are often served perched on top of pieces of good bread or toast so you can eat them with your fingers while standing up – though it requires a bit of dexterity to eat neatly and hold a drink at the same time.

If you want to make a more elaborate rice stuffing, a favourite at Brindisa is the squid black rice on page 359.

Makes 4

300ml chicken stock
150g risotto rice, such as Carnaroli,
  or Bomba (see page 341)
150g wild or chestnut mushrooms,
  finely chopped
80g spinach, washed
80g Manchego cheese, grated
sea salt and freshly ground black pepper
4 *piquillo* peppers

Bring the stock to the boil in a pan, add the rice, turn the heat down to a simmer and cook for 10 minutes, stirring regularly. Add the mushrooms and cook for 5 minutes, then add the spinach and continue cooking for another 5 minutes. Add the cheese for 2 more minutes. Season to taste.

Very gently open out the peppers and, holding each one with the thumb and forefinger of one hand, use a teaspoon to stuff them – very carefully, taking care not to split the peppers. Transfer to a serving dish.

Pimiento de piquillo con crema de queso y mojo verde

Piquillo pepper stuffed with goat's curd, mixed herbs and mojo verde

These are really quick and colourful: great for summer parties and picnics. Josep, our executive chef, who came up with the combination, uses goat's curd from La Bauma, but you could substitute cream cheese or cottage cheese.

Makes 4

150g goat's curd, cream cheese or cottage cheese
1 teaspoon mixed herbs, such as thyme, rosemary, chives, parsley and lemon thyme, finely chopped
4 piquillo peppers
150ml *mojo verde Brindisa* (see page 298)

Mix together the cheese and chopped herbs. Very gently open out the peppers and, holding each one with the thumb and forefinger of one hand, use a teaspoon to stuff them very carefully with the cheese mixture, taking care not to split the peppers. Top each one with a spoonful of *mojo verde*.

Pimiento de piquillo con morcilla de cebolla

Piquillo peppers stuffed with *morcilla* with onion

These have become a classic at our London Bridge tapas bar, where we present them in little terracotta dishes.

Makes 4

2 tablespoons olive oil
1 shallot, finely chopped
1 clove of garlic, finely chopped
1 tablespoon pine nuts
1 tablespoon raisins
170g *morcilla* with onion (see page 76), skin removed, crumbled
4 *piquillo* peppers

To serve (optional)
a little hot tomato *sofrito* (see page 316)

Heat the olive oil in a frying pan. Add the shallot and garlic and cook gently until soft but not coloured. Add the pine nuts and raisins, and let the pine nuts colour and the raisins expand a little. Add the *morcilla* and cook until it is heated through.

Very gently open out the peppers and, holding each one with the thumb and forefinger of one hand, use a teaspoon to stuff them – very carefully, taking care not to split the peppers. Transfer to a serving dish, and if using, spoon some hot *sofrito* around.

Bierzo peppers (fresh or jarred)

The valley of El Bierzo in León has a privileged climate of many hours of sunshine, rainfall, great humidity and late frosts that enables the harvest of amazing vegetables and fruit right through to mid-November. These large, bell-shaped peppers are particularly succulent and fleshy, usually twice as long as they are wide, and orange-red, occasionally with streaks of green. Fresh Bierzo peppers are perfect for dishes such as *pollo al chilindrón*; however, one of our biggest surprises at Brindisa was discovering the juiciness and freshness of the peppers when roasted and jarred.

How to use

For a simple tapa, just warm the jarred peppers in a pan with a film of oil and a clove of garlic, as you might do with a *piquillo* pepper, and serve them with anchovies, or add them to a lentil salad.

Another of our favourite things to do is combine the peppers with a fresh, 20-day goat's cheese such as Tiétar Fresco, and eat them just as they are, or on toast.

Ñora (dried)

Our dried *ñora* peppers are grown by the García family in Murcia. The planting takes place in May, the fruit ripens and turns red over the warm summer and is harvested in the autumn, when only the fully ripened peppers will be picked, then dried on trays in large ventilated ovens. Drying is a slow process, taking about eight days, with the peppers being turned every 2 days, and the trays rotated, to ensure consistency in the drying. Then, once dried, one of the six elderly lady stringers will thread them on to *ristras* of 20 to 100 peppers.

How to use

You need to soak the dried peppers for half an hour to an hour to rehydrate them. Typically, the peppers are then roasted whole in oil, aromatising it ready to sauté onions and garlic to make a base for slow-cooked dishes. The pepper is then taken out, the flesh is scraped from the skin and then pounded to make a *picada/majada* (see page 320) for adding at the end of cooking. The peppers are not very fleshy, but what scrapings of flesh there are give an important, peppery sweetness to a dish.

Choricero (dried)

In Spain you can buy huge strings of around 100 dried red *choricero* peppers – we always have one, made by the García family's network of stringers, hanging in the kitchen at home and many visitors think they are giant raisins or prunes, as they are so dark and wrinkled.

These large, mild, fleshy peppers grow in the Basque country as well as in La Rioja and once rehydrated in water have a deep, rich pepper flavour and subtle smokiness.

How to use

Choriceros are often used in place of *pimentón* (paprika), sometimes made into a pure *choricero* sauce or *gazpacho*, or typically added to lentil dishes, *rancho riojano* (Riojan stew) and, in the Basque country, salt cod *a la vizcayana*.

Pimientos de cristal (jarred)

Fully ripened crimson-red *cristal* peppers are some of the most delicate and sought-after peppers, with the thinnest skins of all – hence the name. They come from a small but very select harvest in the same region as the *piquillos* – Lodosa in Navarra – and are long and slender, wood-roasted and hand-peeled, then put into jars. So delicate are they that each kilo of fresh peppers will end up filling only a small 170g jar.

How to use

Sweet and smoky, the peppers are best eaten just as they come, with only a light dressing of olive oil and vinegar and a sprinkling of sea salt. Their sweetness combined with a salty ingredient such as bacon or anchovies is a match made in heaven. So try them straight from the jar with fried egg and bacon for a brunch dish, or on crusty bread with a fat, freshly-filleted cured anchovy.

Life and Cooking with Mark and Arbell

Perhaps the area of Catalunya that I have come to know best in recent years is Moianès, about an hour's drive from Barcelona. This is where my brother, Mark, chose to settle with his second wife, Arbell, and family after years of living in the city of Barcelona, in order to pursue their dream of producing wine – a passion he always shared with my father. Their ancient stone farmhouse is in an area full of natural beauty overlooking the village of Santa Maria d'Oló, with the mountain of Montserrat to the south and the snow-capped Pyrenees to the north. It is a favourite with birdwatchers, since it is full of bee-eaters, woodpeckers and nightingales, and the house is called Can Coll Tor, which means House of the Wryneck, a sparrow-sized bird that lives on the ground and eats ants.

There are terraces of almond trees and groves of olives which Arbell cures herself, and they keep hens so they always have fresh eggs, but the main project is the wine: Vinos Colltor.

For the last ten years Mark and Arbell have been acquiring small tracts of land, planting, pruning, harvesting, dry-stonewalling and building a small *bodega*. Their land is within the Pla de Bages Denomination of Origin where neighbouring *bodegas* such as Abadal and Celler el Molí have blazed the trail, growing in prestige and encouraging recognition for the fine wines of this area.

The reds of the region tend to be very dark-coloured, full-bodied *crianza* wines (aged in oak) and the popular grapes are Merlot, which thrives in the area, the sturdy and reliable Cabernet Sauvignon, and Syrah, the wild card. Since this is a grape that likes a hot, dry climate, Mark and Arbell have high hopes for it. In addition, with a view to creating more distinctive wines over the coming years, they are planting white Picapoll and red Mando, indigenous varietals to blend with their established international ones.

Wine-making is a tough but exciting challenge, and while the first two vintages were barely drinkable, by 2011 the results were very good. In 2016 they not only produced around 10,000 bottles of their two red wines (in Catalan red wine is known as *vi negre*), but they achieved the mark of the Pla de Bages DO.

Their white label is predominantly Merlot, with some Cabernet Sauvignon, aged in American oak, and the black label is almost all Syrah, aged in French oak to create a very distinguished wine. I feel that we have created the perfect circle in that we are now able to sell their wines in London and on the menu of our restaurant, La Bellvitja, in Barcelona.

When we visit Mark and Arbell in winter a favourite family event is to char *calçots* over a fire bolstered with vine trimmings, as this is also vine-pruning time.

Calçots are the famous sweet, delicate Catalan onions that look like thin leeks or large spring onions and are the great February treat. The word *calçot* means 'shoed' in Catalan, which refers to the fact that the onions are kept tender, white and juicy by piling the earth over and around them to create a shoe-shaped cover that keeps out the light as they try to push through the soil.

You buy the *calçots* in bundles of about 20 and traditionally, for a proper, traditional *calçotada* session, large groups of family and friends get together to cook them outside over a fire made inside a ring of stones with a grill on top. Mark and Arbell have converted a couple of shepherd shelters into *calçotada* venues, which can be used for an entire day in February–March to celebrate the season; however, we like to char them over the huge fireplace in the farm-house kitchen.

As soon as the *calçots* come off the fire, we wrap them in newspaper like fish and chips, to let them steam a bit, then strip them of their charred casings and dip them into great bowls of *romesco* sauce. It's a delicious, messy business that ends up with bits of ash-covered outer skins and dribbles of sauce everywhere, so we use more newspaper for a tablecloth, so that all the leftovers can just be bundled up and disposed of.

CALÇOTS CON ROMESCO

Calçots are snapped up as soon as we begin to sell them and during their season you see them in restaurants all over London. At our own Shoreditch restaurant we serve an entire *calçotada* menu in February, which also features a selection of the grilled meats and vegetables that the Catalans love so much.

The traditional accompaniment is *romesco* sauce, and it is always worth making plenty of this, as it is also good spooned over any grilled vegetables, potatoes or meats such as *botifarra* and lamb chops, or mixed into certain rice dishes, to add texture and flavour. As usual in Spain, everyone has a slightly different and favourite version of *romesco*. See pages 304–305 for three quite different versions.

You can cook *calçots* on the barbecue in the traditional manner, or under the kitchen grill. Allow around six per person if you are serving them with other foods. Trim off the extra-long green leaves and any excessive outer casing, but leave at least one protective layer – you want the *calçots* to be roughly the diameter of a baby leek. Grill them on a high heat for 2–3 minutes, until the outer layer chars. Peel this off before eating, then dip into whichever *romesco* sauce you choose (my favourite is on page 304).

Escalivada
Catalan roasted vegetables

In essence, this is just a collection of vegetables, oven-roasted or flame-grilled in their skins – most commonly red peppers, aubergines and onions – which are taken off the heat, skinned and cleaned of seeds, sliced, then eaten warm or allowed to get cold, dressed with oil and vinegar. However, every household will have their own way of enhancing the taste experience or stretching the dish with extra ingredients. María, the mother of my friend Núria Mayans Pla in Osona in Catalunya, makes a wonderful *escalivada* that unusually includes baked potatoes, which soak up the dressing beautifully and make the dish a little more filling, so I have given them as an option in this recipe. Other people add goat's cheese, anchovies or sardines, which go very well with the juicy, fruity, roasted flavours of the peppers, onions and aubergines. Or you could add some roasted *piquillo* peppers from a jar (see page 275).

Whatever you use, the success of the dish depends on the quality of your ingredients. Ideally, you want sun-ripened peppers and aubergines, which soften easily, and super-sweet onions. Out of season, or even if you are short of time, it is sometimes better to use jarred peppers and aubergines, which might have a better flavour. And equally important is the dressing: if you use an exquisite vinegar such as a Moscatel this will enhance the taste enormously.

Serves 4

2 medium baking potatoes (optional)
2 medium onions, skin on
2 aubergines
4 cloves of garlic, cut into slivers
2 medium red peppers

For the dressing
2 tablespoons extra virgin olive oil
1 tablespoon good vinegar, such as Moscatel or Chardonnay
2 cloves of garlic, finely chopped
sea salt and freshly ground black pepper

To serve
a handful of good black olives or 1 teaspoon Empeltre black olive pâté (or some good black olives, stoned and crushed)
a little extra virgin olive oil

Optional
8 tinned cured anchovy fillets in oil, or sardines, or 100g crumbly goat's cheese
a little chopped parsley (optional)

Preheat the oven to 200°C/gas 6.

If using the potatoes, put them into the preheated oven and bake for 45 minutes to 1 hour, until tender. Wrap the onions in foil and put into the oven for 45 minutes. Cut slits in each aubergine, and push a sliver of garlic into each one. Place on a baking tray in the oven for 30 minutes. Add the peppers to the tray for the last 20 minutes.

Remove the skins from all the vegetables and cut into rough strips.

Combine the oil, vinegar, garlic and seasoning for the dressing, toss through the vegetables and leave in the fridge for 3 hours, so that the flavours can mingle.

To serve, arrange the vegetables to make the most of the different colours: either lay them out separately on a long plate with the potatoes to one side, or, if you are not using potatoes, you can layer them up in a more delicate presentation.

If using olive pâté, or crushed olives, add a little extra virgin olive oil to loosen, then drizzle this over the dressed vegetables. Otherwise, add the olives to the plate. If using the anchovies or sardines, arrange them on top, or if using goat's cheese crumble it over and, if you like, scatter with a little chopped parsley.

Pisto manchego de Ana Barrera con huevos rotos
Ana Barrera's tomato and courgette '*pisto*' with fried eggs

Throughout Spain you will find different interpretations of *pisto* and it can be very, very good, or extremely dull. Ana's version is very, very good: full of warm colours and rich flavours. It is similar to ratatouille, but cooked slowly, for longer, with fewer ingredients, so it relies heavily on their quality, in particular the abundance of ruby ripe tomatoes which Ana first makes into a sauce. It is this that gives the *pisto* its lovely colour, which ratatouille often lacks.

Ana serves her *pisto* in the traditional way, with 2 eggs very lightly fried, so that the white is not crispy and the yolk is still runny. She breaks them up with a knife and fork and mixes them in – they will cook a little more in the heat of the vegetables. You barely see them in the finished dish, but they really enrich it.

At Brindisa, we add just the yolks – 3 are enough for 6 people – as this is where the flavour is concentrated. We break the eggs and slide each yolk into a teacup, then heat some olive oil in a pan and pour just enough into the cup to cover and lightly cook the yolk (you could do this with boiling water if you prefer). Then we lift out the yolks with a slotted spoon and arrange them on top of the vegetables, ready to be mixed in. If you want to be quite smart you could serve the *pisto* in individual bowls with an egg yolk perched on the top of each one.

Serves 6

a little olive oil
600g green peppers, finely chopped
300g onions, finely chopped
1.2kg courgettes, peeled and finely chopped
sea salt
a little sugar
2–3 eggs, lightly fried, or yolks
 cooked as above (optional)

For the sauce
1 onion, chopped
2kg very ripe tomatoes
3 tablespoons olive oil
a little salt or sugar as necessary

To make the sauce, put the chopped onion and whole tomatoes into a large pan and drizzle with the olive oil (rather than heating the olive oil first). Bring to a simmer, then turn down the heat and cook very, very slowly for 2 hours. Put through a fine sieve and taste. You are looking for a rich tomato flavour nicely balanced between sweetness and acidity. If it tastes too acidic, add a touch of sugar, and if too sweet, counteract this with a little salt.

Heat a little olive oil in a frying pan, put in the peppers and cook for about 30 minutes, very gently, until they are quite soft, then add the onions and cook very slowly for about 30 minutes, until completely soft.

Meanwhile, heat some more olive oil in a separate pan, add the courgettes and, again, cook gently for about 30 minutes, then add to the pan of onion and peppers and cook for a further 30 minutes.

If too much oil has come to the surface at the end of this time, drain it off, then add the tomato sauce and cook for at least 15 minutes more. Taste and again season with salt and/or sugar, if necessary. If serving with eggs or yolks, arrange these on top.

Cigrons guisats a la catalana
Chickpeas Catalan-style with saffron and almond *picada*

My friend Jordi Puigvi lent me a wonderful book called *La Cuina que torna*, written by Josep Lladanosa, who was the chef at the very famous and respected 7 *Portes* restaurant in Barcelona, which has been there for 170 years and specialises in Catalan cooking, particularly rice dishes. Lladanosa is now in his seventies, and is a prolific writer of fascinating books that delve into the history and techniques of Catalan cooking as far back as the Middle Ages.

La Cuina que torna means 'the dishes that come back', i.e. old favourites, and it particularly caught my eye, as it is divided into chapters such as Food of the Poor (which includes pulses and offal; Food of the Rich, which includes meat; and Food of the Gods, which features game and fowl. I particularly like the Food of the Poor chapter, with its economical dishes designed to stave off hunger and give you strength, such as this chickpea dish which combines many different flavours.

The tomato flavour in this dish should be present, but not overwhelming; however, it does rely on sweet, ripe, seasonal tomatoes, or cherry tomatoes. If you really don't feel you are getting enough flavour from your tomatoes, you could add a jar of bought *sofrito de tomate* or about 300g of homemade instead (see page 318 for the recipe).

Serves 6

250g dried chickpeas, such as the small pedrosillano, or 600g jarred, cooked chickpeas
10g bicarbonate of soda (if using dried chickpeas)
6 eggs
125ml olive oil
2 onions, finely chopped
10 ripe medium tomatoes, grated
50g blanched almonds, chopped
10 threads of saffron, soaked
a big handful of parsley
4 cloves of garlic, peeled
sea salt and freshly ground black pepper

If using dried chickpeas, soak them the night before in warm water with the bicarbonate of soda. Drain and put into a pan, cover with cold water, bring to the boil, then turn down to a simmer for about 1½ hours, until tender. Drain, again, reserving the cooking water.

Put the eggs into cold water and bring to a simmer gently so that the shells don't crack, then cook gently for 10 minutes. Drain and run under cold water, then peel and slice.

Heat the oil in a heavy-based pan, add the onions and cook very, very gently for about 20 minutes, until translucent and sweet, then add the tomatoes and cook for a further 20 minutes.

Add the cooked chickpeas (or jarred ones) together with about 200ml of the reserved cooking water, or liquid from the jar, topped up if necessary with water, and heat through.

With a pestle and mortar, pound the chopped almonds with the saffron, parsley and garlic. Blend with another 50ml of the reserved cooking liquid (or water if using jarred chickpeas), then add to the pan of chickpeas and sauce. Stir through, taste and season.

Serve topped with sliced eggs.

PATATAS
Potatoes

One vegetable that really comes into its own on the tapas menu is the potato – often with some lardons, or slivers of *chorizo* or black pudding added. Spain was the gateway to Europe for the potato when it arrived from the Americas, so it is well loved. And the Spanish can be as obsessive about varieties as we often are in the UK, extolling the virtues of their local crops, such as Bufet from Cerdanya in the Pyrenees. The mountain potato has grown there since the end of the nineteenth century, when the seeds were brought in from Brittany of a variety called Institut Beauvis, which became Bufet in Catalan. It can be white or purple and has a creamy flesh and a fabulous, slightly sweet, almost chestnutty flavour, but because the production, especially of the purple potatoes, is very small, it can be expensive. Bufet is the preferred potato for *trinxat de la Cerdanya*, the Pyrenean potato, bacon and cabbage patty that always reminds me of bubble and squeak.

Then there is Bonita, the ancient potato from the Canaries that is of Andean origin and comes in a range of colours from black to red, yellow and white, each of which might have its own descriptive name, such as 'partridge-eye'.

Across Spain there are endless variations of *patatas a lo pobre* – 'poor man's' potatoes with whatever else a family had in the larder added to them – perhaps some mushrooms and garlic, green pepper or tomatoes. Our friends Pepe and Mercedes (see page 80) told us a story that I particularly like about a version known as *patatas a lo pobre estilo merluza*, poor man's potatoes hake-style, in which the potatoes are cooked in fish stock, then mixed with green peas, parsley and coriander and finished off with chopped cooked egg white and grated egg yolk. Who knows whether it is true or not, but the idea was apparently that if you were eating outside, when your neighbours walked past, the aroma and look of the dish might convince them that you weren't eating a humble dish of potatoes, but hake in green sauce.

Patatas enmascaradas
'Masked' or 'dirtied' potatoes

Not very photogenic, but delicious, this Catalan dish is also called *patatas ensuciadas* (tainted). The rather unflattering names refer to the changing and blackening of the white potato by the black pudding (*morcilla*, see page 76), or *botifarra negra* (see page 450), so the first time I made this and took it to our warehouse kitchen to share with my non-Catalan Brindisa colleagues I was afraid they would be horrified, but in fact they loved it and wolfed it down. Even so, I find that if you cream the potatoes and thoroughly mix in the black pudding, as is the tendency in Catalunya, the resulting dish can have a look of cowpat about it, so I prefer to mash, almost chop, the potatoes very roughly, and mix in the black pudding quite lightly, so that the effect is of black and white, with some texture to it.

Patatas enmascaradas is a regular home-cooked combination of the kind known as *de toda la vida*, literally 'of always', among Catalans living inland, especially in the mountainous area of La Berguedà. It is a firm favourite with our friend Enric, the chocolate wizard of Rovira Chocolates (see page 34), and his uncle Francésc – I always find it comforting to discover that even great aesthetic artists such as Enric like nothing better than to sit around the table at their home in Castellbell i el Vilar and share simple, traditional potato dishes like this one.

This particular version was perfected with the help of my friend Boojum.

Serves 4 as a side dish or 6–8 as a tapa with other dishes

30g pine nuts
1kg floury potatoes
2 tablespoons olive oil
100g *panceta* or bacon, chopped, plus 1 slice of *panceta* or whole rasher
200g *botifarra negra* or *morcilla* with onion, skinned and broken up
1 tablespoon chopped parsley
1 tablespoon chopped mint
sea salt

Toast the pine nuts in a dry pan until golden and keep to one side.

Cook the potatoes until just tender in just enough boiling, salted water to cover, then drain through a colander and place this back over the still-hot pan, to allow them to steam a little and dry off.

Meanwhile, heat the olive oil in a pan and fry the chopped *panceta* or bacon, plus the whole slice of *panceta*/rasher, until crispy, then lift out, drain on kitchen paper and keep to one side. Put the black pudding pieces into the same pan and cook for about 3 minutes, moving them around, but also letting them catch a little on the base of the pan until you have crispy little nuggets.

Crush the potatoes roughly, add the black pudding, chopped *panceta* or bacon, parsley and mint, and just draw them through the potatoes with a fork. What you are aiming for is a contrast of white and black rather than the potatoes and black pudding all merging into one colour. Taste and season with salt if necessary. Serve with the whole crispy slice of *panceta*/rasher on top, and sprinkle with the reserved toasted pine nuts.

Patatas a la importancia
Potatoes with tomatoes and almonds

The almonds really add character to the potatoes and make this a filling winter dish, especially good alongside small plates of grilled fish. Typically, you would serve them in a terracotta *cazuela*, the famous round or oblong dish that can be used on top of the stove or in the oven.

Serves 4

50g blanched almonds, preferably Marcona (see page 90), plus a few extra to garnish
1.5kg potatoes, such as Vivaldi
salt
3 eggs, beaten
a little plain flour
around 200ml olive oil
1 onion, finely chopped
2 cloves of garlic, finely chopped
200g tomato *sofrito* (see page 316)
a handful of parsley, finely chopped

Preheat the oven to 180°C/gas 4.

Lay the almonds on a baking tray and put into the preheated oven for about 10 minutes, until golden. Remove from the oven, cool, then pound in a pestle and mortar.

Cook the potatoes, whole and unpeeled, in salted water until just tender when pierced with the tip of a sharp knife. Drain, and when cool enough to touch, cut into slices about 1.5cm thick.

Have the beaten eggs and some flour ready in separate shallow bowls. Coat the potato slices first in egg and then flour, shaking off the excess.

Heat the olive oil in a pan. Make sure it is big enough so that the oil doesn't come further up than halfway. Put in the potato slices and fry them gently until golden. Lift out and drain in a single layer on kitchen paper, then transfer the slices to a wide, flameproof casserole or *cazuela* (the traditional terracotta dish).

Pour away some of the oil from the pan in which you cooked the potatoes, leaving a couple of tablespoons only. Put the pan back on the heat, add the onion and garlic and cook gently until soft, but not coloured. Add the tomato *sofrito*, the pounded almonds and chopped parsley and cook briefly. Add 200ml of water to the mixture, stir well, then spoon over the top of the potatoes in the casserole. Cover with a lid (if using a *cazuela*, use foil) and cook over a low heat until the potatoes are completely tender, adding a little extra water if the sauce becomes too thick.

Serve garnished with a few crushed almonds.

Patates estofades amb rossinyols
Potato and girolle sauté

Another warming and autumnal combination adapted by our executive chef, Josep, from a recipe by Llorenç Petrás, the wild-food man from Barcelona (see page 268). Whenever we make it at home for the family it just flies off the table. The best surprise when you combine potato and mushroom is how aromatic the dish becomes.

Traditionally for certain one-pot dishes such as this, the potatoes are chopped in a particular irregular way, using a technique known as *cascada*, or 'cracking' (from the verb *cascar*). The potatoes are first cut into quite big chunks of about 4–5cm, then you insert a small, sharp knife halfway into each chunk and twist the blade until the potato breaks into jagged pieces (*cascadas*), making a cracking sound as it does so. Because the potato breaks unevenly, as if along fault lines, the cell walls stay more intact and less exposed than if you sliced through them with a knife. So as they simmer, less starch is released and the potatoes cook evenly all the way through rather than being slightly softer on the outside.

If using a green pepper, it is best to find a thin-skinned variety, which will usually be less bitter.

Serves 4

3 tablespoons olive oil
1 clove of garlic, peeled
1 onion, diced
300g girolles or other wild mushrooms,
  roughly chopped
1 sprig of fresh thyme or 1 teaspoon dried thyme
1 bay leaf
1 sprig of rosemary, about 2cm
½ a small green pepper (optional),
  roughly chopped, about 2cm
½ teaspoon *pimentón dulce* (mild paprika)
2 ripe tomatoes, grated
freshly ground black pepper
250g potatoes, peeled and broken *cascada*-style
  into rough 2cm pieces (see above)
sea salt (if necessary)
½ teaspoon sugar (if necessary)
about 6 blanched almonds
1 teaspoon chopped parsley

Heat the olive oil in a deep frying pan, then add the whole garlic clove, frying gently until golden brown. Add the onion and cook gently over a medium heat until it also begins to turn brown, but not crispy. Remove the garlic clove and keep to one side.

Add the mushrooms to the pan along with the thyme, bay leaf and rosemary and fry over a medium heat for around 5 minutes, until the mushrooms release their juices, but don't let them boil.

Add the green pepper, stirring in well, and continue to fry over a medium heat for about 5 minutes until just tender. Sprinkle in the paprika and let it fry for 30 seconds before adding the grated tomato. Cook on a steady simmer for 3 minutes, add a twist of black pepper, then stir in the potatoes, making sure they are well covered with oil, mushrooms and tomato. Continue to cook until the edges are beginning to brown, then add 250ml of cold water and bring the contents of the pan back to the boil. Taste and if necessary add a pinch of salt and the sugar.

Turn down the heat to a simmer and cook for around 20 minutes, until the potatoes are tender.

Meanwhile, make a simple *picada* (see page 320). Crush the reserved garlic using a pestle and mortar. Add the almonds and mash into a paste. Loosen with 4 tablespoons of water, then add the mixture back to the pan of mushrooms and potatoes at the end of the cooking time. Let the *picada* heat through briefly, sprinkle with the chopped parsley and serve hot.

Patatas revolconas
con sus torreznos

Paprika tumbled potatoes
with lardons

I love the name of this dish: *revolconas* is derived from the word *revolcón*, which means a tumble or roll around in the hay, kissing and canoodling, so there is something very romantic and fun about the idea of the lardons (*torreznos*) and the potatoes frolicking together.

I first ate *patatas revolconas* way back in the early heady days of Brindisa when I and my great school friend Tara O'Connor were on a trip to see Julián Sánchez García, our bean supplier in Ávila.

We walked high up into the Gredos mountains, where icy cold lakes irrigate the growing beans, and as Tara and I were wearing shorts, we were frozen. So on our way back to the village of El Barco, where Julián sorts and grades the dried beans, he took us to a mountain bar, where they served up this wonderful dish of creamed potatoes, reddened and flavoured with smoky *pimentón*, with chunky bacon pieces in it. Central heating in a bowl!

Since then I have eaten it many times at Ana Barrera's restaurant in Madrid (see page 442), where it is a staple, loved by all her regulars. It is typical of her style of cooking that she takes these kinds of dishes you would make at home – but raises them to a highly exacting level.

She makes the dish with *papada ibérica*, slabs of pork jowl from Ibérico pigs, which she buys semi-cured and prepared to her own specifications, from a particular butcher. The *papada* consists mainly of silky-white, acorn-fed, beautifully sweet and tasty fat, with the thinnest streaks of lean pork running through the base. There is nothing visually delicate about Ana's *torreznos*; she cuts them into quite doorstep-like chunks – about 2cm x 1cm thick – which she sautés in olive oil to which they add their own fat, until they are crispy-crunchy on the outside and delicate and melting – almost liquid – on the inside. Then she uses the oil from cooking them, flavoured with paprika from La Vera, near to her native Ávila, to make the most delicious, warming crushed potato.

This idea of flavouring oil with paprika is something many people do, especially in northern Spain, when cooking all kinds of vegetables. For example, you might blanch some cauliflower, then sauté it briefly in oil, just enough to colour it, lift it out, then flavour the oil with paprika and pour it back over the cauliflower. My friend Ambrosio in Burgos (see page 154) calls this oily paprika 'sauce' *salsa preve*, and it can be enhanced with garlic, dried peppers, parsley and vinegar. It is also used to flavour meats or fish from the barbecue. Just a note of caution: be careful not to burn the paprika, as it will give the oil a bitter flavour.

If you can't find *papada*, you can use *panceta* instead. Ana also recommends you use a quite neutral potato with a floury texture, as the potato flavour shouldn't dominate; instead it should really absorb the oil and paprika, and take on its smoky, bittersweet flavour.

Serves 4

1kg potatoes, peeled
salt
2 cloves of garlic, peeled
1 bay leaf
2 tablespoons olive oil
about 250g *panceta* or *papada ibérica*,
  cut into chunks
¼ of an onion, roughly chopped
1 tablespoon bittersweet paprika,
  plus a little extra to finish

Cook the potatoes gently in just enough salted, boiling water to cover, with the garlic and bay leaf.

While the potatoes are cooking, heat the oil, put in the chunks of *panceta* or *papada ibérica* and seal quickly, then reduce the heat and keep moving the pieces around so that they cook slowly and take on a golden colour, but don't burn. This will take about 5 minutes. They should be crispy on the outside and very soft inside. Lift out and drain on kitchen paper. Add the onion to the oil and cook for a few minutes, just to flavour the oil, then remove it. Take off the heat and let the oil cool a little, then add the paprika, stirring well.

Patatas bravas Brindisa
Fried potatoes with Brindisa *brava* sauce

When the potatoes are tender, drain them over a bowl, so that you reserve the water. Discard the garlic and bay leaf.

Add the potato water, a little at a time, to the oil and paprika, being careful to avoid spitting, and stirring well. Crush the potatoes, then gradually work in the flavoured oil and potato water a little at a time. The potato should taste strongly of the paprika.

Serve topped with the lardons and sprinkle, if you like, with a little more paprika.

If I am honest, I have never quite understood why this particular potato dish is so much more popular than others – especially as I have frequently encountered it done very badly, with potatoes that are crunchy on the outside, but not cooked properly inside, or a sauce that is either weak, watery and separating, or overpoweringly hot. However, since it is probably the most famous Spanish potato dish and we do have it on the menu at Brindisa, I couldn't write a book without including it.

Of course, once you start talking to Spanish cooks about *patatas bravas*, like *tortillas* and *croquetas*, everyone has a critical viewpoint on the way to make it 'properly', but in my experience, the best way to achieve the right crunch and cooking of the potatoes is to use King Edwards, cut them into squares and blanch them briefly first, as you would for roast potatoes, then drain, dry and deep-fry them. Potatoes done this way are also good served just with *alioli* (see page 136).

The original *brava* sauce, which was typical of Madrid, was actually quite thin, with a meaty background flavour as it was made with the stock left over from a *cocido* (stew), to which tomatoes and peppers were added. However, I think it should be thick enough to properly cling to the potatoes. We like to give ours a freshness by using a whole red chilli, which can be topped up with dried varieties to adjust the heat to your preference – though the aim is not to make the sauce so hot that you can't appreciate the other flavours.

Serves 4 as a tapa with other dishes

400g potatoes, preferably King Edward, peeled and cut into squares of about 2.5cm
500ml vegetable or sunflower oil, for deep-frying
sea salt

For the salsa brava
1 fresh red chilli pepper or a pinch of dried chilli flakes (plus extra flakes if required)
2 tablespoons olive oil
½ a large onion, finely chopped
1 carrot, finely chopped
¼ a large leek, finely chopped
1 clove of garlic, finely chopped
500g ripe medium tomatoes, chopped
1 tablespoon tomato purée, if needed
a pinch of sea salt, or to taste
a pinch of sugar, or to taste

First, make the *brava* sauce. If using a fresh chilli pepper, preheat the grill, roast the pepper for 2 minutes on each side to bring out the flavour, then leave to cool and remove the stalk.

Heat the oil in a pan, add the onion, carrot, leek, garlic and the whole roasted chilli pepper, if using, and cook very slowly for 25–30 minutes, until the vegetables are soft, but not coloured, stirring from time to time to make sure they are not catching.

Either grate the tomatoes or, if you prefer, de-skin and de-seed them (see page 206).

Add the tomatoes to the pan. If you are using chilli flakes instead of a fresh chilli, add them now. Simmer over a very low heat for 1¼ hours, stirring frequently. Taste and add extra dried chilli if necessary to give more heat. The sauce should be a rich, deep orange colour, but if your tomatoes aren't the ripest, you might want to help the colour – and flavour – with a tablespoon of tomato purée.

When you are happy with the spiciness, take the pan off the heat and blend the sauce in a food processor until it is as thick as mayonnaise. Taste and if necessary season with salt and/or a pinch of sugar.

Cook the potatoes in boiling water for 10 minutes, until tender if pierced with the tip of a sharp knife, then drain in a colander and leave to dry.

Heat the oil in a deep pan (making sure it comes no further than a third of the way up). It needs to be around 180°C, but if you don't have a thermometer, put in a small piece of potato and if it sizzles the oil is hot enough.

Put in the potatoes and deep-fry for about 3 minutes, until they are golden and crunchy all round. Drain on kitchen paper.

Sprinkle with salt and serve with the *brava* sauce. You can spoon this over the top of the potatoes, or do as I prefer and serve it on the side, so that people can take as much or as little as they like.

Papas arrugadas
Salt-wrinkled potatoes

Every visitor to the Canary Islands will be offered *papas arrugadas*, which is their famous dish of wrinkled potatoes (*papas*), served with a red and/or green *mojo* sauce (see pages 298–300) – though I also think the potatoes are wonderful with *romesco* sauce (see pages 304-305). Sometimes some crumbled goat's cheese and fried almond slices will be sprinkled over the top, in which case the dish is known as *papas garrapiñadas*.

The variety of potato they use is Bonita, which is small, irregular in shape, with dark yellowy insides, quite floury in texture and with a strong flavour. For a small potato it has a thick skin, which does actually wrinkle away from the flesh, though you may find you don't get the same effect with English potatoes.

You need to cook the potatoes in lots of salty water – originally it would have been sea water, so the idea is to recreate the same ratio of salt to water (sea water is 3.5 per cent salt). The locals say that if you have enough salt in the water the potatoes will float.

Serves 4

1kg Canarian *papas*, or English new or baby potatoes
sea salt
about 150ml *mojo rojo* and/or *mojo verde*, to serve (see pages 298–300)

Put the potatoes into a pan with enough salted water to cover (use a ratio of 50g sea salt to 1.5 litres of water). Bring to the boil and let the potatoes cook until they are just tender. Drain them, leaving just a little water on them (as you would when draining pasta), then put them back into the pan over a very low heat. Don't cover them, just let them dry off for about 7 minutes, rolling them around in the dry pan so that they don't burn. You will see the salt crystallize around the potatoes.

Remove from the heat and cover with a tea towel for about 20 minutes, until there is a fine patina of salt on the skins of the potatoes. If you are lucky, they will also have wrinkled a little.

Serve with the *mojo rojo* and/or *mojo verde* drizzled over.

SALSAS

'everyone has their own variation'

Many regions have their own favoured sauces, for example the *salmorreta* of Alicante, made with *ñora* peppers, tomatoes and garlic, which is added to the local rice and seafood dishes and stews.

The mojos of the Canaries
Some of the most famous, however, are the Canarian *mojos* – these are more like a pesto than a sauce – which are inevitably served in traditional fashion alongside salt-wrinkled potatoes, *papas arrugadas* (see page 296), or grilled fish such as the local *cherne* (sea bass), but are also increasingly being used in more imaginative ways. On one trip to Gran Canaria, at Restaurante Nelson in Agüimes, I ate a starter of the local, delicate white Palmero goat's cheese, grilled lightly on the *plancha*, so that it had a little bit of crust on the outside, but was soft and gooey inside, served with a green coriander *mojo* (see page 300) and tomato jam (see page 533), and it was really delicious.

The two most typical *mojos* are made with either green or red peppers (*mojo verde* or *mojo rojo*), but there is no standard recipe: everyone has their own variation, using different herbs, garlic, a drop of vinegar, perhaps, and like an Italian talking about pesto, every Canarian islander will tell you *theirs* is the only true way.

Mojo verde Brindisa
Brindisa Canarian green sauce

This is one of the *mojos* we make all the time at home – it is slightly more delicate than its red counterpart, made with a sweeter vinegar and less garlic, but it still punches quite hard.

It really suits potatoes, cooked in any style, and goes especially well with tapas of squares of firm white fish such as *cherne* (sea bass), floured and lightly fried.

Again, because you are dealing with small quantities, you could use a pestle and mortar – but this *mojo* is designed for making in a blender.

Makes about 300ml

4 cloves of garlic, peeled
100g bread, fried in olive oil
  and broken into small pieces
2 teaspoons ground cumin
6 tablespoons sherry vinegar
4–6 heaped tablespoons chopped
  coriander or parsley, to taste
a pinch of sea salt
300ml olive oil

Blend all the ingredients apart from the salt and the oil, then add the oil slowly and season to taste.

Mojo rojo picón Brindisa
Brindisa Canarian hot red sauce

Mojo rojo is the typical sauce for serving with *papas arrugadas* (see page 296), though you could also choose *mojo verde* (see page 298). This is the version we make in our Brindisa kitchens, using the hot *guindilla* pepper in equal quantities with garlic cloves. We make it often at home and use it to add to a tapa of grilled cutlets of lamb, beans and pulses, or even a burger, steak slider or sandwich. If you want to reduce the heat of the sauce you can add a little fresh or roasted red pepper to the blend (see below). Some people add pieces of fried bread to thicken the sauce, but I feel that it is fresher without.

With such small quantities it is easy to make by hand using a pestle and mortar, but if you want to use a blender, put in all the ingredients, except the oil, and blend to a paste, then slowly add the oil while continuing to blend.

Makes 300ml

4 long *guindilla* chilli peppers (see page 275)
1 teaspoon cumin seeds
4 cloves of garlic, roughly chopped
½ a red pepper (or the equivalent roasted
  and peeled pepper from a jar) (optional,
  to reduce the heat)
¾ teaspoon fine sea salt
75ml wine vinegar, such as Cabernet Sauvignon
200ml olive oil

First, prepare the peppers by soaking them in warm water for 20 minutes. Drain them and scrape out the flesh.

Grind the cumin seeds using a pestle and mortar and put through a fine sieve. Return to the mortar with the rest of the ingredients, except the olive oil, and pound to a paste. Add the olive oil slowly and work it in until well combined.

Mojo verde con pimiento y cilantro
Coriander *mojo* with green peppers

This recipe was given to me by Miguel García, one of our Soho chefs who is from Tenerife and always has the calmness and smile typical of island life. It is a variation on the green sauce recipe for serving with *papas arrugadas*. A softer, herby *mojo*, it is good with fish, cuttlefish and squid tapas, as well as pan-fried semi-cured or even lightly smoked goat's cheese.

Makes 300ml

2–3 cloves of garlic, peeled
1 teaspoon sea salt
3 tablespoons chopped coriander
1 tablespoon chopped parsley (optional,
  if you want to soften the coriander flavour)
½ teaspoon ground cumin
¼–½ a fresh green pepper, roughly chopped
½ a fresh green chilli (optional)
180ml olive oil
about 2 tablespoons white wine vinegar

As with the red version of this, the traditional way to make the *mojo* is using a pestle and mortar, but the easy way is to whiz everything, except the oil, in a blender, then add the oil slowly at the end to allow it to emulsify properly.

If using a pestle and mortar, first crush the garlic cloves with the salt (the salt helps to smash the garlic). Add the chopped coriander, parsley, if using, and the cumin, and grind until you have a paste. Add the fresh green pepper and chilli, if using, and continue to grind, until you once again have a paste.

Add the oil, a little at a time, until it is all incorporated. Finally, mix in the vinegar. Do this just before serving, to keep the powerful green colour that the coriander gives to the sauce. If it feels too thick, add a few drops of water.

Mojo de naranja
Orange and coriander sauce

My good friend Boojum is a great cook who ran a National Trust café in Stackpole Quay in Pembrokeshire, Wales, but has also spent a great deal of time in Spain and the island of Mallorca, where she and her family have a home. Living so near the sea she has access to very fresh fish, so is constantly looking for good ways of serving it – and when she and I were testing sauces for this book, we were intrigued by a recipe for a *mojo* made with bitter oranges in a little book of Canarian cooking that I found in a shop at Las Palmas airport. We thought it would be amazing with tapas of grilled fish. In fact, the rather sketchy recipe in the book ended up as just a starting point from which we departed quite a long way, changing the bitter oranges for sweet ones, but we loved the result: fragrant with orange, coriander and soft Moscatel vinegar yet pungent with garlic (though you can reduce the number of cloves if you prefer a milder taste). As well as being great with fish, it is lovely spooned on to chicken casseroles.

Makes 300ml

4 tablespoons olive oil
**2 small slices (about 20g) stale country-style/
    sourdough bread with the crusts cut off**
4 cloves of garlic, peeled
a pinch of salt
4 tablespoons chopped coriander leaves
2 juicy oranges
4 teaspoons Moscatel vinegar

Heat 2 tablespoons of the olive oil in a small pan, put in the bread and fry briefly until just golden. Remove and set aside. Pound the garlic to a paste with the salt, using a pestle and mortar, add the bread and keep pounding, then put in the coriander leaves and pound to a smoothish paste.

Cut the oranges in half across the middle and squeeze the juice into the mixture in the mortar, working it in with the pestle all the time. Tear out the remaining pulp from the oranges (avoiding the pith and seeds) and incorporate. Work in the remaining olive oil, and then the vinegar.

Pour into a bowl and then leave to stand for 30 minutes to 1 hour, to let the flavours develop.

Almogrote Brindisa
Canarian cheese sauce

We make this chunky cheese sauce in our Food Rooms in Brixton to serve as a dip with little breadsticks, and everyone seems to love it. What is especially pleasing is that when we first started offering it almost no one had previously heard of *almogrote*, so it has been rewarding to introduce something so simple but quite intriguing.

Sometimes called *mojo de queso*, *almogrote* can be used in a similar way to the *mojo rojo* and *mojo verde* (red and green sauces, see opposite) which you find all over the Canary Islands, and though its texture is heavier, it is equally fantastic with potatoes.

Historically, *almogrote* is related to the Roman *moratum*, a sauce made with cheese, pounded with garlic and herbs, and more recently the *picada* (see page 320) or even an *alioli* (see pages 136–139). There are versions of *almogrote* all around Spain. In Castilla they call theirs *almodrote*, and in Catalunya, where it is known as *almedroc*, the sauce appears in two of the region's ancient cookery books: *Llibre de Sent Soví*, the oldest manuscript of its kind, which details dishes from the kitchens of the wealthy in the fourteenth century, and the sixteenth-century *Llibre del Coch* (literally 'The Cookery Book'), the first edition of which is attributed to 'Master Robert', cook to King Ferdinand of Naples.

Despite this tie to Catalunya the sauce seems to have found its long-term home on the Canarian island of La Gomera, where I have eaten many different versions, some with chilli and tomatoes added, or, more adventurously, cooked egg yolk, cinnamon, nutmeg or ginger. It can be spooned on to *papas arrugadas* (see page 296) or small, halved potatoes that have been boiled in their jackets; served simply with crackers for tapas; or added to grilled meats or vegetables.

Originally it was a subsistence recipe designed to make use of old and dried-out pieces of cheese, though if you grate some good cheese it will be much tastier. It is usually made with a mature goat's cheese – at the Food Rooms we use Majorero (see page 531) – however, it would also be good with a semi-cured goat's cheese such as Payoyo from Andalucía (see page 524) or Tiétar from Ávila. We also make it with Manchego (sheep's milk), and you could even use the cow's milk Castellot (see page 510).

The sauce has to emulsify in the same way as mayonnaise or *alioli*, so you have to add the oil or water carefully and slowly. In *Sent Soví* there is a tip which suggests that if the sauce doesn't bind, the thing to do is take a spoonful of it, warm it through, then mix it back in.

Makes 300g

2 *choricero* peppers
1 clove of garlic, chopped
½ teaspoon *pimentón dulce* (sweet paprika)
2 medium tomatoes, chopped
250g hard goat's or sheep's cheese, grated
80g olive oil

First prepare the peppers by soaking them in warm water for 20–30 minutes. Drain them well, then scrape out the flesh.

It is best to use a blender for this, so put in all the ingredients except the oil, and blend, then add the oil slowly, continuing to blend, to allow the sauce to emulsify properly.

Almond sauces of Catalunya

There is a big debate among cooks over the difference between the more famous *romesco* sauce, used mainly to dress grilled vegetables, potatoes and fish, and the extremely similar Catalan *xató* sauce, which is used for *xatonada* salad, made with salt cod (see page 198). There is also a third, similar sauce known as *salvitxada*, which is made with raw, rather than roasted garlic (as used in the other two) and is more like a dressing or Canarian *mojo* (see page 298).

In all the discussions I have had with Catalan home cooks and chefs I have never found any consensus over texture, ingredients, or their quantities. Everyone has their own recipe that they insist is the one and only, and the arguments are perpetuated particularly in the Catalan villages of San Pedro de Ribes, Sitges, Vilanova i la Geltru, and Villafranca del Penedès, where annual competitions are held to judge the best of the various sauces.

Some say that bread should be used in *romesco* but not in *xató*. Others dispute this, but say instead that *romesco* doesn't contain parsley, whereas *xató* does. Sometimes the garlic and tomatoes – used in both sauces – are roasted in the oven before peeling, or sometimes they are held over a gas flame to blacken them, which adds a smoky characterful flavour. The verb that describes this charring over a flame is *escalivar*.

There are many variations of *romesco* alone, and since one of the best known ways of serving it is with *calçots* (see page 283), some people even distinguish their recipes as *salsa de calçots*. I have included three favourite versions, which illustrate the subtle differences you can achieve with a small set of ingredients. They are pretty interchangeable, and all are good with vegetables, fish or chicken. However, I think that if you are serving *romesco* with *calçots* you need a sauce with a creamy texture such as our own Brindisa recipe on page 304.

Xató sauce

This is specifically designed to go with the *xatonada* (salt cod) salad on page 198, and has less garlic than the romesco sauces.

Makes 200g

8 blanched almonds, preferably Marcona
8 hazelnuts
1 clove of garlic, skin on
1 tomato
1–2 baguette slices or 2 *picos de pan* (mini breadsticks), broken into small pieces
a pinch each of salt and freshly ground black pepper
1 teaspoon roughly chopped parsley
50ml olive oil
1 tablespoon sherry vinegar

Preheat the oven to 170°C/gas 3.

Roast the nuts on a tray in the preheated oven for 8 minutes, keeping a careful eye on them and turning the tray if necessary to keep the nuts at the edges and the back from getting burnt. Give the tray a gentle shake every now and then. Once the nuts are dark golden in colour, take them out of the oven and keep to one side.

Turn the oven up to to 200°C/gas 6.

Wrap the garlic clove in foil, place on an oven tray with the tomato and put into the oven. Roast the tomato for about 15 minutes, until its skin is beginning to blacken, and leave the garlic clove in for a further 15 minutes.

Remove the skins from both, chop the tomato and crush the garlic and keep to one side. Crush the nuts and bread with the salt and pepper, using a blender or a pestle and mortar, then add the parsley and reserved tomato and the garlic and blend or pound further. Slowly add the olive oil a little at a time, blending or pounding well after each addition so that the sauce doesn't split. Finally, stir in the vinegar.

Romesco sauce Brindisa

This is the sauce we serve in our restaurants and tapas bars, with grilled fish and/or *calçots* in season. The difference here is that the garlic, almonds and bread are fried to give a deeper flavour, and the sauce has a smoother texture.

Makes 250g

2 *ñora* peppers (see page 280)
2 medium tomatoes
80ml olive oil
2 cloves of garlic, peeled
75g blanched almonds, preferably Marcona
1 thin slice of bread
1 tablespoons sherry vinegar

About 2 hours ahead, split open the *ñora* peppers and put into a bowl, then pour a little boiling water from the kettle over them to rehydrate them (alternatively, if you are pushed for time, put the peppers into a pan of boiling water and simmer for 10 minutes to soften them). Once the skin has softened, scrape out the flesh with a knife and keep it to one side, discarding the skins.

Preheat the grill or the oven to as high as it will go (220°–250°C/gas 7–9) and grill or roast the tomatoes whole for about 15 minutes, until the skins are shrivelled and charred. Peel, if you like, and put into a blender or mortar.

Heat the oil in a frying pan, put in the garlic and fry gently, without colouring, then lift out and keep to one side. Put the almonds into the pan and fry until golden, then lift out. Finally, put the bread into the pan and fry until well browned, then lift out. Make sure you don't let any of the ingredients burn.

Put the reserved pepper flesh, garlic and bread into the blender or mortar, and pulse/pound until well mixed. Next add the reserved almonds and pulse/pound briefly, then add the rest of the oil slowly, a little at a time, blending or pounding well between each addition. Finally, stir in the vinegar.

Romesco sauce Montserrat Fruitos

This is from Montserrat Fruitos (see page 406) and is unusual in that it contains no sun-dried *ñora* peppers, which most Catalans insist upon. Instead Montserrat uses only unsmoked *pimentón* (paprika). I like this with potato dishes, salt cod *brandade* and grilled white fish.

Makes 200g

15 blanched almonds, preferably Marcona
10 hazelnuts
1 thin dry slice of country bread, about 10cm x 10cm
1 tablespoon good white wine vinegar, preferably Moscatel
2 small ripe tomatoes
4 cloves of garlic, skin on
a pinch of sea salt
2 flat tablespoons chopped parsley
1 flat teaspoon *pimentón dulce* (sweet paprika)
a tiny pinch of freshly ground black pepper
around 8 tablespoons olive oil

Toast the nuts in a dry pan until golden, then take them out and keep to one side.

Soak the bread in the vinegar for 10 minutes.

Hold the tomatoes with tongs or a toasting fork over a gas flame (or grill them) until they char on the outside. Repeat with 3 of the garlic cloves. Allow to cool slightly, then peel them and keep to one side.

Squeeze the vinegar from the bread and put into a blender or mortar. Peel the remaining clove of garlic and add to the blender or mortar along with the reserved peeled garlic and tomatoes and all the remaining ingredients, except the olive oil. Pulse-chop or pound a few times to mix the ingredients briefly, as you don't want the sauce to be too smooth at this point. Now add the olive oil slowly as you blend or pound, until you have a thick, emulsified sauce that is quite smooth but still retains some texture.

Romesco sauce Joan Puigcercós

This is the sauce favoured by Joan Puigcercós, our former politician friend in Santa Maria d'Oló in Catalunya (see page 138). It is really delicious, very nutty, quite thick and rough-textured, with all the flavours of peppers, tomatoes, garlic and mint coming through. It is good with _escalivada_ and grilled meats.

Makes 200g

50g blanched almonds, preferably Marcona
30g hazelnuts
1 _ñora_ pepper (see page 280)
2 medium tomatoes
2 cloves of garlic, skin on
80ml olive oil, or more if needed
1 teaspoon white wine vinegar,
  preferably Moscatel
2 tablespoons fresh mint, finely chopped
about ½ teaspoon each of sea salt and freshly
  ground white pepper

Toast the nuts separately in a dry pan until golden, then take out and keep to one side. If they have skins, rub these off with a clean towel while the nuts are still warm. When cool, pulse-chop them into small pieces – again do this separately, so that you keep a consistent texture.

About 2 hours before you want to make your sauce, split open the _ñora_ pepper and put it into a bowl, then pour a little boiling water from the kettle over it to rehydrate it (alternatively, if you are pushed for time, put the pepper into a pan of boiling water and simmer for 10 minutes to soften it). Once the skin has softened, scrape out the flesh with a knife and keep it to one side, discarding the skin.

Either use tongs to char the skins of the tomatoes and one of the garlic cloves over the flame of a gas ring, or put them under a hot grill for 15–20 minutes. Allow to cool slightly, then remove the skins and discard the tomato seeds.

Put the tomato flesh and garlic into a blender or a mortar. Add the reserved pepper flesh and the remaining raw garlic clove, peeled, and pulse-chop or pound together, then slowly add the oil a little at a time, blending or pounding well between each addition.

Mix in the chopped nuts with a spoon, to give texture to the sauce. Finally, stir in the vinegar and mint. Season to taste.

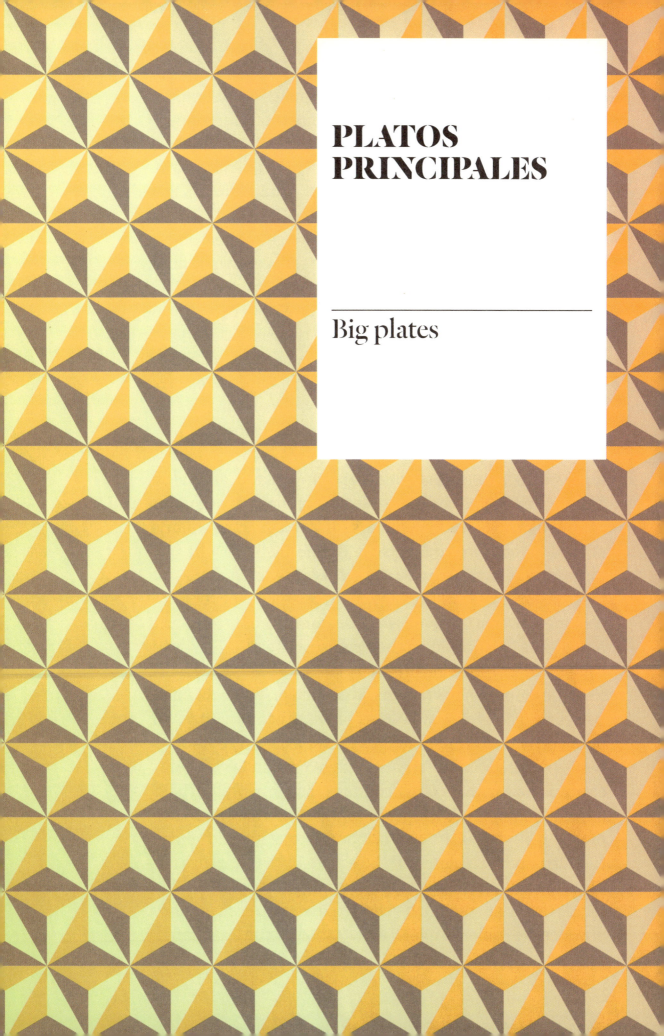

PLATOS PRINCIPALES

Big plates

During my first summer in Spain, when I worked for Pepa Salvador at her restaurant, La Salsita, on the Costa Brava, I had no concept of the way Spanish families ate at home or during the working week. It was so hot that everyone seemed to be living outside in the sunshine and the waves, and only going home very late. I imagined kitchens to have breakfast foods and a chiller full of cold drinks, and that was it. It was only really when the summer ended and I went on to study in Barcelona that I realised the biggest meal of the day was lunch, and the biggest meal of the week was Sunday lunch, when everyone would be involved in the cooking, and the main course would often be more elaborate. On one occasion in Catalunya I helped a friend marinate a wild boar in the bath overnight ready for a big family gathering.

As always, Spain's big dishes vary from region to region, from the fire-grilled meat feasts that are famous in the Basque country to hearty coastal fish and shellfish soups or stews (call them what you will, as they are somewhere in between), to *bacalao* (salt cod) further inland, and rice dishes: *paellas* and the more risotto-like *melosos* or quite soupy *caldosos*. Less known outside of Spain is the tradition of *fideo* (or *fideu* in Catalan) – short, fine pasta, which is used in a very similar way to rice. Then there are the big one-pot meat dishes that traditionally would be started off, or left cooking slowly in the oven while the family went to church, ready to be finished off on their return and shared following drinks and a procession of small plates.

In the mountainous regions, in particular, these might be hearty dishes of slow-cooked game, or beans with pork and *chorizo* or *morcilla*. The grandest – symbols of wealth or celebration – are the mixed meat and vegetable extravaganzas, which often contain chicken as well as beef and pork dumplings. There are versions all over Spain, the most famous being the *cocido madrileño* 'of Madrid' and the surrounding region, and the *escudella* of Catalunya (see page 447). Almost every region of Spain has its own *cocido* recipe that is adapted to its climate, local preferences and produce. Not quite so charmingly named is the Castilian *olla podrida,* which dates back to medieval times. Though it translates roughly as 'rotten pot', it was actually a rich man's stew, so it is sometimes thought that its original name was *olla poderida,* or 'powerful pot'. It combined beans (most typically *alubias de Ibeas,* from the hills of Sierra de la Demanda in La Rioja) with any available pieces of meat, from chicken to mutton, beef, pork and sausages – it was even usual to add whole eggs in their shells.

At the opposite end of the scale are the waste-not-want-not sharing stews that either made use of the leftovers in the days following the big Sunday *cocido,* or were born out of poverty and making the most of whatever ingredients were available and affordable. Many years ago in the market in Las Palmas de Gran Canaria in the Canary Islands I first came across dishes of *ropa vieja* – 'old clothes' – at the *tratoría* stand. Such a great descriptive name. For me it conjured up childhood memories of polishing the furniture with dad's old vests, rather than throw them away, but in food terms it is a generic name for any one-pot dish made with snippets of leftover chicken, beef, sausages or pieces of octopus, cooked up with onions, garlic, tomatoes, *pimentón* (paprika) and chickpeas or whatever handfuls of potatoes, carrots, peppers or herbs you might have. In hard times it might be only a pot of vegetables, coloured deep gold with a little saffron or *colorante* (colouring).

On a similar theme, in Catalunya you have *lentejas poti poti. Poti poti* is the glorious phrase for 'bits and pieces', i.e. the bric-a-brac you might find on a stall in the flea market. In this case it is about leftovers added to a pot of cooked lentils, thickened and seasoned with a *picada* (see page 320) of garlic, the juice of a lemon and fried bread, pounded using a pestle and mortar.

PESCADO

Fish

Suquet de pescadores de l'Empordà
Fishermen's stew
Empordà style

To translate *suquet* as a stew hardly seems to do justice to the dish, since a good *suquet* is one of the classics of Catalan cooking and enjoys almost legendary status among seafood lovers.

Originally it was a one-pot meal made by fishermen on board their boats, using sea water to cook the fish with a few potatoes and pieces of bread, flavoured with parsley and garlic. Or it would be a way of using up the fish that was left at the quay at the end of the day's trading.

Over the centuries, though, it has been considerably enhanced, enriched with *picadas* (see page 320) of almonds and garlic, or made golden with saffron – additions which give a distinctive flavour that helps set the *suquet* apart from similar French fish stews.

At weekends along the Costa Brava, families and groups of friends will make an expedition to a favourite waterside restaurant especially to share a *suquet*, partly to make an occasion of it and partly because these dishes take time to prepare at home and the ingredients are expensive. So I would say think of it as something quite special to make for a celebration.

As a family, we love *suquet*, so I have included two different versions. This first one is the most popular in the Empordà: hearty, but not too heavy, and slightly more humble than the more elaborate one which follows. It uses a whole head of garlic, which softens out during the slow cooking, creating a mellow savoury base. It is inspired by a recipe featured in a tiny gem of a book, *Cuina Casolana Empordanesa*, which my friend Pepa Salvador (see page 371) lent me, since she often took inspiration from it at her restaurant, La Salsita, on the Costa Brava. Originally printed in 1981, in two volumes, it is a collection of recipes gathered by the French gastronomic society Chaîne des Rôtisseurs, from the fine kitchens of the Girona coastline.

We worked on the recipe a little at Brindisa, and came up with this version using a lighter *picada*. The fish is cooked on the bone for added flavour, and the flesh will easily fall off once it is ladled into bowls – but it is good to warn people that the bones are there.

Serves 6

5 tablespoons olive oil
1 head of garlic, peeled and finely chopped
2 tomatoes, roughly chopped
sea salt
1kg potatoes, ideally peeled and cracked *cascada* style (see page 292) into 5cm chunks
1kg gurnard (about 2–3 whole fish), cleaned but still on the bone, cut into chunks (about 5cm) – keep the heads to flavour the cooking water

For the picada
4 threads of saffron
2 tablespoons olive oil
2 cloves of garlic, peeled
2 tablespoons chopped parsley

To serve
6 slices of toasted bread
1 clove of garlic, cut in half
a little olive oil (optional)

Heat the oil in a casserole or large pan, put in the garlic and fry gently until it begins to turn golden. Add the tomatoes and a good pinch of salt, stir, and allow the tomatoes to soften and sweat for 5 minutes.

Add the potatoes and stir into the mixture, so that they are well covered with oil. Put in the fish heads (these will be removed before serving) and cook over a medium heat for a further 5 minutes, stirring occasionally to prevent sticking.

Pour in 2 litres of cold water and bring slowly to the boil, to ensure that the potatoes cook through evenly. If they are cooked too quickly the outer edges will begin to break up and make the stew too thick and starchy. Once it has begun to boil, turn down the heat and simmer gently for around 15 minutes, until the potatoes are just tender.

Remove the fish heads and add the fish, then bring back to a low simmer and allow to bubble for 10 minutes. Again, by cooking slowly and

Suquet de peix a l'all cremat
Fishermen's stew with toasted garlic

gently, the flavour of the stew will develop but the fish won't lose its texture and start falling off the bone.

Meanwhile, make the *picada* by pounding all the ingredients into a smooth paste, using a pestle and mortar.

The stew is ready when the fish is cooked through and can be lifted lightly off the bone. Take the pan off the heat and add the *picada*. Taste and season with a little more salt if necessary – the fish will have added their own salt so you may not need much.

Ladle the stew into 6 large bowls. Rub the toasted bread with the cut clove of garlic, drizzle with oil, if you like, and serve alongside.

En route to my brother's farmhouse in Catalunya on one occasion, I stopped off in Bigas to see Ángel, the master *coquero* who makes our wonderful *coca* bread (see page 70). He and his great friend and colleague Josep Pujol made this *suquet* outside over an enormous gas ring, and since there were ten of us, they used a heavy-based frying pan 50cm in diameter. Lobsters on a camping stove, that's Spanish picnicking for you. But then the word picnic is supposed to have come from the Spanish court, who loved elaborate meals outside on tapestry-covered tables, with music and dancing.

The art of making this *suquet* is in patiently sautéing each fish, and the potatoes, separately, so they keep from breaking up before being combined in the final cooking. Marcona almonds are not cheap, but neither are lobsters, so it is worth investing in superior nuts, as they are so creamy they really add richness to the *picada*.

Serves 4

2 medium prepared lobsters
100g clams
100g mussels
olive oil, for frying
200g monkfish, cut into rough 4cm chunks
200g gurnard fillet, cut into rough 4cm chunks
300g potatoes, peeled and cut *cascada* style
   (see page 292) into rough 4cm chunks
50g cuttlefish, cut into small squares, about 2cm
1.6 litres hot *fumet blanco* (white fish stock,
   see page 466)
salt, to taste
1 teaspoon chopped parsley (optional)

For the toasted garlic picada
4 blanched almonds, preferably Marcona
8 hazelnuts
4 cloves of garlic, skin on
4 tablespoons olive oil
a pinch of salt
2 tablespoons hot *fumet blanco*
   (white fish stock, see page 466)
1 slice of good white bread, crusts cut off

Preheat the oven to 180°C/gas 4.

Cut the lobsters in half lengthways and separate the halved heads from the tails. Keep the halves of the heads intact, as the flavours found there will contribute to the sauce. Separate the claws and crack them.

To start the *picada*, spread the almonds and hazelnuts on a baking tray, put into the preheated oven and roast for about 8 minutes, until lightly browned, making sure you watch carefully, gently shaking the tray and turning it if necessary to keep the nuts from getting burnt. Take out of the oven and keep to one side.

Leave the garlic cloves in their skins, but bash them with the flat of a knife to crack them. Heat 2 tablespoons of the olive oil in a small frying pan and add the garlic cloves, tilting the pan so that they are well covered and can sizzle steadily in the oil. As they cook, press down on them with the back of a spoon. The skin of the cloves will become crisp and peel off, so you can remove it with tongs. By cooking the garlic this way the thinner parts of the cloves will turn a quite deep golden brown, and the thicker parts will become lightly golden, with a soft interior. Check for this by pushing them down with a spoon. As soon as there is some give, the cloves are ready. Take them out of the oil, and when cool enough to handle, remove any remaining skin and cut off the root base. Keep the pan of oil for use again in a minute.

Using a pestle and mortar, grind the garlic cloves with a pinch of salt, to a smooth paste. Add the reserved nuts, grind to a paste once more, then slowly pour in 1 tablespoon of the oil, a little at a time, working it well in until it is all incorporated. Finally, stir in 1 tablespoon of *fumet blanco*, to loosen the paste a little.

Heat the reserved pan of garlicky oil, adding the rest of the oil, then put in the slice of bread and fry gently to a golden toffee colour and rich, savoury flavour. Remove and, when cool enough to handle, break into pieces and add to the nuts in the mortar, grinding again to a smooth paste, adding the rest of the stock to loosen it slightly. Keep this *picada* to one side.

To make the *suquet*, wash the clams and mussels in plenty of water, cutting off any beards from the mussels. Discard any that are not closed, or won't close if tapped against your work surface.

Start by heating a couple of tablespoons of oil in a large, high-sided pan, at least 40cm in diameter, until it shimmers. Put in the monkfish and fry for a minute on each side, just to seal – treat it gently, as you don't want the fish to break up later and turn the *suquet* into a gloopy fishy paste. Lift out and keep to one side. If necessary, add a little more oil, but keep it to just a fine film as you cook the different fish.

Put the gurnard into the pan, skin side down, for 1 minute, then lift out and reserve.

Now put in the cracked lobster claws and cook for 2 minutes on each side until they turn dark red, then lift out and reserve. Next put in the split lobster heads, shell down, for another 2 minutes, without turning them over, then take them out of the pan and reserve. Now cook the tail pieces, shell side down, for only 1 minute, until the shells turn red. Remove and reserve.

Put the potatoes into the pan, adding another tablespoon of oil if necessary, sauté until they are brown at the edges, then lift out and reserve. Put in the cuttlefish and cook until it turns translucent, then add the mussels and clams together with 50ml of water. Cover the pan and steam the shellfish until the shells have opened. Remove and reserve, discarding any that fail to open.

Return the potatoes to the pan, stirring them well to coat them in the juices released by the shellfish, then add the stock and bring to the boil. Taste and add a pinch of salt if needed, then simmer the potatoes for around 12 minutes, until tender.

Stir in the *picada*, taste again and adjust for salt if necessary, then add the monkfish and the lobster heads, with the shell side upwards. Add the rest of the reserved lobster, fish and shellfish, boil steadily for about 2 minutes, until the fish and shellfish are just cooked through, and serve immediately. Remove the lobster heads and finish, if you like, with the chopped parsley.

SOFRITO Y FRITADA

'a base for sauces, stews and pulses'

The word *sofrito* comes from the verb *sofreir*, which means to sauté or fry lightly, and so it is used to describe the process of making a base for sauces, stews and pulses. Classically, this will be made with tomatoes and onions, but these can be enhanced with green and/or red peppers, bay leaves or herbs; or leeks might be used instead of onion, according to taste or context. Sometimes the ingredients are sautéd relatively quickly but more often they require long slow cooking. Then they might be puréed or pounded until smooth; sometimes not.

When this base is made up in advance, either commercially or at home, if it is primarily made with tomatoes and onions it is known as *sofrito de tomate,* and if peppers are added it will be called *fritada*.

In Spain families will typically spend a week or two each summer cooking up different combinations of tomatoes and peppers when they are at their best, storing the *sofrito* or *fritada* in the freezer or under oil in jars ready to use later.

You can also buy good-quality, ready-made tomato *sofrito* or *fritada* in jars, tins and cartons in the same way as the Italian *passata*; however, these will usually contain a high level of water and so should be reduced to the intensity you prefer for your dish. It is also worth noting that in these preparations the tomato tends to dominate over the onion or pepper, whereas in some of the recipes in this book you will see that only a small quantity of tomato is used in the base, as in some regions, particularly the Mediterranean coast, the feeling is that too much can overwhelm other flavours, especially in more delicate fish and vegetable dishes. It is good to be aware of this, as a jarred *sofrito* is not always a straightforward substitute for a homemade one.

Sofrito de tomate
Tomato and onion base

This is our Brindisa recipe for the traditional onion and tomato base that you will see referred to time and again throughout this book. Although it is simple to make, it isn't a quick fix, as the secret is to first cook the onions very, very slowly in just enough oil to stop them burning, but not so much that they drown in it. As they cook, their water content reduces, their natural sugar becomes intensely concentrated and the onions become very sweet, which really helps to bring out the flavour of the tomatoes once you add them. Because the heat needs to be really low, it is best to use a diffuser. When we cook large amounts of onions in this way in the restaurant it can take many hours, but for the kind of quantities you are likely to be using at home, it should normally take no more than an hour for the onions to reach the right stage.

In the UK I would say it is only really worth making *sofrito de tomate* yourself during that brief moment in summer when there is a glut of tomatoes at their absolute best. Ideally, choose a mix of very ripe and soft tomatoes and some slightly harder ones. Then I would do as our friends in Spain do, and make plenty of *sofrito*, seal it in jars, then pasteurise these in boiling water, or store it in containers in the freezer. Alternatively, it will keep in the fridge for a week.

It is best to season the *sofrito de tomate* only very lightly with a little salt and sugar as necessary, as when you come to use it in a recipe you will usually add more seasoning.

Makes about 600g

50ml olive oil
200g sweet white onions (around 1 large whole onion), finely diced
1kg good, fresh red and ripe tomatoes, grated
sugar and sea salt to taste

Heat the oil in a heavy-bottomed pan, add the onions and cook gently for at least 30 minutes (even better for 45–60 minutes, if you have the time), using a diffuser, until the onions are light golden, soft and very sweet. Add the tomato and cook gently, stirring regularly, for 30–40 minutes, until you have a deep red sauce that has a thick, pouring consistency. Taste, and add a little sugar and/or salt if necessary. Pass through a fine sieve.

Keep in the fridge and use within a week, or put into a freezer bag or box and freeze.

Fritada de tomate y pimientos
Tomato and pepper base

Fritada is very similar to *sofrito de tomate,* but with peppers added, and it is their sweet-savoury flavour that distinguishes it.

Our executive chef, Josep, uses long red peppers, as well as green ones which are known as *italianos* and come in from Barcelona. The red ones weigh in at about 500g each, and are deep red with wide streaks of rich green, and very sweet. In the UK the long, pointed red Romano peppers that you can find in supermarkets are the best equivalent. While the green peppers are meant to add piquancy, you don't want the bitterness that often comes with hydroponically grown ones, so look out for long, Mediterranean peppers that will have seen sun.

If a recipe should call for red pepper *fritada*, use 1½ long red peppers and omit the green one.

Makes 700g

50ml olive oil
2 cloves of garlic, finely chopped
200g onions (around 1 whole large onion), finely chopped
1 large long red pepper (about 400g), finely diced
½ a large long green pepper, finely diced
1 sprig of rosemary
1kg tomatoes, grated
1 teaspoon sea salt, to taste
a pinch of freshly ground black pepper
1 teaspoon sugar, to taste

Heat the oil in a heavy-based pan, then add the garlic and fry lightly.

Add the chopped onions and cook very gently for about 15 minutes, until the onions are light golden, soft and very sweet.

Add the peppers and the rosemary sprig and continue to cook gently for another 15 minutes.

Stir in the grated tomato and cook for another 40 minutes over a low heat, stirring often to keep the mixture from sticking to the pan. Taste and add salt, freshly ground black pepper and sugar as necessary. Remove the rosemary sprig.

If not using immediately, keep in the fridge and use within a week, or put into a freezer bag or box and freeze.

Cebolla caramelizada
Caramelised onion base

The origin of this is French, but it is typical of Catalunya. It is a very intense base that is made predominantly with onion and only a little tomato. Our head chef at Brindisa, Leo Rivera, who is Catalan, always has a big pot of it on the go, and uses it to give depth to all kinds of recipes. Whenever we cater at events he seems to have a vial of it secreted about his person, like a wizard with a magic potion. Leo uses it as a base for Catalan rice and pasta dishes; however, in other regions there is an ongoing debate about whether or not onion should be used in dry rice dishes (see page 347).

As with *sofrito de tomate*, it is best made using a diffuser, which will allow you to cook the onions very, very slowly for hours with garlic and oil, so that, as with all these bases, the onions become beautifully sweet.

Makes around 300g of drained onions

3 onions, grated
150ml olive oil
1 medium tomato, grated, or ¼ of a tin (i.e. 100g) of chopped plum tomatoes

Put the grated onions into a sieve for 10 minutes to allow excess juice to drain away.

Warm the oil in a pan, add the onions and cook very gently until transparent, then add the tomato. Cook very gently over the lowest heat possible, preferably using a diffuser, for at least 45–60 minutes. The onions must not burn, but they will darken as they cook, and will look very dark and taste very sweet when ready.

If using straight away, drain off the oil and use only the darkened onions in whatever recipe you choose. Alternatively, store under the oil in the fridge for up to a week.

PICADA/MAJADA

'where sofrito leads, picada finishes'

The inspired idea of combining ingredients pounded together into a paste to thicken, flavour and aromatise a dish, typically a stew, is an ancient idea.

In Catalan the name is *picada,* while elsewhere in Spain it is *majada* – though for the purposes of this book, I have referred to *picada* throughout, to avoid confusion. There is a saying that where *sofrito* leads, *picada* finishes, i.e. the *sofrito* – typically a mix of onions and tomato, to which peppers and other ingredients may be added – forms the base of a dish, while the *picada* is added towards the end of cooking to give an extra dimension of flavour and texture.

The ingredients vary, often according to region, but there will be something starchy like nuts (almonds, hazelnuts or pine nuts), bread or biscuits, combined with aromatics, such as saffron, herbs, peppercorns, chillies, *ñora* peppers (see page 280), tomatoes, fresh peppers, garlic, or even chocolate.

Where nuts are used these will almost always be roasted but unsalted (packaged roasted and salted nuts are too overwhelming). You can easily buy toasted unsalted hazelnuts, but it is usually best to buy plain blanched almonds and pine nuts and toast them yourself without any salt, as I have indicated in the recipes.

In general, when you make a *picada* you crush the harder ingredients first, and work through to the softest, finally adding some liquid to bind: usually olive oil, stock or *vi ranci* wine (see page 373). Sometimes there may even be a touch of cuttlefish liver or rabbit liver, fish eggs or egg yolk, to add another deeper layer of flavour.

Whatever the combination, the ingredients thicken sauces with a freshness and lightness that is very different from the heavier butter and cream used in traditional French cooking, and more varied than Italian pestos.

Sépia amb mandonguilles
Cuttlefish with meatballs

Mar i muntanya (sea and mountain dishes) – the equivalent of surf and turf – can often sound very odd, but many of these traditional Catalan recipes are brilliant, as they are not fussy or overworked, and so make for really hearty and nourishing family meals. This is a recipe from Montserrat Fruitos (see page 406). Of all the *mar i muntanya* combinations I have tried, this, for me, is the most forthright, as the contrast of meat and fish is more striking and the flavours and aromas heartier than, say, a more classic lobster and chicken (see page 416) – so you either love it or hate it.

Always with one eye on the next dish, Montserrat used the main body of the cuttlefish for this, keeping the wings and tentacles (*potes i aletes*) in the fridge, or freezing them to put into another rice dish, or *croquetas*, to serve at the big family house in the country at the weekends. There was never any waste in Montserrat's kitchen.

She would insist on peeling off the outer greyish skin of the cuttlefish so that the pieces were tender and white, and would also keep the soft pouch of liver attached behind the head. It has a strong taste, so you don't need to use it all, but a little adds strength to the colour, and gives depth to the fish flavours within the thick stock.

Montserrat used to prepare the cuttlefish herself, but you might find it easier to buy yours cleaned and ready for you.

If you prefer, you can use a light red wine, rather than white, but it will make the dish darker in colour. You can also make up the meatball mixture the night before and leave it in the fridge overnight.

Montserrat's way of serving the dish was to scatter sprouting seeds on top of the meatballs or add some fresh peas. She would either put these into the cooking pot for the last 5 minutes or so, or cook them separately and serve them on the side.

Serves 4

olive oil
1 medium onion, chopped
2 cloves of garlic, chopped
1 large tomato, grated
sea salt
sugar, to taste
½ a cuttlefish liver (optional)
250ml white wine
½ a cinnamon stick
250g cleaned cuttlefish, cut into
    pieces about 2cm x 0.5cm
1 litre *fumet blanco* (white fish stock,
    see page 466), or water

For the meatballs
160g very lean minced beef
480g very lean minced pork
20g breadcrumbs, soaked in a little milk
2 eggs, beaten
5 cloves of garlic, chopped
2 dessertspoons chopped parsley
sea salt and freshly ground black pepper
plain flour, for dusting
olive oil, for frying
100g peas (optional)

To make the meatballs, mix the minced meats together. Squeeze out the milk from the breadcrumbs and add to the meat, followed by the beaten eggs, garlic and parsley, and mix well. Season and leave to rest for an hour.

Have the flour ready in a shallow bowl. Form the mixture into 16 balls each slightly smaller than a golf ball and pass them through the flour.

Heat the oil in a large pan, making sure it comes no higher than a third of the way up. If you have a thermometer it should be 180°C, otherwise drop in a little flour, and if it sizzles gently the oil is hot enough.

Put in the meatballs (in batches if necessary) and fry for 2–3 minutes, until brown on all sides – they will cook fully later – then lift out and drain on kitchen paper.

Heat a little olive oil in a pan, add the onion and cook gently for a few minutes. Add the garlic and after 3 minutes, when it has released its aroma, put in the grated tomato. Cook for 30 minutes over a very low heat. Taste and season with salt to taste, adding a little sugar if necessary to balance the acidity. If using the cuttlefish liver, add it now and cook for another 10 minutes.

Meanwhile, warm the wine in a separate pan with the cinnamon stick and put in the cuttlefish pieces. Poach for about 5 minutes, until all the alcohol has boiled away. Take off the heat and keep to one side.

Add the fish stock or water to the pan of onions and tomato. Bring to the boil and add the reserved cuttlefish and wine, turn down to a simmer for 15 minutes, then add the meatballs. Add the peas, if using, and continue to simmer for a further 10–15 minutes, then serve.

Bonito escabeche Barrera
Ana Barrera's *escabeche*

The origin of the word *escabeche* is Persian, and the idea of putting a cooked piece of fish, chicken, game bird or rabbit into an acidic marinade before serving was brought to Spain by the Arabs during the Moorish conquests.

This is our version of a dish that Ana Barrera (see page 442) makes with a fresh *bonito*, but this can be hard to find in the UK. If there is none available, use another oily fish like mackerel, or *melva*, which is sometimes known as frigate or bullet mackerel, and has a darker flesh and slightly drier texture.

The wine Ana uses is Chardonnay, and she loves to use fruit as a garnish for dishes like this. Perhaps surprisingly, mango turns out to be an amazing complement to *escabeche*.

Ana serves this with *ensaladilla Barrera*, her variation on Russian salad (see page 207).

Serves 4

1 small *bonito* (about 800g), Spanish mackerel,
   frigate tuna or *melva*, butterfly-filleted,
   i.e. the fillets are still joined on one side
sea salt and freshly ground black pepper
a little plain flour
a little olive oil
6 cloves of garlic, peeled, 3 of them crushed
1 tablespoon *pimentón dulce* (sweet paprika)
about 10 peppercorns
about 10 bay leaves
3 cloves
175ml white wine, such as Chardonnay
175ml white wine vinegar, such as Chardonnay
1 orange, unpeeled and sliced
1 lemon, peeled and sliced
about 6 strands of saffron, infused in warm water

To serve
sliced avocado or mango (optional)
red *piquillo* peppers (see page 275)
Russian salad (see page 207, optional)

Make sure you have a pan that is big enough to take the fish, or cut off the tails. Season the fish, then dust with flour.

Heat a little olive oil in the pan, put in the fillets and the whole garlic cloves and sauté until the fish is golden, taking care not to burn it. If you feel that it is beginning to burn, drain off the olive oil and replace it with new oil.

When the fish is golden, lift it out and keep on one side. Drain the oil through a sieve into another pan.

Add the paprika, crushed garlic cloves, peppercorns, bay leaves, cloves, wine and vinegar, with a dash of water, and bring to a simmer. Add the fish, the orange, lemon and saffron, with its soaking water and cook gently for 5 minutes.

Turn off the heat and leave to cool down to room temperature before serving. Remove the skin from the fish, garnish, if you like, with avocado or mango, and serve with *piquillo* peppers and Russian salad.

BACALAO

'a mindset I have come to value'

Salt cod, or 'stockfish', is the most famous *salazón* (salted fish) and known to everyone in Spain, though it is not very well understood in the UK, probably because it involves an unfamiliar mindset; however, it is a mindset I have come to value as a great way of getting to eat fish more often, without having to go out and find a good fishmonger or buy frozen fish.

Before the invention of refrigeration, if you wanted to eat fish in the most remote inland areas of Spain, salting was the only option, which is why it is sometimes known as the 'mountain fish', and recipes for it abound. Now, of course, everyone has access to either fresh or frozen fish, but the tradition of cooking with salt cod, often in quite inspirational ways, has remained strongly woven into the culinary fabric of Spain and other parts of the Mediterranean, with discerning cooks stocking up on it, planning ahead and buying from specialist sellers, and inventive chefs coming up with ever newer ways of using it.

Spanish salt cod is done with a quite gentle cure, sometimes known as a green cure (*bacalao salado verde*), which involves keeping the fish in salt in large barrels for four months and gives soft flakes of white fish, a clean, fresh aroma of the sea and a delicate flavour, albeit more pronounced than fresh cod. This is in contrast to the style of salt cod that is more popular in Portugal, the Caribbean, Africa and Brazil, where it is air-dried (sometimes it is salted first, sometimes not), so it becomes drier, tougher and chewier in texture, tending to be more stringy and fibrous, with a much stronger fish taste and a light yellow colour.

Ready de-salted cod
Of course, before you cook with salt cod you have to de-salt it by soaking it in water. While aficionados will stock up on it and keep the soaking process going continually in the fridge so they always have some ready to go, there is an increasing market for ready de-salted cod that you can use straight away, or that you can keep in the fridge for about three weeks, and you can also buy it pre-packed.

The de-salting may be done at a specialist salt cod shop, and many markets, especially in Catalunya and the Basque country, have dedicated stalls where the fish will be soaking in stone or marble basins. Or it will be done by the original salting factory. In the Basque country our supplier, Iban Alkorta, has a special long blue de-salting room, filled with lines of tanks, each one with its own taps for changing the water, in which the various cuts are carefully labelled and monitored as they soak for varying lengths of time according to the size of the pieces.

Iban will often offer chefs and catering businesses a bespoke service tailored to their

style of cooking, so that they have a consistent ingredient that will always behave the same way in a recipe. On one occasion when I visited, Iban's father was skilfully tearing fat de-salted cod *morros* into strips in the traditional manner for the Catalan salad *esquiexada* (see page 200), for a customer who requested that only he should do the tearing.

De-salting cod yourself

If you are able to buy salt cod and are prepared to de-salt it yourself, here are some guidelines:

Spanish salt cod is only lightly cured and not dried like its Portuguese counterpart, so it barely gains in weight once soaked. So although I have given weights for de-salted cod throughout this book, if you choose to do the de-salting yourself the starting weight of the fish will be roughly the same.

Before de-salting, wash the cod under running water, as you can remove quite a bit of salt at this initial stage.

Always do the de-salting in the fridge, because as you soak out the salt you are also losing its preservative properties, and without it the fish will begin to deteriorate.

Put the cod, skin side up, on a rack in a dish of very cold water, so it isn't in contact with the base of the dish, where all the salt will be deposited, and so that the gelatine that is released from under the skin penetrates the flesh as well as the water. It is the gelatine that enables the fish to retain its unctuous texture when cooked and to contribute to the creaminess of any sauce that is involved in the dish.

The water you use for the actual soaking is very important – at this stage the taste and smell of tap water can be transmitted to the cod, so it is better to use spring or mineral water, as people would do in Spain. Ozonised water is the absolute ideal: no chlorine, no micro-organisms and no minerals.

Using very cold water is important. If you use warm water the gelatine will seep out too soon, and the flesh of the fish will separate and also become yellow.

Soaking times obviously depend on the size and thickness (pieces can be from 0.5–3.5cm), but small pieces of fillet up to 500g can be de-salted relatively quickly, say for 24 hours, changing the water 2–3 times. Larger pieces might take up to 36 hours, again changing the water 2–3 times. Don't be tempted to change the water more regularly, as every time you do so you disturb the cod and risk losing some of its vital properties, particularly the gelatine. The cod whitens slightly as it de-salts and the texture softens. If you want to check that it has lost enough salt, taste a small corner of fish, remembering that you will probably be adding fresh salt when you use it in a recipe.

How to choose and use salt cod

Salt cod isn't just salt cod: there are many specific cuts which are used for different dishes. Spanish cooks can be quite obsessive about the subject and know when it is worth spending money on the best loin cuts and when this is a complete waste of money, as cheaper pieces will do a particular job better. While the various cuts are known as *bacalao*, a whole salted cod is called *una bacalada*, and can be up to 60cm long and weigh 4–5kg. These huge cod give fat fillets which provide the finest and most sought-after cuts, and then, as the fish scale down in size, there is a whole science behind defining the cuts to be taken from them, all the way down to the smallest cod, weighing less than a kilo, which provide two fillets only.

The fishmonger will get out what looks like a paper-cutter and if you don't know which pieces to buy, he will invariably ask you what you are going to cook and cut the fish accordingly – at which point anyone else waiting to be served will usually pitch in and offer some tips.

Because I am on something of a mission to spread the message about salt cod, at Brindisa we have spent a long time researching the whole subject, and I invited our supplier in the Basque country, Iban Alkorta, to come over and give a workshop for colleagues in my kitchen at home. We packed everyone in, piled the table with ingredients, and spent an entire day with Iban and Leo Rivera, our head chef, making all kinds of dishes using the various cuts, many of which appear throughout this book in everything from big dishes to salads and omelettes.

However, I am aware that salt cod and de-salted cod are only slowly gaining an audience in the UK, so unless you seek out a specialist supplier, you may have a more limited choice, and sometimes might only find fillets taken from small fish, but it is worth keeping an eye out for the following:

Lomo
Loin

The best loins come from the central part of the very biggest fish (up to 4 kilos). They are boneless and cut square or rectangular, for dishes where you really want to show off the perfect *láminas* or flakes of the fish, which stay beautifully intact during cooking, then fall apart elegantly as you eat. You can lightly steam them and add a sauce, or poach and then grill them, and they are ideal for recipes such as *bacallà amb mel* (salt cod with honey, page 331).

Morro
Cheeks

If you can find these, they have the longest and largest *láminas* (flakes) of all, and are especially popular in Catalunya. Juicy and aesthetically quite beautiful, they are best broken up and shown off in salads such as *remojón* (see page 198), *esquieixada* (see page 200) and *xatonada* (see page 198).

Pil pil

This is the special cut for the famous Basque dish of the same name (see page 332). It is the most muscular part of the fish, behind the loin and before the tail, and has the greatest gelatine content from bones and skin of all the central cuts – it is this gelatine that is needed to form the emulsion that is essential to *bacalao al pil pil*. When the cut is taken from a smaller fish it is known as *txiki* (small) in the Basque language.

Kokotxas
Jowls

Salt cod jowls are considered a delicacy. Known as *kokotxas* in the Basque language and *cocochas* in Castilian, these used to be eaten fresh by the fishermen after the fish had been filleted. Now everyone else has woken up to how delicate, tasty and textural they are: very gelatinous, and juicy, they slip down almost like oysters, and salted jowls are much sought after. Quick to cook, they make perfect light and tasty bite-sized tapas. In Basque bars they are popular as *kokotxas rebozadas,* coated with flour and egg, then deep-fried until lightly golden and dressed with chopped parsley, garlic and lemon juice.

Kokotxas al pil pil is another favourite, in which the jowls are cooked in the garlic and olive oil sauce that is also used for salt cod loins (see page 332). Of course the drawback is that jowls aren't that readily available, as there is only one per fish.

Cuts that are worth knowing about if you are in Spain, but that you are unlikely to come across in this country are:

Colas recortes
The tails

These are high in gelatine and too good to waste. Those from the smaller fish, in particular, are juicy and delicious breaded and fried for tapas, or used in *buñuelos de bacalao* (see page 248), omelettes, or for making fish stock (see *fumet blanco*, page 466).

Recortes
The edges

Also called skirt or belly pieces, these are trimmings from fillets, which tend to be drier, and are used in recipes where the quality of the fish is less detectable – so, like the tail pieces, they can be used for *buñuelos de bacalao* (see page 248).

Migas
Crumbs or pieces

These vary in quality according to the cut they come from, but are mostly used in dishes where their appearance isn't crucial (as they are more randomly shaped and not so elegant as the shreds from the *morro*), such as *buñuelos* (see page 248), *tortilla* (see page 267), *empedrat* (see page 201) and *porrusalda* (see page 226).

Tripet
Tripe

Tripet in Catalan, or *tripa* in Spanish, this is not the intestines, but the breathing pouch which comes from the underside of the fish. It is bigger than you might expect and contains high levels of gelatine. Once de-salted it is usually blanched so that its grey skin can be peeled off easily, after which it is put into cold water, brought to the boil, then taken off the heat and left to cool. After that it is usually diced, and typically cooked in a tomato *sofrito* with pieces of *chorizo* or *panceta*, chickpeas and a *picada* added at the end.

Some salt cod notes
Although it might sound strange, it is still necessary to season the cod to taste during cooking, as once de-salted it needs to be treated like a fresh fish.

Since salt cod isn't as readily available in the UK as in Spain, some recipes I have seen suggest substituting fresh cod, and salting it overnight; however, the fish won't gain the flavour or perfect flaking of salt cod, so I wouldn't recommend it.

Bacallà amb mel
Salt cod with honey

When you buy your salt cod or de-salted cod, make sure that the pieces are long enough to cover the apple slices which form the base layer of the dish.

Serves 4

2 eating apples
a little olive oil
120g sugar
1 heaped tablespoon pine nuts
200g *alioli* **(see page 136)**
30g good honey, preferably rosemary
4 x 300g pieces of de-salted salt cod loin or tail
plain flour, for coating
olive oil, for deep-frying
100ml PX sherry vinegar (see page 188)
  (optional), to finish

Preheat the oven to 220°C/gas 7.

Peel and core the apples and cut into eighths.

Heat a little olive oil in a frying pan, put in the apple slices and sugar and cook gently until caramelised.

In a separate pan, dry fry the pine nuts until they are lightly toasted, then keep to one side.

In a bowl, mix the *alioli* and honey together.

Coat the cod pieces in flour, then heat a generous amount of olive oil in a pan, making sure it comes no further than a third of the way up the pan. If you have a thermometer it should be 180°C; otherwise, drop in some flour and if it sizzles gently then the oil is ready.

Put in the floured cod and deep-fry for around 2 minutes until golden, depending on the thickness. Lift out and drain on kitchen paper.

Arrange the apple slices in the base of an ovenproof dish, and place the fried cod on top, skin side down. Spread a thick layer of the *alioli* and honey mixture over the top. Sprinkle with the pine nuts and bake in the preheated oven for 4–6 minutes, until golden brown (if it doesn't brown enough, you could put it under a hot grill to finish for 2–3 minutes).

Heat the PX vinegar in a pan and let it bubble up until reduced by just over half, then drizzle over the dish before serving.

Bacalao al pil pil
Salt cod in olive oil

Salt cod is one of the famous treasures of Basque cuisine and *pil pil* is a very Basque dish. Made with only four ingredients – salt cod, olive oil, garlic and peppers – its name seems to come from the sound that the sauce makes as the gelatine from the fish, olive oil and garlic emulsify around the cod pieces, almost like an *alioli*, as the dish cooks slowly over several hours.

The story goes that the dish has its origin in a peculiar circumstance during the Carlist wars of the 1800s, when the people of Bilbao were cut off from supplies by the second siege and faced starvation. Miraculously, just before the siege a tradesman who had ordered around 20 pieces of salt cod unaccountably received more than 20,000. So the people had salt cod, as well as olive oil, which sustained them over a long period – and *pil pil* was born.

Two important things: you need cod with the skin on, as this is where the gelatine is concentrated. Ideally, this will be a special *pil pil* cut of loin, from the most gelatinous tail end; and also you need to cook it over a gentle heat (around 50°C and no higher than 60°C), otherwise the emulsion won't form properly, or will break down if you overheat it once it has formed. This is a dish that can't be served piping hot for that reason.

There are two ways of making the dish. The traditional one involves putting all the ingredients into the pan and gently shaking it continuously over a low heat to create the emulsion – a skill, like making *alioli*, that most Spanish cooks are comfortable with. Some restaurants use *pilpileras*, which are small electric cookers which move the *pil pil* pan gently in a circular motion so that you do not have to do this manually; however, where these are used, sometimes milk and flour are also added if the sauce is not thickening itself enough. There is also a more contemporary way, which involves cooking the de-salted cod first, then whisking the sauce separately until it is thick; I favour the traditional version I have given here, which comes courtesy of my friends Ambro and Asun in Pedrosa de Duero in Burgos (see page 154).

Ambro made it for us for Sunday lunch using a big, wide but light enamel pan with two handles, which he could shake backwards and forwards without too much strain on the wrists.

Asun and I bought three whole *bacalada* with bones, fins, skin and tails, as Ambro was cooking for ten, going on a hundred. The fishmonger sliced each fish into eight pieces so that we ended up with 5kg of fish, ready for the soaking over 1–2 days in a series of big buckets. This was serious cooking, with 1.2 litres of olive oil and 30 cloves of garlic. Ambro does sometimes like to use a shocking amount of garlic – he had 20 cloves for the pan and ten for decoration; plus five peppers. Despite his off-the-scale portions, over a long slow lunch everything was devoured!

Serves 4

350ml strong olive oil (with a deep colour)
10 cloves of garlic, peeled
2 peppers, de-seeded and sliced
  (or dried red chillies)
4 de-salted *pil pil* cod loins, around 800g

Heat the oil in a light, wide, two-handled pan.

Slice 2 of the garlic cloves and fry in the oil until golden, then lift out and keep to one side. Put in the peppers or chillies and fry for 30 seconds, then remove these, too, and keep to one side. Let the oil cool down – if you drop in a small piece of bread it shouldn't fry – then put in the cod loins, skin side down. Slowly heat the oil up again to a slow bubbling. Crush all the other garlic cloves and place them in the oil, dotted around the loins, making sure they are well submerged in the liquid.

Now you need to move and gently shake the pan continuously for all of 30–45 minutes (yes, really) as the sauce warms and cooks – making sure it doesn't get too hot and burn. The fish should remain whole and intact, so that it will break into shards later as you eat it, and the sauce will slowly begin to thicken and emulsify, until after about 30–45 minutes it will have formed into a silky yellow sauce which has folded itself around the fish.

Sprinkle with the reserved toasted garlic and peppers or chillies and serve.

AZAFRÁN

'the planet's most expensive spice'

The *manto*, the day the saffron flowers come into bloom in the fields around the villages of Castilla La Mancha in central Spain, is a beautiful sight. It usually happens around the last week in October. One day you can drive through the region and see only barren hillsides, and the next, you are surrounded by a gorgeous blanket of deep purple petals shimmering in the late sunshine: a spectacle that will last only about two weeks before the landscape returns to brown earth and mud. It really is one of the wonders of nature and there is something magical about it.

Saffron, which comes from the dried stigma of *Crocus sativus*, has been grown in La Mancha for at least 1,000 years, and the region, which encompasses part of the provinces of Cuenca, Toledo and Albacete, as well as the majority of Ciudad Real, is still the most famous for the spice. It also used to be grown in small quantities in Galicia, Asturias and Jaén, and is now cultivated in a tiny area of Aragón near Teruel, known as Jiloca, where it has been championed by Slow Food, but not, strangely, in Valencia, the land of the *paella*, although this is where most of the packers, distributors and exporters are based. Here, as in other regions of Spain, people often use food colouring (*colorante*) instead.

The planet's most expensive spice, a pound of which, in the eighteenth century, was quoted as being literally worth its weight in gold, saffron was introduced by the Moors, originally from Iran, and the name La Mancha is probably derived from the Arabic *al-mansha* (meaning a dry area or wilderness). Saffron's fascination lies not only in its unique flavour and aroma but in its colour. In ancient times it was used as a dye in the finest fabrics and carpets – Buddhist monks dyed their robes with it, and Irish chiefs their cloaks. The fact that it can only be harvested by hand adds to its worth, and it is not only an ingredient for our kitchens but also a remedy. Like honey, it is often seen as a natural source of goodness that can help to ward off illness and ease conditions such as asthma, assist digestion and stimulate appetite. I heard of an opera singer who insisted on drinking warm milk infused with saffron before singing, as a way to wake up her larynx.

At one time in La Mancha, most villagers would cultivate an area of saffron flowers, however tiny, to boost their income at a time when other agricultural work tended to be quite quiet – for a few weeks of intensive work, even the smallest pocket-handkerchief patch of flowers would earn a family enough to buy a new washing machine or a small luxury. There are stories of families keeping saffron in a special *guardazafrán*, a locked chest, to form part of a young girl's dowry, or of flowers being stolen from the fields on a Sunday during harvest time when the villagers were all at church.

However, in the last decade Iranian saffron has taken over the market, so much so that it now satisfies 80 per cent of the world's demand. Spain, like everywhere else, began importing Iranian saffron in the late eighties, when trade embargos were lifted. The market flooded, the price went down, and there was little motivation for the growers in La Mancha to carry on, so the production shrank and people began abandoning the crocus fields for the building trade, or to work in the cities. Then, ironically, the building trade collapsed, unemployment rose, and locals began looking to plant saffron once again. La Mancha was granted its own PDO and began finding new markets.

The reality, however, is that Spanish home cooks who use a great deal of saffron baulk at the price of the La Mancha spice, preferring to keep it for special dishes. The rest of the time they might buy saffron from Iran or design their own blend of imported and home-grown. At Brindisa we sell saffron from Iran as well as from La Mancha – but both are selected for us by our saffron specialists, the Sotos family, in Albacete in La Mancha. Antonio Sotos has run the current operation since 1958 with his wife, Encarnación González Tolosa, who comes from a saffron dynasty going back four generations, to 1912. Their son, also called Antonio, is involved in the business as well, and the two generations live and work out of a large, elegant town house in the centre of Albacete.

I am often asked if saffron from La Mancha is worth its high price. Well, I believe it is, partly because its deep brick-red colour and intense aroma mean that you can add less of it to your cooking than Iranian saffron and achieve a much greater impact. To highlight the differences between the two, at Brindisa one day I asked some of our chefs to make two batches of ice cream, one flavoured with saffron from Iran, the other with saffron from La Mancha. Then we held a blind tasting. The Iranian saffron did the job very well, but the ice cream made with Spanish saffron had the most incredibly rich flavour, colour, and above all aroma that hung like a little cloud in the air and made for a much fuller experience (see recipe on page 496).

The dedication to quality in La Mancha begins with the cultivation of the crocus bulbs in June (each 5–8cm bulb produces a new one the following year). The specifications of the PDO insist on the bulbs being planted 15–20cm apart, so that they can fatten up properly and produce the prized long threads. By contrast, in Iran planting tends to be more intensive, which can result in threads that are shorter and thinner. Also in La Mancha new bulbs are planted on a four-year cycle, whereas in Iran this refreshing of the bulbs might happen only every ten years.

As soon as the first flowers bloom they have to be picked, signalling the start of around two weeks of back-breaking work, since each crocus blooms up to three times. The pickers begin early in the morning, sometimes in the autumn mist, before the sun has a chance to warm the petals and make them limp and more difficult to pick without damaging the threads, which, of course, are the precious part of the flower.

In the town of Consuegra a famous saffron festival takes place each year. This is pure Don Quixote windmill country, and the last time I visited I went out into the fields with Encarnación in the early morning. By midday the pickers had already harvested a piece of land the size of an Olympic swimming pool. Most of the villagers and neighbours of the growers will join the harvest for free, and children are even allowed to take time off school in order to help.

Once the baskets are filled to overflowing, they are taken indoors to the *mondadores* and *mondadoras*, the men and women – but mostly women – who settle down for the afternoon around tables piled high with the flowers to carry out *la monda*, the separating of the stigmas from the petals. The skill is to do this with one quick but delicate turn of the thumb and index finger, removing the three stigmas in one go but keeping them joined at the base. As the *mondadores* work, their fingers become stained a deep red-yellow, the mound of deep red-orange filaments gets higher, and pillows of purple flowers drop to the floor. It seems such a scandal that no one yet has seemed to find a use for the discarded petals.

Certain villages and areas of La Mancha have different reputations for the quality of their saffron, and particular *mondadores* are renowned for being the most skilled. One of the highlights of the Consuegra festival is a race in which competitors from different villages are each given 100 flowers, then the *monda* begins, against the clock, to find the champion who can produce the quickest perfect batch of saffron threads, in their threesomes. I believe the record is around ten minutes, and I'm sure the locals have been known to have a bet or two on the outcome.

Once the threads have all been removed, they must be dried or 'cured', either by the sun, by fan (a more intensive method) – or the gentler, old-fashioned dry-toasting in small batches favoured in La Mancha and known as *el tueste*, which preserves the aroma better.

A big round sieve is filled with the threads, placed over the low heat of a gas heater and shuffled from time to time so that they are toasted slowly and evenly. The room is filled with the heady aroma and as you watch over 20 minutes or so, the volume of threads sinks as the moisture rises off, and a flat dry red disc of saffron is left in the sieve.

For every kilo of stigmas just 200g of saffron is produced, and since you can only expect to harvest around 12 kilos of threads per hectare, it is clear why the saffron is considered so valuable.

In La Mancha the local people traditionally cook with whole threads of saffron, but for use elsewhere around Spain and abroad, the spice might be powdered. In this form it is popular, since it gives a more uniform colour, without the blotchy spots of intense colour that the threads create. So, many of the best saffron selectors are now selling ground saffron, as well as the threads, packed in little paper envelopes, known colloquially around Asturias, Galicia and Murcia as *sardinetas* (the name for the ceremonial stripe on military uniforms), which contain enough saffron to put into most dishes for four people.

Among the younger generation, the packets of powdered saffron are becoming increasingly popular because of their convenience and approachability; however, you often find that older home cooks trust threads more, as they remember times when the powder has been adulterated because of the greed to make money from saffron. Although some unscrupulous saffron dealers attempt to pass off the threads of the safflower as *Crocus sativus,* it is far easier to mix the powdered spice with inferior saffron, powdered safflower or paprika.

How to choose saffron

Saffron consists only of the three red stigmas of the saffron crocus and none of the rest of the flower.

Quality is measured by the flavour, aroma and colour that the saffron produces when put into warm water. The flavour should be hay-like with a hint of bitterness, its aroma a combination of honey with grassy tones, and the colour it imparts should be a luminous, delicate yellow-gold.

When buying threads, look for long, whole ones with no broken bits.

Check the country of origin on the packaging or look for the PDO (Protected Denomination of Origin) mark of La Mancha. If you see neither listed, only the country where the saffron was packed, then you cannot be sure of what you are buying. It could be Iranian saffron or a blend of Iranian and Spanish (since these two countries account for 80 per cent of the world production it is unlikely to be from anywhere else).

The price of Spanish, and especially La Mancha, saffron can be high, so if you are using it for stocks, or rice dishes, especially those containing meat, even the most ardent supporters of La Mancha saffron agree that the Iranian spice is fine. It is worth splashing out on more expensive threads for sauces and dishes where these will be very visible.

You also need to be aware of the possibility that in order to increase the weight, improve the look, and demand a higher price, the saffron might not be what it appears. Safflower threads are often sold as saffron, and past scandals have involved padding out genuine saffron with beet or pomegranate fibres, even red-dyed silk fibres. More recently, in 2011, consignments of saffron were found to have been bulked out with other parts of the crocus flower that had been dyed.

You can recognise safflower threads, as they will look more like dry, golden, wide-stemmed grass with no distinctive aroma, whereas a genuine, good-quality saffron thread will most likely be deep crimson red, and will have a marked trumpet-shaped end. Some genuine saffron threads, however, have a more yellow appearance, so the real test is to put them into water. Real saffron will keep its own colour but turn the water golden, and the threads will float. Fake saffron will lose its colour into the water, and will usually sink. Ultimately, the safest thing is to stick with a clearly labelled brand or supplier that you trust.

Powdered saffron, too, has been known to have been adulterated with turmeric, paprika – even brick dust. So the same advice about trust applies.

How to keep and use saffron

All saffron should be protected from the light so it retains its properties for longer. So avoid packaging that doesn't recognise this.

Although saffron, once packaged, has a 5-year date code, time is not its friend, so it is best to buy it within the first year of its lifetime, and then use it quickly.

Remember that although saffron has the potential to add a powerful and specific flavour to a dish, it is not meant to dominate, but to enhance the key ingredients. Most recipes tend to leave the quantity of saffron quite loose: a pinch, or a few strands; however, I feel that it is helpful to have a guide as to how much to use, at least when experimenting for the first time – then you can vary the quantity if you wish. So I would say as a very rough guide, for a dish that serves 4–6 people you need around 0.1g, which equates to 15–25 threads, depending on their size and weight – but meat dishes usually require more (María José San Román, who is the major contemporary researcher of saffron, often uses double this quantity). Also, drier, baked dishes which rely on aroma might need a little more, and dishes based on fats, such as ice cream, might also need larger amounts for colour.

While I would usually favour strands over powder in general cooking, María José recommends that a good, authentic powdered saffron is better in baking, where you are adding it to flour, and want the colour to diffuse evenly.

While the most popular way to awaken the character of the saffron before you add it to your dish is either to toast the threads or powder in a dry frying pan (just long enough for it to release its aroma), unless a dish is very dry, María José prefers the infusion method, putting the stigmas into warm water (65°C) often for 4 hours before using.

ARROCES

Rice dishes

Just as I always say tapas are not the only Spanish food, *paella* is not the only rice dish. Rice plays a big part in everyone's life in Spain, whatever the region, but rice dishes come in one of three styles. The relatively dry styles are called either *paellas* or *arroces secos* (see page 346). Then there are creamy risotto-like dishes known as *melosos* – usually cooked in a *cazuela* (terracotta dish) – and soupy *caldosos*, made in a deep casserole. All might be eaten communally, straight from the pan or earthenware pot, or served in individual portions.

Rice dishes are the food of the people, not the elite, however elaborate they might become in the hands of a creative chef. As always, the recipes reflect the season and locality, so the added ingredients might be wild mushrooms, seafood, rabbit, *chorizo*, garlic shoots or snails.

On rice menus you might also see 'a banda' – which means 'on the side', so a fish pot arrives first, in which there might be langoustines, red snapper, large chunks of monkfish and potatoes in a rich stock. Rice will follow, quite alone, but its taste will be sumptuous because it will have been cooked in stock from the cooking of the fish.

Across the world there are in excess of 40,000 varieties of rice, but the basic divide is between lowland tropical types and higher-altitude cooler varieties, although there are crosses and hybrids in between. In Spain the traditional rice is of the Japonica type, which is plump and slightly opaque with a bright white concentration of starch in the centre of the grain.

The starch in rice is made up of amylose and amylopectine, and it is the ratio of these that determines the way the grains behave during cooking. At one end of the scale, strains that are high in amylose and low in amylopectine will be more resilient and the grains will stay separate and springy, as with Indian Basmati rice. At the opposite end, those that are low in amylose and high in amylopectine are more fragile and will become more sticky as they cook, so at the extreme end of the scale, you have sushi rice. In between are the Mediterranean rices, whose grains swell up and glisten, enriched by the stocks, oils and ingredients that are introduced to them, and then deliver all these flavours, intensified, in each spoonful, while at the same time retaining a little bite. Spanish rice and Italian risotto rice, which is also of the Japonica strain, are very similar; however, the Italian varieties are even more absorbent. Interestingly, a Spanish strain of the Italian risotto rice Carnaroli is being grown in Catalunya and it works very well in soupier dishes like *melosos* and *caldosos* (see pages 359 and 362).

Of the Spanish varieties, the most popular, Bomba, has achieved almost mythical status, partly because it is one of the oldest varieties (first identified in the eighteenth century) but also because its production is limited and its purity as a strain remains intact. For this reason Bomba is the only varietal you are likely to see identified on a label, as producers want to extol its reputation and its heritage. Otherwise rice is usually just marketed under brand names.

The Bomba grains are very small, almost a perfect round, with a tiny tail at one end. This is the most resilient and tolerant of Spanish varieties, with 23 per cent amylose (compared to 28 per cent for Basmati), so, while it has the ability to absorb enough liquid to double in size, the grains remain loose, making it easier to cook the rice well. Other varieties, such as Senia, Bahía, and the Balilla x Sollana from Calasparra all have their fans, but with only 17 per cent amylose they are more sensitive, and if you are not used to them, there is more of a risk of overcooking and releasing so much starch that they become gloopy. As expert rice grower Juan Trías (see page 342) puts it, *Bomba tiene un espacio de cocción en vez que un momento de cocción*: 'Bomba has a space in which to cook perfectly, rather than just a moment.'

So, although I give some alternatives in the recipes that follow, and I would favour Carnaroli for the soupy *melosos*, as the variety releases more starch, I would say if you want to choose one rice and stick with it, it would have to be Bomba, or a rice from Calasparra (especially for *paellas* or in soups).

THE RICE REGIONS

'numerous and varying dramatically'

Originally from Asia, rice came to Spain with the Arabs in the eighth century and they used the large fresh-water lagoon in the region of Albufera in Valencia to plant and grow it. These days the rice-growing areas across Spain are numerous and vary dramatically in the volume they produce, from Andalucía, which is the largest, then Extremadura, through to the Delta del Ebre in Tarragona, Catalunya; Albufera de Valencia; Zaragoza, Navarra, Calasparra in Murcia; and Pals, down to the tiniest 500-acre paddy field in Mallorca. However, the most famous areas are measured by quality, rather than quantity, and these include the Delta de l'Ebre; a small area in Gerona; Albufera; and Calasparra, each of which is very different.

In most of these regions you find a mix of large and small producers. The big concerns may use industrial processes and chemicals in the cultivation and processing of the grains and are geared to producing more cost-efficient crops. But there are also smaller family businesses and co-operatives that concentrate on one exceptional, pure varietal, or a carefully cultivated cross, and use more alternative or traditional methods of growing, cropping that encourages biodiversity and protects wildlife, sun-drying of the grains and in some cases even stone-milling. Many things can have an impact on the quality of the grains, from altitude, to the water used to irrigate the fields, or the use of sun-drying; however, the most important element is the varietal, its genealogy and the care with which it is cultivated, harvested, dried, milled, and carefully selected for intact grains.

Tarragona

In Tarragona the rice-growing region stretches over some 20,000 hectares of coastal delta, populated by growers large and small, producing some excellent rice. When we were developing the rice menu for our restaurant in Shoreditch, I went to visit the flat delta land, stretching to the sea, with Josep, our executive chef. It is an area dotted with small, very Mediterranean-looking villages with white-washed houses and gardens full of colourful flowers. We visited a family estate, Illa de Riu, where Juan Trías del Romero focuses on single varietals, mainly Bomba (see page 341), and it was a joy to see the understanding and empathy between chef and grower.

Juan is the third generation of this rice-growing family. This is a difficult area to cultivate, as its proximity to the sea makes the salinity high, and irrigation is done by a network of channels and gates which allow the movement of water. The fields are waterlogged for at least 10 months of the year, which helps to support wildlife.

Ducks and eels abound in this area and both are favourites cooked with rice. All around the fields you see one-storey white cottages with thatched roofs that are hunting lodges for duck shooting, and lines of eels, cleaned and drying in the sun ready to be preserved, in which case they are known as *xapadillos*.

In the great white estate house next to the rice stores you can still see the room with the blackboard where Juan's mother taught the children of the estate workers to read and write. A crocheted rice calendar, made by one of Juan's sisters, runs along the edge of a dresser, showing the yearly schedule of draining the fields in January, levelling the soil, flooding, sowing and, finally, harvesting the tall, golden plants in October, before the fields are mulched and filled with water and the cycle begins again.

The rice varieties they cultivate are Tebre, Senia, Bahía, Carnaroli and Bomba (which now accounts for 40 per cent of the crop). It was harvest time when we visited and rice was flowing in every direction – trailers brought in fresh grains from the field which waited in a vast aerated tunnel, to be sucked up into the old drying machines, upgraded, but still a maze of moving wooden beams, pivots, funnels and towers. The flames beneath roared and reflected deep orange on the brick walls as the hot air was funnelled through the turning cylinders of rice, until the right humidity levels were achieved. Then the rice passed into cooling silos and, finally, the storage chamber, with its cool air vents and thermometers buried deep in the mountains of rice to ensure no rogue grains ruined the valuable stock.

The production of rice in this area has changed over the years and many small growers no longer have mills, so they rely on the benevolence of larger establishments to mill their rice. Fortunately, in the Delta de l'Ebre area of Tarragona there are still two co-operatives, one on each side of the river, that work with small-scale growers. The rice is milled bright white, packed, then returned to the estate to sell.

Gerona

In Pals in Gerona, there is a smaller rice-growing area that covers just over 900 hectares, irrigated by the river Ter. The land mass is small, and the labour cost high, as, although the rice is harvested using modern machinery, in order to ensure it is collected quickly and efficiently the weeding and replanting is all done manually, and the crops are kept healthy without chemicals. The rice is excellent, and at the Molí de Pals mill varieties go by old local names, so the Bahia variety, mainly used for *caldosos* and *melosos*, is known as Rodó Perlat, and Semillarg Cristal is the name given to the Loto variety, which is the favourite locally for dry *paella* dishes.

Valencia

In the Valencia region there are about 15,000 hectares under cultivation in the massive still-water lagoon, which stretches over 50,000 acres at sea level. It is an amazing sight with herons swooping over the fields of water which reach as far as the horizon, bordered by the bright green leaves of the citrus groves. All varieties grow here, on a large and small scale, but the main crop is Senia and Bomba.

Murcia

In Calasparra in Murcia, along with Bomba, a variety that is a cross of Balilla and Solana is grown across 400 hectares of land, high up, with elevations that vary from 1,150 to 1,650 metres above sea level. Since this medium-grain rice usually features the name Calasparra on packets, I find that people often tend to think this is the variety rather than the region where it is grown.

The Arabs recognised that this point where the Segura and Mundo rivers meet would make an ideal rice-growing area, and built terraces and irrigation channels which remain unchanged, so that exceptionally clean water irrigates the fields and is never still or stagnant.

The landscape around Murcia is almost lunar, but the dry rocky hills change to wild flower meadows the closer you get to Calasparra, and the rice fields feel like an oasis in the midst of the surrounding barren land. Most of the rice is harvested by a co-operative of 160 members, and only half the area is planted each year, so that other crops – fruit trees and vegetables – can be rotated systematically, in order to keep the level of nutrients in the soil at its best and maintain the ecosystem for the birds and wild life.

Outside the village is a sanctuary dedicated to Our Lady of Hope, and her statue is carried on the shoulders of robust locals at Easter time and other festivals. In the local restaurant they make seafood, rabbit and chicken *paella* using the Bomba rice, and people arrive in coachloads for a day out looking at the rice fields and having lunch. The last time I visited, a large group of elderly nuns were lunching and singing hymns and dancing around the tables in between courses.

ARROCES SECOS Y PAELLAS
Dry rice dishes

When we were developing the rice menu for our Shoreditch restaurant, we decided not to use the word *paella* at all, primarily because it isn't representative of all the dry rice dishes of Spain that make good use of many different ingredients. The name *paella* doesn't refer to any specific recipe, but to the wide flat pan typical of Valencia that was first used by farm workers to cook a meal of rice with snails or maybe rabbit, and vegetables – typically green beans – over an open fire. Because of the association with Valencia, the word *paella* has often been avoided in other regions, except on tourist menus, and rice dishes made in neighbouring Alicante, Catalunya and the Balearic Islands are rarely if ever called *paella*. Instead, dry rice dishes are simply known as *arroces* and sometimes the word *paellera* is used to describe the cooking pan, to distinguish it from the dish.

Confusingly, even in Valencia they also have dishes labelled *arroces* – just don't ask me to explain the difference, as no one I have met in that region or anywhere else has been able to come up with a definitive answer. One explanation is that a true *paella* includes not only meat and green beans, but also dried white beans; however, there are endless exceptions, and people just seem to know instinctively whether a dish is a *paella* or an *arroz*.

The other reason for our avoidance of the word *paella* on the Shoreditch restaurant menu was that the concept has become so misunderstood, thanks to a touristy experience of badly made dishes, often containing frozen mussels and prawns, indifferent chicken, and electric yellow food colouring. And the experience hasn't only been confined to coastal resorts. My husband Rupert remembers eating atrocious stodgy reheated *paellas* in motorway restaurants when he was growing up in Spain.

At the opposite end of the scale, traditional restaurants would often rather sniffily insist on 45 minutes warning to prepare the dish. However, a new, exciting wave of appreciation for the *paella* is sweeping around Spain, re-interpreting it as something contemporary, fun and accessible. Smart specialist restaurants are springing up, serving many different, and often experimental, contemporary recipes, such as Thai mussel or salt cod *paella*, so that if you have a party of people going out for lunch or dinner, you can order a selection and share. Often these new-style *paellas* are quite shallow, the equivalent of thin-crust pizzas; and the use of heritage, rare and organic rices with individual characteristics, as opposed to blander hybrids, has become a selling point in the most progressive restaurants. There is even a new and popular fashion for ordering *paella* to be delivered to your home on a moped, like pizza.

Some *arroz seco* notes

It is hard to give exact cooking times, because as well as the varietal and the quality of the grains, there are other important variables, such as the softness or hardness of the water, the temperature of any stock added, the cooking vessel, and the type of heat used for cooking. So I would say, cook by eye and by taste, and use proportions and cooking times only as a guide.

There is an ongoing debate about the use of onions in a dry rice dish – should you use them in the base or shouldn't you? Our Catalan chef Leo adds his special *cebolla caramelizada* – onions reduced right down with a touch of tomato (see page 319) – to rice dishes, but in other regions the thinking is that because onions have a high level of humidity they can interfere with the cooking time. Certainly if you were to add onion to a dry rice dish in Valencia or Alicante, you would be upsetting the purists.

Making an *arroz seco* is a different process from that of a *risotto* or its Spanish equivalent, *meloso*. In a risotto, the hot stock is added ladleful by ladleful and you let the rice take it up before adding any more, stirring constantly to release the starch from the rice, at the same time as allowing it to absorb flavours. In an *arroz seco* the hot stock or water is added at the beginning – initially you put in enough to bring the level to just below the handle studs of the pan, holding some back in case you need it. The liquid is brought to a gentle simmer, but then isn't stirred during cooking, though the pan is shaken occasionally to meld the ingredients a little and a little extra hot stock can be added as necessary to ensure the rice cooks perfectly.

Where an *arroz seco* is similar to risotto or *meloso*, however, is in the need for good-quality stock. The rice will absorb it all, so you can't use a feeble stock and expect a dish full of flavour.

Paella pans are wide and don't always fit conveniently over a domestic hob. If it looks like the rice is cooking unevenly, rotate the pan clockwise every minute and a half or so, taking it off centre too if necessary.

There are two approaches to cooking an *arroz seco*: either you let it cook on the hob all the way through, or you start it off on the hob and then transfer it to a hot oven at 200°C/gas 6.

If you cook the rice entirely on the hob, towards the end of the cooking time the thin metal of the pan causes a crusty layer of toasted rice (the *socarrat*) to form on the base and edge of the pan. This *socarrat* is one of the characteristics that most aficionados adore. Once the liquid is absorbed and the rice is ready the pan should be taken off the heat and covered with a clean tea towel or foil for a couple of minutes before serving to even out the texture of the rice by allowing the upper layer to steam and finish cooking.

If you put it into the oven the rice cooks through more evenly without the need to steam it at the end, but you need to keep an eye on it, and if it is getting too dry pour in a couple of ladlefuls of stock around the edges in a circular movement.

Which method you prefer is up to you, but in the recipes that follow, we have suggested the one we

Arroz de alcachofas con bacalao
Artichoke and salt cod rice

This is the dish that Leo, our head chef, made for us after a meeting one day, and it was so good it spurred us on to develop a serious rice menu for our Shoreditch restaurant. The base is the intense Catalan *cebolla caramelizada* – onion and garlic paste, made with a little tomato added (see page 319) – and in this case the *arroz* is finished off in the oven, to dry off the rice a little more, but without the crunchy base, or *socarrat*, that is produced by cooking on the hob. Because there is more rice and liquid involved, the cooking time is also a bit longer. The dish uses a *picada*, made with nuts, for added flavour interest.

Serves 4

4 medium globe artichokes
a squeeze of lemon juice
3 tablespoons olive oil
2 cloves of garlic, chopped
6 young garlic shoots or mild spring onions, roughly chopped
40g *cebolla caramelizada* (see page 319)
400g Bomba or Calasparra rice
1.25 litres hot *fumet rojo* (red fish stock, see page 468)
a pinch of salt
350g salt cod (fillet or loin), cut into 2.5cm chunks (skinned and boned)

For the picada
5 blanched almonds
5 hazelnuts
1 clove of garlic, chopped
1 tablespoon flat-leaf parsley, chopped
12 strands of saffron
1 tablespoon olive oil

Preheat the oven to 200°C/gas 6.

Put the nuts for the *picada* on a small tray and roast them in the preheated oven for 5 minutes. Keep to one side.

Prepare the artichokes (see page 350) and cut each one into 6 pieces, keeping them in a bowl of water acidulated with a squeeze of lemon juice until you are ready to use them.

Make the *picada* by pounding the roasted nuts with the rest of the ingredients, using a pestle and mortar, until really smooth. You should have about a tablespoon of paste. Keep to one side.

Heat the oil in a 38cm paella pan, add the chopped garlic cloves and cook for a minute, then add the artichoke pieces and cook for 2–3 minutes, stirring frequently over a medium heat. Add the garlic shoots or spring onions and cook for a further 2 minutes, stirring from time to time.

Add the *cebolla caramelizada* and stir well, then add the *picada* and stir for about 30 seconds.

Add the rice and stir around for a few minutes to 'toast' the rice, taking care not to burn the *picada*.

Add the hot stock, all in one go, then sprinkle with a pinch of salt and stir. Leave to bubble over a medium heat, and when the stock has reduced by half (about 10 minutes), quickly stir in the pieces of cod and leave to cook undisturbed for 2 more minutes.

Transfer the pan to the preheated oven for about 15 minutes, until the grains of rice are quite dry and still slightly *al dente*. Remove the pan from the oven, leave to sit for 2 minutes, then serve.

Arroz a la zamorana
Rice Zamora style

The province of Zamora is in north-west Spain, close to the border with Portugal – a region which couldn't be further from the rice-producing area of Valencia, where the *paella* is said to have originated. Nevertheless, they have their regional interpretation, which is all about the pig, and can be a real nose to tail affair. This is a dish that our former chef Roberto's mother makes regularly at home and she will include any part of the pig she happens to have, from minced pork or sausages to ears, cheeks, trotters or tails, all boiled until tender and then cut into tasty chunks. This version, however, sticks to easily accessible cuts.

Serves 4

2 tablespoons olive oil
150g *panceta*, cut into 6–8 chunks
150g pork ribs/chops *adobado* (i.e. marinated in *adobo* spice mix, see page 398), cut in half
150g fresh cooking *chorizo*, sliced into 1cm rounds
1 small onion, finely chopped
1 clove of garlic, chopped
1 small red pepper or ½ a large one, cut into medium strips
1 small green pepper or ½ a large one, cut into medium strips
250g Bomba or Calasparra rice
500ml vegetable stock or water
sea salt
1 teaspoon *pimentón de La Vera picante* (smoked hot paprika)
1 teaspoon dried oregano
50g Serrano ham, finely chopped

Ideally, use a wide, flat-bottomed heatproof terracotta dish about 6cm deep or so. You can also use a *paella* pan or a wide, high-sided casserole.

Heat the olive oil in the dish, put in the *panceta* and the ribs and cook until browned on all sides, then add the *chorizo* slices and fry for 2 minutes. Lift out all the meat and keep to one side.

Now add the chopped onion and garlic and allow to fry gently, stirring frequently, for about 5 minutes (remember that if you are using a terracotta dish, it will retain the heat more than a metal or enamel one, so be careful not to burn the ingredients).

Add the strips of red and green pepper, stirring and pushing the vegetables about for a few more minutes.

Now return the meat to the dish, add the rice and stir for a couple of minutes, then add the stock or water and bring to the boil. Add a pinch of salt, the *pimentón* and the oregano. Allow the rice to bubble gently for about 15 minutes, by which time all the liquid should be absorbed.

Take the dish off the heat and stir in the ham. Cover with foil (or a clean tea towel) for about 4 minutes to retain the heat and finish cooking the upper level of rice grains, before serving.

ALCACHOFAS

'preparing an artichoke is second nature'

For most Mediterranean home cooks, preparing an artichoke is second nature and in Spain market stalls will be piled high with them in season. Whenever one of my former colleagues at Brindisa, Sandra Jarauta, would return from visiting her family in Navarra, she would bring us wonderful artichokes grown by her mother on their allotment, which she had picked fresh and fried in a light batter that morning – they were just amazing: bursting with flavour.

The main variety in Spain is the Blanca de Tudela, cultivated in the Ebro valley around Navarra and La Rioja, across Catalunya, the Levante and Andalucía, where the harvest starts in October and lasts until the first frosts. It is small and round, with green-grey leaves which remain open at the top of the flower. They are excellent trimmed and then cooked whole, either grilled on an open fire, steamed or boiled. Then you can peel off the hard outer leaves to get to the inner yellowish-green leaves, whose bases are soft and smooth with a delicate flavour, before you get to the tender, meaty heart, excellent with homemade mayonnaise or melted butter.

Most Spanish recipes, however, require the artichokes to be cut into four or six pieces, depending on their size, or sliced. First you need to snap off the outer leaves at the base near the stem. Once you get to the lighter-coloured leaves, tidy up the stem by trimming it where the leaves

have been snapped off. Next, lay the artichoke on its side, and chop off the top two-thirds of the leaves. Now cut the artichoke into quarters, or into sixths.

In all but baby artichokes you will see the fuzzy layer of choke above the heart in each section – in small artichokes it will be very small. Take this out with the tip of a knife.

Either keep the artichokes in quarters, or slice them thinly, depending on the recipe. Whichever you do, put them into a stainless steel, glass or terracotta bowl of water acidulated with lemon juice (3 tablespoons to 1 litre of water) to stop them turning black, until you are ready to use them.

Jarred artichokes

The texture of an artichoke lends itself very well to cooking/char-grilling and then preserving in jars in brine or olive oil. The Spanish, however, tend not to char-grill them, preferring to allow their pure flavour to come through. Also they usually cook artichokes destined for jarring a little longer than the Italians, who prefer them a little more *al dente*. As a result they have a softer texture, and are more delicately flavoured.

Drained of their brine and dressed with lemon juice, oil and salt, they make a good, quick and easy tapa on pieces of toasted bread.

Arroz de pollo y conejo con pimentón

Rice with chicken, rabbit and paprika

This is a fine rice dish from Imanol Jaca who supplies us with our wonderful buttery beef, and which he made for me at his gastronomic club, Txoko el Sauco, in San Sebastián, where the men cook, and then the families come to eat. Compared to the layering of some *paellas*, it was a simple, almost one-dimensional dish – quite macho really: just meat, rice and copious amounts of paprika, but very, very tasty. While we have remained true to his macho aesthetic, we have added another dimension, using the heart, liver and kidneys of the rabbit to make a *picada*, which in this part of Spain would be known as a *majada*.

Imanol likes to spread out the rice in the *paella* to keep it very shallow (2cm maximum) so although this recipe is for 4, he uses a pan that would be big enough to serve 8 people.

Serves 4

5 tablespoons olive oil
2 rabbit saddles, cut into 8 pieces
2 rabbit legs
1 rabbit head, cut into 2 pieces (optional)
2 chicken thighs
2 chicken drumsticks
1 level teaspoon *pimentón dulce* (mild paprika)
about 10 threads of saffron, infused in 4 tablespoons warm water
a sprig of thyme
380g Bomba rice
800ml warm *caldo de pollo* (dark chicken stock, see page 468)
salt

For the picada
3 tablespoons olive oil, plus a little more if necessary
4 cloves of garlic, skin on
a pinch of sea salt
1 rabbit heart
1 rabbit liver
2 rabbit kidneys
1 *ñora* pepper (see page 280)
1 tablespoon chopped parsley leaves
3 tablespoons chicken stock (see above)

To make the *picada*, heat 3 tablespoons of oil in a small frying pan. Crush the garlic cloves, still in their skins, and put them into the pan, then take it off the heat and tilt it, so that the cloves cook in deep oil without running the risk of burning. The reason for cooking the garlic this way is that the irregular shapes develop more complex garlic flavours. When the cloves have cooled a little, remove any remaining dry skin and transfer to a mortar with a pinch of salt.

Put the pan of oil back on the heat, then add the rabbit heart, liver and kidneys and fry well for 5–10 minutes, breaking up the liver if necessary to make sure it is cooked well through and will crumble easily, as its powdery consistency is an essential quality of the *picada*. Lift out all the offal and keep to one side, leaving any remaining oil in the pan.

Crush the garlic and salt in the mortar with the pestle, and when it is creamy add the kidneys and gently work them into the paste. Use your fingers to separate the lobes of the liver and remove any gristly bits, then add the lobes to the mortar and continue to pound. Add the heart and pound a bit more. Again, remove any gristly bits. The finished paste should have the consistency of pâté.

Cut the stalk from the *ñora* pepper and remove the seeds, breaking the pepper into 2 or 3 large pieces. Heat the oil in the pan again, adding a drop more if necessary, then add the *ñora* and tilt the pan in the same way as for the garlic earlier, so that the pepper fries in the deeper oil for just a few seconds, otherwise its thin skin will burn. It should just turn crisp and the flesh white. Take off the heat and clear a space at the bottom of the mortar so that there is a hard surface on which to pound the *ñora*. Crush it, piece by piece, gradually blending it into the paste, until all the *ñora* has been incorporated. Don't worry if there are flakes of skin left in, as the *picada* will be passed through a sieve.

Return the pan of oil to the heat one last time, add the parsley and cook until crisp, then blend into the paste. Add the 3 tablespoons of stock to the *picada*, to give it the consistency of a thick soup, then pass through a coarse sieve into a bowl, in order to remove any flakes of *ñora* skin and any stray bits of connective tissue. Keep to one side.

To start the dish, heat 4 tablespoons of the olive oil in a large *paella* pan (46cm if you have one, otherwise 38cm). Add the rabbit (and the head, if using, cut in half lengthways) and chicken pieces and brown well over a medium heat for about 15 minutes, until the skin is crisp and toffee-coloured on all sides.

Make a space in the centre of the pan and heat another tablespoon of olive oil, then add the paprika, saffron, with its soaking water, and thyme and take the pan off the heat, to make sure the paprika doesn't burn and turn bitter. Stir quickly for a minute, then mix the chicken and rabbit pieces into the red-coloured oil, making sure they are well coated.

Add the rice and stir well, again making sure each grain is coated with oil. Ladle in the chicken stock in a circular motion until the level reaches just below the handle studs.

Bring to a fast boil for 5 minutes, then reduce the heat to a simmer, taste and season with salt as necessary. Add the *picada*, sprinkling it around into the stock.

Simmer for 11 minutes, then test the grains of rice around the edge of the pan. The finished texture needs to be just *al dente*, so if it looks like the stock is going to evaporate before the rice is cooked, add another ladleful.

If you like a *socarrat* (crunchy crust) to form on the base of the pan, turn up the heat for a few seconds at the end of the cooking time, until you begin to hear a crackling sound and start to smell gently toasted rice.

Take the rice off the heat and let it rest for 4 minutes, covered with foil or a clean tea towel. This will allow the rice to absorb any excess liquid but leave the centre moist.

Gastronomy and Trade Societies and Clubs

The north of Spain, particularly the Basque country, is known for its often sophisticated cooking, which is related to that of the nearby region of Biarritz. Aristocrats would often spend some of the summer season at these seaside spa resorts, and those who cooked for them (mostly women) would take their knowledge of haute cuisine home with them and apply it to local ingredients. While in the largely matriarchal society the women ran the domestic arrangements, the men set up *txokos,* gastronomic clubs, where they would gather to cook (the word *txoko* means a small space or corner and is often also used for a den or cellar in the home). Only through knowing an existing member would you be allowed to join the *txokos,* which are places of great camaraderie, yet usually pretty macho, competitive environments, in which the communal kitchen is inevitably brilliantly equipped with big ovens, big burners and *planchas,* with every conceivable knife and pan housed in specially made shelves.

Each society has its own rules. Some don't allow wives, girlfriends or families in at all; in others the men cook together on a Sunday and then join their families in the dining room, where everyone eats together outside the forbidden bastion of the kitchen. In areas where people live in flats with quite small kitchens, this must still be quite a practical answer to feeding large families for the traditional Sunday meal.

In San Sebastián our meat supplier, Imanol Jaca, cooked for us at his club, Txoko el Sauco, where each member had their own locker, and there was a communal stock of wine and key store-cupboard ingredients, with each member being trusted to write down what they had used on a chit. Imanol laid our table with cloths and school-style cutlery and served his wonderful rice dish with rabbit and chicken. I think on this occasion the women were allowed in after the meal to clean up!

The Pots
of Zamora

When we opened Casa Brindisa in South Kensington, the space felt so like a house with its different rooms and levels that I thought this was the chance I had been waiting for, to fill one of our restaurants with some of the beautiful old *arcilla* (clay) cooking pots, jars and jugs, hand-made by the local women of the villages of the Zamora region. If you are lucky you can find wonderful ancient, traditional and collectable decorative pots – enormous, many of them – in local antique markets and shops, each with a specific purpose. There might be *ollas* or *pucheros* (different names for stew-pots), *barriles* (ceramic urns for wine storage), *barrilas* (double-handled water-carriers used by workers in the field), *cantimploras* (water bottles), *botijos* (drinking jugs), *cántaros* (pouring vessels) and *tinajas* (jars) or *jarrones* (shaped like a vase) that were once used to store meat preserved in silky white pork fat.

Rupert, our cheese-maker friend, Félix Pastor (see page 432) and his friend Ramón, a ceramicist and collector, set off to scour Zamora and the surrounding villages of Moveros de Aliste, Carbellino de Sayago, Pereruela and Toro. After ten days Rupert arrived home with the car packed with antique vessels and a story to tell about each one. I love those pots. They make a real connection between the ingredients of the region that we have come to know at Brindisa and the local families who once used them.

Such pots are still made in the villages of the region in the traditional way. They are fashioned by *alfareras* (women craft potters), while the men are delegated the jobs of stacking firewood, preparing the ovens and collecting the local clay, which gives beautiful tones of biscuit ranging through to fudge, depending on where a piece has sat in the kiln. The pots include the famous *cazuelas*, the terracotta-coloured dishes which are glazed inside and can be used on the hob or in the oven, as well as other traditional pieces, still made to the old shapes, and more contemporary styles which are often more decorative than practical.

Especially beautiful are the pieces from Moveros de Aliste, where there is still a communal oven in the middle of the village, dating back to Arab times, fired with rock rose and heather woods. In the face of competition from ceramic factories, the village community is still optimistic that by holding firm to the ancient roots of their craft, their pottery can flourish on its reputation.

Arroz con costillas y morcilla
Rice with pork ribs and black pudding

This was one of our earliest recipes for the Shoreditch restaurant. We started out with only rice dishes made with fish and then felt that, especially in winter, people would also like the choice of some more hearty, sustaining dishes, with a generous dose of pork – and this one, created by our head chef, Nico Modad, is exceptional. Preferably make it with Ibérico pork ribs, but otherwise use the best ribs you can find that have tasty nuggets of meat on them. In the finished dish they will emerge from the rice a bit like the circle at Stonehenge.

Serves 4

around 5 tablespoons olive oil
8 good pork ribs, preferably Ibérico
2 medium onions, very finely chopped
3 cloves of garlic, finely sliced
1 medium red pepper, very finely chopped
sea salt, to taste
400g *morcilla*, peeled and sliced (2cm pieces)
a sprig of fresh thyme or 1 teaspoon dried thyme
300g tomatoes, chopped
1–2 teaspoons sugar, if necessary, to taste
360g Bomba rice
2 litres hot *caldo de pollo* (dark chicken stock, see page 468)
1 teaspoon *pimentón dulce* (sweet paprika)

Heat 1 tablespoon of the olive oil in a 38cm *paella* pan, tilting the pan to ensure the oil covers the surface as far as possible, put in the ribs and brown them on all sides, then lift them out and keep to one side.

Add 3 more tablespoons of olive oil to the pan, and, keeping it on a low heat, add the onions and garlic and cook gently until the onion is translucent. Add the red pepper and stir and coat well in the oil, adding another tablespoon if necessary, then season with a pinch of salt and cook very gently for 10 minutes.

Add a quarter of the *morcilla*, along with the thyme, and continue to cook gently for a further 10 minutes. Add the reserved ribs and stir and coat them in the ingredients in the pan for about 4 minutes.

Preheat the oven to 200°C/gas 6.

Add the tomatoes, stir well and bring to the boil, then taste and if necessary add 1 or 2 teaspoons of sugar to counteract the acidity of the tomatoes. Turn the heat down and simmer for another 10 minutes, until the sauce thickens to the consistency of a runny jam.

Add the rice and stir until the grains are well coated. Stir in 2 ladlefuls of the hot stock and the paprika, then ladle in around 1 litre of the stock in a circular motion until it reaches just below the handle studs. Bring the stock to a fast boil, taste the liquid and adjust for salt if necessary. After 5 minutes push the reserved ribs into the *paella* and lower the heat to a simmer for another 5 minutes.

Arrange the remaining *morcilla* on the rice in a decorative pattern, then add another ladleful of stock, sprinkling it in as before, in a circular motion, working in from the edges of the pan.

Simmer for a further 2 minutes – the *morcilla* will begin to break up – then transfer to the preheated oven for a final 4 minutes. During this time the *morcilla* will cook through, and any excess stock should have reduced, leaving the rice moist and dark and the top slightly crisped.

Remove from the oven and gently stir the *morcilla* through the rice before serving.

MELOSOS
Risotto-like rice dishes

These are much stickier than *paellas* and are made with either Bomba rice or an Italian risotto rice such as Carnaroli, which is now grown in Spain. As in a risotto, the stock is added ladleful by ladleful, letting the rice absorb it before adding more, but there is no butter and cheese beaten in at the end.

Meloso de arroz negro con calamar
Black rice with squid

This is a long-standing favourite at our Borough tapas bar that we can't take off the menu. It is served in terracotta bowls and the colours are wonderful: black-stained grains of rice, on a copper background with the straw-coloured squid on top.

Any of this that you have left over makes a wonderful stuffing for *piquillo* peppers as a tapa (see page 276).

Serves 4

olive oil, for frying
1 onion, finely chopped
300g squid, finely chopped, plus 4 medium whole squid tubes
400g Bomba or Carnaroli rice
½ teaspoon squid ink
1.1 litres hot *fumet blanco* (white fish stock, see page 466)
200g *alioli*, to serve (see page 136)

Heat a little olive oil in a large pan, add the onion and the chopped squid and cook briefly until they colour, then add the rice and the squid ink and stir well. Add the hot stock a ladleful at a time, stirring in and waiting for each ladleful to be absorbed before adding the next one. Cook in this way for 15–20 minutes, until the rice is still *al dente*, but quite creamy, like a risotto.

Meanwhile, preheat the grill until very hot. Open out the squid tubes and with a sharp knife make diagonal scores on them one way and then the other (taking care not to cut all the way through), to give a criss-cross effect. Put under the grill for 4–5 minutes. They will probably curl, so turn them until they are golden all over. Serve on top of the rice, with the *alioli* alongside.

Arroz meloso de setas
Creamy wild mushroom rice

This dish was created by Josep Carbonell, Brindisa's executive chef. We make it with Carnaroli rice, grown on the Illa de Riu estate in Tarragona.

Serves 4

3 tablespoons olive oil
1 clove of garlic, finely chopped
150g wild mushrooms, sliced chunkily
400g Bomba or Carnaroli rice
800–850ml hot vegetable stock
6 threads of saffron
½ teaspoon sea salt

For the picada
1 *ñora* or other mild dried pepper,
  de-seeded (optional)
1 tablespoon olive oil
2 cloves of garlic, peeled
4 mini breadsticks or ½ a slice
  of white bread, crust cut off
1 tablespoon flat-leaf parsley leaves

To make the *picada*, soak the *ñora*, if using, in hot water. Once softened, scrape the flesh from the skin and set aside. Heat the oil in a pan, put in the garlic and fry gently until golden-yellow, then lift out and keep to one side. If using bread, add it to the same pan and fry until golden in the same oil, then remove and also keep to one side. Put the reserved garlic into a mortar with the breadsticks, or fried bread, and the rest of the ingredients, and grind to a very smooth paste. Keep to one side.

Heat the 3 tablespoons of olive oil in a deep-sided frying pan, add the garlic and mushrooms and cook lightly for 3–4 minutes.

Add the rice and stir for a minute. Add the hot stock a little at a time, stirring constantly so the rice can release some starch and thicken the stock. During 10 minutes of cooking you should have added half the stock.

Add the *picada*, saffron and salt and cook for another 10 minutes, stirring and adding the rest of the stock until the consistency is creamy. Serve in soup dishes.

CALDOSOS
Soupy rice dishes

These are the soupiest of all rice dishes, served in deep bowls so that the rice is only just visible beneath the level of the soupy stock.

Though traditionally *caldosos* would be made with Bomba rice, again you can use the Italian Carnaroli, as it releases more starch but absorbs the liquid less.

The important thing with a *caldoso* is the timing: when it is just *al dente* and only a tiny dot of starch remains inside each grain, you need to take the dish off the heat and eat it straight away, as if you leave it for any length of time, the rice will carry on absorbing liquid and the dish will lose its essential soupiness.

Beware leaving the table for a moment in a restaurant specialising in *caldoso*, as if the chef has cooked the rice to the point of perfection he won't be amused if you are not ready to eat it immediately.

When we opened the doors of our Shoreditch restaurant, this was one of the most popular dishes on the menu. One of our neighbours loved it so much he came and ate it twice a week for about two months. It is similar to the Menorcan *caldereta*, made with spiny lobster, which we have enjoyed so many times on the island.

If you prefer not to use lobster you could use 8 langoustines instead.

Serves 4

2–3 prepared lobsters (allow 500g per person)
2 tablespoons olive oil
2 medium onions, finely chopped
1 medium red pepper, finely chopped
3 cloves of garlic, finely chopped
sea salt
500g cuttlefish, finely chopped into 1cm pieces
1 large tomato, grated
a little sugar to taste, if necessary
¼ of a sachet of squid ink
360g Bomba rice
3 litres warm *fumet blanco*
  (white fish stock, see page 466)
1 teaspoon finely chopped parsley
sea salt and freshly ground black pepper

For the picada
1 clove of garlic, finely chopped
1 tablespoon finely chopped parsley
2 threads of saffron, toasted in a dry pan
2 tablespoons olive oil

Cut each lobster in half lengthways and remove the claws. Wrap them in a tea towel in case of flying shards, and crack the shells with a hammer or the handle of a heavy knife. Cut each lobster tail into four pieces and leave the rest of the lobster uncleaned.

Heat the olive oil in a large pan or ceramic dish and fry the lobster tail and claws quickly for a minute on each side, so that their juices flavour the oil. Lift out and reserve. Add the onions, red pepper and garlic, together with a pinch of salt, and cook steadily for 15 minutes, until the onion is translucent and just beginning to turn a light golden brown.

Add the cuttlefish and fry for 10 minutes, allowing any liquid it releases to bubble up until the pan is almost dry. Add the grated tomato and let the mixture simmer for a further 20 minutes. Taste, and if the tomato is too acidic add a little sugar.

Meanwhile, pound all the ingredients for the *picada* together, using a pestle and mortar.

Add the squid ink and a tablespoon of the *picada* to the pan, stirring briefly to heat through, then put in the rice and stir thoroughly for 1 minute, ensuring each grain is coated. Now begin adding 400ml of the warm *fumet blanco*. Let the rice simmer quickly until the stock is almost all absorbed, then continue to add more stock by the ladleful for another 6 minutes. Don't stir, as the dish should have the consistency of soup and if it is stirred, the grains will begin to break up.

In between adding the ladlefuls of stock, scoop out the creamy green liquid from the lobster's thorax and add it to the pan. It will dissolve and flavour the rice.

Return the lobster pieces to the soup, ensuring they are covered with the *fumet*, and keep on a steady fast simmer for another 6 minutes. Taste the rice regularly, to see how quickly it is cooking. It should take 16–18 minutes in all, and when you estimate that there are about 2 minutes to go, stir in another tablespoon of the *picada*.

Check the rice again. It should be just *al dente* – bite a grain in half and you should see just a tiny pinprick of white at the core of the grain. Take the pan off the heat and leave to rest for a minute. Sprinkle with the parsley and season to taste with a pinch of sea salt and a twist of black pepper.

Serve immediately, as the rice will continue to cook in the hot soup.

Arroz caldoso de alcachofa, guisantes, sepia y gambas
Soupy rice with artichokes, cuttlefish and prawns

Many of the dishes from the Levante coast have a generous amount of vegetables, which gives them a certain lightness. Our friend Pilar, of Gutiérrez de la Vega wines in Alicante (see page 190), insists on using smaller amounts of onion and tomato than many Spanish cooks, so that the other flavours in the dish can find their way to the forefront, and I love this *caldoso* that she makes with two kinds of seafood, artichokes and peas, finished with a superb stock.

In season you can add fresh broad beans. If they are big, Pilar suggests peeling them, but this isn't essential.

If, when you buy the fish for the stock, the liver of the cuttlefish is intact, keep it and add about a third of it to the dish, as it gives another layer of flavour.

Choose deep wide bowls to serve it in, as there will be lots of wonderful soupy stock, and serve some good bread with it, to soak this up.

Serves 4

4 large artichokes or 8 small ones
a little lemon juice
2 ripe medium tomatoes
2 tablespoons olive oil
120g cuttlefish or squid, chopped
1 shallot, finely chopped
2 cloves of garlic, finely chopped
2 litres warm *fumet blanco*
  (white fish stock, see page 466)
4 threads of saffron
80g peas, podded
80g broad beans (optional)
200g Bomba or Carnaroli rice
1 teaspoon sea salt
½ teaspoon cuttlefish liver (optional)
200g small prawns, peeled

Prepare the artichokes (see page 350), and chop each one into 8 pieces (into 4 if small). Put into a bowl of water acidulated with some lemon juice to stop them discolouring.

Either grate the tomatoes or, if you prefer a smoother, more elegant texture, de-skin and de-seed them (see page 206).

Heat a tablespoon of oil in a deep pan. Put in the cuttlefish or squid, fry for a few minutes, until it turns white, then remove and reserve. Put the artichoke pieces into the pan and cook for about 3 minutes, just to soften them, then remove and set aside.

Heat the rest of the oil in the same pan and add the shallot and garlic, then the tomato. Cook gently over a low heat for about 10 minutes, until the onion is soft but not coloured. Add half the warm *fumet* and the saffron and bring to the boil, then turn down the heat and simmer for 3 minutes.

Add the peas and beans, if using, to the pan. Then add the rice and the rest of the *fumet*, the salt, reserved cuttlefish and the cuttlefish liver, if using. Add the artichokes and continue to cook for another 14 minutes. Stir a little occasionally to release the starch in the rice. Finally, add the peeled prawns and cook for a further 3 minutes, or until the rice is tender but still has some bite and the stock has reduced by about half.

Serve immediately so that the rice doesn't absorb any more stock.

FIDEUS

Pastas

Particularly in Catalunya and all along the Levante coast, there is quite a tradition of using pasta, possibly because the Catalans ruled Sicily in medieval times and there would inevitably have been an exchange of ideas. So when I first began living in Catalunya I shouldn't really have been surprised to see *macarrones* and *canelones* (macaroni and cannelloni) being enjoyed in homes and restaurants – originally these were created as a way of using up the meats left over from a big family meal, of roast chicken or even *escudella* (stew, see page 447).

Cannelloni was actually made fashionable by an Italian chef at the Barcelona restaurant Rossini in La Vila de Gràcia, who made *cannelloni a la Rossini*, named after the composer and great food lover in the 1920s (the dish is still served today), and it has passed into the Catalan cooking tradition. Cannelloni followed by roast chicken is a popular Sunday lunch.

Pasta was first introduced to Spain by the Moors around the eighth to ninth centuries. It was called *aletria* and appeared in the first Catalan cookbook, published in 1323, *Llibre de Sent Soví*. In fact, the name is still used in Murcia in a pasta dish called *costillejas con aletria*, made with thick noodles and pork.

Less well known outside Spain is the thin pasta known as *fideos* (*fideus* in Catalan), originally a Moorish pasta whose name comes from the Arab word *fada* (meaning abundance), and which appeared in Catalunya as early as 1429. It can be added to soups, but is more typically used in the same way as the rice in an *arroz seco* and with the same combinations of ingredients, from seafood and chicken to pork and sausages. Usually the pasta is toasted in a dry pan for about 3 minutes or lightly baked in the oven (at 180°C/ gas 4 for about 5 minutes) until it turns golden before cooking.

Whereas the Italian way of cooking dried pasta is to plunge it into masses of boiling water in which it can swirl around, *fideos* goes into hot stock – and not much of it – so that the pasta absorbs the flavours and becomes completely coated in the stock from the beginning. Then, in a similar way to the rice in a hob-cooked *arroz seco*, it is allowed to become a little crusty on the base of a pan. At the end of cooking you take the pan off the heat and put a damp cloth over the top, again as you would do with an *arroz*, and the extraordinary thing is that the moistness pulls up the little pasta 'hairs' so they stand on end, giving an intriguing spiky look.

Fideos comes in various diameters, the finest being similar to angel hair pasta and the thickest almost like macaroni. The finest are most likely to be added to light stock soups, such as *sopa cubierta*, or 'cupboard soup', which is like a minestrone and is a household staple in Valencia. For *fideuà* with seafood I would recommend the sizes No. 1 or No. 2, broken into short pieces, as the larger diameter ones (No. 3) can look clumsy and suit meat versions much better.

Like *paella*, *fideuà* is a dish that has often been very badly represented in tourist resorts, but done well it is elegant, delicious and a little lighter than a *paella*.

I have included two versions here which, though they may appear to have similar ingredients, are actually incredibly different. The first is a quite substantial, garlicky, vibrant dish made with prawn stock and Cognac; the second is a much lighter, more subtle and seductively delicate affair.

Fideuà Casta Diva
Fideus with seafood,
spinach and fennel

This is a delicate, very original version of *fideuà* from Pilar Sapena, whose husband Felipe makes the beautiful Casta Diva wines in Alicante (see page 190). It is a dish typical of Pilar's imaginative cooking: light, balanced and delicate, with the unusual addition of spinach and fennel fronds.

Pilar always buys her fish whole, and uses all the trimmings to make her stock, but in Spain there is also a way of shopping for ingredients that is known as '*muy señorito*'. It means 'gentlemanly', indicating you don't get your hands dirty, because the fish, or meat, will be cleaned and prepared for you – I would say go for this option, and ask your fishmonger to do the work for you.

You need 700g of fish and shellfish in all – the proportions below are Pilar's suggestions, but you can vary it according to what you can find that is good and fresh.

Pilar serves this with *alioli* to mix in as you eat, but she makes an interesting variation by cooking a small potato and mashing it into the *alioli*, which, she says, softens the garlic and also adds some texture.

Serves 4–6

400g *fideu* No. 1 or No. 2
6 tablespoons olive oil
200g monkfish or sea bream fillets,
  cut into pieces about 2cm square
200g cuttlefish, chopped,
  or baby cuttlefish, cut in half
100g small prawns, peeled
2–4 of the largest prawns you
  can find, kept in their shells
100g red mullet fillet
½ a green pepper, very finely chopped
1 medium onion, chopped
1 bay leaf
about 1 teaspoon sea salt
1 teaspoon *pimentón dulce* (sweet paprika)
1.8 litres hot *fumet rojo* (red fish stock,
  see page 466)
40g baby spinach (or chopped large leaves)

For the picada
1 whole *ñora* pepper, seeds
  and stalk discarded
3 cloves of garlic, skin on
2 tablespoons olive oil
10 threads of saffron
a pinch of sea salt
1 teaspoon chopped parsley
2 teaspoons chopped fennel fronds
2 medium tomatoes, grated
2 tablespoons *fumet* (from quantity above),
  if needed

To serve
alioli (see page 136)

Have ready a large tray or plate for putting the cooked ingredients on as you go, keeping each one separate.

Put a 38cm *paella* pan on a low to medium heat. Add the pasta and spread it out thinly over the pan, stirring and turning it for 3 minutes to stop it burning, until it 'toasts', i.e. turns golden brown. Turn out into a bowl and keep to one side.

Heat 2 tablespoons of the oil in the pan, add the monkfish or sea bream and sauté for about 4 minutes, turning with tongs, to ensure it has browned a little on all sides, then remove from the pan to your tray or plate. Next, add the cuttlefish to the pan, along with the *ñora* pepper. The *ñora* is going to go into the *picada*, but needs to be briefly fried first, so it makes sense to do it now. As soon as the *ñora* flesh turns white or chars, take it out, or it will become bitter, and put into the mortar ready to make the *picada*. Allow the cuttlefish to cook for another 4 minutes, then move the pieces to the edge of the pan where it is cooler. Turn down the heat, add another tablespoon of oil to the centre of the pan, and when it is hot put in both the peeled and unpeeled prawns and sauté for a minute on each side. Stir the prawns and cuttlefish together, then lift out and add to your tray or plate in a separate mound.

Finally, heat another tablespoon of oil, if necessary, put in the red mullet and fry for a minute on each side, then lift out and add to the tray or plate. Scrape any crisp bits of fish from the base of the pan to avoid burning, then add another tablespoon of oil. Put in the green pepper, stir for 30 seconds, turn down the heat to medium, and cook for another 4 minutes until browned and beginning to caramelise. Lift out and keep to one side, taking the pan off the heat.

To make the *picada*, crush the garlic cloves with the flat of a knife. Return the pan to the heat and add the oil. Put in the garlic cloves and fry for a minute, tilting the pan, so that they cook in a depth of oil, and removing the pieces of skin as they separate from the cloves. Lift out, chop and put into the mortar. Put the saffron into the pan in a small pile, then take the pan from the heat to stop the threads from burning. As soon as they start to release their aroma, lift them out with a teaspoon and add to the mortar. Take the pan off the heat, but keep to one side for use again in a few minutes.

Add a pinch of salt to the *ñora*, garlic and saffron in the mortar. Crush with the pestle, then add the parsley and the fennel fronds and continue to work everything into a paste. Add the grated tomato. The *picada* should have the consistency of a thick soup. If you need to loosen it some more, add a tablespoon or two of *fumet*. Keep to one side.

Heat another tablespoon of oil in the *paella* pan and add the chopped onion, along with the bay leaf (lightly crushed first in your fingertips). Cook gently, until soft but not coloured, for about 5 minutes. Taste and season with salt if necessary.

Add the reserved green pepper and pasta and the paprika and stir together over a high heat. When the mixture begins to sizzle, add around 850ml of the stock, a ladleful at a time, in a circular motion around the edge of the pan until the level is just below the studs that connect the handles. Add the spinach and let the pasta boil vigorously for 1 minute before turning the heat down to a steady simmer. Add the *picada* in tablespoonfuls so that it is well spread out throughout the pan. Add another 200ml of stock and stir gently. Taste and add a little salt if necessary. Let the pasta simmer for 5 minutes, testing regularly until the *fideu* is cooked, but still *al dente*, with the strands around the edges becoming crisp and dry, and most of the stock has been absorbed or evaporated.

Arrange the reserved pieces of fish and seafood decoratively in a circle around the *paella* pan and cook for a further 3 minutes, until these are cooked through. To finish off, rotate the pan off-centre, so that any wobbly areas which are holding too much liquid around the edge can cook through, too (remember that *paella* pans are big, and the centre will always be hotter than the edges).

When a light crackling sound emerges from the pan it means that the crusty base is just beginning to form and that it is time to take the pan off the heat and cover it with a clean tea towel for 4 minutes. The trapped steam allows the top layer of pasta to steam and dry a little more, and the pasta will curl upwards.

Serve with the *alioli* to mix in as you eat.

Fideuà bandera
Fideus with prawns and cuttlefish

This is based on a recipe from one of my oldest friends and my first boss in Catalunya, Pepa Salvador, who ran La Salsita restaurant on the Costa Brava. *Fideuà* is something we never cooked at La Salsita, because so many other restaurants around the coast served it, and Pepa always wanted her menus to be a little different, but in the 1980s she and her husband, Sergi Medir, and brother Oriol built their own boat, a beautiful schooner called *Pepa Bandera I*, which Sergi and Oriol sailed around Cape Horn and the islands of Chile, and on to the Galapagos and the Arctic Circle, before returning home through the Panama Canal. Pepa would close the restaurant in the low season to join them and she found *fideuà* to be a perfect one-pan dish to cook in the galley or out on deck.

She makes her *fumet rojo* (red fish stock, see page 468) in advance, then enriches it by making an extra little stock with the heads and shells of the small prawns she has peeled for the *fideuà*, plus a generous amount of Cognac.

Pepa's local port is Palamós in the Empordà, and she has the luxury of being able to select the famous local large, deep pink prawns, *gambas de Palamós,* which are brought in on the day boats. These are so outstanding, they are always eaten on their own or used, shell-on, to adorn *fideuà* or rice dishes, so while Pepa uses smaller prawns to mix into the pasta, she arranges these big ones on top so the dish looks stunning. In the UK it isn't so easy to find the equivalent, so when we make the dish at home we use tiger prawns throughout. We buy them shell on, so we can still use the shells for the stock.

When Pepa made this *fideuà* for us she served it with *alioli* and a simple leaf salad. As is her custom, Pepa first put some finely chopped sweet young onions into the bottom of the salad bowl to marinate in oil and vinegar for a while before putting in the leaves and tossing the oniony vinaigrette through them.

Serves 4–6

30 tiger prawns, shell on
5–7 tablespoons olive oil
125ml Cognac
1.5 litres hot *fumet rojo*
  (red fish stock, see page 468)
4 cloves of garlic, skin on
700g cuttlefish, cleaned and
  cut into 2cm squares
around 2 medium tomatoes, grated
  (you need about 150g of pulp)
400g *fideus* No. 1 or No. 2
8 threads of saffron

To serve
***alioli* (see page 136)**

Remove the heads and shells from 20 of the prawns and reserve the tails in a bowl in the fridge.

Heat 2 tablespoons of olive oil in a large pan over a high heat and put in the heads and shells. Stir with tongs, pressing the heads to get as much juice out as possible, then turn down the heat and cook for 4 minutes, continuing to stir and press.

Turn up the heat again, so that the shells begin to sizzle and release their aroma, then move the pan off the direct heat and add the Cognac. Stand away from the pan, as there is a lot of alcohol and it may well ignite. Put the pan back on a low heat and let it bubble and reduce until almost all the liquid has evaporated.

Add the hot *fumet*, bring to the boil and skim off any foam from the surface. After a couple of minutes of boiling, take the pan off the heat and leave the shells to infuse in the stock for another 5 minutes. Don't leave it longer, as the shells can start to release sulphurous flavours.

Pour the stock through a fine sieve into a clean pan, pressing the shells with the back of a spoon as you do so, to release every last drop of tasty juice. Keep the enriched stock hot on the hob.

Crush 3 of the garlic cloves, still in their skins, with the flat of a knife. Heat 3 more tablespoons of oil in a 40cm *paella* pan (or larger), put in the garlic and stir for a minute, then put in the peeled and unpeeled prawns – spread them out well, so that they have space to fry for a minute on each side until coloured (if you overcrowd them, the temperature will lower and they will boil). Remove the prawns and keep to one side.

Add the cuttlefish to the pan and stir to coat in the oil (you may need to add another couple of tablespoons). Sauté over a high heat until translucent.

Add the tomato and 150ml of the reserved stock and bring to the boil. Turn down to a simmer for another 10 minutes, until the liquid has reduced by about half – this may take a bit longer if the cuttlefish release water (this can happen especially if they have been previously frozen). When the cuttlefish are tender, transfer the mixture to a bowl and keep to one side.

Crush the remaining garlic clove in the same way as before. Wipe out the *paella* pan with kitchen paper and put it back on a low to medium heat. Add the pasta, together with the crushed garlic, and spread it out thinly over the pan, stirring and turning it for 3 minutes to stop it burning, until it 'toasts', i.e. turns golden brown.

Add the saffron and continue to toast for another minute.

Add the reserved cuttlefish and tomato mixture, turn up the heat and stir continuously for a minute, then begin adding the hot enriched stock a ladleful at a time in a circular motion around the edge of the pan until the level is just below the studs of the handles (around 850ml to 1 litre). Keep some stock in reserve in case the *fideuà* becomes dry. With a spoon, make sure the ingredients are spread evenly around the *paella* pan, then don't stir it again. Turn up the heat and boil fast for a minute, then turn down to a simmer for another 5 minutes.

Push in the reserved peeled prawns and arrange the unpeeled ones like the spokes of a wheel on top (tails pointing inwards). Add more stock if necessary, and continue to cook for another 3 minutes, until the *fideu* is cooked, but still *al dente*, with the strands around the edges becoming crisp and dry, and most of the stock has been absorbed or evaporated.

When you hear a light crackling sound it means that the crusty base is just beginning to form and that it is time to take the pan off the heat and cover it with a clean tea towel for 4 minutes. The trapped steam allows the top layer of pasta to steam and dry a little more and the pasta will curl upwards.

Serve with the *alioli* – which should be mixed in as you eat.

Cassola de fideus
Fideus with Catalan sausage
and Ibérico pork ribs

This meaty *fideuà*, made with a fatter *fideu* (sometimes called *perla*) and rich with hearty stock and tasty meats, is more of an inland dish, which I often enjoyed when I lived in Vic, Catalunya. Our head chef, Leo, whose family are from an inland village near Manresa, put this version on the menu in our South Kensington tapas bar and restaurant, and it is especially popular in the winter. I like it with Savoy cabbage.

Vi ranci is a traditional Catalan ingredient. Literally 'rancid wine', it is fortified wine made from white or red grapes that is allowed to oxidise as it ages. It can be drunk like a dessert wine if you dare, or used in cooking. It isn't easy to find in the UK, so you can substitute a dry or *amontillado* sherry.

Serves 4

160g *fideu*, No. 3 (or *perla*)
4 pork or Ibérico pork ribs (ask your
 butcher to cut them in half)
plain flour, for dusting
2 tablespoons olive oil
2 large, fat sausages such as *botifarra*,
 or good-quality Toulouse sausages,
 cut into chunky pieces
2 cloves of garlic, finely sliced
2 small onions, finely chopped
1 ripe tomato, grated
½ teaspoon sugar, if necessary (optional)
50ml *vi ranci* or *palo cortado*
 or *amontillado* sherry
750ml hot *caldo de pollo* (chicken stock,
 see page 468)

For the picada
10g blanched, unsalted almonds
10g blanched hazelnuts, in their skins
8 threads of saffron
1 heaped tablespoon finely chopped
 flat-leaf parsley

First toast the *fideu*. Put a 38cm *paella* pan on a low to medium heat, add the pasta and spread it out thinly, stirring and turning it for 3 minutes to stop it burning, until it 'toasts', i.e. turns golden brown. Turn out into a bowl and keep to one side.

Dust the ribs with flour. Heat the oil in the *paella* pan. Fry the ribs until well browned, then remove from the pan; put in the sausages and fry them until they colour. Lift out and set aside with the ribs. Put the garlic into the pan, then add the onions and fry gently for a few minutes until softened but not coloured. Add the grated tomato and cook for 10 minutes, until most of the liquid has evaporated. Taste, and add the sugar if the tomatoes are too acidic.

Put the ribs and sausages back into the pan, add the *vi ranci* or sherry and cook for 1 minute before adding the hot stock, a ladleful at a time, in a circular motion around the edge of the pan until the level is just below the studs of the handles. Bring to the boil, then add the *fideu* and simmer for 10 minutes.

While the *fideu* is cooking, make the *picada*. Crush the nuts in a pestle and mortar. Heat a dry pan and briefly toast the saffron, then add it to the nuts with the parsley and grind to a paste.

Once the *fideu* is soft but still a little *al dente*, scatter the *picada* over the surface, stir in and cook gently for 2 minutes, until the stock has reduced and coats the ingredients generously.

To finish off, rotate the pan off-centre, so that any wobbly areas which are holding too much liquid around the edge can cook through too (remember that *paella* pans are big, and the centre will always be hotter than the edges).

When a light crackling sound emerges from the pan it means that the crusty base is just beginning to form and that it is time to take the pan off the heat and to cover it with a clean tea towel for 4 minutes. The trapped steam allows the top layer of pasta to steam and dry a little more, and the pasta will curl upwards, giving the dish its spiky look.

LEGUMBRES

Legumes

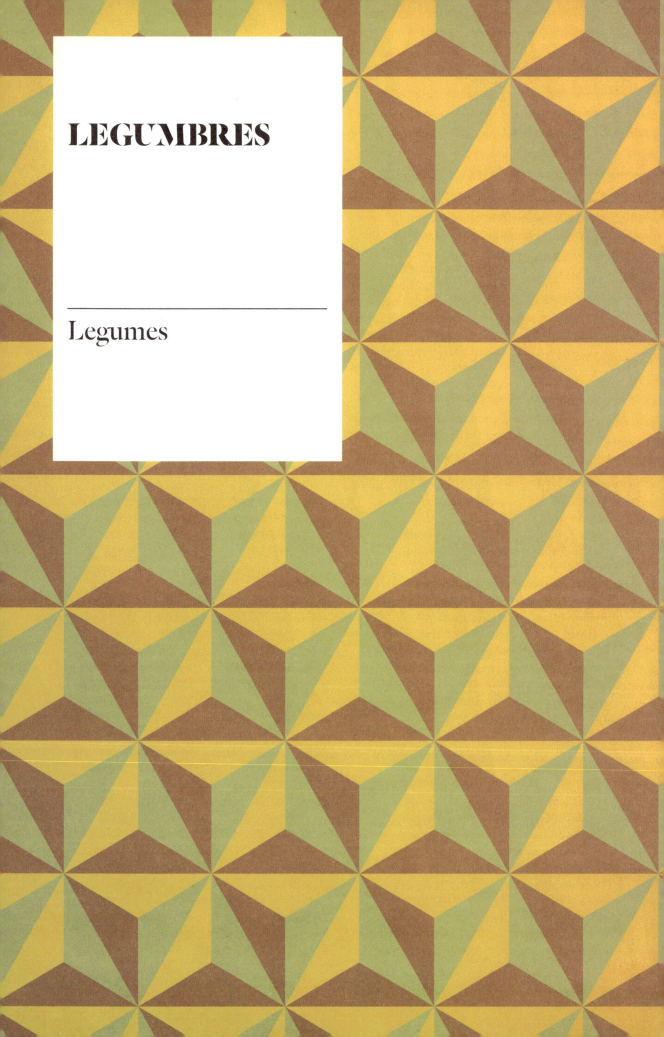

On a visit to the Villarejo dairy in Castilla La Mancha, from which we buy one of our Manchego cheeses, the owner, Francisco Antonio Moral Sánchez, took us to a roadside truckstop for lunch, and on the menu of the day was a huge choice of white bean, lentil and chickpea stews. It really highlighted for me how fundamental all these legumes are to Spanish cooking. Such dishes were usually born in times when meat was a luxury but legumes could be relied on for their ability to absorb tasty stocks and sauces, so that you could pack a dish full of flavour and provide hearty, cheap nutrition on a shoestring.

The nineteenth-century writer Pérez Galdos gave a snapshot of this in his novel *Miau*, in which he portrayed a relatively well-off family in Madrid in the nineteenth century who lived on a stew of chickpeas and cabbage almost every day. If the father was lucky enough to get a bone to make the stock a bit more juicy and flavoursome, it was a cause for celebration.

Over the centuries hundreds of legume recipes have been handed down through the generations, which feature added ingredients from clams to partridge, cabbage to pumpkin and almonds. The classic partner for legumes, however, must be cured pork, from *panceta* to vibrant, spicy red *chorizos* and *morcillas*, particularly those from Asturias, with their dark smouldering flavours.

Chickpeas, lentils and broad beans were originally cultivated in the Middle East and have been grown in Spain since at least Roman times, while most of the other beans typical of Spanish cooking originate in Latin America: *pinto* and *frijol* from Mexico and large white varietals from the Andes. On small plots in regions such as Tolosa, the old Latin American way of planting beans around the stems of maize is still practised, since the two crops are complementary, with the beans fixing nitrogen in the soil to nourish the maize.

Most households in Spain will use both dried and prepared (i.e. cooked and jarred) legumes and you can usually buy both in the markets and *ultramarinos* (grocers) shops. In the specialist *cansaladerias* that you still find in some towns, they sell beans and pulses freshly cooked in their own kitchens, along with their own stocks and cured produce, so you can buy everything you need for a quick and easy, nutritious meal.

For over 20 years at Brindisa we have been buying superb-quality prepared legumes from Navarrico, the company started in the 1950s by José and Amalia Salcedo in San Adrián in Navarra. Their artisan philosophy still prevails, and rigorous selection and careful cooking are the key. Their *alubias blancas* (haricot beans), in particular, are creamy, delicate and quite special.

'in some recipes only dried beans, chickpeas or lentils will do'

There are some recipes in which only dried beans, chickpeas or lentils, soaked overnight and cooked from scratch, will do. For example, in a rich stew such as a *fabada* or *cocido*, the beans need to absorb the stock and fats to an extent that ready-cooked beans can't match.

Beans

In the UK we love baked beans from tins, and fresh runner beans and broad beans in the spring, but beans dried naturally on the plant haven't figured very highly in our culture since medieval times, when they were grown for subsistence and cooked up in potages. These days our climate is considered too damp to allow most varieties to dry well in this way without risk of mould and mildew, and as a consequence we haven't retained the tradition of soaking and slow-cooking them that prevails in Spain and the Mediterranean, where certain heritage varieties will often be so cherished that they are granted the mark of a PDO and championed by the Slow Food movement.

So I'm sure it isn't usual in British households to talk about beans for hours on end as we seem to do in our family, but as Rupert and I both lived in Spain for many years, we have a healthy respect for all legumes, and a working lunch when we are both at home will often be a bowl of home-cooked beans, just dressed with oil and vinegar and salt and pepper, perhaps with some Spanish sardines for me, and chunks of bread.

I find dried beans quite entrancing. Visually they are splendid: their colours, shapes and shiny skins are so beautiful and tactile that I always want to plunge my hands into the sacks and run my fingers through these jewels.

In Spain dried beans are ideally bought loose from a trusted market stallholder, preferably local to the area of cultivation. I have a vivid memory of an old lady sitting on a step in the tiny village square of Castellfollit de la Roca in Catalunya, carefully podding pale yellow pods of *mongete* beans (see page 381) for sale.

When the beans are harvested in the autumn you can buy and cook them immediately: an experience beyond compare, as the virtually 'fresh' bean will cook through within about 30 minutes and be as smooth as cream, with the tenderest of skins that melts away. I love to see the women shopping in the markets, so knowledgeably weighing up the qualitative features of the different varieties piled on trestle tables, and have been lucky enough to be in San Sebastián at just the right time to pick up armfuls of 'fresh' *pochas* in their mottled mauve pods.

In some regions there are heritage varieties that are so local you won't see them anywhere else, and they may have evocative names and nicknames that vary from village to village.

Sometimes the beans are produced with great care and attention in such tiny quantities that they become rare and very expensive, for example, in the villages outside Madrid there is a bean called Rascafría, which is so highly prized that bags of them are given as presents. Occasionally at Brindisa we bring over the most incredible beans that really do cost a lot of money because a small farmer has only a field of them to sell, but they will cook to clotted-cream silkiness, and incredibly their skins will appear not to have moved at all, because they will have swollen in tandem with the bean inside, without a single split or tear.

How to choose and store beans

It isn't only the way it is grown that marks out a high-quality dried bean, but its age. It is easy to forget, when dealing with dry produce, that beans, like vegetables, are seasonal: every year the crop is harvested, dried and then sold. And the idea, among societies that have a strong culture of eating beans, is that you finish up the dried beans from one season and then move on to the next – something that is a little alien to us in the UK. In the last 20 years or so at Brindisa our sales of new-season beans have been mostly to chefs, and rarely beyond, so most people have yet to discover the pure pleasure of cooking and eating them.

The newer the dried bean, the more elastic the skin, which means you can happily slow-simmer or bake the beans over many hours and they will hold up – or as chef Jeremy Lee, one of our earliest bean friends at Brindisa, puts it, as only he can: 'the skins behave impeccably, stretching and expanding as the beans swell up in the water, holding their structure superbly, so they can withstand long, long, one-bubble-on-the-surface cooking over many, many hours and develop an amazing intensity of flavour and creaminess – but you can still put in a spoon and lift them out, or decant them from one pot to another and they will stay intact, and their stock will never be overly soupy. If you tried to cook older, poorer-quality beans for the same length of time, they would just break up and produce a much more starchy stock.'

In Spain, because of this bean culture, there is a quick and diligent rotation of stock in the shops as well as the markets, so beans are not allowed to get old and stale, and a Spanish home cook is highly unlikely to come across a forgotten packet bought on a whim and languishing in the kitchen cupboard (often they are sold loose, or in beautiful cloth bags in shops with a high turnover). Whereas, even if you buy a packet of supermarket beans in the UK and use them straight away, the chances are that the slow customer turnaround means that the beans will have been stored for a long time. It can be so frustrating to buy a packet of dried beans, soak them diligently overnight, cook them for the correct amount of time stated in a recipe, and then find that the skins are tough and the beans won't give when you bite into them, however much longer you cook them for. Or, alternatively, the skins will split and the beans turn to mush.

There isn't an obvious way to tell by looking at a bean (unless it is excessively wrinkled and discoloured) whether it is recently dried and at its best, or older. Ideally, you want to buy your beans from a reliable supplier who can assure you that they have been harvested in the previous season – and I would say to enjoy them at their best, consume them within a year of harvest; eighteen months maximum. So if you are buying beans in a packet, check the 'best before' date – if it is years ahead, avoid them.

In the UK most beans are sold in cellophane packets and will have been sterilised, to close off any danger of finding weevils. Weevil eggs will hatch in warmth. When high-quality beans are kept properly at low temperatures this is not a problem, but since there is no telling what temperature the beans will be kept at once people take them home, large-scale packers won't take any chances. However, the sterilisation process can be brief, gentle and graduated according to the variety of bean; or more aggressive, with the beans blasted at a higher, indiscriminate temperature which can harden their skins and reduce the creaminess of their texture. Unfortunately, the difference is indiscernible to the eye; however, if you can find them, it is worth buying beans in vacuum packs, as this is usually an indication of good quality. The beans will still have been sterilised, but as vacuuming is an extra cost to the producer/supplier, it is a sign that they are considered worthy of extra care and the process will have been done more considerately, producing fresher, more delicate beans that deserve not to be kept for too long.

Always store your beans in a cool dry place (the optimum temperature is less than 18°C), not under bright lights – at home this could be a cellar or larder. Otherwise their skins will harden. A fridge is fine in the summer, as long as the beans aren't allowed to get wet.

Cooking dried beans

Apart from the white *pochas* (see page 380), which can be bought virtually 'fresh' in the summer in Navarra and the Basque country, and need no soaking and only 20–30 minutes cooking, the beans suggested for the recipes in this book are dried, therefore they need to be soaked for a minimum of 12 hours or overnight. Make sure you do this in plenty of cold water in a spacious bowl – the water should cover the beans by at least 5cm – as larger beans such as *judiones*, especially, can plump up to double their size.

Transfer them to a pan of fresh cold water before cooking (some recipes call for you to keep the soaking water).

Calculate 70–80g of dried beans per person for a main dish.

Long, slow cooking is best and a terracotta pot is often a better option than a metal pan, as it helps you to slow-cook the beans to a creamy texture, without the risk of the beans catching on the base. Even better, put a diffuser underneath the pot to keep the temperature stable and even. Since so much depends on the age of the bean, the important thing is to keep watching and testing. I have bought beans a few months after harvesting that have cooked through in 20 minutes, while much older ones have sometimes needed 5 hours.

You need to cook the beans without salt, which will toughen their skins and, as Harold McGee, expert on science in the kitchen, explains in his book, *On Food and Cooking*: 'salt reduces swelling of starch granules within beans creating a mealy texture rather than a creamy one'. Only salt them at the end of cooking.

Finally, a trick for cooking beans that are being really slow to absorb liquid: you need to 'frighten' or blast the beans (the verb is *asustar*), so once they break into their first boil, throw in some cold water to halt it. This allows the bean to begin to rehydrate better. Once should be enough, but if the beans show no sign of softening, you can repeat the process.

When you drain them, rinse them with tepid water, to prevent the skins peeling back as they change temperature.

This is my guide to some of the most interesting of Spanish beans, and the best way to use them.

Alubias blancas
White beans

Faba

Not to be confused with the dried *fava* beans of the eastern Mediterranean/north Africa, *fabas* are long, lozenge-shaped white beans traditionally grown in the Picos de Europa mountains of Asturias, around the municipalities of Villaviciosa, Pravia and Cangas de Narcea, and above the port of Luarca in the municipality of Valdés. They are probably the most expensive legumes in Spain, since they are grown on small allotments and mountain terraces that are often only accessible on foot, and must be tended and harvested by hand.

Fabas are the classic ingredient in the local bean and sausage stew, the luxurious *fabada asturiana*, which provides much-needed winter fuel in the high mountain villages. One January when Rupert and I were staying in the village of Sanabria, we were snowed in and it was the big bowls of *fabada*, with the white beans luxuriating in rich, glossy molten pork meat and fat, that gave us the strength to walk through six kilometres of deep, deep snow to the nearest garage to find chains for the car. I remember passing a frozen stream where a white stork was serenely stepping over the ice, trying to peck its way through to find food, and thinking how much luckier we were to be fuelled with beans and pork fat.

There is also an exceptional, similar and equally lovely bean, also named *faba*, grown in small plots over the border from Asturias in Lourenza, Galicia, but here the beans are used in a different way, often cooked with fish, especially octopus.

Pochas

These young round white beans inside purple and white streaked pods are similar to fresh Italian borlotti beans and are harvested in August and early September, most typically in Navarra and La Rioja. Since they have not been allowed to fully dry on the plant, they are treated like fresh beans that need no overnight soaking and cook through in about 20 minutes, after which time they just melt in the mouth.

In Navarra they are cooked with quail, eel, crab and/or even lamb's tail. They can be equally good with vinaigrette or accompanying a vegetable dish.

Like fresh borlotti, they can be difficult to find in the UK, but if you do come across them, for four people, you need around 300g of beans.

Put them into a pan of cold water, bring to the boil, then turn down the heat to medium and add a red and a green pepper, roughly sliced, a couple of tomatoes, and a couple of whole garlic cloves. Simmer for 20–30 minutes, until tender, then take off the heat, take out the peppers and tomatoes and put them into a bowl, with 2 tablespoons of beans and 2 tablespoons of their cooking water. Mash these together roughly, then mix in the rest of the drained beans, season, stir in a couple of tablespoons of good olive oil, such as Arbequina, and enjoy.

Alternatively, you can buy jarred cooked *pochas*, which can simply be heated through in a pan. Sauté the peppers, tomatoes and garlic separately and then combine with the beans in the same way.

Fesols de Santa Pau

These are white and round, similar to small navy beans. They are grown in the volcanic soil of the national park of Garrotxa in Catalunya and so contain an exceptionally high level of minerals. On the edge of the famous beech forest, La Fageda d'en Jordà, which is rooted in lava, we had a dish of *fèsols* with pork scratchings – which was a bit hairy in texture – but the combination of pork skin and beans was very tasty.

Mongetes del ganxet

These are the beautiful little white Catalan hooked beans (*ganxet* means 'little hook' in Catalan), which have exceptionally delicate, almost indiscernible skins. In Catalunya people often grow *mongete* beans in the garden, picking them either quite fresh or leaving them to dry on the plant until the pods are wrinkled. You can also buy them cooked, in jars, and they are lovely, just heated through and served with some grilled fresh *botifarra* sausages (see page 450). They are also typical in *empedrat*, a salad which combines the beans with salt cod or white tuna (see page 201). However, their production is relatively small and so they are quite expensive, especially the exceptional ones from the PDO of Vallès-Maresme, whose territory includes villages within the beautiful, wild and hilly areas of Vallès Occidental and Vallès Oriental just outside Barcelona and whose sunny, dry microclimate encourages the best beans to be grown.

Alubias arrocinas

Tiny, round, white beans which are an elegant addition to soups and leaf salads, *arrocinas* are also ideal for homemade baked beans (see page 74). One of my favourite ways of cooking them is in the same way as for *pochas* (opposite). Being fully dried, they just need longer to cook – about an hour.

Blancas redondas

This is a very similar bean to *alubias arrocinas*, but bigger.

Alubias planchadas

Long, white, slightly flat beans – *planchada* means flattened or ironed – these are excellent in hearty stews or as an accompaniment to roast meats, especially lamb, in which case the beans are cooked quite plainly in bay-scented vegetable stock. You might also come across *blanca riñón*: white, kidney-shaped beans, which are similar, but not as flat, and often cheaper.

Alubias pintadas
Coloured beans

Tolosas

These shiny, deep coppery-purple, oval-shaped beans are now protected by a Slow Food Presidia. They come from the Basque town of Tolosa, where the water is low in calcium, and the locals insist that if you don't have the good fortune to live there you should cook the beans in mineral or rain water instead. Tolosa chefs also recommend cooking them in a terracotta pot until velvety, sometimes enriched with *panceta* and *chorizo*. Typically, they are then served with the local pickled peppers, known as *langostinos de Ibarra* (see page 275), on the side.

I ate a special lunch at the home of Pello Urdapilleta and his wife, Maite Izaquirre, who farm black and white Euskal Txerria pigs in the region. In 1981 the breed was close to extinction with only 50 animals left. They were saved by a French Basque stockbreeder and butcher, Pierre Oteiza, who began making high-quality hams in the Aldudes forests in Pyrénées-Atlantique. Then in 1997 Pello and Maite began their own project, nurturing a small herd on their farm in Bidegoian, in the north-eastern Basque province of Gipuzkoa. Pello's surname actually means 'load of pigs', and when he started researching the history of his family, who had lived in the same house for generations, he found that they had pig-farming roots going back to the sixteenth century, so his mission is a personal, as well as an ethical one.

The animals roam around 54 hectares of verdant forest where they can feast on chestnuts, cobnuts, hazelnuts, walnuts, grasses and herbs, a diet as privileged and complex as that of their distant Ibérico cousins in the Dehesa of Extremadura. For the last two-month fattening phase they are fed corn, beans and bran until they reach the required weight, and the resulting ham and its fat have a beautiful nutty and buttery character.

Following plates of their stunning home-cured ham, lomo (loin) and *salchichón* (sausage) made with pepper, and before the main dish of *pollazo* (free-range roast chicken with *piquillo* peppers), Maite served up the silkiest, creamiest *Tolosa* beans, cooked very gently for a long time in the traditional way, which she believes gives the beans such a full-bodied flavour that the addition of meat is unnecessary.

For four of us she soaked 300g of *Tolosa* beans overnight, then drained them and put them into a casserole with enough fresh cold water to cover by two fingers, maximum. She added a large red onion, chopped finely, and a medium potato, roughly cut into chunks, brought the water to the boil, then turned down the heat, skimmed off any foam that had come to the surface, and simmered the beans very slowly for 2–3 hours, before seasoning them with sea salt. She told me that some people insist on not stirring the beans at all as they cook, while others say you must stir very occasionally (Maite prefers not to stir). Again, if you can use a diffuser under the pan it helps the beans cook evenly without sticking or burning. As is traditional, she served the beans with pickled green *guindilla* peppers.

Moradas

These can be either *redonda* (round) or *larga* (long). The small *redonda* are similar to the *Tolosa* (left) and very delicate, but are expensive and hard to find, while the bigger *larga* are closer in appearance to the red kidney bean. Both are traditionally used in pork stews.

Frijoles negros

These mild, sweet, black haricot beans are loved across Spain, particularly in rice dishes, as well as in Latin America and the Caribbean. They are good cooked with bay leaves and whole dried peppers to give them a touch of aromatic spice. In the Balearic Islands they are famously used in a dish called *moros y cristianos*, in which the black beans are mixed with white rice to symbolise a sixteenth-century battle between the Moors and the Christians.

Verdinas

These are very similar to the more well-known green flageolet beans. Picked before they are ripe, they have a pale green colour which they manage to hold as they cook. Unusually for a bean, they are enjoyed a little *al dente*, and their delicate flavour goes very well with seafood such as clams and prawns, and also small game, like partridge.

Canelas

Quite rare beans, local to León and Burgos in Castilla y León, these are the colour of ground cinnamon, and turn more salmon-pink as they are cooked – typically with local *chorizos*.

Pintas leonesas

Although these pale, oval, purple-streaked coloured beans are often more associated with the Texas/Mexican border, where they are known as *pinto*, there is a traditional production area in León. The beans are often served with meats such as *chorizo*, but in order to aid digestion the locals like to add greens, such as cabbage, turnip tops, chard, or the Andalusian speciality, *pintas con tagarninas* (common golden thistle).

Caparrones

In the village shops of La Rioja and Burgos you see baskets full of these medium-sized, oval aubergine and beige-white beans, which are typically cooked with cured meats such as *chorizos*, *panceta* and black puddings.

Judiones
Butter beans

Judión really just means a large white bean, and when you see these in Spain they will have different names attached, e.g. *judión de La Granja, del monasterio, del Barco*, which mostly indicate where they are grown. They are characteristically plump, ivory white and creamy in texture, very versatile and especially delicious with meat, clams and grilled vegetable salads. (See Barny Haughton's salad on page 208). You could also use them for the *fabada* on page 390 if you cannot find *fabas* (see page 380).

Garbanzos
Chickpeas

A good chickpea, properly cooked until it is creamy and tender, is a delight, traditionally paired with *chorizo* and vegetables, such as Swiss chard, and there is a famous Andalusian dish in which the chickpeas are cooked with the stalks of an edible thistle. Spain has specific varieties of chickpea grown in different regions which are used for local dishes, but they are all interchangeable.

Garbanzo pedrosillano
Known as *cigronet* (little chickpea) in Catalan, this is a small, very fine, golden-yellow-coloured chickpea with a small pointy tail and a smooth exterior. It does not increase much in weight as it soaks or cooks, so it looks very elegant in a dish. It is cultivated in a number of provinces in Castilla la Mancha and Castilla y León, most significantly in Salamanca and Zamora in Castilla y León, and takes its name specifically from the village of Pedrosillo in Salamanca. Here the combination of altitude, high mineral content in the soil, clean mountain water for irrigation, and dry cold winters and sunny summers gives the perfect growing conditions, and the chickpeas that come from Pedrosillo and Fuentesaúco in Zamora, in particular, are supreme.

Garbanzo castellano
Cigron in Catalan, this is the most popular chickpea. It is larger in size, ochre in colour with clear ridges, and it often cooks to a softer texture than the *pedrosillano*. It is cultivated across the central *meseta* (plateau) of Castilla y León and Castilla La Mancha as well as in Andalucía. It is excellent in *contundente* (hearty) dishes such as *potaje de quaresma*, a spinach and salt cod stew, and *escudella* (see page 447). It also combines brilliantly with *chorizo* (see *cocido montañes*, page 449). Its nutty taste and firm texture makes it perfect with combinations such as *morcilla* and pine nuts, aubergine and red pepper, tomatoes and fresh cheese, clams (see *garbanzos con almejas,* page 396) pork and cabbage, and white tuna and peppers (see *ensalada de bonito con piquillos huevos y garbanzos,* page 206).

Garbanzo blanco lechoso
The *lechoso* is grown in the southern regions of Andalucía and Badajoz. It is a fatter chickpea which is bone white, so it is a favourite in clear soups along with *fideu* pasta and vegetables.

How to choose, store and cook chickpeas
Like beans, chickpeas are typically allowed to dry in their pods on the plant and are then harvested at the optimum point, but, also like beans, if they are stored for too long and become old, their skins may never soften properly however long you cook them; whereas a fresher chickpea will have a delicate thin skin which will become very tender, allowing the chickpeas to become beautifully creamy.

An old chickpea is more obvious than an ageing bean, however, as it will have become wrinkly and hard. Look for a clean colour, with few or no marks or wrinkles, a shine to the skin and a smooth feel.

Store in the same way as beans (see page 378). Chickpeas need to be rinsed well and soaked, for at least 12 hours. Our friends Sam and Sam Clark at Moro swear by adding a pinch of bicarbonate of soda to help soften them. Always drain and rinse them well after soaking, and never cook them in the soaking water, or they will give you terrible wind.

To cook, put them into a pan, cover with twice their quantity of cold water, and for every 200g of dried and soaked chickpeas add a carrot, halved lengthways, half an onion, 4 cloves of garlic, a stick of celery, a sprig of thyme and a bay leaf, if you like (but no salt initially, as it will toughen the skins of the chickpeas). Bring to the boil, skim off any froth that rises to the surface, then turn down the heat and simmer very slowly until tender. This can take anything between 40 and 90 minutes (depending on the variety, quality and age – the older the chickpeas, the longer they will take to cook), so start checking after about half an hour. When the chickpeas are *al dente*, you can add a pinch of salt and cook them for another 10–20 minutes, to the point where you can lift out a chickpea, press it between your fingers and it will split in two.

As with beans, chickpeas that are very hard can be helped by bringing them to the boil, then 'shocking' them by adding cold water, before continuing to cook gently – you can do this again from time to time if they are failing to soften.

Lentejas
Lentils

Rich in iron and minerals and very versatile, lentils are a crucial staple food in most Spanish homes – in our house, too, they are almost sacred and we are never without at least a couple of varieties in our larder. Their cooking time is shorter than other legumes, soaking is rarely needed, and the best ones will hold their shape as they cook. Equally good eaten hot or cold, they can be humble, but it only takes the addition of some diced vegetables and aromatics such as bay leaves, peppers and garlic and they can pair with more luxurious ingredients to great acclaim.

Castilla y León and La Mancha are the heartlands of lentil cultivation, where growers with long experience select varietals valued for their quality over quantity.

Lenteja pardina
These are tiny, brown lentils which are favoured for their earthy flavour, have a good texture and retain their shape well during cooking. They are excellent with most meat, fish and vegetarian dishes.

Lenteja verdina
Small, dark green lentils with dark purple speckles, very similar to Puy lentils from France.

Lenteja rubia castellana
Larger, pale-pinky green lentils, shaped like little flat flying saucers, that grow mainly in La Mancha. These are the most popular varietal across Spain and will be found in *menús del día* up and down the country.

How to choose and cook lentils
Lentils don't need to be soaked before cooking but they must be thoroughly rinsed. For four people as part of a dish, or for a salad, you need around 300g. Start them off in cold water – enough to cover – preferably with finely chopped onion, carrot and celery, plus a bay leaf and some peppercorns, then bring to the boil, turn down the heat, skim off any froth that comes to the surface, and simmer for about 20–25 minutes until tender, depending on the variety. Just don't overcook them – if anything they are better slightly *al dente*.

Julián and the Beans of El Barco

One day during the autumn of 1989, in the fledgling days of Brindisa, the phone rang. It was Sally Clarke, chef/proprietor of Clarke's restaurant, famous for her fixed menus of elegant dishes made with fresh seasonal ingredients – something of a revolution at the time. She was asking if we could supply her with some new season's beans from Spain. 'Yes, of course. We have some on the way. They will be with us next week,' I told her. As I put the phone down I yelped with delight – only a month earlier, after researching Spanish bean suppliers and discovering Julián Sánchez García in Castile, the man who still supplies us, I had decided to invest in some truly superior beans at what seemed like a terrifyingly high price, especially as at the time I had no customers for them and no real plan for how to gain any. But now, not only did I have a customer, but a chef famous for her insistence on the best produce, someone I knew would understand and appreciate a good bean.

The village of El Barco (the Ship), where Julián is based, and where he also roasts coffee beans and grinds cocoa beans for the family chocolate business (see page 34), is so called because it sits on the flat plain at the foot of the Gredos mountains, and in the days before it expanded with new houses, when you approached the village it looked like the body of a ship with its castle and church steeple resembling two funnels.

The beans are grown in neat rows in fields and smallholdings outside the village, and Julián gives his own names to some of the varieties, which often relate to the colours of his stunning horses – for example, he has a speckled bean which he calls Appaloosa.

He is involved with each grower from the moment they plant their seeds to the point of harvesting. An outstanding dried bean has a delicate skin, a hearty size and a creamy texture that is able to absorb stocks and flavours, and in Julián's view the key to growing such superior beans is loose soil, well irrigated, in this case with the exceptionally clean Gredos mountain water, and a dry climate, cold in winter and hot in summer. If the bean suffers from an absence of good water, or is subjected to humidity, combined with high temperatures during the growing season, this can create a hard outer skin which is very water-resistant, so the beans can refuse to soften during cooking.

The growers know how to harvest the beans at just the right moment when they have dried on the plants. In the case of the more delicate varieties, this can often mean collecting them by hand on a pod by pod basis, a special skill which sets Julián's operation apart from more industrial systems where the beans would be dried using mechanical methods.

Back at the plant, the shiny, sleek dried beans are sorted by hand and graded in wooden sieves in an astonishingly simple operation. Much of Julián's equipment is a collector's dream – antique machinery kept running by a network of friends throughout Spain who supply spare parts and expertise – and hung on the wall, like the trays used for panning for gold, are old-fashioned *crivas*, sieves made from animal hide.

After my first inspirational trip to El Barco, as I headed back to Madrid I was firmly convinced that beans would one day be the next pasta in the UK. It didn't happen then, but as this is the International Year of Pulses, as declared by the WHO, and the health-giving properties of beans are better understood all the time, I can still hope.

Changurro con alubias
Cantabrian white crabmeat
with white beans

Agustín Bedía, who has a wonderful fish restaurant in Somo, near Santander, makes a rich and stunning signature dish of crab in a sauce made with tomato *sofrito*, wine and Cognac, to which he adds large *judión* beans. It is so well-loved and in such demand that you have to pre-book it, as it takes time and planning to prepare. One time when our family turned up at the restaurant after snow-shoeing in the Picos de Europa mountains, I had completely forgotten about this, so we missed out on being able to order it: heartbreaking!

As some compensation Agustín generously gave me a version of the recipe made with smaller beans for ease. In the restaurant he uses a cock crab (which is bigger than the female) and breaks out all the white meat from the body and legs; however, I have simplified the recipe further by suggesting you just use white crabmeat.

Serve with good bread to soak up the sauce.

Serves 4

200g butter
1 medium onion, finely chopped
2 small leeks, finely chopped
1 medium carrot, finely chopped
60ml Cognac
60ml white wine
400g good tomato *sofrito* (see page 316),
  either from a jar or homemade (see page 318)
sea salt, to taste
500g good white crabmeat, plus some
  clawmeat (optional), sautéd in a little butter

For the beans
300g small white beans, such
  as *arrocina* or *planchada*
1 medium potato, peeled
½ an onion, chopped small
½ a green pepper, chopped small
½ teaspoon *pimentón dulce* (mild paprika)

Soak the beans overnight. Next day put them into a pan of cold water, ensuring that it covers them by three fingers. Bring to the boil, scrape away any foam from the surface, then turn down the heat and simmer for about an hour. At this point, chop the potato into medium pieces and add to the beans, along with the onion, green pepper and *pimentón*. Leave to cook for a maximum of another hour, until the beans are just tender. Keep checking as they cook, as the timing will depend on the variety of beans; for example *planchada* will take longer than *arrocina*.

Meanwhile, heat the butter in a wide pan, add the onion, leeks and carrot, and cook gently until soft but not coloured. Add the Cognac and flame it, then add the wine and the *sofrito*. Stir well and allow the sauce to bubble for a few minutes, then turn down the heat and simmer for 20 minutes or so, until it has reduced by half. Blend with a hand blender until the sauce is smooth. Taste and season with salt as required.

Drain the beans, reserving a little of the cooking water. Mix the crabmeat with the tomato sauce and beans in a terracotta dish or dishes, loosening with a little of the cooking water if necessary, and serve straight away.

Fabada asturiana
Asturian white bean pot
with *chorizo* and black pudding

This is quite a rich and heavy dish, a medieval-style stew really, not for eating late in the evening as you need several hours to digest it. Amazingly, we once saw it as a starter on a provincial restaurant menu of the day, to be eaten before the main meat course.

When I first came across this bean pot it was interesting to me that saffron should be a key ingredient, given that Asturias is on the other side of Spain from the Castilian saffron fields, and it is a dish full of such big flavours that you wonder why such a delicate spice would be added. Then I discovered that saffron used to be cultivated in the allotments of central and north-eastern Galicia next door, which may explain it. And in fact, even up against *chorizo* and *morcilla,* as well as pork shoulder and *panceta,* it makes its presence felt.

Ideally, this is made with *faba* beans, but since these can be both hard to find and expensive, we often use *judión* (butter beans) or other large white beans, such as *planchada* (see page 381), as they behave in the same way, absorbing the fats and flavours and holding their integrity during long slow cooking.

Asturian *morcilla* is semi-cured and highly spiced, so it holds up to long slow cooking without falling apart and adds a bigger flavour than other *morcillas.* If you can't find it, and are using a softer, poached *morcilla,* such as the one from Burgos, a *boudin noir,* or an English black pudding, then I suggest you slice it, fry it gently and add it at the end of cooking instead.

The key to this is the very long slow cooking, and since it shouldn't be stirred, it is a good idea to use a heat diffuser, especially if you are using a saucepan rather than a terracotta dish, to make sure that the beans cook gently and evenly with no risk of burning.

If you like, you can make this the day before you need it, as it will improve massively with a night's keeping in the fridge. Just reheat very gently before serving.

Serves 8

1kg *faba* beans, butter beans or *planchada* beans, soaked overnight
300g *panceta,* in a single piece
3 lightly smoked cooking *chorizos,* from León or Rioja
2 lightly smoked Asturian *morcillas* (see page 76)
1 head of garlic
1 bay leaf
1 dried red *guindilla* pepper (see page 275)
4 strands of saffron
sea salt, to taste

Drain the beans and put them into a casserole with all the ingredients except the saffron and salt. Cover with fresh cold water and bring to the boil. Skim off any foam that comes to the surface, then turn down the heat. If possible, place a diffuser under the casserole, as from now on the dish shouldn't be stirred at all since moving the beans around will break them up as well as the *morcilla.* Cook very gently – just the occasional bubble breaking the surface will be enough – then, after an hour, pour in 50ml of cold water. This is the traditional process of 'shocking' the beans, to stop the boiling, causing the cell walls of the beans to contract and allowing the whole process of developing flavours to begin again as the water comes back to a bare simmer. If you like, you can repeat the shocking process again after an hour or so to help the flavours develop.

Because the quality and age of dried beans is so variable, it is impossible to give precise cooking times, so it is a good idea to try a bean after the first hour and at regular intervals, in order that you can begin to assess how long the cooking process might be. Ideally, if you keep the cooking really slow and gentle, it should be 3–4 hours.

About 15 minutes before the beans are ready, lightly toast the saffron in a small dry pan and add to the casserole. The *panceta* and *chorizo* will add salt, but taste just before serving and add a little more if necessary.

Alubiada de Tolosa
Tolosa bean stew with *chorizo*

Judiones a la cazuela estilo Jeremy
Jeremy Lee's slow-cooked butter beans

Sandra Salcedo's family have been preparing Navarrico jarred legumes since the 1950s, and we have worked with them for over 20 years. This is her recipe for Tolosa beans, which is really simple and good eaten with some pickled *guindilla* peppers on the side. The idea of resting the beans for half an hour or so before serving is a personal touch that she believes improves the flavour.

Serves 4

500g Tolosa beans or other coloured beans,
   such as *caparrones* or *canelas* (see page 383)
1 onion, chopped
1 leek, chopped
1 carrot, chopped
100g *panceta*, whole
100g fresh or semi-cured *chorizo*
1 tablespoon olive oil
1 clove of garlic, sliced
½ teaspoon *pimentón dulce* (sweet paprika)

Soak the beans in cold water overnight.

Drain the beans and put into a pan or terracotta pot with the onion, leek, carrot, *panceta* and *chorizo* and cover with fresh cold water. Bring to the boil and skim off any foam that comes to the surface. Turn down the heat and preferably place a diffuser underneath the casserole. Simmer very, very slowly, ideally for 2 hours, until the beans are cooked, but still intact and creamy inside, though not mushy – start testing after 45 minutes.

Heat the olive oil in a frying pan, put in the garlic and paprika and fry briefly, then add to the bean pot. Continue to cook slowly for about 10 minutes, to allow the flavours to mingle, then take off the heat and leave to rest for 30 minutes, so the beans settle before serving, to help them absorb the flavours a bit more. Warm through if necessary before serving.

When Jeremy Lee, now of Quo Vadis, launched the Blueprint Café on the banks of the Thames, he was one of Brindisa's earliest customers. Spanish anchovies, oils and hams all featured on his menu, but above all he loved the beans. For Jeremy there is 'something miraculous' about a bean. 'A beautifully braised, silky bean, holding its shape, with a bit of pork is an absolute joy that can bring grown men to tears,' he says.

This is Jeremy's way of cooking *judión* beans, one of his favourite varieties, with vegetables, *panceta* and lots of whole garlic cloves that melt over the slow cooking time and become beautifully sweet. 'I follow the same method for chickpeas, even lentils – you would be amazed how long good lentils hold their shape for,' he says. 'The key is to curb your instinct to stir. Leave them alone.'

If you like, once the beans and vegetables have come to the boil, instead of turning them down to a bare simmer on the hob, you could put the pot into a very low oven (120°C/gas ½) or even the slow oven of an Aga overnight. You could also sprinkle the surface of the near-finished dish with breadcrumbs and bake at 180°C/gas 4 for 30 minutes, until the crumbs are golden and crunchy.

Serves 4–6

500g good-quality dried *judión* beans
   (see page 383)
6 tablespoons olive oil
1 piece of *panceta*, about 300g, coarsely chopped
1 onion, coarsely chopped
1 medium carrot, coarsely chopped
1 small stick of celery, chopped
about 6 garlic cloves, peeled
a bundle of thyme, rosemary, sage sprigs
   and about 3 bay leaves, tied with string
   (or a *farcellet*/bouquet garni)
sea salt and freshly ground black pepper
a little *pimentón dulce* or *picante*
   (sweet or hot paprika, as you like, optional)
good extra virgin olive oil, to finish

Garbanzos salteados con berenjena y pimiento rojo
Sautéd chickpeas with aubergine and red pepper

Soak the beans overnight in plenty of cold water, then drain them and wash them thoroughly under the cold tap until the water is crystal clear.

Put the drained and washed beans into a large pan. Cover them generously with fresh cold water, bring quickly up to a furious boil, then drain and rinse them again under the cold tap to get rid of the excess starch.

Warm the olive oil in a large, heavy-bottomed pot and throw in the *panceta*, vegetables, garlic and herbs, together with a large shot of black pepper – but no salt. Put the lid on and cook quickly, just to soften and colour everything a little.

Add the drained beans to the pot of vegetables and cover with enough cold water to clear the beans by 8–10cm. Put the lid on and bring to the boil. Spoon off any froth that comes to the top, then turn down the heat and cook half-covered very, very gently – the water should just tick over with the odd bubble on the surface – for as long as you can: preferably at least 3–4 hours, but really anything up to 12 hours. The beans are ready when they yield completely when you bite into them, and they will be enrobed in their own sauce – rich and delicate and full of character.

Now you can taste and season them with salt if necessary. The beans can be served just as they are, finished with some good extra virgin olive oil, or you could heat a little paprika in olive oil quickly in a small pan and stir it in.

During the writing of this book, my husband, Rupert, donned chef whites and shared many cooking days (and consequently good lunches) with our head chef, Nicolás (Nico) Modad, who was then at our Shoreditch restaurant, in order to test the restaurant recipes for the home cook, and also to experiment with more vegetarian choices for the menu. This is a light, fresh combination that they particularly liked.

Serves 4

1–2 tablespoons olive oil
1 red pepper, finely chopped
1 medium courgette, sliced lengthways
  into thin strips, about 5mm wide
a pinch of sea salt
1 medium aubergine, chopped, into 1cm pieces
200g tomato *sofrito* (from a jar,
  or see recipe on page 318)
200g chickpeas (jarred or cooked as on
  page 384 and still in their cooking water)
a big handful of spinach leaves, finely shredded
about 10 mint leaves, finely chopped

Heat 1 tablespoon of oil in a large pan, then add the red pepper and fry for 3 minutes, until sizzling and browning at the edges. Add the courgettes and a pinch of salt, plus another tablespoon of olive oil if needed, fry for a further 2 minutes, then add the aubergine and fry for another 2 minutes.

Add the *sofrito* and heat through, then add the chickpeas along with 200ml of their cooking water, so that they are half submerged. If using jarred chickpeas, add their liquid, topped up if necessary to 200ml. Bring to the boil, taste the liquid and add a little salt if needed, then turn down the heat to a simmer until the liquid is reduced by half. Take off the heat and stir in the spinach. Leave to rest for a minute, then stir in the mint and serve.

TOCINO Y PANCETA

'no fat no cooking'

There is a saying in Spain, '*sin el cerdo no hay tocino y sin tocino no hay cocina*', which translates as, 'no pig means no fat, and no fat means no cooking'. *Tocino* is fat from the back of the animal, and usually has no lean at all, whereas *panceta* is slightly streaked fat from the belly button upwards.

Tocino is mostly used in dishes of beans, chickpeas and lentils, stews and *cocidos* (see page 446) while *panceta* is used more on grills and barbecues. However, since *tocino* is impossible to find in the UK, we have substituted *panceta* in this book.

When *panceta* comes from the Ibérico pig it is extra special, though this too can be hard to find, even in Spain, if you are outside the designated production areas, as most goes into cured sausages, rather than being sold in its own right. However, it is well worth seeking out.

One of my most memorable experiences of Ibérico *panceta* was on a visit to the Dehesa, the vast expanse of forest in south-west Spain where the pigs roam freely. I took a band of chefs to visit José Gómez of Joselito, one of Spain's most eminent and legendary ham producers, whose great grandfather began the business over a century ago, and at one of the *cortijos* in the area (houses with a courtyard where the tenant family and workers live) the woman of the house cooked her silky home-cured *panceta* for us for

breakfast. The hens in the yard provided the freshest eggs, with yolks of the most beautiful rich gold colour, which were fried until the edges were crisp like a lace mantilla – I doubt if I've had a better egg, ever – and the combination of those eggs and the *panceta* was simple but heavenly.

Often Ibérico *panceta* is cut into very chunky *torreznos,* or lardons (sometimes pork neck fat, known as *papada*, is also used), which are cooked slowly in very little oil at first, then the flame is increased so that the *torreznos* become brown and crunchy and irresistible. One of the classic ways to serve them is with roughly crushed potato (see page 293). My daughter, Daniela, is the greatest bacon eater of our family, and on one occasion when we were staying with our friends Ambro and Ásun (see page 154), Ambro brought out a great side of the pork belly, then meticulously trimmed off the tough outer skin, and instead of chunky pieces he cut slender pillars of about half a centimetre wide which consisted of fat with just a small speck or two of lean pork at the base. This time, rather than starting off the *torreznos* slowly, he reversed the cooking process and sealed the pieces quickly in hot fat so that they were crisp on the outside, then turned down the heat until they were cooked to a silky texture inside. The wait was agonising and we were practically drooling at the smell of the *panceta* cooking, but when the

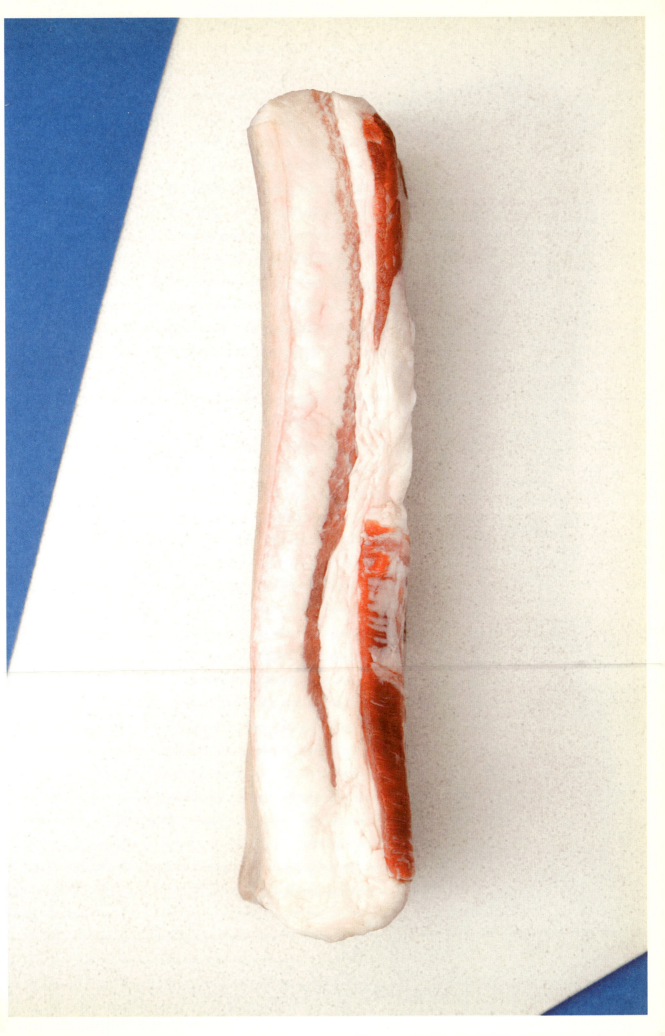

Garbanzos con almejas
Chickpeas with clams

torreznos eventually found their way on to our plates they were devoured in seconds.

Our executive chef, Josep, has another method for *papada,* which involves first poaching and then frying. He puts whole fresh *papada* into a large pan of water, brings it to the boil and spoons off any foam or impurities that rise to the surface, then he changes the water to fresh, puts in a bay leaf, brings it back to the boil and turns down the heat to a simmer for 2 hours. At this point he lifts out the *papada*, dries it off, cuts it into chunks, and fries it in hot oil for 2–3 minutes, so that the *torreznos* are almost melting in the middle, like warm caramel.

Alternatives to Ibérico *panceta* include the lightly smoked *panceta ahumada* from León, which can also be paprika-coated, in which case it is known as *adobada*. You could even use chunks of good British streaky bacon, though none of these options will have the intensely sweet and unctuous fat of the Ibérico *panceta*.

While testing recipes Rupert and Nico were keen to pair chickpeas with seafood, a combination often favoured in Asturias, as an alternative to the more traditional *chorizo* (see opposite).

Serves 4

800g clams
200g tomato *sofrito* (from a jar, or see recipe on page 318)
600g chickpeas, cooked as on page 384 and drained of their cooking water
200ml hot *fumet rojo* (red fish stock, see page 468)
½ teaspoon sugar (optional)
1 tablespoon finely chopped parsley, plus a little extra to finish
freshly ground black pepper

Wash the clams well, discarding any shells that are open, or that won't close if tapped against your work surface.

Heat the *sofrito* in a pan and add the cooked chickpeas. Heat together for 2 minutes, until the mixture comes to a simmer. Add the *fumet rojo* – there should now be enough liquid for the chickpeas to begin to float. Taste the liquid and add the sugar if the *sofrito* tastes a little too acidic.

Add the clams, bring to a vigorous boil, and put the lid on the pan for 1–2 minutes, just long enough for the clams to open and release their juices (discard any that don't open).

Take the pan from the heat, stir in the parsley, and add a twist of black pepper.

To serve, lift out the chickpeas and clams with a slotted spoon and put into small bowls, then cover them with a ladleful of the cooking liquid. Garnish with a final sprinkling of parsley.

Garbanzos con chorizo
Chickpeas with *chorizo*

Of all the ingredients we offer at Brindisa, the classic combination of good jarred chickpeas that can be heated and served with sautéd or poached *chorizo* is something that people love for a quick, satisfying, tasty meal.

This particular, colourful version is one of Scott Boden's super-easy recipes, devised to warm up Clerkenwell folk at lunchtime when we had our shop in Exmouth Market. Since we had only a tiny kitchen area, with a single electric ring to cook on, it was a way of showing how to make the ultimate hearty, convenience lunch, using the best Spanish store-cupboard produce.

We use beautifully creamy Navarrico chickpeas, *panceta adobada* (cured pork coated with paprika), plus the jarred *fritada* (tomato and pepper base) which is made especially for us in the Ebro Valley. The point of the dish is really the ease of putting it together, though of course you could cook your own chickpeas (see page 384) and make your own *fritada* (see page 318).

There is no salt in this recipe, as the idea is to use the brine from the jarred chickpeas, which combined with the *chorizo* should make the dish salty enough. A little red wine gives it a dash of luxury.

Serves 6–8

1 tablespoon olive oil
200g diced *panceta adobada*,
 or lardons, dusted with paprika
2–3 *chorizo* sausages or 1 cooking
 ***chorizo* hoop, diced**
1 medium red onion, chopped
1 x 400g jar of *fritada*
 (or homemade, see page 318)
100ml red wine (optional)
3 large cloves of garlic, crushed
black pepper, to taste
2 tablespoons chopped fresh oregano
2 x 660g jars of good prepared chickpeas,
 undrained, as you will use the brine

Heat the oil in a large pan. Add the *panceta*, *chorizo* and red onion and sauté until they are all beginning to brown.

Add the *fritada*, then fill the empty jar with water (or measure 400ml) and add it to the pan, together with the red wine, if using. Stir well and bring to a gentle simmer.

Now add the crushed garlic, black pepper, 1½ tablespoons of the oregano and the chickpeas in their brine and stir again. Bring back to a gentle simmer for 5–10 minutes, then serve, scattering the rest of the oregano over the top.

Lentejas Asunción
Ásun's lentils with pork

This is a recipe inspired by Asun Gordo (see page 154), who uses *pardina* lentils from her home region of Burgos in Castilla y León, which have a very creamy texture. She uses a wet marinade for the pork, but our head chef, Nico, preferred to make the dish with a drier combination of herbs and spices and Rupert came up with the inspired idea of finishing it with a *picada* that would echo the same flavours. The potatoes are cut *cascada*-style (see page 292).

Lentil dishes such as this tend to improve if you make them a day in advance, keep in the fridge and then reheat before serving.

Serves 4

6 pork ribs (350g)
250g *pardina* (or Puy) lentils
2 tablespoons olive oil
100g diced onion, diced as finely as possible
70g leeks, white part only,
  diced as finely as possible
1 clove of garlic, chopped
1 bay leaf
a pinch of sea salt
2 cooking *chorizos* (200g), cut in half lengthways
  and then crossways into quarters
75g tomato *sofrito* (see recipe
  on page 318, or from a jar)
140g carrot, cut in half lengthways
  and then again crossways into quarters
10cm of the green part of a leek, very finely diced
1 green pepper, chopped
500g potatoes, cut into uneven chunks
  (see above)

For the adobo marinade
4 black peppercorns
½ teaspoon chilli powder
1 teaspoon finely chopped rosemary
1 teaspoon finely chopped thyme
2 tablespoons finely chopped parsley
2 cloves of garlic, crushed with the back
  of a knife, then roughly chopped
2 teaspoons *pimentón dulce* (sweet paprika)
½ a lemon

3 tablespoons olive oil

For the *picada*
1 teaspoon finely chopped rosemary
1 teaspoon finely chopped thyme
1 teaspoon finely chopped parsley
½ a clove of garlic
juice of ½ a lemon

For the *adobo* marinade, crush the black peppercorns and put into a bowl along with the rest of the ingredients. Mix together, then put the ribs into the bowl and rub them well with the marinade, making sure they are covered all over. Leave in the fridge for 3–4 hours or overnight.

Rinse the lentils well in a sieve under the cold tap.

Heat the olive oil in a casserole pan. Lift the ribs out of their marinade and put them into the pan (discard the marinade). Sizzle the ribs for a minute on each side to brown them, then move them to the outer edges of the pan.

Put the onion, leek, garlic and bay leaf in the centre of the pan and stir to coat them well in the oil and meat juices. Add a pinch of salt, then turn down the heat and let everything cook gently for another 10 minutes.

Turn the heat up again, put in the quartered *chorizos*, meat side down, and stir for about a minute to brown. Add the *sofrito*, stir for another minute, then add 1.2 litres of cold water and the carrot, lentils, green leek and the pepper.

Bring slowly to the boil, skimming off any foam that comes to the surface, then turn down the heat to a simmer for 40 minutes, adding the potatoes after 25 minutes, until both lentils and potatoes are tender. Pound the ingredients for the *picada* together in a pestle and mortar, then take the pan off the heat and stir in a tablespoon of the mixture (or more to taste). Taste and adjust the salt if necessary before serving.

EMPANADAS Y COSTRADAS

Spanish 'pies'

Empanada de atún
Tuna parcel

A slice of this 'pie', or parcel, is fast food in Spain. In many cafés you can simply buy a wedge, like tortilla, to eat on the go. I like to use good tinned white *bonito del norte*, and if you can find *migas* (small pieces) they are excellent. You can also use this filling to make a variation on the crab *empanadillas* on page 251.

Choose the black olives carefully. You are looking for the clear flavour of a genuine black olive (see page 97), so I would recommend Empeltre from Aragón or Kalamata black olives in brine only, as you don't want to introduce random flavours by using olives in a strong marinade.

If you like, you can add a layer of hard-boiled egg (one per *empanada*) over the top of the *bonito* or tuna and pepper mixture before putting the lid on the 'pie'. You can also make the dough in a food processor or blender.

Makes 2 *empanadas* about 20cm x 40cm

50g tomato *sofrito* (from a jar)
500g strong white flour, plus extra for dusting
120ml olive oil
sea salt
1 egg

For the filling
390g *piquillo* peppers (see page 275),
  cut into strips
500g *bonito del norte* or tuna in olive oil
150g tomato *sofrito* (from a jar)
½ teaspoon fresh thyme
½ teaspoon fresh oregano
1 tablespoon chilli flakes (optional)
sea salt and freshly ground black pepper, to taste
1 teaspoon sherry vinegar
120g pitted black olives in brine, finely chopped

To make the pastry, first put the 50g of *sofrito* into a pan and bubble up briefly to reduce it and remove some of the water.

Put the flour in a mixing bowl, add the reduced *sofrito*, the oil, a pinch of salt and 120ml of water and mix and knead to a homogeneous dough that comes away easily from the sides of the bowl (you may need to add a little more water or flour). Roll into a ball, cover the bowl with clingfilm and leave in a warm place to rest for 2 hours.

Preheat the oven to 180°C/gas 4.

For the filling, put the *piquillo* strips into a bowl. Drain the *bonito* or tuna, and add, along with the *sofrito*, herbs, chilli flakes, if using, and a twist of pepper. Mix in the sherry vinegar, taste and add salt if necessary.

Line 2 baking trays with baking paper (alternatively, you can bake the *empanadas* one at a time).

Lightly flour a work surface and roll out half the dough into a square roughly 40cm x 40cm. Cut this in half, so that you have 2 bases, each approximately 20cm x 40cm.

Roll the first sheet of dough around your rolling pin, then unroll on to the baking paper on the baking tray. Repeat with the second sheet.

Roll out the rest of the pastry in the same way to give 2 more sheets of dough 20cm x 40cm. These will form the tops of the *empanadas*.

Divide the olives between the dough bases, leaving a 2cm border, then sprinkle the *bonito*/ tuna and *piquillo* mixture on top.

Beat the egg and use some of it to brush the borders of the dough, then cover each base with a dough lid. Fold the edges of each base up over the edges of the lid to form the traditional thick *empanada* crust, and press down firmly, creating a dimpled rim by pushing down with your finger all around the edge.

Paint the top of each *empanada* with the rest of the beaten egg, prick with a fork several times and put into the preheated oven for 20 minutes, until the dough is golden brown.

Costrada de setas
Wild mushroom pie

Before I encountered Pedro Roca, the famous Galician chef and restaurateur, all I really knew about *empanadas* was that they originated in Galicia, the pastry was actually more of a dough, and the most popular one you could find in almost every café in Spain was filled with tuna and sold cold, in neat squares (see page 401). Then one year I attended the Fórum Gastronómico in Santiago de Compostela, a modest trade event for chefs that was founded by Pep Palau (see page 84). There I joined in an *empanada* workshop hosted by Pedro, who showed us three of his fantastic, but very different recipes, each done with a particular flour.

There was an open-style sardine and pepper *empanada* similar to the Catalan *coca* (see page 142), and the two that I have included here, the game pie on page 405 and this *costrada*, a slight variation on the theme. We were given only the recipe outlines but when I came back from Galicia we worked on them many times in our kitchen at home until we got them as we wanted, much to the delight of various neighbours who were called in to help us test them.

This is a more elaborate variation on *empanada*, which works fantastically well – layering the mushrooms with pancakes is a brilliant trick that stops the filling from collapsing to the bottom of the 'pie'. You will need to make your pancakes in a frying pan the same diameter as your tart tin, so that they fit exactly.

You can use whatever wild mushrooms you like, but the idea is to have three different types in separate layers. Ideally, choose ceps (*hongos porcini*), oyster mushrooms (*champiñones ostras*) and *trompettes de la mort* (*trompetas de la muerte*).

As usual, if you prefer, you can make the dough in a food processor or blender.

I like to serve the *costrada* with Catalan-style chard. For around six people you need about 600g of chard. Separate the stalks and leaves and blanch the stalks briefly in salted boiling water, then drain and chop both stalks and leaves. Heat 3 tablespoons of olive oil in a large pan or wok; add a chopped medium banana shallot, 50g each of pine nuts and raisins and cook until golden. Add the chopped chard and toss with the other ingredients until the leaves just wilt. Season to taste and serve immediately.

Makes 1 x 22cm round pie

500g strong white flour, plus extra for dusting
50g tomato *sofrito* (from a jar)
120ml olive oil
sea salt
1 egg, beaten, for brushing the pastry

For the filling
2 onions, sliced in rings
around 8 tablespoons olive oil
a pinch of sugar or sea salt, if necessary
200g ceps, cleaned and sliced into strips
200g oyster mushrooms, cleaned and torn into strips
200g *trompettes de la mort* mushrooms, cleaned and sliced into strips
a little cumin (optional)
a little *pimentón picante* (hot paprika, optional)

For the pancakes
125g white flour
1 egg, beaten

Put the flour into a mixing bowl, add the *sofrito*, oil, a pinch of salt and 120ml of water, and mix and knead to a homogeneous dough that comes away easily from the sides of the bowl (you may need to add a little more water or flour). Roll into a ball, cover the bowl with clingfilm and leave in a warm place to rest for 2 hours.

To make the filling, put the onions into a 22cm heavy-based frying pan (which you can use for the pancakes later) and drizzle with 2 tablespoons of olive oil. Stir the onions to ensure they are well coated. Place the pan, preferably on a diffuser, over a low heat and allow the onions to slowly caramelise for up to

1 hour, stirring occasionally. After an hour taste the onions and adjust with a pinch of sugar or salt if necessary. Take off the heat, lift out the onions and keep to one side. Wipe out the pan and keep it for cooking the mushrooms.

Preheat the oven to 180°C/gas 4.

For the pancakes, put the flour into a bowl, then gradually whisk in the beaten egg and 100ml of water until you have a smooth mixture. Leave the mixture to rest for 20 minutes.

Meanwhile, for the filling, heat 1–2 tablespoons of olive oil in the frying pan, put in the ceps and sauté for 1–2 minutes until just golden, sprinkling with a pinch of cumin and paprika, if using. Lift out and keep to one side. Repeat with the oyster mushrooms and then the *trompettes de la mort*, keeping each variety separate and seasoning each with another pinch of cumin and paprika, if using. Wipe out the pan and keep for the pancakes.

Have ready a tart tin 22cm in diameter and 5cm deep.

Wipe the frying pan with a thin film of olive oil, then pour in half the pancake mixture and tilt the pan so that it covers the base. Cook very briefly until the underside is set and just golden, then flip over and cook the other side in the same way. Slide on to a plate and repeat with the rest of the mixture.

Lightly flour a work surface. Divide the dough in two – not quite in half, as you will need slightly more to line the tart tin than for the top. Roll out the larger piece into a circle big enough to line the tin and leave an overhang. Roll the dough around your rolling pin and then unroll it into the tin.

Spoon in the caramelised onion and spread it out evenly, follow with the ceps and a sprinkling of salt. Lay one of the pancakes over the top. Put in the oyster mushrooms and season with salt. Lay the second pancake on top, and finish with the

trompettes de la mort, again seasoning with salt. Roll out the remaining pastry into a circle big enough to cover the pie and lift it over the top using your rolling pin, as before. Fold the overhang from the base pastry over the edges of the lid and pinch together to seal.

Brush the top with the beaten egg and prick it a few times with a fork. Bake in the preheated oven for around 20 minutes, until the pastry is golden brown. Take out, allow to cool briefly, and serve warm.

Empanada de castañas con perdiz
Partridge pie with chestnut pastry

Reminiscent of an English game pie, this is good with a simple lettuce and tomato salad and a chilled white Verdejo wine from the Rueda region. If you can't find *trompettes de la mort*, you could use oyster or shiitake mushrooms.

Again, if you prefer, you can make the dough in a food processor or blender.

Serves 4

150g strong white flour, plus extra for dusting
100g chestnut flour
15g fresh yeast
25g melted butter
½ teaspoon salt

For the filling
4 onions
5 tablespoons olive oil
a pinch of sugar or sea salt, if necessary
1 carrot, cut in half
1 tomato, cut in half
1 sprig of thyme
1 teaspoon salt
2 oven-ready partridges
200g *trompettes de la mort* mushrooms, cleaned and torn into strips
1 egg, beaten

To make the filling, slice 3 of the onions into rings, put into a heavy-based frying pan and drizzle with 2 tablespoons of the olive oil. Stir the onions to ensure they are well coated. Place the pan, preferably on a diffuser, over a low heat and allow the onions to slowly caramelise for up to 1 hour, stirring occasionally. Taste the onions and adjust with a pinch of sugar or salt if necessary. Take off the heat and keep to one side.

Put 2 litres of cold water into a large pan. Halve the remaining onion and add to the pan, with the carrot and tomato, thyme and salt. Bring to the boil, then put in the partridges, turn down the heat and simmer for 30 minutes. Open up each partridge with a knife to confirm it is cooked through and the meat comes away from the bone. If not, leave to simmer for a few minutes longer. Lift out and cool enough to strip out the meat and shred it into similar-size pieces to the mushrooms. Keep to one side. Discard the vegetables from the pan.

Heat the remaining olive oil in a frying pan and sauté the mushrooms for around a minute – take off the heat before they release their juices into the pan, as you want these to flavour the filling as the mushrooms finish cooking inside the pastry.

To make the dough, mix the two flours together in a large bowl. Dissolve the yeast in 100ml of warm water and add to the flour along with the melted butter and salt, then mix and knead to a homogeneous dough that comes away easily from the sides of the bowl (you may need to add a little more water or flour). Roll into a ball, cover the bowl with clingfilm and leave in a warm place to rest for 90 minutes, until risen a little.

Preheat the oven to 180°C/gas 4.

Lightly flour a work surface, turn out the dough and knead it briefly, then divide in half.

Line a 60cm x 30cm baking tray with baking paper. Roll out half of the dough into a rectangle roughly 20cm x 40cm, roll it around your rolling pin, then unroll it on to the baking paper.

Spread the caramelised onions over the pastry, leaving a 3cm border around the edge. Next, add the shredded partridge meat, and finish with the mushrooms.

Roll out the rest of the dough into a rectangle big enough to make a lid, and use the rolling pin to lay it over the filling. Fold the border of the pastry base up over the edges of the lid and pinch to seal. Brush the top with the beaten egg and prick it a few times with a fork. Put into the preheated oven for around 20 minutes, until golden brown, and serve hot.

Life and Cooking with Montserrat Fruitos

It was always a joy to be shopping and cooking with Montserrat Fruitos, who gave me so much inspiration for this book. She was a wonderful matriarch, stunningly beautiful and with a glorious smile, even though I met her when she was already in her eighties. She had cooked all her life, launched a pioneering cookery school, and knew exactly what she wanted to buy and where to find it. She passed away before this book was finished, but in her last weeks she read these words, and was happy that I wanted to include this small testament to her life, family and food.

She lived, during the week, in Barcelona, where her first-floor apartment was a stone's throw from Plaça Catalunya. It was an amazing place, with one whole corner that was an enormous balcony, the size of a living room, facing the sun and full of pots of plants, succulents and flowers, and just one block away from the famous Mercat de la Concepció, where she did most of her food shopping.

Montserrat was born in 1930 and grew up living above a dairy in Caldes de Montbui in Catalunya after the civil war. One of her many cousins still owns a curing house there, from where she would get her excellent *salchichón de payés* (country sausages). Her father was a lawyer who worked as the Town Hall Secretary and helped the poor as much as he could, giving his services free. He was also a great gourmet, and her mother would spend hours preparing endless dishes and titbits for the table. Unusually, she even had three styles of cooker to work with: a wood-burning stove, a sunken burner for long, slow cooking, and separate gas rings. During the post-war years of the 1940s there was immense poverty and it was hard to get food in the city, but people would leave gifts of milk, butter, pulses and bread from the Empordà at the back door to say thank you to Montserrat's father. And at Christmas they would never have to find a goose, because one would always miraculously and mysteriously arrive on Christmas Eve, though the family never saw who brought it.

When a little more affluence came back to the city, Montserrat's father would always be very specific about the things he bought: his cigars came from a special shop, and almonds had always to be bought from Casa Gispert, the famous store which has been in Barcelona since 1851 and still has its own roasting stove for hazelnuts. Montserrat remembered that when she was young, she swore she wouldn't spend so much time in the kitchen as her mother, but she ended up following in her footsteps – and from her father she inherited that particularity about shopping, buying her ingredients only from specific market stalls and shops.

When she was thirty, and a young married woman, she found she had some free time, so she and two friends decided to go on a cookery course at a Women's Institute in Barcelona. Twenty years later, when she was widowed with four children all studying, and a pension that didn't cover their expenses, the trio of friends started up a home-based cookery school called Mi Cocina, with classes for up to 30 people, and three sessions daily, very much inspired by the food culture of Montserrat's family.

This was something novel and they were incredibly successful. Often their pupils were young men who had never been taught to cook, or those who had been brought up before the war, when wealthier families employed a cook and maids.

Soon after the cookery school was set up, a cousin commented on the poor food at a primary school in the city, where she worked. The children went home for lunch at 2.30 p.m. but the teachers, over 25 of them, stayed on and were given a meal while they prepared the work for the next day. Montserrat was invited to take over the lunch preparation and ended up in charge for 18 years: buying all the ingredients, hopping on and off buses with bags of provisions, in between teaching at the cookery school and looking after and cooking for the family.

Her meticulous food shopping followed the same routine each week. At the Mercat de la Concepció, which was first opened in 1888, she would buy fresh fish, meat and fruit and vegetables, plus cured ham for breakfast and *panceta* for flavouring stews, from particular trusted stallholders she had known for most of her life. They used to give her special cuts and portions, and offer recipes for soups and special dishes to give her strength if she wasn't feeling well.

Another essential on her market trip was to buy prepared white beans, chickpeas and lentils from the ladies who cooked them freshly each day and dispensed them by weight from large bowls.

Salt cod was another ingredient that she was very particular about. Two or three times a year she would travel to a favourite warehouse, a bus trip away from home, to buy two whole fish (*bacalada*), cut to her specifications, so she had a mixture of superior loin cuts and lesser ones for certain dishes, as well as some traditional hand-torn cod to make the Catalan salad *esqueixada* (see page 328). At her apartment she always had a particular cut de-salting in a bowl of water in her fridge, and once she had used it, she began soaking the next batch.

There was no waste in Montserrat's kitchen. For every meal she cooked she was thinking about the next one, and how leftovers could be extended.

Once she retired, like many a Spanish grandmother she spent much of her time during the week helping her three sons and a daughter, by looking after and cooking for her five grandchildren, with whom she was in touch daily.

What is lovely is that the youngest generation all love their food and have their favourites among her dishes – her eleven-year-old grandson loved her salads of goji berries, apples and cheese and she would make her *crema de verduras*, vegetable soup, especially for her granddaughter, using vegetables from local growers. She would chop up the vegetables quite small, and then meticulously sauté them briefly in olive oil, in groups, so as not to overcook them: a couple of cloves of garlic first, in and out of the oil to flavour it, then onions and leeks until they softened and were lifted out. Then she would repeat the process with carrots, green beans and potatoes, then courgettes, and chard. Finally, she put all the vegetables back in the pan, added enough chicken or vegetable stock to cover by two fingers and let the pan bubble for about 10 minutes, until all the vegetables were just tender. Then she blended the soup, seasoned it, and served it with a squeeze of lemon juice, a spoonful of double or soured cream, and a decoration of lamb's lettuce.

At weekends, however, and for much of the summer, Montserrat became the *grande dame* of La Roca, a large isolated house – more of a small hamlet, really – in the woods near the village of Sant Llorenç Savall, north-west of Barcelona, that has been the family hideaway for generations. There are hardly any other villages in the area, with its hillsides covered in aromatic herbs, neighbouring the wild mountains of the Parc Natural de Sant Llorenç de Munt i l'Obac. Montserrat's mother was born at La Roca and Montserrat spent her childhood summers there. Now sometimes three generations of her family – up to twenty people – carry on the tradition, in a complicated but very happy arrangement of eleven apartments – a *conjunto de familia*.

Each family has its own living space. Montserrat shared hers, filled with her wall-to-ceiling collection of traditional ceramic pots and *botijos* (earthenware jars for storing water or oil), with her daughter Nuria and her family. But there are also communal areas in which they all grow fruit and vegetables, or get together to cook and eat generous meals made to family recipes.

There is a Roman wood oven for roasting whole lambs and suckling pigs, and Ramón, one of Montserrat's many cousins, does a stunning *paella*.

They have neighbours with allotments who share their harvests and some of the uncles hunt, so in June there is a big family celebration of *civet de jabalí*, a large, slow-cooked, wild boar stew which Montserrat always prepared.

Every Friday Montserrat packed up and got ready to go to the country, and it was only when I went to visit her there that I really understood what this amazing retreat was all about. On the day I arrived lunch was *macarrones* (pasta) with a meat sauce, followed by *pollo a la vinagreta* (chicken braised in wine vinegar), which she made with two chickens. It was so good that when I came home we reproduced it on a smaller scale, following her instructions.

The meal at La Roca was finished off with her daughter Nuria's apple pastry twists and homemade blackberrry jam mixed into local yogurt, and then – there was still more – Montserrat's amazing chocolate tart. All washed down in the warm autumn sunshine with *cava*, red wine and, finally, *ratafía* liqueur.

POLLO A LA VINAGRETA

Cut up a single chicken and then put it in a pot with a couple of chopped carrots and onions, 4 cloves of garlic, a small handful of peppercorns, a few sprigs of thyme and a bay leaf. Add 100ml of white wine and 60ml of Moscatel vinegar, 5 tablespoons of olive oil and enough water to cover the chicken. Put a layer of baking paper over the top, bring everything to the boil, then turn down the heat to a slow simmer for an hour and a half – so simple and so good.

POLLO, PATO Y CONEJO

Chicken, duck
and rabbit

Pollo
Chicken

In Spain a good *pollo de corral* (a large free-range chicken which has tougher and tastier meat than an industrially raised bird) is seen as the passport to several meals. One of the most spectacular examples of these big chickens is the rare breed Rojo Campero, grown very slowly and allowed to forage and eat corn, a diet which gives the birds a startlingly red gamey flesh. Because of their size, such chickens can be as festive as a turkey in Britain.

In Burgos, Asun Gordo (see page 154) typically buys two at a time, takes off the breasts and tenderises them by rubbing them with a dry marinade (*adobo*, see page 398), before cooking them on the *plancha* (flat grill) or *la carmela*, a flat, round, ridged frying pan, like a shallower griddle pan.

The drumsticks will go into *pollo al chilindrón*, a homely casserole made with peppers and tomato, then she makes a stock from the carcasses, using leeks, carrots, onions and sometimes celery, even adding a ham bone to give a stronger flavour. Once the stock is made, she strains it for serving as a light soup before the main meal, perhaps with some *fideu* (thin pasta, see page 366) added.

The vegetables from the stock won't be wasted either, as she will add them to a rice dish (made with a *sofrito* and the vegetables simply added at the end).

Alternatively, she might roast one of the chickens and then the leftover meat will go into *croquetas* with some mushrooms (see page 245).

Since these Spanish free-range chickens are almost gamey in their flavour and texture they need around three hours' cooking in a casserole-style dish; however, in the recipes that follow I have adapted the times in line with the more tender free-range chickens we are used to in the UK.

Pollo en cazuela de barro
Chicken cooked in an earthenware pot

This is a recipe from Juani González of the Pérez Pascuas *bodega*, who is also the Mayoress of Pedrosa de Duero in Burgos and with whom our family has shared many a meal together with our friends Ambro and Asun. She makes it to celebrate Christmas and uses a *pollo de corral* which would weigh 3–4 kg; however, I have adapted the recipe to the size of free-range chicken normally found in the UK. The festive green and red of the peppers is in keeping with the Christmas spirit and the sauce, thickened with bread, is quite substantial, designed to combat the bitter cold of a typical Burgales winter.

If possible, cut the chicken into ten pieces, so that you have the drumsticks, thighs, wings and each breast cut in half.

Serves 4

1 x 1.8–2kg chicken (the bigger the better), cut into small pieces, 10 if possible (see above)
sea salt
1 medium onion, finely chopped
1 red pepper, finely chopped
1 green pepper, finely chopped
100ml Cognac

For the picada
100ml olive oil
50g bread, chopped
3 cloves of garlic
50g blanched almonds
2 tablespoons chopped parsley

Start the *picada* by heating the oil in a heatproof earthenware pot, if you have one, otherwise a casserole, then add the bread, whole garlic cloves and almonds and cook for a few minutes until golden brown. Lift these out with a slotted spoon and keep on one side.

Season the chicken pieces just before they go into the same pot, then colour them well on all sides. Lift out and keep to one side.

Lower the heat, put in the onion and peppers and cook gently for about 20 minutes.

Return the chicken to the pan and add the Cognac. Let it bubble for about 10 minutes and then, once the chicken has taken the flavours of the Cognac and the other ingredients, add about 500ml of water, or enough to cover all the chicken pieces. Season with a generous pinch of salt and leave to simmer over a low heat for about 1 hour.

Meanwhile, finish the *picada* by pounding the reserved fried bread, garlic and almonds with the parsley, into a paste, using a pestle and mortar or a blender. Add this to the pan 20 minutes into the cooking time and stir well. The bread and almonds will thicken the sauce. Taste and season with salt again if necessary, then serve.

Pollo a la catalana con ciruelas y piñones

Catalan chicken with
prunes and pine nuts

This is an all-time favourite, as I love the
combination of poultry and fruit, and the syrupy
juices that result from cooking them together.
My ultimate experience of this dish was in a
rustic restaurant in Pallars Sobirà in the High
Pyrenees, where the chicken was cooked in a vast
wood-burning oven with oven-baked potatoes
(al caliu) and it was just beautiful.

Serves 4

2 tablespoons olive oil
sea salt and freshly ground black pepper
4 chicken drumsticks
4 chicken thighs
1 large white onion, diced
2 ripe tomatoes, halved horizontally
1 head of garlic, skin on but separated into cloves
20 prunes
50g pine nuts
200ml white wine
200ml hot chicken stock

Heat the olive oil in a large casserole or deep
wide pan that will transfer to the oven. Season
the chicken pieces, add to the casserole or pan
and brown on all sides, then remove and keep
to one side.

Put the onion, tomatoes and garlic into the
casserole or pan and cook gently for 20 minutes,
until the onions and garlic cloves have softened
and the tomatoes have browned.

Soak the prunes and pine nuts in 200ml of boiling
water for 10 minutes, then drain, reserving the
liquid.

Return the chicken to the casserole or pan along
with the drained prunes and pine nuts. Raise
the heat, season to taste, and add the white wine.
Bubble up to burn off the alcohol and reduce the
liquid slightly.

Meanwhile preheat the oven to 200°C/gas 6.

Add the hot chicken stock along with the
reserved liquid from soaking the prunes and pine
nuts. Simmer gently for 20 minutes over a low
heat, to reduce the liquid by half and concentrate
the flavours.

Transfer to the preheated oven for 20 minutes,
until the chicken is cooked through and tender.

Pollastre amb bolets
Braised chicken with wild mushrooms

For me this is a very special dish which holds wonderful memories of when I shared a flat with a friend, Núria Mayans Pla, in the village of Roda de Ter. On Sundays her mother María would prepare lunch at the family home nearby, and I would always be invited to join in. Of all the dishes she treated us to, this was my favourite.

The combination of almond, hazelnut, garlic, rosemary, mushroom and white wine is one of the great traditional tastes of Catalunya. In autumn the forests are carpeted with wild mushrooms, such as *rossinyol de pi* (yellow chanterelles), which grow out of bright green moss beds under pine trees, large *rovellons* (saffron milk caps) and *llenagues negres* (herald of winter) – these black mushrooms are known as *mocosos,* as their caps are covered with a glutinous layer of slime, unlike their white equivalent, *blancas.* You might also see small *fredolics* (grey knights), which are used in the classic *sopa de frédolics; cama de perdiu* (brown slimecaps or copper spikes), which are brown and turn pink when cooked; the cep-like *pinatells* (related to the saffron milk caps that grow in pine forests), and *llores* (charcoal burners), which are a little peppery in flavour.

For this dish you need quite meaty mushrooms, which won't release dark juices into the dish, so that the sauce stays clear and golden in colour. And, ideally, stick to one variety, to make cooking easier and more consistent. Chanterelles are a good choice. If you can't find wild mushrooms, use chestnut mushrooms, or you could even use dried chanterelles. Soak them in water first to rehydrate them, and keep the soaking water to add to the cooking liquid.

Cut the chicken into eight, so that you have the breasts, drumsticks, thighs and wings, then cut each breast into small pieces (about five per breast) so you end up with around 16 pieces in all.

Serves 4

400g wild mushrooms in season (see left)
1 x 1.8–2kg chicken (the bigger the better), cut into about 16 pieces (see left)
sea salt and freshly ground black pepper
3–4 tablespoons olive oil
1–2 sprigs of rosemary, according to taste
3 bay leaves
50ml wine
50ml Cognac
3 tablespoons Moscatel vinegar
2 cloves of garlic, unpeeled

For the picada
8 raw almonds
8 raw hazelnuts
3 cloves of garlic
a pinch of sea salt
1 tablespoon olive oil

Preheat the oven to 180°C/gas 4.

For the *picada*, spread out the nuts on a baking tray and roast for 7 minutes (shaking them to turn halfway through) until golden. Using a pestle and mortar, crush the garlic cloves with the salt, then add the nuts and continue to pound, adding the olive oil, until you have a paste.

Clean the mushrooms with kitchen paper (avoid using water), and cut away any decaying parts of the stalks and caps. Slice any very meaty mushrooms, such as chestnut mushrooms or large chanterelles.

Season the chicken pieces with salt and pepper. Heat 2 tablespoons of the olive oil in a lidded sauté pan or large casserole. Put in the chicken pieces and brown on all sides for about 10 minutes. Add the herbs, wine, Cognac, vinegar and 100ml of water and bubble up, uncovered, for 5 minutes, then turn down the heat, cover, and cook slowly for 15 minutes, turning the pieces of chicken from time to time to prevent them drying out on one side.

Bash the garlic cloves with the back of a knife, to crack them. Heat another tablespoon of olive oil in a separate pan, put in the garlic and fry for a minute before adding the mushrooms. Cook briefly until coloured, then take off the heat and keep to one side. If you have a mixture of mushrooms, cook the meatiest first, set aside, then cook any more fragile ones separately, being careful to not let their moisture evaporate. You may find you need another tablespoon of olive oil if cooking the mushrooms in batches. The cooking time varies with different types of mushroom but none should take more than 2–5 minutes.

When all the mushrooms are cooked, remove the garlic and add the mushrooms to the chicken, then add the *picada* and stir well.

Taste the sauce and add a pinch of salt if you feel it is necessary.

You may need to add some more water at this stage – perhaps another 100ml – so that there is enough sauce.

Allow to simmer, uncovered, over a low heat for a further 10 minutes while the *picada* thickens the sauce and the flavours mingle. If on the other hand the sauce is too liquid, take off the lid and let it bubble up and reduce for a few more minutes.

Pollastre amb llagosta de Begur
Chicken and lobster Begur style

When, in the nineteenth century, it became possible to separate cocoa butter and powder to make solid chocolate rather than consuming it only in drinks, it became popular, not only in desserts, but in savoury dishes of chicken, game, beef and oxtail. This dish, which features chocolate in the *picada* (see page 320), is from Pepa Salvador's colourful repertoire at La Salsita, the restaurant she used to run on the Costa Brava (see pages 9–10). Chicken and lobster is the most classic of *mar i muntanya* (sea and mountain) combinations.

Serves 4

1 prepared lobster, about 1.5–2kg,
  or 8–10 very large prawns, shell on
1 free-range chicken, cut into 8 pieces
sea salt and freshly ground black pepper
1 teaspoon ground cinnamon
olive oil, for frying
1 onion, finely chopped
1 leek, finely chopped
1 carrot, finely chopped
4 tomatoes, grated
125ml dry sherry
125ml Cognac
500ml *caldo de pollo* (chicken stock,
  see page 468) or water
1 *farcellet* or bouquet garni (bay,
  thyme, parsley, oregano, orange peel,
  tied together with string)
a handful of chopped herbs of your choice
  for garnish (optional)

For the picada
30g hazelnuts
30g almonds
30g grated dark chocolate
8 strands of saffron, soaked in
  1 tablespoon warm water

Take off the head of the lobster, if using, and put to one side for later. Discard the body, then cut the tail lengthways, remove the meat and cut it into 1cm pieces. Keep to one side.

Wrap the claws in a tea towel in case of flying shards, and crack the shells with a hammer or the handle of a heavy knife. Remove the flesh and save it along with the tail meat.

Season the chicken pieces with salt, pepper and cinnamon. Heat a little olive oil in a casserole, put in the lobster head, if using, or the prawns, along with the chicken, and brown all over. Remove the chicken from the pan and keep on one side. Remove the lobster head, if using, and discard. If using prawns, lift these out and keep for later.

In the same pan that you cooked the chicken, fry the onion, leek and carrot, and when they begin to colour add the grated tomatoes and cook until the liquid has mostly evaporated. Put back the chicken and add the sherry and Cognac. Bubble up to reduce the liquid and when it has reduced, cover the chicken with the stock or water, add the *farcellet* or bouquet garni, and simmer for 30 minutes.

Meanwhile, make the *picada*. Toast the nuts in a dry pan, turning regularly, until golden (take care not to let them burn), then leave to cool and rub off the skins with a clean tea towel. Pound the chocolate, nuts and saffron (with its soaking water) using a pestle and mortar until it forms a smooth paste.

Add the *picada* to the chicken along with the reserved lobster, if using, and simmer gently for about 10 minutes, until the sauce has thickened. Alternatively, add the reserved sautéed prawns to the pan just for the last couple of minutes until heated through. Serve, garnished, if you like, with herbs.

Guiso de pollo con albóndigas
Braised chicken with meatballs

A warming, nourishing, golden stew, this is another family recipe from Pilar Sapena of the Gutiérrez de la Vega wine estate in Javea (see page 190). Pilar's oenologist daughter, Violeta, has spent time with us in London, bringing over the estate wines, and when I asked her which were the family recipes she most treasured from her childhood, she chose this, along with *gazpachos manchegos* (see page 456). For the meatballs Pilar uses a mixture of beef and pork, as, she says, the addition of pork makes them more juicy.

The dish is delicious with braised greens.

Serves 4

**500ml *caldo de pollo* (chicken stock,
  see page 468)**
**½ a chicken, cut into 6 pieces
  (or 2 drumsticks, 2 thighs and 2 wings)**
1 tomato, grated
**400g potatoes, peeled and cut into
  cubes of about 2cm**

For the meatballs
170g stale bread
100ml milk
**around 100g flour, for coating
  the chicken and meatballs**
250g minced beef
250g minced pork
1 egg
2 cloves of garlic, finely sliced
1 tablespoon chopped parsley
30g pine nuts
a pinch of nutmeg
sea salt and freshly ground black pepper
olive oil, for frying

For the picada
20g roasted almonds, with skin
3 cloves of garlic, sliced
**1 tablespoon chopped parsley,
  plus a little extra to finish**
**1 *ñora* pepper (optional), soaked
  in water for 30 minutes**
a pinch of saffron, briefly toasted in a dry pan

First make the meatballs. In a bowl, soak the bread in enough milk to cover, for at least 10 minutes. Squeeze out the milk and discard it.

Have the flour ready on a deep plate. Add the minced meats to the squeezed-out bread, along with the egg, garlic, parsley, pine nuts, nutmeg, salt and pepper and mix well. Form into around 20 balls just smaller than a golf ball (around 40g each) and coat these well in the flour.

Heat some oil in a frying pan and put in the almonds for the *picada*. Move around until they are golden, then lift out and keep to one side. Put in the meatballs (in batches if necessary) and fry until golden on all sides. Drain on kitchen paper and keep to one side.

To make the *picada*, pound the garlic, parsley, almonds and 2 tablespoons of the hot stock into a paste using a pestle and mortar. Keep to one side. If using the *ñora* pepper, scrape out the flesh and work into the paste along with a little of the soaking water and the saffron.

Heat 2 tablespoons of oil in a large, deep, wide pan or casserole. Season the chicken pieces, add them to the pan, and sauté for about 10 minutes over a medium heat until browned all over. Lift out and keep to one side.

Put the grated tomato and cubed potatoes into the pan and cook for about 2 minutes, until the potato takes on some colour. Put back the reserved chicken, then pour in enough stock to cover (if necessary, top up with water) and bring to the boil. Turn down to a medium heat and simmer for 20 minutes, then add the meatballs and stir in the *picada*. Cook for another 10 minutes or so, until the golden-coloured stock has reduced and thickened a little and the chicken is cooked through. Take out a piece and pierce it to check that the juices run clear.

Serve sprinkled with chopped parsley.

Pato con peras y calabaza
Duck with pears and butternut squash

Duck is more often associated with France, but in northern Spain and Catalunya, in particular, it is very popular for its cured breast meat and its liver, as well as this classic casserole made with a whole fresh duck.

In autumn in the forests of Catalunya, alongside the mushroom hunters and chestnut foragers, you can still bump into ladies from the villages looking for the wild pears which grow there and have a quite woody and tough texture that can withstand longer cooking than their more delicate orchard cousins. We have adapted this family recipe, which was given to me by Mari Carmen Ruiz, mother of our Catalan head chef Leo Rivera, to include the more familiar fruit.

Serves 4

sea salt and freshly ground black pepper
1 duck, about 1–1.5 kg (cut into wings, breasts and legs, and keep the carcass)
1 cinnamon stick
1 star anise
3 medium sweet white onions, finely chopped
3 medium tomatoes, finely chopped
1 glass (100ml) port
350ml *caldo de pollo* **(chicken stock, see page 468)**
4 pears
¼ of a butternut squash
50g sugar

For the picada (optional)
10 almonds
10 hazelnuts
a slice of toasted bread
3 cloves of garlic
3 tablespoons roughly chopped parsley

Preheat the oven to 150°C/gas 2.

On the hob, heat a heavy-based deep casserole (one that will transfer to the oven and has a lid). Season the duck pieces, put them into the casserole and brown each piece on all sides. You shouldn't need any oil, as the duck is fatty enough. Once golden brown, remove and keep to one side, then put in the carcass and brown it all over. Add the cinnamon and star anise and colour briefly, then remove both the carcass and the spices. Discard the spices and keep the carcass to one side.

Leave the residual duck fat in the pan, put in the onions and cook gently until golden, then add the tomatoes and cook gently for about 20 minutes, until the tomatoes have lost most of their water. Add the port and bubble up for 10 minutes to burn off the alcohol.

Return the carcass to the casserole, add the stock and cook for 10 minutes. Take out the carcass and blend the sauce, then pass it through a fine sieve. Return the duck to the pan, pour the sauce over the top, cover and put into the oven for 1 hour.

Towards the end of the cooking time, peel the pears, cut them in half, and cut the squash into 2cm squares. Put the sugar into a frying pan over a low heat and let it melt, then add the pears and squash and keep moving them around until they are nicely caramelised. Keep to one side.

If making the *picada*, toast the nuts until golden in a dry pan, then crush along with the rest of the ingredients, using a pestle and mortar or a small blender.

Remove the casserole from the oven. Put in the caramelised pears and squash and cook on the hob over a low heat for a further 10 minutes. Add the *picada*, if using, to the casserole for the last 5 minutes, lightly stirring it in.

Conejo al 'jas'
Jazzy rabbit with brandy and carrots

Conejo
Rabbit

Wild rabbit, along with hare, has long been on the menu in Spanish homes and restaurants, and these days rabbit is also farmed in a big way to satisfy demand. Our family, including the children, have always enjoyed rabbit, as it is very lean and often has more flavour than chicken.

The cooking times I have given are for farmed rabbit, but if you are using wild rabbit I would recommend adding more liquid and cooking for around double the time.

This was one of Pepa Salvador's dishes at La Salsita on the Costa Brava (see pages 9–10) and we make it regularly at home. When rabbit is cooked at a very low temperature over three hours you end up with meltingly tender meat, very sweet carrots, and soft caramelised onions which all meld together in a thick and really delicious sauce. Of course, you could substitute chicken for the rabbit.

Serves 4

4 tablespoons olive oil
sea salt and freshly ground black pepper
1 rabbit (about 1.6kg), cut into 10–12 pieces
100ml Cognac
3 large carrots, cut thickly like chips
3 medium onions, sliced in rings
3 medium tomatoes, diced

For the picada
50g almonds
3 cloves of garlic

Preheat the oven to 180°C/gas 4.

Spread the almonds over a baking tray and roast in the oven for 8–10 minutes. Take out and keep to one side. Turn down the oven to 120°C/gas ½. Heat a tablespoon of olive oil in a frying pan, season the rabbit, brown on all sides, then flambé with the Cognac. Lift out and put into an ovenproof dish with a lid.

Put another tablespoon of oil into the frying pan, add the carrots and sauté for a few minutes, then lift out and add to the rabbit. Add yet another tablespoon of oil to the pan, sauté the onions for a few minutes, then add to the rabbit and carrots. Put the last tablespoon of oil into the pan, sauté the tomatoes for a few minutes and add to the rabbit.

Make the *picada* by pounding the almonds and garlic in a mortar, dilute with 250ml water, add to the rabbit, cover with the lid and put into the oven for 3 hours.

Conejo al ajillo con patatas a lo pobre
Rabbit in garlic and wine with 'Poor Man's potatoes'

There are many, many versions of rabbit with garlic – originally the rabbit would probably have just been fried in a pan with peppers and potatoes, a quite dry affair – but now every cook or chef has their own interpretation of how the meat should be, from deep-fried and toffee-coloured to slow-cooked. This is our executive chef Josep's twist on the theme, a variation on the Canarian stew *conejo al samorejo*, and it is very tasty. You need a litre of oil to cook the potatoes, which might seem wasteful, but it will be beautifully flavoured, so you could strain it through a fine sieve and keep it for sautéing meat and vegetables in other dishes.

Serves 4

5 tablespoons olive oil, plus a little extra
2 heads of garlic, trimmed of roots and loose skin
sea salt and freshly ground black pepper
1 rabbit (about 1.6kg), cut into 10–12 pieces
1 rabbit liver
125ml dry white wine
400ml *caldo de pollo* (chicken stock, see page 468)
3 black peppercorns
1 *farcellet* (see page 80), or 1 bay leaf and 5 sprigs of thyme
juice of 2 lemons
2 tablespoons roughly chopped parsley

For the potatoes
1 litre olive oil
4 cloves of garlic, peeled
1.5kg potatoes, thinly sliced (5mm)
1 green pepper, thinly sliced

For the potatoes, pour the olive oil into a deep pan, making sure it comes no higher than a third of the way up. Put it over a medium heat and put in the cloves of garlic. When they begin to sizzle, put in the slices of potato.

Now you need to keep the oil at a gentle simmer for about 40 minutes, so that the potatoes cook slowly and become soft and lightly golden around the edges. Don't stir the potatoes or they will break up, and don't worry if the lower level of potatoes becomes more well-browned.

Add the green pepper, gently pushing the slices into the oil and carefully giving the pan a shake to help them settle. Continue frying gently for a further 10 minutes.

Take the pan off the heat, allow to cool slightly, then carefully lift out the potatoes and green pepper with a fish slice, put into a sieve to drain off the oil and keep to one side.

About halfway through the cooking time for the potatoes, heat the 5 tablespoons of oil in a deep, heavy-based sauté pan or ceramic dish over a medium heat and put in the heads of garlic, tilting the pan so they just sizzle lightly and begin to brown.

Season the rabbit pieces and begin by adding the legs to the pan, letting them sizzle in the oil on a medium heat until browned on all sides, and remove. Next, put in the loin pieces, again brown on each side and remove. Put in the ribs, and repeat. Lastly, drizzle a little more oil over the liver, put it in the pan and again fry until browned, then remove.

Return all the rabbit pieces to the pan, add the white wine and stir until it begins to bubble. Pour in two-thirds of the stock along with the peppercorns and the *farcellet* or herbs, and simmer for 5 minutes.

Add the remaining stock and the lemon juice and cover with a lid for 2 minutes, then take off the lid, stir in half the parsley and cook uncovered for a further 10 minutes, until the sauce has reduced. Sprinkle with the rest of the parsley and serve hot with the potatoes.

CARNE

_____

Meat

Solomillo con castañas
Roasted pork tenderloin with chestnuts

Cerdo
Pork

The pig is the great popular animal of Spain, used from nose to tail and prepared in every possible way. There is even a factory near Madrid which specialises in ready-meals with pig's ears as the main ingredient.

The large European white pig has for many decades been the stuff of everyday eating all over Spain but now the fresh meat from the famous Ibérico pig, better known for its luxurious dried hams, is becoming much better known both in Spain and beyond (see page 172).

This is a favourite dish developed at our London Bridge restaurant, and is very easy to make at home. In winter I like it with something green alongside, such as blanched cabbage, other brassicas or long beans, but it is a recipe that suits summer too, with a fresh green salad and some new potatoes. If you can find Ibérico meat, then it will be extra special.

Serves 4

1 large pork tenderloin (preferably Ibérico), about 800g
2 tablespoons honey
3 tablespoons olive oil
1 teaspoon freshly ground black pepper
sea salt
100g peeled and cooked chestnuts
125ml white wine

Preheat the oven to 220°C/gas 7.

Line a roasting tray with baking paper to prevent the sauce from burning as you roast the meat. Put in the tenderloin.

Mix the honey and oil together in a small bowl, smear this over the meat, then season.

Arrange the chestnuts around the meat and pour the white wine over the top. Put into the preheated oven for 10 minutes, then turn down the heat to 180°C/gas 4 for another 20 minutes, until the meat is browned on the top and the chestnuts have darkened.

Take out of the oven, leave to rest for a few minutes, then slice the meat and serve.

Rancho riojano
Riojan pork, *chorizo* and potato pot

On one occasion when I visited the Alejandro brothers, suppliers of our Riojan *chorizo*, they cooked this up outdoors on an open fire in a big pot – and generously gave me their recipe.

It expands the famous Riojan potato and *chorizo* dish *patatas a la riojana* further into a bigger one-pot stew that includes pork chops, peppers, wine and mushrooms – in spring in Rioja, you find *perrechicos* (St George's mushrooms), which are excellent. It makes a great weekend lunch with crusty bread and a good Riojan wine.

This is one of a number of dishes in which the potatoes are traditionally cut *cascada* style (see page 292), and it will be even better if you have the time to rub the chops first with a dry *adobo* marinade (see page 398).

Serves 4–6 people

2 tablespoons olive oil
500g single pork ribs
300g cooking *chorizo*, roughly chopped
2 medium onions, finely chopped
½ a leek, finely chopped
4 cloves of garlic, crushed with the back of a knife
½ a green pepper, finely chopped
2 tomatoes, grated
100ml white wine
800g potatoes, *cascada* style (see page 292)
2 teaspoons *pimentón dulce* (sweet paprika)
2 *choricero* peppers, halved, stems and seeds removed
100g St George's mushrooms in season, or chestnut mushrooms
a few sprigs of thyme, to garnish

Heat the oil in a large, wide, deep pan or casserole. Put in the ribs and *chorizo* until browned, then lift out and keep to one side.

Put the onions and leek into the pan and cook gently for about 5 minutes, until softened and golden, then add the crushed garlic and the green pepper and continue to cook gently for another 5 minutes. Add the grated tomatoes and simmer for another 10 minutes.

Pour in the wine and bubble up to burn off the alcohol. Then turn down the heat and simmer for another 5 minutes.

Add the potatoes and stir to ensure they are well coated, then return the ribs and *chorizo* to the pan, stir briefly, and add the paprika, 800ml of water and the *choricero* peppers. Lower the heat and simmer for about 25 minutes. Once the potatoes are tender, add the mushrooms and continue to cook for another 15 minutes.

Serve each plate with a half of *choricero* pepper on top – the idea is to scoop out the flesh and mix it into the stew – and garnish with thyme.

IBÉRICO PORK

'quite sublime'

Ibérico pork is something quite sublime. Historically, it was always eaten in the south-west of Spain, where small quantities would be left after the butchering of the pigs for hams, sausages and other cured produce. Abattoirs would usually sell this meat to local restaurateurs and butchers. However, as the clamour for Ibérico hams has risen and risen and their production has expanded to satisfy a growing global market, more fresh meat has naturally also become available, and modern packaging and transport allows it to be frozen and to travel efficiently to more distant markets. Especially in tough financial times, it is both an attractive, and often necessary, proposition for a ham producer to also sell fresh meat, which can help keep the cash flowing while he waits three or four years for each vintage of hams to cure.

Of course, the down side to the expanding market for both hams and pork is that more Ibérico pigs are being farmed intensively, rather than running around the hills and forests, and you won't necessarily be able to tell, since the labelling of fresh Ibérico meat is less rigorous than for cured products (see page 172). It isn't compulsory to declare the upbringing of the animal or the feed on which it has been reared, so provided a pig has 50 per cent Ibérico in its genes the meat can be labelled *ibérico*, but you won't necessarily know any more about its life than

that. Even if it has been fattened on acorns, there may be no mention of this on the label, however if the *de bellota* status *does* appear, the supplier needs to be able to offer full traceability.

The price is no real indicator either, as it varies little, since the reality is that the gulf between fresh meat from an Ibérico pig that has been fattened on industrial feed and *de bellota ibérico* meat from an elite animal that has run free, eating acorns, is far smaller than in the case of hams. This is because it is the long curing process for hams that allows the acorns time to fully work their magic, imparting all kinds of silky, complex nuances to the meat.

That said, *de bellota ibérico* is the carnivore's ultimate meat, all the more enticing because it is only available fresh (rather than frozen) from around January to March, when the acorn-fed animals are slaughtered. We celebrate this short season every year in our shops and restaurants, where the chefs put on a *'menu matanza'* in January, using different cuts of the fresh meat. The 'noble' ones, richly marbled with fat, are usually grilled and can be cooked slightly pink, since to overcook them would blast the delicacy, balance and complexity of flavours.

Secreto

This is the most expensive cut, a fan-shaped muscle located next to the shoulder socket and under the back fat. It has a very silky texture and its thinness makes it suitable for slicing into strips, grilling and serving in salads. In the Brindisa bars and restaurants we serve *secreto* with *papas arrugadas* (see page 296) and *mojos* (see page 298).

Pluma

The end of the loin, sometimes called feather loin, this attaches to the neck of the animal and is also expensive. We like to sear it in a pan over a high heat until the fat almost caramelises, then serve it with onion confit and oven-baked sliced potatoes, *patatas panaderas*.

Solomillo

Solomillo, or tenderloin, is the leanest cut, which is more popular in the UK than in Spain, as to the Spanish taste the lack of fat just means it is less juicy. We might serve it with *piquillo* peppers, pomegranate and a red wine sauce, or with chestnuts (see page 425).

Presa

A big and precious muscle, marbled with fat, between the top of the shoulder and the head of the loin. It weighs about 700–800g and is usually around 1–2cm thick. It is very juicy, with a distinctly gamey flavour, and can be roasted – or it is superb barbecued over an open flame. At Brindisa we pan-fry a whole 800g *presa* – enough for eight people – until slightly pink-medium in a little olive oil in a heavy-based pan. We cook it for 15–20 minutes, turning it every 3 or 4 minutes until it is well coloured all over. Then we leave it to rest in a warm place for 10 minutes before serving, and it is tender, moist and succulent.

Carrillera

This is the cheek, which we often use for long, slow cooking as it becomes very tender over a couple of hours or more. Typically in the Brindisa kitchens the cheeks are cooked with red wine, and are often served with butter beans or mashed potato (see opposite).

Carrilleras estofadas
Pork cheeks braised in red wine

Pork cheeks need longer cooking than other cuts, but will become rich, dark and juicy in the sauce and the meat will just fall apart when you eat it, especially if you can find Ibérico pork, which is rich in fat and incredibly tender. This is another dish created by our executive chef, Josep, who put it on the menu the moment we were able to bring Ibérico pork to London. It is good with mashed potatoes or with white beans. You could also make it with beef cheeks.

Serves 4

1kg pork cheeks, preferably Ibérico
around 50g plain flour
sea salt and freshly ground black pepper
3 tablespoons olive oil
2 onions, finely chopped
2 carrots, finely chopped
1 leek, white part only, finely chopped
1 stick of celery, finely chopped
200ml red wine
1 litre warm beef stock

Clean the cheeks with a sharp knife, taking off what you can of the thin layer of fat and network of nerves. The rest will just melt and disappear.

Put the flour into a shallow bowl and season it with salt and pepper. Dust the cheeks with it.

Heat the oil in a deep pan and put in the cheeks. Colour on all sides, then lift out and keep to one side.

Put all the vegetables into the pan, add a pinch of salt and cook gently until golden brown, but take care not to let them burn.

Return the meat to the pan, add the wine and bring to the boil, to burn off the alcohol. Pour in the warm stock and bring back to the boil. Turn down the heat to low, cover and leave to cook gently for at least 2 hours, or until the meat is very tender.

Have the oven on low and put in a serving dish. With a slotted spoon lift out the cheeks and put them into the warm dish in the oven.

Pour the contents of the pan through a fine sieve into a clean pan, pressing the vegetables through, then bubble this up on the hob until reduced to a thick, silky consistency.

Pour this sauce over the cheeks and serve.

Wood-fired Meats

From chops to whole suckling lamb, kid or pig, baked in an *asador* (wood-burning oven), there is a big tradition of the Sunday roast in the north of Spain, especially in northern Castilla, around Burgos – but not as we would recognise it in the UK. Usually the meat is the hero, presented on its own, with vegetable dishes such as *escalivada* (see page 284) or grilled artichokes served first.

The old practice of lighting a fire and roasting suckling animals, especially (lambs and goats may be as young as four or five weeks and a suckling pig usually less than three), makes for meat that is incredibly succulent and delicate in flavour, and the idea that we could roast such meats in London was the inspiration behind the launch of our own Brindisa *asador*, in Piccadilly. Once I knew that we could bring over lambs from the herds farmed by Félix Vicente Pastor and Isidora Llamas Vicente, whose milk goes into their Zamorano cheese (see page 516) along with suckling pigs from Castilla y León, we were up and running.

In Spain the grilling, roasting or baking of the meat is frequently a male thing, when the men of the family take huge pride in preparing the meal and often build or convert some kind of den, or *merendero,* equipped with a big, serious grill, for cooking copious amounts of delicate chops of milk-fed lamb (*lechales de cordero*) or sausages, such as *botifarras* (see page 450); and/or a wood-burning oven for roasting vast pieces of meat or whole suckling animals at the weekends and on feast days and holidays.

Some of our friends have built quite luxurious communal cooking and eating spaces that are like gourmet playrooms for entertaining, attached to their homes or businesses, with shelves of cookery books, slicing machines for hams, and racks of vintage wines. Others are more rustic, lined with hunting trophies.

Félix and Isidora and their family live in one of three adjoining terraced houses in their village. His two brothers and their families live in the others, and in an ingenious arrangement, a cellar runs beneath all three houses, with staircases leading up to each home. As well as allowing the young cousins to run from house to house without using the front doors, the space has been transformed into a *bodega*, with a grill, eating area and wine store, for everyone to gather around the table while the men do the barbecuing. And in Burgos our friends Ambro and Asun have a typical *merendero,* transformed from an old storage cave in the hills, where they roast lamb over vine trimmings, to be eaten with the local country bread, *pan de hogaza.*

Families and friends will also gather together to go out for the big meat meal. There is a medieval town called Lerma, about two hours' drive from Madrid in Burgos, which is famous for its ancient convents and monasteries. At Easter especially, you see the cars snaking up the mountain to any number of *asador* restaurants where they roast whole suckling lambs over wood fires. There is no menu, everyone is given the same thing: wonderful milk-fed lamb, salad – maybe some potatoes – good bread, and dark red wine.

One of the most memorable roasted meat meals I ever had was in Catalunya, with a group of friends from a local theatre group called La Gabia. We went up into the mountains to a vast farmhouse in Pruit, a tiny hamlet next to the famous shaped workshop space used by the troubadour group Els Jogleurs: a hexagonal bubble sitting on the side of a hill by a stream and medieval bridge, which looked completely alien in this quiet wooded corner of Catalunya. The farmhouse had a long, rough wooden table that could sit at least 25 people and the troupe of actors had bought three suckling pigs, which we roasted slowly in three separate ovens.

After drinks and tapas, and much ad hoc performing of comedy and singing, the pigs were brought to the table on vast plates, and carved – head, ears, tail, everything. A neighbour on one side sucked on trotters and on my other side a chap with a pig's head on his plate dug away at the cheeks, while I rather demurely tucked into a piece of lovely fillet and delicious crackling.

Cordero

Lamb

In the central regions of Spain, *lechal* (unweaned or suckling) lamb is a big favourite for roasting in the *asador* (wood-burning oven). There are five protected production areas: Castilla y León, Extremadura, Navarra, Aragón and La Mancha. The dominant ancient breeds, capable of surviving in harsh conditions, are the Churra (in the north), Manchega in the central region south of Madrid, Merina (known as Merino in the UK) in the south, and the Aragonesa in Aragón, where the herds are raised in the hills and fed on herb-rich pasture which give a certain 'bouquet' to the meat.

Because of my long association with our cheesemaker friend Ambro in Burgos, the Churra, whose milk he used in his cheeses, is the breed that I know best. It is the prettiest of all the Spanish breeds: bright white, with a short coat and black markings on its ears, eyes and hooves. Despite its beauty, however, it is a very hardy animal which adapts very well to the wind, cold, rain, frost and storms that can prevail in its home provinces of Burgos, Palencia and Valladolid in northern Castile – where the rainfall produces very aromatic, fine grass pasture that reshoots over a long season.

While in Aragón the lambs are typically slaughtered at 70–90 days, after being reared on a mixed diet of milk and grass, in the two Castillas they might be as young as 28–30 days. Many of the towns in Castilla y León, such as Lerma and Aranda de Duero in the province of Burgos, are full of restaurants which specialise in roasting them (as well as kid goats and suckling pigs), whole or quartered, covered with chunks of lard, in ceramic dishes. Then they will be served perfectly plainly, with local Ribera del Duero wine, such as Viña Pedrosa or Carmelo Rodero, to cut through the sweet fat.

To some, slaughtering a lamb of just 12 kilos as opposed to around 20 kilos, the average weight of a British lamb at slaughter, might seem shocking, brutal even, but the *lechal* tradition is deeply rooted in the farming and sustenance cycle of the region, where the typical cheeses such as Manchego, Zamorano and Castellano are made with sheep's milk, and so the flocks are primarily dairy. In order to keep the animals producing milk, they have to continue to breed, and the suckling lambs must be taken away from their mothers so that the milk can go into the cheese-making. The consequence is plenty of young animals for the table, whose meat is so much more delicate in flavour than the lamb we are used to in the UK that it seems wrong to distract from its purity. I once took a jar of mint sauce out to Isidora Llamas Vicente, the wife of shepherd and artisan cheesemaker Félix Pastor in Zamora (see page 432) for her to try, since young lamb provides their staple diet, but instantly regretted it as it was far too aggressive for the subtle meat, and I suspect it is still sitting in the larder untouched.

Older lamb or mutton, known colloquially as *macanco* (though it can also mean an elderly donkey), is rarely seen, though you will occasionally come across *la borra*: a female sheep that is barren and 'has to go': *hay que borrarla*. In Burgos, the children of our friends Ambro and Ásun (see page 154) have often managed to save the occasional *borra* from certain dispatch by giving her a starring role in the village Christmas play, where she would become *la religiosa* instead.

There is, however, a big tradition of long, slowly cooked lamb stews such as *caldereta* (see opposite), whose origins are in the pots cooked over fires by the shepherds on the *transhumance*.

Caldereta de cordero de la pastora
Shepherd's lamb stew

This, historically, is not really a recipe at all: it is just the humble meal that the *pastores* (shepherds) cooked up in the open countryside, as they travelled the *transhumance* routes (see page 526) of Castilla y León on foot.

They would find some good tree trunks and suspend a rope between them from which to hang a stewpot over an open fire. Then they would slaughter a lamb from their herd and prepare most of it for the stewpot, perhaps keeping thinner pieces for grilling on long forks. Since they were in the wild, little else would be added to the pot, except perhaps a leaf or two of wild bay or thyme, and so the meat would just cook in its own juices.

These days, however, *caldereta* has become 'a dish' and there are all sorts of recipes which include extra ingredients to embellish the flavour of the lamb. When Ásun Gordo (see page 154) makes hers, she uses 80 per cent of leg cuts and 20 per cent of neck to give some fattiness – however, the taste of the meat is much milder than its equivalent in Britain, since Spanish lamb is slaughtered much earlier. This also means that the cooking time in Ásun's kitchen would only be about 40 minutes, but to bring the lamb to the same level of tenderness in my kitchen takes about 3½ hours of slow cooking.

This is Leo Rivera's recipe, and as with all stews, the flavours will deepen if you can leave the pan to rest for an hour before you want to eat it, and then heat it through on the hob before serving.

It is good served simply with chunky bread and a deep red wine such as Rioja, Ribero del Duero or Bierzo.

Serves 4

2 tablespoons olive oil
sea salt and freshly ground black pepper
1kg lamb leg, cut into cubes of about 3cm
50g flour, to coat the lamb
1 onion, chopped
1 green pepper, chopped
2 *guindilla* peppers (see page 275), de-seeded
6 cloves of garlic
the leaves from 2 sprigs of thyme
100ml white wine
100ml Cognac
100ml white wine vinegar
1 teaspooon *pimentón dulce* (mild paprika)
¼ teaspoon *pimentón picante* (hot paprika)
a handful of parsley leaves, chopped

Heat the oil in a large pan, season the meat, coat with the flour, put it into the pan and brown it on all sides for about 10 minutes, then lift out and keep to one side. Put the onion, green pepper and whole *guindilla* peppers into the pan and cook slowly for about 15 minutes.

Pound the garlic and thyme together with a pestle and mortar and add to the pan, then put back the lamb. Add the wine, Cognac and vinegar and stir in, then add the paprika and cover with 800ml of water.

Cover the pan and cook very slowly for about 3½ hours, or until the lamb is tender, tasting and adjusting the seasoning as necessary. Sprinkle with the parsley and serve hot.

Cordero al cava
Shoulder of lamb roasted in *cava*

This is our executive chef Josep's recipe, which works equally well for young and older lamb, as the *cava* keeps the meat juicy. He uses sweet pink onions from Figueres in the Empordà region of Catalunya, but Roscoff onions also work well.

Serve it with braised white beans or fresh *pochas*, if you can find them, fresh minted green peas, or fried potatoes and peppers.

Serves 4

1 x 1–1.5kg shoulder of lamb
sea salt and freshly ground black pepper
4 tablespoons olive oil
4 whole medium-sized sweet onions
1 head of garlic, cut in half horizontally
½ a bottle of cava

Preheat the oven to 180°C/gas 4.

Take the meat from the fridge about half an hour before cooking to bring it up to room temperature, and rub it all over with salt and pepper.

Pour the oil into a deep baking tray.

Cut the foreleg section of the shoulder from the blade section, and rub each piece all over with more salt and pepper. Place next to each other in the baking tray, along with the whole onions and the garlic, cut side down, and put into the preheated oven. Roast for 10 minutes to brown one side of the meat, then take out and turn it over (if the meat is looking a little dry, sprinkle with a little water). Put back into the oven and brown the other side for a further 10 minutes.

Add the *cava* and roast for another 20 minutes, basting and shaking the tray a little to make sure the juices are moving around. The total cooking time should be no longer than 40 minutes.

Rest the meat for about 5 minutes before serving.

Perol de cordero menorquín
Menorcan baked lamb with tomatoes

On our frequent family visits to Menorca, we can't resist this wonderfully hearty one-pot lamb dish, so one of our Menorcan chef colleagues at Shoreditch restaurant showed us how to make it. *Perol* is the name of the pan used, which is similar to a *paella* pan.

Serves 4

5 tablespoons olive oil
3 cloves of garlic
1.2kg potatoes, peeled and thinly sliced
sea salt and freshly ground black pepper
8 large beef tomatoes, thinly sliced
8 young lamb ribs, separated
2 teaspoons fresh thyme leaves
2 sprigs of rosemary, plus a little
  extra for garnish

Preheat the oven to 180°C/gas 4.

Oil the surface of a large oven dish or roasting tin with 1 tablespoon of the olive oil, then cut one of the garlic cloves in half and rub this, too, over the surface. Put in half the potatoes, making sure they don't overlap too much, and season. Lay half the tomato slices on top, again making sure they don't overlap, and season. Place the ribs on top and season again. Slice the rest of the garlic and sprinkle over, along with the thyme leaves. Drizzle with half the remaining oil, then put in the 2 sprigs of rosemary, cover with the rest of the tomato, press the slices down and season again, then layer the remaining potatoes over the top, season again and drizzle with the remaining olive oil.

Cover with foil and put into the preheated oven for 20 minutes, then remove the foil and allow to brown for a further 5 minutes. Serve garnished with a little rosemary.

Ternera
Beef

In the north of Spain there is a great tradition of excellent beef, especially the vast beef steaks of the Basque country. Galicia, Asturias, Navarra, Extremadura, Sierra de Guadarrama, the province of Ávila and the Basque country all have beef production with protected status – for example, the excellent meat that comes from the herds of Raza Avileña (local to Ávila) that are nourished on open lowlands rich in natural pasture and grassland. In most restaurants you will find huge *chuletones* (chops) of Avileña beef which are supremely good, doused in olive oil, seasoned with chunky sea salt and cooked rare.

In the south, mainly in Andalucía, are the big open plains where the great beasts for bullfighting roam, and following the fight, the meat and tail from a slain bull *(carne de lidia)* is often sold to an exclusive network of restaurants which traditionally cook the awesome prime loin steaks on the grill. Other cuts might be marinated overnight in red wine and treated more like game.

Cooking on an open fire does wonderful things for beef and it is an art which the Spanish have long understood. In the Basque country, thick rib-eye steaks from mature animals of up to 156 months old and weighing over 800kg, are typically cooked over coals in the open air, with their yellow waxy fat softening like butter. In Catalunya, too, where the grills are called *parelladas,* steaks might be a part of the traditional big meal of mixed grilled meats.

Our Basque beef supplier and friend in San Sebastian, Imanol Jaca, sources and hangs his beef for 25 days at his San Sebastián warehouse, before selling it to the best Basque restaurants and specialist steak and cider houses. When I first met him many years ago at a festival of food I was amazed at the vast sides of deep red meat on display at his stand – some of the biggest I had ever seen. The meat is from selected farms on which the cattle have been allowed to grow to maturity on grass, enjoying a natural and varied diet, with fresh air and plenty of exercise, and are not slaughtered until they have led a long life, which could be 15 or 20 years. Imanol chooses the farmer before the animal, valuing those who look after their cattle as if they were the family treasure. The beef is comparable to an Ibérico ham, in that the age and lifestyle of the animals determines the quality of the best meat, marbled and enriched with generous, golden buttery fat that gives the cooked steaks the silky texture and sumptuous flavour that the Basque people love.

The last time I visited Imanol he filled a bag with cuts of his top-of-the-range 18-year-old rump and rib-eye and we headed to his gastronomy club around the corner from his shop, Don Serapio, where, on the *plancha*, he grilled a massive rib-eye steak of around 700–800g, taken from the upper rib with the full bone on, followed by a 400g piece of topside which he seared for just two minutes on each side. He finished with *txogitxu tartare pasado por la plancha* (seared Basque steak tartare) – a cross between a steak tartare and a very rare burger – in which the joy of the tender, smooth-flavoured meat from these older cattle really shone through. The only seasoning Imanol used was a little rock salt sprinkled on for serving, as he insisted that when meat is this flavoursome you barely need any.

Equally, great pieces of meat, simply barbecued or grilled, require little in the way of sauces; however, various regions have their favourites. In Burgos our friend Ambrosio (see page 154) bastes the meat as it grills with his *salsa preve,* olive oil heated gently with smoked *pimentón*. The Catalans will serve a bowl of *alioli* (see page 136), with every plate of grilled meats, and the Canarians will often accompany the meat with *mojo rojo* (see page 300).

Blue cheese from the Picos mountains can make a rich accompaniment, dotted on a hearty rib-eye steak; and one of the best early combinations we put on the menu at Tapas Brindisa was a fillet of beef on a bed of sweet caramelised onions, topped with melted Torta de Barros sheep's cheese from Extramadura (see page 524).

Rabo de buey a la cordobesa
Cordoban oxtail stew with potatoes

I am including two ways with oxtail – first, this quite light southern recipe which we serve at Tapas Brindisa. What is special and unusual about it is that it is made with sweet Moscatel wine and tomatoes, which results in a sweet-savoury sauce wonderfully enriched with the gelatine from the oxtail. We serve it with very thinly cut sautéd potatoes, but boiled potatoes or slices of chunky bread are just as good.

Serves 4

**a little plain flour, seasoned with sea salt
  and freshly ground black pepper**
1.5kg oxtail, cut into medallions 4cm thick
around 4 tablespoons olive oil
2 medium onions, finely chopped
2 medium carrots, finely chopped
2 cloves of garlic, finely chopped
1 teaspoon *pimentón dulce* (sweet paprika)
2 bay leaves
500ml Moscatel wine
600g tomatoes, grated
around 1.5 litres beef stock (see page 469)

Put the seasoned flour into a shallow bowl and dust the oxtail pieces in it, shaking off the excess.

Heat 2 tablespoons of olive oil in a wide pan (that has a close-fitting lid), put in the onions, carrots and garlic and cook gently until softened but not coloured. Lift out and keep to one side.

Turn up the heat, add another 2 tablespoons of oil, put in the pieces of oxtail and brown and seal on all sides, then lift out and keep to one side.

If the pan contains any burnt flour, lift out the oxtail and clean the pan before putting it back on a gentle heat with a little fresh oil.

Return the vegetables to the pan, add the paprika and cook for another minute, then return the oxtail to the pan, add the bay leaves and wine and bubble up to burn off the alcohol. Add the tomatoes, season, and pour in enough stock to cover by 1cm.

Put on the lid, turn the heat down very low and simmer extremely gently – just the occasional bubble disturbing the surface – for 2–2½ hours (if possible use a diffuser underneath the pan). Top up with stock as necessary. The stew is ready when the meat comes readily away from the bone and the sauce is thick and glossy.

Rabo de buey al vino tinto con chocolate
Slow-cooked oxtail in red wine and chocolate

This second recipe for oxtail is inspired by a dish that Ana Barrera makes at her restaurant (see page 442) and has a darker sauce than the Cordoban-style dish on page 439, as it is made with red wine. It does take longer planning, as the oxtail needs to tenderise in the wine for a day before you cook it, and it is at its best if you serve it the day after it is cooked. It is good served, as Ana does, with chunky chips.

Serves 4

1.5kg oxtail, cut into medallions 4cm thick
2 large onions, cut into chunks, about 3–4cm
2 medium carrots, cut into chunks, about 3–4cm
2 leeks, cut into chunks, about 3–4cm
2 medium parsnips, cut into chunks, about 3–4cm
1 litre red wine
a little plain flour, seasoned with sea salt and freshly ground black pepper
2 tablespoons olive oil
2 bay leaves
1 sprig of thyme
12 black peppercorns
4 cloves
8–10 threads of saffron
sea salt and freshly ground black pepper
5cm cinnamon stick
1 head of garlic, whole but trimmed top and bottom
50g dark chocolate
2 tablespoons Cognac (optional)
1.5 litres beef stock (see page 469)

Put the oxtail and vegetables into a bowl with the red wine, ensuring that the liquid covers the meat. Leave in the fridge for 24 hours.

Take out the oxtail, reserving the vegetables and marinade. Put the seasoned flour into a shallow bowl and dust the oxtail pieces in it, shaking off the excess.

Heat the oil in a large casserole, put in the pieces of oxtail and brown and seal on all sides, then add the reserved vegetables and sauté briefly. Add the reserved wine marinade and bubble up to reduce a little before adding all the rest of the ingredients and enough stock to cover all the ingredients by 1cm.

Allow to simmer extremely gently – just the occasional bubble disturbing the surface – for 2–2½ hours (if you have a diffuser, use this underneath the casserole). Add a little more stock if necessary during cooking and towards the end, taste and adjust the seasoning if needed.

The stew is ready when the meat will come away from the bone easily, but keep checking that you don't overcook it, as you want the bone to stay in for serving. Take off the heat, cool and then leave for 12 hours in the fridge to rest.

The next day, turn the oven on to low, and put a serving dish in to warm. Scoop the fat off from the surface of the stew, return the pan to the hob and gently heat through.

Carefully lift out the oxtail, arrange in the warm serving dish and put into the oven while you strain the vegetables and liquid through a fine sieve into a clean pan. Bubble up gently for about 10 minutes, stirring all the time until you have a sauce that is the consistency of a thick syrupy gravy. Pour over the oxtail and serve.

Life and Cooking with Ana Barrera

It is thanks to our friend and buyer/expert in Ibérico hams, Germán Arroyo Duque, that I got to know his friend Ana Barrera and her lovely restaurant in Madrid. Germán has spent many years working in the world of excellence, from tobacco to the finest of *de bellota ibérico* hams, and the circle of people he knows in the food world have great integrity and dedication to doing things the right way. Ana's Restaurante Barrera has long been one of his favourite, almost secret places to eat, as there is no obvious sign that directs you to the townhouse on the corner of an ordinary block in central Madrid. Inside, the dining room feels more like being in Ana's home, with its pictures and well-read books collected over the years. Pale yellow curtains give privacy from the passers-by, and cast a soft light over the handful of tables, carefully laid with beautiful linen.

When first we went there Ana and her late mother, who taught her to cook, were running the kitchen together. Between them they had built up a loyal and long-standing clientele who appreciate traditional cooking, but done with a light and contemporary hand and perfectionist attention to detail.

Ana is originally from Ávila, north-west of Madrid, and their first restaurant, near the famous monastery of San Lorenzo del Escorial, is still run by her brother Pablo, who also buys wine and distributes it to a small network of restaurants, including Ana's.

In the country and in Madrid, the focus of mother and daughter was always on bringing out the ultimate flavour, colour and texture of a relatively small portfolio of excellent and carefully sourced ingredients. There is no regular menu at Restaurante Barrera; the dishes change daily and when something runs out, that is it. Ana has no interest in the cult of the celebrity cook, or even in the idea of *guarnición*, the dressing up or garnishing of a dish, but she is a stickler for just the right ingredient and has a wonderful appreciation of flavour, so that unusual marriages such as pheasant with pomegranate or strawberries (see page 460), or mango with an *escabeche* of *bonito* (see page 324), live in the memory and feel comfortable and true, rather than experimental.

The kitchen of the restaurant is tiny, and Ana needs almost to be a mathematician and magician as well as a cook, in order to divide up the limited work-and-storage area and find space enough to conjure up lunch and dinner every day.

She rarely leaves her kitchen, but finally I managed to convince her to come to London for a few days to see Brindisa and cook some dishes for this book at our home, along with our top chefs, Josep and Leo. We scurried from fruit and vegetable market to fish market, searching for the ripest tomatoes, fruits, wild mushrooms, and the best fish, and once we got cooking it was both a joy and challenge to keep up with her, as she would have four recipes on the go, with the three of us peering over her shoulder asking questions at every stage and scribbling notes. Of course, she has never written down a recipe: everything is in her head, and, as she insists, nothing can ever be set in stone, because you are working with ingredients which vary every time you shop and cook with them, so you must always adjust, taste, smell, and work *al ojo*: to the eye.

ROAST BABY GOAT

One of the specialities I order almost every time I go to Ana's restaurant is *cabrito asado*, baby goat. It is a simple, wonderful dish that is rarely off the menu. Ana feels that goat meat is much more interesting than beef for roasting. It is full of flavour, healthily low in fat and, since relatively few goats are reared industrially – instead they are brought up on the kind of barren shrubby land that characterises certain parts of Spain, the meat is very natural. She likes to roast quite big pieces of young goat – leg/shoulder or a rack – just coated in olive oil and sea salt, perhaps with some halved garlic cloves tucked into slashes in the skin, and some thyme leaves sprinkled over, until the skin is toffee-coloured and caramelised and the meat very tender and juicy.

She starts off with a really hot oven, 220°C/gas 7, then puts the meat in a roasting tin with some water – just enough to come halfway up the pieces of meat, and puts it into the oven. Once the water boils, she turns down the heat to 180°C/gas 4, pours a glass of wine over the meat, and then allows it to cook for 2–3 hours. While it roasts, she turns the pieces as they begin to brown, adding more water and wine if necessary. Then before serving she turns up the temperature again, to finish the bronzing of the meat, by which time the juices should have thickened into a sauce.

Estofat de buey amb xocolata
Catalan beef stew with chocolate

This is a favourite recipe from Colman Andrews's book *Catalan Cuisine*, which was published by Grub Street back in 1997 and has kept our family nourished and centrally heated through many a winter. What is really satisfying is that when you look into the pan towards the end of cooking time, you think, 'Mmm, a bit grey and plain looking,' and then you put in the chocolate and cinnamon, and in front of your eyes it turns into a rich, dark, velvety and aromatic sauce. Sometimes I cook the stew without the potatoes, but serve boiled ones on the side; at other times I serve it with rice, or root vegetables. Colman suggests you can substitute the *botifarra* with three good English sausages if necessary.

Serves 4

60g thick bacon, sliced
750g braising steak, cut into chunks about 4cm
250ml *vi ranci* (see page 373) or dry sherry
2 onions, chopped
4 cloves of garlic, finely chopped
1 *farcellet* or bouquet garni (a bay leaf, a sprig each of thyme, marjoram and savory, if you can find it, tied together)
1 tablespoon chopped parsley
1 tablespoon flour
sea salt and freshly ground black pepper
20g good dark chocolate, finely grated
¼ teaspoon cinnamon
500g new potatoes
1 tablespoon olive oil
1 *botifarra* sausage, cut into 1cm slices (optional)

Sauté the bacon in its own fat in a heavy-based casserole over a low heat until golden brown but still juicy. Remove with a slotted spoon and keep to one side.

Put the beef into the pan of bacon fat and lightly brown on all sides, then return the bacon pieces to the casserole.

Pour in the *vi ranci* or sherry and bubble up, stirring and scraping all the bits from the base of the casserole. Add the onions, garlic, *farcellet* and parsley and stir in the flour. Then pour in 500ml of water and season.

Bring to a simmer, then cover the casserole and cook gently for around 2½ hours, stirring occasionally. Add the chocolate, cinnamon and potatoes and continue simmering for another 30 minutes or so, until the potatoes are tender, adding more water if necessary.

Just towards the end of the cooking time, heat the oil in a frying pan and sauté the slices of *botifarra* until golden. Lift the bouquet garni from the stew and serve, garnished with the fried *botifarra* slices on top.

Albóndigas con salsa de tomate y aceitunas de Aragón
Meatballs with tomato sauce and black olives

Our executive chef, Josep Carbonell, initially created this recipe, which uses both beef and pork, for our pop-up tapas bars at events. It goes down a storm and is a great, quick dinner.

Serves 4

For the meatballs
160g minced beef
480g minced pork
20g white bread, crusts cut off,
  soaked in a little milk
2 eggs
5 cloves of garlic, finely chopped (optional)
1½ tablespoons finely chopped parsley
sea salt and freshly ground black pepper
100g plain flour, for coating
vegetable oil, for deep frying

For the tomato sauce
5 tablespoons olive oil
1 onion, finely chopped
2 carrots, finely chopped
1 leek, finely chopped
1 clove of garlic, finely chopped
500g tomatoes, chopped
sea salt and freshly ground black pepper

To finish
8 black olives, such as Aragón, stones removed
1 leaf of chives, chopped

To make the meatballs, mix together all the ingredients except the flour for coating and the vegetable oil for frying and leave for an hour. To check the seasoning, take a little of the mixture and fry it, tasting and adjusting the seasoning if necessary.

While the meat mixture is resting, make the tomato sauce. Heat the oil in a pan, add the onion and carrots and cook gently until the vegetables have just started to turn golden, then add the leek and garlic. Cook for around 5 more minutes, then add the tomatoes. Simmer for 20 more minutes, then blend with a hand blender and season to taste.

While the sauce is simmering, make the meatballs. Have the flour ready in a shallow bowl. Form the meat mixture into about 20 balls (each should be about 40g, smaller than a golf ball) and pass each one through the flour.

Heat the oil in a large pan, making sure it comes no higher than a third of the way up. If you have a thermometer it should be 180°C, otherwise drop in a few breadcrumbs, and if they sizzle gently the oil is hot enough.

Put in the meatballs (in batches if necessary) and fry for 2–3 minutes, until golden on all sides. Lift out and drain on kitchen paper.

Add the meatballs to the pan of sauce. Simmer for 6 more minutes, then add the olives and cook for 3 more minutes. Take off the heat and leave to rest for 15 minutes, then add the chopped chive leaf and serve.

Cocido
The big stew

This is central heating in a pot, the big winter dish that you see in various guises all around Spain, definitely not recommended for late in the evening, as at its richest it is a very hearty litany of ingredients: meat, meatballs and sausages, chickpeas and cabbage.

Cocido is similar to the French *pot au feu* and the Italian *bollito misto*, in that the rich cooking liquor is often served as a soup (*sopa de cocido*), with the meats and vegetables eaten separately. In general the soup comes first; however, in the Maragato area of León they prefer to start with the meat, and in Galicia there tends to be a split between those who like the soup first and those who prefer it last. Here, the *cocido gallego* usually contains beef, chicken, salted pork ribs, *chorizo*, chunks of local *lacón gallego* (short-cured ham shoulder), white *faba* beans (see page 380), cabbage or *grelos* (turnip tops) and potatoes.

If the soup is eaten first, it normally has some pieces of pasta cooked in it, then the meat, vegetables and beans will follow. If the meat comes first it is usually eaten on its own and then the vegetables and beans are added to the soup, which is known as the *caldo de cocido*, 'the broth that follows the stew'. In some cases – though not at a Catalan table – homemade tomato sauce will be on the table to add to the meat or vegetable course.

Often the meal is split over different days. The big tradition that my Galician colleagues at Brindisa remember was that the mother or grandmother of the family would have a massive pot of *cocido* cooking while the family went to church. When they returned, the meat and potatoes would be taken out and eaten and the *caldo de cocido* would be boiled up again in the early part of the week and served with other foods and wedges of *pan de millo* (heavy cornbread).

While almost every region has its own variation, the roots of the *cocido* appear to be in the Jewish community of Murcia in the nineteenth century. Originally it was a simple dish of chickpeas and cabbage, with the extravagant mix of meats being added later when these became more generally affordable. Given the Jewish origins of the *cocido*, the meat was likely to have been chicken, goat and game, rather than the pork, *panceta*, *chorizo* and *morcilla* that most modern-day *cocidos* contain.

The most famous *cocidos* are the *escudella*, typical of Catalunya (see opposite), and the *cocido madrileño* of Madrid and the two Castilla regions surrounding the city. *Chorizo* is one of the distinguishing features of the Madrid recipe, and the cabbage is usually taken out of the pot at the end and sautéd in *pimentón* and olive oil.

One of Madrid's smartest restaurants, Lhardy, which first opened in 1839, is famous for its *cocido madrileño* and its *cocido* soup stock, which is sold every day in their shop from a vast ornate silver urn, and in times gone by many of the city's restaurants would have had three different *cocido* sittings at different prices: 12.30 p.m. for the labourers, 1.30 p.m. for the office workers and 2.30 p.m. for artists and politicians.

One of the most memorable versions I have eaten was with a table of friends in Madrid at the home of Raul Domingo and Carmen Dalmau on an exceptionally cold but crisp, bright sunny day just before Christmas.

Though Raul is the main, highly accomplished cook in the household, who rules the shopping and quality of ingredients, *cocido* is Carmen's speciality, and the meal was quite splendid. Interestingly, instead of meatballs, she included dumplings made only with parsley, breadcrumbs and egg, and she used a bean net to hold the chickpeas as they cooked, which also allowed her to scoop them out easily to serve separately from the pieces of meat and vegetables.

Escudella i carn d'olla
Catalan stock and meat pot

Like all the *cocidos* across Spain, the *escudella* of Catalunya is a strong, sustaining dish whose roots are in providing energy for families who earned their living working the land. It is not particularly colourful, since the meats, chickpeas, vegetables and stocks turn dull-ish after long cooking; however, the hearty aromas and flavours make for happy folk around the table. *Escudella barrejada* (which means 'all mixed up') is a quite rustic version, made with whatever vegetables, bones and pieces of meat are to hand. However, it is the much more elaborate *escudella i carn d'olla* that is more widely known, as this is the big Christmas dish in many Catalan families, carefully prepared in stages and featuring either one big celebratory meatball (*pilota*) in among the other meats, which is divided up between everyone, or lots of smaller ones. And in a similar way to the big turkey dinner in the UK, it is calculated to last for a few more meals, with the leftovers being used for *canelones* (cannelloni) and *croquetas* (see page 241).

Home cooks put different interpretations on the dish; some prefer to have everything in one pot, while keeping the chickpeas corralled in a bean net; others will cook the vegetables separately. Some will brown the meat first, others won't. Whatever the preference, the basic principle holds good of starting off with the ingredients that need the longest cooking and then working through the list to the most delicate.

I had a splendid version at Casa Riera Ordeix, makers of superb cured sausages, when I visited with Rudi von Vollmar, one of my longest-standing colleagues. Rudi is a charismatic, hugely entertaining character who has befriended chefs around Britain and enticed them to buy all sorts of ingredients over the years, so he is always on the lookout for new ideas and eating experiences to introduce to them. After our visit we were invited to stay for supper. The *escudella* followed small plates of the sausages, tortilla and *pà amb tomaquet* (Catalan tomato bread) and was rounded off with *mató* and homemade plum jam for a pudding. Not a meal for the faint-hearted.

The *escudella* I have included here, however, is based on the family recipe given to me by a colleague at Brindisa, Arantxa Monsalve, which she looks forward to enjoying every year when she goes home for Christmas. With two of our head chefs, Leo and Fran, we adapted and reduced down the quantities of the big Monsalve household meal (which requires a fabulous selection of beef bones – a salt beef bone, two beef knee bones and a large shin bone) to a more easily manageable dish for four.

We excluded the traditional potatoes, so that it is not too filling, and made small meatballs which can be served more delicately in the soup, along with the pasta shells – but there is no reason not to include whole small potatoes, or even chunks of parsnip or celeriac, if you like (add them with the carrots and celery).

Although the list of ingredients looks long, it isn't a complicated dish. It just needs some time and planning, but no more so than the traditional British roast, and I think it makes a great alternative winter Sunday lunch.

A bean net is handy for containing the chickpeas as they cook, as then you can easily retrieve them to serve separately. If you don't have one, you can lift them out with a slotted spoon and simply serve the vegetables and chickpeas mixed up together.

Serves 4

150g *pedrosillano* chickpeas
a pinch of bicarbonate of soda
1 beef marrow bone
2 chicken thighs
1 whole carrot
1 small stick of celery
1 leek, white part only
1 whole head of garlic
300g whole rump steak (leave whole
   and slice once you serve)
250g large *galets* (pasta shells)
½ a Savoy cabbage, cut into thin strips (optional)
45g *panceta*, kept in a chunk
2 fresh *botifarra* sausages
   (or good pork sausages)
2 poached black *botifarra* sausages
   (or *boudin noir*)
2 poached white *botifarra* sausages
   (or *boudin blanc*)

For the mini pilotas (meatballs)
3 slices of white bread, crusts
   cut off and soaked in a little milk
2 eggs, beaten
375g beef mince
125g pork mince
1 clove of garlic, crushed
4 tablespoons finely chopped parsley
sea salt
a little plain flour, for dusting

Soak the chickpeas overnight in cold water
with a pinch of bicarbonate of soda.

Fill a large stockpot with 3 litres of cold water
and put in the beef bone and chicken thighs.
Bring to the boil, then pour away half of the
water and replace it with fresh cold water. Bring
to the boil and repeat this process twice over –
this eliminates the usual impurities that rise to
the surface in the form of foam, and means that
you don't need to keep skimming this off during
cooking.

When you bring the water to the boil for the
fourth time, drain the chickpeas and add them
to the pot (if you have a bean net, put them inside
this first, so that you can easily scoop them out
later). Put in the carrot, celery, leek, garlic and the
whole steak and simmer gently for 1 hour.

Put the oven on to low and put in a big shallow
dish to warm.

Make the meatballs. Squeeze out the excess
milk from the bread, put into a bowl with the
rest of the ingredients – apart from the flour –
and a large pinch of salt and work into a paste
with your hands.

To check the seasoning, fry a little of the mixture
in a pan until the meat is cooked, then taste and
adjust if necessary.

Put the flour into a shallow bowl. Form the
mixture into 16 small meatballs – they will each
be about the size of a cherry tomato – then roll
in a little flour, shake off the excess and keep
to one side.

Strain off about a litre of stock from your pot
into a smaller pan, put in the pasta shells and
cook until *al dente* (about 15 minutes depending
on the size of the shells and the particular pasta),
adding the meatballs and the cabbage strips,
if using, for the last 2 minutes of cooking.

Meanwhile, add the *panceta* and *botifarras* to
the main pot and cook for 10 minutes, then lift
out the *botifarras* and the rest of the meats,
chickpeas and vegetables from the main pot,
and arrange them on the warmed serving dish,
keeping the meat separate from the vegetables.
If you have used a bean net, mound the
chickpeas separately, too.

Add the remaining stock to the pot containing
the meatballs and pasta and ladle into bowls,
for people to eat first, then follow with the dish
of meat and vegetables.

Cocido montañés
Mountain meat and chickpea stew

This is a slightly simpler *cocido* recipe from Ismael Playan Paul, who was the chef in charge of our Soho kitchen for many years and has since returned to his home in the amazing Aragonese mountain town of Benasque, where this dish will have originated. It should be eaten with hunks of bread to soak up the juices.

Serves 6

**350g dried chickpeas, preferably *pedrosillano*
   or *castellano***
4 tablespoons olive oil
**150g fresh belly pork or *panceta*, cut into
   chunky slices, at least 1cm thick**
**100g hot cooking *chorizo*, chopped into
   chunky slices**
**80g semi-cured *morcilla*, such as Asturian
   or Ibérico, chopped into chunky slices**
**½ a head of garlic, peeled and cut
   in half horizontally**
2 medium white onions, finely chopped
½ a green pepper, finely chopped
½ a red pepper, finely chopped
**3 medium tomatoes, grated (you need about
   250g of grated tomato)**
a little sugar and/or sea salt
1 litre good chicken stock
**250ml ham stock (if you don't have this,
   just use more chicken stock)**
¼ a Savoy cabbage, kept in one piece

Soak the chickpeas in cold water overnight.

Heat 1 tablespoon of the oil in a heavy-based deep casserole, add the belly pork or *panceta* and fry until golden brown, then lift out, keep on one side and discard the excess fat.

Put another tablespoon of oil into the pan and fry the pieces of *chorizo* and *morcilla* until they brown a little. Then again lift out, put them to one side with the belly pork or *panceta* and discard the excess fat from the pan.

Add 2 more tablespoons of oil to the casserole, put in the garlic and fry gently until it begins to brown, then lift out and keep to one side. Add the onions and cook very slowly for at least 30 minutes, but ideally an hour, until completely caramelised. Now add the peppers, return the garlic to the casserole and cook slowly for about 20 minutes. Add the grated tomatoes and continue to cook slowly until the liquid has come out of the tomatoes and has reduced down. Taste and, depending on the flavour and ripeness of the tomatoes, you may need to add a little sugar and/or salt.

Heat the two stocks (if using both) together in another pan. Once boiling, put in the chunk of cabbage and cook for around 5 minutes, taking care not to overcook it. Lift out and keep to one side, leaving the stock in the pan.

Add the chickpeas and all the reserved meats to the casserole and cook gently, stirring for about 5 minutes to meld the flavours. Add enough of the hot stock to cover, keeping some back, so that you can top up the level if and when needed.

Simmer gently for about 1½ hours, adding stock as necessary, according to how much of it the chickpeas absorb. For the last 15 minutes of cooking time, slice and add the cabbage – if you leave the pieces on top of the casserole rather than mixing them in, they will steam and reheat, taking on the aromas of the stew, but keep their fresh colour.

Serve with hunks of good bread.

EMBUTIDOS

'so many different shapes and styles'

In Spain, the generic name for sausages is *embutidos*. The verb *embutir* means to stuff or pack into a tube, and *embutidos* can refer to sausages of many different shapes and styles. They might be freshly made in a butcher's shop, or *oreado*, which means they have been allowed to dry for a few days before being sold. Sometimes they will be pre-cooked, usually poached, especially in northern Spain where the damper climate isn't conducive to curing meat.

Trekkers on the pilgrims' route through Galicia to Santiago de Compostela may come across *botillo*, as they pass through El Bierzo. The *botillo* is a large, round sausage weighing about 1kg, made from cuts of pork including ribs and sometimes tongue which are chopped, salted, seasoned with *pimentón* (paprika) and garlic, stuffed into a pig's stomach, then smoked over oak and hung up to cure for two days. After this the *botillo* is boiled for about two hours with potatoes, cabbage, or local pulses, and *chorizo* added for the last half-hour of cooking, to make an incredibly hearty one-pot meal. It is one of the most overwhelmingly meaty dishes you are likely to eat, designed to keep you going in bitter, biting winter winds in the foothills of the Picos mountains.

Botifarra negra y blanca

In Catalunya and along the coast southwards you will find these poached sausages, which are similar to the French *boudin noir* or *blanc*, made with pork and pork fat, with the addition of blood in the case of the *botifarra negra*, which can be used in place of *morcilla*. *Botifarra de perol* is a heavily spiced version made with various pieces of the pig that are left over after butchering, and there are others made with egg white (*clara d'ou*), foie gras, rice or truffles, and a very sweet one from the Empordà made with honey to a medieval recipe.

Another of the *botifarra*-style cooked sausages that dominate the cold climate regions of northern Spain, especially Catalunya, is *bull*. In food shops across the Catalan Pyrenees, you will see these not-so-beautiful round stomachs stuffed with minced pork and tongue, hanging from the ceiling. They can be *blanca* (white), or *negra*, made with pig's blood, and there are many other variations, such as *bull amb rovellons*, with wild mushrooms. Cooked or poached *botifarra* and *bull* can be eaten as they are, pan-fried, or added to the end of a dish to warm through. The most popular is the fresh style *botifarra fresca*, which can be fried or grilled – there is a long, fat one typical of Catalunya which is coiled around itself and will fill a large frying pan: a favourite served with white *mongeta* beans (see page 381).

CAZA

_____

Game

So much of Spain's mountainous land is still uncultivated, and hunting is a treasured part of local life, providing much-loved, excellent quality food. Not only that, but in these days when it is less of a necessity and more of a pastime, there is a good income to be made from hunting reserves (*cotos de caza*) catering for affluent city folk. On the islands, too, hunting is a big deal. The emblems of the Canary Islands are the palm tree and the local hunting dog: *perro canario de presa,* which is the pride of the countryside.

I remember going to a rustic restaurant up in the hills in Gran Canaria and seeing five of these dogs caged on a trailer which had been parked outside by their hunter owner, while he had lunch. Afterwards they would be let loose in the hills to bring home shot birds and hunt rabbits and they were clearly raring for action – fearsome-looking creatures, tall and skinny, with massive heads and jaws, and a very strong smell about them. After our lunch, we went into the town of Las Palmas and behind the cathedral there were a number of impressive stone sculptures of these historic dogs, looking down regally on the passers-by. It felt a little spooky looking at them, having just been so close to the live, smelly, ferocious animals in the mountains.

The hunting season all over Spain is, of course, the autumn and wintertime, from October to January, while the spring, when no hunting is permitted, is the breeding season for small birds, such as pheasant, partridge, quail, pigeon – even doves.

Game birds

Faisán
Pheasant

Since it is one of the larger birds, pheasant is often cooked for celebratory meals, particularly in a casserole for Christmas. At the home of our Madrid friends Raul and Carmen (see page 225), the traditional job for their son and daughter is to sit at the kitchen table peeling around 2 kilos of the last grapes that have been left on the vine, and sweetened to a Moscato-like flavour, for the festive dish – it is the equivalent of everyone peeling sprouts in the UK, but far more time-consuming and fiddly. Raul cooks a mass of onions very slowly in a casserole, browns the birds and adds them to the onions with the grape mulch, pours over some white wine, tops it up with water and puts it into the oven for about an hour. Then he carves the birds, reduces and purées the sauce, strains it to get rid of the grape pips, and pours it over the meat.

Perdiz
Partridge

Partridge is often raised in captivity and, although it doesn't have quite the flavour of the wild bird, is very popular as it is a good size and has quite white meat. The female bird is tastier than the male one, and there are many recipes for it, including the one on page 463, in which Madrid cook Ana Barrera (see page 442) uses the sweet flavours of blended onion and carrot with red wine to marinate the birds, which she ultimately serves with soft berries. Chocolate is another great partner to the partridge, as are apples and mushrooms.

Codorniz
Quail

This used to be a very common bird around cereal fields and hillsides, feeding mainly on seeds, grains, grass and insects. However, modern methods of farming have changed the use of land and reduced the population, so now some are bred in captivity. As with all game birds, these never quite compare to the taste of the wild ones. Usually you would need two birds per person, as they are very small.

Paloma torcaz
Wood pigeon

These are greedy birds, and when they are not perched high up in the woodland trees watching the world go by they are constantly eating, so the older the bird the more pungent the meat. There are no special recipes for wood pigeon – they are usually simply plucked, cleaned, cut into four and casseroled with the likes of garlic, chopped carrots, peppercorns, parsley and white wine. Often they will be slowly cooked for around three hours in the oven, then kept in the fridge overnight and cooked again the next day for a further four hours or so until the meat becomes very tender.

Becada
Woodcock

Very well known around the province of Burgos, woodcock is best hunted in October when it is young and tender and its taste is reminiscent of the autumn forest. It is usually hung for three days and can then be roasted in butter (or wrapped in bacon), or stewed with vegetables and a shot of brandy. If you have an older bird it can be excellent for pâtés and terrines.

Larger game

Corzo
Deer

This is an animal native to Asturias that is about the size of a goat. It eats grasses, wild fruit, mushrooms and leaves, and the venison meat of the young animal is tender, but gets tougher the older the animal gets. Typical dishes include baked fillets with chestnuts, roast leg with hazelnuts and prunes and stewed foreleg with wild mushrooms or chocolate. The legs can also be cured to make cecina (see page 178).

Liebre
Hare

Hare has long been one of the most appreciated foods in Spanish cooking – though it is less popular nowadays when most people don't have to rely on game for subsistence. Despite its meat being dark, hare is a herbivore and will have eaten lots of wild herbs, such as thyme and lavender, which makes it quite exquisite-tasting – especially when the hares are young (around six months old) and very tender. Older hares of a year or more need marinating, coating with lard and stewing to tenderise them. Ingredients that reflect the hare's wild habitat bring out its flavours the best, so it is good paired with mushrooms, thyme, bay, walnuts and mint, together with earthy ingredients like lentils, and always, a good slug of wine. See hare with lentils on page 464.

Jabalí
Wild boar

The great trophy for any hunter, the ancestor
of the pigs we have domesticated, this animal
eats everything it finds and loves acorns,
potatoes, beetroot and cereals. Its meat is dark
and very lean and is usually eaten when the
animal is between six months and about a year,
and the loins and legs are the most valued pieces:
they can be stewed, roasted with apple compote,
stuffed with prunes and walnuts and even cured
for *chorizo*. The younger the animal the milder
and more tender the meat; however, *jabalí* is
nearly always best in a long, slowly cooked stew,
as you cannot be certain of the age or the size
of the animals shot in the wild.

Isard
Mountain goat antelope, or Chamois

This is the Catalan word (similar to the French
izard). In Castilian this goat-antelope is known
as *rebeco*. It lives in the Pyrenees, Cantabria
and in the Apennines and was almost hunted
to extinction for its meat and leather. However,
in the Pyrenees they now have a population
of around 25,000 animals and in the Catalan
mountains I enjoyed *izard* roasted – full of
flavour and extremely lean – as part of a fabulous
New Year's Eve dinner.

Gazpachos manchegos Casta Diva
Game and chicken stew Casta Diva style

There are many versions of this classic dish, which is traditional in inland Valencia, Alicante and particularly southern Castilla, around La Mancha. The first time I came across it, it was a complete revelation because even in Spain most people associate the word *gazpacho* with cold summer soup, whereas *gazpachos* in the plural refers to unleavened *tortas* (thin flour and water biscuits or breads), also known as *tortas cenceñas or ácimas)* which are traditionally added to, and also accompany, this homely, hearty winter small-game stew. Presumably, the link between the two dishes is the idea of adding the *torta* in the case of the stew, or bread, in the case of *gazpacho* soups, to soak up and bulk out the other ingredients.

Gazpachos is originally a shepherd's dish, made with any small game (wild rabbits, hare, partridges) that could be shot and cooked in water with lots of garlic and herbs in a ceramic pot or a special pan with a long handle and legs that would sit over a campfire in the countryside or hills. The flour and water *tortas* would be made and baked in the ashes – some would be broken up and added to the pot to bulk out the stew like pieces of pasta which become enriched with the stock, and one big one would be kept to use as a communal plate. Usually there would be more *tortas* made than were needed, so there would always be some left over to add to the next stew.

When the meat was cooked it would be stripped from the bones, cooked further with the *torta* pieces in the stock, and then put out on the communal *torta* 'plate' for the shepherds to scoop up, using yet more *tortas*. Once the meat was finished, they would spread the 'plate' with wild honey, then break it up and share it out for pudding.

At our Brindisa *asador* in Piccadilly, as well as focusing on the roasted meat dishes of northern Castilla, we wanted to introduce people to this less famous small game stew from the south of the region. Our chefs make their own dough in the charcoal oven and, to echo the way the shepherds would have eaten the meal, they add small strips of *torta* to a stew of quail and rabbit and then serve it on a whole *torta*, along with a small bowl of honey for people to spread over it after the stew has been eaten. The result is a lovely contrast of sweetness and savoury gravy flavours.

Here, though, I am giving two slightly simpler recipes which combine game and chicken. This first is from Pilar Sapena (see page 190), and is the recipe that prompted me to ask for a version to be included at the Rupert Street restaurant.

Pilar makes her own *tortas* in her bread oven, which when added to the stew give it the luscious consistency of a lasagne, and one of our chefs, Francisco Juan Martínez Lledo, who is also from Alicante, helped us to perfect the recipe.

Often for this dish the meat is cooked on the bone, but Pilar likes to poach it first, then debone it before cooking in the stock.

Serves 4

4 chicken thighs
2 legs and 2 breasts of rabbit
2 legs and 2 breasts of partridge
1 bay leaf
1 sprig of thyme
1 sprig of rosemary
10 black peppercorns
1 teaspoon sea salt

For the base
1 head of garlic
5 tablespoons olive oil
2 onions, chopped (about 1cm)
1 teaspoon thyme
1 bay leaf
4 tomatoes, grated
sea salt

For the tortas
600g white flour, plus extra for dusting
½ teaspoon salt
a little honey, to serve (optional)
a little thyme, to garnish (optional)

First make the *tortas*. Put the flour and salt into a bowl, make a well in the centre and slowly mix in 250ml of water, kneading well until you have a homogeneous dough that has quite a dry consistency (this can take up to 20 minutes, so you can do it in a mixer with a dough hook, if you prefer). Put into the fridge to rest for 30 minutes.

Lightly flour your work surface and break up the dough into 8 balls. Roll out each ball into a round of about 1mm thick, and of a size to fit the base of a large, heavy-based frying pan.

Put the dry pan over a low heat. When the base is hot, put in your first *torta* and toast it, turning regularly, until there are no uncooked areas left. Lift out and lay on a rack to avoid condensation as it cools. Repeat with the rest of the *tortas*.

Put all the meat in a casserole along with the bay leaf, thyme, rosemary and peppercorns. Add 2 litres of water, plus the salt, and bring to the boil, then turn down the heat and simmer for at least 1 hour, until the meat comes off the bone easily.

Take the pan from the heat, lift out the meat (reserving the liquid), allow to cool, then strip the meat from the bones, trying to keep the pieces as big as possible, so they don't break down into an indistinguishable paste during the next stage of cooking. Keep to one side.

To make the base, take the head of garlic, trim off the roots, peel off any loose skin and give it a good bash with the flat of a knife to crack the cloves. Heat the olive oil in a deep frying pan, tipping it to create a deep pool, then put in the garlic and fry until it begins to brown.

Add the onion, thyme and bay leaf and cook for about 5 minutes, until the onions are translucent and just beginning to brown. Put in the tomatoes and a pinch of salt and simmer steadily until reduced and very aromatic.

Add 1.4 litres of the reserved liquid from cooking the meat and bring back to a simmer, then put in the reserved meat. Resist the temptation to stir too much or the meat will break up. Taste for salt and adjust if necessary.

Break up four of the *tortas* into rough pieces (about 3cm) and add to the casserole. Leave them to soften and absorb the tasty stock for at least 10 minutes.

To serve, put one remaining *torta* onto each of 4 plates and ladle the stew on top. Sprinkle with a little thyme, if you like. When the stew has been eaten and each person reaches the gravy-coated *torta* it will be quite soft, and can be torn or cut into strips and then spread with honey.

Gazpachos manchegos Esperanza
Esperanza's game and chicken stew
with *tortas* (biscuits)

This is a simpler version of the stew without the
torta base, which I worked on at home with our
former chef, Esperanza Añonuevo Heys. In this
recipe the bones are left in, but the meat should
be very tender at the end of cooking and will fall
away from them.

Serves 4

2 tablespoons olive oil
180g Spanish *torta* biscuits, matzos
  or water biscuits, broken up
sea salt and freshly ground black pepper
½ a rabbit, cut into 8 small pieces
½ a chicken, cut into 6 pieces
1 partridge, cut into 6 pieces
2 cloves of garlic, sliced
1–2 *guindilla* peppers (see page 275),
  deseeded and finely chopped
2 medium tomatoes, chopped
2 bay leaves

For the picada
a little olive oil
70g chicken livers
leaves from a sprig of rosemary
leaves from a sprig of thyme
2 cloves of garlic
½ teaspoon each of sea salt and
  freshly ground black pepper

Heat the oil in a wide, deep sauté pan (with a
lid). If you are using matzos or water biscuits,
fry them briefly, then lift out and reserve (if using
traditional Spanish *tortas*, there is no need to do
this, as they are drier).

Season all the meat and put in the rabbit first.
Brown it for 10 minutes, then add the chicken
and brown them together for another 10 minutes.
Finally, put in the partridge and continue to
brown everything for a further 10 minutes.

Add the garlic and peppers to the pan and
fry briefly, then put in the chopped tomatoes
and cook over a moderate heat for another
5–10 minutes.

Add 1.5 litres of hot water, along with the bay
leaves. Break up the biscuits, add to the pan
and cook for 20–25 minutes over a medium heat.

To make the *picada*, heat a little olive oil in
another pan and briefly fry the livers on both
sides (for about 3 minutes in all), until browned.
Transfer the liver to a pestle and mortar, add the
rosemary and thyme leaves, and pound together
with the garlic and some salt and pepper.

Add the *picada* to the stew and cook for 15 more
minutes until all the meat and *tortas* are tender
and the sauce is thick, but not dry.

Faisán a fuego lento con berenjena confitada y granado
Slow-cooked pheasant with sweet aubergine and pomegranate

In this recipe from Ana Barrera (see page 442), she uses wild birds, which are marinated over two days in apple, carrot and onion juice and half a bottle of white wine, then casseroled slowly, so they are really tender. For a farmed bird a day's marinating should be enough.

Ana loves the bitter-sweet flavours that come from serving meats with fruit, and in this case she cooks aubergines in a long, slow process, with sugar, cinnamon and cloves, to serve alongside the pheasant, then scatters everything with pomegranate seeds. Or, in season, she might use cherries, or even strawberries or raspberries.

Serves 4

sea salt and freshly ground black pepper
2 pheasants, oven-ready and legs tied together
plain flour, for coating
olive oil
1 clove of garlic
4 peppercorns
4 cloves
a pinch of cumin
2 bay leaves
2 onions, chopped
2 carrots, chopped
½ a bottle of white wine (optional)
100g pomegranate seeds, to serve/garnish

For the marinade
4 carrots, chopped, for juicing
  (or 200ml bought juice)
4 apples, chopped, for juicing
  (or 200ml bought juice)
4 onions, chopped (or grated, if you
  are using bought carrot and apple juice)
½ a bottle of white wine
2 bay leaves
1 head of garlic, skin on, roughly chopped
1 leek, roughly chopped
6 cloves
a sprig of thyme
about 6 threads of saffron, infused
  in a little water

For the confit aubergine
1 large aubergine, roughly chopped, around 1cm
250g sugar
½ a cinnamon stick
1 clove

Season the pheasants inside and out and put them into a bowl.

Put the carrots, apples and onions for the marinade, if using, into a juicer, or mix together the bought juices and grated onion. Add to the pheasants, along with the wine and the rest of the marinade ingredients, which should be enough

to completely cover the birds (if not, add a little extra apple juice or wine). Cover with a plate and leave in the fridge for 1–2 days, depending on whether the bird is truly wild, or farmed.

When you are ready to cook, start the confit aubergine first, as this will take about 2 hours. It might seem like a long process, but it concentrates the flavour deliciously into the absorbent texture of the aubergines.

First, just blanch the aubergine in a pan of boiling water for about a minute, making sure you keep pressing it down under the water and turning it over. Drain, and discard the water.

Put the aubergine back into the pan with the sugar, cinnamon, clove and 250ml of water. Bring to the boil, then straight away take the pan off the heat, and leave to get cold (this will take around 30 minutes). Put back on the heat, bring to the boil, then take off and leave until cold again.

Repeat this process about 6 times in all over a period of around 2 hours. The last time, don't leave to get cold as the confit hardens as it cools. Ana would blend it until smooth and then strain it, but this is optional.

Meanwhile, take the pheasants out of the marinade. Pat them dry a little with kitchen paper, season them again, then coat in flour.

Heat some olive oil in a pan, put in the pheasants and the garlic clove and brown the pheasants very lightly on all sides. Add the marinade liquid, together with the peppercorns, cloves, cumin and bay leaves. Add the chopped onions and carrots and the ½ bottle of wine, if using, or 375ml of water. Bring to the boil, then turn down the heat and cook gently, covered, for 1–1½ hours (or even a little longer), although this will depend on the size of the pheasants and whether they are male or female (females are more tender).

Lift out the pheasants on to a warm plate, then strain the liquid through a fine sieve back into the pan and bubble up until reduced by two-thirds to make a sauce. Pour this over the pheasants. Sprinkle with pomegranate seeds and serve with the confit aubergine.

Perdiz estofada al estilo Barrera con fresas y frambuesas
Partridge with soft fruits and baby onions

This is another dish based on one that Ana Barrera (see page 442) serves at her Madrid restaurant. In summer she serves the dish with berries, and in winter with braised *lombardo* (red cabbage). She chops up a small red cabbage, blanches it in salted water, then drains it. Then she sautés a chopped shallot and a chopped clove of garlic in olive oil until soft, adds the blanched cabbage to the pan with some toasted pine nuts and a teaspoon of sherry vinegar, and cooks it gently for 2–3 minutes until the cabbage is deep red. At the last minute she adds freshly chopped apple and seasons everything with sea salt.

Serves 4

4 partridge or 8 quail
about 100g butter (Ana says that the butter should be about half the weight of the onions)
18 baby onions or shallots, peeled
sea salt and freshly ground black pepper
a little plain flour, for coating
100ml olive oil
1 clove of garlic, peeled and crushed lightly with the back of a large knife
100ml Cognac
3 carrots, chopped
2 leeks, chopped
4 onions, chopped
1 parsnip, chopped
2 bay leaves
a sprig of thyme
6 strands of saffron, soaked in warm water
about 1½ teaspoons cumin seeds, crushed
1 cinnamon stick
25g good dark chocolate (70% cocoa solids)
around 32 raspberries and 32 strawberries (you want around 8 of each per person)

For the marinade
4 carrots, to make 200ml of juice (or equivalent bought juice)
3 onions, chopped (or grated, if you are using bought carrot juice)
½ a bottle of full-bodied red wine

If using carrots and onions for the marinade, put them into a juicer, or mix the bought carrot juice and grated onion. Put into a bowl with the partridge or quail, the red wine and enough water to cover. Cover with a plate and leave for 24 hours in the fridge.

Melt the butter in a pan, put in the whole baby onions or shallots and cook on a very low heat for 2 hours to soften and sweeten, stirring periodically.

Meanwhile, remove the partridge or quail from the marinade (reserving the liquid for later) and pat them dry with kitchen paper. Season, then coat them in flour.

Heat the olive oil in a pan, put in the birds and the garlic clove and brown very lightly on all sides. Remove the garlic, add the Cognac, and flame. When the flame has died down, add the marinade liquid, together with the chopped vegetables, bay leaves, thyme, saffron, cumin, cinnamon and chocolate and bring to the boil. Be sure that the liquid covers the birds and vegetables. If not, add more water.

Turn down the heat, cover with a lid and cook gently for about an hour, depending on the size of the birds, removing the lid after half an hour to allow the sauce to thicken slightly. The meat is ready when it comes away easily from the bone.

Lift the partridge or quail on to a warm plate, then put the pan back on the heat and bubble up just enough to reduce the liquid further to a sauce consistency. Strain and pour over the partridge or quail, scatter with raspberries and strawberries and serve with the slowly-cooked onions on the side.

Liebre con lentejas
Braised hare with lentils

The pairing of hare and lentils is inspired: dark, tender and aromatic meat and juices and earthy flavours – delicious. I was first given a recipe for hare with lentils by Josep Bassal, a friend from my early days living in Catalunya. Known as 'Popon', he is a cellist who performs worldwide, and also a great cook whose food always seems to be full of music and drama. I remember dropping by one afternoon and he was preparing a completely 'orange' dinner rounded off with saffron ice cream, for his wife, Isabel Ruiz de Villa, a flamenco dancer whose stage name is La Chamela, an affectionate diminutive of Isabel. Despite the lure of his recipe, though, I never quite had the courage to tackle it.

Then some time later on an Easter visit to our friends Ambro and Asun, a Castilian hunter, Isidro el Bartolo, shared a bowl of braised hare with me and the meat was so incredible that I realised I had to finally go and buy a hare. I decided to amalgamate Popon's method with Isidro's dish and the result is this recipe, which was happily devoured in seconds when I served it up to colleagues at the Brindisa warehouse, both English and Spanish.

In Spain a dish like this is usually served on its own, but I think it is good with winter cabbage or kale.

When you buy your hare, ask for the liver and the blood.

Serves 4–6

500g small dark lentils such as *pardina* or Puy
sea salt and freshly ground black pepper
1 bay leaf
2 sprigs of thyme
2 sprigs of parsley
1 hare, about 1.5–1.8kg, prepared for cooking
    (i.e. skinned and cut into 8–12 pieces,
    depending on its size)
3 tablespoons olive oil
4 shallots, very finely chopped
½ a green pepper, very finely chopped
1 clove of garlic, finely sliced
2 tablespoons plain flour
hare's blood
½ a bottle of white wine
100ml Cognac
1 teaspoon good red wine vinegar,
    such as Forum or Fondillon

For the picada
1 tablespoon olive oil
the liver of the hare, or 100g chicken livers
2 cloves
3 cloves of garlic
½ teaspoon chopped *guindilla* pepper
    (see page 275)
1 tablespoon chopped parsley
½ teaspoon grated nutmeg

Put the lentils into a pan with 850ml of cold water, a teaspoon of salt, the bay leaf, one of the sprigs of thyme, and one of the sprigs of parsley, and cook for 30 minutes, until the lentils are tender but have not broken down. Drain most of the water, leaving about 100ml, and leave the lentils in this. Keep to one side.

For the *picada*, heat the oil in a small pan and fry the liver. Using a pestle and mortar, pound the cloves, garlic, *guindilla* pepper, parsley with the fried liver and grated nutmeg until you have a paste. Keep to one side.

Season the pieces of hare. Heat the oil in a casserole and put in the shallots and green pepper. Cook until soft but not brown, then add the garlic and cook for 5 minutes. Put in the hare and sauté for 20 minutes, until golden on all sides, then add the flour and stir.

Add a tablespoon of warm water to the blood, strain it, then add this to the casserole. Add the white wine, Cognac, the rest of the thyme and parsley and the vinegar, and season with salt to taste. Bubble up to evaporate the alcohol, then add enough water to cover the hare, cover with a lid and cook for at least 3½ hours, until the meat is falling off the bone, topping up with a little water as necessary to keep the hare covered. Stir in the *picada* for the last 30 minutes.

Add the lentils with their remaining liquid. Bring to the boil for a few minutes, to heat them through, then turn down the heat and simmer for about 5 more minutes to allow them to soften a little and to take on the flavour of the hare juices before serving.

CALDOS Y FUMETS

'so simple to make'

A good stock (*caldo*) or fish stock (*fumet*) is at the heart of so many of the dishes in this book, and since these are so simple to make they are really worth doing at home in big batches, as they will keep for up to two days in the fridge, or you can freeze them in containers.

Caldo vegetal
Vegetable stock

Makes around 1.5 litres

1 large carrot, roughly chopped
1 large leek, roughly chopped
tops and trimmings from a fennel bulb
  (if you have some), roughly chopped
2 sticks of celery, roughly chopped
10 peppercorns
1 bay leaf

Put all the ingredients into a pan with 1.5 litres of cold water. Bring to the boil, skimming as necessary, then turn down the heat and simmer for 30 minutes. Cool and strain through a fine sieve.

Fumet blanco
White fish stock

This is a gently flavoured stock that is light in colour and is ideal for dishes such as *arroz de alcachofas* (see page 348) and *suquet de peix a l'all cremat* (see page 312). It is best to use the bones of 'blue' fish such as hake, monkfish, sole, or turbot.

Makes around 1.3 litres

500g fish bones
1 onion, roughly chopped
1 carrot, roughly chopped
2 sticks of celery, roughly chopped
1 leek, roughly chopped
1 bay leaf

Put all the ingredients into a large pan. Add 1.5 litres of cold water and heat slowly until boiling (this will take about 25 minutes), then take off the heat. Strain well through a very fine sieve.

Fumet rojo
Red fish stock

This stock has a stronger flavour than its white counterpart. It is most popular in dishes such as rice or *fideuà*, in which the ingredients benefit from a hint of colour. Select rock fish such as scorpion fish, fresh prawn heads and crab to help give a bigger flavour. If you prefer, you can roast the bones in the oven (at 200°C/gas 6 for around 30 minutes) rather than frying them in the pan.

Makes around 1.3 litres

2 tablespoons olive oil
500g fish bones
125ml brandy (optional)
1 carrot, roughly chopped
1 leek, roughly chopped
1 onion, roughly chopped
2 sticks of celery, roughly chopped
¼ of a head of garlic, topped and tailed,
  but unpeeled, and with some of the
  cloves cut, to release more flavour
¼ teaspoon *pimentón dulce* (sweet paprika)
175ml white wine
6 tablespoons *sofrito de tomate*,
  from a jar or homemade (see page 318),
  or 2 fresh medium tomatoes

Heat the oil in a large pan, add the fish bones and sauté for 5 minutes, then flambé with the brandy, if using. Remove the fish bones and keep to one side. Add all the chopped vegetables to the pan and allow to brown a little, then add the garlic and paprika and stir briefly, taking care not to burn the paprika. Add the wine and bubble up to allow the alcohol to evaporate.

Add the *sofrito* or fresh tomatoes and sauté briefly for 5 minutes, then return the fish bones to the pan and pour in 1.5 litres of cold water. Bring to the boil, skimming off any foam that comes to the surface, then turn down the heat to a simmer for 10 minutes. Take off the heat and strain through a fine sieve.

Caldo de pollo
Chicken stock

Makes around 1.2 litres

1 fresh chicken carcass, or carcass
  from a roast chicken
2 chicken wings
1 carrot, roughly chopped
1 leek, roughly chopped
1 onion, roughly chopped
2 sticks of celery, roughly chopped
1 bay leaf

If using a fresh carcass, heat the oven to 200°C/gas 6, put the carcass into an oven tray and roast it for 30 minutes.

Put the roasted carcass into a large pan with the rest of the ingredients. Add 1.5 litres of water and bring to the boil, skimming off any foam that rises to the surface, then turn down the heat to a simmer for 1 hour. Strain through a fine sieve.

Caldo de jamón
Ham stock

At Brindisa nothing is wasted from our Ibérico hams, so the bones are used to make the most exquisite stocks. Of course, you don't have to use Ibérico bones, but the better the ham bones, the better the stock will be.

Makes around 1 litre

2 tablespoons olive oil
1 carrot, roughly chopped
1 leek, roughly chopped
1 onion, roughly chopped
2 sticks of celery, roughly chopped
500g ham bones, cut into manageable pieces
1 bay leaf

Heat the oil in a large pan, add all the vegetables and sauté lightly, then add the bones, bay leaf and 1.5 litres of cold water. Bring to the boil, skimming off any foam that rises to the surface, and cook for 1½ hours. Strain through a fine sieve.

Caldo de ternera
Beef stock

A robust beef stock is an important element of the cooking of northern Spain, and this one, recommended by our head chef, Leo, involves roasting the bones and vegetables separately first.

This is an ideal stock for soups such as *potaje de berros* (see page 222) and slow-cooked beef and oxtail dishes (see pages 438–444).

It is traditional in Spain to mix beef stock with dishes containing pork and *panceta* to make them more hearty and filling.

Makes around 1 litre

1kg bones, including a calf knee bone
around 3 tablespoons olive oil
1 carrot, roughly chopped
1 leek, roughly chopped
1 onion, roughly chopped
2 sticks of celery, roughly chopped
½ a celeriac, peeled and roughly chopped
4 cloves of garlic, peeled
1 ripe tomato, chopped
½ a bottle of red wine
1 cinnamon stick

Preheat the oven to 190°C/gas 5.

Put all the bones on a baking tray greased with a little of the oil and put in the oven for 20 minutes. Lift out the bones and reserve, drain off the excess fat, put in the vegetables and garlic and return to the oven for another 20 minutes, adding the tomato for the last 5 minutes.

Transfer the roasted bones and vegetables to a large pan and add the red wine and cinnamon. Bring to the boil to allow the alcohol to evaporate, then add around 1.5 litres of cold water (you need enough to cover the bones and vegetables). Bring back to the boil, skimming off any foam that rises to the surface, then turn down the heat and simmer gently for 1 hour. Take off the heat and strain through a fine sieve.

POSTRE

Pudding

Thanks to the sunshine, Spain is blessed with so much exquisite fruit and for me it makes the best end to a meal. When I lived in Catalunya I got used to being offered *fruta del día*, fresh fruit of the day, or a glass of freshly squeezed orange juice as a simple dessert in local restaurants. A remarkably sensible burst of vitamins after a good lunch or dinner.

And what a spectrum of fruit there is to choose from, since Spanish territories span such a wide variety of climates, from the tropics of the Canaries, where you find bananas and paw paw, to the forests of central Spain, where in summer wild *grosellas* (redcurrants), *frambuesas* (raspberries), *moras* (blackberries) and *fresas* (wild strawberries) grow, and in autumn, *zarzamoras* (blackberries) and *arándanos* (blueberries). The central and eastern regions of Castilla y León, La Rioja, the Ebro valley in Navarra, Aragón and Catalunya are also famous for their orchard fruits: cherries, quinces, plums, peaches, figs, pears and apples. And in the south and in Valencia, alongside oranges, brilliant red persimmons (like sweet and fruity tomatoes) have their own PDO, and are excellent mixed with yogurt, or you can just eat them like passion fruit, digging into their juicy interior with a small spoon. Fruits such as pears and peaches are typically poached in wine, and oranges or strawberries are outstanding macerated for a few hours with some sugar and vanilla.

At one time in Catalunya it was traditional for innkeepers to 'pay' minstrels who performed in their establishments with a 'musician's dessert' of dried fruit and nuts and a glass of sweet wine. The idea always makes me think of the children's story of Trubloff the mouse, who ran away from his family in his village in Russia to play the balalaika with a travelling band of gypsies, performing in inns and receiving food and drink in return. I imagine Trubloff and his Catalan counterparts would enjoy the simple combination of a glass of Casta Diva Moscatel (see page 190) with some excellent Spanish pine nuts, hazelnuts, almonds, Moscatel sultanas, figs and apricots. Or, as a variation on a traditional theme, the fresh combination of pine nuts, oranges, honey and mint on page 474.

Other than fruit and nuts, the most typical weekday desserts in Spain tend to be dairy- and egg-based, not unlike our nursery puddings; for example, *torrijas* (fried milk-soaked squares of bread, see page 480), *natillas* (set custards), *cremas* (runny custards) and *leche frita*: cold custard, allowed to solidify, cut into squares, then fried in butter to a golden colour. Then there are the very rich egg-yolk sweetmeats which often originated in the convents of southern Spain, around the sherry-producing cities. The *bodegas* would use egg whites to clarify the sherry then give the yolks to the nuns who would use them in delicacies to sell for a little money, such as *tocino del cielo*, a 'heavenly' (but sinfully rich) dessert made with caramel. Or *yemas de Santa Teresa*, golden-coloured balls of creamy sweetness named after St Teresa of Ávila, founder of the Carmelite convents, which are made with sugared egg yolk, lemon juice and zest and involve a laborious method of overnight baking at a very low temperature.

In various regions of Spain, cheesecakes are popular, and I have given two recipes from the Levante, which use goat's curd or *mató* (see page 525). Creamy rice pudding is also a favourite all over Spain, not cooked in the oven so that it forms a roasted brown skin in the way of the traditional British pudding, but gently simmered on the hob, infused with citrus peel and cinnamon, allowed to cool, and served chilled. I have given two versions, which might sound similar but turn out quite differently.

At weekends, when friends and family gather for big meals, there will be more elaborate almond or chocolate tarts, cakes, mousses and ice creams, perhaps made with saffron (page 496) or *turrón* (page 497) depending on the region.

For the selection of recipes in this chapter I have simply homed in on my favourites and some of their many variations.

Fresas con vinagre PX y chocolate
Fresh strawberries with PX vinegar
and chocolate

These are fun and colourful.

Serves 4

250g strawberries
50ml Pedro Ximénez vinegar
10g butter
100g dark chocolate (at least 70%
 cocoa solids), broken into squares

Wash and carefully pat dry the strawberries,
leaving them whole with the stalks still on.

Pour the vinegar into a pan and let it bubble up
until reduced by two-thirds. Take off the heat
and leave to cool.

Put the butter into a bowl over a pan of
simmering water, taking care not to let the base
of the bowl touch the water. Let it melt, then
add the chocolate and stir as it melts into the
butter. Take off the heat and dip each strawberry
into the chocolate (so they are only half covered
in chocolate), then place on a rack with the
chocolate side upwards and put into the fridge
for an hour, until the chocolate has
set completely.

Drizzle the vinegar over the strawberries
and serve.

Naranja fresca con menta
Orange carpaccio with fresh mint

In season, navel oranges are excellent combined
with the freshness of mint leaves and the
creaminess of pine nuts. I also like the oranges
simply sliced and drizzled with a dressing of olive
oil, orange juice, orange liqueur and a sprinkling
of sugar. Choose good Mediterranean pine nuts.

Serves 4

40g pine nuts
4 ripe oranges
8 fresh mint leaves, finely sliced into strips
4 teaspoons clear neutral honey, such as
 '1000 Flowers'

Toast the pine nuts in a dry pan and allow to cool.

Peel the oranges and remove as much pith as
you can, then slice them very finely horizontally,
using a sharp knife.

Arrange on a plate or in a bowl, then sprinkle with
the mint, drizzle with honey and scatter the pine
nuts over the top.

Peras al vino con helado de regaliz
Pears poached in white wine with liquorice ice cream

Macedonia con alineo de vainilla y aceite de oliva
Fruit salad with vanilla and olive oil dressing

Pear in red wine is a classic combination across Spain but we wanted a variation on the traditional, so our head chef, Leo, uses white wine to poach the fruit and adds the complementary flavour of liquorice, then serves the pears with liquorice ice cream. The flavour of liquorice reminds him of his childhood, when he and his friends would chew the sweet sticks of natural liquorice known as *palo duro* or *palo dulce*, very different to the 'sweets' which contain artificial colour and sweeteners. Here you can usually find these in health food shops.

At home in Catalunya Leo would also use the small round *peras de San Juan*, which appear in the markets in June for a short season of 30 to 40 days and are crunchy but juicy and sweet. In London we use the larger Conference pears, which work very well.

Serves 4

**4 medium Conference pears or
  8 San Juan pears, peeled
1 bottle (750ml) of fruity white wine
  such as Albariño or Verdejo
40g sugar
1 stick of natural liquorice root
liquorice ice cream, to serve (see page 496)**

Put the whole pears into a pan and add the wine, sugar and liquorice root, then lay a sheet of baking paper over the top to trap in all the flavours. Simmer for around 15 minutes, until the pears are tender, testing them occasionally by inserting a skewer.

Lift out the pears, put them into a freezer container and freeze for 30 minutes to halt the cooking process, then transfer to the fridge.

Meanwhile, continue simmering the wine until it has reduced by half, then take off the heat, transfer to a bowl and put into the fridge to cool.

Halve each pear and put into a bowl with a scoop of liquorice ice cream and drizzle with the syrup.

Our chef Leo likes to infuse olive oil with a vanilla pod and combine it with juice and honey to make a dressing for a selection of fruit. It makes a good, fresh and healthy finish to a meal, and the combination of olive oil and vanilla is unexpectedly luscious.

Serves 4

**125ml olive oil
1 vanilla pod
2 teaspoons honey
juice of 1 orange
2 peaches, cut into small pieces
250g strawberries, quartered
¼ medium melon, cut into small pieces**

Pour the oil into a small pan, then slice the vanilla pod lengthways and scrape all the seeds into the oil, as well as adding the halves of the pod. Warm the oil as gently as possible (don't let it boil) for half an hour, ideally keeping the temperature of the oil below 65°C to prevent the aroma of the vanilla from disappearing. Take off the heat and allow to cool and continue infusing. Any surplus can be stored in a sterilised jar – leave in the vanilla pods – for a week.

Gently heat the honey and orange juice in another small pan until the honey melts. Take off the heat and leave to cool. Mix with the reserved vanilla oil in equal proportions to make the dressing.

Put the fruit into a bowl, pour the dressing over it and allow the flavours to develop at room temperature for an hour before serving.

Melocotón caramelizado con helado de Manchego
Caramelised peach with Manchego ice cream

The perfect ripe peach for this has a beautiful aroma and is properly ripe with generous natural sugars, but still has a slight crunch. Probably the best peaches I have ever eaten have come from Spain, grown in the regions of La Rioja, the Ebro Delta or Calanda in Aragón, where the popular variety is the Amarillo Tardío. These cosseted late-harvest fruits are individually wrapped in paraffin-coated paper bags while still on the tree, to protect them from disease and abrupt climatic shifts through the summer. Out of season, you might also find preserved Calanda peaches, which you can warm through, caramelising them in their own syrup before serving with the ice cream.

Serves 6

6 fresh peaches
300g sugar
4 cloves
1 cinnamon stick
Manchego ice cream, to serve
 (see page 495)

Peel the peaches and put into a small pan with 1 litre of water, the sugar and spices, then cover and cook over a very low heat for 20 minutes, until tender. Take off the heat and allow to cool.

Cut each peach in half and serve with some of the cooking syrup and the ice cream.

Crema catalana
Catalan burnt custard pudding

This is probably Catalunya's most famous pudding, so it is impossible to leave it out – and besides, I am a sucker for such milk puddings, so I am always tempted to choose it from a menu.

It is very close to the French *crème brûlée*, except, typically of Catalan and Spanish milk-based desserts, it is not cooked in the oven, but on the hob, and as a result tends to be less set and more custardy. A homemade *crema catalana*, using excellent eggs with deep yellow yolks, and aromatised with lemon and cinnamon, is a world apart from the mass-produced ones, which can often be quite bland in flavour and slightly gelatinous in texture. We like to add vanilla, but Catalan purists wouldn't do this, so I have made it optional.

Serves 6–8

1 litre milk
½ a cinnamon stick
grated rind of 1 lemon
½ a vanilla pod (optional)
6 large or 8 medium egg yolks
40g cornflour
250g caster sugar
about 1 tablespoon demerara
  sugar per person

Put the milk into a pan with the cinnamon and lemon rind and, if using, put in the vanilla pod and scrape in the seeds. Heat until the milk starts to rise, then take the pan from the heat, cover, and leave for about 2 hours at room temperature so that the flavours infuse.

In a bowl, whisk the egg yolks, cornflour and sugar. Strain the reserved milk through a fine sieve on to the egg mixture, whisking continuously. Pour into a pan and stir continuously over a low heat until the mixture thickens into a custard. Be careful not to overheat, as the mixture will separate if it reaches more than 80°C.

Pour into small, individual dishes, leave to cool, then put into the fridge for 3–6 hours to set.

Just before serving, sprinkle the top of each dish with demerara sugar and caramelise with a blowtorch or a brûlée iron. Alternatively, put under a preheated, very hot grill, very briefly, making sure the caramel doesn't burn.

Torrijas
Sugared egg-fried squares

An almost childish Castilian treat, similar to eggy bread or French toast. I made the mistake of mentioning to my chefs at Brindisa that I might not include the recipe, as it is not a usual kind of dessert in the UK, only to be met with a look of anguish on their faces! So here it is.

When we spent Easter with our friends Asun and Ambro in Burgos, Asun made a generous batch of these on Maundy Thursday, keeping them in the fridge to see us through to Easter, and I was surprised how delicious they were even when fried and eaten cold.

This is an amalgamation of Asun's recipe and one from Nico, chef at our Tramontana restaurant. Use a stale loaf or brioche that will absorb the flavours in the milk without disintegrating.

Serves 4

250ml milk
50ml double cream
80g sugar
the peel of ½ a lemon
the peel of ½ an orange
1 cinnamon stick
1 vanilla pod
4 slices of stale bread, from a tin loaf or brioche
2 eggs
2 tablespoons olive oil, or 40g clarified butter
1½ tablespoons sugar, to finish
1 teaspoon ground cinnamon, to finish (optional)

Warm the milk and cream in a pan with the sugar, peel, cinnamon stick and vanilla pod (seeds scraped in). Heat gently and just before it comes to the boil, take off the heat and leave for 30 minutes to infuse.

Arrange the slices of bread in a wide, shallow dish and pour the infused milk and cream over them. Leave for at least 10 minutes, to allow the bread to soak up the mixture.

Break the eggs into another wide, shallow dish and beat them with a fork. Once the slices of bread are soft with milk, coat each slice on both sides in the beaten egg.

Heat the oil or clarified butter in a large frying pan and fry the slices, no more than one or two at a time, on both sides for about 2 minutes, until they brown around the edges. Then serve, or keep in the fridge and eat when cold, sprinkled with sugar and, if you like, ground cinnamon.

Mousse de turrón
Turrón mousse

Josep Carbonell created this dessert for our first tapas bar menu and it has been a signature pudding ever since. It looks good served in glass tumblers.

Makes 8

100g raisins
200ml good sherry, such as Pedro Ximénez
300g soft *turrón* (nougat), broken into pieces
300ml double cream
4 eggs, separated

Put the raisins into a small pan with the sherry and bring to the boil, then take off the heat and leave to cool.

Put the *turrón* into a food processor with the cream and egg yolks and mix for a minute until you have a smooth paste.

In a bowl, whisk the egg whites until they are frothy, then gently fold into the *turrón* mixture.

Put a heaped teaspoon of raisins along with a level teaspoon of the marinating sherry into the base of each of 8 glass tumblers – keeping back a few raisins to decorate – and fill with mousse.

Put into the fridge for at least 2 hours to allow the mousse to set (although it will not become hard), and decorate with the reserved raisins just before serving.

Horchata de piñones
Pine nut *horchata*

Our head chef, Leo, is a genius with sweet things and one summer's day he put this simple dessert on the menu. It's a recipe that dates back to his time working in a restaurant in Arenys de Mar on the Catalan coast, when he and his colleagues were looking for lighter ways to use local ingredients.

Like all *horchatas* (nut milks), it has a consistency that is slightly thicker than regular milk, but it is meant to be drunk, rather than spooned – though if you are using whole berries, or large slices of berry, these can be scooped out with a spoon.

Serves 2

75g sugar
125g Spanish pine nuts
**50g wild strawberries or small slices of
  cultivated strawberries, to decorate**

Put the sugar into a pan with 500ml of water and heat, stirring to dissolve the sugar. Just as the water starts to boil, remove from the heat and add 100g of the pine nuts.

Leave to cool, and then blend with a hand blender. Put into the fridge to chill for 12 hours, or overnight.

Strain the liquid (which will now be a milky colour) through a fine sieve or muslin.

Toast the remaining 25g of pine nuts in a dry pan until golden.

Pour into small glasses and decorate with the toasted pine nuts and strawberries.

Quesada la bauma con confitura de tomate

Goat's curd cheesecake with sweet tomato jam

On a visit to Toni Chueca, who supplies us with Garrotxa goat's cheese from his La Bauma dairy in Berguedà, he gave me some goat's curd to try, explaining that he sells it to Catalan chefs for sauces and puddings. It was so delicious – delicate and sweet, with almost no acidity – that I decided we must bring some to London, and Leo developed this recipe around it for Casa Brindisa. Our chefs, who have the benefit of large ovens, bake the cake in long-handled metal frying pans, but at home you can use a more conventional cake tin.

Makes a large cake, serving around 12

250g goat's curd
8 eggs
200g caster sugar
750ml double cream
icing sugar and ground cinnamon, to decorate
4 tablespoons sweet tomato jam (see page 533), to serve

Preheat the oven to 140°C/ gas 1.

Slowly combine the goat's curd, eggs, sugar and double cream in a bowl.

Line a 22cm, 6cm high ceramic dish or cake tin with foil, making sure you leave no gaps in order to avoid any leakage, and spoon in the mixture.

Place the dish or tin in a deep roasting pan. Pour in enough boiling water to come halfway up the sides of the pan and put into the preheated oven for 1¼ hours until, if you shake it gently, it has a more solid jelly-like texture. Switch the oven off and leave in the oven for another 45 minutes.

Remove and allow to cool fully for another 30 minutes before putting into the fridge to chill for around 12 hours (or overnight). To turn out, place a plate over the top of the tin and turn both over together so that the cheesecake is sitting on the plate.

Dust the top with sugar and cinnamon and serve with the tomato jam.

Flaó d'Eivissa
Ibizan cheesecake

We opened our Tramontana restaurant with this Ibizan cheesecake on the menu. The addition of mint to cheesecakes and almond tarts is a refreshing touch typical of the Balearic Islands. This cake pairs really well with a sweet Moscatel wine or a Malvasia from Sitges.

Makes 1 x 30cm cheesecake

6 mint leaves
4 eggs
250g caster sugar
600g fresh goat's curd or ricotta
icing sugar, to finish

For the pastry
250g plain flour, plus a little extra
  for preparing the tart tin
a pinch of salt
¼ teaspoon baking powder
50g caster sugar
½ teaspoon anise seeds
65g unsalted butter, softened, plus a
  little extra for preparing the tart tin
1 egg
zest of 1 lemon
25ml anise liqueur

Preheat the oven to 170°C/gas 3.

To make the pastry, combine the flour, salt, baking powder, sugar and anise seeds in a bowl. Add the softened butter, the egg, lemon zest and liqueur and mix until the dough comes together in a ball. Wrap in clingfilm and put into the fridge for 30 minutes.

Prepare a 30cm tart tin with a removable base by greasing with a little butter and then dusting with flour, turning the tin to make sure that it is fully coated, and tipping out any excess flour.

Lightly flour a clean work surface and roll out the pastry into a circle around 5mm thick and large enough to line the tin. Roll the pastry around your rolling pin, then lift it up and unroll it into the prepared tart tin. Line with baking paper and baking beans and put into the oven for 5 minutes, so that it is only lightly coloured and not browned. Remove from the oven and trim any overlapping edges.

For the filling, tear the mint into small pieces and keep to one side.

In a bowl, beat the eggs and caster sugar briefly.

In a separate bowl, mix the curd or ricotta with the mint (keep back a few pieces to decorate the top of the cheesecake), then fold into the eggs and sugar until you have a smooth mixture.

Spoon into the pastry case and decorate with some extra mint leaves, if you like. Put into the oven for 35 minutes, making sure that the top of the cheesecake doesn't brown.

Turn off the oven and leave the tart in until it has cooled to room temperature. Remove and chill in the fridge before serving, dusted with icing sugar.

Brindisa arroz con leche
Brindisa rice pudding

This is a big favourite in the Brindisa tapas bars and restaurants. We make it with medium-grain rice (we use a Balilla x Sollana cross, see page 341) grown in Calasparra, and although the pudding is quite loose-textured, the grains of rice retain their feel and shape within it.

When the pudding is first taken off the heat it will be more liquid than you might expect, if you are used to more sturdy British rice puddings. It will look more like a *caldoso* – the soupy savoury rice dish (see page 362), but as it cools down the rice will absorb more of the citrusy milk and become creamier, although it will never be as thick as the British version. You need the peel from one orange and one lemon – half of the peel from each fruit is cut into large strips to go into the pudding, and the rest is cut into thinner, more elegant strips for decorating the top.

Serves 4

1 litre whole milk
the peel of ½ a lemon and ½ an orange,
  cut into large strips
1 cinnamon stick
125g medium-grain rice, such
  as that from Calasparra
50g caster sugar
ground cinnamon, to decorate (optional)

For the citrus peel confit
the rind of ½ a lemon and ½ an orange,
  cut into long, thin strips
50g granulated sugar

First make the confit to decorate the dish. Blanch the thin strips of peel in a small pan of boiling water for 1 minute, just to remove their bitterness, then drain and refresh under the cold water tap.

Put the sugar into a heavy-bottomed pan with 200ml of water over a low heat until the sugar dissolves, then add the blanched peel and simmer for about 20 minutes, until the syrup reduces and thickens. Remove from the heat and leave to cool.

Put the milk, the large strips of orange and lemon peel and the cinnamon stick into a separate pan and bring to the boil, then take off the heat, add the rice and sugar and stir well.

Put back on the hob over a medium heat for 5 minutes, stirring and watching carefully to make sure that the milk doesn't boil over or burn. After 5 minutes, turn down to low and cook for 20 minutes, stirring often, and constantly towards the end.

The texture of the rice pudding will be quite liquid at this stage, but will thicken as it cools (see above). Spoon into a serving dish or individual dishes, cover with clingfilm to prevent a skin from forming, then put into the fridge for at least 3 hours, preferably 24 hours.

Before serving, remove the peel and cinnamon stick, decorate the bowl or bowls with the confit citrus strips and sprinkle, if you like, with a little cinnamon.

LIMONES DE LUNA

'an incredible concentration of aromatic, essential oils'

One of the most exciting additions to the fresh produce we bring in from Spain is the limited production of fabulous organic moon lemons sent to us by the writer Paul Richardson and his Spanish partner Nacho.

They gather them from small family farms and trees planted in the backyards and *huertas* (vegetable gardens) of the stone houses in the village of Hoyos in Sierra de Gata, Extremadura, where he and Nacho live and make their own olive oil, grow their own vegetables and keep pigs to make hams and sausages.

The lemons are an ancient, heritage variety whose name comes from the fact that they flower once a month instead of once or twice a year.

The trees are planted behind stone walls to protect them from frosts, since this area is only just below the northern limit for growing citrus fruit and the temperature changes dramatically between day and night. However, it is this special microclimate that helps to develop the intense flavour of the rough-skinned lemons and the incredible concentration of aromatic, essential oils in the zest.

When Paul first moved to the village 16 years ago, he was astounded at the way the villagers took the lemons for granted, often not even bothering to harvest them, so that the fruit was left to rot on the ground. He made it his mission to knock on the doors of neighbours and villagers asking to buy the lemons in order to bring over boxes of them to show off in London.

They are truly amazing in puddings such as *arroz con leche* (page 485), and in the restaurants we also grill them and serve them with fish; we use them in cocktails and gin and tonics, and they are excellent for the *limonada* and Easter lemons on page 159.

Arroz Bomba con leche y naranja
Ana's slow-cooked sweet orange
infused rice

This version of rice pudding given to me by Ana Barrera (see page 442) is made with pure Bomba rice (see page 341), and is exceptionally creamy, thanks to the absorption capacity of the rice and the long, slow cooking that reduces the milk to the consistency of double cream, fusing it with the rice grains to give a concentrated flavour and a texture similar to risotto. It is such a simple thing to make: all it needs is steady stirring, a watchful eye and patience.

Ana serves it at room temperature, not chilled, and, if you want to be really indulgent, she advises that it is very good paired with a dark chocolate pudding; however, we like it simply decorated with citrus confit (see page 485). As Ana uses only orange peel in the cooking of the rice, you can echo this by making the confit with just the peel of one orange, rather than that of half an orange and half a lemon, if you prefer.

Serves 4

1.5 litres full-fat milk
100g Bomba rice
75g caster sugar, plus a little extra if necessary
rind of an orange (in one or more big pieces)
a small piece (about 1.5cm) of a vanilla pod
1 cinnamon stick
citrus peel confit (see page 485), to decorate
a little ground cinnamon, to decorate (optional)

Put a litre of the milk into a pan and add the rice, sugar, orange rind, vanilla pod (and seeds) and cinnamon stick. Bring to just under a simmer, then keep at this very low heat for about 2 hours, adding the balance of the milk a little at a time, waiting until the rice absorbs each addition before adding more, and stirring regularly to make sure the mixture doesn't stick. Taste and add more sugar if necessary, as the rice cooks.

The pudding is ready when the milk has reduced right down and is thick and creamy, almost like double cream, and the rice is plump. Leave to cool down to room temperature, then remove the vanilla pod, orange rind and cinnamon stick.

Serve, decorated with the citrus confit, and a little ground cinnamon, if you like.

Almond Confections

I really don't know where the Spanish would be without the almonds that the Moors first introduced in the eighth century. In the autumn on city streets, alongside the chestnut roasters, you will see vendors of *garrapiñadas*: beautiful warm, coppery-coloured, sugared almonds in white paper cones.

If I am lucky, in November a little blue box will arrive from our friend Pilar Sapena (see page 190) and underneath a delicate lace doily will be a collection of tiny, exquisite *panellets*, dusted with cinnamon and white icing sugar. These are the little sweetmeats typical of Catalunya and all of the Levante region, made in a similar way to marzipan, but with the addition of eggs. Pilar's are dainty, half-moon-shaped parcels fondly known as *panellets de aire*, since their almond and sweet potato filling is so incredibly light. Traditionally, *panellets* were made to celebrate All Souls' and All Saints' Day on 1 and 2 November, but luckily for addicts like me, these days you can also buy them all year round. Most typically they are encrusted with pine nuts, but you can also find them flavoured with coffee, chocolate and other ingredients, which also lend their own colours – they are a lovely way to finish a meal.

Then, as the season edges towards Christmas, the shops will be filled with all kinds of almond confections, from whole roasted nuts set in bars with caramel or within large rice-paper discs, to soft, egg-rich bars of *mazapán* (marzipan), praline chocolate bars, large *pan de Cádiz* – almond loaves with confit orange rounds set in the centre – and dozens of different *turrones* (nougats). The most famous of these are the soft blocks of *turrón de Jijona,* which resemble the Middle Eastern *halva,* but are made with ground and nibbed almonds crushed together with honey.

In particular, almonds form the basis of so many sweet tarts which, as they often don't have pastry bases, are more like cakes. The most famous is probably the *tarta de Santiago* from Galicia, which has its origins in medieval times when pilgrims first made the journey (which is still followed) to the cathedral at Santiago de Compostela, where the remains of St James are buried. It is made only with almonds, sugar and eggs, and traditionally a stencil of the cross of the order of the saint is laid on the top of the cooled tart before it is dusted heavily with icing sugar, so that when the stencil is lifted the shape of the cross stands out boldly.

Personally, I have never been able to resist any kind of almond cake or pudding, and throughout the Levante and the islands of Mallorca, Menorca, Ibiza and Formentera I have also enjoyed many local versions of the almond tart/cake, some of which do have pastry bases and some have the inspired addition of fruit as well as spice. Often in the islands the filling is aromatised with mint in a similar way to the cheesecake on page 484. So rather than include the usual *tarta de Santiago* in this chapter I have chosen a couple of favourite variations.

While the details of the recipes may differ, the key to success is always the quality of the almonds. We always use Marcona almonds (see page 90), as although they are expensive, they are wonderfully creamy, with a high oil content.

Different cooks have their own preferences as to how to work with them, whether to choose blanched almonds or ones with the skins left on to add more colour, or whether to grind them rather than blitz them, to give the tart more texture. Ultimately, it is up to you to experiment and find the method you like best.

Tarta de almendra con naranja
Orange and almond cake

This recipe from Ana Barrera's Madrid restaurant is in a class of its own: moist, flour-free and citrussy. Ana recommends serving the tart with vanilla ice cream and a glass of Moscatel wine or PX sherry.

Serves 8–12

2 medium oranges
2 tablespoons orange liqueur
3 tablespoons olive oil
300g caster sugar
300g almonds, preferably blanched Marcona
2 teaspoons baking powder
6 large eggs
300g butter, well softened, plus
 a little extra for greasing
icing sugar and/or slivers of toasted almonds

Preheat the oven to 180°C/gas 4. Grease and line a 25cm round cake tin with a removable base.

Grate the zest of 1 orange into a large mixing bowl. Peel the orange, cut into slices, discarding any pips, and add to the zest. Add the juice of the second orange to the bowl along with the orange liqueur, olive oil and 4 tablespoons of the sugar and leave to one side.

In a food processor, grind the almonds with the remaining sugar and the baking powder until very fine in texture, almost like flour.

In a separate bowl, beat the eggs until they are lighter in colour and very creamy.

Transfer the orange mixture to a blender and blend until very smooth, then blend in the butter a piece at a time and return the mixture to the mixing bowl. Whisk in the beaten eggs until smooth, then gently but thoroughly stir in the ground almond mixture

Spoon this batter into the prepared cake tin, then put into the preheated oven for about 1 hour, until the cake is set and the sides are pulling away from the tin. It should be a rich, deep golden colour.

Remove from the oven and allow to cool completely in the tin before lifting out.

Dust with icing sugar and/or slivers of toasted almonds.

Torta de almendra
Airy almond cake

In the Casta Diva wine estate kitchen in Parxent, in northern Alicante (see page 190), Pilar Sapena makes this very light sponge cake with unpeeled raw almonds, which she puts through a manual grinder attached to her table. The nuts come through in short worm-like forms speckled with dots of brown almond skin. Pilar says that the grinds, being larger and more uniform than anything she can achieve with a blender, give the cake a more interesting texture. You could also pulse-chop the nuts or put them into a freezer bag and crush them with a rolling pin – though you will end up with quite a high proportion of finely ground almonds as well as rough-chopped. When I made the cake with my daughter, we pulse-chopped the nuts and then sieved off the finer grounds – a bit laborious but worth it. If you prefer less skin, you could substitute half the quantity of almonds with crushed, blanched Marconas.

Although I suggest using a cake tin, Pilar makes her cake in a mould with slanted edges, so that when it is turned out and sprinkled with icing sugar, the sides, rather charmingly, resemble gentle ski slopes.

I must admit I like a little addition of spice in an almond cake, especially as it gives an amazing aroma during baking – so as well as dusting the cake with cinnamon, you could also try the variation that our head chef, Leo, makes at the South Kensington restaurant, replacing the lemon zest with two teaspoons of ground cinnamon and two teaspoons of ground star anise, added with the flour.

Serves 10–14

12 eggs, separated
480g caster sugar, plus ½ teaspoon
grated zest of 1 lemon
2 level tablespoons strong white flour
1 teaspoon baking powder
tiniest pinch of salt
500g ground almonds, skin on (preferably grind your own, see left)
icing sugar and ground cinnamon, for dusting

Preheat the oven to 180°C/gas 4.

Line the base and sides of a loose-bottomed or release-spring cake tin (30cm in diameter and 6cm deep) with baking paper.

In a large bowl, beat the egg yolks with the caster sugar and lemon zest until they are quite light in colour.

In a separate bowl, whip the egg whites until they form snowy peaks, then add the ½ teaspoon of sugar slowly, continuing to whip, until firm and glossy.

Gently fold the egg whites into the egg yolk mixture. Sift in the flour, baking powder and salt, and fold in, together with the almonds.

Spoon into the prepared cake tin and smooth the top. Bake for around 45 minutes, then turn up the heat to 200°C/gas 6 for a further 15 minutes, until golden and a skewer inserted into the centre comes out clean (the cake will probably colour quite early during baking, so be sure to use a skewer to check so that you know it is ready).

Turn out and leave to cool on a rack, then dust with icing sugar and a little cinnamon.

Helado de Manchego
Manchego cheese ice cream

HELADOS
Ice creams

Spanish-inspired ice creams made with British milk and cream are heavenly, and ever since Rupert and I were given an ice-cream churner as a present, they have become a big feature of our summers at home.

Esperanza Añonuevo Heys originally created this recipe for our London Bridge tapas bar and now we serve it at our Brindisa Food Rooms. Although Manchego cheese sounds an unlikely ingredient in ice cream, it works beautifully, especially if you choose a young, creamy-textured one.

Makes 800ml

250g semi-cured or young Manchego cheese, finely grated
300ml full-fat milk
5 egg yolks (from large eggs)
100g caster sugar
150ml single cream

Put the grated cheese into a mixing bowl.

Pour half the milk into a saucepan and bring to a simmer. Remove from the heat and stir into the cheese. Keep the saucepan to one side.

In a second mixing bowl, beat the egg yolks with the sugar until thick and creamy. Whisk in the remaining milk and the single cream.

Pour this mixture into the saucepan and heat gently, stirring all the time until you have a smooth custard.

Take off the heat and stir into the cheese and milk mixture, combining well. Allow the mixture to cool, then cover with clingfilm and put into the fridge for 2 hours.

Churn in an ice-cream maker. This will produce a soft ice cream. For firmer ice cream, transfer to a container and freeze for 2 hours.

Helado de regaliz
Liquorice ice cream

Our head chef, Leo, created this to go with the poached pears on page 476, but it stands up really well in its own right. Since I have always adored liquorice sweets I happily embraced this recipe. It is best to use a good-quality liquorice candy of the kind you would find at a health food shop or market stall (such as the Calabrian stall at Borough Market).

Makes 800ml

5 egg yolks (from large eggs)
100g caster sugar
50g liquorice candy, cut into very small pieces
450ml full-fat milk
200ml double cream

Beat the egg yolks and sugar in a mixing bowl until thick and creamy.

Put the liquorice, milk and cream into a pan and heat gently, stirring until the liquorice melts, then take off the heat and slowly add to the egg and sugar mixture, whisking continuously until smooth.

Return to the pan and heat gently, stirring all the time until you have a smooth custard. Remove from the heat and transfer to a bowl. Allow the mixture to cool, then cover with clingfilm and put into the fridge for 2 hours.

Churn in an ice-cream maker. This will produce a soft ice cream. For firmer ice cream, transfer to a container and freeze for 2 hours.

Helado de azafrán
Saffron ice cream

When our former Brindisa chef Esperanza worked in the London Bridge kitchen we had fun one day making saffron ice cream with both Iranian and La Mancha saffron and comparing the results. Both were excellent, but the La Mancha saffron had the edge, particularly in terms of the wonderful aroma it gave to the ice cream. So I would say La Mancha saffron is the ideal, but otherwise use whichever you happen to have; just make sure that the threads are not too old or they will have lost some of their power.

Makes 800ml

350ml full-fat milk
350ml single cream
100g caster sugar
20 saffron threads
5 egg yolks (from large eggs)

Heat the milk, cream and sugar in a pan, stirring frequently until the mixture just starts to simmer. Remove from the heat and stir in the saffron.

Cover the pan and leave to stand for 4 hours at room temperature. Strain the mixture into a mixing bowl.

In a separate bowl, beat the egg yolks, then whisk into the saffron mixture. Cover the bowl with clingfilm and put into the fridge for 2 hours.

Churn in an ice-cream maker. This will produce a soft ice cream. For firmer ice cream, transfer to a container and freeze for 2 hours.

Helado de turrón
Nougat ice cream

A delicate, sand-coloured ice cream.

Makes 800ml

150g soft *turrón de Jijona*,
** chopped into small pieces**
200ml double cream
350ml full-fat milk
100g caster sugar
5 egg yolks (from large eggs)

Put the chopped *turrón* into a bowl with the double cream and stir until the *turrón* is coated.

Warm the milk and sugar in a pan over a gentle heat until the sugar has just dissolved. Remove from the heat and whisk in the egg yolks.

Return the pan to the hob and heat gently, stirring all the time until you have a smooth custard. Remove from the heat and pour on to the cream and *turrón*, stirring well to combine. Allow the mixture to cool, then cover with clingfilm and put into the fridge for 2 hours.

Churn in an ice-cream maker. This will produce a soft ice cream. For firmer ice cream, transfer to a container and freeze for 2 hours.

QUESO

Cheese

Brindisa began with cheese, and it is largely through the many wonderful, engaging cheese-makers I have met, listened to for long hours, and become friends with over the years that I have come to know Spain's more secret, remote and hidden landscape, its local traditions and foods. Many are mentioned or profiled throughout this book, as they have introduced me to far more than the skills of cheese-making, inviting me to cook with them and generously sharing their family recipes.

The culture of traditional cheese-making is unique: not only can it keep us in touch with the land and the seasons but it is a constant reminder of the determination, dedication and often courage required of the small-scale farmer or artisan. Nurturing a cheese with real personality and quality is '*muy sacrificado*', a challenge that demands daily uncompromising commitment and often an extended family network.

The history of cheese in Spain varies depending on who you talk to. The Basque country makes the oldest claim, dating it as far back as 8000 BC. Some give credit to Moorish technology, others insist that the real knowledge of cheese-making was spread across the country by monks. What is certain is that by Roman times, the process was already well understood. The writer on agriculture Columella, who was born in Cádiz, includes in his book *De Re Rustica* clear instructions about rennet coagulation using crushed green pine nuts, thistle, fig tree sap or thyme. He explains the pressing of the curds in wicker baskets, the process of salting manually or in brine, then ageing the cheese on wooden shelves, noting that 'this kind of cheese can even be exported beyond the sea'.

Spain boasts hundreds of varieties of cheeses made from sheep's, goat's and cow's milk. Since this is a country of vastly diverse ecological conditions, these often determine both the animal and the breed which can best adapt to a particular area. The local climate and the type of micro-organisms which act on the curds will also traditionally have an effect on the style, appearance of cheese produced and the kind of maturing process it undergoes. Many of the shapes and patterns that pertain to a particular cheese were originally formed by whatever local material was available for making moulds, such as the ceramic bowls typical of the Levante coastline, or the carved wood and sycamore leaves often used in the mountains.

Until the eighties, however, the majority of cheeses were not known or valued beyond the immediate vicinity in which they were produced, let alone in the UK and abroad. After 1975, when Spain opened up to foreign trade following Franco's death, local produce tended to be looked down on in favour of imported, often industrially made foods promoted for their consistency, milder flavours, smooth textures and their aura of improved hygiene. So processed cheese began appearing on shop counters, along with the likes of imported sunflower and soya oils, marketed as superior to olive oil. The first official listing of Spain's cheeses by the Ministry of Agriculture was printed in 1969 and included forty-eight varieties, but the government's food safety authorities continually closed down unregistered or illegal dairies and insisted that any new ones must use only pasteurised milk. As a result, many of the famous cheeses of northern Spain disappeared almost entirely, and indigenous breeds of cows were replaced by Friesian herds which produced higher volumes of milk, but with little of the character needed to maintain the quality of traditional cheeses.

In spite of this repression, however, unpasteurised artisan cheeses continued to be sold in small village markets in rural areas such as Asturias, Andalucía, Galicia and the Canaries, where local authorities would turn a blind eye so long as there were no outbreaks of food poisoning or disease in the herds.

Then, after years of totalitarian government, the early eighties heralded a resurgence of traditional culture, reflected in the formation of the first association of artisan cheese-makers. In 1981 Roncal cheese from the Navarran Pyrenees became the first Spanish cheese to be awarded the status of PDO, the EU scheme which protects particular, distinctive regional and traditional foods, and by 1989 a total of eighty-one cheeses had been officially rediscovered, twenty-seven of which achieved PDO status. In that year the first cheese fair was staged in Trujillo, giving local producers and *afinadores* (specialist maturers) an outlet for their cheeses.

1989 was also the year that, in the fledgling days of Brindisa, my brother, Mark, and I began looking for Spanish cheeses to bring into the UK. We were really ahead of our time, as there was limited distribution beyond the main cities and it was a big challenge to decide what, and how much, to buy, and then where to sell it.

The regulatory council for each PDO determines the rules, standards and controls that will govern its producers according to six basic criteria, which are: that the cheese needs to be recognised by the name of the area in which it originates; it must display qualities that reflect the geography and climate in which it is produced; the cheese and the milk from which it is made must pertain to a particular territory; the raw material needs to have particular characteristics, for example, the dairy animals must be of a certain breed; the milk and cheese must be produced according to particular methods; and there must be a system of control and a guarantee of origin and quality on the label.

Every batch of cheese that is made must be checked and analysed and once approved will be awarded the stamp and/or label that carries the logo of the PDO, and a number relating to the specific dairy, so that each cheese is traceable.

There is no doubt that the PDOs of Spain have helped enormously to give Spanish cheeses the support and identity that they needed, both at home and abroad. However, the system leaves big gaps and pockets of land where very good cheeses are made that do not have the PDO identity. The stamp cannot always acknowledge the difference between a relatively industrial cheese and the produce of an artisan dairy which places great importance on forging an important, sustainable relationship with the environment, and takes great care over the quality of life and feed afforded to their dairy herds. Nor can it recognise the endlessly different and fascinating nuances that a skilled cheese-maker can achieve.

Of course, one of the constant issues facing the cheese industry in Spain, as all over Europe, is how to balance the introduction of modern chilled facilities and provide high-quality products at more reasonable prices, while preserving cherished handed-down traditions and artisan techniques. In many areas, in these tougher economic times, smaller cheese-makers are once again having to fight for their existence against the dominance of the big dairies, who want milk volumes on a massive scale from animals bred to produce quantity over quality. This brings down the price of milk, making it harder for those farmers of traditional breeds who produce lower volumes of higher-quality milk to maintain a viable place in the market. As a consequence, in some areas traditional farming and shepherding jobs are in danger of being wiped out for good.

At Brindisa, we see it as our mission to discover and support these small, often remote dairies wherever we can, and the following is a selection – by no means exhaustive – of some of the ones that we and our customers most enjoy, together with some suggestions for the wines, and/or fruit and nut accompaniments which enhance the eating experience.

Some of these cheeses are only ever with us in the UK for a short seasonal visit and not very widely available, but there has been an explosion of artisan cheese shops in Spain, even in the smallest provincial towns, so if you are there it is worth seeking some of them out and, of course, there will be many, many other local ones to explore.

'traditional blues and some very buttery soft cheeses'

Spain's traditional blue cheeses all come from the north, as do some very buttery, soft cheeses. The green valleys and humid meadows stretch around the coastal regions, and Galicia, Asturias, León and Cantabria in the north-west all benefit from abundant rainfall and plenty of land on which to graze dairy cattle, and small herds of sheep and goats too. The crags of the Picos de Europa mountains, with their unique eroded limestone landscape and some of the deepest gorges and caves in Europe, offer their steep pastures to hardened shepherds.

Picos de Europa blues

The farmers of the Picos de Europa mountains have moved their cattle herds around these rich pastures for centuries, diversifying into mixed herds including sheep and goats. The milk from any combination of these animals can be used to make the cheese – although cow's milk has predominated over time. The cheeses were originally pressed and salted by hand and wrapped in sycamore leaves so they were easier to handle, as their rind became slippery and sticky during maturation in the region's natural, damp mountain caves, rich with the *Penicillium roqueforti* mould which would penetrate the cheese and give it its distinctive blue-green veins.

Some, like Gamonéu, are made in tiny quantities, and are often only found within the Picos de Europa mountains.

As well as serving these blue cheeses as they are, throughout the Brindisa kitchens we use them a great deal in salads with walnuts and beetroot, or endive; in sauces for cuts of Basque beef, or to add to pumpkin soup.

Cabrales PDO (cow's milk or mixed milk, i.e. cow's, sheep's and goat's), raw

This is an artisan cheese still produced in a traditional way, but it is not one for the fainthearted: you love or hate it. The thin, muddy rind of the cheese is sticky and bumpy, with a fetid aroma (think silage and fermented fruit), and although the mottled, yellow-white interior, with its veins of green-blue, can be crumbly in texture when young, it becomes creamy as it ages. It has a strong flavour that can almost burn the palate, with a persistent aftertaste, and as it ages it can become completely blue, with almost no yellow paste. In the old days, there was much *machismo* associated with eating very old, rank Cabrales, and if it had some *gusanos* (maggots) inside, so much the better! Thankfully, those days have gone, but a piece of Cabrales should still always be offered at the end of a selection of cheeses.

The cheeses are matured in deep, damp limestone caves for a minimum of two months, and each cave has natural running water, a south-facing opening and an exit to allow the *soplados* (breezes) to flow through and create the blue veins without the need to pierce the paste. The cheeses are a slightly irregular round shape and can be identified easily, as these days they are wrapped in sheets of deep green foil to evoke the sycamore leaves that were originally used. The sycamore leaf also appears on the PDO label along with the serial number of the cheese.

Cabrales is best paired with a sweet sherry like Pedro Ximénez, or a fruity cider, and we like to serve it with a slice from one of the artisan wheels of pressed prunes and walnuts made for us in Catalunya.

Valdeón PGI (blue, mainly cow's milk), pasteurised

The village of Posada de Valdeón, which gives the cheese its name, is on the south side of the Picos mountains in the province of León, surrounded by high passes, rushing mountain rivers and spectacular jagged peaks, and the dairy is the only industry in its valley.

The cheese has a rough, grey rind with tiny specks of red and blue mould, and inside the paste is a pale creamy colour with veins of greeny-blue mould running through it. It is made all year round, with pasteurised cow's milk blended with a little goat's milk.

The dairy has managed to move very capably from traditional production to a more industrial, modern set-up, so that while the cheese is still wrapped in sycamore leaves, it is matured (for at least a month and a half) in modern curing chambers rather than caves. The conditions are not as humid and although this produces a less intense flavour, the creamy freshness of the cheese has proved very popular. It is outstandingly well balanced, strong but not overwhelming, salty but not overly so, and it is fatty and melts in the mouth, leaving an elegant aftertaste.

Valdeón is best paired with a sweet wine such as port or a robust white Rioja and served with walnuts and dried fruits.

Picón Bejes Tresviso PDO (cow's milk or mixed milk), raw

The name Picón indicates the sharp flavour of this ancient blue cheese, and Bejes and Tresviso are the names of the two villages around which it is produced.

Picón Bejes Tresviso has the lowest production of any PDO cheese, since the area is so isolated and hard to reach. It is made from a blend of cow's, sheep's and goat's milk – predominantly cow's milk – and matured for a minimum of three months. Traditionally, it was matured in abandoned mines and natural, damp caves but our current supplier prefers to exert more control, maturing his cheeses in a small modern curing chamber high in the mountains.

The *Penicillium roqueforti* which forms the greeny-blue veins of mould is allowed to penetrate the paste naturally, and, unusually, the slightly irregular round cheeses (varying from 1–3kg and 12–13cm in height) are never turned, resulting in an uneven blueing, darker at the bottom and lighter at the top. The rind that forms is a beautiful pale orange, slightly sticky with rich yeasty aromas, but the interior is pale yellow and has an open, creamy texture and an enjoyable balance of bite, butter and salt.

As with Cabrales, the cheeses were originally wrapped in sycamore leaves, which has given way to foil – in this case, gold.

Picón Bejes Tresviso pairs well with sweet wines such as Moscatel and dried fruit and nuts.

La Peral (cow's milk), pasteurised

Antonio León's family, now in its third generation, adapted a family recipe in the 1920s when they built the modern La Peral dairy, where the cheese is made on a small scale using pasteurised cow's milk. It is matured for two months and has a sticky yellow rind with a pale yellow interior of glistening curds speckled with blue veins, a gentle omelette-y aroma and a creamy, briny flavour that gradually develops into a clean, fresh, mild blue taste.

La Peral pairs very well with aged white Riojas or Asturian cider, and is excellent with forest fruits such as blackberries and hazelnuts.

Fresh cow's milk cheeses

Tetilla PDO (cow's milk), mostly pasteurised
The original home of this cheese is the Galician province of La Coruña, but now it can be produced throughout Galicia. *Tetilla* is the diminutive of *teta*, meaning small breast, and refers to the cheese's distinctive shape, which comes from the mould, similar to a ladle, in which it is made (it may also be called *de perilla*, 'round pear-shaped'). Most Tetilla is now made in modern dairies, although a number of artisan makers still survive. On rare occasions you might find unpasteurised cheeses made from the milk of Friesian or Gallega cattle which feed on natural scrub and pastures, plus fodder crops such as corn, beets and turnips. It is aged for just seven days and is soft, elastic and straw-coloured, with a smooth, waxy, yellow rind and a mild, milky sweet flavour and buttery aroma that make it very accessible and popular. Tetilla pairs well with fruity white wines like Godello and it is served most often with quince or apple paste. It also makes a very good sandwich with *piquillo* peppers, or try it melted over slices of *lacón* (wet-cured ham from Galicia) or gammon.

Pasiego de Las Garmillas and La Jarradilla (cow's milk), pasteurised
Pasiego is originally made in the Cantabrian valleys through which the River Pas makes its way to the Cantabrian Sea. It is sold at about 15 days old, and has a subtle, beguiling and enticing character. The interior is soft and fatty, with an aroma of fresh yogurt and mountain streams, and the flavour is surprisingly mild.

It comes in different guises. The cheese made by Álvaro Carral at La Jarradilla, his wife's family dairy in Barcenilla near Villacarriedo, is tall, with a slightly firmer texture and the hint of a rind, whereas the one from Las Garmillas in Ampuero is a fragile, primitive patty with no rind that comes wrapped in wax paper.

The cheese is good for breakfast, eaten with crusty bread or fresh fruit. It also combines very well with the savoury flavours of anchovies and *piquillo* peppers, together with a glass of dry cider.

Rey Silo (cow's milk), raw
At the Rey Silo dairy in Pravia, named after the eighth-century king who set up the Asturian court there, Ernesto Madera López has devoted his energies to bringing the ancient Afuega'l Pitu cheese recipes of Asturias into modern times. These are mentioned in texts dating back to the eighteenth century, and the cheeses were usually made on the farm with milk from local dairy herds of Friesians or indigenous breeds. Some were formed by the milk fermenting spontaneously in the heat and were bound in a knotted cloth, while others had animal rennet added and the firmer curd would be shaped in a perforated mould. They could be fresh or briefly matured, pyramid or tri-conical shaped, or they might be rounded like a large ox-heart tomato, with a rippled rind formed using the culture, *Geotrichum candidum*.

Ernesto's cheeses are diligently crafted into flattened cone shapes and matured for up to 20 days in cellars on the banks of the Nalón river. The cheese comes in two styles: white or red (thanks to the addition of *pimentón*), and inside the rinds, with their entrancing patterns, they have a quite unusually compact texture, a little like mashed potato, with a fresh aroma of white cabbage and a sweet flavour reminiscent of white chocolate (the red version also has a pronounced spicy finish): utterly delicious.

Both cheeses are best paired with medium-bodied white wines such as Riojas, while the red cheeses would go very well with bigger whites such as Mas d'en Compte from Celler Cal Pla in Priorat, or Godello whites from Galicia. I also tasted them with local cider, which was an excellent match.

They are fine with fruit, but also excellent in cooking. Many of Spain's leading chefs use them in delicate foams and sauces and pair them with fish and shellfish, from anchovies and sardines, to tuna tartare or mussels.

Mountain sheep's milk cheeses

Idiazábal DOP (sheep's milk), raw

Idiazábal is a shepherd's cheese that is produced throughout the whole of the Basque country and the north of Navarra in the mountains and valleys such as Urbia, Aralar, Urbasa and Gorbea. On a visit to the region in the company of some British and American cheese experts, we ate at a local restaurant, where to finish the meal we were given a cheeseboard of half a dozen Idiazábal cheeses from local makers, which, despite their similar appearance, all tasted remarkably individual. One, in particular, stood out, made with milk from a breed of sheep known as Carranzana, which a father and daughter team were trying to save from extinction – proof of the worth of keeping special breeds for small-scale cheese production.

Originally the shepherds herded the sheep up into the mountains in the summer, to enjoy the fresh pastures. Here they made the cheese and then in October they would guide their herds down again to the valley of Goierri, where they sold the cheeses at the market in Idiazábal village, hence the name.

Since 2008, these small-scale shepherd cheese-makers have established their own Artzai Gazta PDO, which further enhances their Idiazábal identity, setting specific criteria for artisan production. This dictates that a maker can only use milk from his own herds of sheep, he must also make his own rennet and ultimately control the whole cycle from animal husbandry to marketing the finished cheese.

The hard cheeses, pressed in moulds, and distinguished by the red band on their label, are made from the raw milk of the Latxa sheep, a breed found only in the Basque country and next-door Navarra, which are easily recognised by their long straggly coats. They are well adapted to these high, alpine pastures, have a healthy appetite and are excellent producers of milk.

The cheeses are very compact, generally made in 1kg or 3kg rounds. They are aged for a minimum of two months, bone white in colour, and the flavour is pronounced and pleasantly fatty in the mouth, with a caramel sweetness from the ewe's milk which begins modestly and ends with a touch of salt and acidity.

The cheeses can be smoked or unsmoked, but most commercially made ones are smoked. Only natural woods are permitted, and the beech and hawthorn that is typically used gives a bronze colour to the smooth, oily rind and allows the mild sweet taste of smoke to hover over the distinctive flavour of sheep's cheese.

It is said that this style came about almost by accident, because the shepherds would cure and store their cheeses in the rafters of the huts known as *txabolas* that were dotted around the mountains and where the shepherds would stay. The *txabolas* were provided by the Basque government but were not permitted to have chimneys, as this would denote a permanent home. So when the shepherd lit his daily wood fire in the hut on which to cook, the cheeses would become smoked naturally.

Both cheeses also play an important role in local cooking. The smoked version is often used with blue fish or red meats, while the unsmoked one is better in soufflés or cheesecakes.

Idiazábals pair well with the local white wine, Txacoli, or dry cider, and are good served with walnuts and quince paste.

Roncal DOP (sheep's milk), raw

The environment and climate of the Roncal valley is similar to the alpine conditions of the Idiazábal region, in the neighbouring Basque country (see opposite), and shares the same breed of mountain-hardy Latxa sheep, whose milk makes an extremely handsome cheese with a persistent and interesting flavour.

At the Larra dairy, an extraordinary concern run by artisan shepherd-cheese-makers in an ultra-modern, solar-powered environment, the curd, once cut, is manually pressed into moulds, originally of beech wood, then salted and matured – preferably for at least four months, though the best are aged for up to 12 months. Once matured, the rind becomes slightly darkened by the natural moulds that are a sign of an excellent cellar-aged cheese. The interior is very firm and dense, and its sheepy flavour has a touch of burnt caramel and a strong piquancy that lingers on the finish, with hints of dried fruit. Individual cheeses can generally range from 2 to 3 kilos in weight, although smaller cheeses can now be found.

Roncal pairs well with full-bodied red wines from Navarra and La Rioja and is good in cooking, for example, in a gratin of artichokes or grated over asparagus.

Pyrenean cheeses

El Benasqués (cow's milk), raw

The cheese takes its name from the valley in which it is produced, within the national park of Posets-Maladeta in the Huesca area of the Pyrenees, where the flora and fauna of the pasture are exceptional. Amado Ballarín and Carmen Demur use only raw milk from their own herd and mature the lightly pressed cheese for 2–4 months in caves beneath their house. It has a natural velvety rind whose aromas are reminiscent of mushrooms and cool damp wood, while the flavour of the cheese is distinctive and enticing, sweet with milky, buttery tones and a hint of raw hazelnuts.

It is mainly eaten before dinner with drinks, or afterwards, and pairs perfectly with the red wine of the area, such as a Crianza from Enate.

Tou dels Til.lers and Tupí de Sort (cow's milk), raw

These cheeses are made in the town of Sort, in an area of the Pyrenees in the north-west of Catalunya called Pallars Sobirà, which I first discovered in the early nineties. It is a beautiful region, deep in the mountains, where shepherds guide their sheep over the high passes of Los Encantados peaks. It is a favourite place for horse-riding and hiking, where river experts know every turn and rock of the roaring rapids enjoyed by canoeists.

Agricultural engineer Josep Font, together with a group of Pyrenean cattle farmers, started the artisan Tros de Sort dairy in 1995 in order to add extra value to their outstanding unpasteurised milk. The cheeses range from hard, pressed cheese to lactic, soft cheese such as Tou dels Til.lers, which is similar to a Camembert.

One of the most interesting styles is Tupí, named after the little ceramic pot it is presented in. It is a strong, twice-fermented paste, originally designed to use up leftover cured cheese, which is broken up and fermented again with olive oil and alcohol so that the bubbling yeasts turn the dry cheese into a creamy spread.

Tupí can only really be paired with sweeter drinks such as cider or dessert wines, while the creamy, mild Tou dels Til.lers goes very well with the red wines of Navarra or Somontano.

Garrotxa (goat's milk), pasteurised

Garrotxa was created in the eighties by a group of city dwellers who opted for a rural life, re-inventing the style of cheese originally made in the Comarca of La Garrotxa from the pasteurised milk of Murcia–Granada goats. These animals thrive on the green, herb-filled slopes of the foothills of the Pyrenees and the lowlands of Tarragona. The cheeses are now made in a number of small dairies and most are identified by the producer's name. At Brindisa we work with Toni Chueca and his wife, Maria Rosa Heras, of La Bauma dairy, just outside Borredà in the forested mountains of Berguedà.

The Catalan climate is temperate but with significant humidity, which helps create *pell florida*, the fluffy, velvety-grey bloom typical of most Garrotxa cheeses. They are semi-cured and cylindrical. Inside, the compact paste is snow-white with a slightly soft and elastic spring to it. It has a mild goaty, yet floral, aroma and taste. At four weeks old the cheese is very creamy; then, as it ages, the paste close to the rind becomes more complex and intense while the very centre retains its moisture, developing gorgeous savoury notes of herb and mushroom.

Garrotxa is produced all year round and can be served marinated in herb-infused oil, lightly fried, or with hazelnuts and plums. It pairs well with Verdejos and Penedès white wines.

Ermesenda and Castellot (cow's milk), raw

The Mas d'Eroles dairy was founded by Salvador Maura, an engineer who worked for the regional Ministry of Agriculture in Barcelona for many years before deciding to move to the mountains and start his own dairy on a milk-producing farm in Adrall, close to Andorra. He experiments with a range of recipes, putting his own interpretation on to them. All are made with raw cow's milk, and matured in caves.

Ermesenda is a large round cheese, best aged for around three months. It has a natural washed rind and a slightly elastic, close texture. There are aromas of wild mushrooms and the initial sweet flavour is both fruity and honeyed. As the cheese matures the flavours become full-bodied and meaty.

Castellot, also at its best at around three months old, is inspired by the Italian technique used to make Castelmagno cheese (in both Italian and Catalan the name means 'magnificent Castle'). This is known colloquially as *pasta rota*, in which the paste is kept in a mould for a day, then crushed and salt is added before it is pressed a second time.

The paste is yellow and has some small eyes. The taste at the beginning is lemony, with interesting vegetal notes reminiscent of nettles, intensified since the fat and cream has drained away, and the texture is close but crumbly.

All the Mas d'Eroles cheeses are extremely good with red wines from Catalunya, such as those from the Empordà *bodega* Castillo Perelada – my personal favourite is their 5 Fincas Reserva.

Membrillo/Codonyat
Quince paste

Quince is one of the flavours of Spain that my husband, Rupert, says takes him straight back to his childhood in Santorcaz, near Madrid, because when the fruit was in season there would always be a big bowlful and the aroma would fill the house. While in the UK quince might be made into desserts, and in the Middle East it is a favourite ingredient in spiced meat stews, in Spain the fruit is chiefly turned into the rich fruity paste *membrillo*. Thick slices of *membrillo* sandwiched between María biscuits was Rupert's favourite playground snack to take to school.

And while some chefs might use *membrillo* in a more adventurous way – Sam and Sam Clark, of Moro, use a layer in their *tarta de Santiago* (almond tart) – in Spain people generally prefer to eat it in the time-honoured way, with cheese. It is especially beautiful paired with a fresh white Queso de Burgos, made with sheep's milk, a fresh goat's cheese such as Cabra del Tiétar Fresco, *requesón* (pressed ricotta), or yogurt.

I met our very first supplier of *membrillo* (known as *codonyat* in Catalunya), over 20 years ago in Plaza del Pi in Barcelona, which is a small square on the opposite side of the Ramblas to the Boqueria market, where a small group of artisans used to set up their stalls. Among them was Víctor, with his ponytail and big smile, selling blocks of deep coppery-amber fruit paste.

At that time most commercial quince paste was made in the south, around Córdoba, and was quite yellow, smooth and sugary, in the style known as *dulce de membrillo*. By contrast, Víctor's *codonyat* was of the style known as *carne* (meat) *de membrillo* and was much closer to the paste people made at home: deeper in colour, more fleshy and fibrous, with a good grain. It was beautifully balanced and not too sweet. It was the best quince paste I had ever tasted.

Víctor was a real pioneer, who had run one of the best fruit and veg stores in Barcelona, called El Pèsol (the Green Pea), but moved out of the city to make his *codonyat* in Corbera de Llobregat. All he had was a tiny space with a fridge for the quince pulp, a couple of jam-making machines and the help of a beautiful girl who used a domestic iron to gently and very lightly heat-seal the wrapping around the quince once the blocks had set. Finally, it was presented in simple wooden boxes at a time in Spain when to show off a food so elegantly was quite revolutionary.

Víctor has diversified over the years and makes other pastes with fig, or orange and tomato, and I have also seen industrial producers put squares of different flavours together in blocks that look like a Battenberg cake, which I find overly sweet and more about pleasing the eye than the palate. For me, the classic quince *membrillo/codonyat* will always be the best.

How to choose *membrillo*
There is a vast variation in the colour, texture and flavour of *membrillo*, from grainy and dark to light and golden; from fruity to sweet; some so thick you can slice them, some so soft they are spoonable.

You can buy very good quince paste in jars, which can be kept at ambient temperature, but these tend to have higher levels of sugar in them. Personally, I always prefer *membrillo* sliced from a block. Not only does it look more beautiful, but the texture is more unctuous and juicy. Block *membrillo* is best kept in the fridge, as it retains its juiciness better.

More industrially made *membrillos*, generally from Córdoba, tend to be yellower in colour and sweeter than artisan ones, which are usually a deeper coppery orange that feels more reminiscent of the fruit.

You want the paste to have some texture, but not be too fibrous.

Since quince has a very short season, most producers will purée and freeze as much fruit

Membrillo
Quince paste

as possible in order to provide *membrillo* all year round. However, some makers will also buy in quinces from the southern hemisphere, especially Chile (though this won't be apparent from the label). While this isn't necessarily a bad thing, as with the very best jams, the highest-quality *membrillo* will be made with the very best local fruit, in small batches.

Some are made with fructose, rather than sugar, which doesn't taste different but just offers an alternative.

Like making your own jam, there is a special satisfaction in achieving the complexity of flavour and texture of *membrillo* in your own kitchen. It is an amazing way to preserve fruit, and if kept well wrapped in greaseproof paper in a larder or a fridge the *membrillo* should easily keep for up to six months. This recipe is simple, but be prepared for plenty of stirring.

Makes about 1kg

1.5kg quinces
rind of 1 lemon, cut in strips
1 cinnamon stick
about 1kg sugar

Put the quinces (which will be rock hard) into a large pan, add enough water to cover, together with the lemon rind and cinnamon, bring to the boil, then cook for around 40 minutes. When the quinces are tender you should be able to push a skewer easily through the centre of the fruit.

Drain the quinces, leave to cool and discard the lemon rind and cinnamon. Peel and core the fruit, keeping the seeds and skin on one side.

The seeds and skin are high in pectin, which helps the *membrillo* to set, so put these into a sieve and push through with a wooden spoon. Add this pulp to the cooked fruit.

Now weigh the cooked fruit and add the same weight in sugar. Either mash to a smooth paste by hand or use a blender. Put the fruit and sugar mixture back into the pan and heat to just below boiling, stirring regularly for at least 40 minutes to allow any excess water to evaporate.

Meanwhile, line a loaf tin with baking paper, and when the mixture is ready, spoon it in, smooth the top and put into the fridge to set overnight.

If by any chance your *membrillo* hasn't set, put the loaf tin into a low oven (about 90°C) for an hour or so to let more of the water evaporate.

CENTRAL SPAIN

'some of the most recognised cheeses in Spain'

The central area of Spain consists of two high *mesetas* (plateaux) – Castilla y León and Castilla La Mancha – with Madrid sitting between the two. These have always been home to numerous hardy sheep breeds such as the Merina, Castellana, Churra and Ojalada, which thrive in the very dry climate that ranges from -10°C in winter, with icy winds coming off the snowy Guadarrama mountains, to 40°C heat in summer.

The cheeses produced from the milk of these sheep are some of the most recognised in Spain. Hard-pressed and tyre-like, they fall into two main categories: those made with pure sheep's milk, which can be some of the best cheeses you might ever taste; while those made with a blend of cow and goat's milk, much of which is brought in from outside the region, tend to be everyday cheeses. However, newer prize-winning cheeses made by innovative dairies using only high-quality local goat's milk are now emerging too.

Hard sheep's milk cheeses

Manchego DOP (sheep's milk), pasteurised

There are so many Manchegos – or cheeses calling themselves Manchego – that it is quite easy to be overwhelmed. To make sure you have an authentic Manchego, always check for the PDO label and for the serial number of the cheese, which will be on its base and label. Then try to establish the size of the dairy, which can help identify how far production has been industrialised, since most Manchego is now made in factories using milk that is transported long distances, pasteurised and put through a fully automated production line.

The best cheeses, however, are made with raw milk and have a natural rind. There are still some smaller artisan concerns that produce these, combining manual and modern techniques and using milk that comes from within 30 kilometres of the dairy. These will have *queso manchego artesano* on the label.

All the cheeses are pressed and salted and patterned in the traditional Castilian way, i.e. the sides are imprinted with the zigzag weave of the local esparto grass, which was once used as a plaited belt (*pleitas*) to contain the curds, and the tops and bottoms have the imprint of the wooden boards which were used for pressing. These days, however, plastic moulds are used to create these patterns, rather than grass and wood.

The cheeses stand about 8cm high and 20cm in diameter although smaller ones are now made. The rind can range from natural muddy grey on artisan cheeses through darkish yellow on wax-coated cheeses, to the flat dark brown of some industrial cheeses that have been painted with food-grade paraffin wax. The ivory-coloured

paste inside is speckled with small irregular eyes and the texture is compact and dry, yet creamy and rich in flavour.

Manchego is matured to various stages. At 60 days (the minimum curing time) up to five months it is called semi-cured; from 6–11 months it is cured, and from 12–48 months it is *añejo* (meaning one year) or *Gran Reserva*.

The best Manchego tastes of dry summer grasses, with a hint of roast lamb and caramel and a faint earthy aroma of lanolin. Younger cheeses are buttery and slightly oily on the palate, while older cheeses are granular, with crunchy crystals and a more spicy flavour.

This is a cheese that should be eaten simply with good white bread drizzled with olive oil and maybe a hint of tomato rubbed across it. It pairs best with a *cava* or, alternatively, a Riojan wine, either a hearty red such as Sierra Cantabria from the Eguren family, or an aged white such as Viña Izadi.

As well as certified Manchegos, the region produces many cured sheep's milk cheeses that are sometimes coated with lard and rosemary or other herbs, then wrapped so that as they mature the flavour penetrates right through the paste. Despite not being allowed to call themselves Manchego, they are often elegant, aromatic and every bit as good as a cheese carrying the mark of the DOP. In fact, some people prefer them.

Zamorano DOP (sheep's milk), raw

In the Museo Etnografico (Ethnographic Museum) in Zamora you can see cheese-making utensils that date back 4,000 years, and numerous references in local historical documents, including the archives of two important twelfth-century Cistercian monasteries, Santa María de Moreruela and San Martín de Castañeda, confirm that Zamora has been a consistently important area for sheep farming and cheese-making. It is also a region where the skills of the shepherd are still valued (see page 526).

The traditional sheep of the region are primarily the black-and-white-faced Churra and the pure white Zamoran Castellana, and only the raw milk from these can be used in the cheese. The sheep are nourished on the traditional crops of the region: cereals, pulses and vine cuttings, with certain supplementary foods added to enhance their diet. However, the population has been constantly whittled down as more and more high-volume milk-producing breeds, originally from the Middle East, such as the Awassi and the Assaf, are infiltrating dairy herds.

The Zamorano cheese-makers established their own PDO in 1982 to protect and distinguish their cheese from the other Castilian varieties of Manchego and Castellano, so look for the flower-shaped design of the label. Like Manchego, the cheeses are characterised by the design of the traditional grass *pleitas* and wooden pressing boards, but are deeper and bigger, at about 3kg, and 8–12cm in height and 18–22cm in diameter. The rind has a darker yellow colour, often blackened slightly by moulds, while the interior is an ivory yellow, dense and compact, with the tiniest of eyes spread irregularly throughout. The flavour is long and nutty with a pleasant sharpness on the finish.

Maturation must be for a minimum of 100 days, but can be up to 16 months, and once matured, the cheese can also be cut and marinated in herb-infused olive oil.

Zamorano cheeses, particularly the Gran Reserva from Félix Vicente Pastor, go extremely well with the best bold yet elegant red wines made along the Duero river, such as La Ribera del Duero, Viña Pedrosa and Cillar de Silos; or those from Toro, such as Bodegas Vega Saúco.

Castellano (sheep's milk), raw

The pastures around Palencia and Burgos in Castilla y León are incredible: full of mushrooms, wild flowers, camomile, thyme and other herbs, and the long, slender grass re-grows constantly, as there is a good amount of rain. As a result, the local Churra and Castellana sheep produce excellent intense and aromatic milk, and the three Paramío brothers, who set up the Campos Góticos dairy in Villerías de Campos in Palencia in 1994, are determined to keep their herds intact and respect the traditional recipes.

Their Castellano has a natural rind, traditionally imprinted with the pattern of plaited grass, and combines sweet and piquant flavours, honeyed overtones and a floral aroma. The January and February cheeses will be the best of the year, and while we like the subtle grassy, nutty cheeses that have been matured for 2–4 months, the dairy matures the cheeses for up to 12–15 months and you could even eat them up to 17–20 months, as they don't spoil; on the contrary, the flavours are enhanced with maturity.

Castellano pairs very well with big red wines such as El Gordito or Viña Pedrosa and should be served just as it comes, with crusty white bread or with a slice of pressed fig and almond wheel.

Soft and semi-soft cheeses

Monte Enebro (goat's milk), pasteurised

This unique cheese, which has won many gold medals at international competitions, is the creation of the late Rafael Báez (see page 520). It involves a slow lactic coagulation of the milk, the use of a ladle to cream the curds into the cheese moulds, and the introduction of the blue *Penicillium roqueforti* in the maturing chambers. Here the cheeses stay for 20 days, growing the thinnest of natural, light brown rinds with a rich crust of natural bluish-grey mould that helps retain the creaminess of the cheese and give it an earthy, mushroomy aroma.

The cheeses are shaped like a flattish, rounded log or 'mule's hoof' (*pata de mulo*), about 10cm high and 30cm long. The interior is bright white, with a smooth, semi-soft texture, citrusy creaminess and an intense lingering flavour, distinctly goaty, with complex woody aromas and hints of herbs and fresh hazelnuts that give way to a pungent bite as the cheese ages. Although the cheese is made all year round, production levels vary with the seasons, as only the highest-quality milk is selected. The best time of year for flavour is April to June.

Although the Monte Enebro takes priority, the dairy uses any surplus milk to make a pressed goat's milk cheese (Cabra del Tiétar), which is semi-cured over two months, and has a robust ivory rind, cream-coloured paste and a herbaceous and slightly toffeed flavour.

Both these cheeses go beautifully with fruity white wines such as Verdejos or whites from Galicia. Monte Enebro, in particular, suits a white such as Vega de la Reina from Rueda, while a youthful red such as Rudeles from Ribera del Duero combines well with the acidity of the younger Cabra del Tiétar. We serve Monte Enebro with fresh grapes and orange blossom honey and also use it in many recipes and salads on our menus.

Cremoso de Cañarejal (sheep's milk), raw

This is made in Pollos, Valladolid, by the Santos family, who have been growing cereals and farming sheep for many generations. It is a new cheese made with milk from their 1,800-strong herd of Assaf sheep (a cross between the resilient Israeli breed, Awassi, which is used to arid climates and produces high volumes of milk, and East Friesian). The dairy is based in the National Reserve of Las Riberas de Castronuño in Valladolid province, close to the Duero river where the lush pastures are filled with aromatic wild rosemary, thyme and oregano in the spring and summer. During the winter months the animals' diet is supplemented with straw, grains and cereals, many of which the family grow themselves.

The cheese has balanced sheepy aromas, feels silky on the palate and tastes slightly bitter, but since it is made with vegetarian rennet as opposed to the infusion of cardoon thistle typical of other 'torta' styles, it has a sweeter finish.

Cañarejal goes very well with the elegant soft red and rosé wines of Ribera del Duero, and the 250g Cremoso is a perfect size for serving whole. I like to eat it at room temperature, with the top sliced off so you can spoon the creamy paste on to a cracker, and on our menus we serve the creamy cheese with boiled new potatoes and caperberries.

La Setera (goat's milk), raw

This semi-soft cheese comes from the tiniest of dairies in a remote village in the area of Sayago, Zamora. It is staunchly local, with a limited production and season, and is made by Sarah Groves-Raines, an Englishwoman whose husband, Patxi, is a wine-maker from the Basque country. Sarah makes the cheese with goat's milk collected daily at first light from local herders within 10 kilometres of the dairy. It is cured for about three weeks, which allows it to keep its very fresh character, and it has a stone-coloured rind with a fine grey bloom, a bright white interior, mild flavour and a delicate and smooth finish.

The cheese pairs well with the robust dry red wines of the area of Los Arribes de Duero, made with Juan García grapes, as well as Patxi's own La Setera wines, and is good served with tomato jam (see page 533).

Beato de Tábara (goat's milk), raw

Having farmed and shepherded their own flock of goats in the Sierra de la Culebra for over 30 years, Santiago Lucas León and his sons set up a family dairy in San Martín de Tábara in 2001. He makes his semi-soft artisan cheese to a traditional recipe, but using modern facilities and technology, according to his mantra: '*prima la calidad sobre la cantidad*' (quality before quantity).

The paste is compact and smooth and the cheese is aged for about two and a half months. Its light grey rind looks almost like an inscribed goat's skin and its aroma makes you think of dark cellars, while the bright white paste has a coolness on the palate and a character that invokes the floral meadows where the herds graze.

It is an elegant and excellent cheese with a purity about it that should really be enjoyed simply, with just a Verdejo wine from nearby Rueda for company.

Engineering
Cheese

In 1984 Rafael Báez dreamed of bringing a new identity to the traditional Castilian Pata de Mulo cheese, using pasteurised goat's milk in place of the sheep's milk that is typical of the Valladolid province.

Rafa was a force of nature, an enigma, a man of great spirit and conviction, and we had the privilege of knowing him for more than twenty years. Maybe I recognised in him a kindred spirit who took on a slightly crazy challenge, and pulled it off; after all, how many people retire from a career in engineering at the age of sixty, with a family of eight children, decide to learn a new skill at agricultural college, start up an all-consuming, innovative artisan business, and succeed in creating one of the world's most wonderful cheeses?

Enric Canut, a tutor in artisan cheese-making at the agricultural school Torre Marimon, just outside Barcelona, remembers perfectly the day Rafa walked in in 1982: 'In came a very well-dressed, upright and polite man, who had arrived in his BMW sports car – and this was Rafael. However, he proved himself, within days, to be an honest man of few, but sound, words, responsible and with one big decision in his head: to change his life. He learned fast and made radical decisions. He was on his final adventure – *olé tus huevos!* – what tenacity! He chose to leave the course and start the new path he had carved for himself. He wanted to make a delicious but exceptional cheese that would stand out against all the rest. His decision to change his life was a big one and the cheese would be his companion.'

Two years later Rafa set up his own dairy in the valley of Tiétar in Ávila, below the Sierra de Gredos mountain range, a corner of Spain that he loved, where the climate is mild and the Tiétar and Alberche rivers encourage abundant lush pasture.

On the other, north side of the mountains, sheep predominate, and their milk goes into the local semi-hard pressed Pata de Mulo cheese; however, on the south side, where Rafa built his dairy, the local farmers raise Verata goats close to La Vera to the west, and the Serrana breed towards Madrid in the east, which graze on the fine grasses, wild flowers and herbs, producing wonderful rich milk.

When Rafa arrived, however, most were struggling to maintain their herds on the meagre income they could make from selling the milk, and traditional cheese-making was virtually non-existent.

So Rafa's mission was to pay the farmers well for their exceptional milk, which he planned to make into a completely new handmade lactic cheese, with a mould-ripened crust, that had the shape of the neighbouring Pata de Mulo but was made in a different way, using milk from goats rather than from sheep.

As an engineer, he understood the machinery required, he had the wonderful milk, and he had an unstoppable creative energy, wit, generosity and humour. Though he may have sometimes growled, or fixed you with a piercing glare if you asked boring bureaucratic questions, he loved people, especially women, whom he mostly employed in the dairy, as he believed they have a gentler touch with the delicate curds. So it is fitting that it is now Rafa's cheese-maker daughter Paloma, who worked with her father for over 20 years, who is in charge of the dairy.

'traditional breeds produce very aromatic milk'

The cheeses in this section include favourites from the Mediterranean coast. As it turns northwards the land becomes more temperate, with gentler hills filled with wild herbs and floral shrubs, so the many traditional breeds of goat that are pastured here produce very aromatic milk. When you reach Catalunya the dairies tend to be on a smaller scale, with many of the newer styles of cheese, such as Garrotxa and Montsec, being made by people who have left behind city lives, in search of something simpler and more fulfilling.

Tortas and cremosos

Extremadura, in the south-west corner of Spain, is the home of the famous Merino sheep whose milk defines the flavour of *tortas extremeñas*: round, cake-like, luxuriously creamy cheeses that are traditionally eaten with the tops sliced off and the insides scooped out – ideally they should be served between about 18°C and 22°C, at which temperature they are at their most fluid.

Originally the Merino herds (mostly concentrated around Casar de Cáceres, La Serena, Tierra de Barros and Trujillo) were kept for wool, but they would also provide farming families with milk at its very best – full of nutrients, thick, fatty and aromatic – and they would usually take advantage of the breeding season to collect a little extra milk to make cheese for their own use. However, the Merino milk has such a concentrated flavour that it would often be softened with the milks from other breeds, such as Churra and Lacaune.

Over the years these *tortas* have become some of the most expensive and sought-after cheeses of Spain, but ironically, commercial dairies originally considered them to be *atortado* (collapsed), i.e. their runny texture meant they had failed to mature into semi-hard cheeses, and so they were given away to the local people.

In October 2012 the name *torta* was restricted to those that have PDO status in the region of Casar, and so the many very good cheeses that are made using an identical process, but outside this official area, have to go by the name of *cremosos*, or sometimes *retortas*, as in the case of the Trujillo cheese made by Juan Figueroa (see page 524). In drier microclimates such as La Serena, where they are semi-soft, they are simply known as *quesos*.

Made with raw milk and coagulated slowly, using vegetable rennet extracted from the cardoon thistle, *tortas* and *cremosos* have a distinctive earthy flavour and the gentle bitter finish typical of thistle rennet cheeses. They are so in demand that the cheese-makers and shepherds of the region are actively pulling

together to find ways to increase production without compromising quality. They now provide better folds and more abundant food for the animals, and synchronise their breeding periods so that milk is available throughout the year.

We were once told that the way to serve this cheese in Spain is after leaving it in the boot of the car on a hot summer afternoon, but an easier option is to take the cheese out of the fridge overnight, or long enough to bring it to room temperature. It needs to be runny enough so that when you slice off the top, you can spoon it out of its wall of rind on to good bread – or you can dip breadsticks into it.

Barros (sheep's milk), raw

Made in Villafranca de los Barros, this cheese has a deep orange-coloured rind created by the yeasts which impregnate the wooden boards on which it is aged for 60 days in the traditional way. If you slice off the top, the inside is soft and scoopable, the aromas are fruity and fermented, and although the paste is smooth, the flavours are complex and full-bodied, with distinctive bitter artichoke-y notes of thistle rennet.

Casar (sheep's milk), raw

The most famous and widely available of the *tortas*, named after the village of Casar de Cáceres. There are currently six dairies producing this cheese, with its thin, delicate rind and ivory-coloured paste. The texture should be smooth and silky, rich with the sweet flavours of sheep's milk and the complex vegetal notes of thistle.

Pascualete la Retorta (sheep's milk), raw

The cheese is made in Trujillo with milk of exemplary quality from Finca Pascualete's own herds of sheep, which graze on the extensive pastures of this vast estate. The Retorta is one of Spain's most complex cheeses, and the rind is an ochre-yellow with assertive aromas of beer

and mustard. Once the lid has been sliced off, the paste has a soft, oily sheen. Flavours are bold, with notes of bitter thistle, sweet milk and English mustard.

Semi-cured and cured cheeses

Payoyo de cabra (goat's milk) and Payoyo de Oveja Merina de Grazalema (sheep's milk)

In his early forties Carlos Ríos had the vision to leave his job as a salesman in order to form a business partnership with Andrés Piña and start up a ground-breaking co-operative dairy, Quesos Payoyo, in the stunning setting of the natural park of Grazalema in the Sierra de Cádiz. Here the altitude and high levels of rainfall mean that the pastures are of the best quality. Carlos bought some 80 goats and 160 Merino de Grazalema sheep, and he and his wife, Ana Sánchez, now make artisan cheeses that are direct descendants of the traditional ones once made by the region's shepherds.

Both cheeses are called Payoyo after the local Payoya breed of goats, even though some are made with sheep's milk, or blends of the two.

The pure goat's milk cheese has a clean flavour of fresh curd. The unctuous, pure Merino de Grazalema sheep's milk cheese is coated with lard and then with *salvado de trigo* (wheatgerm), which minimises the loss of moisture as it cures, intensifying the complex fermented-tropical-fruit flavour with its toasted caramel finish.

Some of the mixed milk cheeses are coated in rosemary and lard and wrapped for about three months in greaseproof paper to infuse the herb into the cheese.

All the styles pair really well with aged sherries, such as Antique Oloroso from Fernando de Castilla or Amontillado Seco Sacromonte, and the Payoyo makes a good 'butter', melted over grilled steaks.

Tronchón (goat's or sheep's milk), pasteurised or raw

The Catí dairy was formed in 1972 by a group of farmers wanting to pool their resources to preserve and continue traditional cheese-making in the Maestrazgo hills in the south-east of Spain, with its age-old tradition of *transhumance* (see page 526) and raising sheep and goats in mixed herds.

Their Tronchón is a semi-hard cheese, cured for two months and made in an unusual shape which resembles two upturned shallow bowls joined together and indented on the top and bottom, reflecting the vessels in which the cheese would originally have been made. The paste in this artisan cheese is dense, with a flavour that varies according to the milk: the sheep's milk cheese will be sweeter, while the one made with goat's milk has a sharper taste. Both have a floral aroma that reflects the wild, herbaceous pastures where the animals graze.

It pairs well with a dry white wine like Rueda and fresh fruits such as grapes and apples.

The dairy also makes Pañoleta, a semi-soft goat's cheese also made in a distinctive shape, this time square, with rounded corners created by the knotted cloths that hold the curds as the cheese cures for two months. It has a velvety olive-green bloom and is fresh and smooth, with a crisp citric finish.

Fresh cheeses

Mató and Requesón

The fresh cheeses (and yogurts) of Catalunya and the Levante play an important part in the region's cuisine. Mató (which is like cottage cheese) and Requesón (ricotta) are made from the whey that is left after making cheese from cow's milk (though originally it would have been goat's or sheep's milk). They are very mild in flavour and can be eaten with honey, nuts or fruit, and are used in savoury dishes, cheesecakes or the *flaó* (tarts) of the area.

The Contented Shepherd

There is a simple beauty about the shepherding way of life that I have always found very emotive – and it is probably my husband Rupert's dream job. I often find myself stopping the car in the middle of the countryside to chat to elderly shepherds (*pastores*) because I know they are likely to be the last of their line, since in most regions shepherds are a vanishing breed, although in pockets of Castilla y León, especially Burgos and Zamora, and in the Canary Islands, their skills are still valued. Here the language of whistles as the shepherds speak to each other can be heard from valley to valley, like Swiss yodels.

A shepherd understands his land, and will know where to move his animals, depending on the season, between the *páramo* (higher open mountain plains), and richer lowlands in order to feed on exceptional pockets of flowers, tender grass shoots and wild herbs. The animals enjoy a stress-free existence which, together with this diet, gives the milk a wonderful quality.

This movement of animals is known universally as the *transhumance*, and in central Spain the well-trodden routes, dotted with huts where the shepherds would sleep along the way, are known as *las cañadas reales*. Though the routes have inevitably been modified to take into account modern obstacles such as motorways and new urban developments, they are still managed by regional laws, known as *Leyes de Mesta*, that have been in place for centuries and dictate when each official route is open for the movement of herds. Possibly as far back as the thirteenth century, for example, the inhabitants and shepherds of the Roncal valley in the far-eastern corner of Navarra established themselves as an independent political entity – 'the community of the seven villages of the valley of Roncal' – to govern the use of the communal pastureland and control the calendar of the *transhumance*.

In the village of Roa de Duero in Castilla y León, home of our friends Ambro and Asun, there is a herd of beautiful Churra sheep, looked after by a shepherd who is known only as El Suave (the gentle one). This is a village where nicknames (*motes*) prevail, and I was told that El Suave earned his *mote* when he was ten years old and a buyer came to the family farm to collect some lambs. While the other children played truant, he helped to guide the lambs into the trailer with such calm that the buyer slipped him a tip, while praising him for his gentleness. On the day I met El Suave it was lambing season and he was setting off for the plateau lands with his herd of Churras and a donkey with saddlebags to hold any lambs that might need carrying.

Zamora is a province of Castilla y León, the autonomous region that produces the highest volume and best-quality milk in the whole of Spain. In Zamora the tradition was that when shepherds took their herds in search of fresh pastures their families travelled with them, making cheeses wherever they came to rest. And though these nomadic days may be over, this is a region that still values the skills of the shepherd, albeit on a smaller, more local scale.

The aptly named Félix Vicente Pastor is one of three brothers who pasture around 2,000 sheep in Morales del Vino and who still employ shepherds in the traditional fashion for their family business, which produces around 80,000 kilos of artisan queso *zamorano* every year (see page 516). Félix remembers that when the brothers were growing up, the shepherds lived in the family home and would be out with the sheep all day, milking the ewes by hand in the open fields in summer and under cover in the winter. Often they would take their lunch and dinner into the fields with them. Times change, though, and Félix told me that for a long time the young people of Zamora saw the role of shepherd as much less of a pastoral idyll and more a low-skilled, relentless grind, so the family had to rely on Portuguese and Romanian shepherds, who brought the old gifts of experience and dedication to the task. Now, however, tougher economic climates have at least brought one positive outcome, in that local young people are again looking to the role of shepherding.

In Zamora there is also a new system, known as the *Ordenación común de hierbas, pastos y rastrojeras*, which encourages sheep farmers to 'rent' agricultural fields from arable farmers after the harvest, so that the animals can feed on the stubble and grasses. It works well, encouraging the arable farmer to buy more land to cultivate, and the sheep farmer to acquire more sheep. It also means that the herds don't have to be moved so far to graze, so the new breed of shepherd/farmers can pen the animals and, instead of cooking up a pot of stew over an open fire in a remote hut, they can go home for lunch before the afternoon shift.

THE ISLANDS

'a specialist culture of ageing cheeses'

In the Balearic Islands cow's milk cheeses are a speciality, particularly in the most northerly and easterly of the islands, Menorca, where dairy cattle – mainly Friesians which arrived during the British occupation in the eighteenth century – thrive in the climate, which is warm but with generous rainfall, softly salted by the marine winds. As a result of this the pasture is rich and green, from October to spring.

The pale yellow cheeses of Mallorca are very similar, although they may have goat's or sheep's milk added to the recipe, and they tend to have a milder flavour and a buttery texture.

On the Canary Islands, where the land is extremely dry and wild, it is the goat, rather than the cow, that thrives and the dairy industry is an important part of the local economy. Until recently the cheeses have rarely left the islands, and the Canarian people eat more cheese per capita than any other European country. It is like bread to the islanders, particularly in the poorer, remote areas away from the tourist centres. Often it is eaten along with the local grain, *gofio*, and it is present, in savoury and sweet combinations, at almost every meal.

Gran Canaria has the richest cheese culture of all the islands, since much of the land is completely unspoilt and provides exceptional pastures in which shepherds still take charge of flocks, leading them up into the hills to run free.

Often farmers will be doing the milking in the corner of a field under rustic, palm-leaf shelters but the raw milk is excellent and there is no history of disease, so the farmers can use it to make fresh cheeses, as well as those intended for maturing, using simple methods. It is common for people just to buy directly from their neighbouring farmer, whose production might be only half a dozen cheeses, made that morning.

Originally, like Menorca, the Canaries had a specialist culture of ageing cheeses, and you can still see the names of the original *afinadores* (maturers) on old buildings; however, this is a skill the cheesemakers mostly have to perform themselves these days.

Some of the Canarian goat's cheeses, in particular, like the Majorero and the lightly smoked Queso Palmero, are beginning to find appreciative markets abroad, and are gaining in reputation and production. With success, however, comes the temptation to expand and, in some cases, risk compromising the very qualities that have attracted outside attention. Across the islands, the Canarian government has been trying to intensify production, build bigger dairies and make the most of the milk, often at the expense of small farms, many of which already face uncertainty, since the younger generation don't necessarily want to live the same lives as their parents and grandparents.

Menorca

Mahón or Maó DOP (cow's milk),
pasteurised or raw

Mahón, or Maó, to give it its local name, is a square cheese with rounded edges and corners, a tangy, sharp flavour, and characteristic saltiness that reflects the rich maritime *terroir* on which the dairy cattle thrive. Mahón cheeses are sold at different stages of maturation: fresh at 21–60 days, when they are quite elastic, semi-cured at 2–5 months, and cured, or aged (*añejo*) at over five months, when they become more brittle.

While you can still find traditional artisan farmhouse Formatge de Maó cheese produced from raw cow's milk, the bulk of cheeses are now produced by the bigger dairies using pasteurised milk. However, within the PDO classification the two must be distinguished by their labels. A green label denotes artisan Maó, while industrially produced cheese has a red label.

For the green label cheese, originally produced in Menorcan *llocs* (traditional small farms with stone-walled enclosures), the curds are gathered inside a *fogasser*, or cheesecloth, so the cheese is often called *formatge de fogassa*. The mass is pressed manually into a square shape, which loses the bulk of the whey, and the four corners of the cloth are then pulled in tight and tied with a *lligam*, or cord. Next, the cheese is pressed again in a horizontal press, so that the creases of the cloth imprint themselves in a pattern on the upper surface of the cheese. The cheeses are then salted, and originally the farmer would sell them on to the island's skilled *afinadores*, cheese maturers, who would finish them in their own cellars. These specialists are now few and far between, however.

The rind starts off a light straw colour and, as the cheese matures, becomes a matt ochre with a stunning aroma of fresh peaches, as the rind is rubbed with olive oil and paprika to protect it from excessive mould growth, as well as adding colour and character.

Artisan green label cheese can be stunning, with a saline yet fruity taste that is buttery on the palate when young, and becomes more nutty with age. It goes very well with *sobrasada* (see page 260) and honey on toasted bread.

In industrial dairies, the red label cheeses are formed in plastic moulds, which recreate the traditional cloth pattern, and they are pressed in modern vertical presses and salted and matured in special chambers within the dairy. The rind of these cheeses tends to be a waxy orange, created with dyed food-grade paraffin. They can be excellent, but their character is different from that of a green label cheese: piquant and quite sharp in flavour, with a hard, granular texture almost like that of a Parmesan. In addition to *sobrasada* and honey, the cheeses are good with jams and in gratin dishes.

At Brindisa we buy our Maó from one of the last two *afinadores* of artisan Mahón or Maó cheese on Menorca, Nicolás Cardona. Nicolás's grandfather, Josep Cardona, known as Bep de Torralba, founded Quesos Torralba in 1939 in the town of Alaior. This was a time when food was scarce, and Josep would barter with local farmers, offering the likes of oil, salt and sugar in exchange for a turkey, vegetables, tomatoes, milk, and of course Mahón cheese. The cheese was Josep's passion, so he began maturing and selling the cheeses in premises next door to the family home. He named the business after the nearby ancient stones of Torralba d'en Salord, which are the remains of a prehistoric town dating somewhere between 1000 BC and the Roman era.

The Maó Torralba cheeses that Nicolás matures are still handmade and pressed in selected dairies from raw milk. He chooses ones made between November and May, when the island is covered in good lush pasture, and ripens them to his exacting standards, greased with olive oil and paprika, to give the rinds elasticity. They are either semi-cured for around two months, so that they are ivory-coloured with a soft, buttery texture and an orange-brown rind; or aged in small batches for five months until yellow and hard, with a dark brown rind and a flavour that is intense and piquant.

Nicolás and his wife Rosa champion excellence and insist on paying much more than the industrial dairies for the cheeses, as their way of helping to sustain the true artisans and small farmers of the island, whose number is sadly reducing as they find it harder and harder to keep going.

The cheeses are good with fruity white wines and big reds, and we serve them with home-made tomato jam (see page 533) on our menus at Brindisa. The aged Torralba is supremely good with honey.

Fuerteventura

Majorero (goat's milk), pasteurised or raw

Majorero is made on the island of Fuerteventura, which is the closest to Africa of all the Canary Islands. The land is desert-like, has almost no rainfall, and the goat is the only dairy animal that can survive on the scrubby vegetation. This island has its own indigenous breed called Majorera, and its dairies collect their milk from around 100 farmers. The cheese is pressed into large, low rounds decorated with the rhomboid pattern of the traditional belt which was wrapped around the cheese and was made of palm fronds.

The big, flat round cheeses are cured from eight to 60 days. The younger cheeses have a white rind and interior and are creamy and fresh with a mild goaty flavour; the medium-cured cheeses are firm, lightly goaty and sweet; then, as they age, the rind and the interior become straw yellow and the flavour caramelly. As the cheese matures the rind can be coated with a mix of olive oil and paprika, which turns it a burnt orange colour, or it is coated with the local cereal *gofio* (see page 60), which gives it a brown colour.

Majorero pairs well with a minerally white island wine such as Los Bermejos, the dry, crisp and citrusy white made from the Malvasía grape in Lanzarote. In winter the cheese is often grated into vegetable soup and in summer over salads. And in one restaurant on the island,

run by a Swiss-German, I ate one of the best fondues I have ever had, made with buttery young Majorero, blended with *mistela canaria*, the traditional orange liqueur made with *aguardiente* (cane spirit), orange juice and sugar and aromatised with orange peel. The pillowy fondue had specks of fruit peel in it, and when you dipped your bread into it, it was heaven.

La Palma

Palmero DOP (goat's milk), raw

This is a terrific cheese, originally the biggest produced in Spain or any of the islands. Made on La Palma, the greenest of the Canaries, it can weigh up to 15kg and is usually lightly smoked. In the markets the cheeses are a sight to behold, with their rind marked with biscuit-coloured lines from the wooden slats of the smoking room.

The native Palmera goats are well nourished on diverse and lush pasture, and their milk gives the crumbly-textured, bright white cheese a rich flavour, salty and lightly acidic, with a toasted aroma and earthiness. It is often briefly grilled and served, sometimes alongside sliced fish, vegetables and potatoes, with *mojo* sauces (see pages 298–300), but it is also good on its own, paired with one of the local mineral-rich Malvasía wines.

Gran Canaria

Flor de Guía, Media Flor and de Guía (sheep's milk or mixed sheep's, cow's and goat's), raw

The creamiest of all Canarian cheeses, these are gently rounded and shaped inside a cloth which is knotted at the top and leaves a very faint imprint on the rind.

Guía is a region in the north-west of Gran Canaria and the cheeses are usually made with pure sheep's milk, though the recipe allows for blended milks to a minimum of 60 per cent sheep's milk and a maximum of 40 per cent cow's milk and 10 per cent goat's milk.

The local cattle and sheep, now both known as Canaria, are a *potaje*, or mix, of breeds originally from the mainland which have adapted well and are mostly used to work on the land, but the quality of their milk is exceptional. As the animals are not continually drained of every drop of milk in the way of intensive dairy farms, it is very high in fat and protein, and so only a small quantity of it (as little as 10 per cent can be added) gives a fantastic burst of richness.

The cheeses are made throughout the year, but the rennets and combinations of milks will change according to the season or what is available to the cheese-maker.

Cheeses labelled Flor de Guía are exceptional and very rare, as they are made entirely with rennet made from the flower of the local wild *cardo* (thistle), which is harvested and then steeped in water, from January to late spring. The Flor de Guía that is made only with sheep's milk is a real treat. Rich, squidgy and creamy, almost like a *torta* or a Reblochon, it melts in the mouth, releasing its mildly acidic, aromatic flavour, culminating in a spicy finish and the typical bitterness of thistle rennet. When the season for the Flor de Guía is over, a semi-hard cheese, Media Flor, is produced using animal and thistle rennet. Then, moving on into autumn, a longer-cure cheese called de Guía will be made using only animal rennet.

Families might make two or three cheeses a day from a few of their own animals, and the typical Gran Canarian home will often have caves beneath it that burrow into the mountains, where the cheeses can be cured on racks lined with cane matting called *cánizo* – a tradition that artisan makers cling to, but the big dairies want to dispense with.

De Guía cheeses in all their variants marry well with fruity white wines and the mineral red wines of the islands, such as Tinto Negramoll from Viña Norte in Tenerife, as well as berry jams.

Confitura de tomate
Tomato jam

This is our Brindisa tomato jam, which goes brilliantly with cheese. For quick tapas, fill some bought mini pastry cases, or spread crackers with some warm Torta de Barros (see page 524) and top with the jam.

Makes 500g

1kg tomatoes
250g white sugar
250g brown sugar
grated rind of 1 lemon
1 cinnamon stick

Either grate the tomatoes, or, if you prefer, de-skin and de-seed them (see page 206).

Put into a pan and cook for 20–30 minutes over a low heat until reduced by half. Add the rest of the ingredients and cook very slowly – just let the odd bubble break the surface – for 2 hours, and up to 4, stirring occasionally until the jam is really syrupy.

Remove the cinnamon stick and either pot in sterilised jars (see page 52) or keep in the fridge for up to a month.

Confitura de pimientos
Red pepper jam

This is a recipe from Sandra Bascones, a friend of Ambro and Ásun in Pedrosa de Duero, who joined us for a big lunch at which everyone brought or cooked dishes and swapped ideas. One of her many contributions was a starter plate of a log of goat's cheese accompanied by this lovely pepper jam.

Makes 300g

400g fresh red peppers
150g white sugar
50g brown sugar
50ml vinegar

Put the peppers into a food processor and blend until very finely chopped. Add the remaining ingredients with 100ml water and blend again until you have a smoothish paste. Turn out into a saucepan and cook over a medium-to-high heat, stirring frequently, until the mixture is thick and sticky, like jam. The colour will be very beautiful, a rich red that is slightly darker than the raw peppers.

Either pot in sterilised jars (see page 52) or keep in the fridge for up to a month.